Public Speaking 7e

Concepts and Skills for a Diverse Society

Public Speaking 7e

Concepts and Skills for a Diverse Society

Clella Iles Jaffe

George Fox University

Australia • Brazil • Japan • Korea • Mexico • Singapore • Spain • United Kingdom • United States

Public Speaking: Concepts & Skills for a Diverse Society, Seventh Edition
Clella Iles Jaffe

Senior Publisher: Lyn Uhl

Publisher: Monica Eckman

Development Editor: Kate Scheinman

Senior Assistant Editor: Rebekah Matthews

Editorial Assistant: Colin Solan

Media Editor: Jessica Badiner

Marketing Manager: Jason Sakos

Marketing Coordinator: Brittany Blais

MarComm Manager: Linda Yip

Design and Production Services: PreMediaGlobal

Art Director: Linda Helcher

Manufacturing Planner: Doug Bertke

Rights Acquisition Specialist: Jessica Elias

Cover Designer: Infiniti Design

Cover Image: © Tim Timmerman

Library of Congress Control Number: 2011941519

Student Edition:

ISBN-13: 978-1-111-34768-0

ISBN-10: 1-111-34768-9

Wadsworth
20 Channel Center Street
Boston, MA 02210
USA

Cengage Learning is a leading provider of customized learning solutions with office locations around the globe, including Singapore, the United Kingdom, Australia, Mexico, Brazil and Japan. Locate your local office at **international.cengage.com/region**

Cengage Learning products are represented in Canada by Nelson Education, Ltd.

For your course and learning solutions, visit **www.cengage.com.**

Purchase any of our products at your local college store or at our preferred online store **www.cengagebrain.com.**

Instructors: Please visit **login.cengage.com** and log in to access instructor-specific resources.

Printed in Canada
1 2 3 4 5 6 7 15 14 13 12 11

BRIEF CONTENTS

CONTENTS

LIST OF SPEECHES

Please Note: *A transcript or outline of the following additional speeches does not appear in the book, but the text refers to some of these speeches, and a video of each is on the book's website along with transcripts, outlines, and note cards.*

Hillary Carter-Liggett, *Shakespeare [informative]*

Edwin J. Feulner, *Lay your Hammer Down: Defend Your Convictions [commemorative]*

Erica Nelson, *Corporate Social Responsibility [informative]*

Alexandra Reed, *A Fork in the Road [commemorative]*

Anna Reidl, *Pumpkins [informative, visual aids]*

Enriques Ruiz, *Anytown, USA [informative]*

Amara Sheppard, *The Biology of Your Lunch: You Are What You Eat [informative]*

Josh Valentine, *The Dun Dun Drum [informative]*

PREFACE

> The civilization of the dialogue is the only civilization worth having and the only civilization in which the whole world can unite. It is, therefore, the only civilization we can hope for, because the world must unite or be blown to bits.
>
> Robert Hutchins, 1967

IT IS A PRIVILEGE to write the seventh edition of *Public Speaking: Concepts and Skills for a Diverse Society*, a culturally informed text that maintains its fundamental purpose—to train students to be effective public speakers and listeners in an ever changing world. A diversity perspective helps students gain critical thinking proficiencies and knowledge of core concepts, theories, and applications that are essential in the twenty-first century where people from one cultural background increasingly find themselves in dialogue with members of other cultures. This text, like its predecessors, grounds discussions of speaking and listening in an awareness of the impact of culture—ranging from gender differences to co-cultures within the United States to the traditions of other nations.

I originally wrote this book to emphasize the intertwined relationships between public speaking and culture because through public speaking we reinforce, transmit, change, and blend cultures. In fact, the very characteristics speakers aim to influence—beliefs, values, attitudes, and actions—are the basic elements of diversity. In addition, our cultural backgrounds influence our perceptions of our roles as public speakers and listeners. Culture also influences topic selection, research methods and resources, and reasoning styles. Consequently, this text combines 2,500-year-old principles from Western traditions with up-to-date research in a way that is sensitive to our pluralistic society.

The years between the first edition and this, the seventh edition, have seen monumental social, cultural, and technological changes, both in the United States and across the globe. Each new edition provides an opportunity to integrate developing trends into the text as well as to update research findings and pedagogical trends in the field of public speaking. I am grateful to all who have used the first six editions and to the many professors and students who have given helpful suggestions to keep the text practical and current.

New to This Edition

I'm proud to say that this was the first public speaking textbook to focus on diversity, include an interpreted speech (given in Spanish and translated into English), describe invitational rhetoric, discuss receiver apprehension, and show alternative patterns of speech organization. Each edition has maintained several proven emphases:

- Cultural influences on public speaking and public speakers' influence on culture
- Gender, ethnic, and global diversity
- Civility and ethics in speaking and listening

- Communication as dialogue
- The importance of narrative speaking
- Technological advances and public speaking
- Traditions dating back to classical rhetoric
- Nontraditional organizational patterns

This edition retains these features and includes a number of important changes in response to reviewer feedback. Here are some highlights of what's new or revised:

- **Civic engagement.** Because of increased civic involvement within the culture, reviewers asked for material on civic engagement. You'll find a definition in Chapter 1 and references in several chapters. For example, Chapter 3 features a new Diversity in Practice box on social media and civic engagement. The professional speech at the end of that chapter combines themes of civility and engagement, and Chapter 9 features a student speech given for an assignment on civic awareness.
- **Collectivist and individualist cultures.** Reviewers asked for inclusion of information on ways that collectivist and individualist cultures affect public speaking. I've included definitions in Chapter 1 and references to these types of cultures in appropriate places throughout the text.
- **Revised organization within chapters.** In response to reviewer feedback, I've revised some material for better flow of ideas. For example, Chapter 7 is now organized around four basic concepts. Chapter 9 is substantially revised to explain how to support and connect main points, taking some material from Chapter 10 and some from Chapter 11. Chapter 13 is reorganized around three concepts; it also follows a specific student as he makes choices to illustrate his topic. Chapters 17 and 18 are reordered. Chapter 17 now provides foundations for persuasion, and Chapter 18 covers persuasive speeches, reorganized around speeches to convince and speeches to actuate or change behaviors.
- **Oral Style.** Reviewers asked for comparisons between written style and oral style, so Chapter 12 now includes a section on oral style and the section on effective language is reorganized around that concept.
- **Additional figures that summarize information.** Student and faculty reviewers noted the helpfulness of visuals, such as Figure 2.1 that summarizes the five canons of rhetoric, so I added several such features throughout the text. For example, Chapter 7 now has a table comparing Internet research to library research; Chapter 12 features a table comparing oral to written style.
- **Updated research.** Communication scholars continue to expand our understanding of listening and reasoning. Information on historical rhetorical traditions (Diversity in Practice box, Chapter 1), gender and anxiety (Chapter 2), and dual coding theory (Chapter 12) are just a few examples of research updates.
- **Practically Speaking boxes.** I've added or revised several boxes to include a Native American activist (Chapter 1), a Korean American businesswoman (Chapter 9), a discussion of Wikipedia (Chapter 7), and a student who organized a civic engagement project on campus (Chapter 14).
- **Updated references to social events.** Keeping a text current requires frequent updating to include accurate and relevant information. For example, between the sixth and seventh editions, Barack Obama was elected President, Ted Sorensen died, town hall meetings turned rowdy, the Tea Party rallied, and social media became much more involved in uprisings globally.
- **New sample speeches.** I replaced or updated many sample speeches for currency, variety, and even greater effectiveness. Most of the speeches are available on video. For more information about the speech videos for this book, see the Student Resources section.

Proven Chapter-by-Chapter Features

In addition to chapter-opening lists of learning objectives, key term definitions in the margins of each chapter, and chapter-ending summaries, each chapter includes several acclaimed pedagogical features that improve student learning and performance.

- **Stop and Check boxes.** These critical thinking and skill-building exercises help students check their progress throughout the chapter. Often, they refer to an article in the InfoTrac College Edition™ database, which helps students better understand the topic and gives them practice in researching and locating quality supporting material online. These activities are also available in an interactive format on the book's online resources.
- **Diversity in Practice boxes.** These boxes enhance the book's emphasis on diversity by presenting brief summaries of public speaking traditions from a range of perspectives. Examples include ancient cultures (Chapter 1), global groups (Chapters 7, 9, and 18), ethnic groups (Chapter 10 and 15), and co-cultures (Chapter 12).
- **Practically Speaking boxes.** Reviewers asked for more practical applications to situations outside the classroom. Consequently, most chapters feature an example of "ordinary" people (including a student) who share tips on how they use concepts developed in the chapter in their daily lives.
- **Ethics in Practice boxes.** This text has always emphasized ethical speaking and listening. This edition includes an ethics box in most chapters. These boxes present short examples or cases that invite students to contemplate the ethical implications of chapter concepts, using probing questions that are appropriate for class discussions.
- **Build Your Speech boxes.** These skill-building activities help students apply text concepts to actual speechmaking. They can serve as starting points for completing speech assignments. Many of these activities offer students the option of completing the activities by accessing Speech Builder Express™ 3.0, an online speech coach. For more information about Speech Builder Express, see the Resources for Students section.
- **Application and Critical Thinking Exercises.** Suitable for individual or group assignments, and for in-class discussion, these end-of-chapter questions help students better understand and critically evaluate the chapter content and further apply the skills they've learned.
- **Student speeches.** Most chapters include an outline or text of a student speech, accompanied by marginal commentary. These speeches provide models showing how other students fulfilled a typical assignment. Chapter 17 provides a cautionary, negative model, and Chapters 3 and 12 feature speeches by professional speakers. Most of these speeches are available on video. For more information about this book's speech resources, see the Resources for Students section.

Accompanying Resources: An Exclusive Teaching and Learning Package

Public Speaking: Concepts and Skills for a Diverse Society, Seventh Edition, offers a comprehensive array of supplements to assist in helping students succeed and in making the public speaking course as meaningful and enjoyable as possible for both students and instructors.

Resources for Students

Many of these student resources are available when instructors order them bundled with the text for students (or when they order access to these resources). Other users or students whose instructors do not order these resources with the text may purchase them at **cengagebrain.com**.

- **CourseMate.** The CourseMate for *Public Speaking: Concepts and Skills for a Diverse Society* offers a variety of rich learning resources designed to enhance the student experience. These resources include Audio Study Tools chapter downloads, Interactive Video Activities, Speech Builder Express 3.0, self-assessments, InfoTrac College Edition with InfoMarks™, and web resources.
- **Interactive Video Activities.** This interactive tool lets students view video of speeches, and compare the performances to three types of outlines. They can also embed notes on the video, and complete critique and evaluation assignments.
- **Audio Study Tools.** These tools provide a fun and easy way for students to download audio files and review chapter content whenever and wherever. For each chapter, students will have access to a chapter review consisting of the learning objectives for the chapter, a brief summary of the main points in the text, audio of a speech, and critical-thinking questions. Students can download files to their computers, iPods, or other MP3 players.
- **Speech Builder Express 3.0.** This online program coaches students through the entire process of preparing speeches and provides the additional support of built-in video speech models, a tutor feature for concept review, and an online dictionary and thesaurus. Equipped with their speech type or purpose, a general topic, and preliminary research, students respond to the program's customized prompts to complete interactive activities that require critical thinking about all aspects of creating an effective speech. Students are able to specify a specific speech purpose, identify an organizational pattern, write a thesis statement or central idea, establish main points, integrate support material, craft transitions, plan visual aids, compose their speech introduction and conclusion, and prepare their bibliography to complete formal speech outlines. Students are also able to stop and start work whenever they choose. They can complete, save online, export to Microsoft Word, or email their outlines.
- **SpeechStudio 2.0™** is an online speech program for the Public Speaking course. With **SpeechStudio 2.0**, students upload recorded speeches, watch and assess their peers' speeches, and review their grades and instructor feedback. Instructors create assignments, comment on student speeches with a library of comments, and grade them with customizable, editable rubrics. Instructors also can choose to allow peer review. Grades flow into a gradebook so that instructors can easily manage their course from within **SpeechStudio**, or instructors can export the grades to a learning management system. Visit **www.cengage.com/community/speech**.
- **InfoTrac® College Edition.** This online library provides access to more than 18 million reliable, full-length articles from more than 5,000 academic and popular periodicals. For more information about InfoTrac College Edition, visit **infotrac-college.com** and click on "InfoTrac Demo."
- ***A Guide to the Basic Course for ESL Students*** is also available bundled with the book. Specifically for communicators whose first language is not English, it features FAQs, helpful URLs, and strategies for managing communication anxiety.
- **The Art and Strategy of Service Learning Presentations, Second Edition.** Available bundled with *Public Speaking: Concepts and Skills for a Diverse Society*. Authored by Rick Isaacson and Jeff Saperstein of San Francisco State University, this handbook provides guidelines for connecting service-learning work with classroom concepts and advice for working effectively with agencies and organizations.

Resources for Instructors

Public Speaking: Concepts and Skills for a Diverse Society, Seventh Edition, also features a full suite of resources for instructors. The following class preparation, classroom presentation, assessment, and course management resources are available:

- **Instructor's Resource Manual.** The Instructor's Resource Manual provides a comprehensive teaching guide. Written by Miri Pardo, St. John Fisher College, this manual features sample syllabi, as well as suggested speaking assignments and criteria for evaluation. Each text chapter has the following resources: chapter goals, a chapter outline, suggestions correlating supplements and online resources, supplementary research notes, and suggested discussion questions. The manual also includes a printed test bank that features class-tested multiple-choice, true-false, short-answer, essay, and fill-in-the-blank test questions.

- **Instructor's Website.** The password-protected instructor's website includes electronic access to the Instructor's Resource Manual and downloadable versions of the book's PowerPoint slides. To gain access to the website, simply request a course key by opening the site's home page.
- **PowerLecture CD-ROM.** This includes an electronic version of the Instructor's Resource Manual, ExamView Computerized Testing, predesigned and customizable Microsoft PowerPoint presentations, and the book's video footage. This resource is available to qualified adopters. Please consult your local sales representative for details.
- **ExamView Computerized Testing.** ExamView enables you to create, deliver, and customize tests and study guides (both print and online) in minutes using the test bank questions from the Instructor's Resource Manual. ExamView offers both a Quick Test Wizard and an Online Test Wizard that guide you step-by-step through the process of creating tests, while its "what you see is what you get" interface allows you to see the test you are creating on-screen exactly as it will print or display online. You can build tests of up to 250 questions using up to twelve question types. Using the complete word processing capabilities of ExamView, you can also enter an unlimited number of new questions or edit existing ones.
- **Wadsworth Cengage Learning Communication Video and DVD Library.** Wadsworth Cengage Learning's video and DVD series for Speech Communication includes Student Speeches for Critique and Analysis, Communication Scenarios for Critique and Analysis, and BBC/CBS news videos and DVDs for Public Speaking, Human Communication, and Interpersonal Communication.
- ***The Teaching Assistant's Guide to the Basic Course.*** Katherine G. Hendrix, who is on the faculty at the University of Memphis, prepared this resource specifically for new instructors. Based on leading communication teacher training programs, this guide discusses some of the general issues that accompany a teaching role and offers specific strategies for managing the first week of classes, leading productive discussions, managing sensitive topics in the classroom, and grading students' written and oral work.

These resources are available to qualified adopters, and ordering options for student supplements are flexible. Please consult your local Wadsworth Cengage Learning sales representative for more information, to evaluate examination copies of any of these instructor or student resources, or for product demonstrations. You may also contact the Cengage Learning Academic Resource Center at 800-423-0563 or visit us at **cengage brain.com**.

Acknowledgments

Every book is a co-created product in which an author relies on the encouragement of others. I owe a longstanding debt to former Oregon State University colleagues (Victoria O'Donnell, Sean Patrick O'Rourke, Anne Zach Ferguson, and dozens of graduate teaching instructors). My colleagues at George Fox University, Richard Engnell, Craig Johnson, Kevin Jones, and Charles Choi, have consistently and patiently supported my writing, for which I am grateful. I also thank generations of students at Oregon State, St. John's (New York), and George Fox University who provided insights, examples, speeches, and support. I extend special thanks too to Sarah Gibson of George Fox

University, who taped the new student speeches; Melissa Meyer, who created the web quizzes for students on the book's companion website; Sherry Lewis of University of Texas, El Paso, who created the critical thinking questions and outlines for the new student speeches; and Kim Cowden of North Dakota State University, who created the audio study tools.

Likewise, I want to thank the many people at or working with Wadsworth Cengage Learning who helped bring this new edition and its many supplements to fruition: Jessica Badiner, Christina Ciaramella, Jessica Elias, Larry Goldberg, Rebekah Matthew, Kim Mercer, Miri Pardo, Linda Presto, Jen Roach, Joanna Schmidt, Donald Schwartz and Preetha Sreekanth.

I would like to thank the reviewers who contributed valuable comments about this book's sixth edition and offered helpful suggestions for the seventh: Kim Harris, William Jewell College; Terri Main, Reedley College; Anna Roseboro, Calvin College; Ken Sherwood, Los Angeles City College; Elizabeth Simas, Diablo Valley College; Cheryl Skiba-Jones, Ivy Tech Community College; Sheri Strothers, Grossmont College; Ed Sweda, Pasco Hernando Community College; Margaret Wick, The College of Wooster; and Tina Zagara, Georgia Perimeter College.

I would also like to thank the reviewers for previous editions of this book. Reviewers for the First Edition were Martha Ann Atkins, Iowa State University; Dennis Beaver, Bakersfield College; Carol Berteotti, University of Wisconsin–La Crosse; Carole Blair, University of California–Davis; Cynthia Brown-El, Macomb Community College; Ferald J. Bryan, Northern Illinois University; Bruce G. Bryski, Buffalo State College; Jacquelyn Buckrop, Ball State University; Michelle Burch, Clark State University; Kathleen Farrell, Saint Louis University; Norma Flores, Golden West College; Franklin L. Gray, Ball State University; Charles Griffin, Kansas State University; Susan Hellweg, San Diego State University; Mark Hickson, University of Alabama–Birmingham; Janet Hoffman, Southern Illinois University at Carbondale; Susan Huxman, Wichita State University; Karla Jensen, Texas Tech University; Tina Kistler, Santa Barbara City College; Shelley D. Lane, Collin County Community College; Jo Ann Lawlor, West Valley College; Steven March, Pima County Community College; Victoria O'Donnell, Montana State University; Sean Patrick O'Rourke, Vanderbilt University; Patricia Palm McGillen, Mankato State University; Mark Morman, Johnson County Community College; Teresa Nance, Villanova University; Patricia O'Keefe, College of Marin; Mary Pelias, Southern Illinois University; Mark Stoner, California State University–Sacramento; Patricia Sullivan, State University of New York at New Paltz; Marsha Vanderford, University of South Florida; Donald E. Williams, University of Florida; Lee Winet, State University of New York–Oswego; and Anne Zach Ferguson, University of California–Davis. Reviewers for the Second Edition were Thomas E. Diamond, Montana State University; Kevin E. McClearey, Southern Illinois University at Edwardsville; Susan Messman, Arizona State University; Karla D. Scott, Saint Louis University; Jessica Stowell, Tulsa Community College; and Lori Wisdom-Whitley, Western Washington University. Reviewers for the Third Edition were Clifton Adams, Central Missouri State University; Linda Anthon, Valencia Community College; Jay Baglia, University of South Florida; Carol Barnum, Southern Polytechnic State University; Lori Basden Arnold, Rowan University; Julie Benson-Rosston, University of Montana; John Bourhis, Missouri State University; Cheri Campbell, Keene State College; Faye Clark, Georgia Perimeter College; Risa Dickson, California State University at San Bernardino; Hal Fulmer, Georgia Southern University; Matthew Girton, Florida State University; Sherrie L. Guerrero, San Bernardino Valley College; Robert Gwynne, University of Tennessee–Knoxville; Fred Jandt, California State University at San Bernardino; Laura Nelson, University of Wisconsin–La Crosse; Jean E. Perry, Glendale Community College; Susie Richardson, Prince George's Community College; Paula Rodriguez, Hinds

Community College; Scott Rodriguez, California State University at San Bernardino; Cathy Sargent Mester, Pennsylvania State University; Kristi A. Schaller, University of Hawaii; Ann M. Scroggie, Santa Fe Community College; Karni Spain Tiernan, Bradley University; David Walker, Middle Tennessee State University; June D. Wells, Indian River Community College; Nancy J. Wendt, Oregon State University; L. Keith Williamson, Wichita State University; and Marianne Worthington, Cumberland College. Reviewers for the Fourth Edition were James E. Bruce, University of Tennessee at Martin; Ferald J. Bryan, Northern Illinois University; Nanci Burk, Glendale Community College; Helen Chester, Milwaukee Area Technical College; Omar Guevara, California State University at Bakersfield; Janice D. Hamlet, Northern Illinois University; Jeff Przybylo, William Rainey Harper Community College; Diana D. Roberts, Community College of Southern Nevada; Amy R. Slagell, Iowa State University; Lisa Waite, Kent State University; and Diane E. Waryas, Community College of Southern Nevada; and Kathryn Wylie-Marques, John Jay College, City University of New York. Reviewers for the Sixth Edition were Christian Blum, Bryant & Stratton College; Bryan Crow, Southern Illinois University; Linda Czuba Brigance, SUNY Fredonia; Jonathan M. Gray, Southern Illinois University, Carbondale; Roxanne Tuscany, Grossmont College; Alex Wang, University of Connecticut, Stamford; and Melinda Williams, Williams Baptist College.

Writing takes a toll on an author's family. I am grateful for Jack, Sara, Josh, J. C., and all the little ones who make a difference in my life. Wadsworth Cengage Learning has provided a series of editors who have guided this text throughout the editions. Monica Eckman and Kate Scheinman were consistently patient and supportive.

Clella Iles Jaffe, Ph.D.

© Tim Timmerman

CHAPTER 1

Introduction to Public Speaking and Culture

THIS CHAPTER WILL HELP YOU

- Explain the value of public speaking courses
- Define culture in the context of public speaking
- Give reasons for studying public speaking from a cultural perspective
- Explain how public speaking influences culture
- Identify three ways culture affects public speaking
- Understand aspects of the dialogical theory of communication
- Identify elements of the transactional model of communication

MAJORA CARTER is a "visionary voice in city planning" whose "confidence, energy, and intensely emotional delivery make her talks themselves a force of nature."[1] Her speeches about environmental justice in her South Bronx, New York community helped create a waterfront park on the site of an illegal garbage dump. Currently, she speaks about eco-friendly local economic development. She's one of many individuals who now have more opportunities than ever to get messages out, thanks to the Internet where participatory sites such as TED and YouTube and social networking sites such as Facebook and Twitter allow them to share their ideas globally.

Perhaps you think of a *public speaker* as a politician, business leader, member of the clergy, or activist like Carter. True, these people commonly speak, but talks occur in many other contexts. A coach giving a locker-room pep talk, a concerned student speaking to campus leaders, or a camp counselor telling a campfire story are just a few ways people speak publicly. By definition, **public speaking** occurs when one person prepares and delivers a speech for a group that listens, generally without interrupting the speaker's flow of ideas.

public speaking a person delivers a presentation to a group that listens, generally without interrupting the speaker's flow of ideas

During the term you are enrolled in a public speaking class, you will join the ranks of public speakers, however briefly. This course will help you build skills and improve your strategies for thinking through the process of planning, presenting, and evaluating effective speeches. You will assess your current skills, identify areas for improvement, and plan ways to deal with the challenges of speaking and listening in a free society. As you create first one speech and then another, you will improve your skills by adding competencies and by refining those you already have.[2]

Getty Images/WireImage

Majora Carter is just one of millions of people who make a difference in the world because of public speaking skills.

Although this text has *speaking* in the title, speech-*making* is only one element of the course. More often than not, you will be in the audience, listening to speeches in an increasingly diverse culture and world. Consequently, learning to better understand and evaluate the messages you hear daily is another major course goal. The competencies needed for these two roles—speaker and listener—are the focus of this text.

Why Take a Public Speaking Course?

Most universities not only offer public speaking courses, they require them. Why? There are at least two good reasons: they emphasize critical thinking, and they provide instruction and practice in communication skills that are important in professional, civic, and personal contexts.

You Can Increase Your Critical Thinking Skills

A bill in the California State Senate defined **critical thinking** as "the ability to engage in reasoned discourse with intellectual standards such as clarity, accuracy, precision, and logic, and to use analytic skills with a fundamental value orientation that emphasizes intellectual humility, intellectual integrity, and fair-mindedness."[3] These skills are valuable, even essential, in a world that is flooded daily with messages from millions of sources. For centuries, critical thinking has been linked with the study of **rhetoric**, or "the art, practice, and study of human communication."[4] In fact, rhetoric is one of the original seven liberal arts, developed by the Greeks and Romans and continued into today's universities, where researchers study effective and ineffective discourse.

critical thinking the ability to think analytically about ideas

rhetoric the study of persuasion in its various forms; this helps develop critical thinking skills

However valuable rhetoric may be, people today often view the word negatively. For instance, one political candidate issued a press release titled, "Rhetoric vs. Results: this election doesn't come down to change versus experience, but words versus deeds, talk versus action, rhetoric versus reality."[5] Her mindset, shared by many, gives the impression that rhetoric is empty or ineffective, in contrast to actions. But is rhetoric just words? Or is it a way to sharpen critical thinking skills? Here are four additional definitions:[6]

- the faculty of discovering in any particular case all of the available means of persuasion (Aristotle).
- the study of misunderstandings and their remedies (I. A. Richards).
- the use of language as a symbolic means of inducing cooperation in beings that by nature respond to symbols (Kenneth Burke).
- the use of reason and evidence by both sides, who express their opinions on matters and issues, expose their opponent's weak points, and finally achieve a correct viewpoint and mutual understanding (*Modern Chinese Dictionary* definition of the Chinese word, 变 *bian*).[7]

As you can see, most definitions associate rhetoric with some form of persuasion. Because persuasion surrounds you, in speeches, ads, films—to name just a few—this text describes rhetorical principles that will help you develop competencies you can use every day to critically think about information, sort through persuasive appeals, discriminate faulty arguments from valid reasoning, and follow ideas to logical conclusions.[8]

You Can Improve Your Professional, Civic, and Personal Skills

Most employers assume that college graduates have job-related skills, but they want more; they want new hires who can communicate by listening effectively, presenting ideas clearly, thinking critically and ethically, working in diverse situations, and understanding global realities.[9] In one survey, personnel interviewers overwhelmingly agreed that verbal and nonverbal skills are vital for higher-level positions.[10] Many competencies learned here are used daily in occupations as diverse as law, medicine, engineering,[11] teaching, and accounting.[12]

Skills from this course also enable you to participate more effectively in society. Stop and think for a moment. What social issues concern you? Homelessness in your community? The environment? Something else? Instead of remaining silent about significant problems, you can take part in **civic engagement** by contributing your ideas and working with others to seek resolutions to issues of public concern.[13] On blogs, LISTSERVs, social network pages, news sites,[14] and other discussion forums, you can share well-thought-out ideas about everything from sport controversies to movies to politics. The most skillful communicators influence thinking and actions about local, national, and international issues.

civic engagement working with others to help solve issues of public concern

Finally, a course in public speaking can help you personally in two ways. This text gives guidelines on how to create speeches for a variety of social situations; for example, you may be asked to give a wedding toast or funeral eulogy, a tribute, or an inspirational talk. In addition, many—even most—students enter this course with some anxiety;[15] they dread even the thought of giving a speech. If you're one of them, there's good news. Most people feel both more competent and more confident after they complete the course.[16]

In summary, studying public speaking adds to your communication abilities within a culture that values them. You can develop critical thinking skills and presentational skills that will serve you well in almost any profession, while you sharpen your ability to engage in the broader cultural conversation that makes a difference in the world. On top of these benefits, you can gain confidence as you face your fears and meet the challenge of preparing and giving speeches.

What Do I Hope to Gain from Taking This Course?

Stop and think about what you want to get out of this course, considering your previous experiences in public speaking and your educational goals in general.

- Why am I taking this course?
- What knowledge and skills do I bring to this subject?
- What skills do I already have that I want to improve?
- What new competencies do I want to develop during the term?
- What role does public speaking and listening play in my life now?
- What role will good speaking and listening skills play in my future?

culture an integrated system of learned beliefs, values, behaviors, and norms that include visible (clothing, food) and underlying (core beliefs, worldview) characteristics of a society

co-cultures subgroups of culture, characterized by mild or profound cultural differences, that coexist within the larger culture

Why Take a Cultural Perspective?

Media sources daily remind us that we live in a rapidly shrinking global context where people from distinctly different cultures regularly interact. Diversity means that people have different ethnic backgrounds, faiths, economic circumstances, views about social issues, and so on. You will better understand our nation and our world if you understand how cultural diversity affects communication. Consequently, this text, while presenting the most common public speaking norms in the United States, introduces some speaking traditions from other cultures.

What is culture? A **culture** is an integrated system of learned beliefs, values, attitudes, and behaviors that a group accepts and passes along from older to newer members. Don Smith[17] founder of Daystar University in Kenya, compares cultures to onions with outer layers (clothing, art, food, language, and so on) and embedded cores that filter how we view the world (ideologies, folk beliefs, attitudes, values, and so on).[18] In other words, culture exists at both visible and conscious levels and at invisible and subconscious levels; they have relatively stable elements, but they can and do change.

Although members of a society share many commonalities, culture is not spelled C-u-l-t-u-r-e.[19] That is, there's no single "U.S. Culture"; instead, this nation contains many **co-cultures**,[20] groups who share many aspects of the dominant culture, but diverge in some way. The TV show, *Glee*, illustrates co-cultural diversity. Finn is a white, heterosexual male; Kurt is a gay, white teen; Artie is in a wheelchair; Tina is Asian-American, and so on. They work together to create a competitive singing group.

Public speaking matters to cultures, and cultures matter to public speaking, as Professor Charles Conrad explains:

> . . . cultures are communicative creations. They emerge through communication, are maintained through communication, and change through the communicative acts of their members. Simultaneously communication is a cultural creation. Persons' perceptions of the cultures in which they live . . . form the situations that guide and constrain their communication.[21]

David J. & Janice L. Frent Collection/Historical/CORBIS

Many cultural transformations have come about because people willingly argued for change. Women's suffrage was a major theme one hundred years ago; today, the themes are different, but reformers still speak out to create a more just, equitable, and safe society.

Public Speaking in Ancient Cultures

Public speaking has its place in every society. For example, fragments of the oldest book in existence, *The Precepts of Ke'gemni and Ptah-hotep* (ca. 2100 BCE), provided young Egyptians with guidelines for speaking, including (1) do not pervert the truth and (2) avoid speech subjects about which you know nothing.[22]

The medieval Arab scholar, Muhammad ibn 'Abd al-Rahman al-Qzawini (d. 1338), classified the science of eloquence into three parts: (1) *'ilm al-ma' ānī* (the science of meanings), (2) 'ilm al-bayān (the science of clarity), and (3) 'ilm al-badī (the science of ornamentation).[23]

The ancient Chinese scholar, Laozi, advised, "[a] virtuous person does not speak with high-sounding words; one who speaks with high-sounding words is not a virtuous person."[24]

This advice and analysis was practical centuries ago; it's still practical today.

The following sections explain some ways that public speaking and culture interact.

Public Speaking Affects Culture

As Conrad pointed out, cultures can and do change, often because of skillful public speakers who transmit, reinforce, repair, or transform their cultures.[25]

- Speakers who *transmit* cultural resources teach cultural beliefs, values, and behaviors. For example, English language professors teach foreign students how to navigate this culture. Religious leaders teach their beliefs to youth and to converts.
- Those who *reinforce* or support existing cultural elements encourage listeners to persist in positive behaviors or beliefs. Examples include politicians who urge people to keep on voting or inspirational speakers who stress the importance of teamwork.
- Speakers who *restore* matters to a healthy state step in when events threaten to tear apart a community. For instance after a community tragedy, officials provide information essential for re-establishing order and a sense of security.
- Those who *transform* societies become instruments for social change. Prison reform, civil rights legislation, environmental protection—skilled speakers argued for all these changes. Even relatively well-functioning societies can be improved, and people currently argue for hundreds of reforms including reforms in sports and media.

Whether the goal is to transmit, reinforce, repair, or transform culture, we depend on communicators who are willing and competent enough to speak out and perpetuate positive cultural characteristics or, when necessary, who will resist and change cultural elements that need improvement.

How Has Public Speaking Affected Your Campus Culture?

Work with a group to evaluate the role of public speaking in creating and maintaining your college or university.

- What role did public speaking play during the founding years?
- How does your school currently use public speaking to recruit new students and donors?
- What role does ceremonial speaking, such as convocation or commencement addresses, have in maintaining the vision and the values of your institution?
- When issues threaten to divide your campus, how do groups and individuals use public speaking to negotiate differences?

Culture Affects Public Speaking

Some cultural influences on public speaking are obvious. For example, whiteboards are widely used in businesses and schoolrooms but almost never at funerals and rarely in rural Uganda. However, cultures also influence speaking in less obvious ways by providing resources, technology, and cultural expectations.

Cultures Provide Core Resources

core cultural resources beliefs, attitudes, and values (BAV) along with behaviors that provide a logical basis for a culture to define what is necessary, right, doubtful, or forbidden

Each culture offers a pool of **core cultural resources**—systems of intertwined beliefs, attitudes, and values (BAV) that underlie our behaviors in every area of life, including public speaking.[26]

Beliefs are the ideas we mentally accept as true or reject as false. Attitudes are our predispositions to evaluate—either negatively or positively—persons, objects, symbols, and the like. Values are our underlying evaluations of what is important, significant,

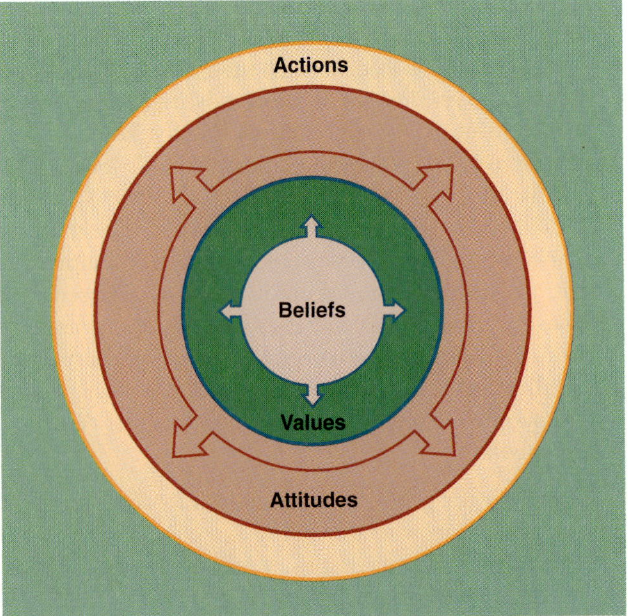

Figure 1.1 Intertwined beliefs, values, attitudes, and actions comprise our core cultural resources.

moral, or right. Finally, behaviors are the actions we consider appropriate or normal. (Chapters 6 and 18 provide more detail about this.) Here are some foundational cultural resources that affect public speaking in the United States:

- A *belief* that we can change society by speaking out and creating public policies instead of giving in to fate.
- Positive *attitudes* toward open forums and negative *attitudes* about suppressing dissent.
- A *value* that places individuality over conformity.
- Standards for predictable speaking and listening *behaviors* that vary according to context.

As you can see, these core resources combine to create expectations for speaking and listening in the United States.

Cultures Provide Technological Aids

The technology available to a culture greatly affects how its members create and exchange messages. A strictly **oral culture** has no way to record, store, or transmit ideas, so speakers and audiences *must* meet face to face. Because everything they know must be memorized, oral groups rely on poems, chants, proverbs, and stories that help them learn and remember their values, beliefs, and traditions.[27]

oral culture culture with no writing and no technology for recording messages apart from face-to-face interactions

In contrast, most cultures today provide at least some access to literacy and to electronic devices that allow people to record their ideas and convey them to audiences separated by both distance and time. You have an almost overwhelming amount of available resources, including printed materials, electronically stored databases, the Internet, and audiovisual resources, to search for speech materials. Additionally, microphones, cameras, sophisticated playback machines, and inventions like presentation software can help you present and record your ideas. You can then post them on a site such as YouTube. Throughout this text you'll find guidelines for using common research and presentation technologies.

Cultures Provide Expectations about Speaking and Listening

According to the Dutch theorist, Geert Hofstede,[28] national cultures vary along an individualistic-collectivist dimension. People in **individualistic cultures** depend on themselves and their immediate families. They're judged on the basis of individual achievement and merits, and they learn to speak up to get their problems solved. The U.S., Australia, and Western European countries score highest on individualism. Members of **collectivist cultures**, in contrast, are born into strong, cohesive in-groups who protect them and to whom they are loyal. They may feel uncomfortable if they, and not the group, are singled out for an honor, and they work hard not to shame others. Many Latin American and Asian countries score highest on collectivism.[29] Compare their pronouns: people from individualistic cultures use comparatively more "I" and "my" words than do people from collectivist cultures who prefer "we" and "our" pronouns. (Have you noticed that English is the only language that capitalizes the word for "I" and not the word for "you"?)[30]

individualistic cultures members of these cultures depend mainly on themselves and are judged on personal merits

collectivist cultures members of these cultures are integrated into an in-group that protects them throughout their lives

Cultures range in the amount and kinds of information they encourage members to express. **Nonexpressive cultures** expect their members to guard their emotions and ideas rather than express them indiscriminately. Japanese, Chinese,[31] Finnish,[32] and many Native American groups are comparatively nonexpressive. As you might guess, someone from these cultures can be overwhelmed at the thought of speaking in public.[33] In contrast, **expressive cultures** encourage people to give their opinions, speak their minds, and let their feelings show. Koreans, Puerto Ricans,[34] African American, and many African cultures[35] are more verbal and confident in speaking out. President Obama is just one example of the many African Americans considered to be a highly skilled speaker.

nonexpressive cultures cultures that value privacy and encourage members to keep their emotions and ideas to themselves rather than to express them publicly

expressive cultures cultures that encourage members to give their opinions, speak their minds, and let their feelings show

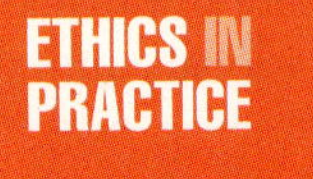

Vir Bonum, Dicendi Peritus

Every culture has sayings that capture cultural ideals in short, pithy statements. The Latin phrase *Vir bonum, dicendi peritus*—"The good person, skilled in speaking"—is a slogan that Quintilian, a popular speech teacher who lived in Rome in the chaotic days of the notorious Emperor Nero, instilled into his students. Roman rhetors knew that persuasive words had power to move people; therefore, they had ethical implications. Put simply, speakers can urge others to act out horrors or to make the world better. Today, "good people, communicating skillfully" are more important than ever in a world where technology opens the possibilities for millions of people to get a wide hearing.

Questions

1. Make a list of individuals, skilled in speaking, who were not "good" persons. (Hitler tops many people's list.)
2. Add to this list Internet sites you think promote negative values or behaviors. (For example, you can find pro-anorexia websites or uploaded videos that demean a specific religion.)
3. How might the principles in the slogan mentioned above apply to the Internet and YouTube generation?
4. Identify situations, real or hypothetical, in which good people want to do something to better their world but lack the skills to present their ideas to those who could support their efforts.

Cultures also influence "who" speaks—and "to whom." Some cultures allow only older adult men who are considered wisest or most knowledgeable to speak, leaving children, young people, non-experts, and women without a voice in public arenas.[36] Sometimes ridicule, misunderstanding, or punishment await the poor, members of minority groups, or people with divergent political views who try to speak out.[37] In addition, access to specific venues is commonly limited. For example, could a minimum-wage worker at a local motel chain enter corporate headquarters and ask for a better retirement plan? Not likely. Can just anyone testify before Congress? No, just those who are invited.[38]

communication style a culture's preferred ways of communicating, given its core assumptions and norms

taboo topics a culture considers inappropriate

Cultures develop a preferred **communication style**[39]—a how-to-speak that's deemed most appropriate. The dominant United States' style includes a *problem orientation*, which means we assume that the world is rational and that we can create solutions to problems by acting on them. The style is *direct*, expecting ideas to be logically organized and go straight to the point. It prefers precise language, not indirect or vague statements. The cultural values of equality and individuality result in *informality*—characterized by conversational delivery—and in *personal involvement*, which leads speakers to share personal experiences that establish common ground with their audiences. Your competency in many public speaking contexts will be judged against these norms.

Sean_Warren/iStockphoto.com

Cultures provide technology for communicating as well as ideas about appropriate speakers, situations, levels of expressiveness, topics, and communication style.

Cultures also influence topics. The Polynesian word *tabu* or **taboo** (inappropriate topics) contrasts with *noa* (discussable topics). Each culture designates some topics as discussable and some as taboo. General topics such as consumerism and the role of media in society are typical of *noa* topics, acceptable in many cultures.[40] However, issues related to human sexuality,[41] personal aspects of religion, death,[42] or criticism of the government—these topics can be considered taboo or confined to an "appropriate" time and place.

Cultural factors such as these can affect how comfortable you feel in a public speaking classroom that teaches Euro-American cultural norms. Appropriate speaking and listening in classrooms or workplace settings may be quite different from your cultural traditions. If so, you can become **bicultural**, knowing how to speak in the dominant culture while appreciating and participating in your own ethnic speech community. In the following example, a Nigerian woman living in the United States explains how she accomplishes this:

bicultural knowing and applying different rules for competent behaviors in two cultures

> At work, . . . I raise my voice as loud as necessary to be heard in meetings. At conferences where I present papers on "Women from the Third World," I make serious arguments about the need for international intervention in countries where women are deprived of all rights. . . . Yet as easily as I switch from speaking English to Ibo [her Nigerian language], . . . I never confuse my two selves.
>
> Hundreds of thousands of women from the Third World and other traditional societies share my experience. We straddle two cultures, cultures that are often in opposition. Mainstream America, the culture we embrace in our professional lives, dictates that we be assertive and independent—like men. Our traditional culture, dictated by religion and years of socialization, demands that we be docile and content in our roles as mothers and wives—careers or not.[43]

As you can see, students from many traditions bring contrasting expectations of "how to" speak into the college classroom. If you judge other traditions by your own culture's standards, misunderstandings and negative evaluations can result.

Recognize Your Cultural Speaking Traditions

What public speaking traditions does your cultural heritage provide? How expressive were you encouraged to be? Were you encouraged or discouraged from speaking because of your ethnicity, your age, your socioeconomic class, or your gender? If so, when and how? What topics are sensitive or taboo? How might your cultural traditions affect your participation and your comfort in this course?

To investigate this topic further, log on to InfoTrac College Edition; find and read Celeste Roseberry-McKibben's article "'Mirror, Mirror on the Wall': Reflections of a 'Third Culture' American." The author was raised in the Philippines, where she was considered a "third-culture" child—not exactly American and not exactly Filipina. As a speech pathologist with a diverse clientele in the U.S., her third-culture status follows her because she looks at customs here at least somewhat through the eyes of a Filipina. Compare and contrast her list of "mainstream American" values with the information presented throughout this chapter.

A Theory and a Model of Communication

The word *communication* is so common that you may not think much about what actually happens when people communicate. However, scholars continue to probe the interrelationships among speakers, messages, listeners, and situations. Current theories and models typically emphasize both speakers and listeners who jointly and actively co-create meaning. We'll first look at the dialogical theory and then turn to the transactional model of communication.

The Dialogical Theory of Communication

dialogical theory of communication theory proposing that face-to-face conversation is the prototype that is foundational to all other communication

Theories are explanations by which scholars provide the general or abstract principles of a field of study. The **dialogical theory of communication** is common in communication studies. Think back to how you first learned to talk. Chances are you spent a lot of time listening and then practicing words and phrases with parents and older relatives. According to the dialogical theory, the give-and-take quality of these first conversations form the foundational pattern for all other communication activities, even public speaking.[44] In this theory, conversation and public speaking share many similarities along with some differences:

respons-ibility speakers' and listeners' mutual engagement with ideas, which allows them to jointly forge meanings

speech genres cultural forms we rely upon when we participate in a specific type of communication

- In both types of communication, nonverbal cues such as facial expressions, gestures, eye contact, and vocal emphasis on specific words add meaning to the message.
- In both types, everyone involved actively engages the ideas presented; they must take ***respons*-ibility**[45] to interact and mutually respond in ways that that co-create meanings. For example, conversation partners have to work together to confirm that what is said is being understood. You might hear something like: "Let's go get coffee." "You mean at Coffee Cottage?" "Yeah, where else?" In public speaking contexts, audiences also engage speakers directly, but they usually wait until the end of the speech to participate in a question-and-answer period.[46]
- Conversations and public speeches each have predictable structures, functions, and lengths. The Russian scholar Mikhail Bahktin explained, "We 'pour' our speech into ready-made forms or **speech genres**. These forms are given to us in the same way in which our native language is given."[47] In other words, we have cultural ways to propose marriage or greet a friend (interpersonal genres or forms), and we have cultural norms for giving an award or a eulogy (public speech genres).
- Meaning in both contexts depends on factors such as "[w]ho says what, where and when, why and for what, in what manner, with and for whom? . . . [A]nd who understands what, where and when, how, why, and for what, in what manner, with or from whom."[48] A conversation with your best friend about a speeding ticket differs from the conversation you have with the police officer and then your parents about that same incident. A resident assistant's report about a specific student incident given in a walnut-paneled boardroom to the university's board of trustees differs from a similar report by the same resident assistant given in a dorm lounge where students munch snacks and sip drinks as they listen. Each situation affects the multiple meanings in the speech act. In short, meanings lie in people[49]; for instance, the resident assistant, the trustees, and the dorm residents will probably differ about the meaning of the incident. The purpose of communication is to get the other person to come to understand and accept your meanings.[50]
- As a general rule, the language and organizational structure of public speeches are more formal, and speeches are more carefully prepared than conversations (although conversational delivery is desirable in public speaking).

Theories, in short, explain a phenomenon or process, and the dialogical theory helps explain the communication process. This theory builds on the prototype of dialogue as foundational to all other communication. However, because theories are generally abstract, many people prefer a diagram or model to help them better understand the concept.

transactional model of communication represents communication as a process in which speakers and listeners work together to create mutual meanings

The Transactional Model of Communication

The **transactional model**[51] shown in Figure 1.2, is one of many ways to think about what happens during communication, and it is the most common. It includes the following components, described by showing how they interact when you give a speech.

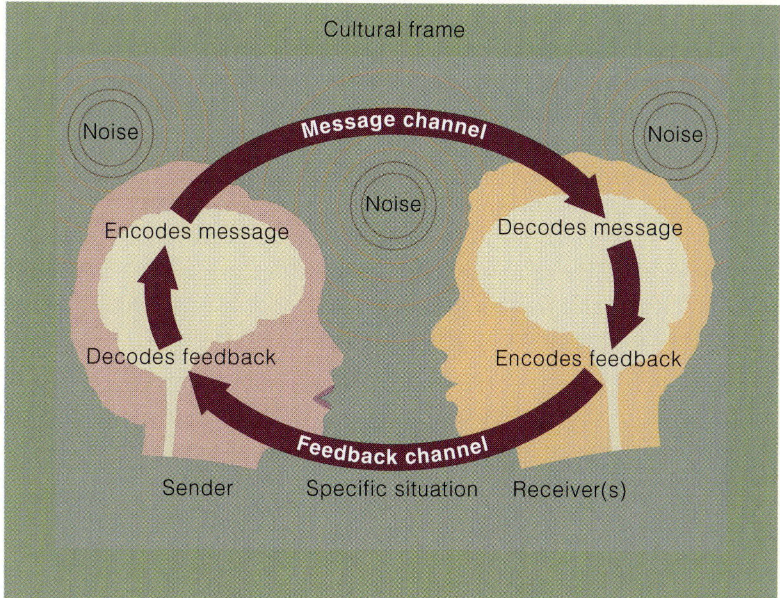

Figure 1.2
The transactional model depicts communication as a dialogical process in which communicators co-create messages in culturally appropriate situations.

- As a *sender-receiver* (or source), you originate or *encode* a message by selecting words (a verbal code) to represent your ideas. As you prepare, you consider your audience, reflecting on what you know about them and their knowledge of and interest in your topic. For instance, you may do a survey to discover their interests, past experiences, their need-to-know, or other pertinent information beforehand.
- Your *message* has a purpose. In your speech classroom, you might be assigned to inform or persuade. In other settings, you might give a report, honor another person's achievements, or try to make your audience laugh. You craft your message in language your audience will understand, using reasoning they accept and illustrations that relate to their lives.
- The face-to-face, voice-to-ear *channel*, along with nonverbal channels such as gestures or tone of voice, is the most common in classrooms. In other settings you might speak in a video conference or record your message digitally and upload it to a fileserver or Internet site where your audience can listen at their leisure.
- *Receivers-senders* hear your words and *decode* or interpret them. They create meanings out of their personal backgrounds and heritages, plus their individual beliefs, values, worries, and judgments. Each listener filters your words through his or her individual perceptions, thoughts, and feelings, and sometimes through the influence of other listeners.
- Your audience sends *feedback*. With face-to-face audiences, some may ask questions, some may nod, frown, smile, or clap. Some may even heckle you. You decode their feedback and adapt to it. For example, if you see confused faces, you might add details to clarify your point. If your listeners seem bored, you might regain attention with an interesting example. Were you to use another channel, such as YouTube, feedback would come in the form of written remarks below your video. In this transactional process of mutual sending-receiving-responding, you and your listeners cooperate in creating meaning.
- *Noise*, or static, can interfere with both the message and its reception. A sore throat that causes you to speak softly might make your words difficult to hear. A leaf blower roaring outside the window (*external noise*) might overwhelm your words. *Internal noise*, such as listeners' worries about being overdrawn at the bank or their hunger

pangs, can also disrupt the process. Finally, *cultural noise* occurs when cultural differences make the message irrelevant or offensive, as when the topic or the manner of the presentation runs counter to a listener's cultural norms.[52]

- Each speech takes place in a specific situation. During the term, you'll speak in a classroom setting. But in the workplace or community, the situations will be more varied. Regardless, room temperature, lighting, room decor, available technology, and seating arrangements all can affect your presentation.
- Finally, as this chapter explained, each speech takes place within a larger cultural framework. Classroom speeches come with expectations about higher education. Other organizations have their ideas about public speaking, and these affect what is considered appropriate and inappropriate in the context.

Although it is not perfect, the transactional model effectively depicts communication as a complex, dynamic process. It further identifies and clarifies some of the many variables that affect the way we cooperate with one another to co-create meanings.

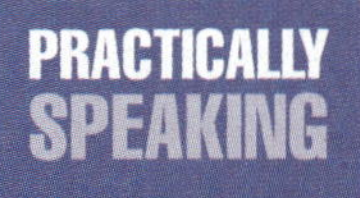

Bruce McQuakay, Native American Activist

Bruce McQuakay is a Native American activist. I first heard him explain some Native American rituals and traditions to a group of school children and their parents.

On what kinds of occasions do you speak? I actually rarely find myself outside of my community, and I'm of very little importance to the big picture. I am but a servant, and I do as asked of me. What I say is solely representative of my own experience, and I have no authority to speak on anyone else's behalf.

Did you ever think you'd be a public speaker someday? As a profession? No. However, I do happen to find myself in front of an audience on occasion, and I find it not much different than a small group. Just more people.

What are some of your cultural groups' views about public speaking? Anyone who has been asked to speak has a purpose for speaking. It is considered extremely rude to talk out of turn or to interrupt. I have mostly witnessed that only those people who are chosen to speak are the ones who speak.

Questions

1. One theme of this chapter is that culture influences public speaking. How do McQuakay's answers reflect this theme?
2. Another chapter theme is that public speaking influences culture. How might sharing your cultural traditions and speaking from your own experience—which McQuakay emphasizes—help build a stronger society?

Summary

This chapter introduced some benefits you can gain by studying public speaking from a perspective of cultural diversity. The study of rhetoric, a cornerstone of a liberal arts education, can equip you with critical thinking skills that are useful in everyday interactions. Along the way, you will learn skills that are personally and professionally valuable in a culture that relies on skilled speakers and listeners.

By definition, cultures emerge, maintain themselves, and change through communication. Cultures include both the visible and the underlying (embedded) aspects of a society; they are complex and contain many co-cultural groups, which often have different norms for speaking and listening. Culture affects public speaking, and public speaking affects culture. Through public speaking, we transmit core cultural beliefs, values, and attitudes to newcomers who must learn appropriate behaviors in specific contexts. Public speeches reinforce or support culture as it is, and through speaking we repair or restore community when it is threatened. We also change or transform cultural elements that are outmoded or dysfunctional.

Our cultures also affect our public speaking in a number of ways. They provide us with core beliefs, values, attitudes, and behaviors that shape our own speeches and our responses to others' messages. In addition, our technologically advanced society provides a variety of resources we can use to research topics and present our speeches. Finally, our cultural heritages provide expectations regarding the *how*, the *who*, and the *what* of public speaking. Of course, within each culture, individual personalities and preferences also shape the ways we communicate.

The chapter closed with a comparison of conversation and public speaking, followed by the transactional model of communication. Dialogical theory assumes that face-to-face conversations are foundational for all our other communication activities, including public speaking. Although public speaking shares similarities with conversations, it also differs in significant ways. The communication model depicts in visual form the transactional nature of communication. It emphasizes that both the originator of the message and the receiver must cooperate if they are to *transact* or negotiate meaning. Although public speakers originate messages, they should remember that meanings lie in people, so they must adapt to feedback both as they prepare and as they speak. Listeners participate by actively decoding information and encoding feedback. All this communication, which can be negatively affected by both internal and external noise, takes place within a specific situation and cultural frame.

STUDY AND REVIEW

Your online resources for *Public Speaking: Concepts and Skills for a Diverse Society* offer a broad range of tools that will help you better understand the material in this chapter, complete assignments, and succeed on tests. Your online resources feature the following:

- Speech videos with critical viewing questions, speech outlines, and transcripts.
- Interactive versions of this chapter's Stop and Check activities, as well as Application and Critical Thinking Exercises.
- Speech Builder Express and InfoTrac College Edition.
- Weblinks related to chapter content.
- Study and review tools such as self-quizzes, an interactive glossary, and downloadable audio summaries.

You can access your online resources at the CourseMate for *Public Speaking: Concepts and Skills for a Diverse Society.* Log in at **http://www.cengage.com/login**, using the access code that came with your book or that you bought online at **http://www.cengagebrain.com**.

KEY TERMS

The terms below are defined in the margins throughout this chapter.

bicultural 9
civic engagement 3
co-cultures 4
collectivist cultures 7
communication style 8
core cultural resources 6
critical thinking 2
culture 4
dialogical theory of communication 10
expressive cultures 7
individualistic cultures 7
nonexpressive cultures 7
oral culture 7
public speaking 2
respons-ibility 10
rhetoric 2
speech genres 10
taboo 8
transactional model of communication 10

APPLICATION AND CRITICAL THINKING EXERCISES

1. If people define the word *public* too narrowly, they may think of public speakers as politicians speaking at conventions but not as teachers making an announcement at a PTA meeting. Write your definition of "public." Then, make a list of specific publics you have already addressed and those you may address someday.
2. To gain experience in speaking publicly, prepare an announcement using the guidelines in Appendix B and deliver it to your classmates. Look for upcoming campus or community events that would interest your audience.
3. To understand the importance of critical thinking skills, work with a group to select a short video on YouTube, a news report, or an ad to analyze. Begin by giving your first impressions. What does the piece you've selected say or suggest? Then probe deeper and identify the assumptions on which it relies. Next, ask question about those assumptions. Finally, compare your first impressions with your impressions about the selection after you've examined it more carefully. Discuss with your classmates the value of critical analysis.
4. What stereotypes do you hold about the word *rhetoric?* The Internet has many sources of information on this topic. Visit **weblink 1.1** and do some of the "Cool Exercises" or watch a couple of speeches. This will help you understand the value of rhetoric. You can access this link through your CourseMate for *Public Speaking,* Chapter 1 resources.

5. Throughout the term, listen for the word *rhetoric* as it is used in public discourse. Each time you encounter the word, decide whether it's being used negatively, positively, or neutrally. Note if any of the sources speak of rhetoric as essential in a free society.
6. Interview a person working in the career you hope to enter after you graduate. Ask what opportunities exist for public speaking within that occupation. Ask if and how public speaking is related to the higher-paying, more prestigious jobs within that career.
7. Many online speeches can help you see the relationship between public speaking and culture. One such example is Barack Obama's speech on race, "A More Perfect Union," given in response to widely disseminated video clips of controversial statements by his pastor. It's available online. Watch it outside of class and then come to class prepared to discuss how it might function to transmit, reinforce, restore, and/or transform culture.
8. Elaborate on the transactional model of communication by selecting a communication event from your own life and analyze it by identifying and explaining each element of the model.

© Tim Timmerman

CHAPTER
2

THIS CHAPTER WILL HELP YOU

- Acquire skills to overcome process anxiety
- Explain the five canons of rhetoric: invention, disposition, style, memory, and delivery
- Develop strategies to deal with performance anxiety
- Develop strategies to deal with physiological anxiety
- Develop strategies to deal with psychological anxiety
- Learn skills for effective rehearsal

Giving Your First Speech: Developing Confidence

KING GEORGE VI OF ENGLAND faced two major problems: Hitler's masterful but evil oratory was mobilizing the German army to conquer England, and King George VI was a stutterer, not only fearful of communicating, but also incapable of speaking fluently. The movie *The King's Speech* tells how he faced his fears and inadequacies, hired a speech coach, and effectively learned how to motivate the British people during World War II. (You can hear one of the king's speeches, full of pauses, on You Tube.)

Like most people, even kings can experience communication anxiety in at least some situations. We may focus on inadequacies—real and perceived; we may focus on our lack of experience or on an intimidating audience. We don't always know what to say. In short, many communication contexts are scary. Consequently, researchers have conducted thousands of studies looking for causes, effects, and cures of **communication apprehension (CA)**,[1] which is commonly defined as "the fear or anxiety associated with either real or anticipated communication with another person or persons."[2] It is the dread of possible negative reactions you might experience when you communicate.[3] CA is linked to inborn temperament traits such as shyness.[4]

communication apprehension (CA) the fear or dread of negative responses you might experience because you speak out

One context that strikes fear into many, even most hearts is public speaking. Call it stage fright or **public speaking anxiety (PSA)**, whatever name you prefer, the term refers to the common feelings of dread people experience at the thought of facing an audience and performing a speech.[5] Here are some specific reasons students gave for their PSA:

public speaking anxiety (PSA) fear or dread specifically related to speaking in public

> Standing in front of people, knowing that they are judging you.
>
> CLAIRE

> Knowing what to speak about.
>
> JONATHAN

> I am very shy, and I don't like to talk much to a single person, let alone a group.*
>
> REESE

Their comments reveal two types of anxiety: **process anxiety** (not knowing how to create a speech) and **performance anxiety** (nervousness about actually giving the speech). The goal of this chapter is to help you decrease both types by

process anxiety fear due to lack of confidence in knowing how to prepare a speech

performance anxiety fear of forgetting or of poorly presenting a speech

Hulton-Deutsch Collection/CORBIS

The award-winning movie *The King's Speech* tells the story of how the stammering King George VI of England learned to speak in spite of his fears, when his role as monarch demanded that he encourage and motivate his nation to resist the German war machine during World War II.

*Used by permission of Reese Wilson.

demystifying the speechmaking process and by giving you strategies for dealing with nervousness, including ways to manage both its physical and mental manifestations. Putting this information into practice will increase your overall speaking competence.

Develop Skills to Overcome Process Anxiety

"I'm counting on you to give a speech next week, so here's your assignment . . ." When you first hear these words—whether at work, at school, or in an organization you belong to—you may begin to experience tension. This is called **anticipatory speech anxiety**,[6] and it is highest just after the speech is announced.[7] Why? Perhaps it's fear of the unknown—like finding yourself in unfamiliar territory without a map.[8] Fortunately, studying speech principles, observing others speak, and actually speaking yourself removes some of the mystery from the process. As speechmaking becomes more familiar, most people experience less process anxiety and the panicky feelings that accompany it.[9]

anticipatory speech anxiety tension experienced at the mere thought of giving a speech

Think of it this way: Those basketball stars you see so effectively playing the game learned the fundamentals step-by-step. They worked on free throws, practicing just the right wrist movement. They watched good players, studied basketball terminology, and developed their personal skills. Although their performance on the court may seem effortless, a lot of hard work got them there. Public speaking is similar; polished performers spend time learning the fundamentals of speech. This text and your course are designed to help you develop your skills and learn the terminology associated with public speaking.

As Chapter 1 pointed out, classical Greek and Roman academies focused on developing public speakers. There, early speech educators identified five major categories of good speechmaking—each category contained a set or **canon** of principles, standards, or guidelines that students should master to become effective orators. The five **canons of rhetoric**[10] are: (1) invention—creating speech content; (2) disposition or arrangement—organizing speech materials; (3) style—choosing effective language; (4) memory—learning the major ideas; and (5) delivery—actually performing the speech. (See Figure 2.1) Learning the principles in the canons will help you understand the process of speech creation.

canon a set of principles, standards, norms, or guidelines

canons of rhetoric principles, standards, norms, or guidelines for creating and delivering a speech

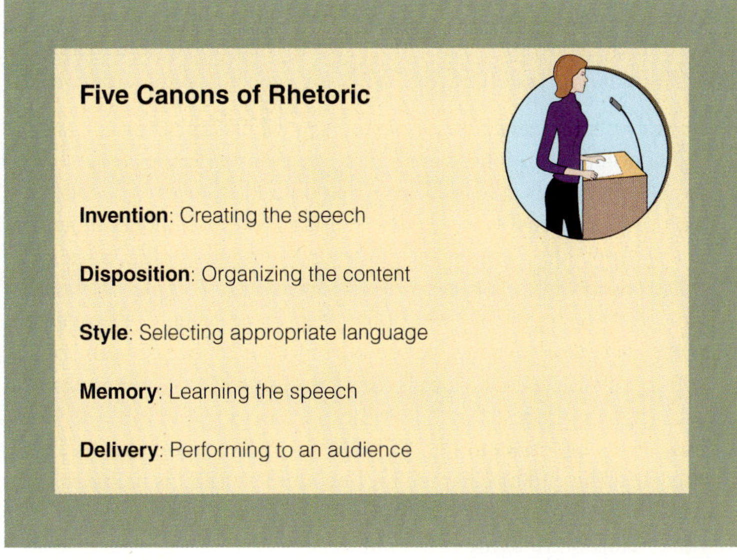

Figure 2.1
The Romans identified five canons of rhetoric. Each canon contains principles, standards, norms, or guidelines for one aspect of speechmaking.

Create Your Speech: The Canon of Invention

canon of invention principles for designing a speech that meets a need of a specific audience

The **canon of invention** provides guidelines for creating the content of your speech. Just as an inventor designs a product to meet a particular need, you will design a speech to meet a need for a specific audience in a specific situation. Principles in this canon help you analyze your audience, select an appropriate topic and purpose, gather evidence, and develop reasonable and logical arguments and explanations. This text devotes nine chapters to this vital canon, but as a general introduction and to help you prepare your first speech, each principle is briefly summarized here.

Consider the Audience and the Setting

Your first task is to think about your audience and their needs. Do they need information? Do they need motivation to act? Thinking about your audience in three general areas will help you select your topic and choose interesting supporting materials. Examine their demographic characteristics, their psychological perspectives, and the situation in which you will speak. (Each area is covered more fully in Chapter 6.)

- Demographic information includes such things as gender and age. Notice, also, features such as religious jewelry or clothing that suggest particular interests, affiliations, and perspectives. Even the region you live in can give ideas for topics that need to be addressed.
- Psychological information includes their attitudes and beliefs about your topic. Strike up conversations with people as a way to learn more about them.
- Finally, consider the situation in which you will speak. Lighting, ventilation, acoustics, and room layout make a difference. Other factors, such as time of day, matter as well. Is your audience typically hungry or sleepy during the time you're scheduled to speak?

Being mindful of details such as these will help you move to the next task—choosing your subject and purpose.

Choose a Topic

"I don't know what to talk about." This may be your first thought when a classroom assignment is given. (In some contexts, such as in an organization or workplace, your topic will be more obvious.) However, the first class assignment is usually either a self-introduction or the introduction of a classmate. If so, topic choice is partly done for you, but finding an interesting focus is still a challenge. If you must introduce a classmate, set up an interview that will uncover one or more unusual facts about the person, and focus your speech around these details. A self-introduction may create more anxiety because *you* are in the spotlight. The information you choose to reveal will create your classmates' initial impression of you. With any speech assignment, consider these guidelines:

- *Be sure you understand the expectations.* You will be embarrassed—and perhaps penalized—if you prepare carefully only to discover that you've misunderstood the assignment. So pay special attention to guidelines that describe the general requirements and time limits for the speech. If you are confused, ask questions. The examples at the end of chapters and in Appendix C, as well as those on the book's online resources provide numerous illustrations of how other students successfully completed classroom assignments. In workplace situations, knowing what's expected will help you avoid unpleasant surprises.
- *Reveal something unusual.* Avoid boring your audience with something everyone has experienced; instead, search for a unique focus. Students have described unusual jobs (fighting forest fires), travel experiences (going on a service trip to Haiti), and humorous events (singing "My Girl"—in German—in a high school play). In the speech at the end of Chapter 15, Benjamin shared his memories of 9/11; his father, an Air Force pilot who often flew Air Force II, was in Florida with President Bush at the time planes were flying into buildings.

- *Select a significant topic.* Have you had life-changing experiences? Have you learned important lessons that others could also learn? Consider incorporating your personal adventures or insights into a speech. For her first class assignment, Mona described her decision to return to school after a divorce, and Britney told of her experiences growing up deaf.
- *Consider a story format.* Sharing a story is often a good way to connect with your audience. In fact, Chapter 15 describes narrative speaking in detail; there, you'll find the exemplum pattern that is especially effective for introductory speeches. At the end of this chapter, you'll find Natasha's story of her parents' intercultural marriage.
- *Consider your listeners' sensibilities.* Your purpose is not to shock your audience by revealing highly personal information or potentially embarrassing details. This is an opportunity to try to think from the diverse perspectives of audience members.
- *Try out your ideas on people you trust.* Discuss your audience and your assignment with close friends or associates. If you have two or three ideas, elicit opinions about each one.

If you have been considering your audience all along, you should have a pretty good sense of what would and would not be appropriate topics.

Identify Your Purpose

After you have selected your topic, identify your reason for speaking, given your specific audience. What response do you want from them? Your answer to this question determines your general purpose. Most speeches focus on one of the following four goals:

- Do you want your audience to learn something? If so, your general purpose is *to inform.*
- Do you want them to respond by believing or doing something? Are you trying to reinforce their beliefs or behaviors? If so, your general purpose is *to persuade.*
- Do you want them simply to laugh and enjoy themselves? If so, your major purpose is *to entertain.*
- Do you want to highlight and reinforce a particular cultural ideal? If so, your general purpose is *to commemorate.*

Chapter 5 describes these purposes in greater detail.

Charles Choi

Interesting and unusual personal experiences often make good speech topics. Natasha told of growing up as a child in an intercultural marriage.

Gather Speech Materials

Although you are probably familiar with the topic you choose, you may need to fill the some gaps in your knowledge by doing research. A reference librarian can help you design a research strategy, or log onto your library's website to search for information in print, online, and media resources. These resources have been scrutinized for accuracy and usefulness before they are added to the collection. Television and radio programs can also provide useful information. And of course, the Internet is a major source of data for people who know how to think critically about what they find there. Finally, this text has online resources to help you do your research.

Although an introductory speech generally relies less on outside research and more on personal experiences or on an interview with the subject, you may need to consult some sources. For example, before Brent introduced himself by talking about the most interesting job he ever had (working at the Oregon Garden), he read brochures from the garden and studied its website for information. Chapters 7 and 8 describe research and supporting materials.

If you are assigned to introduce a classmate, schedule an interview for an uninterrupted time in a quiet place—and then be on time. Bring a list of questions and record your conversation (with permission only) or take notes as you talk. Be sure you understand what you are told by asking questions such as, "Could you explain your German class in more detail?" To avoid any misunderstandings, summarize the major ideas as you conclude.

Organize Your Ideas: The Canon of Disposition or Arrangement

canon of disposition or **arrangement** guidelines for organizing a speech

Once you have your information in hand, your next step is to arrange your ideas so that they make sense. The principles of speech organization make up the **canon of disposition** or **arrangement.**

Most speeches in the Western speaking tradition have three major parts: the introduction, the body, and the conclusion. An introduction orients your audience toward the subject. The body of the speech, which generally takes up most of your speaking time, follows; here, you explain and develop your major ideas. Finally, a memorable conclusion rounds out the speech. Taken as a whole, the outline looks like this:

I. **INTRODUCTION** In general, introductions have these four major functions which were identified by the first-century Roman educator Quintilian:[11]
   A. Draw audience attention to the topic.
   B. Relate the topic to their concerns.
   C. Link yourself to the subject.
   D. Preview the major points.

II. **SPEECH BODY** Here, you present and develop your major ideas, using enough evidence to clarify and support each point. There are many ways to organize speeches, and patterns such as topical, problem-solution, and chronological will be discussed in more detail in Chapter 9. These patterns result in a linear arrangement, as shown by this speech outline:
   A. First main point
      1. Support
      2. Support
   B. Second main point
      1. Support
      2. Support

III. **CONCLUSION** Good speakers don't stop abruptly. Instead, they provide a sense of closure that ties the ideas together and leaves the audience with something to take away with them. Conclusions typically have these elements:
   A. A transition to the conclusion
   B. A reference to the introduction
   C. A summary of the major ideas
   D. A final memorable statement

Connect Your Ideas

Your major work is done; now it's time to weave your ideas together so that your speech flows smoothly from point to point. Words and phrases that link your ideas with one another are called **connectives**. Simple connectives include words such as *first*, *next*, and *finally*. More complex connectives, such as "After I failed to talk my German teacher out of making me perform, I decided I had no choice but to embarrass myself miserably in front of the entire student body," summarize where your speech has been and where it is going. Connectives help your listeners keep their place in the speech by linking the various points to one another and to the speech as a whole.

connectives words and phrases used to tie the ideas together

Once you have gathered materials and selected an organizational pattern, you can then choose precise wording and learn your speech well enough to deliver it to an audience. The principles for these aspects of speechmaking are found in the final three canons of rhetoric: style, memory, and delivery.

Choose Suitable Language: The Canon of Style

When asked "What do you think it means when someone says, 'I like your style?'" two students responded:

> You would most likely mean that you like the way I carry myself or the way I act.
>
> MATT

> It would probably mean that you like something about my personality or the way I handle things and people.
>
> JOSH

A dictionary would say they're right. Style can mean your individuality as expressed in your actions and tastes.[12] However, in rhetoric, **style** refers to language. Because the **canon of style** contains principles for using language effectively in both speaking and writing, you have probably consulted a style manual for your writing classes.

style in rhetoric, style refers to language

canon of style principles for choosing effective language

Put the finishing touches on your ideas by polishing the words of the speech, always with an ear tuned to your listeners. Here are a few general guidelines for effective use of language in public speaking:

- Choose vocabulary and grammar that fit both the occasion and the audience. This means adapting to audience characteristics such as occupation, age, or educational level.
- Omit offensive language such as swear words or demeaning language.
- Choose understandable words. Either define technical jargon or replace it with more familiar terminology.
- Minimize slang expressions. Language used in public speeches is generally more formal than language used in everyday conversation.

More detailed information on the canon of style is provided in Chapter 12.

Learn and Present Your Speech: The Canons of Memory and Delivery

canon of memory guidelines to help you remember your ideas

memorized delivery learning the speech by heart, then reciting it

manuscript delivery reading a speech

impromptu delivery speaking with little advanced preparation

extemporaneous delivery preparing a speech carefully in advance but choosing the exact wording during the speech itself

Because they lacked index cards, teleprompters, and other memory aids, Roman educators taught their students elaborate techniques for learning a speech by heart. However, the **canon of memory** is often called *the lost canon* because so few people in this culture rely on memory alone and because **memorized delivery** can be risky. Forgetting even a few simple words can lead to public embarrassment—something you definitely want to avoid. **Manuscript delivery**, in which you write out your entire speech and then read it to your audience, helps you remember your ideas, but it is generally more useful for formal talks than for classroom or workplace speeches where reading might mean you lose important eye contact with listeners. Also, spur-of-the-moment **impromptu delivery**, where you stand up and speak with little advanced preparation is not recommended for most classroom assignments, although it is common in workplace settings or social events for someone to be asked to "say a few words" on a familiar topic.

Instead, most classroom and workplace settings prefer **extemporaneous delivery**, in which you carefully prepare your remarks in advance but choose the exact wording as you speak. With this method, you gather your materials, organize them carefully, and then jot down key ideas, single words, phrases, and statistics on note cards that you later use to jog your memory during the talk itself. In short, you arrange your main ideas, but you choose the exact wording as you go. Chapter 14 elaborates on these four delivery methods, and Chapter 11 further explains content outlines and speaking outlines.

Rehearsal is a vital part of the preparation process, but the amount of time needed for rehearsal depends on several factors including your level of experience, your familiarity with the topic, your speech length, and your level of anxiety. Interestingly, in a recent study researchers had students log the amount of time they spent in each of the canons. The area that made a difference in grades was rehearsal.[13]

Here are a few rehearsal tips: Find a quiet place where you can practice your speech orally and silently, using your note cards. Recruit friends or family—basically anyone who can act as an audience, provide feedback, troubleshoot problems, and let you deliver your speech to actual listeners. Go through the speech several times, each time selecting slightly different words. Focus on looking away from your notes and communicating conversationally. Although practice may not make perfect, you can at least have the confidence that comes from careful preparation.

canon of delivery rules or standards for presenting a speech

Principles found in the **canon of delivery** provide guidelines on the four delivery methods described earlier and on nonverbal behaviors, such as gestures and eye contact. In brief, these tips make a more skillful performance:

- Make eye contact with your listeners.
- Maintain pleasant facial expressions.
- Avoid speaking in a monotone voice.
- Smile at appropriate times.
- Assume a posture of confidence.
- Incorporate appropriate gestures.
- Speak conversationally.
- Stay within the time limits.

Focus throughout, not on giving something *to* your audience, but on creating something *with* them.

The guidelines found in the five canons of rhetoric build process competence. You learn the skills of audience analysis, topic and purpose selection, and research

Gender Differences in PSA[14]

Do women experience more PSA than men? In a variety of stressful situations, such as test taking, numerous studies indicated that females in general have stronger physical and psychological reactions than males. Consequently, communication researchers wanted to know if this trend carried over into public speaking contexts. They found that females do, in fact, report more communication anxiety than males. In the public speaking classroom, both males and females went through all four milestones of speech anxiety, but females were more likely to react more strongly than males, possibly because they tend to be more cautious about communicating when they know they will be judged on their performance. One of the best ways for both males and females to lessen high levels of anxiety is to reduce uncertainty about the assignment—in other words, to develop process competence.

Photos.com/Jupiter Images

(invention). Then you develop skills in organizing or arranging your ideas into meaningful patterns (disposition), choosing appropriate language (style), and learning your major points (memory), so that you can present them effectively (delivery). For additional information on the canons of rhetoric, follow links on the website The Forest of Rhetoric. Go to **weblink 2.1**. (You can access this through your CourseMate for *Public Speaking*, Chapter 2 resources.)

BUILD YOUR SPEECH

Your First Speech

Using the five canons of rhetoric, prepare a self-introduction or the introduction of a classmate. Throughout your preparation, consider the following questions:

1. Do I understand the assignment?
2. Is my topic somewhat unusual? If not, do I have a unique or novel approach?
3. How will I adapt this speech to this audience?
4. Which friends can I ask to listen to me rehearse?

For additional help building your first and subsequent speeches, use your online resources to access Speech Builder Express.

Develop Strategies to Overcome Performance Anxiety

physiological anxiety bodily responses to a perceived threat (increased heart rate, adrenaline rush)

psychological anxiety mental stress about a perceived threat

Performance anxiety comes in two forms: physiological and psychological. **Physiological anxiety** is your bodily response to the feared event. **Psychological anxiety** is your mental worry, dread, and feelings of inadequacy about the performance itself. This section discusses a number of specific skills you can use in combination to overcome both kinds of nervousness.

Develop Strategies to Deal with Physiological Responses

fight-or-flight mechanism physiological mechanism your body automatically activates when threatened; helps you fight or flee

You know from experience how your body responds to dangerous situations. You might have a "deer-in-the-headlights" response in which you freeze or become rigid in the face of danger. Or you might experience the **fight-or-flight mechanism**—a rush of adrenalin that prepares you to race away from the danger or stay to fight the threat. Unfortunately, your body doesn't distinguish between physically threatening situations (where you actually need extra physical energy to escape) and psychologically threatening experiences (where your increased heart rate, butterflies, and adrenaline rush only add to your stress). Ralph Behnke and Chris Sawyer[15] identify four milestones of anxiety-producing events: (1) *anticipation*, the prespeaking period; (2) *confrontation*, beginning the speech; (3) *adaptation*, completing the speech; (4) *release*, the period lasting one minute after the speech. Anxiety peaks in the anticipation period and steadily decreases, virtually disappearing in the release milestone, although some symptoms may linger.[16] (See Figure 2.2.)

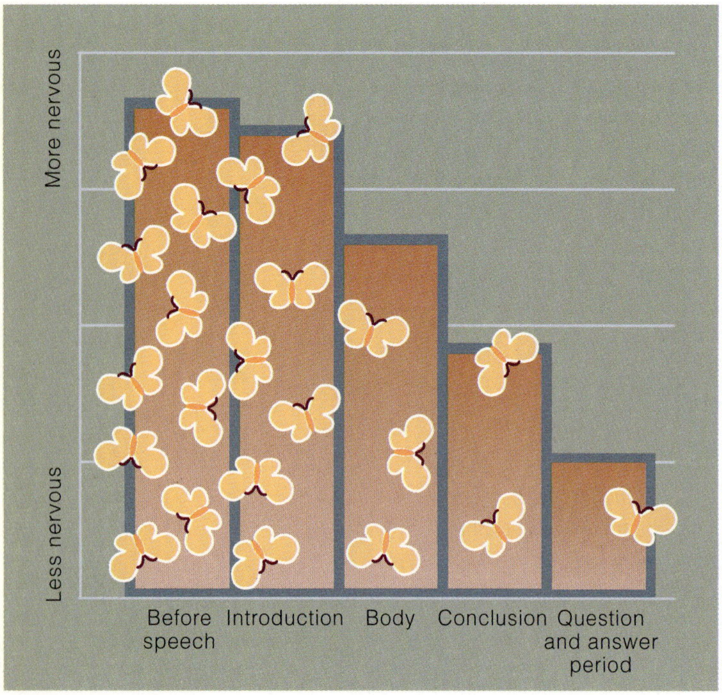

Figure 2.2
Performance Anxiety Knowing that anxiety is greater at certain periods can help you control your nervousness by planning strategies that enable you to get through these periods.

Here's how a beginning speech student described the process:

> As I sit in class, my anxiety level increases by the minute. Right before and as I walk to the front of the room, I use all my power to hide how nervous I am. I take a deep breath and start talking. During the beginning of my speech, anxiety is the worst. My nervous habits show through most in the beginning. As I continue my speech, it gets easier and I become more comfortable. By the conclusion, I'm usually cool, calm, and collected!
>
> EMILY

To counteract this type of tension, prepare beforehand by getting a good night's sleep and then on speech day, work off your excess energy by engaging in some form of physical exercise such as weight lifting, brisk walking, or running. Try to relax by listening to soothing music. Don't skip breakfast or lunch, and limit your sugar and caffeine intake if these substances make you feel wired. Just before you speak, focus on relaxing your major muscle groups and breath slowly and deeply.

Systematic Desensitization

If you are extremely nervous, you can try **systematic desensitization**,[17] a technique designed to minimize the physical effects of PSA when you can't escape or avoid speaking. The underlying concept is that you can't be relaxed and tense at the same time, so this process teaches you how to relax physically as you think your way through increasingly intense scenarios. Psychologists developed it to deal with irrational fears of nonpoisonous snakes, but researchers have also found that the techniques help alleviate public speaking anxiety.

systematic desensitization process designed to lessen physical reactions to stress; teaches how to relax while thinking about frightening speech events

There are three basic activities: (1) construct a list of frightening activities and put them in order, from least to most frightening, (2) learn some principles of relaxation, and (3) learn to relax as you think your way through your list of progressively threatening situations.

To apply the techniques, first, list about fifteen public speaking activities and order your list, from the least to the most frightening. A list might range from reading about a speech in the newspaper (not threatening) to giving a live speech on national television (terrifying). Receiving a speech assignment and giving a carefully prepared classroom speech will lie somewhere in between. Include things you can imagine happening but that you've never seen, such as fainting in the middle of the speech. Make each incident detailed and vivid. Interestingly, researchers have found that humor is helpful, so something as crazy as "during my speech a puppy runs into the room and bites my leg" can go on your list. Sort your list into five piles: low, medium low, medium, medium high, and high, then order items from lowest to highest within the pile. Set this aside for a day.

Next, practice some progressive relaxation techniques. First, breathe deeply . . . hold the breath . . . release it . . . repeat several times. Next tense and relax muscle groups, starting with the legs. Tighten your leg muscles . . . hold . . . hold . . . relax. Breathe, hold, and release your breath again. Continue the tighten-hold-relax process as you move up your body, from foot to head. Breathe-hold-release between each group of muscles. After you have tensed and relaxed all your muscle groups, completely relax, breathing deeply.

While you're still relaxed, pull out an anxiety pile; start with the lowest item, and imagine yourself doing it for a tolerable time. (This may only last ten seconds for very high anxiety items.) Stop. Assess your anxiety level (1–10 scale). Relax again. Go back to the item and repeat the process, assessing your anxiety level each time you end. When you no longer feel anxious about one item, move on to the next. Do just a few per day. When you begin the next day, start with the last item from the previous session.[18]

As you might imagine, this technique only works if you have developed the skills described earlier in the canons of rhetoric. Without learning the process of creating a speech, you may still be very nervous.

Develop Strategies to Deal with Psychological Anxiety

Although you may know better, you might hear an internal voice saying, "I don't know what I'm doing. I'll forget halfway through. I probably won't get my ideas across. They'll see my knees shake." Researchers have identified two areas of vulnerability: your level of confidence (I've never done this before; I'm embarrassed about my looks; I'll flunk) and your expectations regarding the audience's reactions (they'll make fun of me; they won't pay attention; they'd rather be somewhere else). Self-talk is called **internal monologue** (I-M).[19] Negative I-M contributes to negative stress, which, according to Mt. Sinai Medical Center, occurs when you believe the demands of the situation exceed your ability to cope.[20] Although negative self-talk adds to your discomfort, it's not fatal.

internal monologue (I-M) self-talk

Control Your Internal Monologue

cognitive modification identifying negative thoughts and replacing them with positive ones

Mt. Sinai experts suggest that one way to manage stress is to change your perceptions. That is, learn to control your I-M by a process called **cognitive modification**. Identify negative thoughts and replace them with positive ones[21] in four areas: the message, the audience, yourself, and the assignment:

- To think positively about the message, select an interesting topic that your audience will find relevant. Give yourself enough time for research and organization, and check the dictionary to make sure you know how to pronounce unfamiliar words. Keep in mind your goal for the speech. Do everything you can to feel confident about the speech content.
- To promote positive thoughts about the audience, think of each listener as an individual with personal quirks. Specific individuals are not threatening, so why should the group be intimidating?[22] Remember that audience members are probably just as nervous when they speak and that they are not experts in your subject. Assume that they want you to succeed. (If your first language is not English, think of how your audience would feel if they had to give a speech in *your* native language.)
- Maintain a positive self-image by concentrating on things you do well. Remind yourself that your worth as a person is unrelated to your skill as a novice public speaker and that competence develops with experience.
- Finally, think realistically about the assignment.[23] Don't take a world-class orator as a model of what your classroom speech should look and sound like. Instead, watch examples of beginning public speaking students fulfilling an assignment. This book and its accompanying materials provide many sample speeches that will give you reasonable expectations for student speeches.

Remember, too, that being nervous does not mean you're doing a bad job. Most students who watch videos of their speeches are surprised at how calm they appear, knowing how nervous they felt. The fact is that some nervousness can energize you and make you appear more vital and enthusiastic.[24]

Use Visualization

visualization rehearsing by using your imagination to envision your speech from start to finish

A form of positive self-talk or mental strategizing that athletes and musicians use regularly is called **visualization**. Here, you see yourself successfully performing a complex task. Professors Joel Ayres, Theodore Hopf, and their associates have taught thousands of students how to use visualization techniques to ease their anxiety. They found that people who use these techniques during their preparation are less apprehensive and report fewer negative thoughts during their speeches.[25] This is true even for speakers who tend to freeze under stress.[26] The suggested process goes like this:

1. In a quiet place, picture all the details from the beginning to the end of your speech.
2. Mentally place yourself in the audience and pretend you are watching yourself give your speech.
3. Imagine yourself as a competent, well-prepared performer who stands confidently, stresses important words, pauses effectively, and makes appropriate gestures.
4. Think about the audience responding positively with nods, smiles, and interest.

Assess Your Public Speaking Anxiety

Take this test to self-assess your anxiety regarding public speaking. In the blank beside the statement, write the number of the response that best reflects your feelings.

0 = Rarely
1 = Sometimes
2 = Usually
3 = Almost always

______ 1. I begin to get nervous the moment the speech is assigned.
______ 2. I feel panicky because I don't know how to create a speech.
______ 3. I usually feel nervous the day before I have to speak.
______ 4. The night before the speech I can't sleep well.
______ 5. I'm afraid people will think I'm dumb or boring or weird.
______ 6. On the morning of the speech, I am really tense.
______ 7. I find it difficult to think positively about giving a speech.
______ 8. I think my physical reactions are greater than those that other people experience.
______ 9. During my speech I think I'll actually faint.
______ 10. I continue to worry even after the speech is over.

Add Your Scores

______ Total score
0–5 You are virtually fearless.
6–15 Your level of anxiety is quite normal.
16–25 Your level of anxiety may give you problems.
26–30 Consider making an appointment with your professor. Go back and look at the areas that bother you the most, and develop specific strategies from this chapter to help you with your unique stresses.

5. Continue to visualize yourself completing your speech, gathering your notes, making final eye contact with the audience, and returning to your seat.
6. Finally, imagine yourself back in the audience, delighted to be through!

Two key elements accompany successful visualization: You must create vivid images, and you must control the images you generate.[27]

Believe it or not, research shows that most highly anxious students finish their speech class feeling less anxious[28] because of the process of **habituation**. This means that anxiety lessens when an experience is repeated over time and the anticipated negative outcomes are not as bad as expected.[29] Jennifer's comments support this idea:

habituation lessening anxiety by successfully repeating an experience over time

> I think it was really good that we did so many speeches because when we did it so many times, I was less nervous each time.

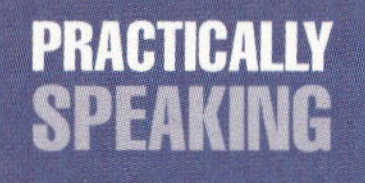

Manfred Tschan, Health Professor and Soccer Coach

Traci Filtcraft

Manfred Tschan

Manfred Tschan, has coached numerous soccer teams and taught many stress management classes about sports psychology. One assignment is to write journal entries about personally stressful situations, and public speaking regularly comes up—by many, many students. Tschan says his students can't think of anything harder to do than to give speeches in other classes.

What do you teach them about dealing with their anxiety? I use a model from Rainer Martens, a sports psychologist from Michigan State, who says stress derives from the relationship between your uncertainty about the outcome and the importance of that outcome. I use four points:

Perception of an imbalance

between an *objective demand*

and your perceived *response capability*,

where failure is perceived to have *serious consequences.*

This gives students four areas to manage, change, or improve:

1. Sometimes they can change the *objective demand*; sometimes they can't. Some people put themselves in situations above their response capability. For example, we sometimes set goals in life that *should* stress us out because they are above our ability to handle. This may not very useful in speech class because students don't make the assignment. But it might happen if they put themselves in the position of starting to prepare the speech the night before it's due.
2. They can increase their *response capability* for whatever tasks they must do. So they can study harder, prepare better, and improve their ability or capability for giving speeches. I draw a little old-fashioned scale where we pile the demand on one side and on the other side we pile the response capability. One way of balancing is to add to the response capability. Study harder, practice harder.
3. Changing *perceptions* is the third strategy. Sometimes students exaggerate the objective demands or they don't give themselves enough credit for their response capability. There are all kinds of techniques for changing perceptions such as using positive language and not thinking in black and white (10: I'm great, or 0: I'm terrible—with nothing in between). Not using magnification and not making mountains out of molehills also helps. If they think, "I must not make mistakes, and if I do it's terrible," they should remember it's human to err. If they mess up, it's not desirable, but it's normal. We don't perfect everything.
4. *Reevaluate the consequences* and see if they really are that serious. There's a difference between not succeeding and not succeeding completely. In the big scheme of things, doing poorly on a speech probably won't change their lives or make them have to drop out school or change their majors or send troops to the border. Some students tend to overestimate every assignment or every grade—at least those who care enough to get nervous.

Does this help conquer public speaking anxiety? Often students will come to me and say, "I gave my speech, and it went great, so I shouldn't have been so nervous."

Questions

1. If Professor Tschan wanted to incorporate material from this chapter into his presentation, where might he put the idea that it's important to learn the process of public speaking by understanding the guidelines in the five canons of rhetoric?
2. Where would he talk about cognitive modification?
3. Where might he include the guidelines relating to visualization?

Used by permission of Manfred Tschan.

Summary

It is not enough simply to get up in front of an audience and talk; good speaking requires thought and preparation. The Greeks and Romans identified principles or standards in five areas of speechmaking (the five canons of rhetoric): invention, disposition, style, memory, and delivery. Use guidelines from the canon of invention to consider your audience's characteristics and interests, and take into account their responses to the specific situation. After that, select a unique, significant, and appropriate topic and focus. Decide whether your major purpose is to inform, persuade, entertain, or commemorate; then gather information from oral, print, or electronic sources that will support your topic adequately.

Organize your ideas to create an introduction, body, and conclusion using norms from the canon of disposition. Choose appropriate wording (canon of style), and learn your major ideas (canon of memory), so that you can extemporaneously deliver your speech (canon of delivery).

Finally, plan strategies for dealing with your nerves. Know when to expect the highest levels of physical symptoms, and prepare accordingly. Plan specific activities to counteract the physical tension brought on by the fight-or-flight mechanism. Systematic desensitization works for some people with extreme physical reactions. Then work on your psychological stress. Control your internal monologue by cognitive modification, substituting positive thoughts for negative ones. Visualize yourself performing your speech successfully from beginning to end. Use vivid images and control your imaginary scenario.

Doing these steps thoughtfully and thoroughly can give you confidence on speech day, and they equip you with the necessary knowledge and skills to be a more competent public speaker.

STUDY AND REVIEW

Your online resources for *Public Speaking: Concepts and Skills for a Diverse Society* offers a broad range of resources that will help you better understand the material in this chapter, complete assignments, and succeed on tests. Your online resources feature the following:

- Speech videos with critical viewing questions, speech outlines, and transcripts.
- Interactive versions of this chapter's Stop and Check activities, as well as Application and Critical Thinking Exercises.
- Speech Builder Express and InfoTrac College Edition.
- Weblinks related to chapter content.
- Study and review tools such as self-quizzes, an interactive glossary, and downloadable audio summaries.

You can access your online resources at the CourseMate for *Public Speaking: Concepts and Skills for a Diverse Society.* Log in at **http://www.cengage.com/login**, using the access code that came with your book or that you bought online at **http://www.cengagebrain.com**.

KEY TERMS

The terms below are defined in the margins throughout this chapter.

anticipatory speech anxiety 17
canon 17
canon of delivery 22
canon of disposition or arrangement 20
canon of invention 18
canon of memory 22
canon of style 21
canons of rhetoric 17
cognitive modification 26
communication apprehension (CA) 16
connectives 21
extemporaneous delivery 22
fight-or-flight mechanism 24
habituation 27
impromptu delivery 22
internal monologue (I-M) 25
manuscript delivery 22
memorized delivery 22
performance anxiety 16
process anxiety 16
physiological anxiety 24
psychological anxiety 24
public speaking anxiety 16
style 21
systematic desensitization 25
visualization 27

APPLICATION AND CRITICAL THINKING EXERCISES

1. Many factors affect communication apprehension (CA). An interesting study found that athletes have less CA than nonathletes, and those who play team sports have less CA than individual athletes.[30] From your own experiences, does this seem true? What factors might contribute to these differences?
2. Rank from 1 to 5 (easiest to hardest) the five canons of rhetoric in order of difficulty for you.

   ___ Invention: audience analysis, topic selection, purpose, research
   ___ Disposition: organization or arrangement and connection of ideas
   ___ Style: choice of appropriate language
   ___ Memory: remembering what you want to say
   ___ Delivery: actually presenting your speech

   Why did you rank them in this order? Identify some strategies you can use to work on the areas that challenge you most.
3. Work with a group to analyze your classroom audience, using the suggestions on page 18. In light of material from Chapter 1 and from your own experiences, discuss some adaptations you might make to speak successfully to your class. For instance, how might your classmates influence your choice of topics? How might you adapt to diversity? How might the classroom itself, the time of day of the class, and other outside factors affect your speaking?
4. At the top of a sheet of paper, write down an occupation that interests you. Then, along the left side of the page, list the five canons of rhetoric, leaving several spaces between each one. Beside each canon, identify ways that the skills developed within that canon will be useful in the job you named. For example, how will identifying a purpose or doing research help in a career such as nursing or engineering? How might organizing ideas help in teaching or computer programming?
5. Often persuasive speeches require informing, and informational speeches have persuasive effects. Think about the goals of two speeches about the same general topic

of study abroad programs. An informative goal could be to describe the various study abroad opportunities on campus; a persuasive goal could be to urge audience members to study abroad. With a small group of your classmates, identify at least three other topics and write down an informative goal and a persuasive goal for each.

6. Classroom speakers generally use extemporaneous delivery; however, the other modes of delivery are sometimes more appropriate. With a group of classmates, write down the four modes: memorized, manuscript, impromptu, and extemporaneous. Beside each, identify specific instances in which that mode would probably be the most effective. For instance: impromptu delivery goes with most wedding toasts; manuscript delivery works with commencement addresses. After you have identified several examples, discuss with your group some guidelines that you think speakers should follow for each type of delivery.
7. Memory is often considered the "lost" rhetorical canon because so little emphasis is placed on memorization in our digital age. Discuss these questions in your class: Is there any value in learning how to memorize speech information? If so, when and where might memorization be useful?
8. Consider the ways that careful preparation and adequate rehearsal contribute to your speaking competence. What effect does last-minute preparation have on competence? What effect does it have on anxiety? Knowing this, how do you plan to prepare for your next speech?
9. Make a list of your top ten suggestions for overcoming public speaking anxiety. My list would start with knowing how to create a speech, because I'm always less comfortable when I don't know what to do. Develop a personal strategy for dealing with your anxiety.

SPEECH VIDEO

Go to your online resources to watch and critique Natasha delivering a speech about a significant aspect of her life. The transcript of her speech appears below.

Student Speech with Commentary

INTERCULTURAL MARRIAGE*

By Natasha Bevis

Intercultural marriage occurs when two people from different countries, cultures, or nationalities marry, often creating multicultural children. I'm a result of an intercultural marriage; my father is Caucasian-American from Texas, and my mother, from India, has been in the States since she was 13. Today, I'll tell their story.

Natasha chose this topic because her multicultural experiences are foundational to her identity.

When my mother was 13, she came from India to St. Louis, Missouri, which she calls her hometown. She was the youngest of eight children. My relatives in India are Christians; however, they maintain many traditions and cultural values of India, practiced by Hindus or Christians or Buddhists or Muslims. The cultures and customs are still very significant in India. All my mother's family in India have arranged marriages. In fact, when she came to the States with her older sister, her older sister was married—at age fifteen—to a man who was almost twice her age.

She sets up the characters, focusing more on her mother and her mother's experiences in the U.S.

My mom came to the States to study, and she went to middle school and high school and learned English here. She really became used to the U.S. culture, including its ideas about marriage. After high school, she attended college in Missouri. The summer they were both 20, my dad, who was born and raised in Texas in a variety of foster homes, came to St. Louis for a conference at her college.

They first saw each other at a meeting. My dad—he was the new guy in the group—looked over and saw this beautiful Indian girl who was there with some of her girlfriends, and he asked someone, "Who is that?" Eventually, the group went around, saying their names and what they want to do. My dad said, "My name is Michael and I want to live and work overseas." And my mom thought, "That's really interesting." As they continued introducing themselves, she said, "My name is Ruth, and I also want to live and work overseas." And my dad thought, "Oh! That's the person I'm going to marry!" And although she was a different color, from a different culture, (I don't really believe in love at first sight) but my dad saw her and their shared passion and their shared same goals, and despite their cultural differences, he decided she was someone he wanted to pursue.

The plot or decision point comes with the grandmother's death in India and the grandfather's decision to find a wife for his youngest daughter.

That summer, they got to know one another and fell in love. But my grandmother in India wasn't well, so my mom had to return to India. Sadly my grandmother died. Because she was the youngest of eight, it was really important to my grandfather that my mom get married while he was still alive. Most of her older siblings were married—through arranged marriages—but my mom and my dad definitely didn't want her family to arrange her marriage. So my dad bravely went to India by himself and married my mom, surrounded by her entire family in India. He had never been to India before, but he went, married her, and they returned to the states. They were able to see past their cultural differences. They've now been married 25 years, and we've lived in India and China, as well as the U.S.

Natasha explains the challenges and then the benefits of a family that must blend two distinct sets of cultural traditions.

Even though their marriage is successful, we have had to face some difficulties because of cultural differences. The language barrier is one. My mom speaks English fluently, but English is still her second language. There are also differences in values and such things as expectations about family roles. I've seen that my parents have had to have more communication, more understanding, more patience with one another. Luckily, my parents share religious beliefs.

Some people might say they would never get into an intercultural marriage because marriage is hard enough without trying to marry someone of a different culture, which is a whole step above! But I think the diversity that intercultural marriages bring to a society is beneficial for all of us. See how much diversity there is in the world, and how we're reaching out to different countries, and embracing each other's differences, and learning from one another?

Knowing that most people in her audience will marry within their own cultures, she at least challenges them to make intercultural connections.

So there are a lot of things to overcome through intercultural marriages, but they can be very beneficial. I have learned a lot through having parents from two cultures. I'm not suggesting that you marry someone from a different culture, but I would suggest that you don't be afraid to reach out to someone of a different race or a different culture.

© Tim Timmerman

CHAPTER 3

THIS CHAPTER WILL HELP YOU

- Define ethical communication
- Describe three responses to diversity
- Explain three democratic principles for public speaking
- Identify characteristics of dialogical speaking and listening
- Discuss ethical responsibilities of listeners
- Define two kinds of academic dishonesty: plagiarism and fabrication
- Explain three types of plagiarism
- Paraphrase and cite sources correctly

Ethics in a Diverse Society

FREE SPEECH. It's the cornerstone of the United States society. The nation's founders knew that limiting our right to express ourselves freely would limit our ability to engage fully in a representative form of government. So they crafted the First Amendment to the Constitution to read:

> Congress shall make no law . . . abridging the freedom of speech, or of the press; or the right of the people peaceably to assemble, and to petition the Government for a redressing of grievances.[1]

This does not mean freedom of speech is total. We can't legally yell "FIRE!" in a crowded theater, nor can we legally damage another person's reputation by

Figure 3.1
This is the minimum-to-maximum scale of sociocultural differences.

Source: Porter & Samovar, 1994

spreading information we know to be false. Instead, we must balance our rights with our responsibilities into what Professor Vernon Jensen calls our **rightsabilities**.[2] Jensen further defines **ethical communication** as the conscious decision to speak and listen in ways that you, in light of your cultural ideals, consider right, fair, honest, and helpful to others as well as yourself.[3] And, although we may have legal rights, we arguably have human rights such as the right not to be called hate names.[4]

Focusing on both rights and responsibilities can be challenging and give rise to a number of ethical questions. On what basis should we determine right and wrong in public discourse? Should some things be left unsaid? When? Who decides? What responsibilities do you have as a listener or as a researcher? This chapter presents some principles that have emerged out of discussions about these ethically challenging questions. We will first examine common responses to diversity and then discuss guidelines for ethical speaking, listening, and researching in a complex culture.

Responses to Diversity

Figure 3.1, the minimum-to-maximum scale of sociocultural differences, shows the range of diversity between individual and national groups.[5] At the minimum end, environmentalists and developers might share a bank, school, neighborhood, and religion but differ in their ideas for balancing environmental and business interests. Further up the scale, the people and groups have fewer things in common. Differences, even at the lower end of the scale, can seem irreconcilable, leading to tensions that can overshadow the many things that might otherwise bind the groups together.[6] Put simply, diversity is frequently divisive. However, diverse people and groups can and do come together in productive, civil ways that highlight ethical choices. Common responses to diversity include assimilation, resistance, and accommodation.

"rightsabilities" phrase coined by Professor Vernon Jensen to highlight the tension between our right to free speech and our responsibility for our speech

ethical communication the conscious decision to speak and listen in ways that you, in light of your cultural ideals, consider right, fair, honest, and helpful to all parties involved

assimilation response to diversity in which you surrender some or most of your ways and adopt cultural patterns of another group

Assimilation happens when groups or individuals meet up with diversity and reject or surrender their ways of believing and acting to embrace other perspectives and behaviors.[7] At one time, this was thought of as a good thing. For example, in the early 1900s, the United States was often called a "melting pot," and a major goal was to "Americanize" immigrants. A century later, however, we've found that assimilation is rarely total, so we have updated our metaphors to include "tossed salad" (a whole comprising distinct entities) or "stew" (distinguishable entities, but changed and merged into a whole) to describe this country's multiethnic reality.

In the United States where choice is a dominant value, people are free to change their ideas and lifestyles, but ethical implications arise when individuals allow themselves to be coerced or manipulated into changing without critically examining good reasons for the change.

Resistance to diversity comes in many forms. Some groups or individuals resist by bolstering and defending their beliefs and traditions. Others withdraw from situations that challenge their cherished ways of thinking and behaving. Still others attack their opponents[8] with an intensity ranging from mild challenges that ignore, discount, or ridicule divergent ideas to physical assaults, death threats, terrorism, or armed conflict. Resisters commonly attack with words, so much so that Deborah Tannen, a professor of linguistics, calls our culture an "argument culture."[9] Tannen is especially sensitive to the war metaphors that frame much public discourse. To illustrate, think about all the battle terminology you hear: culture *wars*, *fighting* for your ideas, *battleground* states. We *arm* ourselves for arguments; we *shoot down* ideas; we *target* our political enemies. There are hundreds of additional examples.

resistance response to diversity in which you refuse to change, and you defend your own positions or attack others

Resistance is not inherently bad. In many cases, both in the United States and around the world, conscientious resistance leads to positive outcomes. Activists often confront social, environmental, and global injustices and bring about necessary reforms. However, consider the ethical implications of activists who justify using questionable means for a good cause. (For more information about resistance, do an Internet search for "protest movement," and read about two or three movements that interest you.)

Finally, **accommodation** means adjustment or adaptation. Accommodating groups or individuals show a willingness to hear and evaluate diverse ideas with an open mind. They allow themselves to rethink their ideas and surrender some, modify others, but hold still some relatively intact. Accommodation helps create a **multivocal society** that seeks out a variety of ideas, opinions, and visions and gives them an open, recognized voice. In such a society, co-cultural groups recognize their diversity yet work together to forge a civic culture that accommodates both differences and commonalities.[10] However, accommodation has its challenges:

accommodation response to diversity in which you listen and evaluate the views of others; both sides adapt, modify, and bargain to reach mutual agreements

multivocal society society that actively seeks expression of a variety of voices or viewpoints

> Participating in this form of communication requires a set of abilities, the most important of which is remaining in the tension between holding your own perspective, being profoundly open to others who are unlike you, and enabling others to act similarly.[11]

Study the speech at the end of this chapter and notice the ways the speaker calls for accommodation on his college campus.

Resistance, assimilation, and accommodation all have ethical implications. It's easy to label extreme forms of resistance (terrorist attacks, for example) or even taunting as unethical, but what about simply ignoring people who differ from you? What about cruel remarks in anonymous posts on Internet sites? Your decision to resist new ideas or to embrace

Reistlin Magere/shutterstock.com

In an "argument culture," a war of words is a common form of resistance by those who are unwilling to assimilate or to accommodate diverse ideas.

them with relatively few questions, to block voices from being heard or to invite dialogue—all of these have ethical implications for both speaking and listening in a diverse society. Let's now turn to specific cultural resources that can help you be a more ethical speaker.

Your Responses to Diversity

Examine your personal responses to diversity.

- In what areas, if any, have you changed your beliefs or behaviors and assimilated diverse perspectives into your personal life? What process did you go through?
- Where do you resist diverse ways of believing and behaving? What *wars* or *battles* do you wage? When, if ever, did you march or openly protest? What perspectives, if any, do you ignore or put down? Have you ever left anonymous comments on websites you disagree with? If so, what kind of comments did you leave?
- When and how have you made an effort to be accommodating? What tensions have you experienced between holding your own positions and being open to the perspectives of others?

Speaking Ethically

Your concern with ethics should begin as soon as you receive your speech assignment because you have responsibilities to your audience, your topic, and yourself. So it's important to consider some guidelines for ethical speaking. These principles fall into two major categories: democratic and dialogical.

Practice Democratic Principles

Events over many decades have highlighted tensions in the United States between free expression and responsible expression. McCarthyism in the 1950s, antiwar and civil rights protests in the 1960s, recent rancorous political campaigns, disputes over social issues like abortion and gay rights, and the recent rise of Internet users spouting widely varying opinions—these, and similar events, continue to bring First Amendment issues into focus and call for citizens who can think carefully about important matters. After the uprisings in Egypt in February 2011, one *CNN* commentator said, "It takes citizens to make a democracy. Protestors can make a revolution, but it takes citizens to make a democracy."[12] The United States has always relied on citizens to continually renew our democracy. The National Communication Association (NCA) has responded by stating widely accepted principles for ethical communication within a democracy; you'll find the latest version in the Practically Speaking box.

Develop a Habit of Research

Because you are your listeners' primary source of information during your speech, you owe it to them to know what you're talking about, and it's important to do your homework beforehand. Let's say you decide to discuss a complex energy issue such as nuclear power plants. Don't just settle for a surface understanding; instead, examine

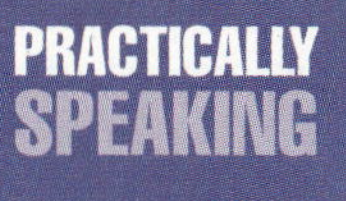

PRACTICALLY SPEAKING NCA Credo for Ethical Communication

Questions of right and wrong arise whenever people communicate. Ethical communication is fundamental to responsible thinking, decision making, and the development of relationships and communities within and across contexts, cultures, channels, and media. Moreover, ethical communication enhances human worth and dignity by fostering truthfulness, fairness, responsibility, personal integrity, and respect for self and others. We believe that unethical communication threatens the quality of all communication and consequently the well-being of individuals and the society in which we live. Therefore we, the members of the National Communication Association, endorse and are committed to practicing the following principles of ethical communication:

- We advocate truthfulness, accuracy, honesty, and reason as essential to the integrity of communication.
- We endorse freedom of expression, diversity of perspective, and tolerance of dissent to achieve the informed and responsible decision making fundamental to a civil society.
- We strive to understand and respect other communicators before evaluating and responding to their messages.
- We promote access to communication resources and opportunities as necessary to fulfill human potential and contribute to the well-being of families, communities, and society.
- We promote communication climates of caring and mutual understanding that respect the unique needs and characteristics of individual communicators.
- We condemn communication that degrades individuals and humanity through distortion, intimidation, coercion, and violence, and through the expression of intolerance and hatred.
- We are committed to the courageous expression of personal convictions in pursuit of fairness and justice.
- We advocate sharing information, opinions, and feelings when facing significant choices while also respecting privacy and confidentiality.
- We accept responsibility for the short- and long-term consequences for our own communication and expect the same of others.

To see the NCA's Credo for a Free and Responsible Communication in a Democratic Society, visit the organization's website at **weblink 3.2.** You can access this link through your CourseMate for *Public Speaking*, Chapter 3 resources.

Source: Endorsed by the National Communication Association, November 1999. Reprinted by permission of the National Communication Association.

a variety of credible sources and search for diverse viewpoints. Find the positions taken by supporters and by critics. Seek out scientific facts and perspectives from community members where plants are located, and identify relevant social class issues. Although you may end up arguing for one position over another, make sure it is well-reasoned. Presenting your listeners with a wide variety of perspectives gives them the breadth of information they need to form their own reasonable conclusions.

This approach contrasts with an "argumentative mentality" that Deborah Tannen says "obscures the complexity of research"[13] and creates oversimplification, disinformation, and distortion of issues.

Be Honest and Fair

Speaking honestly means that you present your information as truthfully as you know how. Don't exaggerate a problem to make it seem greater than it actually is. Don't distort or twist evidence. Statistics can be particularly misleading, so find out as much as you can about the numbers you present. For instance, you might discover a study showing that nuclear power plants are safe, but you find that the research was partially funded by companies who specialize in nuclear energy. Does this mean the numbers are inaccurate? Not necessarily, but probe further and see if sources with nothing to gain from the data, financially or otherwise, come up with similar findings.

Strive for fairness, balance, and evenhandedness rather than presenting one side—the one that favors your position. Avoid the slanted approach of various talk show hosts, political spinmeisters, and Internet sites that only provide a one-sided view of their topics. For example, compare and contrast how the following groups—Greenpeace, the Nuclear Energy Institute, and the US Department of Energy (Office of Nuclear Energy)—present their information. (These sites can be found on **weblink 3.1**. (You can access them through your CourseMate for *Public Speaking*, Chapter 3 resources.)

Practice Civility

Talking heads on all-news cable channels interrupt their guests who are noisily talking over one another; politicians dig for dirt and create negative ads to use against their opponents. Rowdy audiences sometimes loudly boo or heckle speakers with whom they disagree. This all-too-common lack of civility in public discourse led one commentator to coin the term *drive-by debating* to describe this rudeness.[14]

civility self-control or moderation, contrasts with arrogance; civil speakers persuade, consult, and compromise rather than coerce and manipulate

Civility is a social virtue that involves self-control or moderation instead of pride, insolence, and arrogance. Civil speakers and listeners are more than simply polite; they *choose* to persuade, consult, advise, bargain, compromise, and build coalitions. Civility is related to the accommodation response to diversity. It requires communicators to strive for understanding, appreciate opposing perspectives, and accept the outcome when their own position loses. Cultures from the ancient Greeks to modern Asian societies have promoted civility as an ethical principle.[15]

President Obama issued a call for civility at a January 2011 service in Tuscon, Arizona, honoring the six people killed and the nineteen wounded—including Arizona representative Gabrielle Gifford—by a crazed gunman. President Obama did not blame or finger point, but invited thoughtful consideration of the state of public discourse:

> [A]t a time when our discourse has become so sharply polarized . . . it's important for us to pause for a moment and make sure that we're talking with each other in a way that heals, not in a way that wounds. . . . As we discuss these issues, let each of us do so with a good dose of humility. Rather than pointing fingers or assigning blame, let's use this occasion to expand our moral imaginations, to listen to each other more carefully, to sharpen our instincts for empathy and remind ourselves of all the ways that our hopes and dreams are bound together. . . . And if . . . their death helps usher in more civility in our public discourse, let us remember . . . only a more civil and honest public discourse can help us face up to the challenges of our nation in a way that would make them proud.[16]

AP Photo/Gerry Broome

These concerned citizens are taking advantage of a town hall forum where they have an opportunity to dialogue with the city's mayor about public concerns. All speakers should enact dialogical and democratic principles and be mindful of their ethical responsibilities to other speakers, to audience members, and to themselves.

Habits of research, honesty and fairness, and civility—these are by no means all of the democratic principles related to public speaking. However, this list gives you a starting point for thinking about ethical speaking in a pluralistic culture. Since diversity is pervasive, you must create your own way to best respect (and live comfortably with) cultural differences.[17]

Does Facebook Encourage Civility?[18]

In February 2011 young Egyptian activists spray painted "Facebook" on walls as a way of acknowledging the social network's role in helping them organize to protest against the government. In the United States, researchers are currently exploring how digital media is helping or hindering high school and college students' civic engagement and involvement in issues of public concern.

Early studies are discovering that online groups based on common interests are not just "echo chambers" that only reinforce the participants' views. Instead, the more time young people spend in online groups, the more exposure they have to diverse perspectives. These people are more likely to volunteer, give to charitable causes, and express their opinions about community issues, compared with youth who don't participate in online groups.

Researchers will next explore questions related to civility. How do young people respond online to diverse viewpoints? When, how, and why do they attack the opposition? Do they present reasoned support for their own views? Rethink their perspectives? The answers, when they come, may be surprising. (To read more, go to InfoTrac College Edition and search for Article CJ249927176.)

(continued)

Questions

1. Are you a member of online groups? If so, what are they? Do any of them deal with controversial social or political topics? Do you find diversity of participants and of opinion in the groups? Read through some recent messages. How do the participants, in general, interact?
2. Go to an online news or opinion site and find an article about a controversial topic. Read the comments below the article. How do they support or contrast with the NCA's Credo for Ethical Communication?

Use Dialogical Principles

If you log onto InfoTrac College Edition and search for the key word "dialogue," you will get more than 15,000 links, reporting on dialogues between nations and religions, as well as interpersonal dialogues. Taking a dialogical perspective can help you be a more ethical public speaker. It's not a set of "rules" for speaking; instead, a dialogical perspective is a mindset linked to cultural values of honesty, openness, and freedom of choice.[19] In *The Magic of Dialogue: Transforming Conflict into Cooperation*, Daniel Yankelovich[20] identifies three essential components of dialogue: equality, empathy, and examination.

- *Equality* means you and your listeners respect one other and regard each other's opinions as important enough for consideration. This mindset contrasts with the belief that *your* opinions are the most important and that you have the right or the obligation to impose them on others, even if this requires trickery or manipulation.
- *Empathy* means you show compassion and a willingness to identify emotionally with others in an attempt to understand other perspectives. Empathy contrasts with self-centered absorption with your personal needs and perspectives.
- *Examination* means you put aside a know-it-all attitude and willingly scrutinize both your assumptions and those of others with an open mind. Examination doesn't mean you must abandon your personal biases or strong beliefs; in fact, you may *never* agree with some people, or they might eventually be persuaded to adopt your views. But, in the process, you've challenged your own ideas.

Seeds of Peace

Founded in 1993, Seeds of Peace's mission statement says, "Treaties are negotiated by governments. Peace is made by people."[21] Organizers first brought together forty-three young people from Egypt, Palestine, and Israel to communicate face-to-face at a three-week international camp in Maine. Since then, its mission has expanded to include young leaders from three additional regions of conflict: South Asia, Cyprus, and the Balkans. The goal remains the same: to empower future leaders with the communication, negotiation, and leadership skills they need to advance coexistence and reconciliation between combative groups in their home regions. Empathy and respect are fundamental aspects of the program, which aims to reach youth "before fear, mistrust, and prejudice blind them from seeing the human face of the enemy."[22]

To date, more than 4,000 young leaders are working in hot spots around the world. For example, one "Egyptian Seed" helped create a music video called "The Voice of Freedom" during the 2011 protests in Cairo's Tahrir Square. Within the first few weeks after he uploaded it on YouTube, it had more than a million hits.[23] Other "Seeds" wrote news stories or organized fundraisers and clean up days to help repair the damage caused by rioting.

Donald Bowers/Getty Images

Seeds of Peace promotes dialogue among young people from mutually hostile groups.

Whether or not they knew it, Seeds of Peace founders built upon Arab customs relating to dialogue. Traditionally, Arabs met in tents to discuss socially important issues; participants were required to respect other's opinions, to listen carefully, to speak their minds, and to negotiate divisive social issues. Thus, these contemporary dialogues perpetuate longstanding cultural traditions.[24]

To learn more about this organization, visit its website at **weblink 3.3**. You can access this link through your CourseMate for *Public Speaking*, Chapter 3 resources.

A dialogical perspective relies on three skills: (1) the ability to engage in dialogue in response to another's invitation; (2) the ability to invite others into dialogue; and (3) the ability to create contexts that facilitate dialogue.[25] It's a way to create multivocal society. What does this look like in practice? Amitai Etzioni,[26] who experienced Nazi persecution during his childhood, emphasizes both rights and responsibilities in communication. He identified several rules of engagement that make dialogue more productive when people have major differences:

1. Don't demonize the other side or depict it as completely negative.
2. Don't insult or offend the deepest moral commitments of other people or groups; don't bring up dark moments from a group's history.
3. Talk less about nonnegotiable "rights" and more about negotiable needs, wants, and interests.
4. Don't feel you must deal with every issue; it is okay to let some things drop.
5. Don't abandon your convictions, but balance your beliefs and passions against those strongly held by others.

A Dialogical Attitude

Equality: respect others; consider their opinions

Empathy: show compassion and identify emotionally with others

Examination: consider your assumptions and theirs with an open mind

Figure 3.2
These are the three essential components of dialogue.

Internationally, groups are involved in dialogues about issues such as migration, population, sustainable development and hundreds of other global issues. The Seeds of Peace project described in the Diversity in Practice box on pages 40 and 41 is an example of a program that brings together people with very divergent opinions for honest discussions of their prejudices and conflicts. Leaders aim to give participants the tools they need to live with diversity without settling for stereotyping, name-calling, or violence.[27] Furthermore, the principle of dialogue underlies the United Nations, as former UN Secretary General Kofi Annan explained.

> The United Nations itself was created in the belief that dialogue can triumph over discord, that diversity is a universal virtue, and that peoples of the world are far more united by their common fate than they are divided by their separate identities.[28]

Finally, dialogue also helps resolve campus problems. For example, Bruce Mallory and Nancy Thomas developed The Democracy Project to facilitate campus dialogues because they believe that teaching and learning dialogical principles is critically important in colleges and universities. This project develops "intentionally designed, permanent spaces on campuses for identifying, studying, deliberating, and planning action regarding pressing issues with ethical or social implications."[29] Other groups, such as Study Circles and the Difficult Dialogues initiative, provide places for people from various perspectives to come together in reasoned dialogue about contentious issues.

Listening Ethically

Although political differences in the United States have historically generated impassioned gatherings, recent events show that really listening to and thoughtfully considering opposing viewpoints is difficult for many Americans. Here are just a few examples:

- In 2009, many lawmakers who voted for controversial legislation returned to their congressional districts and held town hall meetings to explain the plan and their votes. Some protestors were so disruptive that the lawmakers stopped meeting this way, moving instead to smaller settings or to phone meetings.[30]
- In 2010 a contentious immigration bill in Arizona resulted in outbursts from audiences, who booed and shouted down speakers on both sides of the issue.
- In 2011, a "week of rage" in Wisconsin followed the newly-elected governor's move to follow through on his campaign promises to cut taxes by what his opponents labeled as "an assault on unions."[31]

heckler listener who disrupts a speech or confronts a speaker during a speech

These events, and others like them, illustrate some listeners' reactions to differences of opinion. In these examples, **hecklers** confronted speakers while they spoke, trying to embarrass them, make it difficult for others to hear what they have to say, and shut them down. In less dramatic settings, audience members walk out in the middle of a speech, or whisper and laugh, showing disrespect for the speaker, the ideas, and other listeners who want to hear what's being said.

What ethical principles apply to listening? Obviously, you can't listen to everyone. You simply don't have time. But polite listening affirms the other person's right to speak, and giving others your respectful attention is one way to empower them. Think about how positive you feel when someone who disagrees with you still takes time to ask how you came to your conclusions. Sincere questions that are not meant as personal attacks show that the listener is really trying to understand your viewpoint.

This is not to say that you should listen to just anything, and you might face ethical dilemmas as a listener. When you hear someone saying something you know is false or

In the movie, "O Brother, Where Art Thou?" the politician, Homer Stokes, gives an impromptu speech full of racist comments. His audience heckles him and cuts him off mid-speech. Are their actions justifiable? Why or why not? (You can view the movie clip on YouTube.)

arguing for a viewpoint that does not seem well reasoned, what should you do? Should you confront the speaker in front of others? Should you prepare a speech to present more accurate information or provide a different perspective? Should you ask questions that help other listeners detect the misinformation or bias? These are all possible responses.

To think about your ethical responsibilities as a listener, ask yourself these questions:

- Do I keep myself informed about significant issues by exposing myself to a number of arguments, or do I listen only to the side with which I already agree? In short, do I listen with an open mind?
- Do I fulfill my ethical responsibilities to other listeners by not distracting them?
- Do I fulfill my responsibilities to speakers by letting them know they are being heard?
- Do I encourage speakers to meet ethical standards? This may mean that I ask for further information about their sources or that I point out relevant information they omit.

Ethical Listening

It's easy to listen to someone you agree with, but when you face diverse perspectives and opinions, ethical issues can arise. With a small group of classmates, consider these questions:

- What ethical responsibilities do audience members have toward a speaker, in general? Toward other listeners? Toward their own opinions? Which should assume the most importance in settings such as those described at the beginning of this section? Explain your choice.

(continued)

- After one heckling incident in 2008, candidate John McCain appealed to his audience by saying, "One of the things Americans are tired of . . . is people yelling at each other in America. Have you noticed that? They want us to respect each other's opinions. . . . Americans want a dialogue."[32] Is this a good way to respond to heckling? Why or why not?
- In order to control meetings, many politicians today speak before carefully selected audiences, comprised of people chosen to prevent unwanted interruptions. What do you think of this practice?
- Have you ever been in a situation where a speaker was heckled? If so, discuss the situation and your responses to it.
- What would you list as your five top principles for ethical listening?

Academic Honesty

Kari's introduction was fine until she got to her thesis statement:

> The National Collegiate Athletic Association (NCAA) is the main governing body of collegiate sports, where students look to further their athletic careers. . . .
>
> Today, I will share with you the rule I would like to see changed—and that is athletic scholarships for Division III schools.

Students listened and took notes, but the professor thought, "Wait a minute! I don't assign a change-a-rule speech, but my colleague down the hall does." A quick check with him turned up an identical opening submitted by a student in another class. Kari's speech was plagiarized. She admitted that she had changed a couple of lines, but basically she'd given her friend's speech. In a speech about drug cartels, Aaron made up a statistic—an act of fabrication, a second type of ethical breach. In the United States, plagiarism and fabrication are specific ethical violations, punishable by a failing grade, being fired from a job, and sometimes public humiliation. (Not every culture shares these concepts. See Diversity in Practice: Plagiarism and Culture for other cultural notions about intellectual property.) To avoid ethical problems with plagiarism or fabrication, it is important to understand what they are.

Avoid Plagiarism

plagiarism presenting the words, images, or ideas of others as if they were your own

When you cross the platform during commencement and receive your college or university degree, you'll have in hand your school's official recognition and certification that you have personally grappled with important ideas and learned the practical skills associated with your degree.[33] Because they have a vested interested in their students, colleges and universities crack down hard on **plagiarism**. They reason that, when you plagiarize, you don't personally do the work; instead, you present other people's ideas, words, or works as your own, without giving credit to the originators. It's somewhat like sending your roommate to the weight room to do your weight training; you don't benefit from the exercise.[34] Furthermore, it's not fair to your classmates who *are* doing their own work.[35]

Plagiarism is easier today than ever before because of the Internet, which makes it simple to download text, pictures, diagrams, and other information without citing it.[36] Consequently, a student, who would never consider ripping a paragraph out of a *Washington Post* newspaper column and cutting a sentence out of a *Newsweek* magazine and then gluing the two onto a piece of paper and turning it in, finds it easy to cut and paste the same paragraphs from those sources online and combine them into a paper written with a word processor. And because the material is electronically stored, it might be easy to conceptualize as somehow different in kind from hard copies of the same material.[37]

To avoid plagiarism, you should understand its various forms:[38]

- **Deliberate fraud.** This happens when students borrow, buy, or steal someone else's speech or outline and present it as their own work; they knowingly and intentionally do this. Because Kari's speech on changing a rule, mentioned above, was deliberately copied, she was subject to her university's penalties for plagiarism.
- **Cut-and-paste plagiarism.** Here, plagiarists copy entire sentences or paragraphs, word-for-word from various articles and piece them together into an outline or speech. They omit quotation marks around the copied words and fail to cite the sources in the speech or next to the material on the outline, even though they often supply a list of resources at the end of the outline.
- **Improper paraphrase.** This type of plagiarism occurs when the plagiarist changes words or moves phrases around but keeps the basic organizational structure and ideas of the original intact and fails to credit the source next to the material. For example, an MIT instructor made national news (and tainted his reputation) when a literary magazine accused him of plagiarism for this paragraph in his book about the poet E. E. Cummings:[39]

deliberate fraud knowing, intentional plagiarism

cut-and-paste plagiarism copying material word-for-word and then patching it together without quotation marks or citations

improper paraphrase changing some words of a source but keeping the basic structure and ideas intact without citing the source

> *From a 1980 biography of Cummings:* "Esther Lanman organized a cocktail party for Cummings with as many of the old Cambridge crowd as she could locate. Amy Gozzaldi was there, her jet-black hair now grey. She and [Cummings] looked at each other and grinned self-consciously, feeling what the years had done to them. He raised his hand to his bald head."[40]
>
> *From the professor's 2004 biography about Cummings:* "Lanman even organized a cocktail party for Cummings, inviting every member of the 'old gang' she could round up, including Cummings's first crush, Amy de Gozzaldi. Her hair, once jet black, was now gray and Cummings, now fifty-eight, had finally gone bald. They looked at each other self-consciously, then grinned."[41]

The professor didn't think he plagiarized because he credited the 1980 biography throughout. However, he failed to cite the original source for this specific section, which is very close to the original in content and flow of ideas.

As the professor found out, plagiarism can be intentional or accidental. **Accidental plagiarists** don't know all the rules about plagiarism, so, without intending to cheat, they fail to properly paraphrase or give credit to their sources. Intentional or not, the consequences are still serious. For example, Allison created a series of PowerPoint slides with pictures of an athlete that she'd cut and pasted from the Internet. She omitted the URLs of the websites where she found the pictures. However, it never occurred to her that she was supposed to credit the source of a photograph. Accidental though it was, because her school's policies were easily available in student handbooks and in library and writing lab resources, she was held responsible for knowing the rules relating to plagiarism. Similarly, because you have access to information, you are responsible to be academically honest.

accidental plagiarist plagiarist who lacks knowledge about the rules

What are some of the rules? Your university library or campus writing center provides guidelines for source citations. Here's an example from Purdue University's Online Writing Lab:[42]

- Give credit whenever you use somebody else's words, ideas, or creative works directly—whether you take them from library resources, the Internet, films or television shows, audio recordings, advertisements, letters from friends, or elsewhere.
- Provide sources for information learned in interviews, conversations, or email.
- Tell your audience the source of any unique words and phrases that are not your own.
- Identify the sources of diagrams, illustrations, charts, photographs, and figures.

Yoruba drum with stick, n.d., Wood, string, and hide/The Trout Gallery/Dickinson College, Carlisle, Pennsylvania

Some students accidentally plagiarize because they don't know they must include the source of a downloaded image on the slide itself.

You do not need to document:

- Personal experiences, observations, conclusions, or insights.
- Results of experiments you personally conduct.
- Common knowledge, including folklore or traditions within your cultural group such as Cinderella or Robin Hood.
- Generally accepted facts—the kind of information almost every source provides or information your audience already knows or could easily find in reference material. For example, many sources will tell you that Presidents John Adams and Thomas Jefferson both died on the fourth of July, 1826, so citing just one may be unnecessary. To be on the safe side, however, the Writing Center at the University of North Carolina says to cite information that is new to you.[43] Maybe "everyone" knows about Adams's and Jefferson's death dates, but if you first learn it in a specific history book, cite that source.

Sources can be either published or unpublished. You know that books and magazines are publications; you may not know that paintings, websites, and movies or audio recordings are also considered publications. Unpublished sources are things like letters and email, speeches, personal interviews, personal photographs, class lecture notes and handouts—even papers you've submitted for another class.[44]

To avoid plagiarism, name your sources within your speech. For example, when you use a direct quotation, introduce it as such. When you paraphrase someone else's ideas, cite the originator. When you present a diagram or chart on a PowerPoint slide or an overhead transparency, write the source somewhere on the slide. Here are some specific examples:

- *Published source, book.* Products can be added to shows even after they've initially aired. In a February 1, 2008, article in *Teacher Librarian*, Keith McPherson reported that a scene from the *Friends* sitcom originally showed Ross sitting at a bare table; now a rerun shows a package of Oreo cookies in front of him.[45]
- *Published source, Internet.* Citation in small font at the bottom of the PowerPoint slide showing a photograph of a *dun dun* drum and featuring a sound clip downloaded from the Internet: Source: Yoruba drums from Benin, West Africa: The world's musical traditions, Vol. 8. [online]. Accessed April 25, 2002. [URL][46]
- *Unpublished source, personal conversation.* [by a filmmaker] The other day my friend Glen Basner told me that everything we've learned about financing films over the last 15 years we have to forget.[47]

Chapter 11 describes ways to document sources on your outline. Be sure to list your references at the end using a standard format such as MLA (Modern Language Association) style or APA (American Psychological Association) style. These style manuals and others are available on the Internet or in the reference section of your library, and they show you how to cite just about any source, from a book to a personal letter, from a CD to a website. Because these manuals are often updated, look for the latest version. Many articles in your library's databases also show how to cite the article in a variety of formats. You can also go to **weblink 3.4**, sign up for a free account, and use its citation tool to create your reference list. (You can access this link through your CourseMate for *Public Speaking*, Chapter 3 resources.) Be sure to check the citations manually to make sure they meet the criteria your instructor assigns.[48]

As noted earlier, plagiarists, accidental or intentional, are subject to severe penalties. Typically, intentional fraud results in an "F" for the assignment—at the very least. Other serious breaches may result in temporary suspension, permanent expulsion, and/or a notation on the student's permanent record, which can seriously affect the plagiarizer's life. Accidental plagiarists may be asked to redo the assignment, or they may lose points.

Plagiarism and Culture

Individualistic cultures like the United States consider plagiarism to be a serious intellectual breach.[49] First, writing something down is thought to be a concrete way to demonstrate your knowledge and skills; consequently, instructors expect you to do your own assignments. Turning in someone else's work does not show what *you* know.

A second concept is linked to the cultural value of individuality. You should develop yourself to your highest potential and do creative, original thinking. Turning in someone else's work does not demonstrate your originality.

Third is the cultural notion that ownership of personal property includes ownership of intellectual property. You can patent, copyright, or sell your ideas, creations, musical works, unique words, and writings. They are legally yours. Consequently, if someone else uses your original work or even a portion thereof without crediting you, you can charge that person with "stealing" your intellectual property.

However, collectivist cultures view intellectual property differently. Consider a society that values the group over the individual, one in which words and ideas belong to the culture as a whole, not to any one person. Would stealing or pirating works be viewed with the same perspective? What might happen when a business headquartered in the United States moves into such a culture? Also, consider the impact of the Internet on notions of "ownership" of words and ideas. For example, hypertext allows people to "write collaboratively and use nonlinear connections to create products that show few indications of who said what."[50] Wikipedia is just one example of a jointly created resource. Who "owns" a Wikipedia entry?

For more information about culture and plagiarism, read the speech, "Confessions of an Academic Honesty Lady," by Judy Hunter. You can find it online by doing a Google search for the title.

Avoid Fabrication

Plagiarism is but one form of academic dishonesty. Another is **fabrication**, which happens if you make up information or guess at numbers but present them as factual. Fabrication has serious consequences. For instance, a well-known researcher faked scientific data linking autism to vaccines. He was eventually disgraced, but not until the information was widely disseminated, frightening many parents away from vaccines for their children.[51] Until he was exposed, students had no way of knowing that his data was falsified, and many used it in their speeches on childhood vaccinations. After the news broke, however, the truth became widely available to everyone who double checks their facts, and speakers who continue to pass on the faked data as true can be held liable.

fabrication making up information or repeating information without sufficiently checking its accuracy

Citing a reference you did not actually read or passing along rumors or other unsubstantiated information are types of fabrication common in public speeches.

For example, when Barack Obama first began his bid for the presidency, facts competed with exaggerations and misinformation regarding his background. Here are just a few: His middle name is Hussein (correct); therefore, he is a Muslim (incorrect; he's a Christian); during his childhood, he attended a radical Muslim school (his biography says he went to a Muslim school in Indonesia, but it was not radical; he also attended a Catholic school, but he is not a Catholic); he refuses to recite the Pledge of Allegiance (false, although one photographer once caught him without his hand over his heart during the playing of the national anthem). These rumors, and others like them, swept across Internet blogs, emails, talk radio, and whispered conversations. Some persist in the present. However, accurate information was always available to those willing to search for it, so people who pass along unsubstantiated rumors are guilty of fabrication. (Hypothetical examples, described in Chapter 8, are in a different category because the audience understands that these examples are not real.)

The best ways to avoid fabrication are to use a number of sources and to be alert for conflicting data. Thoroughly check out your information before you present it as factual. If something seems suspicious, don't use it. Many Internet sites exist to uncover hoaxes and false claims and to expose urban legends of all kinds, from food to computers, holidays to weddings.

Good Versus Bad Paraphrasing

Many students think that changing a few words of the original equals a paraphrase, but according to the *Academic Integrity Handbook* published by the Journalism Department of the University of Arizona,[52] it's unacceptable to directly use even three to eight words of a source. They cite Judy Hunter, director of the writing lab at Grinnell College, who says this about paraphrasing:

> In a bad paraphrase, you merely substitute words, borrowing the sentence structure of the organization directly from the source. In a good paraphrase you offer your reader a wholesale revision, a new way of seeing the text you are paraphrasing. You summarize, you reconstruct, you tell your reader about what the source has said, but you do so entirely in your own words, your own voice, your own sentence structure, your own organization.[53]

Here is an example:

> *Original* (from an Associated Press article about Dr. Wakefield, whose faked data linked autism to vaccines): "It was a small series of observations, wrapped in a hypothesis—not even a full medical study. But it exploded in the media, prompting a wave of parental concerns in England, as well as the United States.
>
> Researchers have estimated that as many as 125,000 US children born in the late 1990s did not get the MMR vaccine because of Wakefield."
>
> *Inappropriate Paraphrase:* A small series of medical observations—a hypothesis, really—not a complete study, was all it was. But the media took it and ran, prompting concerned parents in the United States and in England to panic, so much so that researchers think 125,000 or so US children weren't vaccinated in the late 1990s because of Dr. Wakefield's findings. [Analysis: Although many words are changed, the sentence structure and organizational pattern is similar.]

Appropriate Paraphrase: An Associated Press article posted January 6, 2011, noted that many parents in the United States, influenced by data from a study in the United Kingdom linking autism to vaccinations, did not vaccinate up to 125,000 children in the late 1990s. Although the study was small and incomplete, with the help of media hype, it affected parental decisions, both here and in England. [Analysis: This version summarizes the ideas in the speaker's words; it also cites the source.]

Source: Stobbe, M. (2011, January 6). Vaccine-causes-autism study results were faked. Associated Press. *Press-Telegram,* Long Beach, CA. [Online]. Retrieved from http://www.presstelegram.com/news/ci_17029862?source=rss

Now try your hand at it. Here's a quotation about the same general topic of Dr. Wakefield's research. First, write an inappropriate paraphrase by making a few substitutions and changing around a few phrases. Then write an appropriate paraphrase by summarizing the material into your own words.

[From *The Age*, an Australian newspaper] "Now, the *British Medical Journal* reports that Dr. Wakefield, who was paid more than $US 675,000 . . . by a lawyer hoping to sue vaccine makers, was not just unethical but falsified data in the study, which suggested children developed autism after being vaccinated against measles, mumps and rubella."

Source: MCT. (2011, January 7). Data "faked" on vaccine dangers. theage.com.au. Retrieved from www.theage.com.au/world/data-faked-on-vaccine-dangers-20110106-19hju.html

Summary

People in pluralistic cultures differ in beliefs, values, attitudes, and behaviors to degrees that range from superficial to fundamental, and responses to diversity vary. If you assimilate, you surrender some aspect of your own beliefs or cultural traditions and replace it with something new. If you choose to defy or resist, you defend or bolster your position and (perhaps) attack or ignore diverse perspectives. Finally, if you choose accommodation, you accept differences and work with others to create a society in which all can live together.

Our culture provides both democratic and dialogical resources that you can use to speak and listen ethically. Democratic principles remind you to develop a habit of research, to present your materials honestly and fairly, and to respond to diversity with civility. When you choose a dialogical relationship with your listeners you respect them as equals, have empathy with their perspectives, and examine both your own and your listeners' assumptions in an honest, open manner.

Listening also calls for ethically responsible actions, which many people violate. Allowing people to speak empowers them, giving them a voice and enabling others to hear their ideas. However, when speakers present incorrect or misleading information, you face an ethical decision, in which you must balance your rights and responsibilities against the rights and responsibilities of the speaker and other listeners. The term *rightsabilities* highlights this tension.

As you present your materials, be sure to cite your references and check a variety of sources to avoid the ethical problems of plagiarism or fabrication. Plagiarism occurs when you present the ideas, words, organizational pattern, or images created by another person as your own without giving credit to the original source. Fabrication occurs when you make up material or present something as factual when it is not.

STUDY AND REVIEW

Your online resources for *Public Speaking: Concepts and Skills for a Diverse Society* offer a broad range of resources that will help you better understand the material in this chapter, complete assignments, and succeed on tests. Your online resources feature the following:

- Speech videos with critical viewing questions, speech outlines, and transcripts.
- Interactive versions of this chapter's Stop and Check activities, as well as Application and Critical Thinking Exercises.
- Speech Builder Express and InfoTrac College Edition.
- Weblinks related to chapter content.
- Study and review tools such as self-quizzes, an interactive glossary, and downloadable audio summaries.

You can access your online resources at the CourseMate for *Public Speaking: Concepts and Skills for a Diverse Society*. Log in at **http://www.cengage.com/login**, using the access code that came with your book or that you bought online at **http://www.cengagebrain.com**.

KEY TERMS

The terms below are defined in the margins throughout this chapter.

accidental plagiarist 45
accommodation 35
assimilation 34
civility 38
cut-and-paste plagiarism 45
deliberate fraud 45
ethical communication 34
fabrication 47
heckler 42
improper paraphrase 45
multivocal society 35
plagiarism 44
resistance 35
"rightsabilities" 34

APPLICATION AND CRITICAL THINKING EXERCISES

1. Conduct an Internet search for the phrase "hate speech," and come to class prepared to share an example you found. With your classmates, discuss the importance of First Amendment rights to free speech, balanced against the ethical responsibilities described in this chapter.
2. Draw a minimum-maximum scale that represents diversity on your campus. Identify differences at the minimum end of the range. Work your way up the scale, identifying increasingly greater areas of diversity that create conflicts. When and how do campus speakers address this diversity?
3. With a small group of your classmates, choose a specific international, national, or local situation in which conflicting beliefs, attitudes, values, or behaviors caused a conflict. Identify which of the three ways of dealing with differences—resistance, assimilation, or accommodation—the various participants used to respond. Assess the ethicality of their responses.
4. Using the NCA credo as a guide, work with a small group of your classmates to create a class code of conduct.
5. With a small group in your classroom, discuss ways that people who hold diverse perspectives on a controversial topic might engage in dialogue (for example, pro-choice advocates meeting with pro-life activists; born-again Christians talking with committed Muslims; animal rights activists meeting with research scientists; leaders of NATO meeting with leaders of the African Union). How can each group listen to the other and explore their perspectives with an open mind?

6. Form small groups and choose a controversial issue about which you have moderate to strong disagreement. Discuss the topic within the group, and put into practice the principles for speaking and listening in this chapter.
7. For an example of a famous speech that addresses religious diversity, read or listen to streaming video of John F. Kennedy's Address to the Greater Houston Ministerial Association in June, 1960; it's available on YouTube. Kennedy became the first Catholic president in November, 1960, but five months before the election, some voters worried that his allegiance might be to the Pope, not the American people. Notice how JFK lays out his views on religious diversity and how he affirms core American values.
8. Use your own values and beliefs as well as the guidelines described in this chapter to write an ethical code that states the principles by which you want to speak and listen.
9. Evaluate yourself as a responsible listener. How do you avoid silencing speakers? Use the questions in the section on Listening Ethically on page 43 to guide your self-evaluation.
10. Look up your campus's guidelines regarding academic honesty. What guidelines do they provide to help students learn and practice ethical research procedures? What are the penalties for plagiarism?
11. Look up your campus library's information on source citation. What resources are available to help you format your reference list in the style your instructor prefers?

SPEECH VIDEO

Go to your online resources to watch and critique Rodney Smolla's inaugural address as President of Furman University.

Professional Speaker's Speech with Commentary

ENGAGING THE MIND AND THE SPIRIT*

By Rodney Smolla, President, Furman University, Inaugural Address

. . . I begin my reflections with a moment from a great American work of literature.

In the very last paragraph of Mark Twain's classic, *The Adventures of Huckleberry Finn*, Huck tells us that he is planning to light out for the Western Territory, because his Aunt is out to "sivilize" him, and as Huck laments, "*I can't stand it. I been there before.*" . . . my opening theme this morning is Huck's closing theme, this problem he has with being "civilized."

Smolla has acknowledged the audience and the occasion as a preface to the body of his speech. He opens with an allusion to a text commonly taught in schools that sets out his theme.

I invite you to join me in reflection on the state of *our* contemporary civility, and its discontents.

As a nation we are once again poised on the eve of an important political election. Whatever your politics . . . you cannot help but notice that . . . the discourse has often been highly partisan, highly personal, and highly polarized.

The speech was delivered as campaigning was in full swing for the contentious midterm elections of 2010.

What is true of our politics extends more broadly across our culture, in this nation and around the world. At times it seems as if the whole planet is determined to work a cruel twist on the words of Abraham Lincoln, proceeding with malice toward all, and charity for none.

There is a curiosity to this. We might well expect that the health of our public discourse should be at an all time high. Never have so many channels been open to so many voices. From the new media of Facebook, Twitter, and texting, to such old-fangled modes of communication as e-mail, telephone, television, radio, or cable, today we may express and change views with such breathtaking speed and ease that we *ought* to be living in a "golden age" of public discourse, world-wide.

Yet many of us feel a nagging disquiet. Quantity does not equate with quality. Yes, we may talk more than ever before. But when we talk, particularly about issues that really matter—in politics, in religion, in science or the arts—we have, as a culture, become more strident, more shrill, more angry. Our discussions are increasingly laced with personal attacks, increasingly

Throughout, he is describing "resistance" responses to diversity and judging them to be unproductive.

prone to caricature and superficial slogans and sarcastic sound-bites. Perhaps more fundamentally, we may be talking *more*, but we are listening *less*.

Here are some examples of how NOT to listen.

And when we do listen, we may not be listening with genuinely open hearts and open minds. We may instead be listening tactically, listening for our cues, listening for our chance to pounce, our opening to launch a counter-attack.

No one political party, no one religious viewpoint, no one space on the cultural spectrum, has a monopoly on these bad habits. We are equal opportunity employers when it comes to the employment of devices that diminish the civility of our debates, and in turn sap the strength of our democracy.

After establishing the problem, he turns to the solution—civilized and constructive debate and deliberation.

I urge you, however, to not despair!

We have it in our power to effectuate a rescue. It can begin right now, and right *here*.

To all of us in higher education . . . I issue this challenge: [Let us] take on as an assignment the constructive improvement of the civility of our public discourse . . .

What society sorely needs, and what we are uniquely suited to contribute, are the habits of engaging minds and spirits to the service of civilized and constructive debate and deliberation. Let us be leaders in encouraging such habits as a genuine willingness to listen, an avoidance of gratuitous personal attacks and cheap shots, a commitment to factual accuracy and intellectual honesty in our own advocacy, a de-emphasis on caricature, and a re-emphasis on character.

I know, and I *appreciate*, that many of our students and our faculty members, our alumni and our fellow citizens have passionate feelings about the issues of our day. And in our passions we are often deeply and intensely engaged.

Trust me, I am not . . . asking you to curb your enthusiasm. . . . This is not a crusade for blandness, for a discourse that is sanitized and laundered, so that it loses all its color, humor, bite, and zip. Your passions are admirable; they are the stuff of a vibrant democracy and a vital marketplace of ideas.

Nice alliterated contrast: engaged v. enraged.

There is a critical difference, however, between being engaged and being enraged. . . . and we owe it to the nation, and to the world, to stand up and demonstrate the difference.

And so my challenge is for . . . you to rise above the course and the common, and by your leadership advance the common good.

. . . To that end, let me now speak directly to our students.

Intellect + character. He argues that these will lead to more civil communication.

My hope for you is that every single student . . . will pursue and will receive a dual degree. One in an academic discipline, and a second in the development of character. . . . The purpose of your education here, like the purpose of life itself, is not simply to acquire a credential. . . . It is *not* to say that achievement has no place.

It is to say that the meaning to be drawn from achievement must represent values deeper and causes greater than the achievement itself. [I]ts meaning must extend beyond what appears on your transcript . . . [I]t must touch both your mind and your spirit, shape both your intellect and your character.

This effort must be a partnership. . . . We cannot implore you, our students, to refrain from thinking of your education as a compilation of numbers, as the acquisition of credentials, unless we refrain from defining you as numbers or credentials. . . .

He explains his vision of a diverse campus.

We cannot plausibly claim that we . . . graduate [our] students with an academic degree and a degree in character, unless we intentionally seek out students who yearn for engagement in both. . . . And if, as a University, we are serious about attracting a more diverse student body, a student body enriched by peoples of all the cultures of the world, by members of all the great religions of the world, a student body that transcends lines of nationality, race, religion, ethnicity, sex, disability, politics, and poverty, a student body representative of all parts of our country, and all countries of the world, a student body truly engaged in mind and spirit, then we must fulfill the promise of that diversity and that engagement . . .

Diversity is a shallow and hollow achievement if those who comprise the community do not genuinely engage, interact, and experience one another once here. . . . if as a University community we do not encourage our students, our faculty, our staff, our alumni, to cross divides of generations and geography and faith and politics, to listen to one another, with authentically open minds and hearts.

Let us be a community that moves beyond mere grudging tolerance or forced politeness into the realm of generous and genuine respect. . . .

Finally, he evokes basic values—respect, democracy, freedom.

Respect is at the heart of the liberal arts tradition. Respect is at the heart of American democracy. For all our differences and all our divisions, what we in America may most proudly and with unalloyed unity proclaim, is our collective passion for democracy, for equality, for freedom of speech, for freedom of religion, for respect for human dignity.

Let all of us in higher education be keepers of that flame. As we participate in the global marketplace, in the global community, let us be a beacon of civility, compassion, and respect.

Let that respect come from our deepest beliefs, in the essential dignity, and the essential worth, of every human being.

Source

Smolla, R. (2010, December). Engaging the mind and the spirit. Speech delivered October 22, 2010 at Furman University. *Vital Speeches of the Day, 76 (12)*, 570–573 (edited)

CHAPTER

4

THIS CHAPTER WILL HELP YOU

- Distinguish listening from hearing
- Appreciate the importance of listening skills
- Describe linguistic, cultural, and personal barriers that affect your listening
- Draw and explain four thought patterns that are common during listening
- Use cultural schema to improve your listening
- Discuss diverse cultural listening styles
- Identify strategies to improve your comprehensive listening
- Improve your critical listening skills
- Practice dialogical listening through nonverbal feedback
- Give appropriate verbal and written feedback using the D-R-E method

Effective Listening

TAKE A MINUTE AND THINK about all your communication activities during a typical week. Then rank the following activities in order according to the amount of waking time you normally spend doing each one:

___ reading ___ writing ___ listening ___ speaking ___ email and Internet

If you ranked listening first, you're like the average student, who spends about 50 percent of his or her communication time listening. (Speaking takes up about 20 percent; reading is 6 percent; writing comprises 8 percent; email and Internet take about 17 percent.)[1] An ancient proverb, attributed to Zeno of Citium, emphasizes the comparative importance of this skill: "We have been given two ears and but a single mouth in order that we may hear more and talk less."[2]

If we listen so much, we should be pretty good at it. Right? Unfortunately, we often fail to focus on developing this vital skill as much as we focus on improving our other communication skills. Compare the number of reading, writing, and speaking courses to the number of listening courses your college or university offers. Most schools offer many writing, literature, and speech courses, but few offer even one course in listening to comprehend or in critical listening. Instead, instructors typically incorporate listening into other courses or ignore it entirely.

Perhaps part of our problem is that we fail to distinguish listening from hearing. **Hearing** is the physical process that happens when sound waves hit your eardrum, setting up nerve impulses that go to receptors in the brain. Right now, for example, a refrigerator hums in the background. I can actually *hear* it, but I am not really *listening* to it. **Listening** is an active mental process with at least five elements: (1) receiving sounds, (2) discriminating or distinguishing among them, (3) focusing attention, (4) assigning meaning to the sounds and then (5) remembering the information. Consequently, something that goes in one ear and out the other is hearing, not listening. Listening takes motivation, effort, and concentration.

hearing physical process involving sound waves, eardrums, and brain receptors

listening active process that receives, distinguishes, attends to, assigns meaning, and remembers what you hear

Because listening is so vital, this chapter begins by stressing its importance. Then it looks at several factors that typically hinder effective listening. Finally, it presents some strategies you can use to become a more effective listener.

Listening Skills Are Valuable

If you do an Internet search for "listening skills," you will get links to millions of sites. Obviously, many people value good listening. Internet sites typically promote workshops or listening quizzes, give advice, or suggest activities aimed at improving listening in the workplace, in classrooms, or in relationships. So people definitely see room for improvement. Some don't think very much about how they listen, but many others are overly confident, thinking that they remember 75 to 80 percent of what they've heard, when, in fact, two days later, the average listener can recall only about 25 percent.[3] It's worth developing good listening skills because they are essential for many reasons:

- *Listening takes up much of our time.* Listening is the most commonly used skill in the workplace; understanding and following instructions (skills linked to listening) come in second.[4] And, according to the student handbook of the University of Minnesota, Duluth,[5] the average student spends fourteen hours each week in class listening; this is over and above the hours spent listening to friends and to media.
- *Good listening skills are good job skills.* One study reports that 80 percent of executives rank listening as the most important work skill.[6] Another reported that physicians with good listening skills have fewer malpractice claims.[7] And Madelyn Burley-Allen, author of *Listening: The Forgotten Skill*, says the most common comment about well-liked bosses is: "he or she really listens to me."[8] Dental hygenists,[9] interior designers,[10] roofing contractors,[11] tax preparers,[12] journalists—even politicians—understand the need to listen; in fact, "listening tours" are now indispensable in political campaigns. President Calvin Coolidge once said, "No one ever listened himself out of a job."[13] In short, the most successful people are effective listeners.

- *Good listening skills are good academic skills.* Researchers administered a listening test to all incoming students at one university. At the end of the first year, 49 percent of low-scoring listeners were on academic probation, compared to less than 5 percent of high-scorers. In contrast, 68.5 percent of high-scoring listeners were earning honors, compared to just over 4 percent of low-scorers.[14]
- *You have an investment in the listening situation.* The Student Counseling Services team at Texas A & M University advises students to develop a positive, consumer-wise attitude toward listening. The very fact that you are in the listening situation means that you have something at stake. Choosing to listen well and benefit from what you hear will help you gain the most from your investment.[15]

These are only a few reasons that listening is important; you can probably think of many other ways that good listening makes life easier. Pause now, and ask yourself how your listening habits help or hinder your comprehension of course work. How are listening skills used in a job you currently hold or plan to hold someday? Keep these questions in mind as you study the remainder of the chapter.

Barriers to Listening

The Chinese character for listening (Figure 4.1) combines the symbols for ears, eyes, and heart; it reinforces the idea that good listeners are wholly involved in listening. Most of us don't start our day out thinking, "My goal is to be a terrible listener today." We intend to listen well, but we face linguistic, cultural, and personal barriers that hinder our effectiveness. Understanding these barriers and planning strategies to deal with them will build your listening skills.

Linguistic Barriers

Sometimes the speaker's language is a barrier, and in a diverse culture you'll hear many language variations. Visit a large city in the United States, and the number of languages and accents multiplies; for example, around 170 languages are spoken in New York City alone.[16] Add to these the slang that teenagers invent and the phrases their grandparents use, or the terminology that skateboarders use and the legalese that only lawyers understand. Clearly, the potential for linguistic misunderstandings is great. Linguistic barriers show up in both language and vocabulary differences.

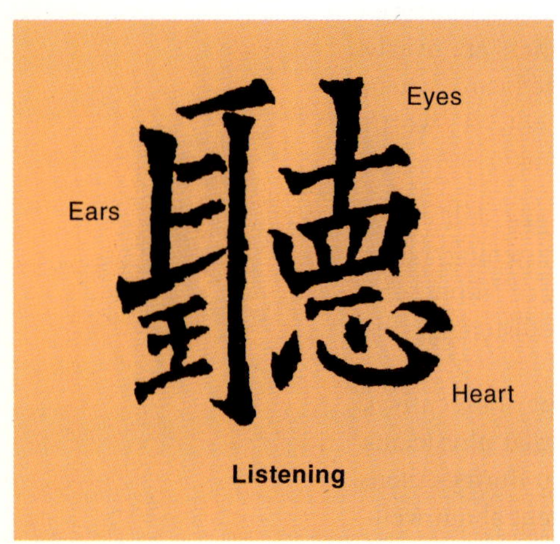

Figure 4.1
The Chinese character that translates as "listening" emphasizes its holistic nature by combining the symbols for ears, eyes, and heart.

- *Language differences.* Obviously, when you don't share a speaker's language, you won't understand without an interpreter. Even then, you'll probably miss some concepts or nuances of meaning, because languages and the ideas they embody are so different. In addition, you may find it hard to figure out words when a person speaks with a heavy accent, whether the accent is regional, ethnic, or influenced by a first language.
- *Vocabulary differences.* Speakers with a more extensive vocabulary than yours may talk over your head. In addition, speakers who use the technical jargon associated with a specific topic such as medicine or engineering will lose lay audiences unless they translate the terminology. And speakers who use slang or other specialized linguistic codes will reach some people but talk past others. Finally, a speaker can say a word, even one as simple as "taxes," that listeners understand differently because each person has a different ideas about and experiences with "taxes." Remember the axiom: Meanings are in people.

To overcome linguistic barriers, listen very carefully and see if you can gain meaning from the general context of the speech. Take notes; jot down words to study later. Speakers can help by translating jargon or slang, explaining how they're using a word, and by displaying words visually when possible (such as on a PowerPoint slide) so that listeners can see as well as hear what they're saying. Chapter 12 provides more information on language differences and comprehension.

Cultural Barriers

Comprehension also depends upon your ability to understand **cultural allusions**, or references to culturally specific historical, literary, and religious sources. You can probably think of many things that are familiar in your culture or co-cultures that would confuse someone from a different group. Here are a few examples:

cultural allusions references to historical, literary, and religious sources that are culturally specific

- A highly educated person whose major interest is art may understand dadaism well but may require a thorough explanation of the most popular Xbox 360 games.
- Most people in the United States would not recognize allusions to the classic Japanese novel, *The Tale of Genji*.
- Although he is one of the most famous sufi poets, many US audiences would need an introduction to Jala-l ad-Din ar-Ru-mi.

In our pluralistic society and multicultural world, each group draws from different resources from their cultural experiences. In pluralistic settings, you may be unfamiliar with these culture-specific references. It is up to each speaker to be sensitive to differences and to explain allusions or choose areas of common knowledge. Listeners can also play their part by jotting down unfamiliar allusions and doing research about them later.

Personal Barriers

A number of personal distractions can obstruct your listening. **Physical factors** (hearing loss, sleep deprivation, hunger pangs, illness) can affect your ability or your desire to focus your attention on a speech. **Psychological factors** can also vie for your attention: you just had an argument with a friend; you have a huge test coming up in your next class; your bank account is overdrawn. The worries that accompany psychological stressors can take your motivation away from listening. You may also feel defensive and anxious about messages that challenge or threaten you in some way. And, if you lack interest in the topic, you may struggle to remain focused.

physical factors bodily conditions that can limit your desire or ability to listen

psychological factors mental stressors or distractions that take away from your desire or ability to focus

Stereotypes and prejudices can also hinder listening. You **stereotype** people when you put them into a category and then assume they fit the characteristics of the category. When you listen with preformed judgments, either negative or positive, you show **prejudice** or bias towards topics or speakers. To illustrate, supporters of gay marriage listened enthusiastically to a speaker who supported that position, but they approached a defense of marriage speaker with suspicion, and vice versa.

stereotype place someone in a category and then assume the person fits the characteristics of that category

prejudice preformed biases or judgments, whether negative or positive

Because the listening process requires attention, maintaining focus is another major listening skill. However, attention constantly fluctuates, as this student explains:

> I'm easily distracted.... It's easy for me to either focus on one particular thing that has been said, and then sort of drift off, exploring it further in my own mind, or—and this applies more specifically to someone whose speaking style or subject does not impress me—float off on unrelated topics ("I wonder where she gets her hair cut?"). Also, depending on the subject, I can get easily bored.

Paying attention can be hard work. For one thing, you can think far more rapidly (about 500 words per minute) than the fastest speaker can talk (about 300 words per

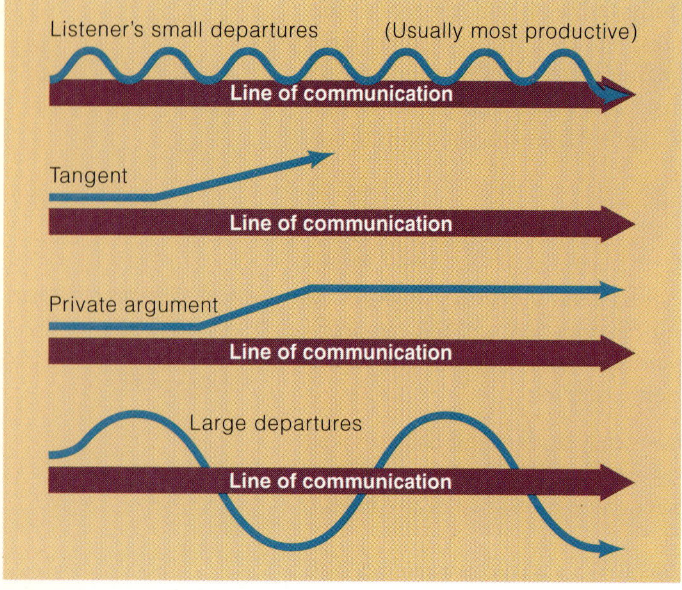

Figure 4.2
Listening Thought Patterns These four thought patterns are typical during listening. The first can be productive, but the rest characterize poor listening.

minute). Most speakers average about 150 words per minute, leaving you with 350 words per minute of a **speech-thought differential.**[17] The following four thought patterns, illustrated in Figure 4.2, are common during listening.[18]

- *Taking small departures from the communication line.* Small departures can be distractions that hinder your comprehension, but they can also help you follow a message if you use them to produce your own examples, relate the material to your personal experiences, answer the speakers' rhetorical questions, and otherwise interact with the ideas during the departure.
- *Going off on a tangent.* When you leave the speakers' line of thinking and seize on one of their ideas, taking it in your own direction, your attention is deflected, and you stop listening. One idea leads to another, and before you know it, you're several subjects removed from the topic at hand.
- *Engaging in a private argument.* When you carry on a running debate or mental argument that parallels the speech, you close your mind and stop trying to understand the speaker's reasoning. Instead, identify arguments that don't make sense, but withhold your final judgment until you have heard the entire speech.
- *Taking large departures from the communication line.* Here, your attention wanders off into unrelated areas; you bring it back and focus on the speech for a while; then, off it goes again, and you find yourself thinking about a totally unrelated topic. This cycle repeats indefinitely.

speech-thought differential the difference between the rate you think (about 500 words per minute) and the average speaking rate (about 150 words per minute)

As you can see, linguistic, cultural, and personal factors can challenge your listening abilities. To assess your skills, complete the test in the Stop and Check box on the following page. After he took the test, Adam reported that his score (72) at first caused him to pout about being "just average," but his score motivated him to develop strategies to improve his skills by developing some of the tips described throughout the remainder of this chapter.

Strategies to Improve Listening

Margarete Imhof, past president of the International Listening Association, says that most students do not think of listening as an active process that they can control. Instead, they find it easier to criticize the speaker's mannerisms and characteristics rather than critically analyze the message. Some of her suggestions for improving listening skills are discussed in this section.[19]

Use Cultural Schemas

schemas mental models that guide your perception, interpretation, storage, and recollection of a speech

Every culture provides a set of cultural expectations or schemas that help its members organize and understand messages (Figure 4.3). **Schemas** are the mental plans, blueprints, or models you use to perceive information and then interpret, store, and recall it.[20]

Listening Skills Self-Assessment

Evaluate your listening by taking this test. First, write the letter that most accurately indicates how often you exhibit the behavior; then tabulate your listening score using the key that follows the questions.

A = Almost always B = Usually C = Sometimes
D = Rarely E = Almost never

How often do you:

_______ 1. Give up trying to understand a speaker's accent and tune the speaker out?
_______ 2. Get lost in a speech because of your small vocabulary?
_______ 3. Stereotype a speaker and let that affect how you listen?
_______ 4. Tune out a speaker whose position is different from one you hold?
_______ 5. Feel angry, defensive, or fearful when you disagree with the speaker?
_______ 6. Become distracted by external factors, such as noises outside the room?
_______ 7. Let internal preoccupations, such as personal worries or stresses, distract you?
_______ 8. Carry on a running argument with a speaker instead of hearing him or her out?
_______ 9. Go off on a tangent?
_______ 10. Give in to your short attention span and lose your place in a long speech?

Key

For every A give yourself 2 points.
For every B give yourself 4 points.
For every C give yourself 6 points.
For every D give yourself 8 points.
For every E give yourself 10 points.

Total score _________

Between 91 and 100	Your listening skills are exceptional.
Between 76 and 90	Your skills are above average.
Between 60 and 75	Your skills are about average.
Below 60	You are probably not as effective a listener as you could be.

If you scored below 80, identify specific strategies from the rest of this chapter to improve your listening.

Think of how you listen to an announcement. You have a mental model of what a good announcement is like, and you use this model to interpret an event announcement—your schema tells you to listen for what the event is about (topic, presenter) and what you need to remember (time, date, place).

Your schemas help you listen to many speeches of various types. For instance, you've heard lots of how-to speeches, and you have a pretty good idea of what they are like because they follow a fairly predictable pattern. Similarly, you've learned what to expect from a news report, a funeral eulogy, or an award presentation because you've heard many speeches in each category. In the classroom, you need a well-developed lecture schema so that you know how to follow a professor's presentation and know

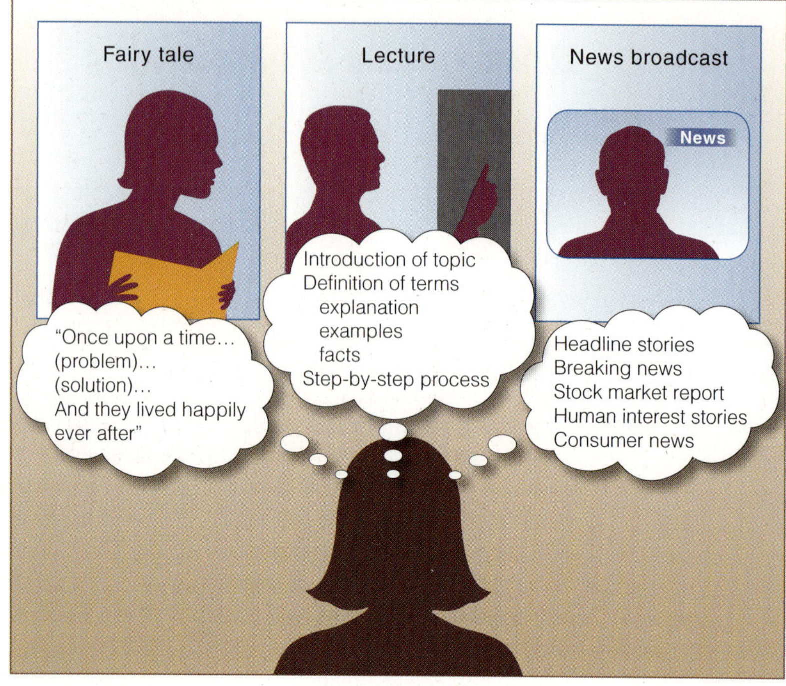

Figure 4.3
Listening Schemas Our minds contain a number of schemas or models that help us listen and respond to specific types of speeches.

how to look for major concepts, even if the lecturer improvises on the general pattern. (The Diversity in Practice box about Cultural Listening Styles identifies some listening expectations that are common in other cultural and co-cultural groups.)

Know Your Listening Purpose

Chapter 2 pointed out some speaking goals, which are related to listening goals. You turn on the TV for entertainment, but when a commercial comes on, you tune out or you critically evaluate the claims, deciding whether or not the product interests you. You listen to a lecture for information, and then you eat lunch with friends and listen empathetically to their frustrations. For each type of listening, you shift strategies to meet your goals. This section focuses on listening to comprehend and listening to evaluate messages.

Improve Your Comprehension

Think of all the times you listen for information: Your professor clarifies a complex process; your boss gives directions for your next project; your physician explains your medical condition; a radio reporter tells where an accident blocks traffic. Listening to learn, or **comprehensive listening**, is a vital skill, and you can employ several strategies to increase your comprehension.[21]

comprehensive listening listening to learn, understand, or get information

Prepare in Advance Before the session, ask some pre-questions such as "What do I already know about this topic? What do I *want* to know? What do I *need* to know?" Your answers to these questions can help you set your learning goals for the session.

- Before a classroom session, review notes from previous sessions and then study the text, noting highlighted concepts, key terms, and headings; read the chapter summary. Look at the pictures and diagrams, or search the Internet for supplementary or background information.
- In the workplace, do your homework before an important session by brushing up on background information. This will help you ask more thoughtful questions and better participate in co-creating meaning.

Use Attention-Directing Strategies A common attention-directing strategy is to take notes. Focus on particular areas of the message; for example, listen for and write down the main ideas, jot down practical "things I must remember," or note examples that will help you recall concepts. Note unfamiliar words to look up later. Use what you know about speech organization to help you remember material. For instance, watch for signals such as "first," "next," or "finally" that help you identify a series of steps. Be alert for words like "therefore" or "in contrast" that connect ideas.[22]

Remember Your Goals It's easier to pay attention when you understand your investment in the topic. For instance, a lecture on anatomy may seem boring, but learning the information is essential in many careers. So try to reframe your attitude about uninteresting material. Think of positive things about the topic and how the information can be of use. In the classroom, try to anticipate what might be on a test; in the workplace, look for the main things your boss wants you to remember.[23]

Cultural Listening Styles

The ways listeners approach public speeches reflect differences in worldviews and behaviors among cultural groups. Knowing some cultural variations will make you more mindful of listening diversity. Here are a few examples:

- *A Javanese listening schema:* On the Indonesian island of Java, listeners turn to their neighbors and repeat phrases they like. The resulting buzz of voices throughout the speech signals the speaker that the audience is receiving it well.[24]
- *Additional listening traditions found in several Asian cultures:* In cultures that emphasize unity, listeners often expect speakers to develop oneness with them rather than present divisive ideas. Both the speakers and their audiences share responsibility for making the speech successful.[25] In some groups, audiences listen in silence, thinking that noise breaks their concentration and diverts their attention. Applause signals suspicion, similar to booing by United States audiences; some cultures do not applaud at the end of the speech so that the speaker can remain modest.[26]
- *An African American schema:* The entire audience participates in a "call and response" pattern that reflects African traditions. The speaker's statements (calls) are punctuated by the listeners' reactions to them (response), and in a real sense, the audience is talking back to the speaker. No sharp line distinguishes speakers and listeners, and everyone cooperates to create the message.[27]
- *Various student preferences:* A cross-cultural study of student listening preferences[28] showed that American students like short, to-the-point messages. They tend to prefer speakers with whom they can identify (women more so than men). German students prefer precise, error-free messages; disorganized presentations frustrate and annoy them. They are much less concerned about identifying personally with the speaker. Israeli students prefer complex and challenging information that they can ponder and evaluate before they form judgments and opinions. The length of the speech is relatively unimportant.

For more on this topic, log on to InfoTrac College Edition and read Christian Kiewitz's study of cross-cultural student listening preferences, "Cultural Differences in Listening Style Preferences: A Comparison of Young Adults in Germany, Israel, and the United States."

Michaeljung/shutterstock

Taking notes and relating the material to your life are two helpful strategies for comprehensive listening.

Use Elaboration Strategies Link the material to your personal experiences and ideas in ways that enhance the meaning. Create mental images or refer to what you already know or have experienced. For example, you might ask questions like: "Who do I know who is like that?" "What comes next?" "Does this match what I learned in another context?" "How does this relate to things I'm doing now?"

Use Strategies That Complement Your Learning Style An auditory learner might get permission to record the speech and replay it later. If your instructor uses **lecture capture** technology to upload class materials into digital formats, you can review them on demand. Replaying complex subjects can be especially helpful. You can skim over parts you understand easily and then replay the parts that are more difficult.[29] If you are a linear learner, outline the main points and the important supporting information. If you are more graphically oriented, make a mind map and draw connections between ideas, or sketch useful illustrations in the margins of your notes. I personally include the speaker's examples in my notes, because I learn and remember abstract ideas better when I can tie them to real-life situations.

lecture capture use of technology to upload class materials in digital formats

Don't Get Hung Up on Delivery Some speakers with important things to say have annoying delivery habits that can take your focus off the main idea.

In summary, listening to comprehend requires you to understand words and ideas, to identify major ideas and supporting materials, to connect new material with old, and to recall information. Comprehensive listening corresponds with the general speech purpose of informing. We now turn to critical listening skills that you should put into practice when you hear a persuasive speaker.

Improve Your Critical Listening Skills

critical listening listening that requires you to reflect and weigh the merits of messages before you accept them

Persuasive messages surround you, urging you to buy something, sign something, donate something, change your beliefs, and so on. Consequently, you must develop **critical listening** skills to sort out competing claims for your allegiance, your beliefs, your money, and your time. A critical approach does not mean that you find fault with everything, but it does mean that you analyze evidence, ponder implications, and evaluate merits of various appeals rather than accept them unreflectively. Critical listening skills build on comprehensive listening skills but add questions such as these:

- What is this speaker's goal?
- Should I trust him or her?
- Is this speaker knowledgeable about *this* topic?
- Does this message make sense?
- Where does the supporting information come from? Are those sources reliable?
- What will I gain or lose if I adopt these ideas?
- What problems, if any, go along with this position?
- Am I being unduly swayed by my emotions?

Critical listening is one way to live out the cultural saying "Don't believe everything you hear." Sharpening these skills will guide you as you sift through all the persuasive appeals each day brings. Chapters 8 and 17 provide tests you can use to evaluate evidence and reasoning.

In a diverse culture, it's psychologically rewarding to seek out those speakers who bolster and affirm your ideas, especially if the dominant society challenges them. The following examples may clarify this concept.

- Scholarship donors gather to hear narratives describing how their gift kept a needy student in school. They want to know that their money is not being wasted, and these stories convince them to continue their donations.
- Religious adherents gather regularly in their churches, synagogues, mosques, and temples to reaffirm their beliefs.
- Members of neo-Nazi groups gather to hear speakers passionately argue the merits of white supremacy.
- Every January 22, the anniversary of the Supreme Court decision of *Roe v. Wade*, supporters on both sides of the abortion issue attend rallies to hear speakers reaffirm their respective positions.

In contexts like these, you might find yourself enthusiastically clapping, nodding, or verbally encouraging speakers who affirm your biases. In fact, you might accept questionable arguments or emotional appeals that support your cause. However, a listener from a different perspective might reject much of the information and arguments. Thus, you should submit these messages to critical evaluation, just as you would any other persuasive speech.[30]

To practice the skills described here, listen to two political convention speeches from the last Republican and Democratic national conventions. Videos from each convention

Develop Strategies To Listen More Effectively

Return to the Listening Skills Self-Assessment (page 59 or on your online resources), and note each question you answered with an "A" or a "B." Using materials from this section, develop a Listening Skills Development Plan that will help you overcome the listening barrier implied in each question.

For additional suggestions, log on to InfoTrac College Edition and search for "listening AND tips." Read one of the latest articles you find there.

Laptops in Lectures[31]

You've probably seen them: students who sit facing the professor with laptops open. In one window they take notes, occasionally glancing at the professor. In other windows they check Facebook pages or play online games.

Back in 2006 law professor June Entman decided that students in her civil procedures class should take notes the old-fashioned way—with paper and pencil. Laptops, she declared, created a "picket fence" between professors and students, discouraging interaction and promoting a mere transcription of her words. She called activities other than note-taking "dishonest and inconsiderate . . . annoying and distracting to other students."[32] Allan Rubin (Princeton, geosciences) says the problem is getting worse.[33]

So Entman and Rubin both banned laptops from their classroom. Entman's students protested that they could type faster than they could write, but she argued that the class required active participation in discussion. Administrators backed her ban. Rubin reported that he now sees "a sea of faces that are looking at me" as he lectures.[34]

Studies show that multitasking, or in this case serial interruptions of attention, actually impedes learning—both for those on their computers and for the people sitting around them.[35]

Questions

1. What has been your experience with laptops in class?
2. Do you agree with Entman that surfing the Web instead of taking notes is "dishonest"? Why or why not?
3. Are there ethical implications in "annoying and distracting" other students who are paying tuition to learn the information, especially if the distraction prevents them from learning effectively?
4. What is your response to this statement: "A student has the right NOT to listen in class"?

are archived online. If you prefer the Republican Party, practice your comprehensive listening skills on a Democrat's speech. Summarize it and show that you understand it. Then listen to a Republican's speech critically and analytically, using the guidelines described above. If you prefer the Democratic Party, do the opposite: make sure you understand the Republican's ideas, and then critically evaluate a Democrat's speech.

Practice Dialogical Listening

Remember the communication model and the dialogical theory introduced in Chapter 1? Because dialogue involves active participation from listeners and speakers alike, your feedback helps co-create the meanings that ultimately come out of the presentation. Feedback comes in combinations of nonverbal, verbal, or written messages. As you read the suggestions that follow, remember that cultural expectations affect what are considered appropriate feedback behaviors.

Give Appropriate Nonverbal Feedback

Your posture, movements, and eye contact, even the distance you sit from the speaker are all ways to provide meaningful feedback.

- *Posture.* Posture communicates involvement and helps focus your attention. Face the speaker squarely and lean forward slightly. When you are thoroughly engrossed, being "on the edge of your seat" is natural. Even if you sit in a corner or off to the side, you can still turn in the direction of the speaker, and let your body assume a relaxed, open position.
- *Eye contact.* Look at the speaker instead of out the window or at others in the room; this not only helps focus your attention, it also establishes rapport and helps the speaker gauge your interest and comprehension. As the Ethics in Practice Box points out, opening your computer and checking Facebook or playing an online game can be perceived as rude.
- *Distance.* Think about the difference in your attentiveness when you sit far away from the speaker where people are passing by an open door versus when you sit closer to the presenter where fewer outside distractions disrupt your focus. Which seat contributes more to good listening? Choose a place where the speaker can readily make eye contact with you; this puts more pressure on you to pay attention and give nonverbal feedback, because the speaker is more likely to look at you more often.[36]
- *Movements.* Avoid distracting behaviors such as fidgeting, shuffling papers, or playing with your pen. Give nonverbal feedback in the form of smiles at amusing anecdotes, nods in support of a major point, or applause when appropriate to further increase your involvement and provide additional interactions with the presenter.

When listeners are attentive, the speaker may actually become more interesting. One campus legend relates that a boring professor always stood at the lectern and read from his notes. His students decided to act *as if* he were fascinating whenever he moved away from the lectern. As he moved away from his notes, ever so slightly, they all leaned forward a bit, made eye contact, and used supportive motions. According to the legend, the professor eventually was walking back and forth across the front of the room, lecturing animatedly.

Give Verbal Feedback

"Where can I get more information?" "One article I read presented very different information." "How is he defining that word?" Questions and comments such as these arise as you listen. Question-and-answer periods provide opportunities to co-create meanings. Here are a few of the most common types of questions:[37]

Stefanie Timmermann/iStockphoto.com

Question-and-answer periods are ways to give verbal feedback and to make the public speaking situation more dialogical.

clarification questions requests to clear up confusing ideas

closed questions requests for brief, specific answers

open questions requests for more lengthy responses

loaded questions questions containing implications intended to put the speaker on the defensive

requests for elaboration questions asking for more information

comments information from personal experience or research

- When you are confused, ask **clarification questions** to gain more information, such as: Again, what's the difference between the Russian Old Believers and the Molokan Russians? What's your threshold level for "poverty"?
- **Closed questions** ask for brief, specific answers such as "yes" or "no." Use them to gain precise information or to verify your understanding. Here are some examples: Have you read C. S. Lewis's *The Chronicles of Narnia* series? Would you buy coffee from a company that did not purchase fair trade coffee beans? Is Bahman Ghobadi the Kurdish director who made the movie *Turtles Can Fly*?
- **Open questions** invite longer answers that could be developed in a variety of ways, as these examples show: What do you think is the best new source of energy? What suggestions do you have for recycling old cell phones? What is your personal plan for paying off your student loans?
- **Loaded questions** put a speaker on the defensive because of what they imply. Try to avoid them. When will you begin to look at both sides of the issue? This implies that the speaker was one-sided, and *when* is not really asking for a time. In other words, you wouldn't expect to hear, "I am going to research the other side tomorrow afternoon at 3:00."
- To get a speaker to expand on an idea, make a **request for elaboration**: You said the Electoral College was modeled on the system used in the Roman Republic; could you elaborate? Can you provide more information about the cost and availability of proton therapy?
- Instead of questions, you can add **comments** or information from your own experience and research. For instance, after a speech on bullying, Tiffany shared statistics she had heard on a television show. Jon told a story about a coach who bullied his team. If you know that data in the speech is incorrect (for example, the statistics are outdated), you could provide supplementary information.

Although question-and-answer periods are common in the United States, not all cultures participate equally in a co-creation of meaning process, as the Diversity in Practice box titled Saving Face explains.

Saving Face

Question and answer periods are rare in some cultural groups. For instance, in the context of traditional Chinese or Japanese public speaking, listeners are supposed to understand the speaker. Asking a question is an admission that they lack the intelligence to unravel the speaker's shades of meaning. Furthermore, a question reflects on the speaker's communication abilities; in other words, if listeners are confused, the speaker has failed to communicate. Finally, to preserve the speaker's "face," it's considered inappropriate to publicly question a speaker's information and, thus, his or her character.[38]

Give Written Feedback

D-R-E method a feedback method that describes content, shares personal responses, and gives evaluation

Your instructor will probably ask you to respond in writing to some of your classmates' speeches. Just writing "I liked your speech" is too vague to be helpful. More effective comments focus on two or three specific elements of the presentation, using the **D-R-E method**: Describe-Respond-Evaluate.[39] *Describe* what you heard; *respond* with your personal interpretations and reactions; and *evaluate* by critiquing what you found effective and what could be improved. Phrase your comments objectively and positively. Here are some examples:

- Description: "You quoted a variety of sources with diverse viewpoints, including *Newsweek*, the *Jerusalem Post*, and *National Review*." (content) "Your speech had clear signposts and transition statements." (organization) "You looked out the window during your introduction, but you looked more directly at us as the speech progressed." (delivery)
- Response: "I really connected emotionally with the story about the grandfather and the little boy." (content) Or, "Because you alliterated your main points, I will be able to remember your ideas better." (style)
- Evaluation: "Using a variety of sources was good, because it showed you sought out opinions from many perspectives. Your use of examples balanced the statistics well. I think your speech would be even stronger if you added a map to your PowerPoint slides." (content) Or, "Your ability to remember your ideas was impressive, but try to eliminate the phrase 'you know.' It became distracting." (delivery)

Specific comments such as these are beneficial because they give the speaker an idea of the overall impression the speech made on you and why. In general, write out as many positive things as you can, and then evaluate the performance by identifying a few things that could be improved.

Write a Critique

Log on to your online resources or the Internet to watch a speech video of your choice. As you listen, take notes on the speech content and jot down some personal responses and observations on the effectiveness of the speech. Then write a critique that (1) describes, (2) responds to, and (3) evaluates the speech. Discuss this critique with a group of classmates.

receiver apprehension (RA) anxiety that people experience while listening

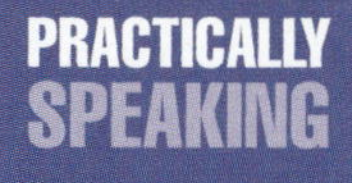

Receiver Apprehension (RA)

Receiver Apprehension (RA) refers to the anxiety people experience during listening. Specifically, RA occurs when listeners fear they'll misinterpret, inadequately process, or fail to adjust psychologically to a particular message.[40] Professor Kaidren Winiecki Sergienko first became interested in RA when she was a graduate student, studying with Dr. Joe Ayres and Dr. Tim Hopf whose extensive research in communication apprehension is discussed Chapter 2. Sergienko finds RA interesting because so many of us experience it so often, and it can have a variety of significant impacts in our lives, but in general it is less visible and less studied than CA.

Is RA a widespread phenomenon? I certainly believe so. If asked, I'm sure most people could recall a situation in which they experienced listening apprehension. Of course, different people experience different levels of RA and in different situations.

Can you give some examples of RA? I sometimes experience RA at work. I feel a level of RA when a student comes to my office upset with

Kaidren Sergienko

Kaidren Winiecki Sergienko

a grade, an assignment, or another student in class. I may also feel RA during a class discussion in which students disagree with each other or are giving each other negative feedback and critiques.

When or where do you see RA in college life? RA is experienced in virtually every part of college life because students are coming to a new place with new people and new norms. Attending orientation, listening to financial aid guidelines, attending the first day of class, hearing a complex or abstract lecture and knowing there will be a test on the material, learning the guidelines for a mid-quarter project, listening to a classmate discuss an opposing opinion, and meeting with a teacher—all of these can result in a low or high level of RA. And these are only a few of the experiences students have.

Faculty, staff, and administrators feel its effects as well. Meeting with colleagues to discuss controversial policy or action plans and attending workshops to learn new technologies are just a few examples of situations that can create RA.

Why did your research focus on RA in the workplace? The workplace is a kind of shared experience that virtually everyone will have. It is where we spend the majority of our waking hours. Many people closely identify with their work. Finally, I believe that our workplace communication can affect our lives outside of work, such as our degree of fulfillment, our self-esteem, and our ability to provide for ourselves and our families. So, if RA is affecting our happiness or our ability for upward mobility within an organization, it is important to acknowledge it and respond to it.

Questions

1. When, if ever, do you fear you'll misinterpret a confusing message?
2. When, if ever, are you afraid you won't understand an abstract or complex message?
3. When, if ever, do you avoid listening to a topic that you find psychologically or emotionally upsetting? (For example, it may directly challenge your beliefs or politics or may be otherwise very disturbing.)
4. How might you overcome your RA in a specific situation where listening fears could have a negative effect on your life?

Summary

Listening is the communication activity that we do most and study least. It involves more than just hearing sounds; listening involves active processing and retention of what you hear. Listening is important in your personal and work life. However, listeners often face cultural as well as personal barriers that impede effective listening. Different languages, vocabularies, and cultural allusions all make comprehension difficult. In addition, personal and psychological factors—such as fatigue, stresses and worries, stereotypes and prejudices, and wandering attention—can hinder listening.

Fortunately, you can devise strategies to listen more effectively. Use cultural schemas or mental blueprints to guide your perception, interpretation, storage, and recollection of what you hear. Know your listening purpose, and identify strategies to help you comprehend information or critically evaluate persuasive messages.

Finally, practice dialogical listening by contributing appropriate nonverbal, verbal, and written feedback. Nonverbal actions communicate that you are interested in the speech; they also help you pay attention. Useful nonverbal elements include a posture that communicates involvement, a distance that helps focus your attention, and movements that support rather than disrupt the speech. When you have an opportunity to interact verbally with a speaker, ask questions or provide comments that elaborate on the topic. However, be aware that after-speech questions and comments are inappropriate in some cultures. Finally, write out comments using the D-R-E method to describe what you heard, respond personally, and evaluate the overall presentation.

STUDY AND REVIEW

Your online resources for *Public Speaking: Concepts and Skills for a Diverse Society* offer a broad range of study tools that will help you better understand the material in this chapter, complete assignments, and succeed on tests. Your online resources feature the following:

- Speech videos with critical viewing questions, speech outlines, and transcripts.
- Interactive versions of this chapter's Stop and Check activities, as well as Application and Critical Thinking Exercises.
- Speech Builder Express and InfoTrac College Edition.
- Weblinks related to chapter content.
- Study and review tools such as self-quizzes, an interactive glossary, and downloadable audio summaries.

You can access your online resources at the CourseMate for *Public Speaking: Concepts and Skills for a Diverse Society.* Log in at **http://www.cengage.com/login**, using the access code that came with your book or that you bought online at **http://www.cengagebrain.com**.

KEY TERMS

The terms below are defined in the margins throughout this chapter.

clarification questions 66
closed questions 66
comments 66
comprehensive listening 60
critical listening 62
cultural allusions 57
D-R-E method 66
hearing 55
lecture capture 62
listening 55
loaded questions 66
open questions 66
physical factors 57
prejudice 57
psychological factors 57
receiver apprehension (RA) 67
requests for elaboration 66
schemas 58
speech-thought differential 58
stereotype 57

APPLICATION AND CRITICAL THINKING EXERCISES

1. Be quiet for thirty seconds and listen to what's going on around you. What sounds can you hear (such as traffic in the background) that you're not really listening to? Choose one of the sounds and really listen to it, keeping in mind the five elements of listening.
2. Listening skills are important in thousands of jobs, ranging from academic advisors or financial aid officers on campus to haircutters and real estate agents. Tell of a time

when someone really listened to you while performing his or her job, and then tell of a time when someone failed to listen well. What was the outcome in each case?

3. Copy the Chinese symbol that stands for listening (see Figure 4.1) onto a sheet of paper, looking at each element. In what way do you use your ears, eyes, and heart when you listen to your classmates? Your professors? People at work? A speaker whose ideas support your own opinions? A speaker with whom you fundamentally disagree?
4. Using the diagrams in Figure 4.2 as models, draw a diagram that depicts your listening pattern during the most recent lecture you heard. Next, draw a diagram that depicts your listening pattern during the last conversation you had with your best friend. Draw a third diagram that shows your listening pattern during your last major conversation with a family member. Compare the three. What conclusions can you draw about your listening in various contexts?

5. Utah State University provides a website (**weblink 4.1**) that provides many student aids. (You can access this link through your CourseMate for *Public Speaking,* Chapter 4 resources.) Link to "Idea Sheets," where you'll find three especially helpful worksheets: (1) "Note taking: Cornell method," (2) "Listening skills for lectures," and (3) "Effective note taking strategies." Use the suggestions in these handouts to create your Listening Skills Development Plan under your online resources for Chapter 4.
6. Practice the nonverbal skills of active listening in one of your courses. That is, use posture, space, eye contact, and movement to help focus your attention on the lecture. Afterward, evaluate how much your nonverbal behaviors helped you pay attention and recall the class material.
7. Verbally interact with one of the speakers in the next round of classroom speeches. During the speech, jot down several comments or questions to ask during the question-and-answer period.
8. Use the Describe-Respond-Evaluate method to give written feedback after a classmate's speech.
9. To face receiver apprehension head on, listen to a speaker who makes you anxious because he or she takes a position that differs dramatically from your views. You may find the person on radio, television, or the Internet (for example, a person whose lifestyle differs from yours, one whose views on a social issue, such as capital punishment, diverges from yours, or a person with different religious beliefs). Describe, respond to, and evaluate the content and delivery, and then assess how your apprehension affected your listening.

SPEECH VIDEO

Go to your online resources to watch and critique speeches of your choice, or link to other Internet sites that offer speech videos, such as TED, YouTube, or C-SPAN.

© Tim Timmerman

CHAPTER 5

THIS CHAPTER WILL HELP YOU

- Choose your speech topic
- Narrow your topic to fit the situation
- Identify a general purpose and a specific purpose for your speech
- Write a thesis statement that states your subject and its importance to the audience
- Write a preview that summarizes your main points

Selecting Your Topic and Purpose

WHAT SHALL I talk about? Many students find that choosing an appropriate topic for a classroom speech is one of their most challenging tasks because the assignment is so open-ended compared to other settings where a topic is often obvious. For example, if you're scheduled to present a report at work, the topic will be related to your most recent project. If you're giving a tribute at a sports banquet, you'll talk about the person being honored. However, in speech classrooms a specific topic is not generally assigned, so you must choose from thousands of potential subjects. Selecting a single topic that's appropriate to the assignment may feel daunting. It can't be too broad or too complex (after all, most classroom assignments are limited to ten minutes maximum); it should be interesting to your audience, as well as to you; it should be relevant; it should be novel . . . you must consider many factors. Topic selection falls into the canon of invention, and this chapter will give you guidelines for choosing your topic, narrowing it to a manageable size, and then selecting your purpose and focus.

Choose Your Topic

Is there a surefire method for selecting a topic that suits you, your audience, and the occasion? Probably not, but many students report that a topic choice can be triggered by a conversation, a news article, or a passionate concern. As you consider a topic's appropriateness, first think of your audience. Is the subject interesting and relevant to them? Then look for topics in four additional places: your personal interests and experiences, other courses you're taking, current events, and international and cultural subjects.

Assess Your Audience's Need to Know

Topics are everywhere. Would you buy a hybrid car? Why, or why not? What historical events took place in your area? What's the latest in technology? What are the causes and the effects of high-priced textbooks? Everyday topics such as these can result in interesting speeches.[1] The key is to find a significant subject—one that *needs* to be discussed because it will increase your audience's knowledge, bring about a desirable change, or highlight important cultural values and beliefs.[2] Evaluate topic possibilities from your audience's perspective (see Figure 5.1). Are they familiar with the subject? What more do they need to know? Do they care about it? Does the subject affect their finances? Their future? Their health? Will it appeal to their curiosity? Chapter 6 provides in-depth information on audience analysis.

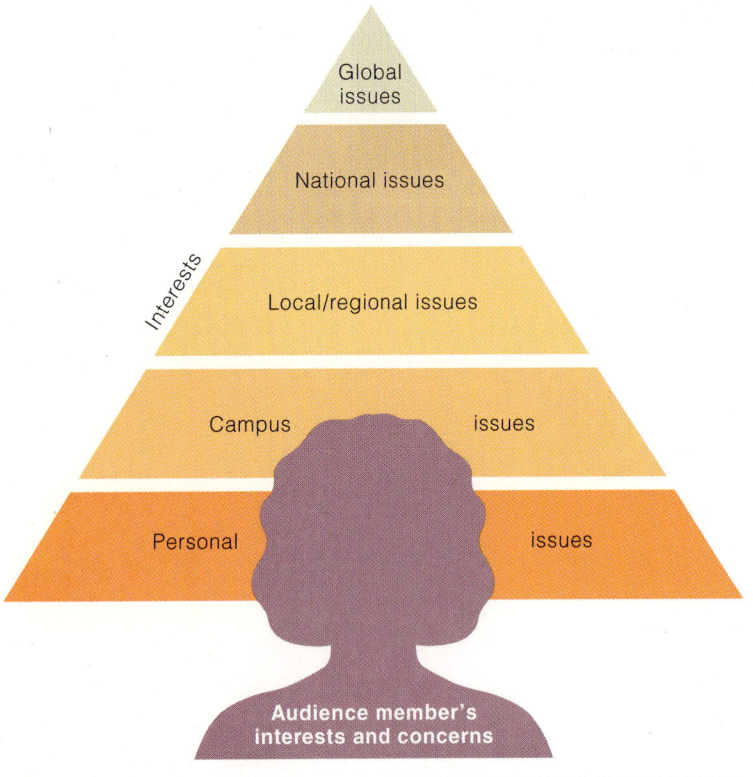

Figure 5.1
Topic Pyramid Topics can be personal or global in scope. People are usually more interested in subjects that are closer to home, although their interest increases when you link the topic to their lives. If you think about why your audience needs to hear about your subject, you can develop your speech in a novel way that connects to their concerns.

Novelty is another general principle for maintaining interest and speaking to a need. That is, either speak about something relatively unfamiliar or present a familiar topic in a creative, new way.[3] Going over familiar procedures such as how to carve a pumpkin, how to make a peanut butter sandwich, or how to brew coffee can waste your listener's time. But can these topics be appropriate? Yes, if you take a novel approach. For example, you might talk about the $850 million[4] peanut butter industry or give a detailed history of peanut butter. Many of these facts would be novel and potentially valuable, even to an audience member who has a peanut allergy.

These two principles—choosing a topic that meets some need in your audience and presenting your subject in a novel way—are fundamental. If you find that your listeners already know a lot about your subject, you'll be more successful if you dig for supplementary information or select another topic. Chapter 16 discusses this in more detail.

ETHICS IN PRACTICE

Are Any Topics Taboo?

In a *BusinessWeek* article, "The Ethics of Talking Politics at Work," Bruce Weinstein argues that people should, for ethical reasons, avoid four topics at work: politics, religion, sex, and money. Discussing them doesn't help workers be more productive because they cause disagreement and raise strong passions. Weinstein bases his conclusion on five ethical principles: do no harm, make things better, respect others, be fair, and be loving.[5] While this may be reasonable advice for the workplace, do topics that cause disagreement, raise strong passions, or make people uncomfortable *need* be addressed in other contexts? For example, some audiences might feel anxious about the topics of race or religion, but *should* race or religion, with their potential for creating discomfort, be addressed publicly? Several politicians have confronted racial and religious issues directly in their campaigns. Their speeches were given to increase understanding of diverse perspectives, invite respect for a variety of viewpoints, and make American society better overall.

Questions

1. Should student speakers avoid topics such as abortion or sexual orientation, which often have political and religious underpinnings and which arouse emotional responses? If so, what topics should be avoided and why?
2. How should students balance First Amendment rights to speak freely—even about culturally taboo topics—against their responsibilities as outlined in Weinstein's five principles or the dialogical and democratic principles described in Chapter 3?
3. Identify a political, religious, sex-related, or money-related topic of your choice that needs to be discussed because honest discussion could actually *enhance* the five ethical principles Weinstein identifies.

Consider Your Personal Interests

Another basic principle is to choose subjects you know and care about. Your personal interests and experiences can generate a number of possible topics.[6] What is your major? Your occupational goals? Your hobbies? Which famous people have you seen in person? What irritates you? What changes would you like to see in society? Unique life experiences also make good topics. You are who you are because of what you know and what you've experienced. Think about your family background, jobs, hobbies, or recreational interests that might interest others.[7] Here are some ways students created speeches around their interests and experiences:

- As an avid gamer, Kelsey began to notice the number of advertisements embedded in video games, so she chose advergaming as her topic. You can find her speech at the end of Chapter 6.
- Because Lishan is from China, his informative speech, given during spring semester, compared and contrasted the Western celebration of St. Valentine's Day with the

Chinese Double-Seventh Festival, sometimes called the Chinese Valentine's Day. Read his speech at the end of Chapter 16.
- David plans to be a nurse, so he explored the topic of male nurses. His outline is at the end of this chapter.

Speaking on a topic that is personally compelling has obvious advantages. When you are truly interested in your subject, you can speak more passionately. Your interest can help you concentrate more on your message than on yourself and your insecurities. Your enthusiasm will also energize your audience—after all, what is more boring than a bored speaker?

Look for Topics from Other Courses

Look for speech topics in your academic major or in other courses you are taking. For example, Casey's engineering professor talked about exciting progress in developing artificial gills. As a child, Casey's favorite superhero was Aquaman, so choosing artificial gills as his topic allowed him to go into more depth on the topic. You'll find his speech at the end of Chapter 13. Jennifer, whose major is cognitive science, discussed neuroimaging. The text of her speech appears at the end of Chapter 7. Preparing a speech on an interesting topic from another class has the added advantage of helping you learn the material for that course.

Don't hesitate to use research you have done for a paper in another course if the subject is appropriate. For example, Bralee wrote a paper on product placement in the media for one course. She also used some of the information from that paper in her classroom speech. However, her speech included information that the paper did not, and vice versa. So, although some of the information overlapped, she adapted her purpose, her organizational pattern, and her language to meet two very different assignments.

Investigate Current Events

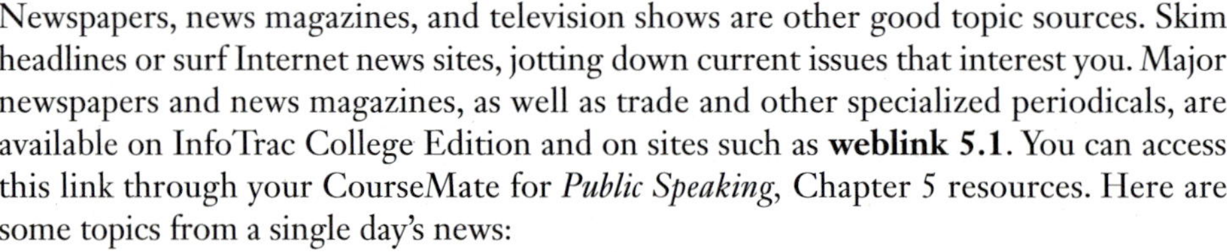

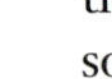

Newspapers, news magazines, and television shows are other good topic sources. Skim headlines or surf Internet news sites, jotting down current issues that interest you. Major newspapers and news magazines, as well as trade and other specialized periodicals, are available on InfoTrac College Edition and on sites such as **weblink 5.1**. You can access this link through your CourseMate for *Public Speaking*, Chapter 5 resources. Here are some topics from a single day's news:

copper wire theft	children with food allergies
military drones	engagement rings
Internet taxes	city parks
nuclear power	mushrooms

Topics from current events usually address a need in society. The fact that they are important enough to discuss in the print or broadcast media means that they are significant to many people. And, because they are publicly covered, you should be able to locate information easily. For example, a topic such as the national debt will have thousands of related links in your library's databases and on the Internet; even a topic such as electric bikes or chocolate production can yield hundreds of links. However, you must carefully examine the credibility of all Internet sources; news outlets and government agencies have a different kind of credibility than blogs and opinion pieces.

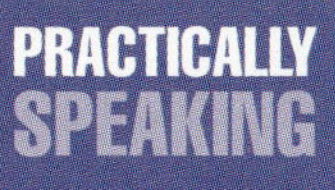

Brad Lau, University Administrator, Student Life

Lau's career requires him to speak to a variety of audiences on a variety of topics. He answered a few questions about the challenges he faces.

Who are your major audiences? I speak to several types of audiences in a given year, and they often come from very different perspectives and backgrounds with diverse interests and needs. My most common audiences include college students in general, student leaders, community audiences, student life professionals (through workshop presentations, and so on), and the press.

How do you find your topics? This happens in a number of different ways:

- Asking people who will be in my audience what they perceive the felt need to be
- Reading books and articles that deal with the needs and interests of a given audience
- Asking others who speak to those audiences what the key issues are and if they have suggestions about specific things that should be addressed
- Keeping a file of articles dealing with relevant issues and topics for the various audiences
- Emailing people I trust and who are credible for that audience for suggestions about topics that need to be addressed
- Looking at publications (online and in print) that seek to reach that particular audience

What are your most stressful topics? It is difficult to speak about very emotional topics. For example, I am the person who must speak with the press when there is a campus controversy or tragedy involving students, such as a fatal traffic accident. Student audiences can also be stressful. Students often hear a lot of speeches, and I feel the pressure of making a topic relevant and timely while also saying what I think they need to hear (sometimes whether they want to or not). In other words, in my job I don't always give an audience what they like to hear; sometimes I must speak to what I think they need to hear, or I must present and defend unpopular administrative policies.

Questions

1. Count the number of times Lau uses the words *need* to discuss topic selection. How could you use the strategies he lists to find a topic your audience needs to know about?
2. Give examples of topics that student audiences might *need* to hear about but might not *want* to hear about.

Used by permission of Brad Lau.

Used by permission of Brad Lau.

In his job, Brad Lau's topics range from pleasant welcomes to new students to unpleasant briefings about campus tragedies.

Consider International and Cultural Topics

You may find it easier to come up with personal or national topics that are familiar and regularly appear in the news. However, don't overlook international subjects. Explore your cultural heritage and experiences; for instance, Bailey, who went on a service trip to Africa, chose the topic of AIDS in Swaziland. Ryan, whose ancestors were Basque, spoke about the Basque artist, Jorge Oteiza. Another possibility is to consider global aspects of your major. A film studies major, for example, might investigate a director or film genre from another country or a different cultural group. International trade, global investments, and international crime—all are topics of increasing importance in the twenty-first century. Contemporary cultural topics are easily found on the Internet on sites such as BBC News World Edition (**weblink 5.2**). You can access this link through your CourseMate for *Public Speaking*, Chapter 5 resources.

Whatever your topic, it's essential to make connections to your listeners' here-and-now concerns. For example, the subject of land mines in another country a continent away might seem far removed from your campus world. But there are ways to link your classmates with the topic. Would they empathize with children and other civilians who lose limbs when they step on a mine? Do any listeners have friends or relatives in the military who might encounter these weapons? What about tax dollars that pay for specialists who detonate the mines? Could you link the topic to fundamental values, such as the desire for a world at peace or for freedom and justice for all? Your challenge is to help your audience understand the significance and relevance of your subject. For additional ideas on how to find topics, check out Professor Ron St. John's Web site: **weblink 5.3.** You can access this link through your CourseMate for *Public Speaking*, Chapter 5 resources.

Does Requiring One Speech on "Communication and Culture" Increase Students' Empathy?

You might think that you'd become more empathetic—better able to understand diverse perspectives—if you chose a diversity-related topic; however, a single speech on a diversity topic probably won't increase your empathy unless you also consider diversity issues throughout the semester.

One study[8] researched four groups of students: the control group took a normal communication course; the second group took an entire course in intercultural communication; the third discussed concepts related to diversity at several points during the term; and the fourth group had a one-shot assignment to give a public speech on a "communication and diversity" topic. Students who studied intercultural communication for an entire term significantly increased in empathy compared to the control group. Those who often discussed diversity issues throughout the semester also showed increases. However, students who gave a single diversity speech made no significant gains.

What does this mean to you? What connections can you see between the ability to understand a variety of perspectives and the diversity concepts presented in this text and in your classroom? How might an increase in empathy make you a more competent communicator?

Narrow Your Topic

Once you have a broad topic, you must then narrow it enough to discuss it within a designated time frame. This principle applies across all speaking contexts, from workplace project reports, sales presentations, and announcements to civic and ceremonial contexts. One professional speaker narrowed his topic like this:

> I'm going to talk about technology and an introduction of technology into developing markets. I'm going to focus on agriculture. I'm going to focus particularly in Africa and particularly in Sub-Saharan Africa . . . in Malawi . . . with a woman named Sabina Xhosa.[9]

Let's consider the general subject of workplace issues as an example. Obviously, you can't discuss "The World of Work" in seven minutes, but you can focus on a specific topic such as how to negotiate a salary, on a controversy such as drug testing, or on a trend such as corporate social responsibility. A mind map is a way to let your ideas flow. Figure 5.2 illustrates how to create a mind map by starting with a broad subject and narrowing it to a series of more realistic classroom topics, including personal, national, or international aspects of the topic.

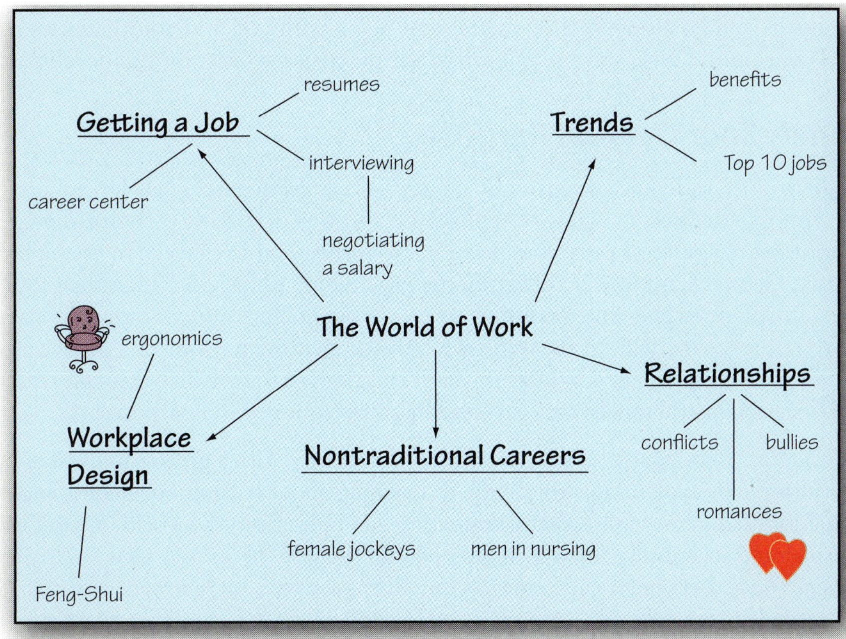

Figure 5.2
Mind Map This mind map shows several work-related topics.

Identify Several Usable Topics

List about ten major topic areas that interest you (such as sports, animals, food). Then narrow your list to two or three, and make a mind map for each of those topics.

By selecting general areas early in the term, you can be alert for information to use in your speeches. For example, someone who chose the topic of workplace bullies could take

(continued)

advantage of the "news alerts" feature at Internet sources such as Google (news) or Yahoo (news) that provide updates on personalized topics of interest. For different perspectives, she might go to carefully-selected blogs related to bullying and use a blog tracker service that lets her know when a particular blog is updated. She could also set up interviews with human resource professionals as well as with people who have experienced bullying. Having the topic clearly in mind gives her plenty of time to gather materials.

Create a file on your computer or in hard copy form for each subject by photocopying, clipping, or downloading articles, taking notes on lectures, and finding relevant video resources. Then at speech time, you should have many resources available for a good presentation that a last-minute scramble might not produce.

Choose Your Purpose and Focus

You don't just "accidentally" give a public speech; instead, you speak to accomplish specific goals or purposes.[10] Consequently, at the outset of your preparation, carefully clarify what you want to achieve by identifying your general purpose and tentatively formulating a specific purpose for that particular speech. Continue to refine your specific purpose as you go along. A thesis statement helps both you and your listeners understand your central idea, and a preview lays out the major points you will develop.

Identify Your General Purpose

general purpose four general purposes are: to inform, to persuade, to entertain, or to commemorate

Teachers of rhetoric have consistently pointed out a few general goals for public speaking. Almost 2,000 years ago, St. Augustine, who was originally a rhetoric professor, identified three **general purposes**: to teach, to please, and to move.[11] In the eighteenth century, George Campbell,[12] reflecting the psychology of his era,[13] identified four purposes: to enlighten the understanding, to please the imagination, to move the passions, and to influence the will. In the mid-twentieth century, Alan Monroe[14] said we attempt to inform, to entertain, to stimulate through emotion, or to convince through reasoning. Today, speech instructors commonly describe these four general purposes:

- *To inform.* Here your goal is to provide your audience with a greater understanding of your topic by explaining, describing, or teaching about it. Announcements and introductions fall into the informative category. Examples from the world of work include explaining accounting fraud or telling how to prepare for an interview.
- *To persuade.* Persuaders attempt to convince, motivate, or reinforce cultural ideals. Persuaders at work sell products, collect donations for worthy causes, nominate someone to run for an office, and urge co-workers to participate in community projects, among other things.
- *To entertain.* Sometimes you just want listeners to laugh at your humorous portrayal of a subject. There are thousands of humorous workplace incidents; funny coworkers, crazy memos, weird customer requests—all of these would make entertaining speeches.
- *To commemorate.* Special occasion speeches highlight and reinforce cultural ideals. Tributes, toasts, awards, and other types of speeches described in Appendix B fall into this category. Farewell speeches, for example, praise the good qualities of the departing coworker, while awards honor people who exemplify an organization's ideals.

Aspects of these speech purposes can overlap because audiences are often comprised of listeners with various levels of information and motivation. Take the example of

Microsoft's Bill Gates, who recently vowed to work for the eradication of polio worldwide. In a single speech, he must tell uninformed listeners about polio's extent and effects globally; he must motivate informed listeners to get involved by donating money to worthy organizations. Throughout, he must hold their interest. Although his talk might not be specifically commemorative, he is reinforcing cultural beliefs about science and health and upholding cultural values on helping others.

Your instructor will probably assign you a general purpose for each speech. When your purpose is informative, focus your research on discovering and presenting factual material that will increase your audience's knowledge or understanding of your topic. When you must be persuasive, select convincing and motivating materials that will influence your listeners to believe and act in the ways you advocate. If you're asked to be entertaining, choose a ridiculous event or situation and use strategies such as exaggeration and wordplay to highlight humorous aspects of the topic. Although giving a speech to entertain is less common in the classroom, each speech should always be interesting, regardless of its purpose. For a commemorative speech assignment, choose a worthy subject and develop it around cultural values. Ryan's tribute to Jorge Otieza in Appendix C shows how to do this. Figure 5.3 shows how to come up with a variety of speech purposes for a broad topic such as the workplace.

Narrow Your Purpose

Practice narrowing your purpose by making a diagram similar to the one in Figure 5.3, using one of the subject-area mind maps you made for the Stop and Check exercise on page 77.

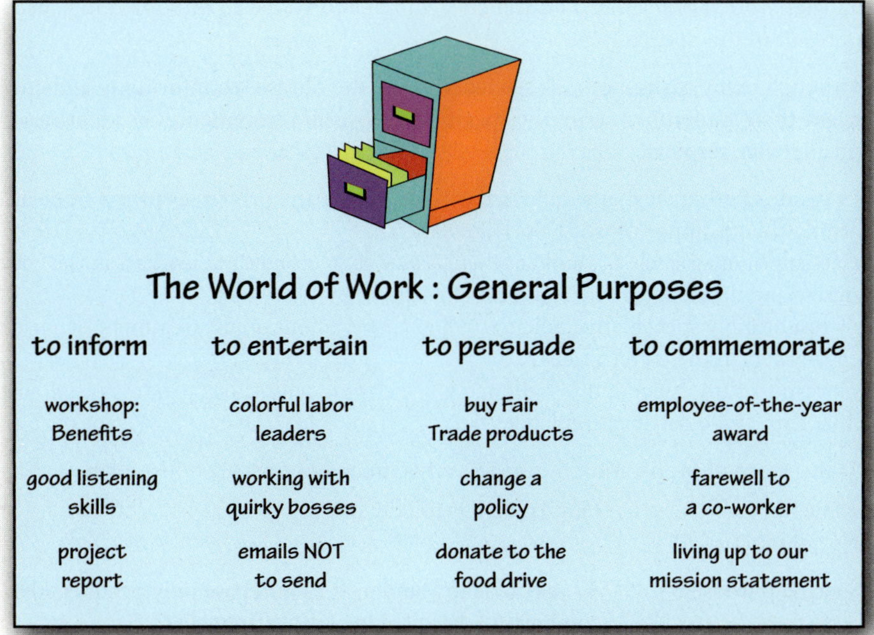

Figure 5.3
General Purposes
A broad topic such as the world of work can generate informative, entertaining, persuasive, and commemorative speeches.

Identify Your Specific Purpose*

specific purpose the cognitive, affective, or behavioral responses a speaker desires

cognitive effects influences on beliefs, understandings, and other mental processes

affective effects influences on listeners' feelings

behavioral effects influences on audience actions

Linnea has become convinced that her morning cup of coffee may mean that a worker in a coffee-producing company is being exploited, so she chooses "Fair Trade certified coffee" as her topic. Her next step is to decide exactly what she wants her listeners to know or do, so she begins to focus on her **specific purpose** statement, an audience-centered phrase or sentence that identifies the cognitive, affective, or behavioral responses she desires from her listeners.[15]

- **Cognitive effects** are influences on the audience's beliefs, thoughts, or understandings. If she chooses this specific purpose, Linnea will focus more narrowly on providing information or on changing her listeners' beliefs about some aspect of coffee production.
- **Affective effects** are the feelings or emotions aroused in the listeners. Fair trade is a potentially emotional topic, and Linnea might hope to instill anger and maybe even guilt feelings over the treatment of workers in the coffee industry.
- **Behavioral effects** are influences on audience actions. She might ask them to sign a pledge to change their purchasing habits and buy only Fair Trade certified products.

In short, Linnea must clarify what she wants her audience to know, feel, or do and then combine her topic and goal into a specific purpose statement. One way to keep her desired response in mind is to write an infinitive phrase that includes the words "my audience." Here are some specific purpose statements that illustrate a variety of general purposes.

- To inform my audience about the meaning of Fair Trade by decoding the meanings in five Fair Trade certification labels. (*Cognitive effect:* The audience will understand how to interpret Fair Trade labels.)
- To convince my audience that agricultural workers in the coffee industry often labor in unfair working conditions. (*Cognitive effect:* The audience will be persuaded that there is a labor problem at the production level of the coffee industry.)
- To persuade my audience to become angry about the abuse of agricultural workers in the coffee industry. (*Affective effect:* The audience will have an emotional response and thus develop a negative attitude toward coffee that is not fairly traded.)
- To persuade my audience to purchase only products that have a Fair Trade certification label. (*Behavioral effect:* The audience will be motivated to do something specific as a result of this speech.)

Although many instructors ask students to use the phrase "to inform my audience," others ask their students to write the specific purpose as a statement that identifies the desired audience response:

- As a result of my speech, my audience will *understand* the principles of fair trade after learning the meanings of five Fair Trade labels.
- As a result of my speech, my audience will *believe* that agricultural workers in the coffee industry and others like it are not treated fairly.
- As a result of my speech, my audience will *feel anger* about unjust treatment of agricultural workers in the coffee industry.
- As a result of my speech, my audience will *purchase* only those products that come with a Fair Trade certification label.

At this stage of preparation, Linnea has this much of her speech formulated:

Topic:	Fair Trade Certified Coffee
General purpose:	To persuade
Specific purpose:	To persuade my audience to purchase only products that come with a Fair Trade certification label.

*Excerpts from Linnea's sample student speech: Used by permission of Linnea Smith.

Formulating her general and specific purpose early on lets her focus her additional research more effectively. She needs facts, descriptions, and explanations for all her speeches, but especially for informative ones. If she wants to prove links between coffee consumption and mistreatment of laborers on coffee plantations, she should look for opinions from experts in global economics. She should search out emotionally compelling examples of exploited workers if her goal is to motivate listeners to care or to act. If she wants listeners to purchase only Fair Trade certified products in general, she should present specific information that will help listeners see this as a realistic goal.

The key is to create specific a purpose statement that is audience-centered, one that focuses your attention on your goal for your listeners. Following this, the next step is to begin formulating a *central idea* or *thesis statement* that captures the major idea of the speech.

Jupiter Images/Getty Images

A topic such as Fair Trade can be developed several ways. A speaker could focus on influencing the audience's knowledge or beliefs, attitudes, or behaviors related to Fair Trade certified products.

Write Your Thesis Statement

If the specific purpose statement is written from your point of view—from what you want to accomplish with your audience—the **central idea** or **thesis statement** is written from the audience's point-of-view.[16] It is a single, declarative sentence that names the subject and establishes your goal.[17] It's like a road map that summarizes the main idea you will discuss throughout your speech. Note the contrast between these correctly and incorrectly written thesis statements:

central idea a synonym for thesis statement

thesis statement a single sentence that names the subject and establishes its significance

Correct: Workers in many countries are exploited by unfair labor conditions, but we can help improve their lives by buying only Fair Trade certified products.

Incorrect: Why should we buy Fair Trade certified products? (This is a question, not a declarative sentence.)

Incorrect: Workers are exploited in many countries. This is unfair, but we can help by insisting on Fair Trade certified products. (Use one sentence, not two.)

Incorrect: Why care about Fair Trade products? (This is a fragment, not a complete sentence.)

Begin formulating your thesis statement when you select your topic and decide on your general and specific purposes. Then allow yourself plenty of time to explore and develop your ideas, narrow the approach, consider the point of view you'll develop, and choose the general direction you'll take.[18] The process of invention takes time and energy. New ideas will emerge and others will seem less important, so don't be afraid to revise your direction as you do additional research, preparation, and organization. As this student explains:

> I tend to have running dialogues in my head, sometimes even out loud. While I talk to myself, I work out particulars. I answer questions I've posed to myself ("Well, really, Gail, if you argue that, where will you go? It's too huge!" or "Now does that really make sense?"). My answers often lead me to modify my central idea as I continue my preparation.
>
> Gail

When you actually give your speech, incorporate your thesis statement into your introduction, and follow it with a **preview**, or short summary of the major points you'll use to develop your thesis. Linnea previewed her speech like this:

preview short summary of the major points you'll develop in the speech

> I will explain some problems associated with coffee production, show how Fair Trade certified products provide a solution, and challenge you to take action to promote and consume only fairly traded products.

The text of Linnea's speech appears at the end of Chapter 18 and on the book's online resources where you can watch it on video. Here is another example that shows the relationship between topic, general purpose, specific purpose, thesis statement, and preview.

Topic:	Males in Nursing
General purpose:	To inform
Specific purpose:	To inform my audience about the history, struggles, and strengths of men in nursing.
Thesis statement:	Men have a long history in the nursing profession, but many factors continue to keep them in the minority.
Preview:	I will first describe the long history of men in nursing, explain how the profession changed after Vietnam, and then tell some current challenges facing men as a minority in nursing.

(An outline of this speech appears at the end of this chapter and on the book's online resources which include a video of the speech.)

In summary, topic and purpose selection are important aspects of speech making. Select a subject that interests you, narrow it to a manageable subtopic, formulate general and specific speech purposes, and then synthesize your main ideas into a thesis statement or central idea that names the subject and alerts the audience to its significance. When you give your speech, state your thesis in the introduction, and add a preview of the main points you will use to develop your central idea.

General Purpose, Specific Purpose, and Thesis statement

Choose three topics from the list below (or select three topics that you could talk about without doing much research). Then quickly write out a general purpose statement, a specific purpose statement, and a thesis statement for an impromptu speech about each topic.

- Online shopping
- Stress relievers for college students
- Simple breakfasts
- Free things to do in this community
- Study tips

Summary

When you choose a speech topic, look for something that interests you and that your audience needs to know. Then, examine your personal experiences, other courses, current events, and international or cultural possibilities for significant subjects. If you do careful work early in the term, you can produce a list or develop a series of files on topics that will interest both you and your listeners.

After selecting your topic, decide on your general intention or purpose for the speech. Will you inform, persuade, entertain, or commemorate? Then write the specific purpose that names the cognitive, affective, or behavioral response you want from your listeners. Focus on the speech's content by writing out the thesis statement, a single sentence that summarizes your major ideas in a way that guides both you and your listeners. Begin to formulate your thesis early in the speech, but revise it if necessary as you proceed in your research and preparation. Finally, write a preview of the major ideas you will develop in the speech.

STUDY AND REVIEW

Your online resources for *Public Speaking: Concepts and Skills for a Diverse Society* offer a broad range of study tools that will help you better understand the material in this chapter, complete assignments, and succeed on tests. Your online resources feature the following:

- Speech videos with critical viewing questions, speech outlines, and transcripts.
- Interactive versions of this chapter's Stop and Check activities, as well as Application and Critical Thinking Exercises.
- Speech Builder Express and InfoTrac College Edition.
- Weblinks related to chapter content.
- Study and review tools such as interactive quizzes and sample quizzes, an interactive glossary, and downloadable audio summaries.

You can access your online resources at the CourseMate for *Public Speaking: Concepts and Skills for a Diverse Society.* Log in at **http://www.cengage.com/login**, using the access code that came with your book or that you bought online at **http://www.cengagebrain.com**.

KEY TERMS

The terms below are defined in the margins throughout this chapter.

APPLICATION AND CRITICAL THINKING EXERCISES

1. Discuss in a small group some ways you could add the element of novelty to the following common topics: seatbelts, making a sandwich, television violence, writing a résumé.
2. Design a mind map on the general topic of education after high school. Identify two or three topics that would be significant to your audience.
3. Work with a small group of your classmates to create a mind map based on a very general international topic such as China, global diseases, ethnic conflicts, or natural disasters. Record your ideas on a blank transparency or a large piece of paper and then display it and explain it to the entire class.
4. For additional information on St. Augustine, one of the great figures of rhetoric, go to **weblink 5.4** (you can access this link through your CourseMate for *Public Speaking,* Chapter 5 resources) and read Chapters 12 and 13 of his treatise on rhetoric. He gave this advice seventeen centuries ago. Which principles still apply?

5. For each of the following topics, tell how you could create one speech to inform, one to persuade, and one to entertain: negotiating a raise at work, attending an opera, cable news programs, spring break, recreational hiking.
6. Choose one of the topics from number 5 and write a general purpose statement, specific purpose statement, central idea or thesis statement, and preview that match the ideas you had for informative, persuasive, and entertaining speeches.

SPEECH VIDEO

Go to your online resources to watch and critique David Boggs delivering his speech, "Males in Nursing."

Student Speech Outline with Commentary

David found his topic in his major.

MALES IN NURSING*
By David Boggs

Topic: Males in Nursing

General Purpose: To inform

Specific Purpose: To inform my audience about the history, struggles, and strengths of men in nursing.

Central Idea: Men have a long history in the nursing profession, but many factors continue to keep them in the minority.

Preview: I will first describe the long history of men in nursing, explain how the profession changed after Vietnam, and then tell some current challenges facing men as a minority in nursing.

Organizational Pattern: Chronological

Introduction

I. Several scenes from the movie *Meet the Parents* show Greg Focker explaining his occupation to his girlfriend's family and friends.
   A. When he says he's "in medicine," he gets respectful looks.
   B. When he confesses he's "a nurse," he gets laughs.
II. How do you respond when one of your male friends says he wants to be a nurse?
III. The Department of Health and Human Services (2010) says there are 3.06 million registered nurses in the US; only 6.6% are men, but I plan to be one of them.
IV. I will first describe the long history of men in nursing, explain how the profession changed after Vietnam, and then tell some current challenges facing men as a minority in nursing.

His preview lets the audience know how he'll develop his ideas.

Body

In this main point he provides many unfamiliar facts about men in nursing.

I. Although women now dominate the profession, males have been nursing for centuries.
   A. According to "History of Men in Nursing: A Review" by Chad O'Lynn (2007), males did nursing duties in ancient cultures.
      1. In Greece, women were restricted to the home, so men assisted the physicians.
      2. Around 250 B.C.E. the first known school of nursing began in India—training only men.
      3. The Roman army depended on male nurses.
   B. O'Lynn (2007) further explains that one function of monasteries and convents was to care for the sick as early as the fourth and fifth centuries, C.E., so both Catholic monks and nuns did nursing duties.
      1. An article in *The Journal of Advanced Nursing* (Evans, 2004) described non-military orders that included the Brothers of St. Anthony, who cared for people with a disfiguring skin disease known as St. Anthony's Fire.
      2. Military knights in medieval times were hospitallers in orders such as the Knights of St. Lazarus and the Knights Templars.

3. The Alexians, an order that nursed the poor and the mentally ill, also buried the dead.
   a. After the plague years, the Alexians worked mainly with the mentally ill.
   b. In 1898, the Catholic Church started a school to train the Alexian Brothers in mental health nursing.
   c. Catholics also started St. Joseph's Hospital School in 1929 to train men in their religious order.

C. In a history of Army nursing, William T. Bester (2007) explained that during the Civil War era men nursed the sick and wounded on the battlefield, while women nursed in military hospitals.

David includes sources in his outline. He can work them in as he delivers his speech.

D. An article "Unheralded Nurses: Male Caregivers in the Nineteenth-Century South" (Sabin, 2007) said that the 1800s the South was devastated with diseases like typhoid, yellow fever, and smallpox, which were rampant.
   1. However, men in the patriarchal society were supposed to provide and protect.
   2. They sent the family to safer areas while they stayed behind to care for the sick.

E. The book *Daring to Care* (Malka, 2007) says Florence Nightingale, the "mother of nursing," changed the demographics of nursing at the turn of the 20th century.

Here, David begins to explain how the nursing profession came to be dominated by women.

   1. Author Susan Malka (2007) said Nightingale rose above the stereotype placed on women and fought for her right to practice medicine just as much as men.
   2. Women then started to flood the occupation, creating gender boundaries in the profession, assuming that men were not needed unless there were male patients.
   3. Thus, men virtually "disappeared" from the profession for half of a century.
   4. By 1940, *The Journal of Advanced Nursing* (Evans, 2005) article said that only 2% of nurses were male, and they were mostly psychiatric nurses.
   5. The Army Nursing Corps did not even admit men until 1955; men who served during war time had to serve as orderlies.

II. Male nursing changed drastically after the Vietnam War.

He moves from the historical to the present day experiences of men in nursing.

   A. *Daring to Care* (Malka, 2007) says that before Vietnam, male nurses got only a reserve commission instead of a full regular army commission.
      1. This discouraged them from joining.
      2. However in June 1967, Lawrence C. Washington, an African American nurse, received the first regular army commission (Malka, 2007).
   B. Sarnecky's (1999) *History of the Army Nursing Corps* stated that in 1971, the National Male Nurse Association was created to fight for workplace equality.
      1. Later, it was renamed the American Assembly for Men in Nursing (AAMN).
      2. A 2007 report on the AAMN (Tranbarger, 2007) says the Assembly gives voice to the men in nursing and has fought and won a number of victories for issues like gender equality in nursing education, clinical assignments for male students in maternity wards, and use of gender neutral language.
      3. Its latest objectives include recruiting men into nursing, supporting them, and advocating for research and study in men's related health issues.

III. Although numbers have increased from 2% (mostly psychiatric nurses) in 1940 (Evans, 2004) to 6.6% today (USDHHA, 2010) male nurses still face challenges.
   A. A Hodes Research poll of 498 male nurses in 2004 said that major factors keeping men from nursing is the stereotype of nurses as women, not men, of male nurses as gay, and of men as "not caring."
   B. Two main factors have contributed to the view of men as uncaring.
      1. In *Men in Nursing* (2007), researchers questioned 111 practicing male nurses in 2003 asking whether the schools that they attended presented a masculine or feminine side of care.
         a. 30.9% stated that they had been taught with an emphasis in feminine styles of caring.
         b. 53.6% stated that no masculine style of caring was taught.

2. A second factor is that men are scared of being falsely accused of sexual inappropriateness.
   a. Between the years of 1992 to 2002, 45% feared being falsely accused.
   b. However, 68% had received no appropriate touch instructions from their professors.

The brief conclusion reviews his points and ends with a reference back to the opening movie example.

Conclusion

I. In conclusion, men have had difficulty gaining significant stature in the field of nursing.
II. However, historically men took leading roles through the church and the military, and since the Vietnam War, the number of male nurses has steadily risen, but men still have a hard time being taken seriously due to stereotypes, stigmas, and training.
III. Hopefully things are changing enough so that a movie character no longer gets laugh lines when he confesses, "I'm in medicine; I'm a nurse."

Sources

Bester, W. T. (2007). Army nursing: A personal biography. In C. E. O'Lynn & R. E. Tranbarger. (Eds.). *Men in nursing: History, challenges, and opportunities* (pp. 83–100). New York, NY: Springer Publishing Company.

Malka, S. (2007). *Daring to care*. Urbana and Chicago, IL: University of Illinois Press.

D'Antonio, P. (2007). *Nurse's work: Issues across time and place*. New York, NY: Springer Publishing Company.

O'Lynn, C. E. (2007). History of men in nursing: A review. In O'Lynn & Tranbarger, *Men in nursing*, 5–42.

Sarnecky, M. T. (1999). *A history of the U.S. Army Nursing Corps*. University of Philadelphia, PA: University of Pennsylvania Press.

Bernard Hodes Group. (2005, January 26). *Men in nursing study*. An Omnicom Group Company.

Tranbarger, R. E. (2007). Assembly for Men in Nursing (AAMN): The first 30 years as reported in *Interaction*. In O'Lynn & Tranbarger, *Men in nursing*, 67–73.

U.S. Department of Health and Human Services. (2010, March). The registered nurse population: Initial findings from the 2008 national sample survey of registered nurses. Health Resources and Services Administration.

Sabin, L. (2007). Unheralded nurses: Male caregivers in the nineteenth-century South. In P. D'Antonio, E. D. Baer, S. D. Rinker, & J. E. Lynaugh. (Eds.). *Nurses' work: Issues across time and place* (pp. 49–64). New York, NY: Springer Publishing Company.

© Tim Timmerman

CHAPTER
6

Audience Analysis

THIS CHAPTER WILL HELP YOU

- Describe various audience motivations
- Tell how demographic audience analysis helps you adapt your topic to a particular audience
- Develop a questionnaire to assess your listeners' psychological profile
- Explain how the situation, including time and place, affect your audience
- Analyze your audience's perception of your credibility

TEACHER of the Year—institutions annually recognize an instructor who is especially skilled at communicating complex concepts to students from various backgrounds. Oregon State University honored Dawn Wright, professor of geosciences (marine and coastal geography), for her ability to make a challenging subject "personal and accessible" to a wide variety of students.[1] Nicknamed "Deepsea Dawn," Professor Wright uses personal experiences from her scientific voyages across the globe, and she incorporates illustrations that are particularly relevant to Oregonians on topics such as wave-generated electricity, coastal erosion, and tsunami preparedness.

Deepsea Dawn also loves to talk to young people, especially girls and members of underserved groups who aspire to science careers.[2] Her effectiveness comes from her sensitivity to each audience at every step of preparation. Using **audience**

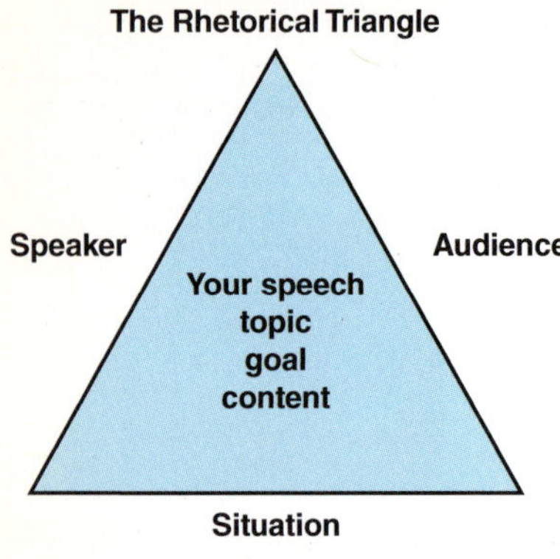

Figure 6.1
The Rhetorical Triangle The audience, the speaking situation, and the speaker come together around the message.

audience analysis identifying audience characteristics to communicate more effectively

listening speaker dialogical speaker who hears audience interests and concerns before, during, and after a speech

analysis skills, Professor Wright thinks carefully about her listeners and then finds the best ways to communicate her ideas, given that group. In doing so, she embodies the dialogical perspective and becomes a **listening speaker**[3] who considers her audience before, during, and after each presentation.

Because your relationship with each audience is complex, this chapter describes some ways to think about the connections between your audience, your topic, your situation, and yourself. Figure 6.1 depicts this as a rhetorical triangle with three sides—audience, speaker, and situation—that come together around a message.[4] The previous chapter discussed the center of the triangle, the topic; however, a great topic, a specific goal, and significant content alone won't make a speech successful. That's why this chapter focuses on the three sides of the triangle—the audience's motivations, the situation in which you speak, and the audience's perception of you.[5]

Analyze Your Audience

A good speech is prepared for a particular group at a particular time. Although some careers such as politics or sales require speakers to present similar material repeatedly, someone who gives an identical speech (also called a "canned" speech or a "stump" speech) to audience after audience, acting as if the listeners were identical, is generally less effective than someone who adapts the material to each audience and each setting. This section explores ways to think about motivations and demographics.

Consider Audience Motivations

Why do audiences gather? What attracts them? What holds them? Answering these questions provides clues about your listeners' motivations and helps you prepare each message more effectively.[6] Here are some general types of audiences:

University Marketing at Oregon State University.

University Marketing at Oregon State University.

Professor "Deepsea Dawn" Wright makes complex science topics personal and accessible to her many audiences—whether they are graduate students, undergraduates, community members, or grade-school students.

1. **Unmotivated audiences** lack a purposeful listening goal. Listeners in **random audiences** are initially involved in another activity, but something attracts their attention, and they pause and listen for a while. A salesman's flashy demonstration of a food processor, the impassioned voice of an activist in an outdoor forum, or the humorous stories of a sidewalk entertainer might draw them in. They may be browsing the radio dial or surfing YouTube when a speaker or topic temporarily captures their interest. Your challenge with a random audience is to attract and maintain attention long enough to present your message. If you communicate through a form of media, remember that your audience can easily change channels or tune you out, so focus on being interesting and relevant, and use conversational delivery as if you were addressing one listener at a time.

unmotivated audiences listeners who lack a listening purpose or goal

random audiences listeners who are initially doing something else but are attracted by a message that catches their attention

2. **Passive audiences** are made up of listeners who are present for a variety of reasons, but *not* because they are motivated to hear a particular speaker or a particular topic. For example, the staff in the sitcom *The Office* sat through "Diversity Day" because their job required it, not out of felt need or real interest. Some people show up at a speech because a parent or a friend drags them there. Most speech classes consist of at least some passive listeners whose goal is to earn academic credit, not to hear you or to learn about your topic. Because their investment in your speech is limited, you must do three things: (1) select a relevant, interesting topic; (2) gain and maintain interest; and (3) help them understand how the topic relates to their lives.

passive audiences unmotivated listeners who listen to accomplish other goals

3. In contrast, **motivated audiences** have a listening goal. They want to know more about a topic, or they want to hear a particular speaker. Consequently, they are **self-selected** in that they voluntarily and intentionally choose to hear a speech. Here are some examples:

   - Students who are interested in studying abroad attend a meeting where speakers give information on available study abroad programs.
   - Entertainers like Ellen DeGeneris and Dana Carvey charge huge speaker fees because they know that hundreds of people will pay to see and hear them in person.
   - A moviegoer who liked *The King's Speech* finds and listens to recordings of King George VI's actual speech on YouTube.

   A special type of audience, such as a campus governance board, a city council, corporate board, or legislative committee, actually invites speakers to voice opinions on issues because these boards have been granted power or authority to act on a situation. Sometimes these meetings are open to ordinary citizens; at other times, only invited experts can gain access to this type of decision-making group.

motivated audiences listen for a reason

self-selected audiences choose to listen to a selected subject or speaker

4. **Homogeneous audiences** can be unmotivated, passive, or motivated. Their defining feature is that they share an attitude, whether positive or negative, toward the speaker, the topic, or both. Speaking to an audience that likes you and is interested in your topic can be fun, but you must still develop your ideas clearly so that listeners can understand and accept them. **Hostile audiences**, in contrast, have a negative attitude toward a speaker or toward that speaker's opinions. Chances are, your audiences won't be hostile toward you as a person—that sort of hostility is generally directed toward controversial public figures. More commonly, listeners would be hostile to your conclusions, especially if your opinions on controversial issues conflict with theirs. Here are two examples: How would a anti-war activist get her ideas accepted by a group of ROTC students, and vice versa? How would a Slow Food advocate get his positions to be taken seriously by listeners who daily rely on prepared dinners and take-out meals? Hostile audiences present unique challenges. Your best strategy is to find as much common ground as you can with those who hold disparate views and then emphasize these commonalities before you address areas of divergence. Chapter 18 discusses additional ways to design speeches for hostile audiences.

homogeneous audiences listeners who are similar in attitude

hostile audiences listeners who are negative toward the topic or the speaker

As you might imagine, a single audience can have listeners from each group. For instance, a mostly self-selected audience may also include passive listeners who are just tagging along with friends. All things considered, you'll be more effective if you consider the fundamental motivation of most people in the audience and design speeches that take their motivations into account.

ETHICS IN PRACTICE

Pandering: Telling Audiences What They Want to Hear

Eric Isselee/iStockphoto.com

During the political campaign of 2008, one editorial writer lamented what he called Congress's "Pander-monium."[7] He chided politicians for sidestepping difficult issues and speaking, instead, about "hot button" topics that energized their base or by playing to voters' unrealistic hopes and ideas. "Pander-Bear" is a term for leaders who tell one crowd one thing and another crowd something different.

Politicians are not the only pander-bears. In the preface to his book, *Our Culture of Pandering*, longtime Illinois senator, Paul Simon, wrote, "In too many areas [including politics, media, religion, and education] we have spawned 'leadership' that does not lead, that panders to our whims rather than telling us the truth, that follows the crowd rather than challenging us, that weakens us rather than strengthening us. . . . Pandering is not illegal, but it is immoral. It is doing the convenient when the right course demands inconvenience and courage."[8]

Many politicians and others panderers have a negative image.

In contrast, a recent book, *The Word of the Lord Is Upon Me: The Righteous Performance of Martin Luther King, Jr.*,[9] tells of King's willingness to speak unpopular sentiments. The famous civil rights leader's decision to speak out against the Vietnam War shocked and upset many civil rights leaders who believed that King's stance could undermine President Johnson, "the president who's done more for Black rights, how can you take him on?"[10] Even the NAACP came out in opposition to his position. However, Dr. King's core values, "the power of his faith, his love of humanity, and an irrepressible resolve to free black people, and other people too,"[11] led him to tell the truth as he saw it.

Martin Luther King, Jr., has a holiday named after him.

Questions

1. In what instances, if any, have you heard a speaker pander to an audience? How did you respond?
2. Do you agree with Simon that pandering is immoral? Explain your answer.
3. Give an example of a current or historical public figure who spoke unpopular truths that upset his or her audiences. What was the result?

Analyze Audience Demographics

How would you reply if someone asked, "Who are you?" Would you tell your age? Your occupation? The ethnic group or religion you most closely identify with? Would you describe character traits or specific talents? Would you talk about your socioeconomic status? These are all overlapping elements of your identity, and these elements exist in complex relationships.

Just as your identity is multilayered, so is your audience's. One way to think about audiences is to do a **demographic analysis** and consider some basic categories such as age or ethnicity. Awareness of demographic factors can help you plan your remarks, but you should avoid classifying listeners into categories and then stereotyping them. No one has a single fixed cultural or social identity.[12] Each person's demographic characteristics become more **salient** (significant or relevant) in some situations than in others.[13] Demographic analysis is very complex:[14]

demographic analysis identifying audiences by populations they represent, such as age or ethnicity

salient relevant or significant

> When we engage in [demographic analysis], we should never lose sight of the fact that (1) any particular woman or man has an ethnic background, class location, age, sexual orientation, religious orientation, gender, and so forth, and (2) all these characteristics are inseparable from the person and from each other. . . . It is also true that . . . we may have to make generalizations about the experience of different groups of people, even as we affirm that each individual is unique.

In short, no one is simply a "professional musician" or a "Japanese-American" or "unmarried," but being a musician, Japanese-American, or unmarried are all elements of the person's identity. And a professional musician may find that her identity as a single person takes prominence in some contexts, whereas being a musician is more salient in others.

The best advice is to consider your listeners' demographic characteristics *in light of the topic and your specific speaking situation.* That is, think about how membership in one category or another might influence their responses to your topic and your goal, given the speech situation. The following categories are common in demographic analysis: ethnicity, race, religion, gender, marital status, age, group affiliation, education, occupation and socioeconomic status, and region. Let's briefly look at each of these.

Ethnicity refers to a group's common heritage and cultural traditions, usually national or religious in origin; it's often linked to language and dialects.[15] Ethnicity is a complex concept, however, because the criteria for grouping people into ethnic categories is neither well-defined nor universally accepted.[16] Ethnicity is often confused with ***race***, but race is a **social category**—meaning the concept is culturally constructed as a way to categorize people by such physical traits as skin color or facial features, despite the fact that humans share 99.9% of their DNA. In addition, millions of people, including President Obama, have mixed backgrounds that further blur the lines.[17] Faulty as racial or ethnic categories may be, being classified as Hispanic or Asian or African-American can have real consequences on the life experiences and the opportunities available to an individual.[18]

ethnicity heritage and cultural traditions, usually stemming from national and religious backgrounds

race categories, often associated with stereotypes, based on physical characteristics

social category culturally constructed category such as race or gender

Religion is another demographic category that can evoke deep emotions. Consequently, disparaging or dismissing a group's sacred texts, heroes, or rituals will likely create intense reactions—even among people who hold their affiliation loosely. As you might expect, a single audience can represent a range and intensity of religious beliefs. Some may be nonreligious; others may claim a particular faith, but their religion is peripheral to their identity. Still others see their religion as a central factor that guides their daily decisions. Be sensitive to the ways your listeners' religious commitments can affect their responses to your topic.

Sex, gender, sexual orientation, marital status and sexual expression extend beyond the simple "M for male" and "F for female" or the "single, married, divorced, or widowed" boxes that show up in demographic surveys. Whereas sex refers to biological categories, **gender** refers to culturally constructed concepts about what is feminine, masculine, or androgynous (not specifically masculine or feminine). Audience members also vary in their sexual orientation and their sexual expression. Some are sexually active; others are not. Some are heterosexual; others are lesbian, gay, bisexual, transgendered, or questioning their orientation. For some topics and in some contexts, categories relating to sexuality become highly salient.

gender clusters of traits culturally labeled as masculine, feminine, or androgynous

Not surprisingly, *age* affects listeners' motivations and concerns. Demographers identify four general groups: mature Americans, baby boomers, Generation Xers, and Generation Y or millennials, sometimes called the "I-generation" (Internet generation). Because

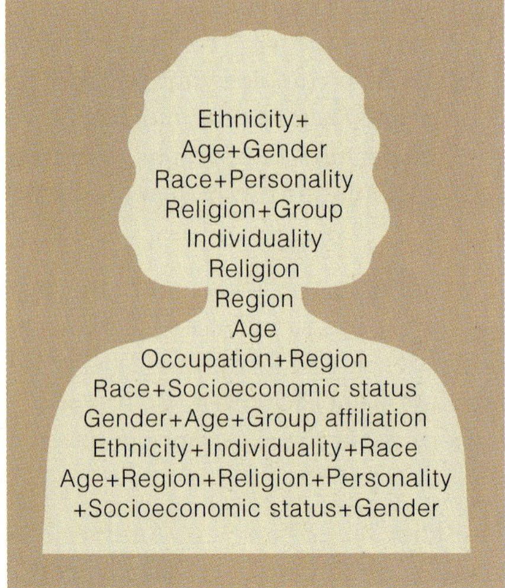

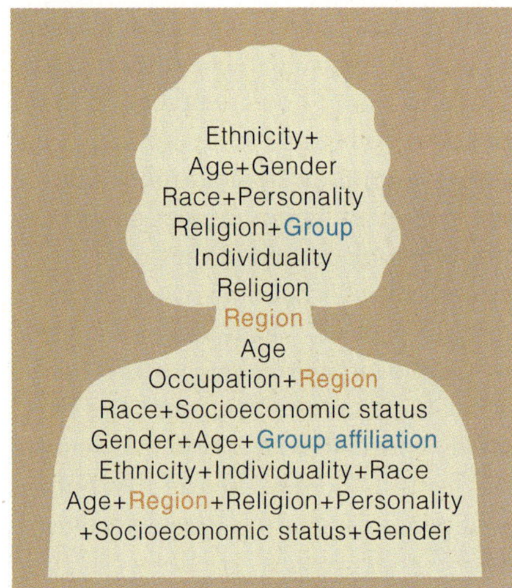

Figure 6.2
Demographic Silhouettes
These silhouettes represent a single audience member who is influenced by many demographic factors that are interwoven with individual traits and personality characteristics. In one situation, her age is the salient factor; in another, her region and group affiliation matter more.

the generational cohorts were raised differently and lived through distinctive historical, cultural, and technological eras, they have different goals and interests.[19] Most traditional college students are millennials; most professors are baby boomers.[20] Although generational gaps can obviously be large, even minor age differences can play out differently in audience concerns. For example, college seniors and first-year students may have varying interest in a topic as seemingly simple as résumé writing.

Group affiliation often matters. Nowadays, some Republicans and Democrats are so committed to their parties that they respond passionately to different topics and policies. But people also join other interest groups as varied as Wheelchair Athletes, Alcoholics Anonymous, fraternities or sororities, and professional business organizations. Obviously, the common interests or concerns of group members determine the topics and appeals that are appropriate in the group's meetings.

Differences in *education* and *occupation* are salient in particular contexts. Members of professions such as law or education share interests, backgrounds, and jargon. Even in the classroom, engineering majors may be more interested in some topics than social work majors. However, a university education aims to inculcate certain values and patterns of thought; this means that MBAs from around the world can interact around business topics because they have learned to share a worldview with certain values. Scientists, similarly, have learned specific ways of doing research that allow them to collaborate across major cultural barriers.[21]

Socioeconomic status is related to educational and occupational opportunities. Comfortably middle-class individuals and those who struggle in minimum wage jobs differ in many important ways. The very wealthy live in a culture very different from the culture of poverty. Don't assume that everyone shares your socioeconomic background.

You know that audiences in different countries require different speaking strategies, but diversity exists between states or *regions* or from area to area within a single state—due to climate, history, language, economic base, politics, and so on. These differences help shape audiences' interests and perspectives (and even the types of cars they prefer).[22] In the state of Oregon, residents along the Pacific Ocean, those who live in the middle "wine country," and inhabitants of the eastern semiarid ranch lands all have different issues, interests, and concerns.

In summary, demographic audience analysis provides insights into your listeners' ethnicity, race, religion, gender concerns, marital status, age, group membership, education, occupation, socioeconomic status, and regional identity. Keep the possible salience of these factors in mind when you select a topic and goal, choose supporting materials, and organize your speeches. However, instead of stereotyping your listeners, try to use the more inclusive model depicted in Figure 6.2. Your major challenge will be to determine which demographic characteristics will be most significant to your topic.

Analyze Your Audience Using Demographic Categories

Use the Audience Motivations and Demographics form shown here to analyze your classroom audience before your speech. In the comments section, list as many reasons as you can for analyzing them the way you did. For example, you might observe engagement or wedding rings, religious jewelry, books related to a specific major, clothing that indicates group affiliation, and so on.

In general, this audience	True	False	Comments
is passive			
is selective			
is positive about my topic			
represent a variety of ethnicities			
is similar to me in religion			
is about equally divided, male and female			
are mostly single			
are close to me in age			
belong to identifiable groups			
represent several majors			
have jobs outside the classroom			
would consider themselves middle-class			
come from this region			

What demographic characteristics can you *not* tell about your classmates by observation alone?

The Audience and the Topic

Just knowing your audience's demographic characteristics does not necessarily tell you how they will react to your topic. Another form of analysis uses direct or indirect strategies to identify their **psychological profile**—their beliefs, attitudes, values and behaviors related to your subject.

psychological profile assessment of an audience's beliefs, values, and attitudes

direct methods asking audience members directly for their opinion by questionnaires, interviews, and so on

Using **direct methods** means you just ask the audience what they think and do, whether by an interview, a focus group, or a questionnaire. For instance, before his commencement address, one speaker interviewed several students about their campus experiences and their expectations for the future. He worked this information into his talk. Focus group consultants, especially in politics, businesses, and other organizations, often invite a small number of people to participate in a group interview where they answer a few questions that helps assess a target audience's response to various products or ideas. Questionnaires are easier than ever to distribute, collect, and analyze through Internet resources such as SurveyMonkey, Zoomerang, or Fluidsurveys. These companies typically allow you to create a limited amount of surveys free of charge. Of course, you could also create a paper-and-pencil test to give to your audience as you begin to gather and select speech materials.

indirect methods assessing audiences by observation or secondhand sources

Indirect methods are less straightforward. Personal observation is one strategy. In the classroom, you can get to know other classmates before, during, and after class. Another indirect strategy is to consult secondhand sources; you might ask other people about the audience or get printed brochures or material from group-related websites. The commencement speaker could have accessed the university's website, read its mission statement, looked at online editions of the campus newspaper, and talked to alumni to get a feel for the makeup of the school. Or he could have asked knowledgeable people about the school's reputation and ethos.

Creating a psychological profile of your classmates' response to your topic helps you assess their beliefs, values, and attitudes about your subject. And it can help you better focus your speech. For example, Terah wanted to give a speech about organ donation, but after she analyzed the results of a questionnaire, she realized that her classmates already knew about organ donation and they had positive attitudes about donating their own organs. They just hadn't registered as donors yet, so she focused on motivating them to sign up to donate their organs by showing how easy it was.

Direct Method: Use a Questionnaire

Kelsey, an avid gamer, wanted to persuade her audience that advergaming has many advantages as a marketing tool that will make it more common in the future, but she wasn't sure how much they knew about the topic or what their attitudes were toward video games. So a couple of weeks before she spoke, she created an online questionnaire to assess what they knew or believed about her topic, what attitudes they'd formed, what they valued, and what they actually did.

As Chapter 1 briefly pointed out, a belief is a mental acceptance of something as true or false, correct or incorrect, valid or invalid.[23] Beliefs are based on study or investigation, as well as on convictions developed without much factual information or knowledge; consequently, misconceptions are common. A series of open questions such as these allowed Kelsey's audience to express their beliefs in a variety of ways:

- What do you know about advergaming (the combination of advertising and gaming)?
- What is your opinion about advergaming?

She added some closed questions such as these:

Do you notice in-game advertisements?

_____ yes

_____ no

_____ I'm not sure

Do you think in-game advertisements are subliminal?

_____ yes

_____ no

_____ I'm not sure

She discovered that most of her classmates didn't know much about advergaming, but they found ads in games annoying.

Attitudes are our tendencies to like or dislike something or to have positive or negative feelings about it. Attitudes include an emotional component that involves feelings and values, a mental component that involves beliefs, and a behavioral component that involves actions. For instance, Americans tend to *feel* positively about recreation because they *believe* that taking breaks are healthy, and they *value* health, so some of them *act* by playing video games to relax—at least occasionally. **Scaled questions** typically measure attitudes along a range or continuum, from highly positive to neutral to highly negative. Listeners with neutral attitudes probably have not thought enough about the subject to form an opinion. These scaled questions relate to advergaming:

attitude our tendency to like or dislike something or to have positive or negative feelings about it

scaled questions asking for responses along a continuum, used to assess attitudes

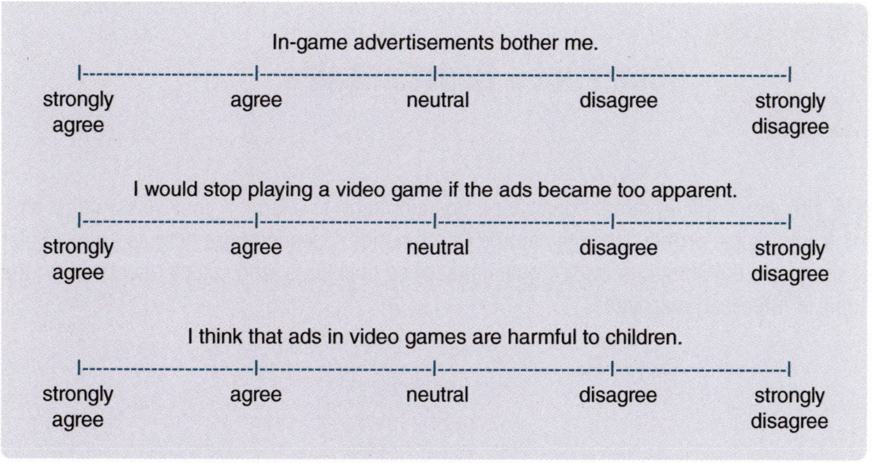

Notice that the first statement is about feelings; the second, about actions; and the third, about beliefs. When listeners share your attitude toward your topic, whether it's negative or positive, your speaking task is usually easier than when audience attitudes are diverse. Kelsey found that most classmates were somewhat negative about, but not hostile toward advergaming. Knowing that her listeners tended to disagree with her positive view helped her plan her speech.

Values are the standards we use to make evaluative judgments such as good or bad, beautiful or ugly, appropriate or inappropriate. US core cultural values include choice, individualism, progress, freedom, and equality. Almost all your topics touch on your values in some way because you at least consider the subject significant enough to discuss. However, when you use words such as *right* or *wrong*, *moral* or *immoral*, *important* or *insignificant*, you are directly addressing value questions. Scaled questions such as this work well for value questions:

values standards used to make evaluative judgments such as good or bad

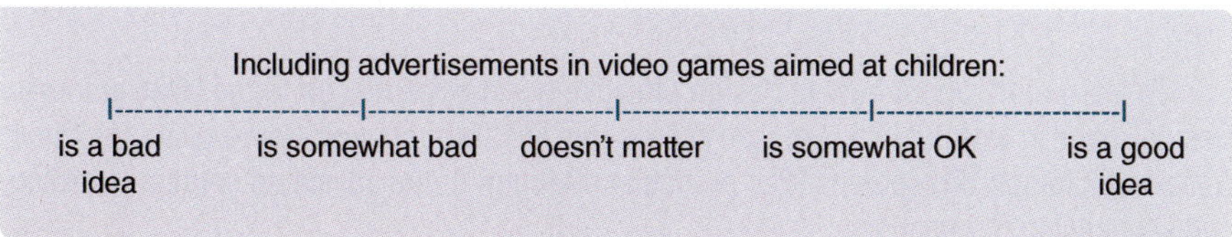

Most of Kelsey's respondents were females, and most rarely played video games. However, half said they'd noticed in-game advertisements, and 80 percent said this bothered them. Most respondents thought advertisements that were relevant to personal interests had benefits. In general, Kelsey learned that her respondents lacked the information they needed to formulate much of an opinion about advergaming. So she knew she had to inform them before she could persuade them that this would be a major marketing tool of the future. Overall, the insights she gleaned from her questionnaire increased her sensitivity to her audience. (Read the text of her speech at the end of this chapter or on your online resources, where you can also watch her deliver the speech.)

Your listeners' psychological profiles affect their interest in your topic. Take a listener who doesn't know what a credit rating is, can't explain why it is important, and has no idea how he can create and maintain a good one. Once you help him understand the importance of the topic to him personally, you've given him a motivation for listening. Contrast him to a listener who understands the need to wear seat belts, who values safety, and who buckles up automatically. Her interest in a "why you should wear a seat belt" speech will be minimal.

Construct a Questionnaire

With your topic in mind, construct a questionnaire to examine your classmates' psychological profile. Use the sample Combination Questionnaire here as an example; it shows a combination of closed questions, open questions, and scaled questions on the topic of inter-faith marriages.

A Combination Questionnaire

Name (optional) ______________________________

Age ______________ Sex ______________ Major ______________

Do you know an inter-faith couple? ______ yes ______ no ______ not sure

Place an X on the point of the scale that best indicates your response to the sentence. Use the following codes:

SA	=	strongly agree
A	=	agree
N	=	no opinion
D	=	disagree
SD	=	strongly disagree

People should only marry when their religious beliefs and practices are similar.

|----------|----------|----------|----------|

SA A N D SD

Most inter-faith couples are less compatible than same faith couples.

|----------|----------|----------|----------|

SA A N D SD

Describe some inter-faith marriages you're aware of.

What effects do you think inter-faith marriages have on children?

What strategies have you seen inter-faith couples use to negotiate their religious differences?

To learn more about how to design effective questionnaires, go to the "Questionnaire Design" page at **weblink 6.1**. You can access this link through your CourseMate for *Public Speaking,* Chapter 6 resources. Pay particular attention to the advice on content, wording, and sequencing of questions.

Assess the Situation

After you consider your listeners' demographic categories and their psychological profiles, assess situational features such as time and the environment that can affect an audience.

Consider the Time

Three aspects of time affect public speaking: the time of day, cultural time norms, and the timeliness of the topic. First, consider the hour when you will speak. For instance, what problems might listeners face in an early morning session? What about an audience just before lunch when everyone is hungry? Or a group just after lunch when they're sleepy? What challenges does an evening session pose? Evaluate these questions, and adapt your talk appropriately. For instance, you might be more animated or use more visual support when listeners are sleepy, or you might shorten your speech when it's very late.

Also, consider the *cultural* time system. In the United States, time is commonly seen as a line divided into segments, each lasting a specific duration, with distinct activities assigned to each segment.[24] Take your speech class, for example. You chose it partly because it filled a time slot available in your schedule. The clock tells you when class starts and when it ends. In this setting, both the date and length of your speech are important. You may be graded down if you don't appear on the assigned date or give a speech of the assigned length, partly because timing is important in work situations. If you're assigned to give a 10-minute briefing at an 11:00 meeting on a Wednesday in mid-March, you could get a lower appraisal or even lose your job if you show up on a Friday prepared with an hour speech—even if the speech is wonderful.

In contrast, listeners from a culture or co-culture with a more relaxed sense of time often focus less on starting precisely on time or on fitting their remarks into a rigid time frame. Professor Robert Levine, who grew up in fast-paced Brooklyn, tells of his experiences in slower-paced Brazil where he went to teach a psychology class that was scheduled from 10:00 a.m. to noon.[25] His cultural expectations traveled with him, so he assumed the class would begin at 10:00 and end at 12:00. To his surprise, students unapologetically arrived as late as 11:00. At noon he was ready to quit, but almost everyone else was still hanging around. At 12:15 they were still asking questions. Finally, at 12:30, Levine himself ended the class and left. The students, however, seemed willing to stay even longer.

Third, consider how cultural or social events might affect the audience's response to various topics. For example, a speech about pumpkins will be more relevant around Halloween than, say, mid-April. Topics such as bullying often follow nationally televised coverage of a situation that got out of hand with disastrous consequences. And topics related to elections may be more interesting and relevant when campaigns are in full swing.

Consider the Environment

Room design and equipment can create a pleasant or unpleasant setting for a speech. Instructors tell horror stories about difficult rooms:

- One class was held in a basement classroom with no windows and three large drain pipes that segmented the room in such a way that not all the students could see one another.
- Another was assigned to a small college theatre that was painted black. Floor, ceiling, chairs—everything was black. The few tiny windows all had heavy black shades. Although it was small for a theatre, the class only took up about 20 percent of the space.
- A third taught in a room that was wider than it was deep. A grand piano sat in the center, and the blackboards were covered with five-lined staffs for musical notations.

credibility listeners' impressions of your character, intentions, and abilities that make you more or less believable

prior or **extrinsic credibility** credibility that speakers bring to the speech because of their experience and reputation

Rooms such as these—windowless spaces, those with awkward arrangements, or other unpleasant features—may all affect your audience, whether or not they realize it. Change the location or the seating pattern if you can. Unfortunately, some things are out of your control, but try to make sure everyone can see you and any visual aid you might use.

Other environmental considerations such as the temperature inside (too hot, too cold), the weather outside (sunny and beautiful, stormy and icy), or noise (an rattling air conditioner or radiator) can also affect audience comfort or distract their attention. You'll be a better speaker if you recognize potential effects on your audience and do what you can to make your listeners comfortable and focused on your speech.

Do a Situational Analysis

Log on to your online resources to complete an interactive situational analysis of your audience. For more information on timing and room problems, read the article "One Speaker's Pet Peeves" on InfoTrac College Edition. What similarities and differences do you find when analyzing a classroom versus a business situation?

Jack Jaffe

This speaker is trying to attract a random audience. Because they don't know her, they initially judge her credibility based on what she is wearing.

Consider Your Audience's Perception of You

While you are forming impressions of your listeners by considering relevant demographic, psychological, and situational factors, they are busily forming perceptions about your **credibility** or believability. They evaluate your knowledge and intelligence regarding the topic, and they make judgments about your motivations and intentions regarding them. Their evaluation begins before your speech, it's modified while you speak, and it leads to a lasting impression after you finish.[26]

Be Aware of Prior Credibility

If a representative of Habitat for Humanity, a group that builds homes for families in need,[27] came to your campus to speak about affordable housing, you would assume that he was an expert on the subject. If you knew that a classmate is on the campus golf team, you'd expect her to have an insider's perspective on golf-related topics. If two coworkers in a business gave a report on a project that has occupied their time for six months, you'd think they would know what they are talking about. This type of credibility—the speakers' reputation or expertise that makes them believable even before they say a word—is called **prior** or **extrinsic credibility**. Practically speaking, you will lack prior credibility in your classroom, unless your classmates know something about you that links you to the topic. Therefore, you should establish some connection between yourself and your topic in the introduction. On the job, this will be a different story. There, you will speak because of your knowledge and expertise on a particular topic. (The Diversity in Practice box provides some cross-cultural information on prior credibility.)

Prior Credibility in other Cultures

Cultures vary in their perceptions of prior credibility. Age and gender loom large in some Native American cultures. When the occasion calls for "saying a few words," younger males and women will seek out older men to speak for them. Researchers Weider and Pratt relate the story of a young woman who spoke for herself and her husband on a public occasion. Her elders scolded her for not knowing how to act.[28]

In Kenya, credibility is linked to wealth, social status, education, age, and ethnicity. Wealth comes in the form of wives, children, cattle, or money, but wealth in itself is not the only criterion for respect. The more credible speakers are people who have used their wealth to help others. Furthermore, unmarried men or men with few children or no sons lack authority, especially in rural areas. In a country made up of forty distinct groups, members of certain ethnic groups have higher overall credibility.[29]

Age can also affect audiences, either positively or negatively. Because US culture celebrates youth and actively looks for fresh ideas, young people often receive as much or more attention than older speakers. In contrast, listeners in cultures that respect the wisdom and experience that come with age may pay less attention to youth and more attention to their elders. Be aware of this potential difference whenever you adapt to a culturally diverse audience.

Demonstrate Credibility in Your Speech

Regardless of your reputation, you must demonstrate credibility as you speak. Not surprisingly, this is called **demonstrated** or **intrinsic credibility**. Think back to the student on the golf team. If she seemed unsure about equipment or about tournaments, you would decide she was no expert. Or consider what would happen if coworkers were unable to answer questions about the material in their reports. Their overall credibility would suffer.

demonstrated or **intrinsic credibility** obvious knowledge the speaker shows during the speech

What does an audience look for when they evaluate your credibility? They look for evidence that you are knowledgeable about your subject. Consequently, it is important to do careful research and cite your sources. Define unfamiliar terminology, give examples, tell your personal experiences with the subject, and otherwise show your thorough understanding of the subject. Finally, be prepared to answer questions afterward.

Listeners also expect you to be calm and poised. Think of it this way: if you're agitated during a classroom presentation, your audience will wonder why you can't control yourself. In contrast, if you appear confident, they will perceive you more favorably.

Take Terminal Credibility into Account

Relief! Your speech is over and you're through. But wait. Your listeners will continue to evaluate you. The overall impression you leave, your **terminal credibility**, is a balance between the reputation you brought to your speech, the expertise you demonstrated as you spoke, and the overall information your audience has or might learn about you or your topic. Thus, terminal credibility is not set permanently. For instance, if your listeners

terminal credibility final impression listeners have of a speaker

eventually discover that some of your information was incorrect or slanted or that you don't act in ways that support your ideas, they will lose confidence in you. A good example is a high profile member of the clergy or of the business community who once had great audiences until they were uncovered as frauds.

PRACTICALLY SPEAKING

What Audiences Do Nurses Address?

Ryan Mortinson

Ron Mitchell

Ron Mitchell, B.S.N., Ph.D., is a nurse educator. He said that nurses have many opportunities to speak to a variety of audiences, and he answered a number of questions about the value of public speaking skills in the nursing profession.

What types of audiences do nurses typically address? Overall, nurses speak to a variety of audiences.

- At the hospital level, they might speak at in-house workshops; for example a nurse who specializes in informatics educates other nurses on the use of new technology for recording patient data. Nurse educators also instruct groups of patients on how to manage a particular medical condition.
- At the professional level, nurses attend conferences, which always include break-out sessions on specific topic areas.
- At the community and civic level, they commonly speak to interest groups such as diabetes or arthritis support groups. A nurse might address the American Association of Retired Persons about home care or other topics of interest. Another big area is prenatal parenting classes. Nurses sometimes speak to teens or to senior citizens in houses of worship.
- Nurses work in specialized fields such as education or industries that have their own clinics. The school nurse might speak to parents at PTA-type events or to the school board if it were considering cutting funding for school health programs. Occupational health nurses address company employees about preventative health care and safety needs.
- At the government level, we also address local, state, and national decision makers on overall health policies. For example, a city council might be considering a development that would impact the water quality—and thus the health—of nearby residents, or the county might be considering closing a clinic, and we would speak out on how that would affect underserved people in the area. At the state level, I just went to the last legislative session and testified about the need to fund nursing education.

How can good public speaking skills help a nurse? In any occupation, if you are able to clearly communicate the needs of the profession, the community, or society, you can get the ear and attention of those people who can support what you are advocating, and you assure the survivability of your cause.

(continued)

Questions

1. Choose at least four of the audiences that Professor Mitchell describes and analyze each audience's major motivation for listening. Which are self-selected? Which are homogeneous? Which are passive? And so on.
2. Identify a specific audience and subject (such as a city council considering an industry in the area), and discuss how a nurse might do a psychological profile on that audience.

Used by permission of Ron Mitchell.

Summary

You and your audiences are involved in an interactive process in which you form impressions of one another. You assess your listeners' motivations as well as their demographic characteristics such as age, ethnicity, race, religion, gender, marital status, group affiliation, occupation, socioeconomic status, and region; however, you also realize that these characteristics are only salient at specific times and in specific circumstances.

Just as focus group leaders analyze a group's psychological profile, you can analyze your audience's opinions about your topic. What do they already know or believe? How do they feel about your subject? What attitudes and underlying values influence their interest? Developing a questionnaire with various types of questions will help you identify their responses to specific aspects of your subject.

Finally, situational characteristics affect your audience. The time of day, the length of your speech, and the noise level or temperature in the room all influence an audience's interest and attention. Do what you can to minimize environmental distractions.

Your listeners actively evaluate you as well. Before your speech, they assess your reputation. During your speech, they form impressions of your credibility and your overall trustworthiness based on cultural criteria such as sound evidence, source citation, overall knowledge, and composure. After you've finished, your listeners continue to assess your credibility, either positively or negatively.

This is one of the most important chapters in this text. As award-winning teachers and other good speakers know, sensitivity to a specific audience is not an option. It is essential to good speechmaking.

STUDY AND REVIEW

Your online resources for *Public Speaking: Concepts and Skills for a Diverse Society* offer a broad range of study tools that will help you better understand the material in this chapter, complete assignments, and succeed on tests. Your online resources feature the following:

- Speech videos with critical viewing questions, speech outlines, and transcripts.
- Interactive versions of this chapter's Stop and Check activities, as well as Application and Critical Thinking Exercises.
- Speech Builder Express and InfoTrac College Edition.
- Weblinks related to chapter content.
- Study and review tools such as self-quizzes, an interactive glossary, and downloadable audio summaries.

You can access your online resources at the CourseMate for *Public Speaking: Concepts and Skills for a Diverse Society.* Log in at **http://www.cengage.com/login**, using the access code that came with your book or that you bought online at **http://www.cengagebrain.com**.

KEY TERMS

The terms below are defined in the margins throughout this chapter.

attitudes 95
audience analysis 88
credibility 98
demographic analysis 91
demonstrated or intrinsic credibility 99
direct methods 94
ethnicity 91
gender 91
homogeneous audiences 89
hostile audiences 89
indirect methods 94
listening speaker 88
motivated audiences 89
passive audiences 89
prior or extrinsic credibility 98
psychological profile 93
race 91
random audience 89
salient 91
scaled questions 95
self-selected audiences 89
social category 91
terminal credibility 99
unmotivated audiences 89
values 95

APPLICATION AND CRITICAL THINKING EXERCISES

1. Identify times when you have been a member of each type of audience: unmotivated, random, passive, motivated, self-selected, homogeneous, and hostile. Select one situation and describe how your motivation affected the way you listened.
2. What occupation(s) most interest you? Think of opportunities you might have to address each type of audience listed in Exercise 1 within your chosen occupational field. Which type of audience is most common in that occupation? Which is least common?

3. To understand race and ethnicity better, read the first-person account of one woman's ethnic and racial identity at **weblink 6.2**. You can access this link through your CourseMate for *Public Speaking,* Chapter 6 resources. Identify the various labels the author has been tagged with. What conclusions has she drawn?
4. How would a demographer describe you? Write a self-analysis using the demographic categories listed in this chapter. From what you observe about your classmates, how are you like others in the class? How are you different?

   Next, identify which aspect(s) of your identity, if any, would be most salient if you were listening to a speech with the following central ideas that came from actual classroom speeches? What should a speaker to do to make the topic appeal to you?

   - To inform my audience about the historical development of the guitar from the early versions to our modern electric guitars.
   - As a result of my speech, my audience will know the history of the foster care system and how it evolved into what it is today.
   - To persuade my audience to broaden their cultural experiences by attending an opera.
   - To persuade my audience to buy a houseplant to decorate their living spaces.
   - As a result of my speech, my audience will be convinced that the $10.5 billion allotted to NASA is essential.

5. Choose one of the topics below, and talk with a small group of your classmates about the different ways you would use demographic factors in your audience to develop a speech for each of the following groups or audiences.

   Topic: Your school's administrators are discussing a policy that will abolish all competitive sports on campus.

   Audiences
   - Your classmates
   - A group of prospective students

- Alumni who are consistent donors to the school
- Basketball team members

Topic: The United States should double its foreign aid budget.

Audiences

- Senior citizens
- A high school government class
- The local chapter of the League of Women Voters
- Your classmates

6. Select a topic that you might use for a speech and then try to see yourself as your classmates might see you speaking on that subject. At this point in the term, what credibility would you bring to this speech? How could you demonstrate credibility in the speech? How do you think your audience would see you after you're finished?
7. In 1981 *Washington Post* reporter Joel Garreau wrote *The Nine Nations of North America*. You can find a summary of his ideas online at **weblink 6.3.** You can access this link through your CourseMate for *Public Speaking,* Chapter 6 resources. Follow the link to your region and see if you agree with his description of the area in which you live. Then link to another region. Do you think the regions have changed in the last thirty years? If so, how? How might a speaker from your region adapt to an audience in the second region?

8. With a small group of students list the physical characteristics of your classroom. Include size, acoustics, lighting, temperature, ambient noise, placement of seats, and distance between speaker and listeners. Then discuss how these physical characteristics might affect the audience's ability to listen effectively. What can you do as a speaker to overcome potential barriers to listening in your classroom setting?
9. Experienced speakers always try to check out the physical setting for a speech in advance. Work with a group of your classmates to develop a checklist of what to look for in any physical setting and then discuss how specific obstacles might be handled.
10. Song lyrics are written with audiences in mind. Analyze the lyrics to Reba McEntire's 1994 song, "She Thinks His Name Was John." You can find them online, or you can watch Ms. McEntire perform this song on YouTube. Who is her target audience? What is her goal? The song came out in 1994. How have audiences changed and/or stayed the same since then?[30]
11. To further your understanding of prior credibility, log on to InfoTrac College Edition and read the article titled "Marquee Speaker Adds Prestige to Engagement." Work with several classmates to identify a campus event such as a commencement ceremony, an alcohol abuse workshop for dormitory residents, or a sports recognition banquet for athletes and their parents. Using information from this article, identify a local, regional, or nationally known figure who would make a good speaker for the event.

SPEECH VIDEO

Go to your online resources to watch and critique Kelsey Bennett's speech. An outline of her speech appears below.

Student Speech with Commentary

ADVERGAMING: THE FUTURE OF ADVERTISING*
By Kelsey Bennett

General Purpose: To persuade

Specific Purpose: To convince my audience that advergaming is one of the best forms of advertising available and that its efficacy will propel it to the forefront of the advertisement strategies.

Thesis Statement: Because of its many benefits, advergaming will become one of the most important advertising strategies in the future.

Preview: Because advergaming is evaluative, efficient, effective, and engaging, it will become more prominent in advertising.

Introduction

Kelsey knows her topic is unfamiliar to many, so she puts the word on a slide so that they see as well as hear it.

[*Behind her is a PowerPoint slide with the word Advergaming and photos of some game packages.*] Consumers today are different than consumers were many years ago. Today, we find ourselves surrounded by technology, such as the Internet. For many, the radio has become largely a thing of the past, and even television is changing as more and more people are switching to services such as TEVO. In many ways, advertisers are having a more difficult time catching our attention than they did fifty years ago. Because of all these technological influences, the messages surrounding us blur. However, advertisers are adapting and finding increasingly creative ways to market to consumers today. Advergaming is one such example. It is leading the way to a new era of marketing strategy.

She links herself to the topic by showing her experience with video games.

Referring to survey results relates to the audience.

As an avid gamer, I've observed an increase in the frequency in which advertisements are incorporated into the video game. And, apparently, so have you. According to my survey, many of you have also noticed the increasing prevalence of in-game advertisements. Well, it was personalizing this observation that drew me to investigate further. Today, I will discuss my finding that advergaming is proving to be an increasingly superior method of advertising. And as its superiority is recognized by various companies, it is rendering it the future of advertising as we know it.

Alliterated main points help audiences listen and remember.

In my research, I've found advergaming can be described by four simple words: evaluative, efficient, effective, and engaging. These four words also provide the basis for my claim that advergaming is the future of advertising. [*She displays a slide with these four words.*]

Body

Because this is unfamiliar, defining the term is essential.

But before we dive in, I want to answer the question that I'm sure is plaguing you all: just what is advergaming? Businessdictionary.com defines advergaming as "a video game, which in some way contains an advertisement for a product, service, or company." [*Displayed on slide, with quotation marks around the quotation, source noted.*] It goes on to distinguish between the two types: one of which the advertisement *is* the game and distributed freely as a marketing tool; and another of which the advertisement is a part of the popular video game—which is essentially product placement within video games.

Advergames are everywhere. For an example of the first type, consider a popular racing game developed by Chrysler Corporation several years ago, called "Island Rally," seen here. [*She refers to her PowerPoint slide, photos of both games, sources cited.*] It was developed to market the new line of Chrysler, Dodge, and Jeep vehicles. The second, perhaps more common type of advergaming is exemplified by the Tiger Woods PGA Tour video game series, in which brands such as Nike and Adidas are commonly incorporated into the game playing.

One of the key elements of advergaming is that it produces evaluative results. In January 2005, a *Newsweek* article indicates such results of the length of time spent at a site and number of visits. Companies can also track the numbers of times a game is downloaded or played. In the case of online sweepstakes, even more information can be obtained. This is information that television, newsprint, and radio ads—all considered traditional forms of advertising—cannot provide.

Source citation, both in the speech and on the slides, avoids plagiarism and builds intrinsic credibility.

Efficiency is demonstrated in the relatively low cost of producing an advergame. The previously mentioned *Newsweek* article cites a range of $30,000 to $500,000. [*She displays a slide with these numbers and a photo of money, sources cited.*] While this may sound expensive, consider the cost of a 2010 Super Bowl ad, which a January 10, 2010, *CBS News* article reported, was about 2.5 to 3 million dollars. As the *Newsweek* article points out, advergames can also run virtually free for years, which is something that commercials cannot do, having only a limited run.

Another important aspect of advergaming is that it is able to be more effective in a number of ways, one of which is in reaching consumers. Gaming is a unique entertainment medium, and certain genres have very distinct audiences. For example, a 2004 *Media Week* article cites that its research demonstrated than men tend to be more drawn to the casino, arcade, and sports games, whereas women tend to be more interested in strategy puzzle or word games, more for stress relief. [*A slide shows this information.*] According to Ronny Lavine, senior manager of product planning at Media Mind–the company that develops digital advertising solutions, this means that casual, downloadable games will have ads targeted more towards women, because they drive that medium. She indicates this in a 2010 article in *CRM Magazine*. In a sense, then, advergaming is more effective than traditional forms of advertising, because it enables companies to reach consumers more effectively.

Additionally, advergaming's efficacy is also demonstrated in the way in which it builds brand loyalty, which drives sales. Few studies have been done so far, as technology is still so new, but many prominent executives seem sold on advergaming. Jeff Bell, vice president of Chrysler Corporation, indicates in a 2004 *Computer Graphics World* article that, "advergaming provides a fresh alternative to the usual marketing approach." It immerses the users in the brand, while delivering key marketing messages. Michael Goodman, director of Yankee Group, a respected marketing research firm, confirms that the medium serves mainly as an awareness builder versus a trigger to buy, in a 2008 *Media Week* article.

Finally, advergaming is engaging. Although 80 percent of you who filled in the survey said that these ads are annoying, they are more engaging than traditional forms of advertising. According to Ya-Ya—strange name, I know—a California-based advergaming firm, in a 2002 *American Demographics* article, the average amount spent on an advergaming site is five to seven minutes, which is 14 times the time spent watching your average television commercial.

Survey findings support her point.

That was eight years ago. It is safe to assume that as gaming has grown in popularity, so is time spent playing advergames. Moreover, with television ads, viewers are passive, whereas with advergaming, users are virtually immersed and engaged, interacting with the company brand or product at a level that far supersedes that of traditional advertising methods. Justin Gavlin, director of business development for the interactive firm, KPE, indicates in the previously mentioned *American Demographics* article that the proof of advergaming's success is in its ability to develop a dialogue between the consumers.

Advergaming provides an ad with a lot more depth. On my survey, a number of you said that ads had value when they were relevant to you, and consumers are interacting with something that actually has value to them. They'll continue to interact with the brand, offering marketers ongoing opportunities.

Despite the clear advantages of advergaming compared to other forms of advertising, it has not escaped its share of criticism–coming mostly from people such as Jeff Chester from the Center of Digital Democracy, who claims in a 2005 *USA Today* article about advergames targeting children, that, "advergaming blurs the lines between content and commercial, and often collects data on consumers playing such games." [*A slide has his quotation, photograph, and sources.*] With this statement, I would agree. It can often be difficult to distinguish between some games and advergames, but is this a bad thing? If anything, it means that advergames are getting better, which will ultimately provide more entertainment value to consumers. Moreover, subtle and not-so-subtle advertising occurs in other forms, such as product placement in movies and on television. And for the most part, no one complains. If anything, people only cry foul when it becomes excessive, and rightly so—I would as well should this ever be the case in advergaming, but I would argue that people *always* have a decision to play or not to play.

Citing a critic is a good way to indicate that she has done her homework and is aware of other perspectives, although she stands by her conclusions. Choice is a fundamental US value.

A rhetorical question invites the audience to respond mentally.

As for the other claim, that advergaming often collects data on consumers playing such games, this is also true. However, it is not for some sinister purpose, but rather to better determine how well the ad is working in the first place, whether the money being spent is money well spent. And again, if this were troublesome to anyone, I would advise for them not to play such games in the first place.

Conclusion

Reinforcing alliterated points at the conclusion tie the speech together memorably.

Critics such as Jeff Chester, however, will be hard pressed to counter the growing popularity of advergaming as a means of reaching consumers. Its evaluative, engaging nature, as well as its obvious effectiveness and efficiency make it the ideal tool for advertisers in this fast-paced world. Consumers today *are* different than the consumers of 50 years ago, and with the gaming industry booming, it is no wonder that advertisers have turned to it as their medium. Advergaming has been a pioneer in communicating to a different kind of consumer, and it is for precisely this reason that it will continue to lead the way to a new era of advertising.

Advergaming is the future of advertising.

Sources

Product Placement. (2010). Got game? *CRM Magazine, 14*(9), 21.

Advergaming. (n.d.). In *Business Dictionary online*. Retrieved from www.businessdictionary.com/definition/advergame.html

Associated Press. (2010, January 11). Super bowl ad prices dip, but still pricey. *CBS News*. Retrieved from www.cbsnews.com/stories/2010/01/11/sportsline/main6082591.shtml

Beirne, M. (2008). Nielsen looks to test ad recall in gaming world. *MediaWeek, 18*(32), 4–6.

Fattah, H., & Paul, P. (2002). Gaming gets serious. *American Demographics, 24*(5), 38.

Mack, A. (2004). Gaming scores with advertisers. *MediaWeek, 14*(26), 18–20.

McCarthy, M. (2005, January 17). Disney plans to mix ads, video games to target kids. *USA Today*.

Moltenbrey, K. (2004). Adver-driving. *Computer Graphics World, 27*(6), 30–31.

Sennott, S. (2005, January 31). Gaming the ad. *Newsweek, 145*(5), E2.

CHAPTER 7

THIS CHAPTER WILL HELP YOU

- Plan your research
- Locate and gather materials from a variety of sources
- Include diverse perspectives in your research
- Critically evaluate your sources
- Record your information in a way that suits your learning style and avoids plagiarism

Researching Your Speech in the Digital Age

COMING UP WITH speech materials is easier—but also in many ways more complex—than ever before. With so many available information and communication technologies (ICT) and with library consortiums that share their holdings, there's no shortage of materials. However, the Educational Testing Service research found that, although typical students are "digital natives" who are skilled at using technology, they don't always know what to do with the materials they find. Librarians say that students too often[1]

> go straight to Google without any thought to their actual research question or the information need. They draw information from questionable resources because they don't know the difference between information they find from

> an ad or a biased source, and that which they find on an authoritative, timely, objective site.... A majority of our students...do not currently have the skills to analyze and synthesize information into something manageable and useful for their needs.

As Chapter 2 explained, principles for gathering effective supporting materials are found in the canon the ancient Romans called *invention*. Choosing the best material and discarding less relevant information combines several skills that increase your competence in speech making and contribute to academic and workplace success. They include the ability to

- Formulate a research plan
- Locate the data you need to support your ideas
- Critically evaluate sources and choose the best materials available
- Record your findings in a systematic way that steers clear of plagiarism

The goal of this chapter is to help you effectively accomplish these four major tasks.

Formulate a Research Plan

If you're a typical student, you have a busy schedule, so you don't want to waste time when you do research. Fortunately, planning a search strategy at the outset will help focus research and save time in the long run. Turn your search into a quest or a pursuit of accurate and little known information about a subject.[2] The following tips have worked for many students.[3]

Start by Analyzing Your Topic to Decide Exactly What You Need Go back to your speech goals from Chapter 5 and consider your audience to decide what materials you must have to engage your listeners. Jot down some questions you must answer in order to create a good speech. Does the audience need big picture information? Definitions? Background information? Here are some examples from Jennifer's speech on neuroimaging, found at the end of this chapter and in your online resources: What is neuroimaging? What is neuromarketing? How does it work? Who uses it? Is it ethical? Identifying these questions at the start helped her focus her research.

Your topic should also guide your choice of sources. A topic such as neuroimaging requires scientific journals and books on ethics, available in the library and its databases. The topic of men in nursing needs personal experiences, historical information, surveys showing attitudes toward male nurses, and statistics about men in nursing. The topic of e-waste (outlined at the end of Chapter 9) requires current information about recycling outdated technology in up-to-date magazine articles and news stories.

Budget Enough Time into Your Schedule The word *research* combines the Latin prefix *re* (meaning "again") with the root word *search*. Good research is time consuming, and if you think you will get high-quality, usable information by spending an hour online or in the library the night before the speech, you will be disappointed. Plan more than one session, and factor in the time it might take to get a book through interlibrary loan.[4]

Include a Librarian in Your Research Plan Part of your tuition money pays your campus librarians' salaries, so plan ways to tap into their expertise. Read the guidelines

Research in Kenya

Although research is expected in US colleges and universities, different cultural groups have different traditions regarding research. For instance, a study compared the public speaking norms in Kenya to the guidelines commonly taught in the United States. Three Kenyan students described typical speech preparation in their culture:

- "Audiences in the African context do not expect researched and memorized speeches, but speeches compiled spontaneously and using the speaker's wisdom."
- "Public speaking in Africa is not . . . something that someone will spend a week researching."
- "In the African context there are less rules to follow, or at least the emphasis is not as much as it is in the West."[5]

Kenyan students, however, admitted that research and preparation is becoming more common in their country.

The type of research described in this chapter is required for many, but not all speeches, even in the United States. The narrative speeches described in Chapter 15 and some of the special occasion speeches described in Appendix B are exceptions.

and informative materials they prepare or consult them directly.[6] **Reference librarians** are the "go-to" people at the reference desk who are specifically trained to help you find information, whether in hard copy or online.[7] In large academic libraries, **subject librarians** have an advanced degree in a specialized discipline as well as a library degree. Despite their availability, a recent study showed that only two in ten students consulted a librarian in their research.[8] But who knows the library better than the people who work there daily?

reference librarian librarian at the reference desk who is specifically trained to help people find information

subject librarian librarian who also has an advanced degree in a particular subject such as law or medicine

OPACs online public access catalogs

Identify Key Terms for Your Topic in Computerized Catalogs, Databases, or the Internet The library's **Online Public Access Catalogs (OPACs)**[9] don't necessarily correspond to terms you'd use in an Internet search, and headings do not always reflect current usage. Internet search engines also suggest spelling alternatives and adjust to abbreviations, but OPACs are less flexible. They use controlled vocabulary, not natural language. Consequently, keyword or author searches are usually more effective than subject searches, because subject terms can be highly specific. For example, to find material on housing for disabled citizens, Marcus logically searched for "disabled" and "housing" with little success until his reference librarian suggested he used the word "handicapped," and he found all the information he needed.[10]

Keep a Running List of all Your Sources as You Search This way, you can easily assemble your final bibliography and return to a source if necessary. If you use the Internet, bookmark each site you search. Carefully noting each source also helps you avoid plagiarism and credit your sources appropriately.

Make Critical Evaluation a Part of Your Plan From the Outset So many resources are available that you might think you're drowning in data—some are highly credible, others are very questionable. Find out as much as you can about every source you use, whether it be a book, article, website, or personal interview. Then compare sources. Some will be okay, some pretty good, and some excellent. Choose the best.

This is not an exhaustive list, but these tips will help you focus your search more effectively.

Begin Your Research Plan

Log on to your online resources for Chapter 7 and begin your research plan by completing steps 1–7 on the electronic form. You'll be guided through the following steps:

1. Write down your topic, general purpose, and specific purpose.
2. Write your central idea.
3. Write questions that you have about your topic.
4. Identify the sources you need to answer each of the questions.
5. List key search terms.
6. List the days and the time periods you plan to set aside to do research.
7. Identify how you'll list your sources.

After you complete sections 1 to 7 of the form, read the rest of this chapter to identify and evaluate the best type of material to use, given your topic and purpose. Additional Stop and Check activities will help you refine your research strategies.

Locate the Data You Need

After you have a general plan, your next step is to actually locate materials, distinguishing between primary and secondary sources, and looking in personal experiences, interviews, oral performances, library, and Internet resources.

Primary and Secondary Sources

primary sources information from people actually involved in the event

original documents evidence recorded by a primary source such as letters or autobiographies

creative works poems, dances, paintings, writings, and other aesthetic creations

relics or **artifacts** culturally significant creations such as buildings, jewelry, or tools

secondary sources summaries or interpretations of an event or a person provided by nonparticipants

Primary sources, materials created by individuals and groups who are directly involved in events as they take place, fall into several categories. **Original documents** are items such as diaries, emails, news footage, autobiographies, and minutes of meetings. **Creative works** include books, paintings, poems, and dance performances. **Relics** or **artifacts** are cultural objects such as jewelry, tools, clothing, and other created items.

Nonparticipants who summarize or interpret original events are **secondary sources**. Some, such as movie reviewers, create their works when the events occur; others, such as biographers, historians, or other authors, create articles, books, textbooks, and so on, at the time or months, decades, even centuries later.

Primary and secondary sources can overlap. For example, an audio recording of the NASA control room made during the *Phoenix* Mars Lander's final touchdown and a photograph that the spacecraft transmitted from Mars are primary sources, but a news article about the landing is a secondary source that summarizes the events and what led up to them. However, the news article *could* be a primary source if your topic were media coverage of the *Phoenix* Mars Mission.[11]

Both types of material take a variety of forms, including personal experiences, interviews and lectures, print materials, and recorded and electronically stored data.

Devan Marchbanks

This student used a variety of sources for her speech about the raku pottery technique. First, she read magazine articles from her library's database that told the history of the process (secondary sources); she then examined several pots and interviewed the potter who made them (primary sources).

Personal Experiences

You probably chose your topic because it relates to your interests and experiences. So think about past experiences that might provide useable speech material. Personal expertise is almost essential for some types of demonstration or how-to speeches. Wouldn't it be unusual if a speaker, who never took a photograph, described photography techniques? Personal experiences with subjects such as drawing cartoons, fighting forest fires, or living with diabetes increase the speaker's credibility.

Interviews

Another strategy is to talk with someone who has personal experience with a topic. A well-planned interview—whether in person, through email, or by telephone—can provide information and clarify confusing ideas. **Experts** know about subjects because of their studies and occupations. The two reference librarians I interviewed when I wrote this chapter are experts. **Laypeople** or **peers** have gained insights and formulated opinions about a topic through ordinary living. The students I interviewed for this chapter gave practical tips about what works and what doesn't work for them.

experts people whose knowledge is based on research, experience, or occupation

laypeople or **peers** ordinary people whose knowledge comes from everyday experience

Because most people have full schedules, keep these factors in mind when you interview someone:

- *Prepare in advance.* Write out your questions so you will remember everything you want to ask and keep the interview on track.
- *Give the person an idea of your topic and the kind of information you need.* This is especially important if you interview nonnative English speakers. Let them think through and prepare their answers by providing them with written questions beforehand.
- *Listen carefully.* Take notes and then read them back to the interviewee, who can then make corrections or additions. Ask questions such as "Is this what you mean?" or "Did I understand this correctly…?"

- *Aim to understand your topic from your interviewees' perspective.* If you find that their ideas and actions clash with yours, practice civility. Listen politely, and try to understand how they came to believe or behave the way they do. Remember that they did you a favor by agreeing to be interviewed.
- *If you want to record the interview, ask permission* in advance, and place the recording device in full view.
- *Be conscious of the time.* When you make the appointment, estimate how long it will take, and then respect those limits. Although different cultural groups have different norms regarding punctuality, be on time, even if your interviewee is late. If you absolutely cannot keep an appointment, give the person as much advanced notice as possible.

To investigate this topic further, search InfoTrac College Edition for the article "10 Tips for Top-Notch Interviews," by Lynn Alfino. Read the author's tips and identify additional pointers you could incorporate into your interviews.

Lectures and Performances

Performances of various kinds are widely available, live and recorded. Check your library's holdings for recordings of lectures and performances. Universities often make significant campus events available through podcasts. Important political speeches and eulogies for significant public speakers are both televised and online; C-SPAN broadcasts live deliberations from the House of Representatives as well as a variety of speakers on topics of national concern. Internet sites such as TED feature "riveting talks by remarkable people, free to the world"[12] categorized by speaker and by topic. TED also provides a transcript of each speech.

Revisit Your Research Plan

Return to your online resources for Chapter 7 to continue your research plan by completing questions 8 to 10 of the form. You'll be guided through the following steps:

8. Identify personal experiences that can support your ideas. Or list places such as museums, hospitals, or schools that you might visit.
9. Identify experts or laypeople who could provide helpful information, and plan an interview.
10. Identify lecture notes you could use from a class you've taken. Or search your library's holdings or Internet sites, such as TED, for usable recordings of lectures and other performances.

Library Resources

Traditional academic libraries are changing in the digital age, but libraries remain as campus centers for information—sometimes renamed as "information commons" or "learning centers." Regardless of terminology, academic libraries still provide carefully selected materials from printed matter in hard copy and in databases to pictures, maps, video and audio recordings in various formats. Library materials have academic credibility because they undergo many screenings by editors, librarians, and professors before they are acquired.

Sue O'Donnell

Library resources have a measure of academic respectability because the materials found there undergo a several-step selection process before they appear in the collection.

Books

Scholarly books advance knowledge in a given field. Experts write them based on research; they are peer reviewed before publication, and they are aimed at specialized audiences of professionals and researchers. Reference books and works of literature also count as scholarly books. **Trade books**, the kind aimed at a general audience, such as bestselling novels or cookbooks are more common in public libraries than in an academic library. Search for a book by subject, author, title, or key words. Many free full-text books, especially classics or books in the public domain, are now available online on **weblink 7.1**. You can access this link through your CourseMate for *Public Speaking*, Chapter 7 resources.

scholarly books books based on research that advances knowledge in an academic field

trade books books aimed at a general audience

Periodicals

Libraries subscribe to general interest periodicals like *U.S. News & World Report* or *Sports Illustrated* and more specialized magazines such as *Hiker's World* or *Vital Speeches of the Day*. They also house **trade journals**, which contain topics related to specific occupations such as nursing or architecture, and **academic journals**, such as *Communication Studies*, which publish research findings of scholars writing in academic areas. When you need to understand both sides of a complex issue, you can save valuable time by consulting the *Congressional Digest: The Pro-and-Con Monthly*. For example, April 2011 is devoted to the high-speed rail controversy. It provides multiple perspectives, including an overview, challenges, a statement by President Obama, relevant subtopics, and pro and con arguments made by members of Congress.

trade journals journals that pertain to specific occupations

academic journals journals that pertain to specific areas of academic research

Most campus libraries purchase access to databases with thousands of periodicals that you can search online. In addition, the InfoTrac College Edition database, one of the online resources available with this text, provides articles from thousands of popular, trade, and academic magazines and journals. Most major magazines and many scholarly journals are also available on the Internet.

News Sources

Newspapers are good at covering current events, because they can provide greater depth than radio or television news. They also provide opinion pieces and syndicated columns. Some are targeted toward various cultural and ethnic groups (see the Diversity in Practice box for more on this). The *New York Times*, the *Washington Post*, and the *Los Angeles Times* are called the "elite media" because of their reputation for high-quality, detailed reporting and because many smaller papers reprint their articles. They are all available on the Internet, some for a subscription fee, along with thousands of local, national, and international news sources. Many newspapers are included in InfoTrac College Edition, or you can find hundreds of news sources through **weblink 7.2**. You can access this link through your CourseMate for *Public Speaking*, Chapter 7 resources.

International and Ethnic Presses

Most libraries carry newspapers from around the world, and many more are available online. Foreign news sources allow you to gain different perspectives and to hear voices other than those found in local or national sources. Check out *World Press Review*. Also look for diverse perspectives within the United States—such as news from labor unions, African Americans, gays and lesbians, Catholics, and Muslims, which all produce news from their perspectives.

If your library doesn't subscribe to the periodicals you need or you can't find them through a search online, go to InfoTrac College Edition and check its list of journal names; you'll find a wide variety of diverse perspectives there.

Reference Materials

Hundreds of reference works provide specific information, such as definitions, dates, and statistics. You're familiar with general encyclopedias that review and summarize information on thousands of topics, but you may be less familiar with the hundreds of **specialized encyclopedias** that provide information about more narrowed subjects. For example, there's an encyclopedia of birds, one for psychological depression, another featuring American Indian costume—the variety is great. Many encyclopedias are available online, some for a fee; however, libraries often pay the fees so that you can freely access the information through your library's website.

specialized encyclopedias texts that summarize information in specific subject areas

Of course, you know to consult dictionaries for definitions, pronunciations, historical sources, synonyms, and antonyms for words. But do you know you can find dictionaries devoted only to pianists or to psychotherapy or to American slang? A quick Web search for the terms "dictionary of" will help you see the wide range of specialized dictionaries, many from reputable .gov or .edu sources.

For statistics, the *Statistical Abstracts of the United States*, a government document, provides numbers on a wide variety of topics, including US population, health, education, crime, employment, elections, the environment, and defense. The *Abstract* shows historical trends as well as current statistics. Almanacs, such as the *World Almanac*, also provide statistical information.

To locate articles easily, use an index such as the *ERIC* index for the field of education (a digital library sponsored by the U.S. Department of Education), the *New York Times Index*, which helps you find articles from that paper dating back to 1851, and the

Readers' Guide to Periodical Literature, which lists popular magazine articles from 1900 to the present. Many indexes provide an abstract or brief summary that helps you decide which articles are worth looking up.

Reference Materials on the Internet

Millions of reference materials are available online. Here are some suggestions for using these resources:

- Look for materials from .edu sources such as *The Encyclopedia of Educational Technology* (San Diego State University) or the extremely specialized *Encyclopedia of Revolutions of 1848* (Ohio University). The *Dictionary of the History of Ideas* comes from the University of Virginia. In contrast, the *Illustrated Dictionary of Jewelry* is from a .com source, so its information will be less credible overall.

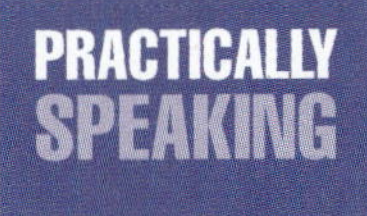

Wikipedia

Although instructors typically distrust or outright ban the use of Wikipedia for speeches and papers, the fact is that students typically consult it at some point in their research; in fact, a survey by librarians found that 85% of students consult it for "big picture" information,[13] partly because Wikipedia entries generally show up on the first page of a Google search. Are there justifications for using it? Tama Lever, writing in *Screen Education*, says yes.[14] Started on January 15, 2001, this user-generated encyclopedia has more than seventeen million entries in 270 languages.[15] Its major innovation was "community-generated knowledge,"[16] so, unlike print encyclopedias, an entry can be updated within minutes instead of waiting for an annual edition. Anyone, even you, can create or edit (or vandalize) an entry, and that's the problem. There's no guarantee that the group-generated material is reliable, although a 2005 study in *Nature* compared Wikipedia articles with *Encyclopedia Britannica* articles and found an average of four errors per Wikipedia article—but also a surprising average of three errors in the *Britannica* articles.[17] Over the years, some Wikipedians (contributors) have proved they can edit in an accurate, neutral manner; others have been banned from editing. Some sites (Chuck Norris is one) are locked because of vandalism. Others, such as George W. Bush and Barack Obama are semi-protected—open only to trustworthy Wikipedians.[18] Users must be careful, especially about controversial topics, but that's true about information from the *Huffington Post* and the *National Review*.[19]

Questions

1. Do you use Wikipedia? Why or why not? If so, when and how do you use it?
2. Find a Wikipedia article on a very familiar subject such as "George Washington." Skim through the article, and check out the references, sources, or external links at the end. Then go to the "view history" link at the top of the page. Describe the kinds of changes that have been made. Then link to some of the wikipedians who have edited the page. See what you can discover about their credibility.
3. What does this make you think about the Wikipedia's overall credibility?

search engine created by computer robots (spiders), matches search terms to words in its database

- Bartleby provides links to well-known and reputable reference works, both contemporary and historical, including a gazetteer (geographical information), a thesaurus (synonyms and antonyms), a style book (grammar), and sources for quotations. It even has the medical textbook, *Gray's Anatomy*.
- For statistics, try FedStats, the site that makes statistics "from more than 100 agencies available to citizens everywhere,"[20] or go to the U.S. Census Bureau's webpage. This user-friendly government site records each new birth automatically; consequently, population figures are updated regularly. These sites are maintained on **weblink 7.3**. You can access this link through your CourseMate for *Public Speaking*, Chapter 7 resources.

Luis Alvarez/istockphoto.com

One study showed that almost all students used their favorite Internet search engine in research, but 9 out of 10 students also consulted library databases, which they saw as credible sources of in-depth information.[21]

Internet Research

Of course, effective Internet research strategies overlap with traditional research strategies, but there are some differences. You should know the categories of search tools as well as tips for using information technology.

Search Tools

Search tools fall into the three general categories: search engines, subject directories, and searchable databases.[22]

- **Search engines**, such as Google, Yahoo!Search, or Ask, are the kind many people consult first. They are built by computer robot programs (*spiders*) that create a database of linked pages. When you type in a keyword or phrase, the search engine comes up with a list of webpages containing terms that match your search terms.
- In contrast, webpages in a **subject directory** are hand-picked by humans, classified by subject, and often annotated. Yahoo is an example. You go to a general category (health), find a more narrowed designation (diseases and conditions), and zero in specifically (liver diseases). You can use fairly broad search terms, because you are searching for categories and descriptions, not for specific words.
- Most of the Web's total documents lie in **specialized databases** that search engines and subject directories do not access. For this reason, they are sometimes called the **Invisible Web** or **Deep Web**. Many databases charge a fee or require you to register before you can access their information. The **Academic Invisible Web** (AIW)[23] consists of databases and collections related to academia. Your library's databases and InfoTrac College Edition are two examples of academic databases that give access only to users who have a password or subscription.

subject directory created by humans; searches the Internet by subject categories

specialized databases databases on thousands of topics, can be accessed by searching specifically for them

Invisible Web or **Deep Web** the vast number of Web pages that are not seen by computer spiders

The websites mentioned in this section are available on **weblink 7.4**, which you can access through your CourseMate for *Public Speaking*, Chapter 7 resources.

Evaluating Internet Resources

Because search tools produce an abundance of information,[24] you'll have a better speech if you exercise critical judgment about each Web source and its content.[25]

Source. Before you even open a document, look for the **domain** suffix, which indicates the provider's primary purpose and tax status. The most common are educational (.edu), commercial (.com), government (.gov), military (.mil), nonprofit organization (.org), and foreign (.ca for Canada, .jp for Japan, and so on). Ask who or what entity published the page. Does a source come from an educational institution (.edu) or one set up to make money (.com)? Is it from a government agency (.gov) or a nonprofit (.org) with an agenda and a need for donations? Choose sites that seem the most appropriate, given your topic. Use .com sites with caution.

Academic Invisible Web (AIW) scholarly databases in the Invisible Web that librarians are identifying

domain the type of site such as .com, .edu, or .org that tells the site's purpose and tax status

On the webpage, look for information about the author, institution, organization, or agency that accepts responsibility for the material on the site. If this is not immediately

TABLE 7.1
Library Resources Compared to Internet Sources[26]

Library Materials	Internet Materials
Monitored: knowledgeable people select and track the information	Not Monitored: anyone can post anything, experts and con artists alike
Reviewed: most materials undergo a systematic editorial review process	Not reviewed: most materials lack a systematic review process
Organized: holdings are systematically classified (Dewey Decimal System, OPACs)	Unorganized: no system to classify contents; even Google changes its algorithms
Non-commercial: materials are not selected for commercial reasons	Often commercial: factual information competes with commercials and advertisements
Guidelines: librarians provide explicit guidelines for evaluating material	No standardized guidelines: No set of explicit guidelines for evaluating materials
Limited amount: the number of documents, although vast, is limited	Unlimited amount: billions of documents are available, with more added by the day

apparent, look for a home page or follow links such as "about us," "philosophy," or "background" to learn more about the site's creators. Distinguish between primary or secondary, expert or peer sources.

Content. Rate the site's content based on the following tips (Note: Table 7.1 summarizes some major differences between library resources and Internet resources):

1. *What's its purpose?* People intentionally put pages on the Internet. They don't just spring up. So yourself ask if the site is designed to inform, to entertain, or to sway its readers.
2. *Is it biased?* Does the material emphasize a particular perspective, or is it relatively objective? Is it free of stereotyping? Does the source have an established position on the topic?
3. *Is it up-to-date?* Is the information (especially factual or statistical data) current? Are the pages maintained regularly? Look for the latest update.
4. *Is it accurate?* Does the material match what you find in other credible sources? Would reputable sources accept the ideas as plausible and accurate? Look for links. Do linked sites appear reputable? Does the document list its sources? Its methodology?
5. *Is it original?* Many webpages use material from other sources, and they sometimes plagiarize. For instance, identical information about the painter John Everett Millais appears on hundreds of .com sites which present the material as if they originated it.
6. *Is it organized well?* If you must decide between two sites that appear to be equal in accuracy and quality of information, choose the one that is better organized and easier to use.[27]

Jennifer's speech on applications of brainimaging required a number of sources. An Internet search for "neuromarketing" turned up more than 600,000 webpages, including the following:

- "Neuromarketing: Is It Coming to a Lab Near You?" by Mary Carmichael is on a Public Broadcasting System (PBS) site under the program, *Frontline: The Persuaders*. PBS has editors and fact-checkers to review articles, and programs such as *Frontline* have a good reputation. This article comes from 2004, so some of the information may be outdated, but it could provide an overview.

- "Neuromarketing: Where Brain Science and Marketing Meet" is a .com blog written by a consultant and entrepreneur who summarizes studies and provides links to companies, articles, and books related to neuromarketing. Jennifer should look for more reputable sites.
- "NeuroMarketing: Top 7 Insights to Unlocking Your Customers' Brains for Instant Sales" is by Denise Corcoran. The webpage is full of advertisements, including a pop up ad that initially blocked the article. Ads break up the text throughout. Ms. Corcoran is a "business and leadership coach" and a former CEO. Jennifer should ignore this .com.

Because your search term can determine the type of webpages you receive, it's a good idea to try more than one term. For example, one study on search terms used to locate information about childhood immunizations or vaccinations discovered that the term "vaccination" resulted in 40 percent provaccination hits and 60 percent antivaccination hits. However, a search for "immunization" resulted in 98 percent provaccination hits and only 2 percent antivaccination hits. Using both terms gave a spread of opinions.[28]

In summary, Internet research is potentially satisfying but frustrating as well, so it's vital to use your critical thinking abilities whenever you log on.

Critical Thinking and the Internet

1. Use the guidelines provided above to assess the reliability of the sites related to brain-imaging shown in Figure 7.1. That is, evaluate the source and the content (the purpose, bias, timeliness, accuracy, and organization) of information you find on each site. Links are available on **weblink 7.5**. You can access this link and the others in this box through your CourseMate for *Public Speaking,* Chapter 7 resources.
2. Then go to the White House's official site and read the biographical information about the president of the United States. Assess the content. What is the purpose, the bias, the timeliness, and the accuracy of this biographical information? Then use your favorite search engine to search for the president by name. Follow at least one link and, using the same tests for site content, compare the biographical information you read there with the information the White House presents.
3. Finally, go into your campus library's database or to InfoTrac College Edition, available through the resources that come with this text, and search for "neuromarketing." Compare the quality and timeliness of the information you find there with what you would find using a search engine.
4. Of these sites, which materials are more apt to be verifiable? Which features more expert contributions? Which materials were probably not screened or edited? What are the strengths and limitations of each type of material? That is, when could you use each source effectively?

Record Your Information

You need a strategy for recording your findings, avoiding plagiarism, and citing sources properly. Then, when you sit down to organize your speech, you will have the necessary information at your fingertips, and you can easily classify your ideas into themes

Figure 7.1
Content Differences by Domain Although a search for "neuroimaging" might turn up both of these Web pages, the .com site is sponsored by a commercial enterprise that sells imaging products; the .edu site is sponsored by a lab at UCLA that does scientific research on brain mapping.

and patterns. Three methods are common for recording information: note cards, photocopies or printouts, and mind maps. Choose the one that matches your learning style or your topic.

Write Note Cards

With all the technology available to copy and print materials, why would anyone use index cards or note cards? Actually, this method has several advantages: it is a structured way to do research; the cards are small enough to handle easily; you can cite your sources directly on each card; and you can easily classify the information into points and subpoints. Better yet, cards can help you avoid cut-and-paste plagiarism because it's easier to jot down key ideas and summarize the material than to copy long paragraphs. For these reasons, we'll first look at source cards and information cards.

Source Cards

Make a separate **source card** for each reference, using a standard bibliographic format. Include the author, date, article or chapter title, book or periodical title, place of publication (for books), followed by the page number(s). For online information, add the title of the website, the sponsoring organization, the date you retrieved the material, and the site's URL. Make source cards for materials gathered from interviews and films as well. It is helpful to **annotate** your bibliography, meaning that you write a brief description of the information you found in the source. See Figure 7.2 for an example.

source cards cards used to record bibliographic information

annotate to summarize a book or article's contents on a source card

Information Cards

Next, use a separate **information card** for each idea, statistic, quotation, example, and so on you find. Use quotation marks around every direct quotation and each uniquely worded phrase, and write down the page number where you got the information, whether directly quoted or not. This practice will help you avoid plagiarism.

information card card for recording and categorizing important data

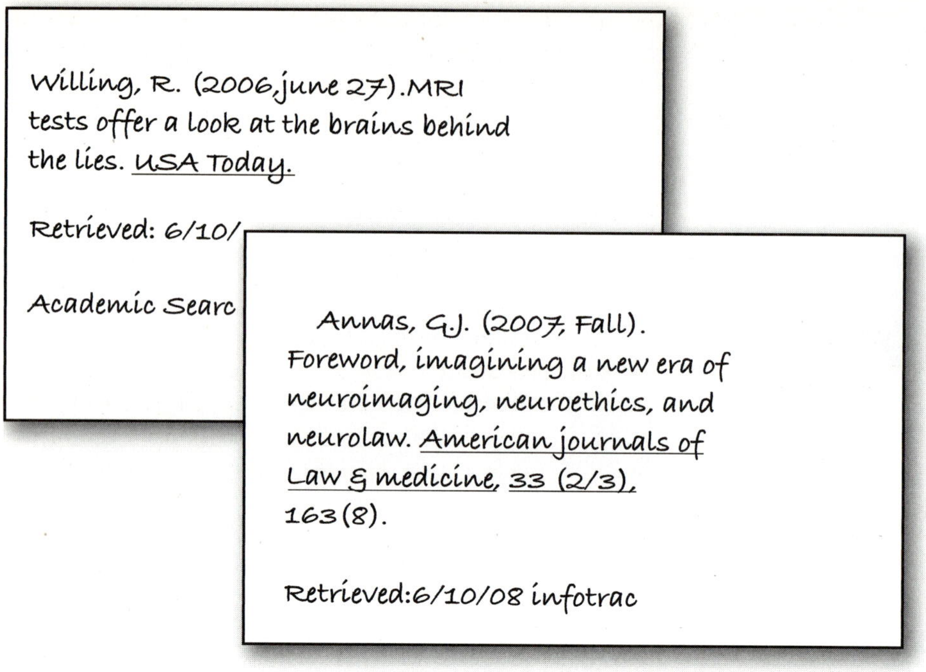

Figure 7.2
Source Cards Source cards contain bibliographic information. Annotated cards also include a brief summary of the material found in the source.

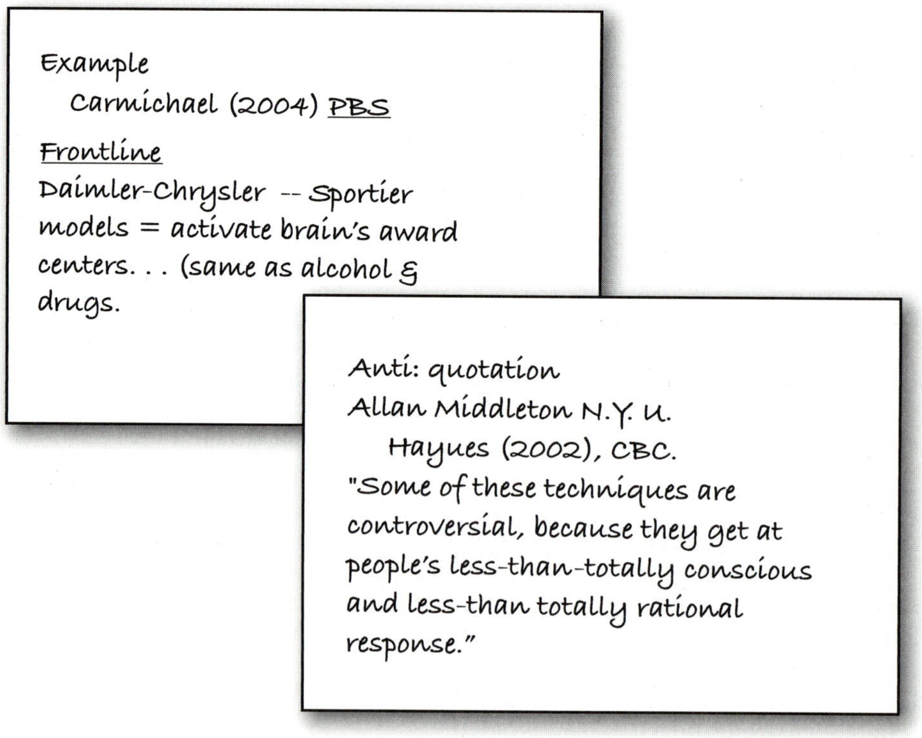

Willing, R. (2006, june 27). MRI tests offer a look at the brains behind the lies. USA Today.

Retrieved: 6/10/

Academic Searc

Annas, G.J. (2007, Fall). Foreword, imagining a new era of neuroimaging, neuroethics, and neurolaw. American journals of Law & medicine, 33 (2/3), 163 (8).

Retrieved: 6/10/08 infotrac

Figure 7.3
Information Cards Use a different information card for each source, and classify each card according to the major idea the information supports. Include an abbreviated source citation, including the page number, on each card.

Example
Carmichael (2004) PBS Frontline
Daimler-Chrysler -- Sportier models = activate brain's award centers. . . (same as alcohol & drugs.

Anti: quotation
Allan Middleton N.Y. U.
Hayues (2002), CBC.
"Some of these techniques are controversial, because they get at people's less-than-totally conscious and less-than totally rational response."

On the top of each card, create a heading that classifies the information into a category you might later use as a main point. Also, label the card with an abbreviated source citation so that when you use the material in the speech, you can cite its source. Figure 7.3 shows examples of information cards.

The advantage of this method is that you can separate your cards into piles and move them around, placing your major point at the top and arranging your supporting information below. You can easily change the order of your points and your relevant supporting materials before writing your outline.

Photocopy or Print Out Your Materials

Photocopying material or downloading and printing an article directly from the Internet has many advantages.

- When you print out an article instead of downloading it to an electronic file, you can more easily avoid cut-and-paste plagiarism.
- Having hard copies of your research can protect you against plagiarism charges and provide materials for future research.
- Many websites are updated daily, and what you find one day might be gone the next. Your printed copy is the only proof you have that it was ever there.[29]
- Photocopying and printing out copies are quick, easy, and readily available, and you can have the entire resource in front of you when you sit down to write your outline.
- Downloaded materials usually have source information on the printout, but also make sure the source (in standard bibliographic form) is on your photocopies. And write the date you retrieved it. Then, use highlighters to mark major ideas and salient information.

When you copy materials, you are using the intellectual property of another person who has a right to profit from its use, so you are obligated to credit your sources. Fortunately, the **Fair Use provision** in the federal Copyright Act allows you to print and use materials for nonprofit educational purposes; therefore, photocopying materials for one-time speech research is within your legal rights as a student.[30]

Fair Use provision the provision in the federal Copyright Act that allows free use of materials for educational and research purposes

Create a Mind Map

If your learning style is more holistic, consider making a mind map. Chapter 5 showed how to create mind maps to generate speech topics, and you can use a similar process to record, subdivide, and categorize information. Although there is no single "right" way to create a mind map, some general principles apply. First, identify your subject in the center of the page, using a diagram or drawing. Write your major points around the subject and then draw a line from each main point to the center. Identify further subtopics and connect each one to the main point it supports. For example, a mind map of the neuroimaging speech, might have a brain drawn in the middle of the page, with lines radiating out to her three major points: neuromarketing, brainimage based lie detection, and brainimage based trait prediction. Each point would then have supporting material linked to it. If you have a lot of material, you can make a separate page for each major point. But always list your sources. If you have room, write references directly onto your mind map; however, if space is limited, make source cards or list your references on a separate piece of paper.

Use a Standard Format to Cite Your Sources

To avoid plagiarism and build and maintain credibility, list each source in a bibliography at the end of your outline. Alphabetize your sources, and use the standard bibliographic format found in the style or publication manual your instructor recommends. Because so many formats are available, this text will not provide specific examples of the various styles.

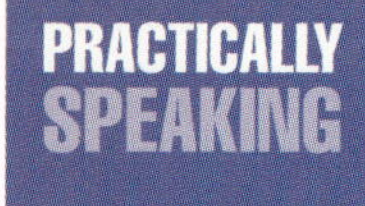

Students and Research

When asked to describe his research strategies, Luke listed five steps:

Devan Marchbanks

1. I start with a Google search and find basic information about the topic. I figure out the difference between important information and superfluous information.
2. Following that, I go to InfoTrac College Edition and find some full-text, primary-source articles about the subject.
3. The library is next. I check out related books for quotations and additional information.
4. Then I outline the speech with information I've collected, looking for gaps in the information. I delete or insert material as necessary.
5. I start typing the outline, doing "spot-research" as needed to fill in gaps.

In contrast, Jonathan used mostly library sources. He described his strategies:

1. First I figure out how much I already know about the subject and try to outline what I might want to write or speak about.
2. Second, I go to the university library or the city library and find credible books on my topic.
3. I flip through and check to see if they will be useful.
4. Usually I check them out or at least take notes and photocopy important pages.
5. I look through and grab the important information for my subject and outline, then start writing and practicing my speech.

Alicia also has her own strategies:

1. I go to the library's online catalog and search for library holdings on my topic. I then request books that library personnel pull from the shelves and leave at the circulation desk.
2. Sometimes I have to order a book through interlibrary loan, which takes a while to get.
3. I end up with a pile of books that I skim for material and mark with little scraps of paper the pages that have useful information.
4. I also go to our library's electronic databases for journal articles, which I save to my computer.
5. I don't use note cards; it's a lot more work.
6. I avoid Google for academic research; too much material conflicts there. I use it for other things (like planning my wedding), but not for class assignments.

Questions

1. After reading this chapter, what would you say are the strengths and weaknesses of each student's research strategies?
2. Which one do you think has the most effective overall strategies? Why?
3. Which student's strategies are most like yours?
4. What suggestions would you give to Luke? To Jonathan? To Alicia?

The basic elements of any source citation include the author(s), date, title, publisher or source, and place of publication or location in a database or Internet site.

A few tips can help you cite sources correctly:

- First, take advantage of your library's reference section or the campus writing center, which has many style manuals; your campus librarians have also created citation guidelines which you should be able to find on the library's website.
- Sometimes the documents you retrieve from your library's database or from academic articles tell you how to cite the material in a variety of styles.
- Finally, easy-to-use online programs are available. For example, WorldCat.org provides a free program created by libraries to help students cite sources. You simply enter information, choose a formatting style, and let the program create the reference list. Of course, you need to proofread the citations to make sure they comply with your course requirements. **Weblink 7.6** shows a tutorial for this program. You can access this link through your CourseMate for *Public Speaking*, Chapter 7 resources.

Whichever style you use, remember two additional rules: (1) use the style your instructor recommends, and (2) use it consistently.

Because so many academic resources are available online, many online sources now have a **DOI**—a digital object identifier, which locates intellectual property online.[31] You can find this series of numbers and letters at the end of the reference. If you retrieve something online that lacks the DOI, write out the URL where it was located. Here's an example (in APA style, with no end punctuation),[32]

digital object identifier (DOI®) series of numbers and letters that locate intellectual property online

Morin, C. (2011, March). Neuromarketing: The new science of consumer behavior. *Society*, *48*(2), 131–135. doi: 10.1007/s12115-010-9408-1

You can see that a vital aspect of research is recording the information so that it is readily available when you need it. If you prefer a structured, linear method, note cards may be your best choice. If you approach the research task holistically, you might download or photocopy your materials and use highlighters to identify important information. If you are a visual thinker, you could make mind maps, using images as well as words to record your findings. Whatever method you choose, always use a standard bibliographic format to list your sources alphabetically.

Complete Your Research Plan

Return to your online resources for Chapter 7 and complete sections 11 to 14 of your research plan. You will be asked to:

11. List usable library and online sources.
12. Tell how you will incorporate sources that provide diverse perspectives.
13. Describe how you will evaluate your sources.
14. Tell how you will record your information.

Make any other alterations that seem justified in light of what you have learned in this chapter.

Summary

Part of your competence in speechmaking is your ability to gather information. To be more effective, set aside plenty of time to explore your topic, and use a research plan that is appropriate for the subject. Distinguish between primary sources—original documents and other firsthand information—and secondary sources, which interpret, explain, and evaluate the subject. Consider also the wide variety of visual and recorded materials that are available. Throughout your research, seek out diverse perspectives from a variety of viewpoints.

In the library, look for materials in books, periodicals, newspapers, and indexes. Consult the reference section for specific information in encyclopedias, dictionaries, sources for statistics, and so on. Many library resources, including reference sources and books, are now available online. Currently, most campus libraries have vast amounts of electronically stored materials, which give you around-the-clock access to their data.

Through the Internet, you can access literally millions of documents from local, national, and global sources—some highly credible, others quite useless. If you want information on unusual topics or if you're looking for specific phrases, use a search engine. Use a subject directory to find human-selected materials on general topics. Or look for academic materials on specialized databases located on the Invisible Web. Sift through the online materials by evaluating each source, the site's purpose, and the bias, timeliness, accuracy, originality, and organization of content.

Consistently record your findings, using a method that meets your learning style preferences, such as source and information cards, photocopying, and making a mind map. Whatever your method, avoid plagiarism by crediting your sources in your notes, in your speech, and on the bibliography that accompanies your outline. Finally, choose a standard source citation format and then use it correctly and consistently throughout your work.

STUDY AND REVIEW

Your online resources for *Public Speaking: Concepts and Skills for a Diverse Society* offer a broad range of study tools that will help you better understand the material in this chapter, complete assignments, and succeed on tests. Your online resources feature the following:

- Speech videos with critical viewing questions, speech outlines, and transcripts.
- Interactive versions of this chapter's Stop and Check activities, as well as Application and Critical Thinking Exercises.
- Speech Builder Express and InfoTrac College Edition.
- Weblinks related to chapter content.
- Study and review tools such as self-quizzes, an interactive glossary, and downloadable audio summaries.

You can access your online resources at the CourseMate for *Public Speaking: Concepts and Skills for a Diverse Society.* Log in at **http://www.cengage.com/login,** using the access code that came with your book or that you bought online at **http://www.cengagebrain.com.**

KEY TERMS

The terms below are defined in the margins throughout this chapter.

academic journals 113
Academic Invisible Web (AIW) 116
annotate 119
creative works 110
digital object identifier (DOI®) 123

domain 116
experts 111
Fair Use provision 121
information card 119
Invisible Web or Deep Web 116
laypeople or peers 111
OPAC 109
original documents 110
primary sources 110
reference librarian 109
relics or artifacts 110
scholarly books 113
search engine 116
secondary sources 110
source card 119
specialized databases 116
specialized encyclopedias 114
subject directory 116
subject librarian 109
trade books 113
trade journals 113

APPLICATION AND CRITICAL THINKING EXERCISES

1. Read the cover story from a current magazine like *Time* or *Newsweek.* Make a list of all the experts and laypeople quoted in the article. Compare and contrast the type of information, primary or secondary, given by each type of source.
2. To learn more about finding credible information on the Internet, do a Google search for "Internet tutorial." Read the material on at least two of the websites. Compare and contrast the two sites in terms of source and content, following the guidelines on pages 116–117. Which site would you recommend to others in your class?
3. Have you heard of the "Mozart Effect" (the idea that babies who listen to Mozart are smarter)?[33] Do an Internet search for this topic. How many Web pages do you get? What kind of domains (.com, .edu, for example) sponsor the sites? Use note cards to summarize the information on at least three sites. Afterward, search for the topic in your campus online databases. How many articles come up there? Summarize the findings in at least two sources there. Bring your findings to class and discuss how you would compare what you find on the Internet with what you find in the library databases. Overall, what would you tell a friend who was playing Mozart to her baby in order to improve the child's IQ?
4. If you have not already done so, visit your campus library. Locate and browse the reference books, the newspapers and periodicals, and the indexes and the guides to their use.
5. If your library provides handouts with instructions for using your campus library, make a file containing the ones you'll use most often, and consult these during your research. Or search your library's online resources for information about research and recording information. (Examples: HOW TO: Locate U.S. Government Documents; HOW TO: Cite References According to the APA Manual; Periodicals Collection: A Service Guide.)
6. Discover the international, ethnic, and alternative newspapers and magazines in your library by making a list of available sources that provide diverse perspectives. Read an article in at least one of the resources.
7. To understand the variety and number of specialized encyclopedias and dictionaries online, do a search for "encyclopedia of" and "dictionary of" and list at least ten titles in each category that may someday be useful to you. Note the source of each. Are they from .com or .edu or another domain's sites? Why does this matter? Bring your lists to class and discuss your findings with a small group of your classmates.

8. Set aside an hour to explore news outlets on the Internet. Try **weblink 7.7** or check Google news for information about current events, noting the variety of papers and television news sources linked there. You can access this link through your CourseMate for *Public Speaking,* Chapter 7 resources. With your classmates, select an interesting, significant current event and surf around, clicking on relevant news links. Then, discuss the value as well as the drawbacks of using the Internet to do research into current events.

9. Browse several weblogs (**weblink 7.8** links you to thousands) on a subject related to your topic. (You can access this link through your CourseMate for *Public Speaking*, Chapter 7 resources.) Assess the quality and bias of each blog. Why or when might you use a blog as a source? Why or when might you avoid them?
10. As a class, research a current event or an issue. Go to the library, find and photocopy a print article, or download information from a website. If possible, interview an expert or layperson. Assign some students to consult mainstream sources and others to seek out diverse perspectives. Bring your information to the next class meeting, and discuss and evaluate the various sources and data by determining the purpose, the source bias, the timeliness, the accuracy, and the organization of the material.
11. Of the three ways to record information presented in this chapter, which method—note cards, photocopies or downloaded material, or a mind map—will you most likely use? Which are you least likely to use? When might you combine methods? Discuss your research style with a classmate.

SPEECH VIDEO

Go to your online resources to watch and evaluate the sample speeches that are research-based. Also, read the text of Jennifer's speech and the accompanying commentary.

Student Speech with Commentary

APPLICATIONS OF NEUROIMAGING*
By Jennifer Blanca Salamé

Jennifer gains attention with thought-provoking statements. She then involves the audience by using "you" words.

You will purchase a 1969 Ford Mustang GT hatchback, candy apple red.

You were lying about the information on your income taxes.

You will not be hired because you brain scan shows an abnormally larger amygdala that may lead to excessive aggression.

The common theme here is that all of these activities are, in one way or another, dependent upon brain function. As humans, we have been given certain mental capacities such as choice and the ability to form opinions. Some of these activities can be monitored in the brain through new imaging technologies.

The ability to influence you to purchase something, to predict your truthfulness with a 90 percent accuracy, or to make a judgment about you based on your brain image are all possibilities lying just around the corner. Welcome to the hot'n'now world of brainimaging and neuroethics!

This topic interests me because I am a cognitive psychology major, and I'm fascinated by how the brain works.

Here she previews the three main ideas she'll develop in the speech.

Today, we will discuss three controversial uses for the recent advances in brainimaging and then discuss some of the ethical questions associated with them. First, we will look at the field of neuromarketing and its potential to influence purchases. Second, we will discuss brainimage-based lie detection. Finally, we will come to terms with the possibility of brainimage based trait prediction.

Let us begin with a definition of neuromarketing. If a company uses a young male model to show off a product, how will their target demographic respond? Will the model encourage or discourage a purchase? What more could be done to stimulate neural activity that could lead to a purchase? These questions are a few that someone in the field of neuromarketing might try to answer. The February 2007 issue of the *International Journal of Psychophysiology* defines neuromarketing as the application of neuroimaging to market research. For decades, scientists have mapped the brain through MRI machines. Now, *Newsweek International,* June 30, 2003, reports they are using fMRI (functional-MRI) machines to pinpoint areas of the brain that are brought into play during a given thought or behavior. For example, PBS's *Frontline,* November 9, 2004,

*Used by permission of Jennifer Salamé.

explained that researchers use fMRI machines to identify which areas of the brain light up when the subject is presented with an ad or a brand name like "Daimler-Chrysler". Reward centers in the brain lit up when sportier models were shown (interestingly, alcohol and drugs also light up those same centers).

A January 2007 article in *Neuron Magazine* called "Neural Predictors of Purchases" provides another example of this technology. Researchers at Stanford University gave participants $20 to spend. When presented with some desirable products, a part of the brain associated with the anticipation of pleasure was activated; however, when shown excessive prices for those products, a different part—the insula—was activated and the medial frontal cortex, the region associated with balancing gains vs. losses, was deactivated. Through imaging which brain regions were activated or deactivated, researchers were able to predict which products would be purchased. This is the general idea behind the services being sold to corporate marketers by up-and-coming companies such as BrightHouse, Neurosense, and SalesBrain.

This section explains neuromarketing and gives some examples. This is her longest point, because there is more information about it than about the other two applications of neuroimaging.

What companies are buying into this method of research into the mind of the consumer? Adam Koval of the Brighthouse Institute of Thought Sciences, a provider of neuromarketing research, told CBC News on February 2, 2002, "We can't actually talk about the specific names of the companies, but they are global consumer product companies. Right now, they would rather not be exposed. We have been kind of running under the radar with a lot of the breakthrough technology." Obviously, there is some controversy surrounding the use of neuromarketing if companies have been reluctant to confirm that they use it.

Is it ethical? Neuroscientists and marketers have lined up on both sides of this debate. From a neuromarketing perspective, selling this new technology to corporations as a resource to boost marketing is similar to using focus groups, surveys, and other marketing tests of days gone by.

Although neuroscientists began the movement, they are also the ones who most vehemently oppose it. A February 2004 article in the *Lancet Neurology* responded to the advent of neuromarketing by stating, "Although many independent experts doubt that fMRI can be meaningfully used [to predict whether a person will respond favorably to a product or brand], this is unlikely to concern marketers wanting to dazzle potential clients with snazzy imaging technology."

Some neuroscientists who have become very passionate about this issue have ethical concerns for the privacy of the brain. A 2005 article in the *Brain Research Bulletin* says that ethical questions are always present when the inner workings of the mind are revealed. The question then becomes, is this research an infringement on the private confines of the brain? Or is it simply a continuation of techniques marketing experts have been using for years? The previously cited *Lancet Neurology* article says that regulations and further discussions must take place to ensure that no one's right to a free choice is endangered. There is a fine line between influencing a decision and manipulating people to do something they wouldn't do on their own, and critics are concerned that neuromarketing could cross that line.

Throughout she demonstrates credibility by citing respectable sources.

Gary Ruskin, retired executive director of Commercial Alert, a nonprofit organization that monitors advertising, is very concerned that governments, not just marketers, could use this technology to manipulate citizens through highly sophisticated propaganda. Researchers at UCLA have already compared brain responses of Republicans and Democrats. Interestingly, one study showed that areas related to fear lit up more in Democrats than Republicans who were viewing ads with images of the September 11 attacks. The scans don't tell why.

Now that we have discussed neuromarketing, we can venture into yet another use of brain-imaging, that is, its use as a lie detector. If you were a prisoner of the government, do you think they should have the ability to force you to tell the truth? We debate methods such as waterboarding, but brainimaging may be much simpler than nearly drowning a detainee to obtain the truth. How about spouses under suspicion? Or candidates for a job? It would be nice to know if they were lying or not. A June 27, 2006, article in *USA Today* reports on an fMRI machine being marketed by companies such as Cephos as a lie detector that is 90 percent accurate. It functions by actually watching your brain as you speak and noticing certain "hot spots" that become more active when you lie.

Cephos says that it appeals only to a specific target audience. According to their Web site, they target the government, "which currently uses a variety of techniques such as the polygraph as part of the process of granting national security clearances to individuals in government and industry." Second, they target the legal system "where truth, integrity, and trust form the foundation."

She emphasizes ethics throughout. True, scientists might be able to map the brain and use information for marketing or other purposes, but should they? Is this an invasion of privacy? She uses many questions for listeners to contemplate.

As you might imagine, neuroethicists see the potential for abuse. Hank Greely and Judy Illes, authors of the article, "Neuroscience-Based Lie Detection: The Urgent Need for Regulating," from the 2007 *Journal of Law and Medicine*, call for better regulations on these tests as well as a demonstration of safety and efficacy. How much of someone's thoughts should be open to search by, say, the U.S. government, and how much is private? Is a forcible brain scan ever warranted? (By the way, much of the research is funded by federal funds, meaning that your tax dollars and mine are supporting this research.) These questions ought to continue to encourage you to take an interest in following the progression of this technology and how it is being used. According to neuroethicists, that may be the difference between maintaining the privacy of your mind and falling into a 1984 scenario where nothing is sacred, not even your mind.

The third point arouses emotions in listeners. Who wants someone else to be able to read their thoughts and then use that against them?

Remember at the beginning of my speech how I presented the possibility of a job applicant not being hired for a job because of the results from his or her brain scan? The use of brain imaging as a trait predictor is our third point of discussion. Here's an example: *Time Magazine*, on January 29, 2007, reported on research done at New York University where neuroscientists studied responses of the amygdale (the part of the brain that is aroused when emotions are stimulated) in a search for racism. Armed with fMRI machines, they scanned subjects' brains as they looked at pictures of unfamiliar White and Black faces. They found that some participants had heightened activity in the amygdala when they viewed unfamiliar Black or White faces. Martha Farah, a University of Pennsylvania neuroscientist, foresees a day when employers, such as police departments, might want to eliminate racist candidates from their applicant pools. However, she cautions, "If we could, in fact, define racism, this would be a potentially useful tool—but with very serious issues of privacy and informed consent." The *Time* article quotes Stanford psychologist Judy Illes, who says, "It's not so futuristic to imagine an employer able to test for who is a good team player, who is a good leader or a follower."

What do neuroethicists have to say about this issue? Does heightened brain activity in response to a different-colored face state definitively that someone is a racist? We are reminded to ask ourselves where the line is between what your brain image says you are predisposed for and what you willfully do. How much of what you do is controlled by the size of your cerebral cortex or the activation of a neural pathway, and how much is will, intellect, soul? Neuroethicists are concerned with the neglect of the self-will factor in the use of brainimaging to predict personality traits or tendencies such as racism. Secondly, neuroscientists admit that any judgment based on an image involves many levels of interpretation, signal processing, and statistical analysis. These separate the imaged brain activity from the psychological traits and states inferred from it. While an image seems authoritative, it may not say what it seems to. This concern is well put by George Annas, author of the "Foreword to Imagining a New Era of Neuroimaging, Neuroethics, and Neurolaw." He says, the images' "potential to provide vivid and compelling, but simultaneously misleading, information is at the heart of many of the articles on neuroimaging in this issue."

Her conclusion summarizes her main points. Because this is an informative speech, she calls for understanding and increased awareness, not action.

Today, we discussed neuromarketing, brainimage-based lie detection, brainimage-based trait predictions and how researchers are striving to maintain high ethical standards amidst the technological advancements brainimage brings. We discussed how companies may use brain imaging to gain further insight into the consumer's mind, how the next frontier of lie detectors may be based on brain imaging, and finally how certain traits may be assessed through these same brainimaging technologies. Will you be persuaded to purchase that Mustang? Will a brain scan prevent you from evading your taxes? Will your brain activity disqualify you from getting that new job? These brainimaging technologies are real, current, and potent. Only through knowledge can we begin to have a true understanding of and a true perspective on these technologies.

Sources

Her bibliography is formatted in APA style.

Annas, G. J. (2007, Fall). Foreward, imagining a new era of neuroimaging, neuroethics, and neurolaw. *American Journal of Law & Medicine, 33*(2/3), 163(8). Retrieved June 10, 2008, from InfoTrac College Edition.

Carmichael, M. (2004, November 9). Neuromarketing: Is it coming to a lab near you? PBS: *Frontline*. Retrieved June 10, 2008, from www.pbs.org/wgbh/pages/frontline/shows/persuaders/etc/neuro.html

Greely, H. T. & Illes, J. (2007). Neuroscience-based lie detection: The urgent need for regulation. *American Journal of Law & Medicine, 33*(2/3), 377–431.

Kelly, M. (2002, December 2). "Troubling science" worries some. CBC News. Retrieved June 10, 2008, from www.cbc.ca/consumers/market/files/money/science_shopping/index2.html

Knutson, B., Rick, S., Wimmer, G. E., Prelec, D., & Lowenstein, G. (2007, January). Neural predictors of purchases. *Neuron, 53*(1), 147–156. doi: 10.1016/j.neuron.2006.11.010

Lee, N. J. (2007, February). What is "neuromarketing"? A discussion and agenda for future research. *Journal of International Psychophysiology, 63*(2), 199–204. doi: 10.1016/j.ijpsycho.2006.03.007

Russo, R. (2007, January 29). Who should read your mind? *Time.* Retrieved June 10, 2008, from http://bioethics.stanford.edu/news/2007/documents/Time1.7.doc

Walter, H., Abler, B., Ciaramidaro, A., & Erk, S. (2005). Motivating forces of human actions: neuroimaging reward and social interaction. *Brain Research Bulletin, 67*, 368–381. doi: 10.1016/j.brainresbull.2005.06.016

Willing, R. (2006, June 27). MRI tests offer a look at the brains behind the lies. *USA Today*. Retrieved June 10, 2008, from Academic Search Premier database.

She includes the URL when a DOI is not available for online material.

CHAPTER
8

THIS CHAPTER WILL HELP YOU

- Identify types of facts and learn how to test factual data
- Use examples effectively
- Select appropriate visual evidence
- Quote authoritative sources
- Select numerical data carefully
- Use comparison and contrast

Choosing Supporting Materials

THINK ABOUT some of today's controversies. Why do intelligent, well-meaning people form such different conclusions that they polarize into opposing camps? Take, for instance, the issue of global warming. Millions of people believe that, unless nations and individuals act quickly to save the environment, human-created global warming will drastically change the planet.[1] They support their claims with data from seemingly reputable sources such as the National Academy of Sciences and the Intergovernmental Panel on Climate Change. In contrast, opposing groups, including scientists and others who've studied the issue in depth, agree that changes are indeed taking place, but that "eco-fundamentalists" overstate the problem, propose ineffective solutions, and neglect other pressing issues such as the global need for pure drinking water.[2] This example shows how reliance on different evidence can lead to very different conclusions about important topics.

Because each culture has rules for what counts as credible evidence, we follow cultural standards for weighing evidence, accepting some information as valid and rejecting other data as inaccurate, inadequate, or irrelevant. This chapter examines six types of evidence that speakers in the United States commonly use: facts, examples, visual evidence, quotations, statistics, and comparisons. Stop and Check sections throughout the chapter will help you think critically about the quality of various types of data or evidence, both when you're selecting materials for your own speeches and when you are listening to the speeches of others.

Provide Facts

Much of the information you present will be factual because audiences typically demand facts before they accept an idea or proposal. **Empirical facts** are data that can be verified by observation, and **established facts** are data that are consistently validated by many observers. We judge factual information as being true or false, accurate or inaccurate. Facts derive from a variety of sources, as these examples show:

empirical facts data verifiable by observation

established facts data verified consistently by many observers

- Bill Shoemaker was the first jockey to win over $100 million. [source: the Kentucky Derby website]
- The program, Puppies Behind Bars, gives prisoners young dogs to train as guide dogs; some of these dogs go to returning Iraq vets who suffer from traumatic stress syndrome. [source: newspaper article]
- The ability for a highway or road to stay intact for a long period of time is directly dependent on keeping the tar seal intact. [source: research reported in an engineering journal]

Generally accepted definitions and descriptions are also considered facts.

Use Definitions

Definitions—the meanings of terms that are generally accepted in common usage—are found in dictionaries and thesauruses. However, definitions also derive from traditions, philosophers, and so on. In a commencement address, communication professor James E. Sayer defined "character" in three ways. He started with the dictionary definition:[3]

> *Webster's* will give you many different definitions for the word character—all the way from symbols used in writing and printing to a person in a play or novel—and lots of other definitions in between. Today I am concerned exclusively with the notion of character as it pertains to our moral and ethical natures, the very core of who we are.

Erik S. Lesser/Getty Images

Listeners need facts about almost every topic, so giving them accurate information on the who, what, when, how, and why about subjects, such as Puppies Behind Bars, is essential to their understanding.

Sayer then added a cultural definition:

> Perhaps you have heard the old axiom that "reputation" is what people think you are, but "character" is really what you are.

He continued with definitions from classical teachers of rhetoric:

> In the fourth century B. C., the great Greek philosopher and rhetorician Aristotle . . . [noted] that character was one of the most important elements in human existence, and that "character is manifested in choice." That is, decisions we make about what to do and what not to do reveal our character, for our character controls those decisions. Other ancient theorists like Cicero and Quintilian also emphasized the importance of character, for they understood that our real being would be demonstrated in everything that we did.

Provide Vivid Descriptions

Descriptions provide details about a subject, such as its size, shape, sound, and color. This description of an earthquake in China was given by a foreign correspondent covering the story:[4]

> We are standing on a pile of rubble. Bricks and wooden rafters are strewn across the ground and much of the roof now lies on the floor of what was [a] restaurant. It is a scene of complete devastation. One bedroom is still standing. Inside there are children's books scattered over the bed and floor.

The details (bricks, wooden rafters, children's books) give facts; the choice of words (*rubble*, *strewn*, *scattered*) makes these facts easy to visualize.

The danger in using factual material is that it is easy to pass along unverified or inaccurate material. If something looks suspicious, double-check it. For example, hundreds of inaccuracies are passed along as "fact," including the following:

- When a park statue features a horse rearing so that both front legs are in the air, the rider died in battle; if one foot is raised, the rider died of battle wounds; four feet on the ground means the rider died of natural causes. [This is mostly true for statues honoring those who fought at Gettysburg, but it is not true in general.]
- Republican presidents over the last 50 years have lower average IQs than their Democratic counterparts. [Two campaign workers supporting George W. Bush's opponent created a list of presidential IQs as a joke—framed as a "scientific study," but it has been widely circulated as factual on the Internet.][5]
- You should drink eight glasses of water a day. [An online fact checking site says no one knows where this number comes from. We should take in as much water as we lose, but that amount varies from person to person and from day to day. As much as four cups of water can come from food.]

With the current explosion of available information, especially through the Internet and other electronic sources, verifying facts is now more important than ever.

weblink 8.1 maintains links to websites useful for investigating bogus "facts" and questionable political information. (You can access this link through your CourseMate for *Public Speaking*, Chapter 8 resources.)

Use Examples

If you're typical, your interest probably increases when a speaker uses a specific instance or example that illustrates how the topic affects someone like you. Examples attract and maintain attention, and we listen for them because they make abstract concepts and

Think Critically about Facts

To avoid passing along misinformation on any topic, apply the following three tests:

1. *Check for accuracy or validity.* Are the facts actually true and verifiable by observation? Has more than one reputable source reported on them? How were the facts derived?
2. *Are the facts up to date?* Perhaps something was true in the past, but do the same conditions hold today? Or have changes over time invalidated the data?
3. *Consider the source.* As Chapter 7 pointed out, the source of information is very important. Use only material from reputable sources, and try to identify any source bias that would cast doubt on the data.

In short, test facts by asking three questions: Is this true and verifiable? Is it timely? Who says so?

ideas more concrete and relevant.[6] Illustrations also help us identify emotionally with the subject as this student explains:

> The speeches that are interesting usually start with an example—often from that person's life. It shows the communicator is human. The story adds credibility . . . and leads the audience into the speech, almost like a conversation; this lets the speaker earn the audience's trust.
>
> David

Additionally, as David points out, your examples let listeners know that you understand real-world experiences and the practical implications of your theories and ideas. Examples can be short or long, real or hypothetical.

Use Real Examples

Because real examples actually happened, they provide concrete, true-life illustrations of your concepts. Consequently, as you gather materials, look for actual events or experiences of real people to illustrate your ideas, and provide names, dates, and places to make your examples more vivid. For instance, to illustrate his persuasive speech about ocean acidification, Kimball gave the following details:[7]

> Five years ago, oyster fishermen in Washington State began noticing something strange. In the waters of Willapa Bay, where nutrient-rich water wells up from the deep and nourishes oyster beds, larvae were dying at alarming rates. They simply weren't building shells and growing into adults. Desperate for answers, the fishermen called the National Oceanic and Atmospheric Administration (NOAA) for help.

He made additional references to this example several times throughout his speech.

Examples from your personal experiences can be very powerful. For example, Carrie spoke on the importance of making a grief support specialist available to students on her campus, based on her own experience. Here's how she began:[8]

> The phone rings. You answer it, and suddenly the world stops. You have just become one of the hundred of thousands of college students experiencing the grief of losing a loved one. September 13th, 2006, my life changed forever when it was *my* phone that rang. My dad was gone. I was 18.

Everett Collection, Inc

In the closing argument of the movie *A Time to Kill,* a young lawyer tells a hypothetical story that makes his point more powerfully than the actual story would have made it.

Personal stories are indispensable in some cultures. Ann Miller's 2002 study of Kenyan public speaking found that focus group participants rated personal stories as the *most* convincing type of example. One Kenyan said, "We believe you only really know about something if you've experienced it."[9] In fact, some Kenyans thought personal narratives should be placed in a separate category because their impact is so different from other types of narratives.

Consider Hypothetical Examples for Sensitive Topics

hypothetical example not a real incident or person, but true-to-life

Hypothetical examples do not actually occur, but they seem plausible because they commonly contain typical elements from several different stories woven together to create believable characters and situations. Our cultural value on privacy makes hypothetical examples more appropriate than real ones for sensitive topics like mental illness or sexual behaviors, so speakers whose work involves confidentiality, such as physicians, members of the clergy, counselors, and teachers, often use them. Family counselors who present parenting workshops, for instance, might tell hypothetical stories of bad parenting skills; however, they would never reveal confidential information about identifiable clients. To distinguish hypothetical examples from true-life events, introduce them something like this: "Let's say there's a 16-year-old girl named Carly; let's put her in a close-knit family in rural Oregon . . ."

Another way to attract attention and involve audience members emotionally is to create an imaginary scenario that invites listeners to personalize your topic. Here's Maria's opening illustration for her speech on the problems lottery winners experience:[10]

> Imagine that you just won the lottery. You can't sleep; you're so excited! You call everyone you know, and for a few days you bask in the joy of being an instant millionaire. Notice I said a few days. A week after you win, relatives you've never seen start asking for loans. A few days later, a friend sues for half the money, arguing that she encouraged you to buy the ticket, and without her urging, you'd still be poor. . . . The demands and the expectations pile up—so much so that you may almost wish you'd never bought that ticket!

Although hypothetical examples and imaginary scenarios work well in informative speeches, real examples are often better for persuasive speeches. Think of it this way: Your listeners are probably more persuaded by something that *did* happen than by something that *might* plausibly happen.

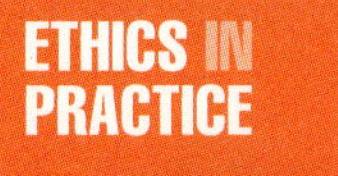

Hypothetical Example or Fabrication?

Margaret B. Jones's 2008 memoir, *Love and Consequences,* told of growing up in Los Angeles foster homes and participating in gangs as a racially mixed adolescent. Turns out, Margaret is not "Jones;" she's Margaret Seltzer, a well-to-do white woman, who was educated in private schools and raised by her biological parents. When confronted, Selzer admitted her story was hypothetical, based on experiences of people she'd met while working in anti-gang outreach programs. But, she explained, "For whatever reason, I was really torn, and I thought it was my opportunity to put a voice to people who people don't listen to."[11]

Selzer is not alone. Recently, a law student wrote a letter to the editor, describing in great detail how campus police manhandled and harassed him, an African-American male, as he walked across campus late at night. He shared his story "to bring attention to the topic of police misconduct."[12] Many fellow students were saddened and outraged, and the university investigated the charges. Turns out, he made them up. The bestseller about overcoming addiction *A Million Little* Pieces turned out to be a "fiction addiction."[13] Didn't happen. Or at least didn't happen the way he said.

Questions

1. What's the difference between a hypothetical example and a fabricated story?
2. What, if any, ethical concerns should you have when you use hypothetical examples?

Create Emotional Connections with Extended Examples

Extended examples include many details; each one gives your listeners an opportunity to identify emotionally with the subject of the story. Longer illustrations are especially useful for clarifying, explaining in depth, and motivating your listeners. Look at how each detail in this example makes the story more engaging. The subject is gastric bypass surgery for teens:

> At 7, Nikki weighed 160 pounds. At 9, she was a veteran dieter whose weight was 250 pounds. By 14, she was up to 363 pounds; her heart was enlarged, her liver inflamed, and her face turned blue when she exercised. Finally, her mother agreed to let her have gastric-bypass surgery—an extreme procedure that costs about $30,000 and sometimes has deadly consequences. Today, Nikki feels "like a whole other person;" she is 6-foot-1, and she is down to 207 pounds.[14]

Listeners can identify with one or more of the details: health issues and money concerns, self-esteem issues during childhood and the teen years. So they become interested in Nikki and the medical procedure she underwent. Because extended examples provide multiple points that engage listeners, they are generally more compelling. In fact, narratives or well-developed stories can function as the entire speech. (Chapter 15 gives detailed information about organizing and evaluating narrative speeches.)

Combine Brief Examples

You may prefer short illustrations to long examples. However, a single, brief example is easily missed, so it's better to string two or three together. Layering them one upon another gives your listeners a number of images they can use to visualize and personalize your subject. The following mentions of women in prison who are training puppies as guide dogs or companions for returning Iraq veterans could be effectively used to introduce the topic:

> Jayme Powers, a convicted murderer, is teaching Devon, a Labrador retriever puppy, to take a box of cereal from a counter and put it into her grocery bag; inmate Sheron Thomas is training a black Lab, Peter, to "speak"; Bliss Edwards, in prison for assault, is working on the "watch me" command with her Lab, Athena.[15]

Think Critically about Examples

To evaluate the usefulness of examples, ask yourself the following questions:

- *Is this example representative or typical?* That is, does the example represent a typical person? Or does it seem like an extreme case? Does Nikki seem typical of obese teens? Do the activities of the puppies and prisoners represent typical tasks? This test relates to the probability of occurrence.
- *Do you have a sufficient number of examples?* Are enough cases presented to support the major idea adequately? Your listeners should be able to see that a significant number of people are affected. Are the Willapa Bay oyster fishermen the only ones facing the problem?
- *Is the example true?* Did it actually happen? How often? For a hypothetical character, does the experience ring true with what you know about the world and how it operates?

Use Visual Evidence

In a culture where visuals are everywhere, we commonly rely on evidence contained in pictures, images, and symbols to support ideas. Images tell a story or put forth an analysis of a topic—or both. In short, visuals allow us to gain information and to "see reasons."[16] How bad is the tsunami's damage? A few photographs tell a lot. What's your university like? Pictures on its website show people, events, and places that promote the school's image. Why should I donate to that organization? A photograph of a child born with a cleft palate provides a reason.

literal image shows the actual subject

Literal images show the actual subject under discussion.[17] For instance, speakers, who are requesting money for physicians or dentists to travel overseas, typically show photographs of people from a developing country before and after treatments. Images can help you fulfill your cognitive, affective, and behavioral speech goals. In her classroom speech on the importance of sanitary procedures for body piercings, Katrina displayed graphic pictures of piercings-gone-wrong to support her goals of increasing her listeners' understanding ("I see what you mean!"), getting them emotionally engaged ("That's repulsive!") and motivating them to act. ("I will never get a piercing under unsanitary conditions!")[18]

Taro Yamasaki/Time Life Pictures/Getty Images

It's easier to raise money for a cause when people see a photograph showing how their money literally changes lives.

Metaphorical images are common, especially in advertising, where fluffy kittens pose beside a box of tissues to imply "softness" or where a flower beside a deodorant implies "pleasant smell." Speakers sometimes use them in talks on subjects such as marriage, where metaphorical images of hearts and flowers suggest love and happiness and support positive attitudes toward marriage.

metaphorical image implies the subject

Margaret LaWare[19] examined the messages conveyed in Chicano/a murals in Chicago. She says these murals make statements or arguments about ethnic pride,

Think Critically about Visual Evidence

Images tell a story, but not necessarily the whole story, and sometimes they tell a misleading story, because editing tools such as PhotoShop allow images to be manipulated or cropped in ways that promote a particular point of view. For example, a photographer with a negative attitude toward an issue might take a wide shot of a sparse crowd at a rally to indicate how few attended; however, a different photographer with a positive attitude might choose a close-up of a single, intensely involved participant to emphasize the importance of the topic.

Analyze the photographs on your college or university's website. Your school uses them to imply messages such as, "you will make lifelong friendships if you come here," or "professors are accessible to students," or "the campus is lovely." Typically, the photographs, while technically "true," fail to tell the entire story. Compare the photographs to your personal experiences by answering the following questions:

- What kind of weather is shown in the photographs? Is that weather typical of the climate where your school is located?
- What students are most typical of the student body? What types of students are shown in the photographs? What types are missing from the promotional materials?
- Which buildings or interiors, if any, are shown? Why do you think they were selected?
- What's left out? Why?

community activism, and cultural revitalization. The images in them combine to define identity, reflect people's needs, and celebrate their histories. LaWare believes "the murals argue that Mexican American people need not assimilate or give up their culture to survive in an urban center that is both geographically and socially distant from Mexico and from the Southwest." (LaWare's article is available on InfoTrac College Edition.)

Quote Culturally Acceptable Authorities

Whatever your subject, think of your audience as asking, "Who says so?" Then support your ideas by citing sources your audience will respect and believe, given your topic and purpose. Each culture recognizes authorities, which vary among cultures and co-cultural groups. Authoritative sources differ in degree (some have little credibility, others have a lot), and their sphere of influence varies (an authority in one subject may be uninformed in another).[20]

Citing culturally accepted sources is especially valuable when your personal expertise on the topic is limited. Integrating the ideas of experts or credible laypeople into your speeches shows that knowledgeable, experienced people support your conclusions. But quoting authorities bolsters your ideas if, and only if, your audience views them as credible on the topic. Therefore, you must provide pertinent information about the authorities you cite, why you believe their testimony, and why your audience should accept their conclusions.

Quote Culturally Accepted Experts

As Chapter 7 pointed out, we look to people whose occupational or educational expertise, career success, and reputation in their field make them experts. Thus, testimony from scholars, elected officials, professionals in various fields, scientists, and so on generally provides good supporting materials. (Keep in mind, however, that experts are often biased. In fact, as a person's expertise increases, his or her bias may also increase. Think of political figures; the longer they're in office, the more partisan they may be.)

Here is an example of expert testimony that would fit well in a speech about puppies in prison, taken from an article published in the *Independent Tribune*, Concord, North Carolina:[21]

- "It's a win-win situation for me, the inmates and the dogs. If everyone does what they're supposed to, everyone gets something valuable out of the program." [Jacqueline Bankhead, Cabarrus Correctional Center case manager and program coordinator]
- The constant interaction with the prisoner trainers gives the dogs almost ten weeks of training in just eight weeks, which would cost about $500 outside the prison. [Tonya Hess, professional dog trainer and prison volunteer]

The first example directly quotes the expert, but the second example paraphrases or summarizes the person's main point. Because most listeners are unfamiliar with both sources, the speaker should state each woman's institutional affiliation or explain her credentials.

We commonly expect people to agree with the general beliefs of others who are similar to them in some notable way. However, people sometimes hold surprising opinions. For example, some well-known conservatives support gay marriage or legalization of drugs, and some well-known liberals take pro-life or pro-nuclear energy positions. Using unexpected testimony like this can be especially powerful in persuasive speeches. Why? Because your listeners will reason that people willing to go against their peers have probably thought through their opinions carefully.

Quote Credible Peers or Laypeople

Often "regular people" who have firsthand knowledge about a subject provide good supporting information. These peer or lay sources may not know scientific facts and related theories, but they can tell you how it feels to be involved as a participant. What do lay people report about prisoners training puppies? For that, you need the prisoners' perspective:[22]

- "It's not all puppy, puppy, lovey, lovey. When I first got Ices [my dog] he did not want to get up. We didn't go for walks. We went for drags. It took a good 2½ months before he got the idea. I kept saying, 'Is it me? Am I doing something wrong?' this is the first puppy in my whole life. It was like we were being trained at the same time." [Caridad Kelly, convicted on cocaine, heroin, money laundering charges]
- "The more time you spend with them, the more you get to see their personalities. I guess it's like kids. Each one is different." [Jennifer Jaramillo, convicted on cocaine and heroin charges]
- "I like the satisfaction of seeing [my pup, Heather,] grow from a rowdy little puppy. She's already showing the signs of being a good guide dog." [Pat Johnson, convicted of Medicare fraud charges]

Each participant's perspective adds important details about the Puppies in Prison program.

Proverbs in a West African Culture

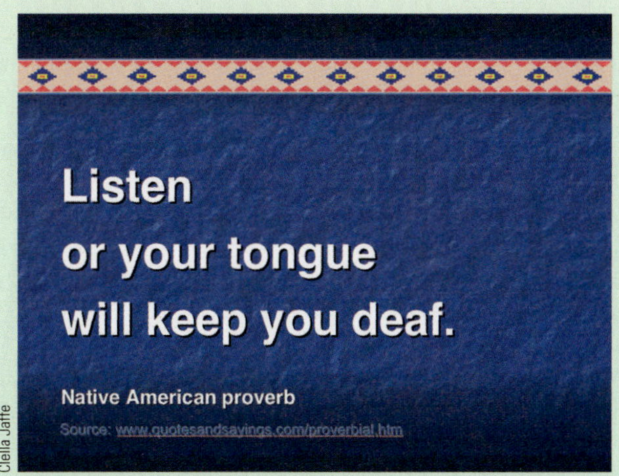

Clella Jaffe

An article titled, "Your Mother Is Still Your Mother"[23] describes the importance of proverb usage among the Igbo people of Nigeria, where proverbs both contain and transmit cultural wisdom. Chinua Achebe, a famous Nigerian author, calls them the Igbo's "horse of conversation." Adults who are considered wise conversationalists invariably use proverbs effectively, and every functioning adult in the village community learned to use them properly during childhood. Each competent user understands each proverb's meaning and discerns the situations in which a specific proverb fits.

(This article is available on InfoTrac College Edition.)

Quote Sayings, Proverbs, and Words of Wisdom

Every culture provides a store of sayings, proverbs, phrases, and other words of wisdom that encapsulates culturally important ideas, beliefs, and values. Words of wisdom come from literary and oral traditions, from well-known and anonymous sources, from philosophical and political treatises. Here are a few examples:

- Ill deeds are doubled with an evil word. (Shakespeare)
- Examine what is said, not the one who speaks. (Arab proverb)
- Judge not, that you be not judged. (Biblical quotation)
- The ignorance of one voter in a democracy impairs the security of all. (John F. Kennedy)
- Scars give you character. (Lamar Odom, "my grandmother used to say")[24]

Religious writings can provide rich sources of material when the audience accepts the text as valid. The Pope, for example, uses the Bible and Catholic teachings in his speeches; by doing so he affirms the authoritative sources of his religion. However, listeners who are not Christians, or Christians who are not Catholics, might question one or both of these sources.

Weblink 8.2 links you to many sources for usable sayings, proverbs, and wise words. (The Diversity in Practice box on previous page provides additional details about the importance of proverbs in some African cultures. You can access this link through your CourseMate for *Public Speaking*, Chapter 8 resources.)

Think Critically about Quoting Authorities

Look back at the quotations from experts and laypeople relating to inmates training puppies in prison, and ask yourself these questions about each source cited.

1. *What is the person's expertise?* For example, what is Jacqueline Bankhead's or Tonya Hess's expertise? Is it relevant to the subject under discussion?
2. *Is the person recognized as an expert by others?* How could you determine the reputation of each woman?
3. *Is the layperson stating an opinion commonly held by others like him or her?* In other words, is it a typical or representative view? Is each prisoner's experience typical? Or is one or more of the situations extreme?
4. *Are the words taken out of context?* Because you don't have the entire article, you cannot assess the context for each person's words. However, whenever possible, ask if the words fairly represent the speaker's intended meaning. Words can be distorted so that the quoted person appears to hold a position not actually held.
5. *Is the quotation accurate?* After the announcement that Osama bin Laden was dead, many Americans celebrated in the streets. The following quotation, attributed to Martin Luther King, Jr., then went viral on the Internet: "I mourn the loss of thousands of precious lives, but I will not rejoice in the death of one, not even an enemy." The quotation expresses noble ideals, but Dr. King never said it. A Facebook user wrote the words as a lead in to some of King's actual words. She included quotation marks to separate his words from hers. However, people who later posted the quotation omitted the quotation marks.[25]

To investigate quotations further, do an Internet search for the exact words "comments taken out of context," and read several webpages to identify the effect of misleading quotations.

Use Statistics Carefully

In the United States, numbers are important. We begin measuring and counting in preschool. We study opinion polls and analyze statistics. Numbers and measurements are typically considered "hard facts" that help us understand the extent of an issue or predict the probability of some future happening. Consequently, numerical support used well may increase your credibility and cause you to appear more competent and knowledgeable.

Although useful, numerical data has unique drawbacks. In general, statistics don't involve listeners' feelings, and too many in a speech can be boring. In fact, better speakers typically balance statistics with examples in order to both clarify and personalize a topic. Finally, numerical information is often misleading, and if you present biased information, your listeners will distrust you. So take extra care to use numerical data both accurately and sparingly.

Provide a Count

Enumeration means counting. A count helps your listeners understand the extent of a problem or issue: the number of Americans who struggle to get food (37 million),[26] the number of miles of U.S. bridges that are obsolete or structurally deficient (about 70,000),[27] and so on. Two tips will help you use enumeration more effectively.

enumeration a count

1. *Round your numbers up or down.* It can be difficult to remember exact numbers; also, numbers related to current topics can change rapidly. By the time they're published, they may be outdated. Consequently, instead of hearing that "New Yorkers spent 16 hours, 43 minutes, and 38 seconds online weekly compared to Clevelander's 11 hours, 57 minutes, 16 minutes," an audience would better understand, "New Yorkers spent more than 16.7 hours online weekly compared to about 12 hours for Clevelanders."[28]
2. *Make numbers come alive by comparing them to something already in your listeners' experience.* How much is a $14.3 trillion dollar US budget deficit? A stack of $1 bills would reach to the moon and back—twice. Think of all the fake money in a Monopoly game ($15,140); the US borrows about 185 times that amount *each minute*. That equals about $40,000 *per second*, more than the cost of annual room, board, and tuition at many universities.[29]

Unfortunately, numerical information can be misleading, as almost every political debate demonstrates. For example, in 2011, Republicans voted not to fund 10,000 *new* housing vouchers for homeless veterans that fiscal year. A leading Democrat then charged that 10,000 homeless vets "literally could be in the streets and die."[30] A Republican responded that 11,000 vouchers were still available from previous years. Who was telling the truth? An online fact-checking site reported that nearly 30,000 undistributed vouchers were carried over from past years, but only 2,400 not 11,000 vouchers, were not spoken for. Clearly, both sides were spinning the numbers.[31]

Choose Statistics with a Critical Eye

Common statistics include the mean, median, mode, percentages, and ratios.

The **mean** is the *average* of a group of numbers. To calculate it, add up the individual measurements and divide by the total number of units measured. The mean is skewed when extreme figures at either end of the range make the comparison less useful. Just average one billionaire's income and the annual incomes of nine people who work for minimum wages to understand the limitations of the mean.

mean average of a group of numbers

median middle number in a set of numbers arranged in a ranked order

mode most frequently occurring number

percentage figure that shows the relationship of the part to the whole, which is represented by the number 100

rate of increase or decrease percentage that uses an earlier baseline figure to compare growth or decline

ratio relationship shown by numbers, such as 1 in 10

The **median** is the middle number in a set of numbers that have been arranged into a ranked order: half the numbers are above and half below. For example, home prices in a particular area are typically stated as a median, which balances the very expensive mansions against the less expensive fixer-uppers.

The **mode** is the number that appears most commonly. For instance, on some college campuses, a few first-year students may be 16 years old, more are 17, some are in their twenties, thirties, or forties, but most are 18—the mode.

Percentages show the relationship of a part to the whole, which is represented by the number 100. Percentages are often stated as **rates of increase or decrease**, which compare growth or decline during a specific period of time to a baseline figure from an earlier period. Treat these rates cautiously, for unless you know the baseline number, the rate of increase or decrease is almost meaningless. Think of it this way: A company that employs two people in the year 2011 and adds an additional employee in 2012 increases its hiring at a rate of 50 percent. However, a company that employs 100 people in 2011 and adds one additional employee in 2012 increases hiring by 1 percent. The actual number of additional employees is the same in each company, but the rates of increase are dramatically different. The reverse is also true: A two-person company that loses one employee decreases by half or 50 percent; there's barely a blip when a larger company loses one worker. As you can see, when baseline numbers are initially very low, the rate of increase is potentially astounding.

Relationships between numbers are often shown as a **ratio**, instead of a percentage because 10% and 1 in 10 are interchangeable, as are 40% and 2 out of 5. Ratios are especially helpful when the percentage is very small; for example, .000001 percent equals 1 case in 100,000. You can see that it's more effective to say, "18 out of 100,000 teens died of gunshot injuries in 1989, up from the 12 per 100,000 recorded in 1979," than to say "eighteen-hundred-thousandth of one percent of teens."[32]

PRACTICALLY SPEAKING Engineers and Evidence

Devan Marchbanks

Good communication skills are vital in engineering because the majority of an engineer's workday is spent writing or speaking. An Engineering Curriculum Task Force identified "effectiveness in communicating ideas" as second in importance to problem recognition and solution skills and above math, science, and technical skills in importance in the career. Good communication is linked to good performance ratings and to career advancement.[33]

Engineers typically speak to two types of audience: technical (such as other engineers and scientists) and nontechnical (such as project managers, public relations personnel, customers, and government regulators).[34]

Let's say a team has designed a handheld device that could tell a blind person what denomination of bill he'd just received in change from a store clerk. The team would present different evidence to different audiences. Engineering audiences respond to numerical evidence and calculations, so using numbers with them is key. They are also visually sophisticated. Show them a visual of the product and they "get it."[35] One engineering professor advised his students, "If you're running out of time the last thing you should give up is the visual—cut other things because having the visual there will make it or break it."[36]

On the other hand, a nontechnical audience might respond better to other types of evidence. Marketers could better develop sales strategies if they knew the number of legally blind people who need a product that would tell them whether they're holding a $20 bill or a $1 bill. And customers would more likely respond to examples of a legally blind person who was ripped off at a garage sale because he was unable to count his change.

Question

1. Identify an occupation that interests you and then list two or three audiences that a person in that occupation might address. What types of evidence would work best with each audience?

Use Visual Aids to Clarify Numerical Data

Because numerical data are sometimes complex, present them in visual form whenever you can. Portland State University's college chaplain poured water out of a large pitcher to illustrate the number of people killed in a tsunami; each drop represented a life. Figure 8.1 shows how a table can help an audience visualize complex numbers. Imagine trying to understand a speaker who simply said:

> Child care workers are underpaid. Male college graduates average more than $59,400 annually, while female grads average $44,700. Men who have some college earn an average of $39,000, and women in the same category average $28,800. Even men with a high school diploma average $33,500, compared to women's average of $25,400. Compare all these salaries to the median child car worker who earns $17,600 annually.[37]

Would you remember any of this data? Now, imagine that the speaker either gives you a handout or projects a slide with Figure 8.1 on it. How is your response different? In what ways does the visual help you grasp the material more easily?

Obviously, different types of data call for different types of visual aids. The Practically Speaking feature in this chapter points out that visuals are essential in some of the speeches engineers give on technical topics. Because visual aids are vital in American culture, this text devotes Chapter 13 to the topic of creating and displaying visual materials.

Comparative Salaries of Child Care Workers

	Average for all men	Average for all women
College graduates	$59,400	$44,700
Some college	$39,000	$28,800
High school diploma	$33,500	$25,400
Highest paid child care worker	$17,600	

Figure 8.1
A table, such as this one presenting salary information, effectively depicts complex numerical data in a format that listeners can easily grasp.

Critically Analyze Numerical Data

Because numbers are easy to manipulate, evaluate them carefully with these questions before you use them.

1. *Are the numbers accurate?* A widely circulated statistic is that 60% of profits in the drug war with Mexico come from marijuana. Both proponents and opponents of legalization of marijuana used the number in their policy arguments. However, the figure, released in 2006 by the federal drug czar's office, is based on "dated" models. Rand Corporation researchers say the figure is closer to 15%–26%.[38]
2. *What is the source of the numbers?* Does the source have an interest such as a possibility of financial gain that would make high or low numbers more desirable?
3. *Are the numbers up to date?* Using a count or a percentage that is old is generally not applicable to current conditions.
4. *Before you use startling rates of increase, look at the baseline figures of the percentages.* Note any other relevant factors that might affect this rate. For example, one source said the rate of US children and teens killed by gunfire is 120 percent higher than in the other twenty-five industrialized countries combined.[39] (Any deaths are lamentable, but what if the other countries only have 10 such deaths? What if they have 20,000?)
5. *Be careful of combined statistics.* The same source from number 4 said that males experience violent crime at rates 28 percent greater than females; however, females are raped and sexually assaulted at 7.5 times the rate of males. Why do you think the authors reported the figure relating to males as a percentage but the figure relating to females as a multiple? What is 7.5 when stated as a percentage?

Find Compelling Comparisons

analogies stating similarities between two things

Comparisons, also called **analogies**, point out similarities between things. We understand new information or unfamiliar ideas better when we find points of comparison to something that's already in our experience. Comparisons can be literal or figurative.

literal analogies comparisons between two actual things that are alike in important ways

Literal analogies compare actual things that are similar in important ways. For example, Pakistani speaker Liaquat Ali Khan,[40] addressing the U.S. Senate, pointed out similarities between his country and ours and helped senators understand why Muslims broke away from India's majority Hindu population to create Pakistan:

> Pakistan was founded so that millions of Muslims should be enabled to live according to their opinions and to worship God in freedom. . . . Like some of the earlier founders of your great country, these Muslims, though not Pilgrims, nevertheless embarked upon an undertaking, which, in aim and achievement, represented the triumph of an idea. That idea was the idea of liberty, which has had its ardent followers in all climates and all countries. When our time came, its call summoned us, too, and we could not hold back.

figurative analogies stated similarities between two otherwise dissimilar things, requires an imaginative connection

Figurative analogies connect less familiar images to well-known images by highlighting similarities between otherwise *dissimilar* things. They are metaphors that require your listeners to apply their imagination and integrate likenesses between two otherwise different things or ideas. For instance, this student compared highways to a familiar food:

> Looking at a road is essentially like looking at a cake. The top layer of frosting is essentially a tar seal that is flexible and resists water infiltration. Once the "frosting" wears off—the road's worst nightmare—water is allowed into the more porous second layer of the road. When it freezes it expands, causing the road to break apart on a micro level. So once the frosting is gone, the rest of the cake deteriorates very fast.[41]

(His speech appears at the end of this chapter.)

Sometimes pointing out *differences*, or showing contrasts between a new concept and a more familiar one, is a good strategy. For example, Andrés explained lacrosse by contrasting it with the more familiar games of baseball and football. You can read the text of his speech in Appendix C.

Think Critically about Analogies

Evaluate your use of comparisons and contrasts. To test literal analogies, make sure the two items are alike in essential details. For instance, you could mislead your audience by comparing the work of a police officer in Houston, Texas, with one in Sioux Falls, South Dakota. Although their duties are alike in many ways, there are significant differences. Comparing the Houston officer to one in Los Angeles or Miami is more appropriate because all three operate in large metropolitan settings with diverse populations. Sioux Falls officers, on the other hand, have more in common with police officers in smaller cities in Michigan or Washington State.

To test figurative analogies, be sure the comparison is clear and makes sense. Can your listeners make the necessary connection of ideas?

To learn more about both literal and figurative analogies, log on to InfoTrac College Edition and do a subject search for "analogies."

Summary

It is vital to support your ideas with evidence that listeners understand and accept so they can see reasons for your major ideas. Select facts, definitions, and descriptions that you can verify in a number of sources. In addition, select up-to-date facts and take care to not pass on distorted or incorrect information.

Almost all listeners respond to examples, and using specific incidents as supporting material helps make abstract concepts more concrete and relevant. Whether real or hypothetical, brief or extended, illustrations also help listeners identify emotionally with your topic. To be effective, examples should be representative, sufficient in number, and plausible.

Visual evidence in the form of pictures, images, or symbols can help your audience "see reasons," which can lead to increased understandings and engaged emotions and can provide a motivation for behaviors.

The use of quotations or testimony also enhances your credibility if you are not considered an expert on the topic. Directly quote or paraphrase the opinions of experts and lay or peer sources. In addition, quote cultural proverbs, written texts, and even words of wisdom from relatively unknown sources that your audience will accept as credible.

In a society that tends to place value on quantification, the judicious use of enumeration and statistics can increase your audience's acceptance of your ideas. However, be sure that your numerical support is understandable, up to date, and used in ways that do not create misleading impressions. Visual aids are often helpful in clarifying complex numerical data.

Finally, use comparisons or analogies as an additional means of support. Literal analogies compare or contrast two actual things; figurative analogies compare two things that are generally considered different but share one likeness. Both types add vividness to your speeches.

As you interweave facts, examples, numbers, visuals, testimony, and analogies, you give your listeners more reasons to accept the conclusions you present.

STUDY AND REVIEW

Your online resources for *Public Speaking: Concepts and Skills for a Diverse Society* offer a broad range of study tools that will help you better understand the material in this chapter, complete assignments, and succeed on tests. Your online resources feature the following:

- Speech videos with critical viewing questions, speech outlines, and transcripts.
- Interactive versions of this chapter's Stop and Check activities, as well as Application and Critical Thinking Exercises.
- Speech Builder Express and InfoTrac College Edition.
- Weblinks related to chapter content.
- Study and review tools such as self-quizzes, an interactive glossary, and downloadable audio summaries.

You can access your online resources at the CourseMate for *Public Speaking: Concepts and Skills for a Diverse Society.* Log in at **http://www.cengage.com/login**, using the access code that came with your book or that you bought online at **http://www.cengagebrain.com**.

KEY TERMS

The terms below are defined in the margins throughout this chapter.

analogies 144
empirical facts 131
enumeration 141
established facts 131
figurative analogies 144
hypothetical example 134
literal analogies 144
literal image 136
mean 141
median 142
metaphorical image 137
mode 142
percentage 142
rate of increase or decrease 142
ratio 142

APPLICATION AND CRITICAL THINKING EXERCISES

1. What facts do you personally believe about global warming? Why? What actual research have you done on the subject? What kind of information would you trust on an issue such as this? When you find conflicting data on a topic, how do you judge which makes more sense? How would you go about forming a reasoned opinion on this topic? Does it matter if you do? Why or why not?

2. Construct a hypothetical example that would be appropriate on a controversial topic of your choice. Come to class prepared to share your example and explain why you chose the details in it.
3. Make a list of topics that almost require visual evidence. (For example: *feng shui*.) Discuss your list with a group of your classmates and explain why a visual is essential.
4. Discuss with your classmates the criteria that determine whether or not someone is an expert on a particular topic. Can students be experts on their speech subjects? How can they communicate their expertise to their classmates?
5. Stalin is alleged to have said, "A million deaths is a statistic; a single death is a tragedy." Examples are the primary tool for eliciting emotional identification with the story. They add drama, emotion, and vividness to any topic. Statistics appeal to the mind; examples appeal to the heart. Be prepared to discuss the differences and how to use each in speeches.
6. Bring to class a news source—whether online or in print. With your classmates, choose a topic from the headlines. Collect and display information by dividing the board into five sections, one for each kind of evidence: facts, examples, quotations, numerical data, and analogies. Contribute information from your news source, cooperating with your classmates to fill the board. Evaluate the evidence using the tests presented in this chapter.
7. Go to the online edition of a newsmagazine such as *Time* or *U.S. News & World Report.* Read one of the featured stories and find examples of a fact, example, visual, expert and peer testimony, statistic, and comparison. Be prepared to discuss how each type of evidence functions to make a more complete story.
8. With a small group of your classmates, evaluate the effectiveness of the following pieces of evidence taken from student speeches. What kind(s) of evidence does each excerpt represent? Is the evidence specific or vague? Does the speaker cite the source of the evidence adequately? Does it meet the tests for the type of evidence it represents?
   - According to the *Natural History of Whales and Dolphins,* dolphins communicate through a system of whistles, clicks, rattles, and squeaks. These clicking sounds are not only used for navigation in the deep waters but they may also be used to convey messages. Pulsed squeaks can indicate distress, while buzzing clicks may indicate aggression.
   - As far as deaths from killer bees are concerned, Mexican officials report that only sixteen people have died in the last three years as a result of their stings. That number is similar to the number who die of shark bite. As one Texan put it, "The killer bee will be no more a threat to us than the rattlesnake."
   - According to New Jersey congressman Frank Guarini, "American families play amusement ride roulette every time they go on an outing to an amusement park."
   - As reported by the *World Press Review Magazine,* the Japanese use of disposable chopsticks has resulted in the destruction of half of the hardwood forests in the Philippines and one-third of the forests in Indonesia. This trend will likely continue as long as the Japanese use twelve billion pairs of throwaway chopsticks a year, which is enough wood to build 12,000 average-sized family homes.
   - Fetal brain cells were implanted deep into the brain of a 52-year-old Parkinson's victim. Traditional treatments all failed this person. Later, he reported that his voice is much stronger, his mind is sharper and not confused, and he can walk without cane or crutches.

SPEECH VIDEO

Log onto the book's website to watch and critique the speeches that are research based. Also, read through Rob's speech and the accompanying comments.

Student Speech with Commentary

AMERICA'S INFRASTRUCTURE PROBLEM*

By Rob Sepich, Mount Hood Community College speech team

What impact does his opening example have on you?

For 45-year-old Gregory Jolstad, August 1, 2007, was a day like any other. He and his crew were resurfacing the I-35 westbound bridge in Minneapolis, when it suddenly and without warning, collapsed beneath them. Once the dust had cleared, 145 people were injured and 13 were found dead, including Jolstad. According to the Minneapolis Department of Transportation's report released in October 21, 2007, the cause of the collapse was a combination of structural weakening over 60 years of use, and components that were half as thick as they were designed to be. The added weight of the construction crew's heavy equipment was, quite literally, the straw that broke the camel's back.

While tragic, this event highlighted a major problem in the United States: our nation's bridges and roads are degrading beyond our means to fix them and causing catastrophic results. The United States government must address this ticking time bomb now. Today, we will examine the weakening of America's infrastructure by, first, looking to the economic issues affecting the maintenance of infrastructure, secondly, exploring the physical deterioration of roads, and finally, discussing some solutions.

How does Rob establish his credibility throughout this speech?

The United States Chamber of Commerce's annual Transportation Performance Index reported September 23, 2010, that if our nation's infrastructure is not able to handle and expand to both the growing transportation and commuting needs, it will directly hurt our nation's economy. Even President Obama recognizes the need to improve our infrastructure before it is too late. In his 2011 State of the Union Address, he pointed out that the US is lacking when compared to countries such as India, China, and Russia, who are seeing exponential growth in infrastructure investment, while our own road and bridge system is falling apart.

Why? Because of neglect. Neglected maintenance of roads and bridges acts as a constant drain on our economy and a scourge on our quality of life. Rough and rutted roads cause accidents, damage vehicles, and trigger traffic jams that lead to countless hours of delay and financial waste. This problem is widespread throughout the country.

According to the California Public Research Interest Group's April 8, 2010 report, over 90,000 miles of roads and 70,000 miles of bridges are structurally deficient or obsolete. This means that while other countries are building up their infrastructure, our own is crumbling. The American Society of Civil Engineers stated on November 15, 2010, that over the next five years, the US will require an additional 550 billion dollars on top of what we are spending just to bring the roads and bridges up to par. Attention must be paid to this problem before it gets swept under the rug and forgotten forever.

What do you think of his analogy that compares the road to a cake? How does this involve your imagination?

The second important thing to examine is the physical wear caused by decades of use. Looking at a road is essentially like looking at cake. The top layer of frosting in this case is actually a tar seal that is flexible and resists water infiltration. Once the "frosting" wears off, the road's worst nightmare, water is allowed into the more porous second layer of the road. Water seeps into the road, and when it freezes, it expands causing the road to break apart on a micro level. So once the frosting is gone, the rest of the cake degrades very fast. Holes in the tar seal result in the familiar alligator cracking and potholes.

The April 2010 *Civil Engineering Journal* tells us that the ability for a road to stay intact for a long period of time is directly dependent on keeping the tar seal intact. It is far cheaper to maintain a road properly over time, according to The Oregon Department of Transportation's annual State of the Streets report (2008), than it is to rebuild from scratch a failing road.

So why is it that states are not able to simply do the necessary maintenance in order to save themselves money in the long run? Quite simply, states do not have the ability to set aside the capital needed to make these repairs. CNN reported on November 15, 2008, that 73 percent of all traffic in the US is on state maintained roads, and state governments simply cannot keep up with the maintenance in most cases. So, in effect, the federal government needs to provide financial support to states to keep our system maintained so we can prevent further cost and safety issues in the future.

He relies mainly on facts and statistics in the speech. Where, if any place, would you advise him to add examples? Where might testimony from experts and from peers be useful? Why?

Now that we have a better idea of the needs facing the Department of Transportation, we can finally look at some realistic answers to this problem. To come up with a viable and sustainable answer, we must act on a national, state, and individual level. One recent large-scale solution that has been proposed is President Obama's National Infrastructure Bank. According to the September 12, 2010 *Atlantic Magazine*, this new infrastructure bank would allot money based on a project's merit and need. The Cato Institute agreed on September 9, 2010 that this new I bank would work well, but only if it is done right. In the status quo, the only way for a state to receive a large amount of money for a project is through earmarks added to Congressional legislation.

The problem with this is that emergency projects are not made the priority and are often pushed aside by more politically popular projects. The *Boston Globe* reports on July 12, 2008 Boston's Big Dig to run Interstate 90 underneath the city cost a record $22 billion—*after interest*. The Big Dig only worsened traffic congestion around Boston and pushed the state into massive debt. Ideally, the I bank could help take the politics out of how projects are prioritized and focus on strengthening the entire country's transportation network instead of just prioritizing one state over the other. The *Washington Post* reported on October 11, 2010 that President Obama asked Congress to approve 50 billion dollars to start this program. 50 billion dollars is NOT a lot of money, considering it is less than ten percent of what the American Society of Civil Engineers states that we need to get our nation's road system back on track.

Does he give enough information about his sources for you to consider them credible? Why or why not?

Unfortunately, bipartisan bickering is holding up a crucial step in solving this crisis. According to the *Congressional Quarterly* of October 21, 2010, the current transportation bill expired September 30, and the House Ways and Means Committee has not yet found an extension that appeals to both Republicans and Democrats. American citizens must compel Congress to act now to protect Americans from an infrastructure that is literally crumbling around us. I encourage you all to write to your senators and congressmen, and tell them it is time to repair our broken system and keep America moving.

Individually, it is important to educate yourself on the issues. I have created a Facebook page to raise awareness and provide links to many of the reports I've mentioned in this presentation. Simply press the like or join group button the next time you are harvesting your Farmville crops. Awareness can lead to action. None of us want to be on the next bridge when it fails or find ourselves alone on the side of the road with a flat tire caused by a pothole. While we cannot bring back Gregory Jolstad, or the twelve others who perished in the Minneapolis bridge collapse, we can take action now to ensure that more needless deaths do not occur. We must face the fact that our roads and bridges can no longer be ignored. It is time to invest, keep Americans safe, and keep it moving!

Overall, what were the strongest areas of this speech? What might he improve and how?

CHAPTER 9

THIS CHAPTER WILL HELP YOU

- Organize your main points
- Identify and use a number of linear patterns, including chronological, spatial, causal, problem-solution, pro-con, and topical
- Develop and support your main points
- Link the parts of the speech to one another through skillful use of connectives such as signposts, transitions, internal previews, and internal summaries
- Identify and use alternative patterns—including the wave, the spiral, and the star—when they are appropriate

Organizing Your Main Points

RECENTLY A COLLEGE-BOUND STUDENT applied for a university scholarship that required a short speech. In his introduction, he clearly stated, "I want to attend your school for three reasons," which he then explained one-by-one. His transition statements helped the decision makers follow his flow of ideas. In his conclusion, he reviewed his main points and restated his reasons for choosing the university. The applicant who followed him had her own good reasons for wanting the same scholarship. However, she did not clearly state them; she rambled from one idea to another, and her ending did not summarize her overall theme. He was awarded the scholarship; she was not.

Good organization is vital. As one student said, "I think of organization as being kind to your audience as well as yourself." Guidelines for arranging your main points and your speech materials fall into what the Romans called the *canon of disposition*, which was introduced in Chapter 2. This chapter begins with general tips for identifying and organizing main points, moves on to explain several common organizational patterns, describes ways to develop, support, and connect main points, and concludes with alternative methods of arranging the body of your speech.

Organize Your Main Points

Although the body is the middle part of your speech, you should plan it before you plan the introduction. Your research has probably turned up several subcategories of information such as a sequence of events or the causes and effects of a problem. Identifying major patterns can help you organize your main points and your underlying supporting material. Here are a few general organizational tips for main points: limit your points, know the major traditional patterns, and choose the best pattern.

Use a Limited Number of Points

Cognitive psychologists say we learn better when we "chunk" information into just a few major units.[1] (For example, notice how you easily learn telephone numbers because they come in three- and four-digit segments). This principle means that listeners will remember your speech better if you limit the number of your main points. Two to five points are common; the key is to keep your basic structure simple.

To identify your main points, return to the thesis statement you developed in Chapter 5. If you've created it thoughtfully, you should have a pretty good idea about how to cover the material.[2] Keeping your goal and the general direction of your speech in mind, you can start fleshing out your content.

Consider Traditional Patterns

Over centuries of speechmaking, several traditional organizational patterns have been developed to fit specific types of topics and purposes. Some patterns work especially well for presenting facts and information, while others are better for persuasive messages. Here, we look at six widely used patterns: chronological, spatial, causal, problem-solution, pro-con, and topical.

Chronological Organization

In the **chronological pattern**, a sequence of events occurs in a given order. Historical topics or biographical speeches describe events as they unfold across a period of years. **Process speeches**, in which several steps, stages, or cycles follow one another in fairly predictable sequences, almost automatically fall into a chronological pattern. Typically, chronological speeches have an informative purpose. Here are the main points in a biographical speech followed by a process speech:

chronological pattern presents points in a sequential or time order

process speech describes a sequence of steps or stages that follow one another in a fairly predictable pattern

King Tut is the most famous mummy found in the Egyptian Valley of the Kings.

I. He was a child king who reigned from his accession at age nine until his death at age nineteen.
II. He died under mysterious circumstances.
III. King Tut again became famous when his tomb and its contents were discovered in 1922.

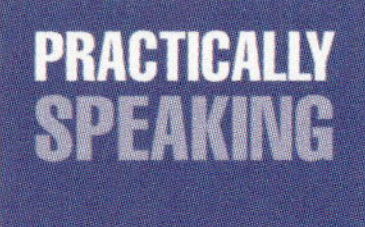

Career Advice

Elisia Choi moved to a new city and entered the work force as an intern in a major public relations firm. Shortly after she gave her first formal project update to a group of clients, she was hired to a full-time position in the company. Choi answered some questions about her workplace speaking opportunities and strategies.

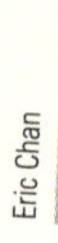

What types of speeches are commonly given in your job? Most of my speeches are informative or persuasive and given in front of clients. We may be informing them of the status of a project or persuading them to adopt new strategies or plans.

How do you typically begin organizing your main ideas? First, I think about my main point. What do I want clients to walk away knowing in the end? I then think about how I will preview my speech to inform the audience of my main points.

Why do you spend so much time in organization? A well-organized speech is easy to understand, follow, and remember. In addition, someone who organizes her speech well is often viewed as an organized thinker and worker. It is important to always portray myself in a positive light and, in essence, market myself as a valuable asset to the company and team. I never know who may be listening to my speech, taking note of my abilities, and considering me for future projects and opportunities.

What advice about organization would you give someone who is new to speechmaking? Work on transitions. Smooth transitions can often make or break a speech. Also, remember that a speech does not mean talking to people—it's about conversing with them. Hence, it's important to be flexible and not prioritize getting through all the main points if you lose the audience's engagement. It is okay to deviate from the speech plan to expand on a point when the audience expresses verbal or nonverbal confusion.

Questions

1. Choi's strategy of thinking about her "main point," or what she wants "clients to walk away knowing in the end," is another way of saying she starts with her thesis statement. Why is this the best strategy to use for deciding on main points?
2. What reasons would you give for saying that speech organization helps an audience remember ideas?
3. How hard do you personally work to understand a speech that is disorganized?
4. Choi says that speech organization, or lack thereof, contributes to a speaker's credibility. What other examples can you give that shows this to be true?

Relational breakups typically go through four stages:[3]

I. In the intrapsychic phase one or both partners ponders what to do about the relationship.
II. During the dyadic phase, they discuss the possibility of breaking up.
III. The social phase is when they tell other people about their breakup.
IV. In the grave-dressing phase, they rationalize the breakup.

The key with chronological speeches is that events *must* occur in a sequence and follow a clear "first, next, finally" pattern. Occasionally, speakers vary the pattern by beginning with the final point before showing the events that led up to it. For instance, a speaker could first describe the discovery of King Tut's tomb and then go back to provide details about his life.

Spatial Organization

A less common way to organize points is spatially—by location or place. The **spatial pattern** is useful for informative speeches about places or things made up of several levels or layers. Patterns could move top-to-bottom, east-to-west, region-to-region, floor-to-floor of a building and so on. Here are two examples of spatial organization:

spatial pattern presents points by place or location

The Louvre Museum in Paris has three major wings.

I. The Denon Wing is on the south.
II. The Richelieu Wing is on the north.
III. The Sully Wing is on the east.

Construct a brick pathway in four layers.

I. Put down gravel for the bottom layer.
II. Next, lay down a heavy-duty weed-barrier fabric.
III. Pour sand over that.
IV. Finally, set the bricks in place.

The construction of the brick pathway must be discussed in order; however, the other topics are more flexible. A speech describing a city, for instance, could be organized by direction (north, south, east, west), by population density (most to least populated, or vice versa), by income level, and so on, depending on the speaker's goal.

Causal Organization

When your goal is to shed light on a problem, a **cause-effect** or **causal pattern** is helpful. This pattern examines both the reasons underlying a problem (the causes) and the implications of the problem for individuals or for society at large (the effects). You can use either a cause-to-effect or an effect-to-cause pattern. Here is a preview for a cause-to-effect speech on campaign ads:

cause-effect pattern presents reasons (causes) and implications (effects) of a topic

Negative ads in political campaigns create a problem.[4]

I. Campaigns use them for several reasons (causes).
   A. Candidates cast suspicion on their opponents.
   B. Negative ads are memorable.
II. Negative ads affect the electorate.
   A. They are linked to decreased voter turnout.
   B. Voters lose trust in politics and politicians.

Some topics are more effectively presented by first looking a problem's effects on an individual or group before exploring its causes. These use an effects-to-cause pattern:

Many Asians are becoming increasingly dissatisfied with their physical appearance.[5]

I. Effects include eyelid surgery and use of skin whitening products.
   A. Eyelid surgery is increasingly popular, especially among Koreans.
   B. Skin bleaching products are sold throughout Asian countries.

II. Critics think that Western media depictions of beauty cause this dissatisfaction.
  A. Ideologies of beauty portrayed in Western media include large eyes, blonde hair, smooth complexions, and skinny or toned bodies.
  B. Multi-national companies use standardized advertising that includes computer-enhanced Western models, even in Asian countries.

Problem-Solution Organization

problem-solution pattern describes a problem and a possible solution to it

As Chapter 1 pointed out, one core US belief is that life presents challenges we can solve through knowledge and effort. Consequently, we often approach global, national, local, and personal issues as problems that require solutions. A **problem-solution pattern** works well for persuasive speeches. Not surprisingly, this pattern requires you to look at the problem—sometimes examining its causes and effects—and then propose a solution. Here is an outline for a persuasive speech on food waste:

Hedda Gjeren/iStockphoto

Topics such as food waste are typically organized in either cause-effect or problem-solution patterns.

Food waste is a problem both locally and globally.[6]

I. Food waste includes uneaten food, scraps from preparation, and produce left after harvest.
  A. Food is wasted everywhere it is produced, sold, and consumed.
  B. Disposal of wasted food leads to environmental and sanitation problems.
  C. Millions of people are malnourished.

II. We can personally help solve the problem in our community.
  A. We can intentionally waste less food.
  B. We can work with groups such as the gleaners who collect food after harvests.
  C. We can support a shift to sustainable agriculture.

This pattern is also useful for informative speeches. Let's say the topic is hair loss. If your purpose were to inform, you'd describe the problem of hair loss and then introduce your listeners to a variety of solutions. (If you were persuading on the same topic, you'd focus on the one solution you believe is best.)

Pro-Con Organization

pro-con arrangement presents arguments in favor of and arguments against an issue

When you need to explore arguments on both sides of a controversial issue, the **pro-con arrangement** is very useful. Classify all the arguments in favor of the issue under the *pro* label, and then list the arguments against it under the *con* label. Here is an example of pro-con organization. The topic is Direct-to-Consumer ads (DCTA) about prescription drugs.

The US and New Zealand are the only two nations that allow the controversial direct-to-consumer advertising of prescription drugs.[7]

I. Proponents make a number of arguments in favor of these ads.
  A. Drug companies say the ads make people aware of potential health conditions.
  B. People are encouraged to talk to their doctors about the conditions.
  C. Early treatment of many conditions can save money later.

II. Critics give many reasons for discontinuing DCTA.
  A. The ads are more emotional than factual.
  B. Some conditions may be over diagnosed and over treated.
  C. Patients may use drugs instead of lifestyle changes to treat the problem.

This organizational pattern is like an investigative report that works best for informative speeches where your goal is to explain the nature of an issue. By hearing both sides, your listeners can weigh the evidence and evaluate the arguments for themselves.

When your purpose is to persuade and you intend to advocate for one set of arguments over another, you should choose a different pattern.

Topical Organization

When your material doesn't really fit into any of these patterns, use the most common pattern—**topical organization**—where you classify the major points into subdivisions, each of which is part of the whole. Although every point contributes to an overall understanding of the subject, the points themselves can be ordered in different ways. For instance, a commencement speaker used these points:[8]

topical arrangement divides a subject into subtopics, each of which is part of the whole

Himagine/istockphoto.com

The major points of a speech on a topic such as travel in Costa Rica could be organized chronologically, spatially, or topically.

There are four simple secrets to becoming very wealthy.

I. Save.
II. Separate needs from wants.
III. Make smart choices.
IV. Give back.

She could easily change the order and start with separating needs from wants and then move to making smart choices, saving, and giving back.

Choose the Best Pattern

Because a single topic can be organized in a number of ways, choose the pattern that works best given your purposes, your supporting materials, your audience, and the assignment. For instance, you could effectively develop the topic of Costa Rica tourism with one of these three patterns:

Chronological: Three days in Costa Rica can be wisely spent.

I. On the first day, explore the capital city, visit a butterfly garden, and take in a soccer game.
II. The next day, take a day trip to the Poás Volcano and the La Paz Waterfall Gardens.
III. On the final day, visit a coffee plantation.

Spatial: Costa Rica has several distinct regions.

I. The Northern Zone includes active volcanoes, hot springs, and cloud forests.
II. The eastern shore bordering the Caribbean is famous for sea turtles.
III. The central valley is most densely populated; it is home to coffee plantations.
IV. The Pacific Ocean in the west contains eight distinct habitats.

Topical: Eco-tourists seek out three famous sites in Costa Rica.

I. Poás Volcano National Park is the number one tourist destination.
II. Tortuguero National Park features nesting sea turtles.
III. Canopy tours in the Monteverde Cloud Forest explore the high-altitude rain forest ecosystem.

Use these patterns to organize the speech as a whole or combine patterns to organize the points within your speech. For instance, a speech on the history of gambling in the United States, could have the main points ordered chronologically with subpoints organized topically.

Develop Your Main Points

After you have decided on major points, evaluate them for effectiveness by making sure they are distinct and parallel. Then develop your main points by adding supporting materials and connecting your ideas so that they flow smoothly.

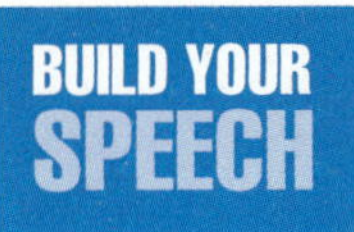

Organize Your Main Points

Write your topic here: ______________________________

Begin the process of organizing your material into main points. Study the evidence you found in your research, and then check all that apply.

___ The topic unfolds in *stages*.
___ The topic unfolds in *steps*.
___ *Ordered dates* are important to this topic.
___ There is a *before, during*, and *after* pattern.
___ The topic takes place in *distinct locations* or *places*.
___ Several *causes* are mentioned.
___ Several *effects* are present.
___ The topic describes a *problem*.
___ There is a *solution* (or are *solutions*) to a problem.
___ There are *pro arguments* for a particular position.
___ There are *con arguments* against a particular position.
___ There are several *topical points* that don't really fit into one of these patterns.

Write your tentative thesis statement here: ______________________________
____
____
____

In light of the boxes you checked and your tentative central idea, select the organizational pattern that would work best with your speech: ______________________________
____
____

Revise your thesis statement, if necessary: ______________________________
____
____

Once you know which organizational pattern will work best for your speech and have confirmed your central idea, log on to Speech Builder Express for help developing the main points of your speech.

Make Points Distinct

Each point should be clear and separate from the others. For example, one student's speech on CPR was so disorganized that her audience had trouble following her train of thought. Her outline identified a number of indistinct concepts, and some of her supporting material overlapped. Here are the main points as she outlined them:

I. Once you have training in CPR, you also have responsibilities.
II. Rules of CPR for an adult.
III. Signs: Something to look for. [Under this point she explained the steps of CPR.]
IV. Statistics from the American Heart Association.

She would have had a better framework for her supporting materials and for her audience to follow if she had used one of the common patterns such as the problem-solution or topical pattern. Here's how her points would look with the problem-solution pattern:

I. [problem] Every year, thousands of people experience sudden cardiac arrest outside of the hospital.
    A. This condition has several causes.
    B. The effects show up in specific symptoms.
II. [solution] More lives could be saved if more people had CPR training.
    A. The American Heart Association teaches people the steps of CPR.
    B. Trained and certified responders have specific responsibilities in crisis situations.

Rhyming or alliterating main ideas are additional strategies that can make points distinct and memorable as these examples show:

Obesity: what dieters don't need, heed, or read[9]
Advergaming is evaluative, efficient, effective, and engaging.

Make Points Parallel

After you have distinct points, make sure they are **parallel points,** meaning that they are similar in kind and in length. Don't write some out as declarative sentences and others as questions. Avoid mixing phrases and complete sentences, and don't put two sentences in a single point, all of which this student did when she originally set out her major points:

parallel points creating points that are similar in kind and length

I. What is Multiple sclerosis (MS)? [a complete sentence in question form]
II. The Big Mystery! [a sentence fragment or phrase]
III. Who? [a single word in question form]
IV. Effects . . . Symptoms of MS. [an incomplete sentence]
V. Three prominent medications are now being used to treat MS. These are talked about in the magazine *Inside MS.* [two declarative sentences]

She should reorganize her points and rewrite them as declarative sentences, as shown here:

I. Multiple sclerosis (MS) is a disease of the central nervous system.
II. The causes remain a mystery.
III. Sufferers tend to share age, gender, and regional characteristics.
IV. The condition affects eyesight and bodily coordination.
V. Most physicians prescribe one of three major medications.

Furthermore, as she looks at these points, she can see that they logically fall into a problem-solution pattern, so her final outline should look like this:

I. Multiple Sclerosis (MS) is a disease of the central nervous system.
    A. Sufferers tend to share age, gender, and regional characteristics.
    B. The causes remain a mystery.
    C. The effects are on eyesight and bodily coordination.
II. Most physicians prescribe one of three major medications.

Support Points with Evidence

Once you've decided on your main points, return to your research and begin to arrange your materials under the ideas they support. Of course, the amount of time you have to speak will help you decide how much information to include, and the amount of previous

Some African Organizational Patterns

In many areas of the world, speakers choose patterns markedly different from those presented in this text. Two such examples come from Africa.

Madagascar

Elders in the Merina tribe use a four-part organizational pattern when they speak:[10]

1. First is a period of excuses in which the speaker expresses his humility and reluctance to speak. He uses standard phrases such as "I am a child, a younger brother." He sometimes relates well-known stories and proverbs.
2. He follows this by thanking the authorities for letting him speak at all. He uses a formula that thanks God, the president of the republic, government ministers, the village headman, major elders, and finally the people in the audience.
3. In the third section, he uses proverbs, illustrations, and short poems as he makes his proposal.
4. He closes by thanking and blessing his listeners.

Kenya

The body of the speech is often organized in a circular pattern, somewhat like a bicycle wheel. The hub or center of the wheel is the single main point that ties the entire speech together. The speaker then wanders out repeatedly from the central point, telling stories and providing other supporting materials and stories that tie back to the main idea. To an outsider, the speech might seem boring or illogical, but Kenyan listeners can easily follow the logic that ties the points together.[11]

knowledge your audience has will help you decide what specific information you must include and what you can leave out.

Here's how Jordan organized the first section of his speech on e-waste. His assignment was a civic awareness speech in which he first described a problem and then told about an organization that exists to combat that problem.[12] A survey revealed that his listeners all had electronic devices, and most intended to replace at least one item within the year. Some knew the term e-waste; all knew that disposal of electronics could harm the environment, but they were less aware of its extent. Everyone wanted to learn responsible ways to dispose of outdated electronic devices. So as he developed the "problem" section of the speech, he selected definitions, examples, statistics, and other evidence with his audience in mind:

I. [main point] First, let's look at the problem of e-waste.
   A. [definition] A Swiss government agency, the EMPA, defines e-waste as any out-of-date or otherwise discarded equipment that uses electricity.
      1. [synonym] Tech waste is another term.
      2. [example] This can be computers, cell phones, or household appliances.
      3. [explanation] If you can plug it in and you throw it out, it's e-waste.

B. [fact] Over the past few decades, the amount of e-waste in the US has grown steadily.
   1. [statistic] Elizabeth Royte, writing in the *Smithsonian Magazine,* estimates that at least 60 million PCs are buried in US landfills.
      a. [fact] That article was from 2005.
      b. [fact] E-waste has only gotten worse since then.
   2. [statistic] A 2008 EPA report said that 80–85% of discarded electronics were sent to landfills between 2003 and 2005.
   3. [expert] In August of 2010, EPA administrator, Lisa P. Jackson, announced e-waste as one of the agency's top priorities.

Jordan similarly supported his next points—specific hazards of electronic wastes and how it affects people—with information his audience was less likely to know. (You can find his entire outline at the end of this chapter.)

Connect Your Ideas

Connectives are words, phrases, and sentences that lead from one idea to another and unify the various elements of your speech. They function somewhat like bridges that link your points to each other or to the whole. With them you can emphasize significant points and help your listeners keep their place as you talk. The most common connectives are signposts and transitions, internal previews, and internal summaries.

connectives words, phrases, and sentences used to lead from idea to idea and tie the parts of the speech together smoothly

Signposts and Transitions

Signposts are similar to highway signs that help you know where you are. Words such as *first*, *next*, and *finally* introduce new points and help your listeners identify the flow of your ideas. Other words and phrases such as *in addition*, *for example*, *therefore*, and *as a result* connect one idea to another. Signposts such as *the main thing to remember* or *most importantly* highlight ideas you want to emphasize. Here are two examples of signposts from Jordan's outline:

signpost connective such as *first, most importantly*, and *consequently* that links ideas, lends emphasis, and helps listeners keep their place in the speech

- *First*, let's look at the problem of e-waste.
- More importantly, electronics contain a bevy of harmful chemicals.

Transitions summarize where you have been and where you are going in the speech. You can use them both between points and within a single point. Here is a simple transition between major points:

transition summary of where you've been and where you're going in your speech

> Now that you have an understanding of the problems surrounding e-waste [where we've been], let's examine possible solutions [where we're going].

Transitions can also lead from subpoint to subpoint *within* a major point. For example, Anne's major point, "Women get more ACL knee injuries than men for several reasons," has three subpoints: wider Q Angle, greater joint laxity, and differing neuromuscular characteristics. After she describes the first two causes, she could transition to the final one by saying:

> In addition to a wider Q-Angle and greater joint laxity [first and second subpoint], women have neuromuscular characteristics that make them more prone to knee injuries [third subpoint].

Internal Previews and Internal Summaries

Internal previews occur within the body of your speech and briefly summarize the subpoints you will develop under one of your major points. For instance, in her speech about amusement park tragedies, Tamara said:

internal preview brief in-speech summary that foretells the subpoints you'll develop under a major point

> Experts agree that there are three main causes of amusement park tragedies: equipment failure, operator failure, and rider behavior.

This internal preview helps her audience identify the framework she'll use to develop her major point about the causes of accidents.

internal summary restatement of the ideas within a subpoint

If you summarize subpoints after you've made them but before you move to another major point, you're using an **internal summary**. Thus, this sentence summarizes the causes before moving on to the effects of amusement park accidents:

> In short, we have seen that equipment failure, operator failure, and rider behavior combine to create thousands of tragedies annually.

Connectives, then, are the words, phrases, and sentences you use to weave your ideas together and enhance the flow of your speech as a whole. They serve to introduce your points, show the relationship of one point to another, preview and summarize material within a point, and help your listeners keep their place in your speech.

Alternative Patterns

organic pattern alternative pattern that provides a clear speech structure in a less linear form

In addition to the traditional patterns examined earlier, researchers have identified several alternative organizational patterns that allow speakers to visualize their speeches in a less linear way. For example, many speakers, because of their cultural backgrounds or personal inclinations, are uncomfortable with the standard organizational patterns.[13] Instead, more **organic patterns**, visualized as a wave, a spiral, and a star, can provide a clear structure for a speech in a less linear form.[14]

The Wave Pattern

wave pattern repetitive pattern that presents variations of themes and ideas, with major points presented at the crests

This pattern, illustrated in Figure 9.1, consists of repetitions and variations of themes and ideas. Major points come at the crests of the waves, which are developed with a variety of examples leading up to another crest, which repeats the theme or makes another major point. Conclusions wind down and lead the audience gradually from your topic; or they begin with a transition and then rebuild, so that the final statement is a dramatic peak. Women and members of various ethnic groups often choose the **wave pattern**.[15] It is common in ceremonial speaking.

Perhaps the most familiar wave pattern speech is Martin Luther King, Jr.'s "I Have a Dream." Throughout, he uses a number of "crests" including "One hundred years later . . ." "Now is the time . . ." and the memorable line "I have a dream. . . ." He follows each repetition of the phrase with examples that develop the idea. His conclusion dramatically emerges from the final wave in the speech—the repetition and variation of the phrase "Let freedom ring."

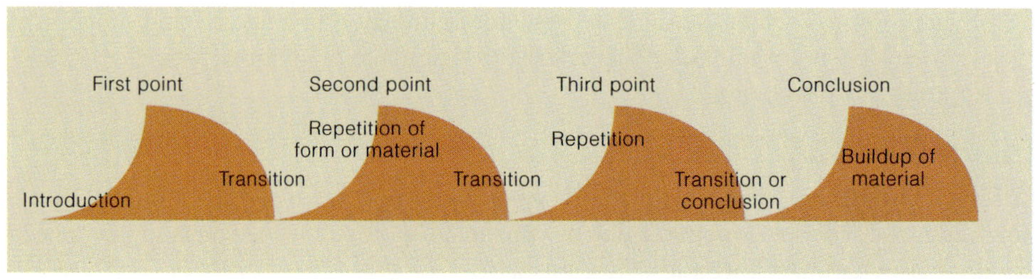

Figure 9.1
The Wave Pattern A wave pattern speech is built around a repetitive theme such as "I have a dream."

The wave pattern shows up in other famous speeches including Sojourner Truth's "Ain't I a Woman?"[16] and Nikki Giovanni's speech, "We Are Virginia Tech,"[17] delivered at the memorial ceremony for the victims of a campus shooter in April 2007. (Truth's speech is in Appendix C; you can read the text and watch the video of Giovanni's speech in your online resources.)

This pattern works well for eulogies. When a popular teacher died while quite young, one of her former students memorialized her, using the repetitive phrase, "Patsy loved us." Here are a few lines from that speech.

> [O]ne theme has emerged from everyone's comments about Patsy. That theme: Love. Simply put, Patsy loved us.
>
> Yes, she taught us English, how to write a full-length essay, how to analyze a poem, how to punctuate correctly. In fact, she taught us so well, that many of our class went on to teach English at the junior high, high school, or university level, myself included. But many more became teachers or leaders in various roles inspired simply because of this woman who loved us.
>
> Patsy loved us . . . and we loved her back . . .[18]

In summary, when you use this pattern, develop a repetitive theme—the crests of the wave—and between these crests, provide specific and general examples. As you can see, repetition with variation can be a powerful strategy to stir audience emotions.

The Spiral Pattern

The **spiral pattern** is a way to visualize points in a topical speech on subjects that increase in magnitude or effect. For example, a student who wanted to speak about food waste by showing how waste occurs on personal, institutional, and community levels, might visualize her points as spiraling in magnitude. In the first loop of the spiral, she would describe food waste in her home. In the next loop, she would move the focus to the university's cafeteria where even more food is wasted. In the third and final loop, she would present information on food waste in the restaurants and other institutions in the community at large. Because each major scenario has greater effects than the preceding one, her audience would see the issue in different contexts. Figure 9.2 illustrates the spiral pattern and how a speaker might sketch and write out her points using it. Notice the increasing sizes of the loops.

spiral pattern repetitive pattern with a series of points that increase in drama or intensity

The spiral pattern is useful for speeches on subjects that build in levels of dramatic intensity. For the topic of workplace bullying, a speaker might tell a series of stories about people who were bullied. The first scenario could be a mild incident of verbal abuse that only happened once. In the second, the bullying intensifies in frequency and type, so much so that the bullied person quits his job. In the final scenario, the bully uses physical violence against the bullied person. Each scene builds in tension, with the most intense scenario reserved for the final spiral.

The Star Pattern

The **star pattern** is another way to visualize a topical speech. Each point in this pattern, illustrated in Figure 9.3, is more or less equally weighted within a theme that ties the whole together. This variation on the topical pattern is useful for speakers who present the same basic speech to a number of audiences. By visualizing their major points as a star, they have the flexibility of choosing where to start and what to emphasize, depending on what's relevant for a specific audience. For example, a wise speaker might begin with a point the audience understands or agrees with and then progressively move to points that

star pattern presents relatively equally weighted speech points within a thematic circle that binds them together; order of points may vary

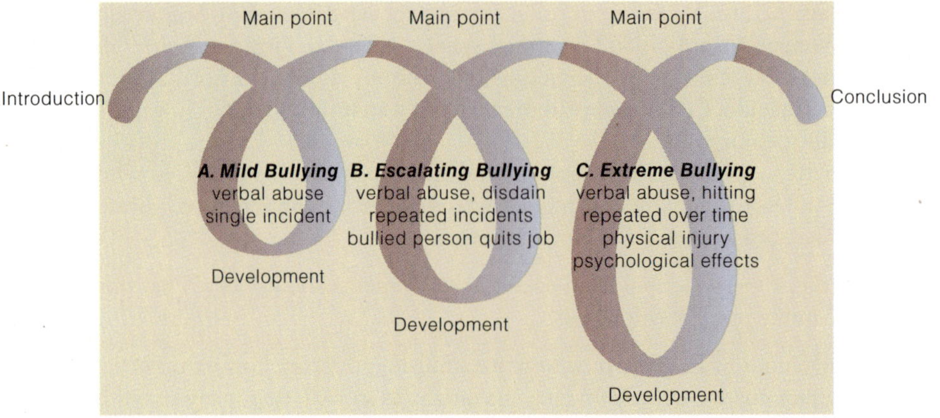

Figure 9.2
The Spiral Pattern Spiral pattern speeches are useful for speeches based on points that build in dramatic intensity.

challenge their understanding and agreement. For inattentive audiences, begin with the most dramatic point to gain attention from the outset. For hostile audiences, begin with the most conciliatory point. This gives the advantage of quickly making audience adaptations and still covering the topics of the speech effectively.

There are two ways to develop the points of the speech. One way is to state the point, support or develop it, and then provide a transition to the next point. Alternatively, you could develop each point fully and then state it. Base your decisions on the type of audience and the nature of your message.

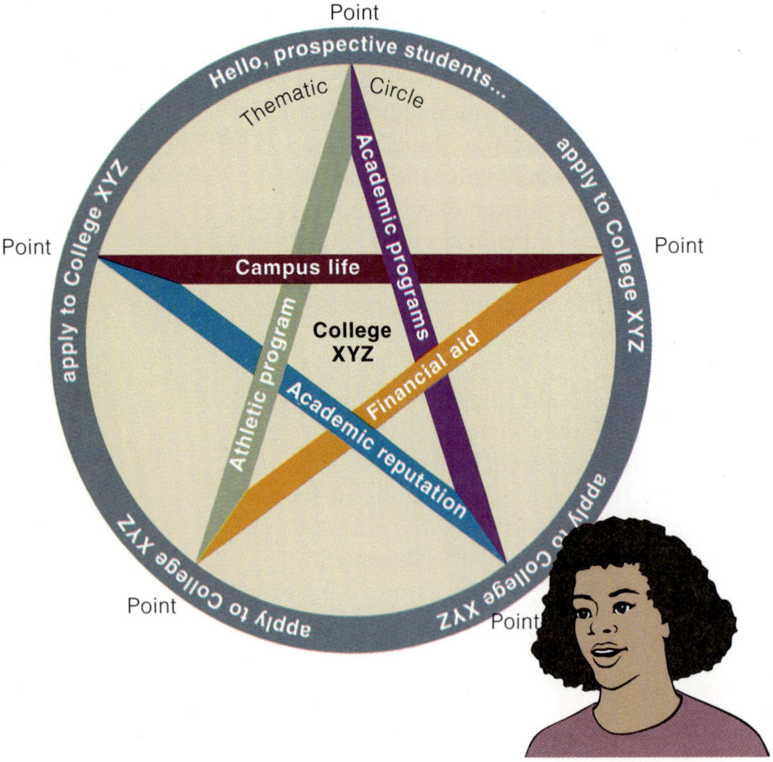

The final element in the pattern is the thematic circle that binds the points together. By the close of the speech, listeners should feel that the circle is completed and the theme is fulfilled. This pattern is common during election years. The underlying theme is "Vote for me!" Then the candidates stake out their positions on various issues. However, instead of giving an identical "stump speech" to every group, they rearrange the issues and target specific points to specific audiences. For soccer moms, a candidate might begin with education and end with crime issues; for elders, the same candidate might begin with Social Security and end with educational policies.

Repetition patterns are probably best seen in songwriting. Each verse develops the song's theme, while the chorus lyrics are repeated unchanged.[19] Although these patterns might appear to be easier to use than a linear format, they require just as much organizational planning.

Figure 9.3
The Star Pattern This college recruiter visualizes her speech as points of a star enclosed within the general theme "Apply to this college." Sometimes she starts with academics, sometimes with campus life, depending on the specific audience's interests.

Develop Your Speech Using an Alternative Pattern

Write your topic here: ______________________________

For a wave pattern:

Draw out a diagram similar to Figure 9.1, and then identify each wave crest that you will develop with supporting evidence. Write the repetitive phrase or idea at the crest of the wave and then list your supporting material below it.

For a spiral pattern:

Draw a diagram similar to Figure 9.2. Write out the main point at the bottom of each loop. Then jot down the supporting material you will use to develop each loop.

For a star pattern:

Sketch out a star within a circle. (Your star does not have to have five points.) Write your major ideas on the points of the star, one idea per point. In the circle that connects your points, write out your speech's central theme.

Summary

After you've gathered speech materials, you must organize them into a pattern. Begin with the body of the speech, and choose a limited number of points from among several traditional patterns. Common organizational frameworks include chronological, spatial, causal, problem-solution, pro-con, and topical patterns. These patterns are appropriate for many types of speeches; causal and pro-con are especially good for informative purposes. Problem-solution works especially well for persuasive speeches.

After you select your points, evaluate them to make sure each one is distinct and they are constructed in parallel form. Support each point with evidence that fits your purpose, the assignment, and the audience. Then weave your ideas together with connectives that link your points and subpoints into a coherent whole.

Although linear patterns are common in the United States, *nonlinear* arrangements are typical in diverse settings, as the examples from Madagascar and Kenya and the alternative patterns show. Some speakers prefer organic patterns such as the repetitive wave, which is especially suited to ceremonial speaking. The spiral pattern is another way to visualize a topical speech in which the points increase in dramatic intensity. Finally, speakers who want flexible points within a major theme can visualize their ideas in the form of a star. Regardless of the pattern, traditional or alternative, you must carefully identify your main points and then develop them with appropriate supporting materials.

STUDY AND REVIEW

Your online resources for *Public Speaking: Concepts and Skills for a Diverse Society* offer a broad range of study tools that will help you better understand the material in this chapter, complete assignments, and succeed on tests. Your online resources feature the following:

- Speech videos with critical viewing questions, speech outlines, and transcripts.
- Interactive versions of this chapter's Stop and Check activities, as well as Application and Critical Thinking Exercises.
- Speech Builder Express and InfoTrac College Edition.

- Weblinks related to chapter content.
- Study and review tools such as self-quizzes, an interactive glossary, and downloadable audio summaries.

You can access your online resources at the CourseMate for *Public Speaking: Concepts and Skills for a Diverse Society*. Log in at **http://www.cengage.com/login**, using the access code that came with your book or that you bought online at **http://www.cengagebrain.com**.

KEY TERMS

The terms below are defined in the margins throughout this chapter.

cause-effect or causal pattern 153
chronological pattern 151
connectives 159
internal preview 159
internal summary 160
organic pattern 160
parallel points 157
problem-solution pattern 154
process speech 151
pro-con arrangement 154
signposts 159
spatial pattern 153
spiral pattern 161
star pattern 161
topical arrangement 155
transitions 159
wave pattern 160

APPLICATION AND CRITICAL THINKING EXERCISES

1. Work with a group of your classmates to make a list of ways that speech organization helps speakers be more effective.
2. Outline one of the speeches available on your online resources. (Don't use a Speech of Introduction; they usually have a slightly different organizational pattern.) Is the organizational pattern easy to discern? What suggestions, if any, could you give the speaker about arranging the points of the speech?
3. With a small group of your classmates, take a topic such as credit cards, divorce, alcohol on campus, or immigration, and identify and organize major points in as many of the following patterns as you can: topical, chronological, spatial, cause-effect, problem-solution, pro-con, and spiral.
4. Using one of the basic outlines you created in Exercise 3, take each major point, and underneath it, identify ways you could use evidence (statistics, facts, testimony, definitions, examples, and so on) to support that point.
5. Using one of the basic outlines you created in Exercise 3, write connectives such as signposts and transition statements for each point.
6. Read or listen to a recording of a speech by an African American such as Vernon Jordan, Barack Obama, or Martin Luther King, Jr. You can find several good examples online. What basic organizational pattern does the speaker use? Can you find examples of alternative patterns within the speech?
7. Do an Internet search for "I Have a Dream" or "Ain't I a Woman?" How many links do you get? Both of these speeches have inspired groups as well as individuals, which shows the power of rhetoric to influence a culture. Follow one of the links and read more about King's or Truth's vision.
8. Take the theme of creativity or the theme of perseverance. Then work with two or three classmates and discuss how you might create a speech organized around the wave, the spiral, or the star pattern. For example, think of three famous people who persevered . . . each one in a more dramatic way. Or use examples from your school's sports teams, your personal lives, lives of entertainers, and so on.
9. Read Dr. Martin Luther King, Jr.'s Nobel Prize acceptance speech, which is available online. Try to outline his speech, using the star pattern. List his main points as well as the thematic circle. Notice, also, the way he uses the wave pattern.

SPEECH VIDEO

After reading and analyzing Jordan Keagle's speech outline below, go to your online resources to watch and critique a video of his speech. In addition to the video of Jordan's speech, your online resources include the transcript of the speech.

Student Speech Outline with Commentary

E-WASTE*
By Jordan Keagle

General Purpose: To inform

Specific Purpose: To inform my audience about the growing issue of e-waste in the United States and of an organization created to combat it.

Thesis statement: E-waste is a mounting problem in the US and around the world, but the Electronics TakeBack Coalition exists to reduce improper technology disposal methods.

Jordan's assignment is to create an informative speech that illustrates civic engagement by describing a social issue and an organization founded to help solve it.

Preview: I will discuss how the problem of e-waste came about, the harms it causes, and how the Electronics TakeBack Coalition helps to counteract the problem.

Introduction

I. Raise your hand if you have a cell phone, computer, or video game system.
II. Raise your hand if you, like me, plan to replace one gadget with a new version.
III. I'm a technophile, so I did some research to discover what happens to discarded technology in the United States.
IV. Today, I will discuss how e-waste came about, the harms it causes, and how the Electronics TakeBack Coalition helps to counteract the problem.

Because everyone will raise their hands on his first question, Jordan says it with a smile. Because most will keep their hands raised for his second question, Jordan shows his listeners that the problem relates to them.

Body

I. First, let's look at the problem of e-waste.
   A. A Swiss government agency, the EMPA (2009), defines e-waste as any out-of-date or otherwise discarded equipment that uses electricity.
      1. Tech waste is another term.
      2. This can be computers, cell phones, or household appliances.
      3. If you can plug it in and you throw it out, it's e-waste.
   B. Over the past few decades, the amount of e-waste in the US has grown steadily.
      1. Elizabeth Royte (2005), writing in the *Smithsonian Magazine*, estimates that at least 60 million PCs are buried in US landfills.
         a. That article was from 2005.
         b. The issue has only gotten worse since then.
      2. A 2008 EPA report said that 80–85% of discarded electronics were sent to landfills between 2003 and 2005.
      3. In August of 2010, EPA administrator, Lisa P. Jackson, announced e-waste as one of the agency's top priorities.
   C. Obviously, piles of electronics are building up in landfills all over the country causing problems.
      1. Sheer space is one concern, as electronics can be heavy and bulky.
      2. More importantly, electronics contain a bevy of harmful chemicals.
         a. Royte's (2005) *Smithsonian* article says that a single CRT monitor contains between 2 and 8 pounds of lead.
         b. Other devices can contain other highly toxic chemicals such as mercury or cadmium.

A definition provides clarity for the rest of the discussion.

His survey showed that a lot of students knew that e-waste created problems, but they did not know the extent or the specifics.

c. A 2009 journal article in *Science of the Total Environment* says that newer devices like LCD screens may seem better than CRT monitors, but they often just trade one harmful chemical for another (Robinson, 2009).

d. Waste services must take apart the devices to remove harmful components.

1. This costs time and money.
2. Companies often discard or destroy electronics, so chemicals enter the environment.

D. Improper disposal of electronic devices can have direct consequences for the environment and the people living near the disposal sites.

1. Obviously, toxic chemicals can't be all that good for the environment.
2. A 2010 study conducted in China, where much of the world's e-waste is processed, compared the health of pregnant women living near an e-waste facility with those living farther away (Zhang, et al., 2010).

Information about pregnant women adds emotion and urgency for finding a solution.

a. Women living close to the facility had up to five times the amount of toxic chemicals in their blood than other women.

b. They also had lower levels of thyroid hormones, which can cause nervous system issues for their developing children.

The transition tells where he's been and where he's going.

Transition: Now that you have a better understanding of some of the problems surrounding e-waste, let's look at an organization that is working for solutions.

Most of the material in this point comes from the organization's website.

II. The organization, Electronics TakeBack Coalition (ETBC) exists to help solve the mounting problem.

A. According to its website (n.d.), the Electronics TakeBack Coalition was founded in 2001 as the "Computer TakeBack Campaign" as a project of the Tides Center.

1. It focused its efforts around Dell Computer Company, which had no recycling program.
2. In 2007 it became the Electronics TakeBack Coalition, reflecting a concern for the wider field of all electronics.

B. According to its website (n.d.). the ETBC has a number of programs and initiatives to change the state of e-waste on a national scale.

1. Its flagship programs centers on producer take back, which urges manufacturers to take back products and properly dispose of them.
   a. In 2007, ETBC ran a campaign called "Take Back My TV," encouraging television companies to offer recycling programs.
   b. Eight companies now offer such programs.
2. The ETBC also provides information to individuals.
   a. Their website offers advice on finding recyclers in your area.
   b. It also has instructions for purchasing more environmentally friendly technology.
3. Finally, the ETBC distributes information and tools to promote and to track implementation of anti-e-waste legislation on federal and state levels.

As a result of his speech, the audience will be more aware of the problem and more aware of ways they can personally be more intentional in purchasing and disposing of electronics.

Conclusion

I. After looking at the facts, it is obvious that e-waste is a mounting problem in the United States.

II. However, despite the harm e-waste poses to both humans and the environment, organizations like the Electronics TakeBack Coalition show that the problem is not insurmountable.

III. So think back to your own pieces of technology: computers, cell phones, iPods, and the like.

His ending statement provides his audience with something to think about.

IV. Next time you are thinking of upgrading, consider the cost of throwing out the old device as well as the cost of purchasing the new.

Sources

Electronics TakeBack Coalition. (n.d.). Campaign platform. Retrieved from http://www.electronicstakeback.com/about/platform.htm

EMPA. (2009). E-waste definition. Swiss Federal Laboratories for Materials Science and Technology (EMPA). Retrieved from http://ewasteguide.info/e_waste_definition

Environmental Protection Agency. (2010, August 17). Administrator Jackson announces EPA's international priorities / agency to work with other countries to curb pollution at home and abroad. Retrieved from http://yosemite.epa.gov/opa/admpress.nsf/0/C94F5F47E03ECC668525778200642318

Environmental Protection Agency, (2008). Fact sheet: Management of electronic waste in the United States. (EPA 530-F-08-014). Washington, DC: Retrieved from http://www.epa.gov/epawaste/conserve/materials/ecycling/docs/fact7-08.pdf

Robinson, B. H. (2009). E-waste: An assessment of global production and environmental impacts. *Science of the Total Environment*, *408*(2). doi: 10.1016/j.scitotenv.2009.09.044

Royte, E. (2005). E-gad! *Smithsonian*, *36*(5), 83–87.

Zhang, J., Jiang, Y., Zhou, J., Wu, B., Liang, Y., Peng, Z., . . . Lu, F. (2010). Elevated body burdens of PBDEs, dioxins, and PCBs on thyroid hormone homeostasis at an electronic waste recycling site in China. *Environmental Science & Technology*, *44*(10), doi: 10.1021/es902883a

CHAPTER
10

THIS CHAPTER WILL HELP YOU

- Develop an introduction that gains attention, motivates the audience to listen, establishes your credibility, and previews your speech
- Develop a conclusion that signals the end, summarizes, provides psychological closure, and ends with impact

Introductions and Conclusions

THE OLD SAYING, you rarely get a second chance to make a positive first impression, is true about speechmaking. Speakers who begin poorly have trouble regaining the audience's attention and confidence. On the other hand, speakers who start strong are more likely to be forgiven for minor slips later. Also, speakers who have otherwise good speeches but trail off or lose focus at the end miss the chance to drive home their point. Consequently, effective speakers carefully research, plan, and practice both their introductions and conclusions, which function like bookends to enclose the body of the speech. Principles in this chapter will guide you in drawing your listeners into your subject and, at the end, concluding in a way that summarizes your thoughts and leaves a memorable impression.

Plan Your Introduction

Chapter 2 points out that the Roman educator Quintilian identified four purposes for an introduction:[1]

1. To draw your listeners' attention to the topic
2. To motivate your audience to listen
3. To establish yourself as knowledgeable about the topic
4. To preview the major ideas of your speech

Here, also, is your opportunity to present definitions or background information that listeners must know if they are to understand your subject. By including Quintilian's four elements in your introduction, you'll answer the four basic questions your listeners are asking up front: What's this all about? Why should I listen? Why should I listen to you? What will you cover? Figure 10.1 depicts these four introductory functions.

Gain Attention

Gaining attention is the first step in the listening process, so it's important to answer immediately your audience's question, *What's this speech about?* Simply saying, "I'm going to talk about product placement," does introduce the topic, but one of the several attention-gaining strategies that follow is more effective.

Ask a Question

Both **rhetorical questions,** those that listeners answer mentally, and **participatory questions**, those that ask for an overt response, such as a show of hands, work well. One speaker, whose topic was emergency preparedness, referred to a major flood in the area and then asked rhetorically:[2]

> Who can forget the images of fifty thousand people being evacuated out of Grand Forks? Who can forget the images of flames engulfing eleven buildings and sixty apartment units before being extinguished? What about those hundreds of volunteers who descended into the Red River Valley filling sand bags, trying to hold back the torrent of water which . . . eventually caused 3.5 billion dollars of damage?

rhetorical questions questions that listeners answer in their minds

participatory questions questions that listeners answer overtly

Figure 10.1 The Audience's Four Questions Your introduction functions to answer these four questions.

When you ask a participatory question, alert the audience to the response you want. For instance, ask for a show of hands or call on a member of the audience to answer a specific question you pose. Here's how Anne opened her persuasive speech about infomercials:[3]

> How many of you admit that you have found your eyes glued to an infomercial for ten minutes or more? (Here she raised her hand and looked expectantly at her audience.) Was it about the snuggie? (She nodded her head and waited for audience nods.) The Bowflex? Proactive? How about the Magic Bullet?

Good rhetorical and participatory questions can help establish dialogue between you and your listeners at the very outset of the speech because they invite audience responses, whether mental or physical.

Provide a Vivid Description

Draw attention to your subject by describing a scene vividly enough that your listeners can easily visualize it. The scene can be either real or imaginary. This opening for a classroom speech on ACL (knee) injuries in female athletes is a good example: [4]

> One jump was all it took. It was the beginning of August and Kristina was already at volleyball camp preparing for her second season on the school's volleyball team. She jumped up to hit a ball during a game when she heard a "pop" in her knee. She had torn her ACL, which meant she could not participate in volleyball that year.

A Navajo (Diné) Speech Introduction

Not every cultural group assumes speakers will gain attention first, relate to audience interests next, and establish credibility following that. Audiences at Diné College (formerly Navajo Community College) expect speakers to first answer the question, "Who are you and what is your clan affiliation?" Upon first meeting, members of Diné (Navajo) culture exchange information about their clan affiliations—first, their mother's clan; next, their father's clan, followed by their maternal grandfather's clan, and finally, their paternal grandfather's clan.[5] This information discloses the roots of the speakers' identity and helps establish their relationship with others in the audience. Only after these personal, identifying facts are shared do speakers and listeners feel comfortable discussing a topic.[6]

Begin with a Quotation

A quotation or a familiar cultural proverb, either *about* a subject or, for a biographical speech, *by* the subject, is a good way to gain attention. Choose a short saying that captures your overall theme—preferably a quotation that is familiar or from a familiar source—and cite that source. A little over a year after he became Archivist of the United States, David Ferriero added humor by beginning his speech with this quotation:[7]

> [As part of my first year on the job] I have become a huge fan of the daily horoscopes in the *Washington Post*. Earlier this month, my favorite, so far was printed: "Many feel limited by the work they do. You won't be in this category today, though. Your work expands you." I do, indeed feel both excited and privileged. Excited every day by the work that we do and privileged to be working with you.

Quotations from song lyrics, poems, and scriptural or literary texts are also common. Family sayings or memorable words spoken by someone such as a coach or teacher also work well. As Chapter 7 pointed out, the Internet contains many sources for thousands of quotations on sites such as those found in **weblink 10.1.** (You can access this link through your CourseMate for *Public Speaking*, Chapter 10 resources.)

Use an Audio or Visual Aid

Photographs, charts, short audio or video clips, and other visual and audio materials also successfully draw attention to your topic. Students have used visuals to gain attention in the following ways:

- Abby played harp music in the background as she introduced her subject, music thanatology—the practice of using music as part of end-of-life care. You can read her outline in Appendix C.
- Kelli began with a photograph and description of a premature baby in a neonatal intensive care unit; her second photo showed him at age two.
- For her speech on "Photoshopped Perfection," Rachel presented a short video clip showing how a model's face was digitally enhanced before the image appeared in advertisements for beauty products.
- Christine opened her speech on child neglect with a pie chart showing the percentage of neglected children compared with other types of child abuse.

Begin with an Example

As Chapter 8 pointed out, examples give your listeners an opportunity to become emotionally involved with your topic, and stories of real people involved in real situations generally make us more attentive. Here, Lauren wove together several short examples to create images of homeless people in the state of Oregon:[8]

> Under the Burnside Bridge in Portland, I had the opportunity to talk with a woman who didn't have enough money to take care of her kids; I talked with a man who had just gotten out of jail; I talked with a man who clearly loved his wife and daughter but couldn't see them any more. I've seen their tears and their trembling emotion, and I've also seen their joys. I've heard their journeys—traveling across the US, hopping trains and biking up from California. These are just a few stories of the almost eight thousand homeless single adults in Oregon.

Start with Startling Numbers

Numbers and statistics can be dry; however, they can also capture and hold listeners' attention if they are shocking enough or if you put them into an understandable context, as this example illustrates:[9]

> In January of every year, the Oregon Housing and Community Services counts the number of homeless families and individuals in the state. In 2010, the January 27 count revealed that, across the state, just over 19,200 were homeless. That's approximately the population of Woodburn or Klamath Falls, Oregon. In the Portland area almost 900 were in the age range of 18–23 years. That's equal to about one-fifth of our student body.

JustASC/Shutterstock

Beginning with an example immediately gains listener attention for a topic such as homelessness. A rhetorical question, startling statistic, photograph, or quotation could also be effective.

Refer to a Current Event

One way to identify with your listeners and establish common ground is to begin with well-known current happenings—airplane crashes, campus controversies, weather disasters, well-publicized trials, elections, and the like. Here's how Bralee introduced her topic about product placement, shortly after *The Social Network* film came out:[10]

> You may have seen the movie *The Social Network*, but you may not have noticed the brands that showed up everywhere. According to Abe Sauer, writing for brandchannel.com on October 4, 2010, the movie featured forty-nine brands, including the Gap, Mountain Dew, Polaroid, Stairmaster, Cambridge University, and the NFL. This is an example of product placement.

Use Humor

If it seems appropriate to the audience, the occasion, and the topic, and if you have good comedic skills, you might try using humor to gain attention while creating a more informal atmosphere. Consider telling a joke or riddle, relating a funny story, or displaying a relevant cartoon on a PowerPoint slide. Of course, subjects such as cyberbullying or homelessness are not joking matters. But many other topics—the importance of speaking a second language, for example—could open with a joke:

> You know the word for a person who speaks three languages? It's "trilingual."
> How about a person who speaks two languages? That's "bilingual."
> And a person who speaks only one language? The correct answer is "American!"

Humor has its risks, however. You can embarrass yourself and make your listeners uncomfortable if the joke flops, and you'll create an overall negative image if your joke is offensive. To avoid humiliation, test your attempt at humor in advance on some friends, and let them decide if it's really funny or appropriate. Also, make sure the joke relates to your topic. Otherwise, you might gain attention, but it won't focus on your subject.

Considering Organizational Culture

Chapter 1 points out that culture includes visible, stated aspects of a group's way of life as well as more embedded beliefs and assumptions that guide group members. The concept of **organizational culture** extends this definition by recognizing that organizations and institutions also have traditions, rituals, folklore, and so on, which make them function as small cultures within the larger society. Insiders know the group's culture; newcomers must learn it.

Before you speak in an organization, learn whatever you can about its culture—even expectations for speech introductions change from setting to setting. For example, on ritual occasions, such as graduation ceremonies or keynote addresses, speakers typically include positive remarks about the organization up front. In fact, audience members would think it strange if the speaker immediately launched into the topic. This speaker included several aspects of the organization's culture that made its members proud:[11]

organizational culture the way of life of a specific organization, which includes its history, traditions, heroes, folklore, vocabulary, rituals, and ways of doing things

Many of you who have trained or visited here in the past know that the Cleveland Clinic is a place where you can hear dozens of languages and meet men and women from every continent. We have a natural diversity of talent that has long been a republic of ideas and one of the best examples of physician-directed health care.

For additional examples, search InfoTrac College Edition for the journal, *Vital Speeches of the Day.* Read the introductions of three or four talks given at ritual events, and analyze how the speakers incorporate elements of the organization's culture into their opening remarks.

Although this is not an exhaustive list of successful opening strategies, these are common approaches used by speakers in a variety of settings. Remember that your opening should not simply gain attention; it must also draw attention to your topic.

Give Your Audience a Reason to Listen

After you gain attention, answer your listeners' second question, *Why should I listen to this speech?* You may think your topic is important and interesting, but your listeners may consider it boring or irrelevant. Bronte wanted to talk about the "hidden poverty" of the elderly poor and the need for retirement planning, but her audience was mostly made up of 20-year-olds. So she related the topic to her audience like this:[12]

> I'm sure we can all think of someone over 65—grandparents, a neighbor, or even a professor. Before we know it, our parents will reach that age. Eventually, we will all be in these "old-timers'" shoes. What will your lifestyle look like?

You can also frame your specific topic within a larger issue. Few people in the classroom will ever spend their weekends training horses to compete in the sport of dressage. However, everyone is familiar with sports in general, and some have trained animals to respond to commands. Here's one way to link this topic to the audience:[13]

> Raise your hand if you have *never* spent part of a weekend participating in a sport of some kind—whether as an athlete or a spectator. The fact that no one in this room raised a hand shows the prevalence of sports in the US. I personally spend my weekends in an unusual sport: dressage—training horses to participate in a series of competitive tasks.

Two important human characteristics are curiosity and the ability to learn new things, so you sometimes will speak to increase your audience's knowledge or to satisfy their curiosity. Instead of linking dressage to sport, the speaker could appeal to curiosity:

> You may have never heard of dressage, but it has a long history. According to the US Dressage Federation website, dressage began with the ancient Greeks, who trained horses for army duty because warriors throughout history have needed obedient, maneuverable battle horses. Today, we no longer train horses for war, but dressage competition continues. Equestrians have competed at the Olympic Games since 1900.

Many issues that don't seem to directly concern your listeners may actually affect their pocketbooks, whether or not they know it. National issues that rely on tax dollars for support are in this category; funding for the arts, agricultural research, and weapons development are just a few examples. Chapter 17 provides more details about needs, wants, emotions, and values that motivate people to listen to speeches.

Audiences relate to some topics easily. But it takes more creativity to link other subjects to your listeners' lives and interests. The cost in time or money, the impact of national or international issues on their lives and future, and an appeal to curiosity are just a few strategies you can use to make connections.

Establish Your Credibility

You have gained the audience's attention and given them a reason to listen to your topic; now, link yourself to your subject so that they can answer the question, *Why should I listen to you?* Typically, you should cite subject-related experiences, interests, and research findings that show your interest and expertise. If relevant, you can mention your major, courses you have taken, television shows that sparked your interest in the topic, and so on. Here are some examples:

> *Topic: Product placement*. I've started noticing product placement in the music I listen to, the movies I attend, the television shows I watch—even in news programs. This awareness motivated me to do further research on this form of advertisement.
>
> *Topic: Hector Berlioz, composer*. As a musician trained in piano, clarinet, and guitar, I attended Fiorello H. La Guardia High School of Music and Art, where I was required to study music history and research the lives of musicians and composers.
>
> *Topic: Retirement Planning*. My grandparents are 80-years-old. My grandmother still works two jobs, and my grandpa was working until dementia forced him to sell his business. Their social security benefits just don't cut it for them. If they had planned for retirement better, they wouldn't struggle so. Concern for them led me to do research on ways to prevent poverty in retirement.

Of course, explicitly stating your credibility is optional when another person introduces you and connects you with the subject or when your expertise on the topic is well established.

Preview Your Ideas

You may have heard the old saying, "Tell them what you're going to say; say it; then tell them what you said." The preview statement, as described in Chapter 5, serves the first of these functions and provides the transition between the introduction and the body of your speech. In the preview, answer the audience question, *What will you cover?* by stating some form of your central idea and indicating how you will develop it.

When appropriate, a creative approach, such as alliterating or rhyming your points, is more memorable. Here are three previews:

> *Straightforward but clear.* Because most people are unclear about multiple sclerosis, I will first define the disease, describe some of its effects, and tell you what is known about the cause, the cure, and the current treatments.
>
> *Alliteration.* In 1990, when Photoshop was first released, the doors opened for a whole new level of media manipulation—creating a perception of beauty that is unhealthy, unethical, and unrecognized.
>
> *Using a metaphor.* Today, I'll retell the story of the boy who cried "wolf," with a few character changes. The boy who cries "wolf" is the American government, and the wolf we are to fear is industrial hemp.

In summary, a good introduction draws attention to your topic, relates the subject to your listeners, links you to the subject, and previews your major ideas.

Create an Interesting Introduction

Select one of the following previews. Then work with a classmate to create an introduction that answers the four questions your listeners ask regarding any subject.

- Arachnophobia, the irrational fear of spiders, has three major causes and two basic treatments.
- Many women, as well as men, experience hair loss, and they try medications, hairpieces, bonding techniques, and transplants to solve the problem.
- You can save money at the market on produce, meat, cereal, and baked goods.
- Thousands of students default on federal student loans every year, leaving taxpayers with their school tabs.

The listener's questions are:

1. What's this about? (Identify several strategies to gain attention to the topics you choose. Which do you think are more effective?)
2. Why should I listen? (How could you relate the topics to audience interests or experiences?)
3. Why should I listen to you? (How might a speaker establish credibility on each subject?)
4. What will you cover? (How would you preview the main ideas of each topic?)

To learn more about introductions, search the Internet for "speech introductions" and skim several results for tips you can incorporate into your speeches. Or watch the introductions of several speech videos in your online resources. Evaluate how well each one fulfills the criteria described here.

Conclude with Impact

Your conclusion leaves your listeners with their final impression of both you and your subject. Appearing disorganized at the end can lessen the positive impressions your audience may have gained during the speech. And failure to restate your thesis and review your main points is a missed opportunity to reinforce your speech goals.

Like the introduction, the conclusion has several important functions: to signal the end, to summarize the main points, to provide psychological closure (often by a reference to the introduction), and to end with impact.

Signal the Ending

Just as your preview provides a transition to the speech body, your ending signal provides a transition to your conclusion. Both beginning speakers and professionals use common phrases such as *in conclusion* or *finally*. However, the following signal is more creative:

> I hope my information about infomercials has given you a higher respect for this often-ridiculed form of advertising. [Here, she transitions to the conclusion and restates her speech goal.]

You can also use nonverbal actions to signal that you're nearing the end. For instance, pause and shift your posture, or take a step back from the podium. A combination of verbal and nonverbal elements generally works well.

Review Your Main Ideas

To fulfill the "Tell them what you said" axiom, briefly summarize or recap your main ideas, but the key word is *brief*. The audience has already heard your speech, so don't repeat or add new supporting material. The following example is an effective review:

> I have explained that infomercials are legitimate ads for products by big-name companies, and even those that appear crazy to us are a result of careful planning and purpose. I also explained that this form of advertising is a logical choice for companies, and we who complain are the very ones keeping them on the air.

One common strategy is to combine your signal with your summary, as this example shows:

> Now that we have looked at the shark as it really is [phrase signaling the end] I hope you realize that its reputation is really inaccurate and that humans present a greater threat to sharks than sharks present to humans [restatement of the central idea].

Provide Psychological Closure

Linking your conclusion to something from your introduction brings the speech full circle and provides your audience with a sense of psychological closure. Consequently, look in your introduction for something that you could repeat at the end. For instance, if you began with an example, you might return to it in the conclusion. Or you could refer to startling statistics or to quotations you presented in the opening. Here's how Bonita began and ended her speech:[14]

> *Opening*. On July 3, 2003, a man and his family are driving their van down the road as it is getting light. An oncoming driver has been driving since midnight; he tries to pass a bus but fails to see the van coming toward him. Because he is tired, the would-be passer cannot react quickly enough to slide back into his own lane, and his car collides head-on with the van, killing the woman in the passenger seat.

> *Ending*. I myself will avoid driving while tired, because the woman who was killed in the van that July morning was my mom. Next time you drive, consider those in the cars around you and think of whose friend, mother, sister, or brother they are. Do you really want others to go through pain and suffering simply so you can get to your destination a little earlier?

Studio DMM Photography, Designs & Art /Shutterstock

A good introduction and conclusion are like bookends that hold the main points of the speech together.[15]

(Read the text of Bonita's speech at the end of this chapter or on your online resources, where you can also watch her deliver the speech.)

End Memorably

Plan your final statement carefully so that you leave a positive and memorable impression. Here are a few guidelines:

- Many of the strategies for gaining audience attention—such as rhetorical questions, use of quotations or examples, and use of humor—are similarly effective at achieving impact in the conclusion.
- Consider using parallel construction. That is, if you began with a story, end with a story; if you began with a rhetorical question, end with a rhetorical question, and so on. Not only is this effective, but it is another way to provide psychological closure.
- In persuasive speeches, it's common to issue a challenge and call people to action.
- Commemorative speakers typically conclude by reinforcing a larger cultural theme or value.

Elisia Choi (see Practically Speaking, Chapter 9) emphasizes the importance of the ending statement:

> I spend a significant amount of time thinking about my concluding statement. Many speakers often don't think about what their last sentence will be and as a result, end their speeches abruptly. I try to set myself apart by making sure my last sentence is powerful, memorable, and impactful.

These three examples show effective conclusions for an informative, persuasive, and commemorative speech:

> *Informative purpose.* Homelessness affects thousands of people in Portland, and Nightstrike is an organization that deals with this issue in the way their motto states: Loving People Because People Matter.

Persuasive purpose. Our media daily bombards us with perceptions of beauty that is unhealthy, unethical, and unrecognizably deceitful—not to mention unattainable. If a picture is worth a thousand words, let's not allow media to fill our minds with thousands of far-fetched lies. Instead, let's be conscious consumers of media who expose media images for what they truly are and who value the beauty of everyday people.

Commemorative purpose [commencement address].[16] Finally, I leave you with a thought from a very brave woman named Harriet Tubman. She said, "Every great dream begins with a dreamer. Always remember, you have within you the strength, the patience, and the passion to reach for the stars to change the world."

In summary, a good conclusion provides a transition, summarizes your major points, gains psychological closure, and closes with a thought-provoking statement. Study some of the speeches and outlines throughout the text and notice the different and creative ways that students memorably end their speeches.

Evaluating Introductions and Conclusions

Here you'll find an introduction and a conclusion for two different speeches. Read through each set and then answer the questions that follow it.

Introduction: Four of the six leading causes of death among Americans are diet related: heart disease, cancer, stroke, and diabetes mellitus, as stated by the *Vegetarian Times* magazine. Everyone here would like to live a healthy life, right? Today, I will explain the advantages of being a vegetarian both to your health and to the environment.

Conclusion: Because I have this information, I have reduced my consumption of meat lately, and I ask you to do the same thing. Being a vegetarian is not that bad; you're improving your health and, at the same time, saving the environment. Don't forget, once you're old and suffering from a heart ailment or cancer, it will be too late. Take precautions now.

- Does this introduction make you want to hear this speech? Why or why not?
- How does the speaker gain attention?
- How does he relate to the audience? Is this effective?
- Do you think he is credible on the topic?
- Could you write a brief outline of his major points from his preview?
- Compare his introduction to his conclusion. Which is more effective? Why?

Introduction: In 1918, one of the worst pandemics ever recorded hit the United States. In her 1999 book *Flu, New York Times* science journalist Gina Kolata, compared the percent of population killed by that pandemic to the number of people who die in one year from heart disease, cancer, strokes, AIDS, and Alzheimer's combined.

However, in the survey I sent out, no one claimed to have more than a moderate amount of concern about the possibility of a pandemic affecting him or her or anyone they knew. According to a 2006 article from the scientific journal *Biosecurity and Bioterrorism*, pandemics occur on average every fifteen years; often twenty-five percent of a population becomes infected. Assuming we all plan to live for fifteen more years and know at least three other people, the likelihood of you or someone you know being affected by a pandemic is very high.

I first became concerned about pandemic preparedness during research for a team scenario analysis competition on pandemics. In the middle of this project, H1N1 surfaced as a major concern, making the research feel even more essential to me, especially when the teams from Singapore had to compete online because their government deemed it too dangerous for them to travel internationally.

Today, I will first describe pandemics and the issues with the United States's current level of readiness to deal with one. Then I will describe one of the government's leading plans to better prepare the country for a very possible pandemic outbreak.

Conclusion: I hope you how have a better understanding of the consequences of pandemics in the United States and how their negative effects can be mitigated. Although many people would become ill beyond our current means to care for them, health departments and organizations are planning for new systems to help as many people as possible. In the chance that one day you could be one of the twenty-five percent of Americans sickened by a pandemic disease, you can now be assured that our government is working to increase its capacity to protect you in the very real possibility of a pandemic.[17]

- This is a very long introduction. Why do you think she put so much into gaining attention, relating to the audience, establishing credibility, and previewing? What, if anything, would you recommend she change?
- What is the most effective part of this introduction?
- What's the most effective element of her conclusion?
- Which part is better: her introduction or her conclusion? Why?

To learn more about conclusions, search the Internet for "speech conclusions" and skim several results for tips you can incorporate into your speeches. Alternatively, watch the conclusions of several speech videos in your online resources. Evaluate how well each speaker signals the ending of the speech, reviews main ideas, provides psychological closure, and ends memorably.

Summary

After you've organized the body of your speech, plan an introduction that will take your listeners from their various internal worlds and move them into the world of your speech. Do this by gaining their attention, relating your topic to their concerns, establishing your credibility on the subject, and previewing your main points. Finally, plan a conclusion that provides a transition from the body, summarizes your major points, gives a sense of closure by referring back to the introduction, and leaves your listeners with a challenge or a memorable thought.

STUDY AND REVIEW

Your online resources for *Public Speaking: Concepts and Skills for a Diverse Society* offer a broad range of study tools that will help you better understand the material in this chapter, complete assignments, and succeed on tests. Your online resources feature the following:

- Speech videos with critical viewing questions, speech outlines, and transcripts.
- Interactive versions of this chapter's Stop and Check activities, as well as Application and Critical Thinking Exercises.

- Speech Builder Express and InfoTrac College Edition.
- Weblinks related to chapter content.
- Study and review tools such as self-quizzes, an interactive glossary, and downloadable audio summaries.

You can access your online resources at the CourseMate for *Public Speaking: Concepts and Skills for a Diverse Society.* Log in at **http://www.cengage.com/login**, using the access code that came with your book or that you bought online at **http://www.cengagebrain.com**.

KEY TERMS

The terms below are defined in the margins throughout this chapter.

organizational culture 172
participatory questions 169
rhetorical questions 169

APPLICATION AND CRITICAL THINKING EXERCISES

1. Before your next speech, partner with someone in your class. Trade outlines and, using the guidelines in this chapter, evaluate each other's introduction and conclusion. Advise your partner on what you think is effective and what could be improved. When you get your own outline and suggestions back, make adjustments that would improve these sections of your speech.
2. Outline a speech given by one of your classmates. Evaluate the effectiveness of the introduction and conclusion. What suggestions, if any, would you give the speaker to improve the beginning or the ending?
3. Review the section on credibility—what your audience thinks of you—in Chapter 6. How and why does a good introduction and conclusion affect your audience's perception of your credibility? How and why does a poor start or finish influence their perception?
4. Read the introductions and conclusions of some speeches you find on **weblink 10.2**. (You can access this link through your CourseMate for *Public Speaking,* Chapter 10 resources.) Evaluate them using the criteria in the text. Does the introduction gain attention, link to the audience, establish credibility, and preview the major points? Does the speaker provide a transition to the conclusion? Review the major points? Provide psychological closure? End memorably? What improvements, if any, would you suggest?
5. Search the Internet for the exact phrase "introductions and conclusions." You should find many sites that were created by both writing and speech instructors. Go to a site for writers, and compare and contrast the guidelines there with the guidelines for speakers that you find in this text. What are the similarities? The differences? How do you account for the differences?

SPEECH VIDEO

Go to your online resources to watch and critique a video of Bonita Persons delivering her speech "Driving While Drowsy."

Student Speech with Commentary

DRIVING WHILE DROWSY*
By Bonita Persons

Introduction

On July 3, 2003, a man and his family are driving their van down the road as it is getting light. An oncoming driver has been driving since midnight; he tries to pass a bus but fails to see the van coming toward him. Because he is tired, the would-be passer cannot react quickly enough to slide back into his own lane, and his car collides with the van, killing the woman in the passenger seat.

Almost everyone will drive while tired at some point in their lives, especially worn out, stressed college students and workers.

I'm guilty of this. I drove tired just last summer when I went to visit my brother in Kansas.

However, drowsy driving is not a good idea. A lot of people are killed because of tired drivers, and the only real solution lies within our hands, but the benefits of avoiding tired driving definitely outweigh the sacrifices one must make.

How well does Bonita fulfill the four major elements of a good introduction? Does her overall introduction make you want to hear more?

Body

Many people have died because of accidents related to tired driving. According to the American Academy of Otolaryngology, driving with sleep apnea is just as bad as driving with an alcohol content of 0.08 percent. In addition, the Pennsylvania Department of Transportation says statistics show that 1,500 people die each year because of drowsy-driving accidents. Finally, the Queensland Transport website on road safety tells us that 1 in 6 fatal crashes in Queensland, Australia, are caused by driving tired. However, these statistics do not include the damage done to cars and other property. All over the world, sleep-related accidents happen.

Underline all the connectives you can find in the body of this outline. Where could she effectively add a transition, internal preview, or internal summary?

The consequences for driving while tired can be fatal, so precautions are important. According to David Jamieson, Road Safety Minister in the United Kingdom, most sleep-related accidents happen on Mondays, although most accidents occur on Fridays.

Dr. Mercola, author of *The Total Health Problem*, says that "After 17–19 hours without sleep, performance on some tests was equivalent or worse than that at a blood alcohol content of 0.05%." This may sound like a long time to be up, but consider that if a college student woke up at seven for this class and did not get to bed until midnight, that is seventeen hours without sleep right there. Going to bed at midnight, for many, is early.

Because sleepiness can be a problem, we need to be able to tell when we are getting sleepy. Signs warning that you are tired are fairly obvious and should not be ignored. Queensland's road safety website outlines several signs of fatigue: sore or heavy eyes, dim or fuzzy vision, "seeing" things, droning and humming in the ears, general tiredness, stiffness and cramps, aches and pains, daydreaming, delayed reaction times, unintentional increases or decreases in speed, fumbling for gear changes, and a car that wanders across the road.

Consequently, if you feel yourself getting tired, PULL OFF THE ROAD! The Pennsylvania Department of Transportation says to pull off and take a 15–25 minute nap when you feel tired and to switch drivers every few hours if the drive is going to be long. Make sure the driver has a good night's rest before driving.

Coffee is a stimulant, but the effects, according to PENNDOT, do not come into play for half an hour after you drink it, and the effects do not last long, so it should not be relied on. Interestingly enough, the Driving While Tired Advice and Checklists from the UK states that certain foods such as turkey, warm milk, and bananas induce sleepiness and therefore should NOT be eaten before or during a drive!

Is there a government solution to this problem? According to ABC News, New Jersey is the first state to make driving tired a crime if a deadly accident occurs when there are signs that it is a tired-related accident. But this still does not cure driving while tired. The solution is a decision each person must make as an individual.

*Used by permission of Bonita Persons.

The benefits for driving when one is NOT tired are obvious: Lives are saved. The downsides are that one may take a bit longer getting somewhere or may not be able to stay at that place for quite as long. However, when one considers the good versus the bad, the good obviously outweighs the negative.

Conclusion

Identify the ways this conclusion signals the end and reviews the main points. How effectively does she create psychological closure? What other ending choices could she have made?

If we ourselves don't want to become a statistic of tired driving, then we need to take steps to protect ourselves and others. Know when you are tired and do your best to prevent driving then. Longer road trips may be inevitable because you avoid tired driving, but it is worth it if you want to live. I myself will avoid driving while tired, because the woman who was killed in the van that July morning was my mom. So next time you consider driving while tired, consider those in the cars around you and think of whose friend, mother, sister, or brother they are. Do you really want others to go through pain and suffering simply so you can get to your destination a little bit earlier?

Sources

ABC News. (2003). N.J. first state to make driving while tired a crime in deadly accidents. Retrieved from www.abcnews4.com/news/stories/0903/104483.html

American Academy of Otolaryngology. (2004). DWT: Driving while tired. Retrieved from http://static.highbeam.com/v/vibrantlife/september012000/dwtdrivingwhiletiredbriefarticle/

Jamieson, D. (2004). Tired of driving? Retrieved from www.sourceuk.net/indexf.html?05568

Mercola, J. (2004). DWT—Driving While Tired. Retrieved from www.mercola.com/2000/nov/26/dwt.htm

PENNDOT. (2003). PENNDOT warns of the dangers of drowsy driving. Retrieved from www.dot.state.pa.us/PENNDOT/Districts/district4.nsf/o3o3310s5-sleep.htm

Queensland Transport. (2003). Road safety. Retrieved from www.roadsafety.qld.bov.au/qt/LTASinfo.nsf/index/rs_driverreviver_home

RAC. (2004). Advice and checklists: Driving while tired. Retrieved from www.rac.co.uk/arcare/advice/general_help/driving_when_tired

© Tim Timmerman

CHAPTER 11

Outlining Your Speech

THIS CHAPTER WILL HELP YOU

- Outline your speech content in a linear form
- Create a heading that summarizes what you plan to accomplish in your speech
- Use standard outlining features including coordination, subordination, indentation, alternation, and full sentences
- Prepare note cards or a speaking outline
- Know how to record your ideas using an alternative pattern

THE PHARMACY STUDENT sat scowling in the front row on the first day of class, arms folded. When I asked students what they wanted out of the course, she said, "Credit." Why would she ever need public speaking as a pharmacist? Day after day, she sat there, grim faced. She even refused to give her first speech. Slowly, she began to turn in outlines and give speeches. One day, late in the semester, she approached me and said, "I want to thank you for this class. I was really mad that I was forced to take it, but I found out how useful it turned out to be—especially learning how to outline. Choosing ideas and supporting materials, organizing my ideas—I've been able to use these skills in many other classes. I just want you to know."

This student discovered what many other students learn: outlining skills are transferable. Nancy Wood, head of a university study skills and tutorial service, reported that some students who come for help have no idea where to start or how to organize their thoughts, but students taking speech classes "confess to us regularly that their speech course is helping them learn to organize and write term papers for their other classes as well."[1]

Although this chapter presents tips for creating full-sentence content outlines, experienced speakers know there's no single way to outline a speech correctly, and there's no set length for an outline. Many factors shape your final product, including the type of speech, the circumstances, and the time limitations. The more speeches you give, the more you'll work out your own method for ordering your ideas, given your individual learning preferences. This chapter explains some foundational outlining principles, followed by a description of how to prepare speaking notes. It concludes with ideas for alternative, more visual methods of recording your ideas that take into account diversity in individual thinking styles.

Creating a Content Outline

content outline formal record of your major ideas and their relationship to one another in your speech

structural elements a speech's introduction, body, and conclusion

logical elements a speech's major ideas with supporting materials and their relationship

script writing down every word of the speech

The **content outline** that most instructors require accomplishes two purposes: (1) it shows the speech's **structural elements**—the introduction, body, and conclusion, and (2) it shows the speech's **logical elements**—the major ideas, the supporting materials, and their relationship to one another. It is not a **script**, where you write out every word you say; it's more like a skeleton or a blueprint of your speech because it provides the framework for the points you will flesh out or develop as you talk. However, using full sentences in the outline ensures that all your ideas are visible and helps you learn the content. Common elements of outline preparation include a heading and standard formatting features.

Begin with a Heading

The heading provides a brief overview of your entire speech. Include your *title*, *general purpose*, *specific purpose*, finalized *central idea* or *thesis statement*, *preview*, and the *organizational pattern* that you've developed using principles found in Chapters 5 and 9. Here is John's heading for his speech on culture shock:[2]

Topic:	The Five Stages of Culture Shock
General Purpose:	To inform
Specific Purpose:	To inform my audience about the stages of culture shock and to demonstrate these with real-life examples.
Central Idea/Thesis:	Culture shock is a psychological process that typically progresses through five recurring stages.
Preview:	The five recurring stages of culture shock are: honeymoon, disintegration, reintegration, autonomy, and interdependence.
Organizational Pattern:	Chronological

mustafa deliormanli/iStockphoto

An outline is like a blueprint that provides a framework on which to build your speech.

Use Standard Formatting

Four features—*indentation* and *alternation* combined with *coordination* and *subordination*—make visible your speech's structural and logical interrelationships.

Alternation and Indentation

Alternation means you use a consistent pattern to vary numbers and letters. Designate your major points with a Roman numeral (I, II, III, . . .), your first-level supporting points with a capital letter (A, B, C, . . .), second-level supporting points with Arabic numerals (1, 2, 3, . . .), third-level points with lowercase letters (a, b, c, . . .), and so on. Also use **indentation** to space various levels of supporting points toward the right and additionally show interrelationships among materials. That is, begin your I- and II-level points at the left margin, but indent your A and B headings to the right. Then space your third-level supporting points even further right and so on. This partial outline shows alternation and indentation:

alternation varying numbers and letters in a consistent pattern for different levels of points

indentation formatting by spacing various levels of points inward

I. US ideologies of beauty are affecting the world.[3]
  A. Many Asian women seek out a surgery called blepharoplasty.
    1. Almost half of all eastern Asians are born with no eyelid crease.
      a. Many Asian women desire a crease.
        1. They think it is more attractive.
        2. A crease makes it easier to apply eye makeup.
      b. However, 25-year-old Tina Quak states, "I think it's a Western idea" (Yee, 2008).
    2. A one-hour surgery can create a crease.
  B. Skin bleaching products are also common.
II. One major cause is standardization of advertising across media. . . .

(*Note:* Some instructors prefer that you use Roman numerals to label your introduction, body, and conclusion and then adjust the labeling of points accordingly.)

coordination arranging points into levels, giving the points on a specific level the same basic value or weight

Coordination and Subordination

Coordination means that you give each major point the same basic value or weight, you weigh second-level and third-level points similarly, and so on. The word **subordination** has two Latin roots: *sub* (under) and *ordinare* (to place in order). All first-level points

subordination placement of supporting points under major points

go *under* the major points they support; all second-level points go *under* the first-level points they support, and so on. The following outline has two major points: problem and solution. Subordinated underneath them are the first-level points, causes and effects, which are coordinated approximately equally. (For purposes of illustration, this outline shows third-level points under the first cause only.)

I. Problem
   A. Causes
      1. First Cause
         a. Support
         b. Support
      2. Second Cause
   B. Effects
      1. First Effect
      2. Second Effect
II. Solution
   A. First Solution
   B. Second Solution

I. People in the US consume too much sugar.[4]
   A. There are several causes for this.
      1. Common foods have unrecognized amounts of sugar.
         a. Even catsup is about 1/3 sugar.
         b. Read labels for fructose, dextrose, molasses, and other forms of sugar.
      2. Carbonated drinks are a major source.
   B. Obesity is on the increase, even in young children.
      1. Obesity is linked to several adult diseases.
      2. Obesity is linked to Type II diabetes in children.
II. Solutions are both national and personal.
   A. We can increase national awareness.
   B. Personally, we can eat less sugar.

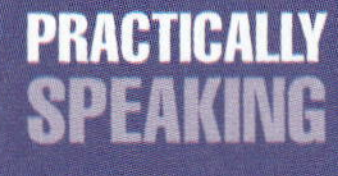

Outlines and Speaking Notes

Several professionals shared their practical experiences with outlines.

Brad Lau: I do background research and gather appropriate materials and then I organize my ideas into a pattern and write them down in outline form. I usually try to speak from a key word outline that I become very familiar with rather than speaking from a manuscript. I occasionally use note cards. (Lau is featured in Chapter 5.)

TebNad/Shutterstock.com

Chris McDonald: Outlining the ideas for my speech topic is helpful because it keeps me on track and ensures that I will get the key message across to my audience. It also enables me to time my speech, which is always a concern in order to run an effective event. (McDonald is the Executive Director for the Oregon and SW Washington Susan G. Komen for the Cure nonprofit organization.)

Jim Endicott: Creating a clear outline is the fulfillment of a silent commitment to the audience. Many professionals use presentation programs such as PowerPoint to help organize ideas. They should first lay out slide titles (main points) and then ask if the flow of the titles create a crisp and logical path through the content. If not, this is the time to change the order and delete non-essentials. The next level of support material can be outlined in bulleted form under the main point, but presenters should *never* write out their outline on slides and then read the points word-for-word. (Read more about Endicott in Chapter 13.)

Questions

1. What do you think Jim Endicott means by the statement, "Creating a clear outline is the fulfillment of a silent commitment to the audience?"
2. Choose an occupation that interests you and interview a person in that career who speaks frequently. What are his or her outlining strategies? Compare and contrast those strategies with the forms of outlining described in this chapter.

In summary, your speech preparation will be enhanced if you create an outline that begins with a heading and uses a standard format that includes coordinated points with subordinated supporting materials, arranged by alternating letters and numbers and by indenting material in a way that shows the relationship of ideas to one another.

Emily's complete content outline, shown below with commentary, pulls all these elements together and provides a model and an explanation of Emily's strategies. As you study this outline, notice that it does not read like a speech script. Instead of putting in each word she'll say, she writes out a sentence that summarizes the contents of each point. She also cites the author and date of specific supporting information in the outline itself; at the end she lists her references in the format required by her instructor.

Student Speech Outline with Commentary

BILIARY ATRESIA*
By Emily Smith

Topic:	Biliary Atresia
General Purpose:	To inform
Specific Purpose:	To inform my audience about liver function and the disease called biliary atresia.
Central Idea/Thesis:	Biliary atresia is a rare congenital liver disease that leads to liver failure and death unless surgically treated.
Preview:	Because of my rare liver disease, biliary atresia, I had the Kasai procedure and a transplant when I was an infant.
Organizational Pattern:	Topical

By writing out her heading, Emily makes sure her speech focus is clear and that her outline accomplishes her stated purposes.

Introduction

I. Do you think about your liver as much as I do mine?
II. Unless you are a transplant recipient, like I am, you may not think much about livers.
III. Every day, I take medications to stay alive.
   A. I was born with biliary atresia, a rare disease that leads to liver failure and death unless surgically treated.
   B. I always wanted to research this topic more, and this was a perfect opportunity.
IV. I will discuss the liver's function and purpose and the disease, biliary atresia; then I will describe my treatment, including the Kasai procedure and a liver transplant.

Identify your speech introduction, body, and conclusion. This introduction gains attention, relates to the audience, establishes credibility, and previews major points.

Point IV is the preview, the transition between the speech introduction and body. It tells the audience to listen for topically organized information.

*Used by permission of Emily Smith.

Body

Emily labels the body of her speech, and she uses the principle of coordination. Points I, II, and III are first-level points that are made up of second-, third-, and fourth-level supporting materials. Second- and third-level supporting points are subordinated by indentation and alternating numbers and letters.

I. Let's first look at the liver's function and purpose.
   A. The American Liver Foundation (updated April 12, 2011), says the liver is one of our most vital organs.
      1. It produces necessary chemicals for digestion.
      2. It breaks down toxic substances and waste and produces bile.
   B. The US Library of Medicine (Dugdale, 2009) says bile is a greenish-yellow substance with many different functions.
      1. It converts food into energy, makes proteins, and cleanses the body of toxins.
      2. Bile also helps get rid of hemoglobin—old red blood cells.
         a. Jaundice is caused when red blood cells get old.
            i. About 1% of old cells go daily to the liver to be destroyed.
            ii. Red cells break into heme and globin; heme converts to bilirubin.
            iii. In a healthy person, bile takes care of this yellow bilirubin.
         b. If bile ducts are hindered, the bile can't destroy bilirubin, and the chemical is turned loose in the body.
         c. Bilirubin causes the yellow-green skin color and eye color of jaundiced people.

All points are phrased as declarative sentences, one sentence per point.

She cites the author or source and date beside the material it supports.

II. Jaundice indicates many diseases including biliary atresia, a rare disease that appears two to eight weeks after birth.
   A. I was diagnosed at two weeks.
      1. For some reason, it affects more girls than boys (Cincinnati Children's Hospital, 2009 last updated).
      2. We were told a virus caused it; my mother, a nurse, says that's a way to say they don't know the cause.
   B. Cincinnati Children's Hospital (2009, last updated) says biliary atresia means the bile ducts are blocked or undeveloped.
      1. The bile can't go into the intestines to perform its usual tasks.
      2. The result is liver failure and eventual death.
      3. The build-up of bilirubin causes symptoms—jaundice, dark urine, clay-colored stools and weight loss—which show up a couple of weeks after birth.
   C. Infants with biliary atresia are very sick because they can't digest food properly.
      1. None of their waste products get destroyed.
      2. Today, I'm a vegetarian because of this.

This is the separation point between her discussion of the disease and its treatment, so Emily writes out her transition statement.

Transition: Now that you know a little bit about the function of the liver and about biliary atresia, let's look at two treatment options.

III. There were then two treatment options: a minor surgery called the Kasai procedure or a complete liver transplant (Cincinnati Children's Hospital, 2009, last updated).
   A. The Kasai procedure removes the damaged bile ducts and replaces them with a piece of the baby's own intestine.
      1. This procedure is effective about 1/3 of the time if done during the first eight weeks of life.
      2. Patients generally need a liver transplant before they turn 20 (Cincinnati Children's Hospital, last updated June 2009).
      3. Doctors performed this procedure on me at six weeks old and at nine weeks old; both were failures.
   B. My only option was a liver transplant.
      1. Doctors didn't expect me to live until my second birthday, but they put me on a transplant waiting list.
         a. This was in the 1980s, and infant transplantation was still fairly new.

Subpoints A and B are first-level points, both with second-level supporting points. B also has third- and fourth-level support.

b. They didn't have the latest methods where they transplant a piece of someone else's liver (Lucile Packard Children's Hospital at Stanford, 2011).
c. Babies like me were put on long waiting lists, and many died while waiting.

2. Liver transplants take between five to about sixteen hours, depending on complications.
   a. My surgery took about six hours with many little miracles during that process.
   b. Transplant patients are hospitalized for 2–3 weeks to take care of any infections and make sure there are no further complications (Lucile Packard, 2011).
   c. Once released, survivors take many medications.
      i. If my body decided the liver didn't belong to me, it would reject it, and I would have to have another transplant.
      ii. I must take an immunosuppressant for the rest of my life (my magical pills of life) to weaken my immune system so it won't think my liver is an intruder.
   d. Liver transplant patients usually bounce back quickly, although it takes time to get used to the medications and the weekly blood tests.

Conclusion

I. I could tell many stories of the miracles that surrounded my transplant, but for now I just wanted to inform you about:
   A. The importance of your liver, take care of it!
   B. The signs and causes of jaundice.
   C. An obscure, but deadly liver disease, biliary atresia.
II. I will leave you with this quotation by Robert Byrne (n.d.), which pretty well sums up the conclusion I have come to after asking God why He let me live: "The purpose of life is a life of purpose."

By setting apart the conclusion, she makes sure that she's crafted a memorable ending that summarizes the speech and is both purposeful and brief.

Sources

American Liver Foundation. (2011, April 12, last updated). Your liver. Retrieved from www.liverfoundation.org/abouttheliver/

Byrne, Robert. (n.d.). *Robert Byrne quotes.* Retrieved from http://en.thinkexist.com/quotes/robert_byrne/

Cincinnati Children's Hospital Medical Center. (2009, June, last updated). Biliary atresia. Retrieved from www.cincinnatichildrens.org/svc/alpha/l/liver/diseases/biliary.htm

Dugdale, D. C. (2009, February 23, last updated). Bilirubin—blood. MedlinePlus. US National Library of Medicine, National Institutes of Health. www.nlm.nih.gov/medlineplus/ency/article/003479.htm

Kaneshiro, N.K. (2009, November 7, last updated). Biliary atresia. MedlinePlus: US National Library of Medicine and the National Institutes of Health. Retrieved from www.nlm.nih.gov/medlineplus/ency/article/001145.htm

Lucile Packard Children's Hospital at Stanford. (2011). Liver transplantation. Retrieved from www.lpch.org/DiseaseHealthInfo/HealthLibrary/digest/livertran.html

UCLA Health System. (2007). Liver transplant: Pediatric liver transplant. UCLA Pediatric Liver Transplant Program. Retrieved from http://transplants.ucla.edu/body.cfm?id=65&oTopID=37

Emily formats her references in the American Psychological Association (APA) style. Ask your instructor which format he or she prefers, but always list the references you consulted during your speech preparation.

How to Create Speaking Notes

Your content outline provides a permanent written record that you can file away after you speak. It is also a good resource to use during rehearsal when you are getting your speech firmly in mind. But content outlines are not **speaking notes**—what you actually use when you deliver the speech. Speaking notes use **key words** for points, including just enough phrases or words to jog your memory as you speak. Use full sentences only for transition statements, direct quotations, and complicated statistics. This section describes two major formats for speaking notes: note cards and speaking outlines.

speaking notes the notes you use to deliver your speech

key words important words and phrases that will jog the speaker's memory

Evaluate Your Content Outline

Return to Speech Builder Express and select Completing the Speech Outline to preview your content outline. Using this complete outline, you can easily prepare your speaking outline or note cards. Evaluate your content outline using the checklist shown here. An electronic version of this checklist is available in your online resources.

yes	no	Did I accomplish the following content outline goals?
		1. My heading provides important summary information about my speech.
		2. My introduction, body, and conclusion are clear.
		3. My organizational pattern is clearly identifiable.
		4. My points and subpoints are properly indented.
		5. I have alternated numbers and letters.
		6. I have written out my transition statements.
		7. I have used complete sentences throughout.
		8. I have cited my sources in the outline.
		9. My references are in the bibliographic form my professor recommends.

Note Cards

Writing out your key words on index cards offers several advantages. For one thing, small cards are less noticeable and easier to handle than standard sheets of paper. And if you must deliver your speech without a podium, you can hold your cards in one hand and still use the other to gesture. Here are some tips for creating note cards:

- Write legibly; print or type key words in capital letters; double- or triple-space your lines.
- Number your cards so that you can quickly put them in place if they get out of order.
- Write on only one side because turning cards over can be distracting.
- Delete nonessential words—use only key, or significant, words and short phrases.
- Use no more than five or six lines per card, and space your lines so that you can easily keep your place. For longer speeches, use more cards instead of crowding additional information onto a few cards.
- Highlight important ideas; circle or underline words you want to emphasize during delivery.
- Include information about your sources so that you can cite those sources as you speak.
- Put delivery advice such as *pause* or *slow down* on your cards.
- Practice in front of a mirror using your note cards. Revise them if they are not as helpful as you would like.

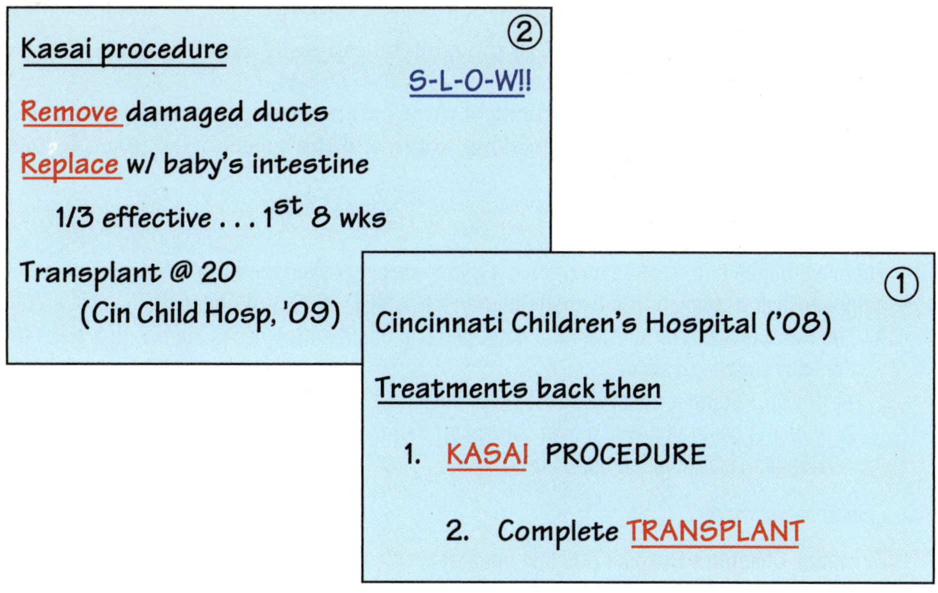

Figure 11.1
Speaking Note Cards Your note cards are a highly individualized set of key term cards that will jog *your* memory.

- During your speech, use your cards unobtrusively. Place them on the lectern if one is available, and never wave them.
- Don't read from your cards unless you are reading a direct quotation or giving complicated statistics; then hold up a card and look at it frequently to show your audience that you are being as accurate as possible.[5]

Figure 11.1 shows two note cards for Emily's speech on biliary atresia.

Speaking Outlines

A second strategy is to write key terms from your outline on a standard sheet of paper. Figure 11.2 shows the first page of a speaking outline. Many of the tips for creating note cards apply to this format, but there are some minor differences:

- Use plenty of space to distinguish between the various sections of your speech.
- Use highlighter pens to distinguish the sections easily. For example, you might underline signposts and transition statements in orange, and use yellow to emphasize the introduction, the body, and the conclusion.
- Use different font sizes and formatting features to break up visual monotony and to direct your eyes to specific places as you go along. For example, Figure 11.2 alternates lowercase and capitalized words.
- If you have several sheets of notes, spread them across the lectern in such a way that you can still see the side edges of the lower pages. Then when you move from one page to another, slip the top sheet off unobtrusively and tuck it at the bottom of the pile.
- If no lectern is available, you can place your pages in a dark-colored notebook or folder that you hold with one hand while gesturing with the other. (Angle the notebook so your audience won't see your pages.)

Cincinnati Children's Hospital ('08)

Treatments back then

1. KASAI PROCEDURE

2. Complete TRANSPLANT

S-L-O-W!!

Kasai procedure

Remove damaged ducts

Replace w/ baby's intestine
1/3 effective . . . 1st 8 wks

Transplant @ 20 (Med Encyc. '08)

Figure 11.2
Speaking Outline On standard sized paper, put key words to remind you of your ideas plus "advice" words to remind you of your delivery.

Speaking outlines help you maintain eye contact with the audience, secure in the knowledge that if you lose your train of thought you can easily glance at these notes to regain your place.

To understand the different functions of these outlines, study this section excerpted from Emily's content outline, her speaking notes, and the speech itself. Each format includes source citations:

From her content outline:

III. There were then two treatment options: a minor surgery called the Kasai procedure or a complete liver transplant (Cincinnati Children's Hospital, 2009, last updated).
    A. The Kasai procedure removes the damaged bile ducts and replaces them with a piece of the baby's own intestine.
        1. This procedure is effective about 1/3 of the time if done during the first eight weeks of life.
        2. Patients generally need a liver transplant before they turn 20 (Cincinnati Children's Hospital, last updated June 2009).

From her speaking notes:

Cincinnati Children's Hospital ('09 last update)
Treatments back then
1. KASAI procedure
2. Complete TRANSPLANT

<u>Kasai</u> procedure
<u>Remove</u> damaged ducts
<u>Replace</u> w/ baby's intestine
1/3 effective . . . 1st 8 wks
Transplant @ age 20 (Cin Child Hosp '09, last update)

From the speech itself: (Note: in extemporaneous delivery, wording will vary somewhat each time):

According to the Cincinnati Children's Hospital website (updated 2009) my parents back then had two options for treating my condition: the Kasai procedure or a complete liver transplant. The Kasai procedure is a comparatively minor surgery where the doctors would remove part of my damaged bile ducts and replace them with a piece of my own intestine. When done within the first eight weeks of life, the procedure is effective about one-third of the time, although the previously mentioned hospital website says patients like me usually need a liver transplant before their twentieth birthday.

Evaluate Your Speaking Notes

When you have finished your speaking notes, evaluate them using the checklist shown here. An electronic version of this checklist is available in your online resources.

yes	no	Did I accomplish the following goals for speaking notes?
		1. My notes have key words or short phrases only, except for direct quotations.
		2. I can't find any other words I could eliminate and still have the notes remain useful.

		3. My structure—introduction, body, and conclusion—are clear.
		4. My transitions are written out; signposts are clearly marked.
		5. I have cited the source next to the material it supports.
		6. I have used color effectively.
		7. I have highlighted (underlined, etc.) words I want to emphasize.
		8. I marked where I want to pause.
		9. I made notes to remind myself to relax and slow down, etc.
		10. I numbered my cards.

Individual Cognitive Preferences

A Diversity Perspective takes into account individual differences in **cognitive preferences** or thinking styles. Because we each have a unique thinking style, every classroom contains "a diverse population of learners."[6] Your thinking style is comprised of the ways you typically prefer to perceive, reason, remember, and solve problems. Our cultures and the technology in them influence our styles to an extent, but your particular way of processing information is unique to you.[7]

In 1981, the cognitive scientist, Roger Sperry, earned a Nobel Prize for his research in brain hemispheric dominance. He found that our right brains process information more globally, intuitively, and artistically, whereas our left-brain processes are more linear, analytic, logical, and computational.[8] Additional researchers have identified "intelligence preferences," our inborn predispositions to prefer particular ways of thinking, including analytical (schoolhouse type), practical (street-smart, contextual), and creative (imaginative, problem solving).[9] Cognitive researchers recognize the value of a whole brain approach that gravitates toward our preferences but flexes as the situation demands.[10]

This text will obviously not describe the finer points of cognitive science research; however, diversity of cognitive preferences and the fact that they reflect both a personal and a cultural orientation fit the emphasis of this text.

Why is this topic in an outlining chapter? Because the linear form of outlining described here and in most public speaking texts is a more left-brained, analytical way to frame a speech, which may or may not match your intellectual preferences. Although you are asked to produce such an outline, your personal style may be more holistic or creative; consequently, when you organize speeches in other contexts, you may prefer alternative, more visual ways of showing your points. Either way, you should ensure that your speeches are structured and your ideas have a logical connection.

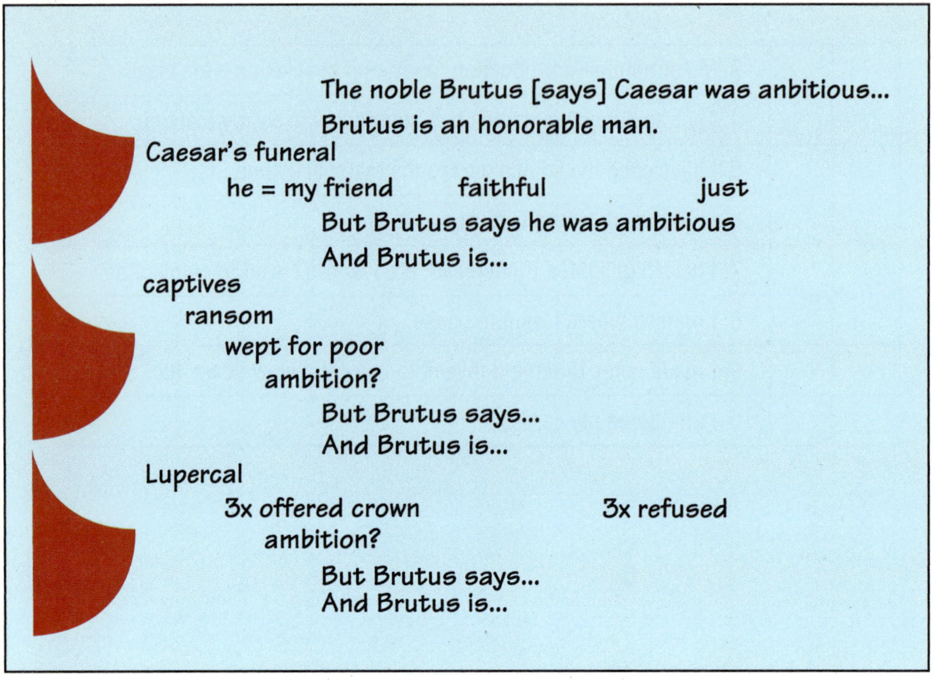

Figure 11.3
Using an Alternate Pattern
This figure depicts the points in Mark Antony's speech visualized in a wave format.

How to Work with an Alternative Pattern

cognitive preference the ways you prefer to perceive, reason, remember, and solve problems; it's culturally influenced but unique to you

The Diversity in Practice: Individual Cognitive Preferences box points out that your **cognitive preferences** may lean toward more visual or imagistic thinking. Consequently, you might prefer an alternative pattern, such as the wave, spiral, or star, described in Chapter 9. If so, your depiction of your speech's content will be less conventional, but you can still design an appropriate representation of your ideas and their relationship to one another by using the tips provided here:[11]

- First, select an appropriate pattern and sketch the diagram.
- With your pattern in mind, write out your main points.
- Next, indicate what you'll use for developmental material and subordinate this material under the main point it supports.
- Indicate how you plan to begin and end your speech, and then write out key transition statements.
- Use standard indentation and numbering only if it's helpful.

Mark Antony's dramatic speech from Shakespeare's play, *Julius Caesar*, features a wave pattern. Figure 11.3 shows how to format it. Antony used a recurring theme, "The noble Brutus says Caesar was ambitious . . . and Brutus is an honorable man." (You can watch this speech on YouTube by searching for "Mark Antony's Speech." Watch the 1953 version, starring Marlon Brando.)

Summary

As part of the speechmaking process, it's important to understand and show the ways that your points and subpoints relate to one another. Consequently, your instructor may ask you to outline your ideas in a linear form, using alternating letters and numbers and careful indentation. Coordinate your main points, and subordinate your supporting materials under them. Write your content outline in full sentences, and include a list of references at the end.

However, don't take this content outline to the podium with you. Instead, use note cards or a key word outline that helps you remember your main points but prevents you from reading your speech verbatim. Content outlines differ from speaking notes or speaking outlines and from what you actually say in the speech.

A linear outline is not the only way to record your ideas; in fact, one way to recognize diversity is to admit that people with various learning styles may actually benefit from using an alternative, more visual way to record speech content. If you have the opportunity to choose an alternative pattern, first sketch out a simple diagram and then arrange your major ideas and supporting materials around it.

STUDY AND REVIEW

Your online resources for *Public Speaking: Concepts and Skills for a Diverse Society* offer a broad range of study tools that will help you better understand the material in this chapter, complete assignments, and succeed on tests. Your online resources feature the following:

- Speech videos with critical viewing questions, speech outlines, and transcripts.
- Interactive versions of this chapter's Stop and Check activities, as well as Application and Critical Thinking Exercises.
- Speech Builder Express and InfoTrac College Edition.
- Weblinks related to chapter content.
- Study and review tools such as self-quizzes, an interactive glossary, and downloadable audio summaries.

You can access your online resources at the CourseMate for *Public Speaking: Concepts and Skills for a Diverse Society*. Log in at **http://www.cengage.com/login**, using the access code that came with your book or that you bought online at **http://www.cengagebrain.com**.

KEY TERMS

The terms below are defined in the margins throughout this chapter.

alternation 185
cognitive preferences 194
content outline 184
coordination 185
indentation 185
key words 189
logical elements 184
script 184
speaking notes 189
structural elements 184
subordination 185

APPLICATION AND CRITICAL THINKING EXERCISES

1. Outline an in-class speech while one of your classmates delivers it. After the speech, give the outline to the speaker, and ask that person to check its contents for completeness and faithfulness to the intended structure and contents.
2. Using the same outline, ask another student to evaluate your formatting—use of indentation, alternating numbers and letters, complete sentences, and the like.
3. Work with another person in your class and create speaking notes for one of the speeches or outlines in Appendix C.

4. Before you give your next speech, work from your content outline to prepare a speaking outline. Let a classmate evaluate both outlines and make revisions that would improve either one or both.

5. To understand how to adapt outlines for situations outside the classroom, visit the website maintained on **weblink 11.1** on your resources. (You can access this link through your CourseMate for *Public Speaking,* Chapter 11 resources.) This online guide to public speaking and presentation skills that shows the general framework for outlines that could be used in a scientific conference talk, a community association meeting, and a business proposal to investors. How are these outlines similar to and different from the content outlines described in this chapter? Why do you think this is so?
6. Experienced speakers do not always prepare a content outline like Emily Smith's, complete with heading and references. Ask your instructor to describe how she or he prepares lectures, informal talks, and speeches to groups outside the classroom.

SPEECH VIDEOS

Go to your online resources to watch and critique two of the speeches outlined in this chapter (partially or in full): "No More Sugar" by Hans Erian or "Biliary Atresia" by Emily Smith. Your online resources include the transcript, outline, and video of each speech under Interactive Video Activities, Chapter 11.

© Tim Timmerman

CHAPTER 12

THIS CHAPTER WILL HELP YOU

- Explain how words are linked to culture and meaning
- Understand the denotative meaning of words including jargon
- Define connotative meanings of words including epithets and euphemisms
- Distinguish between the oral and written style in language
- Choose language that is concise, familiar, concrete, repetitive, vivid, and appropriate
- Use ethical language that is inclusive and positive about groups and individuals
- Give guidelines for listening and speaking in linguistically diverse contexts

Choosing Effective Language

LANGUAGE CONVEYS MORE than just ideas. Your word choices also provide clues about your region of origin, age, educational level, income level, sex, ethnicity, and occupation. For example,

- *Regional diversity:* Oregonians purchase a can of pop, which New Yorkers would call soda; in much of the South, it's a coke (meaning any brand of soda pop).
- *Occupational diversity:* Physicians might say, "The surgical margins for every resected tumor were evaluated proximally, ventrally, and at the postero-lateral aspect. . . ."[1] However, child-care workers or financial counselors don't talk like this.

- *Cultural and gender diversity:* Across many cultures, women use more polite and precise forms of speech than men do. In some languages, such as Japanese, women and men use different words for the same objects.[2]

In the study of rhetoric, language falls within the *canon of style*, which is the focus of this chapter. First, it looks at ways our vocabularies both reveal and express cultural assumptions. Next, it provides tips for effective language choices in public speeches. Finally, it discusses language issues in linguistically diverse settings.

Languages and Culture

languages verbal codes consisting of symbols that a speech community uses for communication

words verbal symbols that stand for or represent ideas

Languages are systems of verbal symbols that members of a speech community use to share ideas. Some symbols are visual; for instance, a country's flag stands for that country. But more commonly we use verbal symbols or **words** to express cultural ideas. Co-cultures often use both the larger culture's vocabulary and terminology that is unique to their group.

Words and Meaning

Think of words as the names we give our "cultural memories." They serve as "markers of cultural attention"[3] or of shared experiences we consider significant enough to name. For example, people notice a phenomenon, formulate a concept about it, and encode their idea into a word, something like this:

Long ago humans:

1. *Noticed a phenomenon*—every morning a shining ball appeared in the east.
2. *Formed a concept*—the sky brightened; the ball emerged gradually and then went up.
3. *Created a label for this event—sunrise* (English), *le lever du soleil* (French), *zonsopgang* (Dutch), and so on.

Devan Marchbanks

Languages name what a culture deems important enough to label. English has many color-related words, compared to many other cultures. The extent of the vocabulary reflects the significance of color in this culture.

The theorist Kenneth Burke explains that when we learn to "name," we assume a perspective on the world[4] because our labels form our social realities. For example, how many mustache-related words do you know? One? Two? An Albanian dictionary gives more than twenty possibilities (along with numerous eyebrow-related words).[5]

How about camel-related words? If you lived in Somalia, you'd have words for a male pack camel (*awr*), dairy camels (*irmaan*), a female camel kept away from her young (*kareeb*), a camel loaded with water vessels (*dhaan*), and so on—more than forty different terms. You'd also have dozens of words for camel diseases, things camels do, and things made from camels.[6]

English has many time-related words such as hours, minutes, milliseconds, tomorrow, or eternity; the Hopi language has no word that means later.[7]

Obviously, our vocabularies show that facial hair or camels are less significant in English-speaking cultures as time is and that time in Hopi culture is less rigid than in English-speaking cultures.

It's easy to understand why we name visible objects such as sunrises or mustaches, but we also name less tangible experiences, actions, feelings, and ideas. Here are a few examples:

Imaginary things: unicorn, Martian, elf

Qualities of objects: soft, generous, wide

Feelings or states: anger, envy, love, happiness, depression

Abstractions: justice, beauty, conscience

Languages change as cultures change. English has adopted many words from other languages, including *giraffe* (Arabic) and *ambiance* (French). Vocabulary added during the last few decades includes *gridlock, serial killer, microchip, and junk food*. Sportscaster Chick Hearn added *slam dunk* and *air ball*. More recent additions include *gluten free*, *phish*, and *blue state/red state*. When your grandparents were growing up, microchips or slam dunks or phish either didn't exist or weren't important enough to name.[8] Languages also change over time, as you notice every time you read a Shakespearean play. You need footnotes to translate the archaic words into contemporary English.

Dialects

A dialect is a variant form of a language that differs in pronunciation, vocabulary, and/or grammar. English dialects include international English, British English, Black English (sometimes called ebonics or African American English—AAE), and a variety of regional and ethnic variations.[9] **Standard English** is the dialect most common in education, business, and broadcasting in the United States; it is the language of print.

If you speak a dialect, you may choose to be bidialectical—using Standard English in public contexts and your dialect around family and friends. This is called **code switching**. Bank officer Pauline Jefferson, for instance, transacts business in her bank and makes public presentations for her coworkers in Standard English. However, with small female audiences in her local church, she switches between Standard English and AAE.

For more information, log on to InfoTrac College Edition and read Jeanette Gilsdorf's article "Standard Englishes and World Englishes." The Internet also has many sources of American slang and idioms. One interesting site, set up for English as a Second Language students is maintained on **weblink 12.1**. (You can access this link through your CourseMate for *Public Speaking*, Chapter 12 resources.)

dialect a variant form of a language

Standard English the English dialect most commonly used in public speaking and in US institutions

code switching changing from one dialect to another

denotative meaning what a word names or identifies

ambiguous word identifies more than one object or idea; its meaning depends on the context

Denotative Meanings

A word's **denotative meaning**, the meaning you find in a dictionary, is what the word names or identifies. **Ambiguous words**, by definition, have more than one meaning, so the context determines which meaning fits the situation. For instance, the word *pot* could denote at least five things:

- A rounded container used chiefly for domestic purposes
- A sum of money, as in the total amount of bets at stake at one time (the jackpot)
- An enclosed frame of wire, wood, or wicker used to catch fish or lobsters
- Slang for cannabis
- Ruin, as in "the business went to pot"[10]

When you cook in a pot, you think of the first meaning. But when you talk about legalizing pot, you know you're not talking about cooking or poker bets. The context helps you discern the meaning. As you plan language for your speech, choose the correct word for the correct context to denote your intended meaning. Consult a dictionary or thesaurus if you are unsure.

Increasing your vocabulary and discriminating among shades of meaning between words are valuable skills, because a larger vocabulary gives you more power to communicate your thoughts precisely. Check your vocabulary prowess by searching the Internet for the list of 100 words that every high school graduate should know. (It's challenging!)

jargon a specialized, technical vocabulary that serves the interests and activities of a particular group

Jargon denotes specialized, technical language that serves special groups (doctors, lawyers), interests (feminism, education), activities (football, gardening), and so on. For example, football has specialized meanings for *drive*, *down*, and *safety*. When everyone in your audience knows the meaning of the jargon, it's appropriate to use it. However, when you're communicating with nonspecialists, you should define and clarify technical terms, or you will exclude some of your listeners.

Connotative Meanings

connotative meaning emotional overtones, related feelings, and associations that cluster around a word

Connotative meanings are the emotional overtones the words carry. That is, words represent feelings and associations related to the ideas they denote. For instance, *chocolate* is not just a food produced from cacao seeds (denotative meaning), it can connote romance or dietary temptation, depending on the individual. Because language is often emotionally charged, people sometimes choose negatively loaded words to demean persons or ideas, or they substitute neutral or positive terms to talk about unpopular ideas.

Kobal-collection

In the movie *Patch Adams*, Robin Williams plays a medical student who treats patients' emotional as well as physical needs. In a key scene, he comes to a dying man, dressed as an angel, and reads him denotative definitions (to expire) and euphemisms (cash in your chips) for death. Eventually, the man contributes his own euphemisms to the list and, thus, accepts his fate.

Epithets are words or phrases, often with negative connotations, that describe some quality of a person or group. For example, politicians use terms such as *flip-flopper* or *corporate welfare* because opinion polls show that voters respond negatively to those terms. Words like *white trash*, *tree hugger*, or *nerd* are negative epithets that function to frame perceptions about people in these groups. Calling anti-abortion advocates *anti-choice* creates a negative image, whereas the group's self-chosen title, *pro-life*, has positive connotations.

epithets words or phrases with powerful negative connotations, used to describe some quality of a person or group

Members of labeled groups often try to lessen the negative power of the epithet by accepting and using the term themselves. For example, *Newsweek* reported on a group of female engineering students who label themselves "Nerd Girls," star in a YouTube video titled "Meet the Nerd Girls," and conduct weekly outreach programs for younger women, where they describe the benefits of being an engineer.[11]

Euphemisms, in contrast, substitute an agreeable or inoffensive term for a more embarrassing, unpleasant, or offensive word. Euphemisms are commonly used for things we hesitate to speak about such as bodily functions (*nature is calling*), religion (*the Man Upstairs*) or weight (*big-boned*). Euphemisms also mask unpleasant situations such as corporate layoffs. It's supposedly easier to be given a *career change opportunity* or be *outplaced* rather than *fired*.

euphemisms words or phrases that substitute an inoffensive term for a potentially offensive, embarrassing, or unpleasant thing

Public speakers, especially politicians, often use euphemisms for controversial actions, ideas, and policies. Planned tax increases become *membership fees* or *revenue enhancements*. Similarly, *shell shock* (World War I) became *combat fatigue* (World War II), which became *post-traumatic stress syndrome* (Vietnam War). Each subsequent term further removes the condition from its cause.[12] Be alert for connotative language in your research. By carefully choosing their wording, speakers hope to create a desired spin or interpretation. (Learn more about this subject by searching the Internet for the word *euphemisms* or *doublespeak*.)

In summary, languages are systems of symbols—words that denote or stand for ideas and evoke feelings or connotative meanings that differ from person to person. Carefully choose your words, making sure you use the correct word in context. Pay attention to connotative meanings, either positive or negative, that listeners might attach to your words. And adapt your dialect and your jargon to your audience and the occasion. As you do this, you take into account the cultural implications of your language choices.

Think Critically About Denotative and Connotative Words

Test your understanding of meanings with these exercises.

1. Before launching new products, marketers carefully select terminology that has positive connotations. Look up two or three advertisements in your favorite magazines, and then list some of the words in each ad. What is the denotative meaning of each word on your list? Now jot down some of your personal connotations for each term. Evaluate the overall marketability of the term.
2. Work with your classmates to make a list of the car models owned by class members (Fiesta, Explorer, Mustang, and so on). Within a small group, identify the denotative meaning of each word. Then discuss the connotative associations that manufacturers hope will sell the car.

Use Language Effectively

Give your speech in an oral style that fits the context, purpose, subject matter of the speech, and your personality. This section first describes elements of an oral style and then explains several principles in the canon of style that will help you choose language more effectively. It closes by discussing ethical aspects of appropriate language.

Use an Oral Style

James Winans, author of an early speech textbook, cautioned his students, "A speech is not an essay on its hind legs."[13] Written texts are more static; writers choose words carefully and they use more complex words and greater diversity in vocabulary because a text can be read and reread. Readers can take their time, stop, look up words, pause to think, and so on.[14] A speech, in contrast, is dynamic; it exists in a specific time frame, and words, once uttered, are gone. However, speakers have the advantage of engaging the audience by using nonverbal gestures, vocal stress, and other nonverbal cues to communicate their ideas.[15] **Oral style** is less formal and more personalized. (Figure 12.1 shows some differences between oral and written style.)

oral style characteristics of spoken language compared to written language

This excerpt from speech given at the Los Angeles Film Festival by an entertainment CEO is a good example of oral style. He is developing his first main point: Rule One: Make Smarter Movies!:[16]

> When I started [my company], I told people I wanted to make movies I'd pay to see twice. Give me *Slumdog* over *Transformers* any day. Give me movies with stories and ideas that people care about.
>
> You say, yeah, but kids today expect special effects. Well, my kids are 9 and 13. My daughter has watched *Twilight* seven times. It has the worst special effects in the world. The ridiculous way that guy runs looks like the track star with blurry legs in that TV commercial. But does she really care that the special effects in the next *Twilight* movie will be any better?
>
> As if.
>
> What she cares about is that Robert Pattinson fights off the werewolf guy for Kristin Stewart.

Figure 12.1
Oral and Written Style[17]

Oral Style	Written Style
Dynamic and interactive	Static
Short, simple, concrete but vivid words	More complex words, greater vocabulary variety
Shorter sentences; fragments acceptable	Longer, more complex and complete sentences
Less formal, more personalized language	More formal, precise language
Repetition of words and ideas	Less repetition; readers can stop, ponder, reread, and look up words
More engaging; speaker adds nonverbal emphasis	Not able to emphasize meanings nonverbally

This excerpt contains several elements of oral style. The speaker uses fairly short sentences—even fragments, and one sentence starts with "but." His vocabulary is familiar and concrete and his words paint vivid pictures. He uses personalized language (you, I) and repetition. The following section describes several basic principles of effective oral language: be concise, choose familiar words, be concrete, build in repetition, use vivid language, and select an appropriate form.

Be Concise

It's easy to clutter a speech with **verbiage**—nonessential or "filler" words. This is especially common in demonstration speeches, as this excerpt from a cooking show on television illustrates:

verbiage nonessential language

The cake chef said: "What you want to do next is you want to take the coffee and pour it over the cake."

He could more concisely say: "Next, pour the coffee over the cake."

Although brevity or conciseness is valued in the United States, many other cultures value flowery words and language. Consequently, what we may consider verbiage, other groups may regard as essential elements of eloquence.

Use Familiar Words

The purpose of public speaking is to clarify ideas, not make them harder to understand. So short, familiar words are part of the oral style. One good way to be clear is to avoid jargon, but because many topics involve technical terms, you may have to look up jargon words to translate them into understandable English. Jesse failed to do this when he said:

We've all been taught that AIDS is perinatal and that it is transmitted through sexual contact.

What does *perinatal* mean? When asked, Jesse didn't know; the word came from an article he had read, and he had not bothered to look it up. (It means "associated with . . . the period immediately before, during, or just after the time of birth.") If he'd used his dictionary, he could have clarified the jargon by saying:

We've been taught that AIDS is transmitted from mother to child perinatally—that is, during the birth process—and that it is transmitted through sexual activity.

Adding a brief definition makes the speech more understandable.

Be Concrete

Another important aspect of style, one that can help your listeners form precise understandings, is to choose **concrete words** that are specific rather than abstract, particular rather than general. Words range along a scale of abstraction such as this:

concrete words specific, rather than general or abstract, terms

abstract/general	animal
	invertebrate
	insect
	butterfly
concrete/particular	Blue Morpho butterfly

When you say, "I photographed a Blue Morpho butterfly," your ideas are much more concrete than when you say, "I photographed an insect." But that is more concrete than "I photographed an animal." The more distinct your word choices, the more vivid your images and the more precise your meanings.

This excerpt from British author Doris Lessing's lecture to the Nobel Peace Prize Committee[18] is exceptional for its use of concrete language:

> [I'm in] northwest Zimbabwe early in the eighties, and I am visiting a friend who was a teacher in a school in London. . . . He is a gently idealistic soul and what he found here in this school shocked him into a depression, from which it was hard to recover. This school . . . consists of four large brick rooms side by side, put straight into the dust, one two three four, with a half room at one end, which is the library. In these classrooms are blackboards, but. . . . [t]here is no atlas, or globe in the school, no textbooks, no exercise books, or biros [ballpoint pens], in the library are no books of the kind the pupils would like to read: they are tomes from American universities, hard even to lift, rejects from white libraries, detective stories, or with titles like *Weekend in Paris* or *Felicity Finds Love*.

Each image in Lessing's carefully chosen language presents concrete sensory imagery that helps you place yourself into the sights and the emotions of the setting.

vague words imprecise terms that have indefinite boundaries

In contrast, **vague words** are imprecise; they have indefinite boundaries. For example, what is *large*? *Small*? Compared to what? A large glass of orange juice is not on the same scale as a large barn. One way to minimize your use of vague words is to choose details that specify or illustrate what you mean. For instance, if you talk about a small inheritance, give a dollar figure that shows how you're defining small. One listener may think $500 is small whereas another has $50,000 in mind.

Choosing More Precise Wording

The purpose of this exercise is to raise your awareness of vague words that we typically use in place of more precise ones. For example, you can often replace *get*, an ambiguous verb, with a more concrete term. In the blank that follows each sentence, replace *get* (or a form thereof) with more precise wording.

What did you *get* your mom for her birthday? ____________

Why did you *get* angry about that? ____________

I'm *getting* ready to outline my speech. ____________

The mayor *got* a thousand dollars just for giving one speech! ____________

The star athlete *gets* excited just before a big race. ____________

After I studied the calculus problem for over an hour, I finally *got* it! ____________

You can *get* information 24 hours a day on the Internet. ____________

After my friend *gets* here, we can leave. ____________

Build in Repetition

Repetition is a common element in an oral style. One strategy is to repeat the same word or phrase at the beginning of clauses or sentences. For example, President Reagan's tribute[19] to the space shuttle *Challenger* astronauts included these repetitive phrases: "We will cherish each of their stories, stories of triumph and bravery, stories of true American heroes." Another type of repetition restates the same phrase at the end of a clause or a sentence. Lincoln's famous phrase "government of the people, by the people, for the people" is an example. This excerpt from a commencement address is full of repetition. You can imagine the speaker gesturing, varying his voice, and using effective pauses to drive home his points:[20]

> I came in the house one day when my younger son Asa was playing the piano. Extraordinary piano player. Playing this Rachmaninoff piece. And I stood at—we had this little small house, big grand piano, took up the whole living room. And I stood in the back door. Couldn't see Asa, he was on the other side of the wall. But the whole house was, like, reverberating like this, just reverberating. And I realized as I stood there that the house was not reverberating with the piano. The house was not reverberating with Rachmaninoff. The house was reverberating with Asa. Asa was filling the house. That piano just sits there. Rachmaninoff is just little dots on a piece of paper until he puts his hands on that keyboard and then the music happens.

Sometimes speakers repeat, but reverse in a second phrase, some words from the first phrase. (The technical term for this is **antimetabole.**) Some examples include:[21]

antimetabole saying words in one phrase, and reversing them in the next phrase

> *The absence of evidence* is not *the evidence of absence.* (Carl Sagan)
>
> *Just because you're born in the slum does not mean the slum is born in you.* (Rev. Jesse Jackson)
>
> *I don't throw darts at balloons; I throw balloons at darts.* (Joe Montana, quarterback)

President Kennedy's inaugural address, printed at the end of this chapter, includes several famous examples of antimetabole including, "Ask not what your country can do for you; ask what you can do for your country."

Use Vivid Language

Colorful, vivid language is a major component of the oral style that helps keep listeners' attention and interest. Vivid linguistic devices include alliteration, rhyming, metaphors and similes, and personification.

Alliteration is the use of words with the same recurring initial sounds. It can occur within a sentence: one activist wondered what "*t*raits, *t*enacity, and *t*alents" make a good environmentalist?[22] Another speaker referred to author Harriet Beecher Stowe as "very *pr*oper, *pr*imly dressed, and *pr*ecisely spoken."[23] Alliteration is also a good way to help listeners remember main points. William Brody alliterated both the title and the main points in his speech, "What's Promised, What's Possible":[24]

alliteration words with recurring initial sounds

> I'd like to tell you about the five C's of healthcare. . . . Two of these five C's you already know—cost and coverage. These are the issues we hear about all the time. . . . And while everyone is talking about the costs of health care and the lack of coverage, meaningful change will only come when we address other issues.
>
> These are the other 3 C's—the issues we're not hearing about: consistency, complexity, and chronic illness. . . .

Rhymes—whether single words, longer phrases, or entire lines—are comprised of words that end in the same sounds. Although rap artists rhyme their entire presentations, most people use rhymes in more limited ways. In his speech about electronic drums, Bob rhymed three words within one sentence: "What or who would you rather have in your band, a *mean* and *clean* drum *machine* or a stereotypical rock drummer?"

rhymes words that end in the same sound

metaphors comparison of two dissimilar things

mixed metaphor combining metaphors from two or more sources, starting with one comparison and ending with another

similes short comparisons that use the word *like* or *as* to compare two items that are alike in one essential detail

Rhymes are also effective for wording your main points to make them more memorable. Here are two examples:

> We are faced with two choices: retreat or compete
>
> Workplaces typically have three generations of employees: boomers, bloomers, and zoomers[25]

A **metaphor** compares two dissimilar things without using the words *like* or *as*. Professor Michael Osborn[26] thinks of speech students as *builders* who frame and craft their speeches, or as *weavers* who intertwine verbal and nonverbal elements into a successful performance, or as *climbers* who scramble over barriers or obstacles such as speech anxiety on their way to a successful speech. Each metaphor provides a different perspective on the subject. Which comparison best describes you as a speech student? Can you come up with a better metaphor for speech making?

One danger in using metaphors is the possibility of creating a **mixed metaphor**, beginning with one comparison and ending with another. To illustrate, one panelist on a news broadcast said, "We must solve the root problem, or the line will be drawn in the sand, and we'll be back in the soup again." Unfortunately, he combined three images, which left his listeners with no clear image of the problem. Should they dig out the root, avoid the line, or stay out of the kitchen?

Similes, like metaphors, compare two different things that are alike in one essential detail; however, they use *like* or *as* to explicitly state the connection. Here are two examples:

Kavram/Shutterstock

Archetypal symbols—such as natural phenomena, journeys, sickness and health, and parents and children—are widely used as metaphors by people all over the globe. Chief Seattle referred to prairies, storms, rain and seas in his speeches.

> When we harbor resentment, it's like drinking poison and hoping the other person dies.[27]

> [The white] people are many. They are like the grass that covers vast prairies. My people are few. They resemble the scattering trees of a storm-swept plain. . . . There was a time when our people covered the land as the waves of a wind-ruffled sea cover its shell-paved floor, but that time long since passed away with the greatness of tribes that are now but a mournful memory. (Chief Seattle)[28]

Some metaphors and similes arise from our experiences of being human, and people the world over understand them. For instance, all human groups experience day and night, sickness and health, seasonal changes, natural phenomena, and family relationships. These form the basis for our most fundamental **archetypal symbols.**[29] We refer to the dawn of civilization and to sunset years, to a cancer that destroys our

archetypal symbols recurring metaphors and similes that arise from shared human and natural experiences

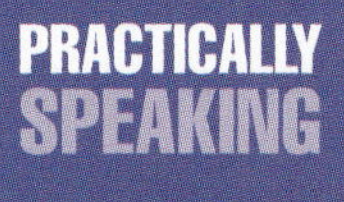

Speechwriters

People whose jobs require them to give important speeches often use speechwriters to craft distinctive language when every word matters. Typically, US presidents have teams of speechwriters, some of whom become famous in their own right. Franklin Roosevelt worked with a playwright; Dwight Eisenhower used a journalist. Comedian Ben Stein wrote for Richard Nixon. TV news host Chris Matthews, wrote for Jimmy Carter. Peggy Noonan became famous for President Reagan's space shuttle *Challenger* tribute and for President George H. W. Bush's "thousand points of light" speech. Even the fictional President Bartlet on *The West Wing* had his team of speechwriters.

While still a candidate, John F. Kennedy discovered his exceptional speechwriter, Theodore "Ted" Sorensen, whom he called his "intellectual blood bank."[30] Sorensen is credited with such memorable lines from JFK's Inaugural as "Ask not what your country can do for you" and "the torch has been passed to a new generation of Americans."

Effective presidential speechwriters frame national issues in memorable ways. They can also influence world affairs. The movie *Thirteen Days*, although not entirely accurate, shows Sorensen's importance as a member of the team that faced down the Soviets during the Cuban Missile Crisis. He also helped pen President Kennedy's speech to a fearful nation, and some historians credit a letter he wrote to the Soviets with saving the world from nuclear destruction during that period. Sorensen joined Barack Obama's team of speechwriters before the 2008 election and put, as *ABC News* phrased it, "Kennedy's touch on Obama's words."[31]

Questions

1. Which, if any, words spoken by a politician do you remember? What about the language was memorable?
2. *ABC News* says political speechwriters "wield untold power over voters."[32] What does the phrase "*untold* power" mean to you in this context?
3. Although you don't have a speechwriter, consult with a few classmates as you prepare your next speech. Ask for specific ways to make your language more memorable. How does this consultation improve your speech?

economy and to a healthy marriage. Other common comparisons relate to cultural modes of transportation (the ship of state) to sports (the game of life), and, as the culture changes, to electronic technology (experiencing static, feeling wired).

personification giving human characteristics to nonhuman entities

Personification means giving human characteristics to nonhuman entities such as animals, countries, natural objects and processes, and social processes. Chief Seattle used personification in an 1853 speech, given before the governor of the Washington Territory:[33]

> Yonder sky that has wept tears of compassion upon my people for centuries untold, and which to us appears changeless and eternal, may change.

Use Appropriate Forms

Generally, language in public settings is more formal, with fewer slang expressions, compared to private settings; however, your audience and the situation should have the final influence over your linguistic choices. For example, the language in a lecture differs from the language in a eulogy. Similarly, you'd use different words and different levels of formality when speaking to teenagers gathered in a park than when addressing members of an alumni association at a formal banquet, even for the same topic.

Use of dialect can be appropriate for some speakers, but not for others. An African American, for instance, might use African American English (AAE) when it's expected and appropriate; however, a Euro-American or an Asian American who used AAE, even in the same setting, would almost certainly be out of line.

Famous speakers such as Martin Luther King, Jr., adapt to various settings, as an excerpt from a biography explains:

> King was . . . a code switcher who switched in and out of idioms as he moved between black and white audiences. But he also made such moves *within* his black talk and his white talk. . . . [He was] a man who blended all sorts of oppositions. The key crossings were not just between black and white but between raw and refined, sacred and secular, prophetic and pragmatic. This mixing suggests . . . a "postethnic" man . . .[34]

Daniel Laflor/istockphoto.com

In cultures where elderly citizens are highly respected, ageist language is not the issue that it is in the United States, where youth is valued. Choose language that presents all groups in a positive, non-dismissive light.

In summary, effective language incorporates an oral style that differs from written language in several important ways. You'll be more effective if you use concise, familiar wording, incorporate repetition and vivid vocabulary, and make sure your language is appropriate to your personality and the audience, topic, and situation in which you speak.

Use Language Ethically

Language choices have ethical implications because words and phrases can include or exclude, affirm or dismiss individuals or entire groups.[35] Emory University's Statement on **Inclusive Language** recommends, "A recognition of the full humanity of all peoples should prompt an attempt to speak and think in ways which include all human beings and degrade none."[36] Choosing inclusive language is not only ethical, it's practical because it can increase your credibility. One study[37] found that speakers who put down persons with disabilities or focus on the disability rather than on the individual lose credibility, likeability, and persuasiveness. Inclusive terminology and positive presentations of groups or individuals are elements of ethical language.

inclusive language ethical terminology that affirms and includes, rather than excludes, persons or groups of people

Choose Inclusive Terminology

Avoid **racist language** that privileges one racial or ethnic group and degrades or devalues others. **Ageist language** portrays older people in ways that demean or devalue their age. Phrases like *over the hill* or *look ten years younger* subtly reinforce the notion that youth is better than age. Finally, **sexist language** gives priority to males, their activities, and their interests.

Nonparallel language is a specific form of sexist language that speaks differently about men and women. It's nonparallel to designate a female by adding a suffix to a male term, as in *actor-actress* or *steward-stewardess*. It's also nonparallel to mark job titles, as in a *female judge*. (Would you ever say a *male judge?*) Similarly, couples may be termed *man and wife* but not *woman and husband*. (*Husband and wife* is parallel because both terms designate roles.)

Use of the "generic *he*" or the use of the suffix *–man* makes women invisible. So substitute inclusive labels such as *chair* for chairman, *mail carrier* for mailman, and *firefighter* for fireman. Other language assumes that relationships are all heterosexual or that *Americans* are synonymous with *US residents*. (Canadians, Brazilians, and Guatemalans are also Americans.)

racist language language that privileges one racial or ethnic group over another

ageist language language that negatively influences the way listeners think about older people

sexist language language that privileges males and their activities and interests

nonparallel language language that does not treat the two sexes equally

Present People and Groups Positively

Phrases like *just a secretary*, *white trash*, or *hypocritical Christians* are put-downs or **dismissive language** applied to people in ways that discount the importance of their ideas. Epithets frame negative perceptions of people or groups. Think about how the negative labels commonly applied to the elderly (*old duffer*, *little old lady*, *old hag*, or *dirty old man*) create mental images that demean seniors. Other examples of slurs include *sissy*, *dumb blonde*, *dumb jock*, and *computer nerd*. In contrast, terms such as *computer genius*, *athlete*, or *retiree* create more positive or more neutral images.

dismissive language put-downs; language that discounts the importance of someone's viewpoint

Mention differences only when they matter in the context of the speech. For instance, say "*my professor*" unless it is somehow important to say "my *Latina* professor." Don't mention someone's competency as if it were unusual for that group: Instead of "an *intelligent* welfare recipient," simply say "a welfare recipient." Don't describe the

The Interplay of Legal Rights and Human Rights

At a hearing on demeaning language in entertainment, congressional representatives quizzed entertainment industry executives about works with explicit and demeaning lyrics. When asked if they counseled artists about their language choices (the answer was yes) or if they refused to produce works with demeaning language (the answer was no), the producers uniformly invoked the First Amendment.

Although free speech is foundational to a democracy, is there a human right *not* to be a victim of demeaning language or hate speech? Chapter 3 introduced the term *rightsabilities:* rights + responsibilities. How should they be balanced? Dolores Frida, writing in the *New York Daily News* (Latino), argues that most songs throughout history have been about women,

> But when, with rhyme but without reason, we are called bitches and ho's and *perras* (female dogs) and *potras* (female horses) in songs heard by millions, and that language becomes part of the culture, it is time to say ¡*basta*! (enough).[38]

She does not advocate censorship, but she says women can walk off the dance floor when demeaning songs play. They can stop buying CDs, and they can start producing and buying their own songs.

Questions

1. Is hate speech the same as demeaning language? Why or why not?
2. How might hate speech violate someone's human rights?
3. What limits, if any, should the government put on speech? How about universities or other institutions? What are your personal limitations?
4. Have you heard "horror stories" about "thought police" going too far? How do you respond?

disabled as helpless victims to be pitied and aided, but don't suggest they are more heroic, courageous, patient, or special than others, and avoid contrasting them to *normal* people.[39]

In short, terminology is not neutral. The words you select have the power to influence audience perceptions regarding issues as well as individuals and groups. The fact that some language choices demean or put down others raises ethical questions and colors your listeners' impressions about you. Choosing inclusive, positive language shows respect for diversity and enhances your credibility as well.

Language and Pluralistic Audiences

Students enter classrooms across the country with many types of linguistic diversity:

- Monolingual (speaking one language only)
- Bilingual (speaking two languages)
- Multilingual (speaking three or more languages)
- Bidialectical (speaking two dialects)
- Multidialectical (speaking three or more dialects)

Communicating in a linguistically diverse setting is often complicated and frustrating, but you can plan ways to adapt to multilingual situations that will be beneficial to everyone involved.

Adapting to Multilingual Situations

Don't assume you'll be instantly understood when you speak to a linguistically diverse audience, so a few simple strategies can help you speak more effectively in multicultural settings. Many of these suggestions are elements of the oral style:

- Before preparing your outline, try to "hear" the terminology and jargon related to your topic in the way a nonnative speaker of English might hear it.
- Whenever possible, choose simple words that most people understand, but don't talk down to your audience.
- Identify words that might be confusing and display them on visual aids as you talk.
- Define difficult words and jargon as you go along.
- Build in repetition and redundancy by saying the same idea in a number of different ways. This way, if listeners are unclear about a concept the first time around, they may grasp it when it's expressed another way.

When you listen to a non-fluent speaker, you must make a more-than-normal effort to create a satisfying experience, both for the speaker and for yourself. Remember that the major goal of any speech is communication of ideas, not perfection of language skills. So concentrate on the main points rather than on each specific word. Use patience and **perspective taking** by putting yourself in the speaker's shoes and imagining what it would be like to give a speech in a foreign language to native speakers of that language. Also, remember that non-fluency is linked to inexperience in English, not to a lack of intelligence or education.[40] These additional tips can help you listen more effectively:[41]

perspective taking trying to imagine something from another person's point of view

- Approach the speech with a positive attitude, expecting to understand.
- Listen all the way through. Make special efforts to keep your mind from wandering in the middle of the speech. It may help to take notes.
- Assume responsibility for co-creating meaning. Give appropriate nonverbal feedback to demonstrate your interest, patience, and support for the speaker.
- Control your negative emotional responses. Let's face it, linguistic barriers are challenging, and people often get frustrated or bored when faced with language differences.
- Don't laugh, even if the speakers do, at their language skills. Often they laugh nervously to relieve tension.

Adapting to an Interpreter

Although using an interpreter may seem remote right now, you may eventually communicate through someone who translates your words into another language, including sign language. If you must use an interpreter, here are a few things to remember:

- Keep your language simple. Avoid overly technical or uncommon words.
- In advance of the speech, give your interpreter an outline or script so he or she can check the meaning of any unfamiliar words. Your interpreter may also refer to it during your speech as a guide to what you will say next.
- Speak in short units, not entire paragraphs. After a sentence or two, allow the interpreter to speak.

- Look at the interpreter while he or she speaks. This encourages the audience to look at the interpreter instead of at you.
- Because it takes two to three times longer to speak this way, shorten your speech accordingly.

Remember that using interpreters is not easy, but without them, you could not communicate effectively. Consequently, work on maintaining a positive attitude throughout the speaking event. (Appendix C provides an example of a classroom speech, delivered in Spanish and interpreted into English by a fellow student. Video of this speech is also available on your book's online resources.) Here is an excerpt:

> *Cuando estaba en mi último año de Preparatoria, yo tuve buenos amigos. Nuestra amistad era muy fuerte que estábamos juntos mucho tiempo.* (When I was a senior in high school, I had some very good friends. Our friendship was so strong that we spent a lot of time together.) *Nosotros éramos como un equipo en todos los aspectos porque está-bamos en las mismas clases, hac'amos juntos nuestra tarea, practicábamos deportes y platicábamos mucho. Nosotros nunca tuvimos problemas serios.* (We were like a team in all aspects because we spent time in classes doing our homework, playing sports, and talking. We never seemed to have any serious problems.) . . .

Summary

Language is a tool that humans use to communicate with one another and build complex societies. We create words to name our cultural memories, meaning that we label those things we notice and need to know in order to survive. Passing on these labels perpetuates our cultural ideas in new generations. Languages are dynamic, and words are added, borrowed, and discontinued in response to social changes.

Words denote or stand for objects, actions, and ideas; jargon, a technical vocabulary common to members of an occupation, can confuse outsiders who don't know its meaning. More importantly, words have connotative meanings that consist of the feelings and associations that they imply. Epithets generally carry negative connotations, whereas euphemisms put negative things more positively.

Oral style contrasts with written language in several ways. It is dynamic, interactive, and engaging because speakers can use nonverbal cues to add emphasis. This style is less formal and more personalized than written language. It uses simpler, more concrete words, shorter sentences—even fragments. Repetition is a hallmark of oral style.

Your speaking effectiveness depends on how well you can put your ideas into words. Thus, there are several guidelines for using language effectively. Be concise, choose familiar words, be concrete, build in repetition, use vivid language, and select a form that's appropriate to you, the topic, the audience, and the context.

In recent years, people have become concerned about the power of words—especially those used in discriminatory ways—and have worked to create inclusive language that affirms individuals and groups and presents them in a positive light.

Finally, you may someday be in a public speaking situation where you either speak in a second language, requiring the use of an interpreter, or, more likely, where you listen to a speaker who is not a native speaker of English. In these situations, it is most important to communicate ideas rather than expect linguistic precision. When you listen to a speaker from another linguistic background, take the responsibility of listening with an open mind in a supportive manner.

STUDY AND REVIEW

Your online resources for *Public Speaking: Concepts and Skills for a Diverse Society* offer a broad range of study tools that will help you better understand the material in this chapter, complete assignments, and succeed on tests. Your online resources feature the following:

- Speech videos with critical viewing questions, speech outlines, and transcripts.
- Interactive versions of this chapter's Stop and Check activities, as well as Application and Critical Thinking Exercises.
- Speech Builder Express and InfoTrac College Edition.
- Weblinks related to chapter content.
- Study and review tools such as self-quizzes, an interactive glossary, and downloadable audio summaries.

You can access your online resources at the CourseMate for *Public Speaking: Concepts and Skills for a Diverse Society.* Log in at **http://www.cengage.com/login**, using the access code that came with your book or that you bought online at **http://www.cengagebrain.com**.

KEY TERMS

The terms below are defined in the margins throughout this chapter.

ageist language 209
alliteration 205
ambiguous word 199
antimetabole 205
archetypal symbols 207
code switching 199
concrete words 203
connotative meaning 200
denotative meaning 199
dialect 199
dismissive language 209
epithets 201
euphemisms 201
inclusive language 209
jargon 200
languages 198
metaphors 206
mixed metaphor 206
nonparallel language 209
oral style 202
personification 208
perspective taking 211
racist language 209
rhymes 205
sexist language 209
similes 206
Standard English 199
vague words 204
verbiage 203
words 198

APPLICATION AND CRITICAL THINKING EXERCISES

1. A webpage by Phil Simborg titled "Incredible Facts" (found at **weblink 12.2**) claims that the English word with the most dictionary meanings is *set*. First, come up with all the meanings of *set* that you can, and then use a dictionary to look it up. Do you agree with Simborg, or can you prove him wrong? Thumb through a print edition instead of an online dictionary, and look for other ambiguous words with more than ten meanings. (You can access this link through your CourseMate for *Public Speaking,* Chapter 12 resources.)

2. Search the Internet for the word *ebonics* or African American English (AAE). Print out at least two articles and bring them to class. In a small group, discuss one of the following questions; then share your group's conclusions with the entire class.
   - Identify some ways that AAE (ebonics) differs from Standard English.
   - What controversies swirl around AAE? Why do you think the dialect is controversial?
   - What do linguists say about the dialect?
   - What are some arguments in favor of instruction in AAE?
   - What are some arguments against instruction in AAE?

3. On the Web site The Word Spy (**weblink 12.3**), technical writer Paul McFedries shares his collection of new words in a variety of subjects, from gadgets and appliances to marriage and relationships. (You can access this link through your CourseMate for *Public Speaking,* Chapter 12 resources.) Technology has created many terms. For example, a *tweep* posts a *tweet* on Twitter; the two have a *tweetup* when they meet in the real world. Go to the site and make a list of six new words you know and six that are unfamiliar to you. Bring the list to class and share it.
4. Interview a member of an occupation that interests you, and make a list of jargon terms associated with the job (for example, carpenters, waiters, foresters, pharmacists, truckers, bankers). Discuss your list with a classmate. How many terms do you know? Which terms are unfamiliar? If you were listening to a speaker from that occupation, what would you want the speaker to do so that you would better understand the speech?
5. A speech can be informative without being interesting. Make a list of not-so-interesting topics and, working with a small group of your classmates, choose one and then think of alliteration, rhyming, repetition, metaphors, similes, or personification that could make the topic more interesting.

6. The speech archives at **weblink 12.4** give you the opportunity to listen to the greatest words ever spoken in the English language. (You can access this link through your CourseMate for *Public Speaking,* Chapter 12 resources.) Link to "Top 100 Speeches" and you'll find Lou Gehrig's 1939 farewell to baseball, General Douglas McArthur's farewell to Congress, Margaret Chase Smith's "Declaration of Conscience," and ninety-seven more. Listen to a speech of your choice and then write a paragraph explaining how the language choices contribute to the effectiveness of the speech.

7. Find a speech by a speaker who represents a culture different than your own at **weblink 12.4**. Locate the metaphors and similes in the speech. Note the similarities and differences between the metaphors of that culture and your own. (You can access this link through your CourseMate for *Public Speaking,* Chapter 12 resources.)
8. When (if ever) might you use an interpreter in the future? When might you listen to a speech delivered with the help of an interpreter? (Include televised speeches.) When (if ever) might you give a speech in a second language? When might you listen to a nonnative speaker of English?
9. If you know a second language, prepare a short speech in that language, and then work with an interpreter who will present your speech in English as you give it in your language. For example, Maria prepared and gave her speech in Italian; an Italian-speaking classmate interpreted when she gave it to the class. Paula prepared her speech in Romanian and brought her cousin to class to translate because all her classmates were monolingual.

SPEECH VIDEOS

Go to your online resources to watch and critique Uriel Plascencia deliver a speech, which Kelly Bilinski interprets. The transcript is in Appendix C and online where you'll also find an outline and video of the speech. In addition, log onto either site listed at **weblink 12.5** and view Dr. Martin Luther King, Jr.'s "I Have a Dream" speech, focusing especially on his language choices. **Weblink 12.6** lets you view Kennedy delivering his Inaugural Address. (You can access these links through your CourseMate for *Public Speaking,* Chapter 12 resources.)

Professional Speech with Commentary

INAUGURAL
John F. Kennedy[42]

President Kennedy's 1960 Inaugural speech, composed with the aid of speechwriter Ted Sorensen, is number two on many lists of 100 best speeches of the 20th century (behind King's "I Have a Dream" speech). It has become the standard to which other presidents aspire.

Vice President Johnson, Mr. Speaker, Mr. Chief Justice, President Eisenhower, Vice President Nixon, President Truman, Reverend Clergy, fellow citizens:

Because of the formality of the occasion, Kennedy begins by recognizing the dignitaries present.

We observe today not a victory of party, but a celebration of freedom—symbolizing an end, as well as a beginning—signifying renewal, as well as change. For I have sworn before you and Almighty God the same solemn oath our forebears prescribed nearly a century and three-quarters ago.

The world is very different now. For man holds in his mortal hands the power to abolish all forms of human poverty and all forms of human life. And yet the same revolutionary beliefs for which our forebears fought are still at issue around the globe—the belief that the rights of man come not from the generosity of the state, but from the hand of God.

We dare not forget today that we are the heirs of that first revolution. Let the word go forth from this time and place, to friend and foe alike, that the torch has been passed to a new generation of Americans—born in this century, tempered by war, disciplined by a hard and bitter peace, proud of our ancient heritage, and unwilling to witness or permit the slow undoing of those human rights to which this nation has always been committed, and to which we are committed today at home and around the world.

Kennedy was the youngest man elected to the office, and he was the first president born in the 20th century. His opening reaffirms the past and points toward the future.

Let every nation know, whether it wishes us well or ill, that we shall pay any price, bear any burden, meet any hardship, support any friend, oppose any foe, to assure the survival and the success of liberty.

This much we pledge—and more.

Note the elements of oral style throughout the speech: familiar words, short phrases, pauses, repetitions, and colorful imagery—especially metaphors.

To those old allies whose cultural and spiritual origins we share, we pledge the loyalty of faithful friends. United there is little we cannot do in a host of cooperative ventures. Divided there is little we can do—for we dare not meet a powerful challenge at odds and split asunder.

To those new states whom we welcome to the ranks of the free, we pledge our word that one form of colonial control shall not have passed away merely to be replaced by a far more iron tyranny. We shall not always expect to find them supporting our view. But we shall always hope to find them strongly supporting their own freedom—and to remember that, in the past, those who foolishly sought power by riding the back of the tiger ended up inside.

His repetition of the phrase, "to those . . .", sets up wave pattern with each crest addressing a different global group, building in intensity from our friends to our enemies.

To those people in the huts and villages of half the globe struggling to break the bonds of mass misery, we pledge our best efforts to help them help themselves, for whatever period is required—not because the Communists may be doing it, not because we seek their votes, but because it is right. If a free society cannot help the many who are poor, it cannot save the few who are rich.

To our sister republics south of our border, we offer a special pledge: to convert our good words into good deeds, in a new alliance for progress, to assist free men and free governments in casting off the chains of poverty. But this peaceful revolution of hope cannot become the prey of hostile powers. Let all our neighbors know that we shall join with them to oppose aggression or subversion anywhere in the Americas. And let every other power know that this hemisphere intends to remain the master of its own house.

To that world assembly of sovereign states, the United Nations, our last best hope in an age where the instruments of war have far outpaced the instruments of peace, we renew our pledge of support—to prevent it from becoming merely a forum for invective, to strengthen its shield of the new and the weak, and to enlarge the area in which its writ may run.

Finally, to those nations who would make themselves our adversary, we offer not a pledge but a request: that both sides begin anew the quest for peace, before the dark powers of destruction unleashed by science engulf all humanity in planned or accidental self-destruction.

We dare not tempt them with weakness. For only when our arms are sufficient beyond doubt can we be certain beyond doubt that they will never be employed.

But neither can two great and powerful groups of nations take comfort from our present course—both sides overburdened by the cost of modern weapons, both rightly alarmed by the steady spread of the deadly atom, yet both racing to alter that uncertain balance of terror that stays the hand of mankind's final war.

Here's an example of antimetabole.

So let us begin anew—remembering on both sides that civility is not a sign of weakness, and sincerity is always subject to proof. Let us never negotiate out of fear, but let us never fear to negotiate.

Let both sides explore what problems unite us instead of belaboring those problems which divide us.

The repetition of "let both sides . . ." is another small wave pattern.

Let both sides, for the first time, formulate serious and precise proposals for the inspection and control of arms, and bring the absolute power to destroy other nations under the absolute control of all nations.

Let both sides seek to invoke the wonders of science instead of its terrors. Together let us explore the stars, conquer the deserts, eradicate disease, tap the ocean depths, and encourage the arts and commerce.

Quotations from the Bible are common in historic addresses.

Let both sides unite to heed, in all corners of the earth, the command of Isaiah—to "undo the heavy burdens, and [to] let the oppressed go free."

And, if a beachhead of cooperation may push back the jungle of suspicion, let both sides join in creating a new endeavor—not a new balance of power, but a new world of law—where the strong are just, and the weak secure, and the peace preserved.

All this will not be finished in the first one hundred days. Nor will it be finished in the first one thousand days; nor in the life of this Administration; nor even perhaps in our lifetime on this planet. But let us begin.

In your hands, my fellow citizens, more than mine, will rest the final success or failure of our course. Since this country was founded, each generation of Americans has been summoned to give testimony to its national loyalty. The graves of young Americans who answered the call to service surround the globe.

This is another Biblical quotation.

Now the trumpet summons us again—not as a call to bear arms, though arms we need—not as a call to battle, though embattled we are—but a call to bear the burden of a long twilight struggle, year in and year out, "rejoicing in hope; patient in tribulation," a struggle against the common enemies of man: tyranny, poverty, disease, and war itself.

Rhetorical questions invite the audience to support his vision.

Can we forge against these enemies a grand and global alliance, North and South, East and West, that can assure a more fruitful life for all mankind? Will you join in that historic effort?

In the long history of the world, only a few generations have been granted the role of defending freedom in its hour of maximum danger. I do not shrink from this responsibility—I welcome it. I do not believe that any of us would exchange places with any other people or any other generation.

The energy, the faith, the devotion which we bring to this endeavor will light our country and all who serve it. And the glow from that fire can truly light the world.

And so, my fellow Americans, ask not what your country can do for you; ask what you can do for your country.

My fellow citizens of the world, ask not what America will do for you, but what together we can do for the freedom of man.

Finally, whether you are citizens of America or citizens of the world, ask of us here the same high standards of strength and sacrifice which we ask of you. With a good conscience our only sure reward, with history the final judge of our deeds, let us go forth to lead the land we love, asking His blessing and His help, but knowing that here on earth God's work must truly be our own.

Five repetitions of the word "ask," developed in different ways, lead to the emotional climax of his speech.

CHAPTER 13

THIS CHAPTER WILL HELP YOU

- Explain the purpose of presentation aids
- Create a plan for visual, audio, and multimedia aids
- Choose specific presentation aids, including three-dimensional and two-dimensional visuals and audio resources
- Determine the advantages and disadvantages of using various presentation technologies
- Apply principles of visual design
- Understand guidelines for using visual aids

Presentation Aids

IN HER SPEECHES, Edith Widder, founder of the Ocean Research & Conservation Association, takes her listeners "on a trip to an alien world"—not to a distant planet, but to the delicate ecosystems of the deepest oceans where glowing animals live in "the weird, wonderful world of bioluminescence."[1] She says words alone are "totally inadequate" to convey her ideas, so she incorporates photographs, video clips, cartoons, and a live demonstration to show dozens of examples of sea creatures that light up when danger approaches. Watch her speech at **weblink 13.1.** You can access this link through your CourseMate for *Public Speaking,* Chapter 13 resources.

As you plan your **presentation aids**, keep in mind the definition of the word "aid," which means to help, assist, or give support. Consequently, presentation aids—whether in visual, audio, or multimedia form—are not just decorative additions to your speeches. Used well, they are a powerful means of support that assists or helps your audience engage, understand, and remember information. Used poorly, and audiences think you either lack the skill to create and present them well, or you didn't take the time to prepare carefully.[2]

presentation aids Visual, audio, and multimedia support that helps audiences understand and remember information.

This chapter discusses the purpose, planning, and principles for designing and using visual, audio, and multimedia support. Most of the chapter focuses on visual support, but it also suggests ways to use audio and multimedia resources as well.

Purposes for Presentation Aids

Presentation aids exist for the audience; their major purpose is to help listeners engage the information and make sense of it by processing it through more than one modality. Using them allows you to appeal to a variety of learning preferences[3] and adapt to audience diversity by providing sensory support for listeners who learn best by seeing, hearing, or doing.

Allan Paivio, a cognitive psychologist, developed the **dual coding theory (DCT)**, which says our brains process material through two separate but parallel and interconnected pathways or codes: imagery and language that we can use separately or together. That is, you can hear words alone or see images without explanations and create meanings, or you can use **dual processing** by combining words and images.[4] (See Figure 13.1.) Researchers have found that hearing words supported by relevant images (such as a map during a talk about a war or a graph during a speech about grade inflation) is easier to process and creates better retention of material than just seeing decorative images (such as clip art or photographs chosen just for their attractiveness[5]) or hearing words while trying to read written words on a visual.[6]

dual coding theory (DCT) theory that our brains process material two ways: through language and through images

dual processing combining words and images to create meanings

The right visual or audio support is vital for presenting certain types of information. So after you prepare your content outline, carefully look it over and identify specific places in the speech that are difficult to express in words alone.[7] Speeches about artists or composers come to mind. For instance, images of Jackson Pollock's paintings were essential for Andrea's speech about the artist's career. Ysenia's audience better understood Hector Berlioz's music only because she played clips from his symphonies. Many complex or technical topics require visual support. In fact, one author says, "Much of modern science can no longer be communicated in print."[8] Casey's speech about artificial gills at the end of this chapter is understandable because of his aids, and the facial expressions of gorillas come to life, not just through words, but through supplementary photographs. A math concept is more easily understood when a formula is written out on a whiteboard, and the results of a campus survey make sense when shown on a pie graph. Demonstrations, similarly, are best understood with visuals. How well could you explain the process of folding a flag in words alone?

Dual Coding	
Language system	Visual system
words	images
More left brain	More right brain
Together → Dual Processing	

Figure 13.1
Dual Coding Theory

A combination of visuals and words can also emphasize or reinforce important concepts, but only when the visual is relevant to the topic, not merely decorative.[9] The mullet hairstyle, for example, is familiar enough that Philip could probably get by just describing it; however, drawings of mullets throughout history added greatly to his presentation. Consider also, where a visual might emphasize or reinforce an idea, show your speech structure, support your concepts, or show relationships between your ideas.[10] Stephanie used a list to preview the three types of listening she would describe during her speech.

Finally, well-placed aids can relieve the monotony of words alone and help maintain audience attention. Consequently, look for places where attention might lag and supporting materials could draw listeners' focus back onto the speech. For her speech on advergaming (found at the end of Chapter 6), Kelsey added photographs of several advergames as she discussed them; later in the speech, she showed a photograph of an expert she was quoting.

In summary, identify the purpose of each visual by asking: Which learning preferences do these visuals support? Is it necessary? Is it interesting but not essential? Is the image relevant to the words, or is it merely decoration? Will it help maintain attention? In each instance, make sure the intellectual content of the visual is challenging.[11]

Begin Your Presentation Aid Plan

Review your speech outline, and decide which ideas must be supplemented by a presentation aid.

What learning styles could you incorporate into the speech?

____

What elements of your speech are difficult to convey in words alone?

____

For which ideas would visual or audio support be helpful, but not essential?

____

What ideas need emphasis?

____

Where in the speech might the audience's attention lag?

____

Use Speech Builder Express to complete this step of the process; its prompts include lists of possible visual aids that you can select. Click on "Presentation Aids" in the left-hand navigation bar.

Planning Your Presentation Aids

After you have identified the concepts you need to support, the next step is to plan which aids to use. Your topic and purpose, the occasion, your audience, and the type of presentation technology available make some types of support better than others. The key is to choose the *best* support, not just the kind that's easiest to create. This section will discuss three basic types of aids: three-dimensional visuals, two-dimensional visuals, and audio or video resources that you can use separately or integrate into multimedia packages.

Three-dimensional Visuals

Three-dimensional visuals in the form of objects, models, or people are helpful when listeners need to experience a subject or see it demonstrated.

Objects

What coach would even try to convey the finer points of shooting free throws without using a basketball? What camp counselor would explain a craft without using actual materials? Some subjects require seeing as well as hearing; consequently, three-dimensional objects are essential, especially in informative speeches that demonstrate a process.

Your topic and the setting determine whether or not an object is realistic. For example, what object could you use for a speech about mortgages? Pandemic preparedness? Grief counseling on campus? However, a little creative thinking applied to other topics can result in ideas for communicating through objects that can add touch, smell, or taste to a speech. Here are some examples:

- Remi brought in a typical tray of food waste, borrowed from the school cafeteria.
- Shelly gave each listener a tuft of unprocessed wool and a piece of yarn to touch as she discussed yarn making.
- Hiroko gave everyone a pair of chopsticks. To make sure everyone could see what she was demonstrating, she used a document camera to project images of her hands holding the chopsticks correctly.

Sue O'Donnell

Casey opened the lid on a bottle of soda to demonstrate a scientific principle—Henry's Law—during his speech on artificial gills.

Some objects are inappropriate or even prohibited. For instance, firearms are illegal in classrooms, and it's unwise to use live animals. Furthermore, some objects are impractical because they're too expensive or too hard to get. Marko couldn't bring his motorcycle into the classroom. (Fortunately, his classmates were willing to walk to a nearby parking lot where he spoke from the seat of his bike.) Bottom line: objects must be legal, accessible, and practical. They should be large enough for everyone to see, or individual listeners should each have an object.

Models

When an object is impractical, a **model** or realistic facsimile can substitute. Scaled-down models depict large objects, such as buildings, dinosaurs, or cars; enlarged models increase the size of small objects such as atoms, ants, or eyeballs. Science teachers often use models of an enlarged human cell or a scaled-down solar system to illustrate scientific concepts. Architects present scale models to decision-makers who decide whether or not to fund a proposed building.

model a facsimile of an object you can't easily bring to the speech

Getting a model can be challenging. You might be able to borrow one from a professional, or you might make your own. For example, one student spoke about his summer job as a pyrotechnician (a fireworks display technician). Because federal regulations and common sense prevented him from bringing explosives into the classroom, he made a model of the spherical explosive device, complete with a fuse. He supplemented the model with several objects: the actual cylinder into which he dropped lit explosives while on the job and the jumpsuit and safety helmet he wore at work.

People

Friends, volunteers from the audience, even your own body are often good ways to demonstrate a concept. For example, Jacinda, an Alaskan of Eskimo origin, used two volunteers from the audience to demonstrate the "stick pull," a native sport. She also wore a T-shirt with the letters W-E-I-O, which stands for "World Eskimo-Indian Olympics." You might incorporate the audience as a whole by asking them to participate in some sort of exercise.

In summary, three-dimensional objects, models, or people are almost indispensable in certain types of speeches, especially demonstration speeches. However, when it's unrealistic to use them, many other types of two-dimensional visuals are available.

Two-Dimensional Visuals

In many cases, two-dimensional visuals are more practical and appropriate than actual objects or models. These types of visuals fall into two categories: text-based and image-based visuals.

Text-based Visuals

text-based visuals carry meaning in the written words rather than in visual images

Text-based visuals, such as lists, rely on written words although you can incorporate art in a minor way. Without the art, the message still comes through, but without the words, it does not. Lists are popular for chronological speeches because stages or steps lend themselves to listing. Listing key words or phrases can also summarize the main points of topically arranged speeches. For example, Kelsey used a list to preview her main points, as shown in Figure 13.2.

A recent study asked students what they thought was the most difficult thing about creating text-based slides and what they disliked about text-based visuals. Typical challenges included, "To put in the most important points in a concise manner." Typical dislikes were "too much text" and "too many lines."[12] Students also disliked having the presenter read directly from the slides.

six-by-six rule limit information to six lines, six words per line

image-based visuals carry meaning in visual images; written words are secondary

Text-based visuals are most effective when you keep them simple and frame your ideas in words, phrases, or short sentences instead of sentences or paragraphs. Although research does not prove the **six-by-six rule**,[13] many experts recommend that you use no more than six lines, no more than six words per line. In addition, always discuss every point in your list.

Image-based visuals rely on some sort of figure or picture to convey meaning. They include charts drawings, diagrams, and maps, graphs, and photographs.

Charts

flowcharts show the order or directional flow in which processes occur; may simply be a series of labeled shapes and arrows

organizational charts show hierarchies and relationships

Flowcharts show the order in which processes occur by using arrows to indicate directional movement. Flowcharts can include drawings (pictorial flowcharts), or they may simply be a series of labeled shapes and arrows. Casey used a pictorial flowchart showing how an underwater breathing apparatus takes oxygen from the water to create "artificial gills." (Read his speech at the end of the chapter, or see the flowchart in his video, which is on your online chapter resources.) **Organizational charts** show hierarchies

Figure 13.2
Kelsey created this list to show the alliterated main points of her speech. (Her speech is featured in Chapter 6.)

Advergaming is . . .

- **Evaluative**
- **Efficient**
- **Effective**
- **Engaging**

and relationships. A family tree, for example, depicts relationships among family members.

Diagrams, Drawings, and Maps

Diagrams are line drawings or graphic designs that explain, rather than realistically depict, an object or a process. Drawings or diagrams can stand alone or be added to lists or other visuals as supplementary support. Substitute them for illegal firearms, inaccessible motorcycles, buildings that are too large or insects that are too small to bring into your classroom. Use diagrams to illustrate processes such as the acid rain cycle or the circulatory system. Consider showing a cartoon that perfectly illustrates your point and adds humor to your talk, but make sure you read the caption to the audience. In the introduction to his artificial gills speech, Casey showed a drawing of the cartoon character "Aquaman," displaying his name in large letters.

Dirk Ercken/Shutterstock

Casey displayed a photograph of an aquatic diving beetle on a PowerPoint slide. He could have substituted a drawing or a diagram of the beetle that were also available online.

Maps are drawings that visually represent spaces such as the heavens, the earth, or the weather. There are several kinds of maps:

- **Political maps** show borders between nations and states. These maps become outdated with changing political developments. For example, any world map dated before 2011 has obsolete sections, because a new country, South Sudan, was added in July of that year.
- **Geographic maps** show mountains, deserts, lowlands, and other natural features. They are updated only when remote or previously unexplored territories, such as Antarctica or the ocean floor, are mapped.
- Other maps include a building's blueprints and floor plan, maps of routes between two points, city maps, and campus maps.

diagrams drawings or designs that explain, rather than realistically depict, an object or process

political maps show current borders for states and nations; can be outdated in a fast-changing world

geographic maps show mountains, deserts, and other natural features; not easily outdated

Photographs

Although photographs show objects, people, and scenes, the saying "A picture is worth a thousand words" is not necessarily true. Pictures are of little value if they are merely decorative or if your audience is unable to see them. However, many students have successfully used photographs. NamKy found photographs of Hanoi to illustrate his speech on the capital of his country, Vietnam. For his speech on aqualungs, Casey projected a large, high-resolution photograph of a beetle that scientists used as a model for aqualung development.

To use photographs successfully, select only high-resolution images. (**Weblink 13.2** links you to two online sources for high-quality photographs. You can access this link through your CourseMate for *Public Speaking*, Chapter 13 resources.) Also find a means to display your photos so that everyone can see them. Avoid passing small photos around; only the person closest to you sees all the pictures and hears them explained, but the last person sees them long after they have been described. Put the source of the photo on the visual, and include it in your list of references.

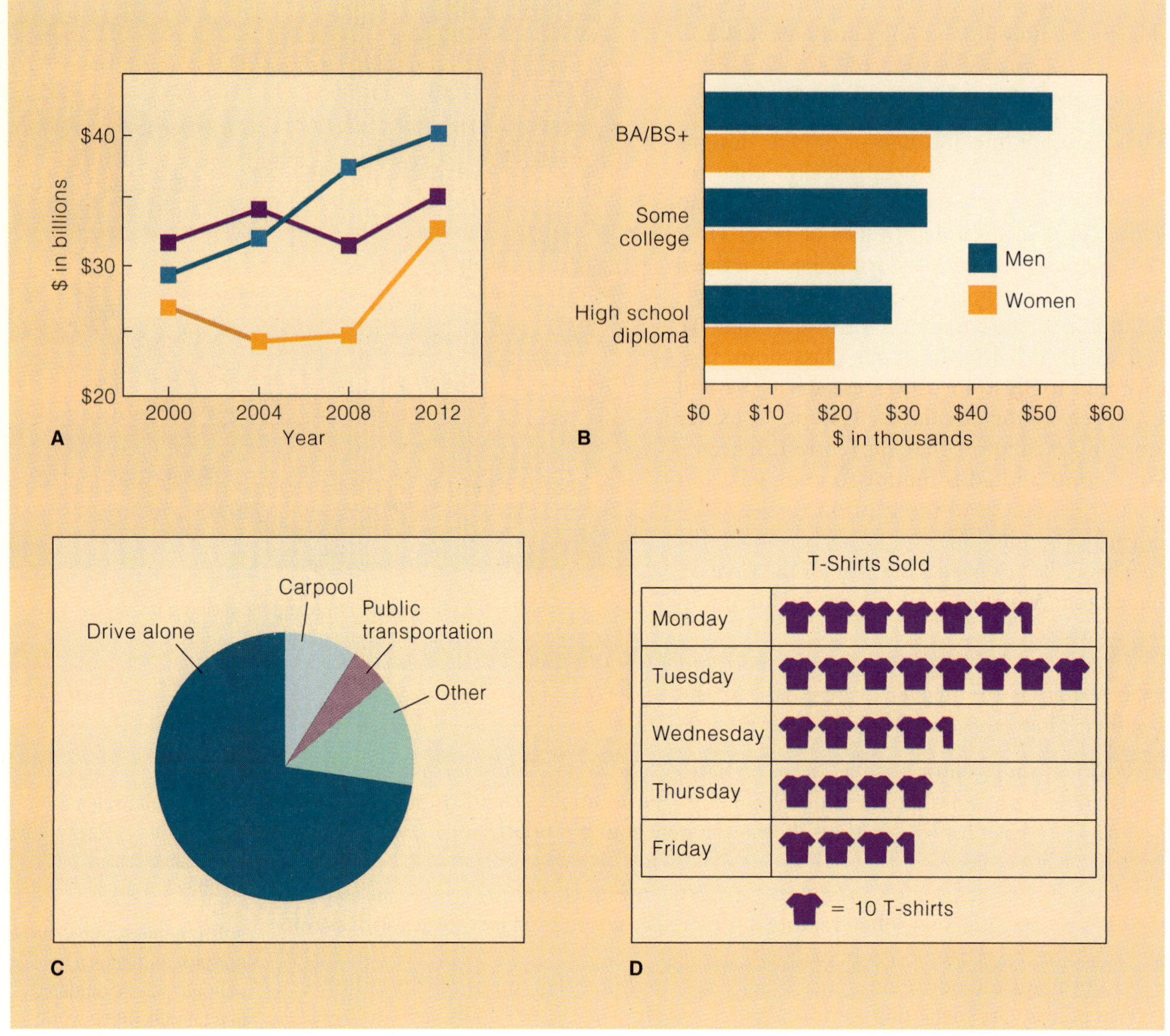

Figure 13.4
Graphs Four major types include (a) a line graph, (b) a bar graph, (c) a pie graph, and (d) a pictograph.

Graphs

As Chapter 8 pointed out, speeches full of numerical data are often boring, difficult to follow, and impossible to remember without some sort of visual. Depicting your material in one of four types of graphs allows your listeners to see how your numbers relate to one another.

line graphs display in a linear form one or more variables that fluctuate over a time period

bar graphs compare data from several groups by using bands of various lengths

1. **Line graphs** present information in linear form; they are best for showing variables that fluctuate over time, such as changes in college tuition over two decades. They are also good for showing the relationship of two or more variables, such as a comparison of state and private school averages during the same period. (Figure 13.4a shows fluctuation in the funding of three projects over a six-year period.)
2. **Bar graphs** compare data from several groups such as the salaries of men and women with differing educational levels. (See Figure 13.4b.)

3. **Pie graphs** are circular graphs that are especially good for showing divisions of a population or parts of the whole. A speech on carpooling or public transportation might feature the pie graph in Figure 13.4c, which depicts ways typical Americans get to work.
4. **Picture graphs** or **pictographs**, the least common of the four types, are especially effective for data related to objects or people. Each picture represents a certain number of individual cases, as Figure 13.4d demonstrates.

pie graphs represent parts of the whole or divisions of a population by circles divided into portions

picture graphs or **pictographs** present data in pictures, each representing a certain number of individual cases

In summary, three-dimensional objects and text- or image-based visuals are useful in visually oriented cultures. However, in some cases, recordings of sounds or images are even more effective support.

Video and Audio Recordings

Audio and video support requires extra preparation and planning, but these resources can help you better convey certain types of information.

Audio Resources

Audio support is particularly important with music- or sound-related topics. Portable electronic keyboards, other musical instruments, MP3 players, and so on let your audience hear the sounds you are explaining, whether your topic is a musical style, a specific instrument, or a particular composer's works. Although less common, you can effectively use sounds other than music. Before her speech on whales, for instance, Mary Beth played a recording of a whale song and asked her listeners to identify the source of the sound. Use your creativity to think of other ways to incorporate short clips, such as sounds from nature or conversations, to enhance your presentation.

Video Resources

You can find massive amounts of video resources, including clips from television shows, feature films, advertisements, and home videos. By carefully selecting short segments to illustrate your points, you can clarify ideas dramatically and memorably, as these examples demonstrate:

- Lisa made the *Guinness Book of Records* for being part of the largest tap dancing group ever assembled at one time for a performance. As she explained ways to get listed in the famous record book, she used a 15-second video clip that her mother had recorded.
- Effie used a scene from the film, *The Importance of Being Earnest*, to illustrate a particular type of territory violation.
- Andrew discussed the differences between men's and women's gestures. In his introduction he played a 15-second commercial showing a male and a female interacting. Then, as he discussed each point, he again played it again, this time with the sound turned off, pausing at various places to illustrate a specific point.

These students succeeded because they preplanned carefully. The short clips they selected illustrated, rather than substituted for their words; they selected the scene in advance; and they planned exactly when to start and stop the visual. (On the downside, Alex's attempt to use a clip from the Internet backfired because it took the video forever to load.)

Enabling listeners to see or hear your topic is important in many public speaking settings. Indeed, it's almost essential in some presentations. Skillful construction and use of visuals distinguish good speakers from adequate ones, and as you learn to work with visuals, your competence will increase. Presentation aids are especially useful with diverse audiences, as the Diversity in Practice Box shows.

Continue Your Presentation Aids Plan

Log on to Speech Builder Express and click on "Presentation Aids" in the left-hand navigation bar for prompts that list possible visual or audio aids you can select, or use the form below to continue your plan:

I need this type of aid ________________ for this idea ________________

I need this type of aid ________________ for this idea ________________

I need this type of aid ________________ for this idea ________________

I need this type of aid ________________ for this idea ________________

Next, using a separate sheet for each aid you plan, make a preliminary sketch of the material. Then edit out every unnecessary word or image.

Visual Aids and Culture

Although technology has changed across the millennia, visual aids have a long history. In oral cultures, speakers have used objects to clarify ideas, help listeners better understand abstract concepts, and dramatize words. For instance, in the sixth century BCE, the Hebrew prophet Ezekiel created a model of the city of Jerusalem and then used a toy army and siege machines to destroy it, symbolizing what the future held.[14] In the days of the Roman republic, noted orators such as Cicero drew his audience's attention to statues and other landmarks in the Forum.[15]

Today, communicators in pluralistic settings, such as international marketers[16] and presenters who must speak in a second language, know the value of visual support. In the classroom, visual aids help nonnative speakers of English understand and be understood in the following ways:

- Nonnative speakers of English often worry that their English is not clear enough or that they will make mistakes when they speak. Putting key words on visuals enables listeners to understand accented English better because they can see as well as hear the word.
- Providing something for the audience to see puts the focus—at least part of the time—on the visual rather than the speaker. This may lessen a nonnative speaker's anxiety.
- Visuals, such as words on a list or figures on a graph, can function as cue cards to remind speakers of their main points—another strategy for minimizing the fear of forgetting.
- Seeing key words, diagrams, and other visuals can help nonnative speakers in the audience. They may be unfamiliar with specific terms, but they can understand the diagrams and visuals and jot down the important words to study later.

In our image-saturated culture, many audiences now expect visual support. Consequently, a good presentation aid package that skillfully uses available technology is culturally appropriate in a diverse society.

Planning the Presentation Technology

The technology for displaying visuals is big business; in fact, giant corporations exist solely to provide machines and materials for creating and displaying visuals. This section covers a number of common ways to display visual aids, along with their advantages and disadvantages.

Presentation Software and LCD Projectors

LCD projectors connect directly to a computer and project what appears on the monitor onto a screen. If you create visuals using a **presentation software program** such as PowerPoint, you'll need a data projector. This technology has so many advantages that it's rapidly making slides and overhead projectors nearly obsolete. The Slide Sorter View feature lets you see your entire deck of slides at a glance, and you can easily edit each slide. You can insert hyperlinks to add audio and video support. During your speech, you simply launch your presentation and move from slide to slide with a click of the mouse. When you discuss material with no visual support, use the "B" key to bring up a blank slide and then return to your presentation with another click.

presentation software programs computer software to create a package of lists, tables, graphs, and clip art

Unfortunately, this technology is often used poorly. For example, an article in *Technical Communication* reports that millions of speakers turn out trillions of slides annually.[17] However, many slides are so ineffective that they detract from the message—but the problem lies in the creators, not the technology. Think of the presentations you've seen. How many were well-done or memorable? To improve your skills with these programs, follow these guidelines:

- Plan the package as a whole. Write out the words you'll use for your text-based visuals, and sketch the visual-based images beforehand. Mentally identify the purpose for everything you include.
- Then go back and remove every unnecessary word or image.
- Choose only high-resolution images that will display clearly.
- Create your text-based slides in black and white at first, and then add color sparingly to emphasize significant ideas.
- Rehearse at least once without the slides to make sure that they don't substitute for your message.

Document Cameras and Overhead Projectors

A fairly recent development in projectors, **document cameras** (also known as visual presenters) have been called "the 21st-century overhead projector"[18] because they are like a scanner, microscope, whiteboard, computer, and projector rolled into one. Some units are compact enough to fold into a notebook-sized carrying case. These high-resolution cameras let you project photographs, slides, three-dimensional objects, a document you've created, and so on. You can zoom in on a painting or enlarge a small object such as a dime or even a microscopic object, so that tiny details are visible.[19]

document cameras high-resolution cameras that display documents and three-dimensional objects

Just a few years ago, overhead projectors were everywhere, and they're still available in many places. These projectors have many advantages. Transparencies are simple and inexpensive to make; they are easy to store and transport. You can draw freehand or photocopy a printed image directly onto a transparency, or you can insert a transparency into your printer and print directly from your computer. However, you cannot create multimedia links, and the transparencies, once made, are not easily revised.

Can a Visual Be Unethical?

Speakers have an ethical responsibility to do their listeners no harm. This includes any behavior that could place listeners at risk for physical or psychological injury or harm. Read the following true examples from classroom speeches and then discuss with your classmates some ethical questions they raise:

- One student killed, skinned, and cleaned a live fish in front of her stunned classmates.[20]
- Another opened his speech on terrorism creatively and dramatically with a role-play scenario. Just as he got up to speak, a couple of his friends, dressed in fatigues and carrying realistic but fake automatic weapons, burst into the classroom and ordered everyone to hit the floor. He didn't anticipate the reactions: Some classmates screamed, others cried. One person, an immigrant from a country where terrorist incidents were common, hyperventilated. Someone called 9-1-1, and she went to the emergency room. Class ended immediately.
- Students have displayed visuals of aborted fetuses.
- One student showed pornographic photographs to illustrate her speech about pornography.
- For his speech on dogs that were half-wolf and half-dog, Denis actually brought in his nervous wolf dog. Wary listeners focused on the animal, not on Denis's words.

Questions

1. Does any example fail to meet the standard of doing no harm, whether physically or psychologically? If so, which one(s)? Why?
2. Try to think from the speakers' point of view. Why might each speaker have chosen that particular aid?
3. What presentation aids could each speaker have substituted?
4. How persuasive do you find shocking or offensive visual aids that stir negative emotions?

If you have questions about the appropriateness or safety of any presentation aid you intend to use, consult your instructor in advance of your speech.

The following guidelines apply to both document cameras and overhead projectors:

- Before you begin speaking, turn on the machine and adjust the focus. Then turn it off until you're ready to use your visual.
- To draw your listener's attention to some part of your visual, point on the visual, not the screen. Place a pointed object where you want listeners to focus, and then move your hand away from the projector.
- If you use a visual repeatedly but want to highlight material each time, place a blank transparency over the material and underline, mark, or write on the blank, using wet erase markers. This keeps your originals clean, and you can easily clean your markings off the top sheet.

Chalkboards or Whiteboards

Chalkboards or whiteboards are standard equipment in most educational settings because of their many advantages. They're great for explaining unfolding processes, such as math problems. They also encourage informality, which is appropriate in some

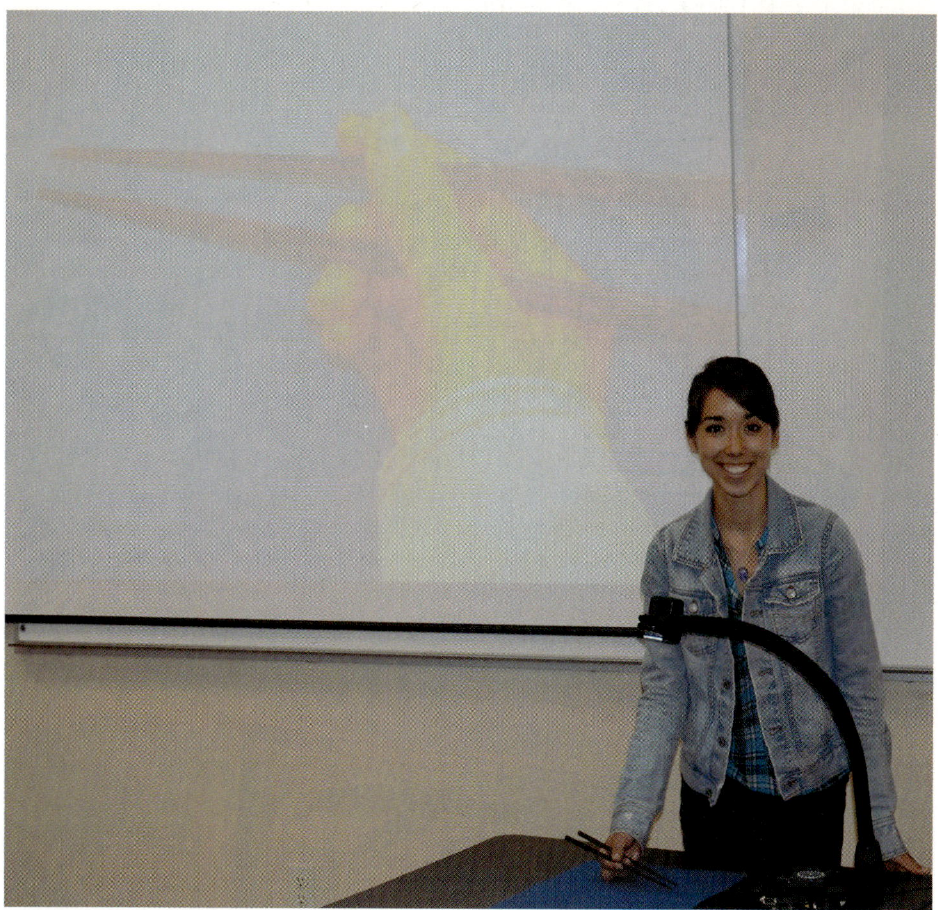

Sue O'Connell

Document cameras are more versatile than many other types of presentation technology because they can easily display written material, photographs, drawings, and objects.

contexts. Finally, they are useful in settings that include speaker-audience interactions such as brainstorming sessions.[21]

Unfortunately, boards have three major drawbacks. (1) You can't prepare your visual beforehand, and unprepared visuals create additional anxiety if you like to have everything ready in advance. (2) Most people don't write well on boards, so the visuals look unprofessional. (3) You must turn your back on your audience while you write on the board. This is probably the major drawback of boards in general.

Boards continue to evolve. **Interactive whiteboards** can now connect to a document camera or to a computer with markup software. You can then use "electronic markers" or even your finger to overwrite material on the board. Finally, you can save your markups to files and later retrieve, email, or print them out.[22]

interactive whiteboards connect to other technology; you can overwrite material and then save your markups

Poster Boards and Flip Charts

For convenience and economy, poster board is a low-tech option. Because it's readily available in a variety of weights and colors at campus bookstores and art supply stores, posters are widely used. Even members of Congress display information on poster board. In the workplace, people who deliver the same speech over and over, such as financial planners, also use professionally prepared posters. Posters are effective with relatively small audiences, but at greater distances they're difficult to see, and small details don't show up. In addition, you need an easel to hold your posters

Traveling and Talking

Today, thousands of professionals use visuals while abroad. Engineers, marketers, physicians, and computer specialists, who once took a required college speech course, are often surprised to find themselves speaking internationally. Someday you may join their numbers. Many have found that taking along visual aids prepared here presents some challenges.

Business writer Dave Zielinski[23] describes "secrets and strategies of speakers on the go." In the light of current security regulations, on-the-road presenters must consider customs agents' or security guards' perspectives on their equipment. Even a collapsible presentation pointer can look suspicious in carry-on luggage. Moreover, expensive equipment tempts thieves in some places. Customs regulations also vary. One sales representative had to post a bond equaling 30 percent of her equipment's cost as a guarantee that she would return with it and not sell it in the country. Overall, Zielinski's advice is: don't assume anything, and have a contingency plan.

during your speech. These tips will help you make more professional-looking posters:

- Use rulers or yardsticks to ensure straight lines and avoid a "loving-hands-at-home" look.
- Use more than one color to attract and hold interest.
- For a more professional look, use adhesive letters or computer created text.
- To protect your posters from becoming bent or soiled, carry them in a portfolio, or cover them with plastic when you transport them.

flip charts tablets you prepare in advance or create on the spot; turn to a new page or tear off and display pages as you finish them

Flip charts are oversized tablets, lined or unlined; they are common in businesses and other organizations but rare in college classrooms. Their name reflects the fact that you can turn pages from one to another. The paper they're made of varies from tablet thickness to stiffer weights. Larger charts work well in conference rooms; smaller ones work well for presentations to just a few listeners.

Flip charts can function like a chalkboard or whiteboard, especially in brainstorming-type situations where you interact with your audience. For example, you might ask listeners to contribute ideas that you later incorporate into your talk. Tear off the lists you create together, and pin or tape them to the wall. When you use a flip chart this way, you must overcome disadvantages similar to those you faced with a whiteboard. Your writing may be messy, and writing on the chart causes you to turn your back on the audience. Many presenters ask a second person to do the writing.

Use flip charts to "build" a diagram in front of the audience. In advance, lightly draw the entire visual in pencil. Then, during your presentation, trace over the lines for a professional-looking diagram that appears to be done on the spot. This way, you can be sure that all the words are spelled correctly beforehand, and you can use the chart as a giant prompt card.

If you repeat the same presentation for different audiences, prepare your visuals on heavier-weight flip chart and use them much as you would use a series of posters, exposing each new visual as you discuss it. The separate visuals will stay in order. In addition, because the cover is stiff, the tablet can stand alone on a table, which makes it a useful display method when other equipment is unavailable.[24]

Handouts

Brochures, pamphlets, photocopies, or other handouts free audiences from having to take extensive notes and give them details they can study later.[25] Handouts can also provide supplementary information you don't have time to cover in your speech. One student distributed professionally made brochures from his campus health services at the end of his health-related speech; another distributed a photocopied diagram illustrating an origami project. Handouts are common in business settings; for example, sales representatives commonly give brochures to potential customers.

Your primary challenge with handouts is to make sure they supplement, not replace, your message. You want your audience to listen to you, not just read the handout. To use them more effectively, do the following:

- Distribute the handout, face down, before you begin speaking; then, when you discuss the material on it, ask your listeners to turn it over.
- Mark the points you want to emphasize with a letter or number so you can easily direct listeners to specific places on the handout. For example, a speaker who distributes a diagram showing how to groom a dog could highlight one area with an "A," a second area with a "B," and a third with a "C" and then draw the listeners' attention to each place as she discussed it.
- Speakers, especially in workplace training sessions, often provide blanks on the handouts for listeners to fill in during the speech; others provide space for notes.
- Put identical material on a slide or transparency and project it as you speak. Highlight the information you want them to find on their handout.
- If the handout provides supplementary information only, distribute it at the end of the speech.

In summary, today's presentation technologies range from high-tech LCD projectors and computer-generated slides to low-tech handwritten flip charts and posters, providing a range of options for displaying visual materials. Effective speakers know how to select and use the types that work best, given their topic and the situation.

Continue Your Presentation Plan

With your visual and audio plan in mind, assess the equipment that is available for your classroom speech. Try to imagine yourself using the various types of display technology during your speech.

- List the presentation technologies available in your classroom: ________________________________
- Which technologies will best display your visual and audio materials? ________________________________

Apply Proven Design Principles

Because of the prevalence of presentation aids, researchers are studying the effects of specific design features on audiences. Not surprisingly, they have found that certain fonts and background color combinations can distract audiences; in addition, sound effects and letters that are too small interfere with audience comprehension.[26] To avoid negative effects on your listeners, follow some basic guidelines for simple, well-designed visuals that use fonts and color wisely.

Design Your Slides

Many books and online resources describe ways to design professional looking, aesthetically pleasing visuals. **Weblink 13.3** links to websites, including Presentation Zen, that provide excellent guidance on designing and using presentation aids. You can access this link through your CourseMate for *Public Speaking*, Chapter 13 resources. Here are four common design principles:

1. *Simplicity*:[27] Professionals such as Garr Reynolds of Presentation Zen and Jim Endicott (Practically Speaking box) put simplicity at the top of their list. Simplify by limiting yourself to one idea per visual and by eliminating everything that does not contribute to the message. Minimize bullet points and text. Keep transitions and animation simple.
2. *Repetition*:[28] Decide on a theme and use the same design elements (fonts, colors, and so on) throughout all the visuals. That is, if you use one font for your title on the first visual, use it on every visual. Do likewise for the subtitle and text fonts. And limit yourself to a couple of complementary fonts such as Candara and Candara bold.[29]
3. *Contrast*: Add visual interest by contrasting elements such as colors or formatting. A variety of formatting features are useful. For instance, centering the title, underlining the subtitle, and bulleting the points can help your audience better see the relationships among ideas. Using boldfaced formatting makes letters show up better on slides. And attributes such as italicizing can highlight and emphasize specific ideas, but use these features sparingly, or the impact will be lost.
4. *Spacing*: Balance your material across the entire visual, but leave plenty of negative (unfilled) space. Many designers recommend the "Rule of Thirds," a principle that artists and photographers use. Divide your visual into thirds horizontally and then vertically. You'll end up with nine areas of the same size. Place important elements along the lines or on the places where they intersect. For additional information and many excellent examples, do an Internet search for "rule of thirds PowerPoint."

Choose a Readable Font

Whether you create your visuals on poster board or use a computer program, *readability* should be your primary concern, so choose a font your audience can read easily. As you consider the hundreds of available fonts, keep in mind some basic tips.

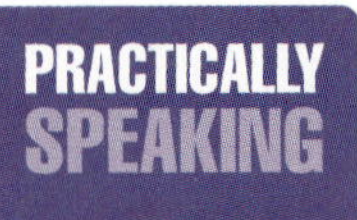

Consult a Consultant

Jim Endicott is a nationally recognized presentation consultant, designer, speaker and award-winning author.

You specialize in "professional presentation messaging." What is that? Today, most organizational communicators "give" a presentation. Unfortunately, mechanical, presenter-focused speakers rarely consider something more important—did anyone actually "get" their message? "Giving" presentations is about slides, bullets, clip art, and projectors. The "getting" piece deals with how the underlying message is shaped to cause an audience to internalize it at a deeper level and take action.

When we grasp that distinction, we can communicate messages that resonate more effectively with the hearts and minds of busy people.

What's the biggest mistake people make in creating and using visual aids? Many presenters have one approach. They pound out screen after screen of text-heavy slides supplemented by a few charts and poor-quality images. These slides then become a crutch that changes the nature of communication. Take away their visuals and most presenters tend to communicate more conversationally. Put them in front of a screen of bullet slides and they often become rigid, mechanical, and impersonal.

What types of visual or audio support is more effective? Audiences reward creativity. They also desire variety. *All* bullets, *all* videos, or *all* charts is a recipe for intellectual and relational disengagement. There are many options: props, video interviews with participants, brief voice-over or audio elements, segments from movies, or on-screen demos of websites. Creative presenters also find ways to use the audience as a visual aid. These approaches take more preparation but produce significantly higher results.

What major design principles do you emphasize in your workshops?

Less is always more. Only put on screen what listeners can assimilate in 7–8 seconds. Too many words force them to choose between reading and listening—they can't do both.

Use less text. Text information is processed on the left side of the brain and rarely moves into long-term memory. The left brain is also most defense-intensive. Never wrap the point into a second line on a bulleted slide. Never utilize sub-bullets, which are typically too small to be read. Presenters use them to "give" information, but audiences don't "get" anything more.

Use images not words. The presentation medium functions most effectively when used to orchestrate simple graphical elements, video, or other visually rich talking points. Presenters need to be better storytellers and less story-readers.

How do you coach people to effectively use their visual aids? We work on specific strategies. Images should transition on screen without fanfare and unfold as a by-product of the speaker's words. We try to take the emphasis away from supporting technologies and put it back on the presenter's unfolding story where it belongs. Know when to turn PowerPoint off. The presenter, the technology, and the visual information should be a well-orchestrated and seamless dance that beckons audiences to join in.

Questions

1. Describe a presenter you've seen who was so tied to technology that the message was lost on the audience.
2. Endicott says, "Audiences reward creativity." What does this mean to you?
3. Describe how the visuals you are planning for your next speech will help your listeners "get" your message instead of helping your "give" it.
4. Design a visual package that illustrates the "well-orchestrated and seamless dance" between you, your technology, your visual information, and your audience.

1. Use title case (Capitalize the First Letter of the Major Words) or sentence case (Capitalize only the words you'd capitalize in a sentence), and avoid using all capitals.
2. Although researchers have not established that one type of font is better than another, they have found that readers prefer **serif fonts** (with cross lines at the top and

serif font a font with cross lines at the top and bottom of letters

sans serif font a simple font with no cross lines on each letter

bottom of letters) for handouts,[30] but **sans serif fonts** (with no cross lines) work well on PowerPoint slides.

3. It goes without saying that letters should be large enough to be visible and that titles and first-level material should be larger than second-level material.

For more information, search InfoTrac College Edition for "fonts." One article described the personality of the font, "Georgia," which a British psychologist called "individual, sophisticated, with a curviness that suggests a little bit of rocker chick."[31] Studies show that fonts with rounded O's and tails are "friendly" but more angular fonts are "cold." Many celebrities and politicians have their own fonts, as do some cities. For instance, both the city of Seattle and President Obama use "the modern classic" Gotham as their signature font.[32]

Use Color for Emphasis

Color adds interest and emphasis and attracts and holds attention. However, carefully plan your color scheme because colors have connotations that vary culturally. For example: red, used sparingly, can be a good emphasis color, but it is "culturally loaded." In the United States it symbolizes anger ("seeing red") or danger (being "in the red"); in China, it symbolizes luck and celebration; in India, it is associated with purity. Red is the most common color found on national flags. Blue may be the "safest" global color. In the United States, it symbolizes stability ("true blue"). In China, it connotes immortality; the Jewish faith associates it with holiness.[33]

For words and images, choose colors that contrast dramatically with the background color. White or ivory-colored posters and slide backgrounds or clear transparencies are generally best, with text material in high-contrasting black or dark blue. Always consider the room lighting and set up, especially when your technology requires dimmed lights; the colors that seemed bright on your computer may look faded on the screen. Experiment until you come up with a combination that works in the specific context.

To avoid a cluttered look, use a maximum of three colors on all of your visuals. To emphasize ideas, use brightly colored bullets to draw attention to a list. Or vary the color of a word or phrase you want to stand out.

The most pleasing visuals follow principles of good design. They should be simple and balanced with fonts that create readability and repeated colors that emphasize important points. These principles will help you remember that your aids are just that—aids. They aren't your message, and they aren't a display of your personal artistic or computer skills.

Complete Your Presentation Plan

Return to your presentation plan. Make any revisions you'd like; next, sketch out each visual—paying attention to the size and spacing of your words and images. Select appropriate colors and decide which words or phrases you want to emphasize. Then go to work on your text- or image-based visuals. Simplify and balance the material, using the rule of thirds. If you plan to use audio or video support, make arrangements now for the equipment you'll need. And have fun!

General Guidelines for Using Presentation Aids

As noted throughout this chapter, each type of presentation aid and technology comes with guidelines for successful use, but the following general principles apply pretty much across the board:

- Whatever type of presentation aid you choose, make sure everyone can hear or see it.
- Display visuals only when you discuss them. For example, use a cover sheet on posters when they're not in use, or press the "B" key on your computer to bring up a blank screen between slides.
- Talk to your audience, not to your visual.
- Rehearse using your aids. If you can't use the actual equipment, you can at least visualize yourself using it—think about where you'll stand in relation to the equipment, how you'll point out specific features, what you'll do when you're not discussing content on the visual.
- Whenever machines are involved, have a Plan B. What will you do if the projector doesn't work or your YouTube video won't load? An alternate plan, often in the form of a handout, can save your speech. In the big picture, demonstrating your composure in case of equipment failure enhances your credibility.[34]

Now that you have read the chapter, go back to the introduction. From the information provided, how effective do you think Edith Widder's visuals were overall? Give a reason for your answer.

Summary

As a speaker in a visually oriented culture, it is to your advantage to use visual and audio support effectively. Presentation aids illustrate your ideas, keep your audience focused on your speech, and make abstract ideas more concrete. The dual coding they offer helps your listeners better comprehend and retain information. Before you make a single visual, sit down with your outline and determine where support is essential, where it would be useful, where variety is needed, and where audio or visual aids would accommodate for a variety of learning styles. If you can state the purpose for every item of support you use, you will have a meaningful package.

Use three-dimensional objects, models, and people when they are legal, practical, and accessible. Or use two-dimensional objects that can be displayed in a variety of ways. These include lists, charts, graphs, photographs, drawings, diagrams, and maps. Finally, don't overlook the potential of audio- or video-recordings that will help your listeners get your message. They are especially helpful for helping nonnative speakers of English understand and be understood.

Choose a means of display that suits your topic and the room in which you will speak. Various projectors—LCDs, document cameras, and overhead projectors—chalkboards or whiteboards, and interactive boards combine with poster boards, flip charts, and handouts as high-tech and low-tech ways to present visual aids. All have advantages and disadvantages, but you should take care to have a Plan B in case your equipment fails.

Emerging technologies have produced sophisticated presentational packages that you can use to create professional-appearing visuals and multimedia presentations to enhance (not replace) your speech. Use proven principles of design, including simplicity, repetition, contrast, and spacing. Choose readable fonts and color that emphasizes ideas. And follow a few rules: Display visuals only when you are discussing them, and talk to the audience, not to the visuals. Make sure your aids are visible and audible to everyone. Rehearse your presentation in advance of your speech.

Remember that competent use of visual materials can enhance your credibility. Professional-looking resources create more positive impressions than those that appear to be scribbled out just minutes before your presentation. Further, the disastrous case of equipment failure may actually increase your credibility if your listeners see you handle the stressful situation with composure. And you can demonstrate good sense and ethical awareness by selecting and presenting only visual support that does not violate your listeners' expectations.

STUDY AND REVIEW

Your online resources for *Public Speaking: Concepts and Skills for a Diverse Society* offer a broad range of study tools that will help you better understand the material in this chapter, complete assignments, and succeed on tests. Your online resources feature the following:

- Speech videos with critical viewing questions, speech outlines, and transcripts.
- Interactive versions of this chapter's Stop and Check activities, as well as Application and Critical Thinking Exercises.
- Speech Builder Express and InfoTrac College Edition.
- Weblinks related to chapter content.
- Study and review tools such as self-quizzes, an *interactive* glossary, and downloadable audio summaries.

You can access your online resources at the CourseMate for *Public Speaking: Concepts and Skills for a Diverse Society.* Log in at **http://www.cengage.com/login**, using the access code that came with your book or that you bought online at **http://www.cengagebrain.com**.

KEY TERMS

The terms below are defined in the margins throughout this chapter.

bar graphs 224
diagram 223
document cameras 227
dual coding theory (DCT) 219
dual processing 219
flip charts 230
flowcharts 222
geographic maps 223
image-based visual 222
interactive whiteboards 229
line graphs 224
model 221
organizational charts 222
picture graphs or pictographs 225
pie graphs 225
political maps 223
presentation aids 219
presentation software programs 227
sans serif font 234
serif font 233
six-by-six rule 222
text-based visual 222

APPLICATION AND CRITICAL THINKING EXERCISES

1. Think about speeches you've heard during the last week. When would visuals have made it easier for you to understand the material? When would visual or audio support have helped you pay better attention? Which support, if any, was best for your learning style preferences?
2. Think about public speakers you know who use visuals. What kinds of visual support are most common? Which do you see used least? Which presentation technologies are

most common? Least common? Do most speakers use visual aids well, or should they follow some tips in this chapter? Explain.

3. Which technology for displaying visuals will you probably use for your classroom speeches? Which would you not consider? In your future employment, what equipment do you think you'll use the most? The least? Why?
4. Do an equipment assessment of the room where you will be speaking. Is there an overhead in the room? An easel? Is there a table or podium? An Internet connection? Where are the electrical outlets? Can the lights be dimmed? If you need equipment, how do you order it? What adjustments will you need to make to accommodate different kinds of audio and visual equipment?
5. Discuss with a small group of your classmates how you would best display a drawing in (1) a large auditorium, (2) a classroom, (3) a speech given outdoors, and (4) a presentation in someone's living room. (Several ways may be appropriate.)
6. Explain what kind of visuals you think would work most appropriately for a speech on each of these topics:
    - The cloud cycle
    - The physical effects on the lungs of smoking
    - The Oregon Trail
    - Ozone depletion
    - Changes in mortgage interest rates over two decades
7. Working in a small group, choose a sample speech from Appendix C or at the end of one of the chapters in this text and design at least three visual aids for it. Show your designs to the rest of the class and explain your choices.
8. Make a visual package using a presentation software program such as PowerPoint. First, draw your slides on paper, spacing the information across the slide, and cutting every unnecessary word or image. Then go to your computer and make the slides. Experiment with layout, fonts, and colors. Use the slide show function to look at the overall balance of the visual; adjust line spacing and font size as necessary.
9. Browse the Internet using your favorite search engine for material about visual aids. Analyze the credibility of several sites. Does the URL contain an .edu or a .com? Why might that make a difference? Who wrote the materials? When? What links are there? With this information, assess the overall usefulness of each site. Take notes and bring them to class to discuss within a small group.
10. PowerPoint is not universally loved. Visit the website of Robert Gaskins, one of its originators, at **weblink 13.4**. (You can access this link through your CourseMate for *Public Speaking,* Chapter 13 resources.) There find the PRESS stories along the right side of the webpage. Read at least two and make a list of negative and of positive aspects of PowerPoint. Come to class prepared to discuss your list.

11. For fun, read Lincoln's Gettysburg address, formatted in PowerPoint at **weblink 13.5**, or read some of the many PowerPoint-related cartoons at **weblink 13.6**. (You can access these links through your CourseMate for *Public Speaking,* Chapter 13 resources.)

SPEECH VIDEO

Go to your online resources to watch Casey Millerick's informative speech, "Artificial Gills," answer questions for analysis, and evaluate the speech. Your online resources also include the transcript of Casey's speech shown below, his content outline, his speaking outline, and sample note cards for the speech.

Student Speech with Visual Aids with Commentary

ARTIFICIAL GILLS
By Casey Millerick

Introduction

Casey' title slide has the words "Artificial Gills" on a blue background with water droplets.

Whether it was super strength, being able to fly, or having laser eye beams, at some point in our lives all of us have probably dreamed about having some form of superhero ability or another. For me, I was always all about Aquaman . . . something about being able to swim underwater, being able to pick up some sunken treasure and what not.

He displays a slide showing the cartoon figure with the words "Aquaman."

The cool thing is that *that* [*pointing toward the slide*] is quickly becoming a reality. People are developing new technologies that will soon allow people to breathe underwater without the use of scuba tanks, which they're labeling as artificial gills.

I first became interested in this whole idea when our engineering teacher read us an article that was described an engineering team that was developing different types of solutions to this challenge.

Today, I'm going to talk with you about the two different types of solutions researchers have come up with, how they work, and the pros and cons of each of them.

Body

He displays a slide showing a very large image of the beetle.

The first solution was developed by an English research team. They based their observations, their data, and the whole idea of this system off of this aquatic diving beetle, and here's a picture of it. Now, it may look like it's an ordinary creepy crawler, but in reality, it's rather remarkable. Its entire body is lined with super rigid hairs, which repel water. So when it jumps into the pond or whatever it's going to be cruising around in, it makes this little air bubble around itself which allows it to get oxygen from the surrounding water without its actually having to inhale the water, which is pretty nifty.

It took the design team three years to finally mimic the beetle's hair-type structures, and according to a September 14, 2006, article in LiveScience [online], they came up with a surface lined with microscopic fibers that basically look like trees, and the tree-like structures work exactly like the hairs in the fact that they repel the water. These "trees" create a thin layer of air between the water and the actual surface of the material.

Here Casey picks up a note card and reads the quotation.

The team tested their model, and it actually worked. But the LiveScience.com article says their big concern with it, according to Glen McHale, the researcher who headed the project, is, "If other gases, such as methane were at elevated levels in the water, such as in stagnant pools, these gases would be transferred into the breathing air as efficiently as oxygen and could potentially cause serious problems." In other words, if you jumped into a pool with bad gases, they would get into your breathing just as easily as oxygen, which would obviously cause you problems!

In January of 2006, the BBC reported on the second solution. It is being developed by a company called Like-A-Fish, which is being headed by an Israeli inventor named Alon Bodnar.

He shows a slide with the title Like-A-Fish and the name "Alon Bodner."

He clicks the mouse and the words "Henry's Law" appears on the slide.

He pulls out a two-liter bottle of soda from behind the podium.

He unscrews the bottle's lid, which produces a "s-s-s-s-s-t" sound.

According to a report on the Discovery Channel, the whole idea works by using Henry's Law, but unless you're a super science guru or something, you probably don't know off the top of your head what Henry's Law is. So it's best to illustrate it by a soda bottle. The principle of Henry's Law is that high-pressure gases will naturally want to travel to lower pressure areas. For example, in a soda bottle, you have a bunch of high-pressure gases trapped in here, but when you give it access to the lower pressure environment, you hear the gas rush from the high-pressure environment to the low-pressure environment. So that's the principle they are using.

Here's a diagram from Like-A-Fish's website that illustrates this. In this process they made a system that pumps water in from the ocean, which is here [*points it out on the diagram*] and then this motor [*points to it*] pumps in the water. Next, it gets put into the air separator [*points it out*], which applies the Henry's Law principle that we just talked about. What happens is that the air gets sucked into this chamber [*points to it*] and then low pressure is applied, and with water oxygen (if you didn't know) is dissolved in the water and oxygen is a gas, so when you apply low pressure, all the oxygen will leave the water and go to the low pressure area [*points it out*]. They trap all the oxygen that leaves and send it this direction [*points it out*], and all the water that's been stripped of its oxygen gets dumped back into the ocean. So then the diver [*points him out*] takes all the air he needs, and all the excess oxygen that he doesn't need gets put into this air tank [*points it out*] for later use. So that's how the whole system that they designed works.

The big downside to that process is battery life. The battery they developed dies really quickly, so they are trying to design a better one, but at this point, Alon Bodnar said that they are coming up with new solutions every day, so they are not too concerned about that hindering them in the future. A June 2008 update on the Like-A-Fish website reports that revisions to the model were successful and the company's next goal was to shrink down the system.

So in the end, we may not exactly be at superhero status yet, but we are certainly on the way to doing what Aquaman does. We've talked about two different types of solutions and the pros and cons of each. Just remember that, even if a dream may sound farfetched, don't rule it out because engineering makes almost anything possible.

A hyperlink on the slide brings up the website which has an animated diagram. Casey scrolls down to the diagram, enlarges it so the audience sees it better, and describes each step of the process as he points it out. You can see the animated diagram on **weblink 13.7**. (You can access this link through your CourseMate for *Public Speaking*, Chapter 13 resources.)

CHAPTER
14

THIS CHAPTER WILL HELP YOU

- List four methods of delivery and explain when and how to use each
- Describe ways to maximize your personal appearance, clothing, and accessories
- Plan ways to gesture effectively
- Build eye contact skills
- Vary your voice effectively in presentations

Delivering Your Speech

SOME PEOPLE BECOME FAMOUS for their delivery skills. Bob Sheppard, "The Voice of the Yankees" for over fifty years, was a speech professor at St. John's University when he decided to make a few bucks on the side as a sports announcer. (His distinctive voice also announced New York Giants' football games for fifty years, and he served as a lector, or scripture reader, in his church.) Because of his legendary skills, he worked well into his nineties before he retired. Sheppard's mantra was "be clear, be concise, be correct."[1] He is only one of two announcers to earn both a World Series ring and a Super Bowl ring.[2] You can watch tributes to Sheppard at **weblink 14.1**. (You can access this link through your CourseMate for *Public Speaking,* Chapter 14 resources.)

Often interesting and intelligent people prepare a well-crafted speech but then deliver it so poorly that the message is lost or ignored. Others could read the phone book and sound impressive. **Delivery**—how you perform your speech—is the topic of this chapter. It first elaborates on the four major types of delivery introduced in Chapter 2, giving tips for developing skills in each one. Next it describes various aspects of nonverbal communication—personal appearance, movements or mannerisms, and vocal variations—that can enhance or detract from your words. The goal throughout is to help you present your speech skillfully and appropriately for the occasion.

delivery the verbal and nonverbal behaviors you use to perform your speech

Select the Appropriate Type of Delivery

A high-ranking government official writes out and reads her commencement address. An inspirational speaker has given his talk so many times that it's memorized. A student, just back from a disaster relief service trip, gives an off-the-cuff summary of her experiences when she's asked to "say a few words about the trip." A prosecuting attorney prepares his closing arguments carefully, but when he actually faces the jury, he relies only on his legal pad with a few scrawled notes. These speakers illustrate the four major types of delivery, introduced briefly in Chapter 2: manuscript, memorized, impromptu, and extemporaneous.

Manuscript Delivery

Manuscript delivery means you write out your entire speech and read it. Because this is the most inactive delivery method, it is generally not recommended for most classroom or workplace situations.[3] Although it can be information rich, it is interaction poor if you read ineffectively and fail to engage your audience.

manuscript delivery reading a speech

This being said, manuscript delivery is sometimes appropriate, especially on formal situations, when precise wording matters or when the speech is significant. Many ceremonial speeches such as eulogies, awards, or important political speeches fall into this category. Manuscripts are also useful for radio or television speeches where exact timing is essential. Finally, speakers who suffer severe speech anxiety often find that a manuscript minimizes their fears.

Consultants give several tips for competent manuscript delivery. First, write the speech out word-for-word in an oral style, using short sentences and fragments and incorporating strategies such as personalized language and rhetorical questions that help you connect with the audience. Rehearse by reading each sentence aloud several times, absorbing the meaning of each phrase.[4] Next, read the entire manuscript aloud and decide which ideas need emphasis (highlight or underline them) and where you want to pause (use slashes to show this). Finally, read the manuscript again, emphasizing words, pausing, and looking up as much as possible. Go back and change any wording that does not sound like you actually speak.[5]

Practice until you can read in a natural, conversational manner. Most people don't like to be read to, especially if it sounds "read"—meaning that you use a monotone or sing-song voice, rush through the words, never pause, and rarely look up. When you are totally familiar with the speech, practice with a podium and place your manuscript high up on it so that you can see the words without lowering your head too much.[6]

Type your final script in a large boldfaced font (20 points). Use double or triple spacing, and number each page.[7] When you deliver the speech, keep two pages visible (like an open book). Read from the page on the right, and when you finish it, slide the page on the left over it and continue without a break.

teleprompter screen, located beneath the camera lens, on which the words of the speech scroll up during a filmed speech

Technology is available to enhance manuscript delivery. Most televised speakers use a **teleprompter** screen, located just beneath the camera lens, which projects the manuscript line by line, somewhat like the credit lines that unroll on a movie screen at the end of the film. If you ever use one, a technician will work with you during rehearsal to match the speed of the lines to your speaking rate. The technician can circle key words or underline phrases you want to emphasize.

To see manuscript delivery in actual use, **weblink 14.2** maintains several sites that feature speakers using written texts or teleprompters. Barbara Jordan's keynote address at the 1976 Democratic National Convention, Barbara Bush's address at Wellesley College, and every important presidential address you find there features manuscript delivery. (You can access this link through your CourseMate for *Public Speaking*, Chapter 14 resources.)

Memorized Delivery

memorized delivery giving a speech you've learned word for word

Memorized delivery was the norm in ancient Rome, where orators learned their speeches word for word. Orators in oral cultures still memorize their tribe's stories and legends, a tradition that ensures that the exact stories are preserved throughout succeeding generations. Memorized speeches are not so common in today's classrooms or workplaces, although professional speakers who repeatedly give the same talk may eventually know it by heart. Students on speech teams often memorize the speeches they deliver dozens of times in competitive tournaments.

Some students believe that memorizing their classroom speech will help them overcome their fears. Unfortunately, the opposite often happens. Standing in front of an audience, a beginning speaker's mind can easily go blank. I once met an elderly woman who vividly remembered her college speech class. She said she was scared to death to give her speech on the topic of spanking, so she decided to memorize it. Unfortunately, memory failed her, and her resulting embarrassment followed her for more than fifty years.

Another drawback is that memorized speeches often sound "recited," not natural or conversational. So, instead of engaging the audience, the speaker appears to be centered on the speech. If you must give the same speech repeatedly, the key is to treat each audience and occasion separately so that you don't just recite words.

If for some reason you must memorize a speech, here are some tips:[9] Write out your talk in its entirety, again using oral style. Vivid language, such as alliterated main points or parallel wording, can aid your memory.[10] Commit your speech to memory line by line first and then chunk by chunk. As you rehearse a line, think about its meaning. Practice speaking conversationally—as if you are talking to each audience member individually. Finally, take note cards with key terms to the podium in case you find yourself forgetting.

Larry Downing/Reuters/Corbis

Although other presidents used teleprompters for speeches given from the Oval Office, they often used manuscripts or note cards in less formal settings.[8] President Obama, however, is known for his use of a teleprompter in almost all settings because he knows that every word he utters as president can have national or international implications.

Impromptu Delivery

Jana Kelsay

Impromptu speeches are common at ceremonial events where guests are often invited to "say a few words." The best impromptu talks are focused and brief.

Impromptu delivery means you speak with little advanced notice; consequently, this mode takes the least amount of preparation and rehearsal. However, in most cases your life, your knowledge, or your experiences prepare you to make the speech. In fact, people are rarely, if ever, asked to talk about totally unfamiliar subjects.[11] Let's say you are suddenly asked to say a few words at a farewell dinner. You don't have time to write out a speech and practice it. Instead, you think quickly and talk about experiences you've had with the person who's leaving.

You may shudder at the thought of speaking without preparation and rehearsal, especially if your performance will be rewarded or punished in some way such as a grade or a job evaluation. However, business consultant Steve Kaye says that impromptu speaking is so common in the workplace that "business leaders are eventually going to be asked to give an impromptu speech at some point in their careers,"[12] and top leaders can count on a 99.9 percent chance that they'll be asked to say a few words at banquets, company picnics, farewells, and so on. (Of course, "winging it" is a bad strategy if you've been assigned to give a carefully prepared speech.)

If the situation arises, don't panic.[13] In fact, expect to be called on when you are in a key position of some sort (a child of parents celebrating an anniversary, a friend of a graduate, a project manager, and so on). Listen carefully to what other speakers say at the occasion, and make mental notes of points they omit. If you have a few minutes of advance warning, apply what you know about speech structure (gain attention, make a couple of points, support each one briefly, make an ending statement). Decide on a couple of points to develop briefly, and jot down key words when possible. Or think of one good story. When possible, tie into things others have said. Finally, conclude with a memorable statement and then sit down instead of rambling on and on.

impromptu delivery presenting the speech as you create it

Martin Luther King, Jr.'s "I Have a Dream" speech is a good example of a speech that begins with manuscript delivery but ends with impromptu speaking. In the final section, he departs from his script and draws from his vast knowledge of the Bible, of song lyrics, of previous sermons, and so on, to deliver some of his most inspirational lines.[14]

Extemporaneous Delivery

Most speeches are not read, not memorized, and not given spur of the moment. Instead, they are delivered extemporaneously. Lectures, briefings, sales presentations, class reports, you name it—most good speakers prepare their ideas carefully in advance but use speaking notes when they talk. Although they lose some precision in language, this frees them to speak conversationally and to make eye contact with listeners. Because **extemporaneous delivery** is the most common method used in workplaces and classrooms, learning how to deliver speeches extemporaneously is important for both school and career success.[15]

extemporaneous delivery preparing and rehearsing a speech carefully in advance, but choosing the exact wording as you deliver the speech

After you've done research, organized your ideas, and created your content outline, make speaking notes or a speaking outline as described in Chapter 11. These notes will help you remember the order of your ideas, but you will choose your exact wording during delivery. (To avoid reading, don't put too many words on your cards. Then you'll have nothing to read.)

As you might imagine, rehearsal is vital to the process, so give yourself plenty of time to learn your material. The key is to memorize the thought patterns, not every word.[16] Try dividing the content into sections and then work on each one separately.

Or concentrate on one element at a time; for example, in one run-through, focus on your visual aids, in another, on the content, on signposts, or on smooth transitions.[17] Time yourself and make adjustments. Conclude with at least two full rehearsals: one to find your errors, the second to correct them.[18] Challenge yourself to practice enough to be really good, not just adequate.[19]

On speech day, review your outline, go over your notes and head off to the speech with the confidence and security that comes from thorough preparation.[20] If you happen to make a mistake during delivery, don't say, "I'm sorry." Just pause slightly, regain your place, and continue as if nothing happened.

Each of the four types of delivery—manuscript, memorized, impromptu, and extemporaneous—is common in the United States. Each has strengths and weaknesses. The key throughout is to think about your listeners not your delivery. The noted orator Sir Winston Churchill, Prime Minister of Great Britain during World War II, always kept his audience in mind. Once when he was rehearsing in the bathtub, his valet heard him through the door and asked, "Were you speaking to me, sir?" Churchill replied, "No, I was addressing the House of Commons."[21]

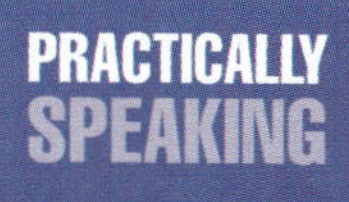

Kendra Phillips, Student Serve Day Coordinator

Kelsey Adent

Kendra Phillips is a recent graduate of a university that begins each fall semester with a campus-wide civic engagement project called Serve Day. On a Wednesday early in the fall semester, the entire institution shuts down and every student and every employee (the president included) participates in community service projects. In her senior year, Kendra was the student Serve Day coordinator.

What kind of speaking opportunities did you have as coordinator of this massive service project? I had several speaking opportunities that promoted and encouraged students to become excited about Serve Day. I did announcements for First Year Student's Orientation and chapel. I also led numerous Serve Day briefing meetings with university staff and faculty.

How did you prepare for these speeches? I first thought about my audience I was delivering the speech to and then thought about the goal and purpose for each speech. I created a speech that would meet that goal with that audience.

How did you deliver these speeches? For most of the speeches I prepared an outline in advance to make sure I covered my main ideas. Then I used key words on the outline when I gave the speech. A few times I was asked to speak impromptu, and at those times I tried to focus my speeches on the heart of Serve Day and make each talk authentic and genuine.

Questions

1. If you had to give an impromptu speech right now about your school or a current project you're working on, what "heart" of the topic could you build upon?
2. Why is speaking from an outline the most practical mode for the type of speeches Kendra gave?

Maximize Your Personal Appearance

Erving Goffman[22] develops the concept of **impression management** in his influential book, *The Presentation of Self in Everyday Life.* Goffman says we attempt to create and maintain impressions of ourselves as if we were on stage, using a combination of props and personal mannerisms. Part of successful delivery includes management of your physical appearance, your clothing, and your accessories to give your audience a good impression of you.

impression management self-presentation, using the metaphor of a staged drama in which we use props and personal mannerisms to create and maintain impressions of ourselves

Images of physically perfect bodies pervade our media, and by comparison, most people have at least one flaw. Features like less-than-perfect skin, crooked teeth, visible birthmarks, above- or below-average weight or height, or use of a wheelchair can cause reluctance to speak publicly; you may feel as if you're in the limelight, being scrutinized.[23] However, audiences don't just see your physical characteristics; they form an overall impression based on things you can control—your facial expressions, posture, gestures, and grooming.[24]

Clothing can also create a positive impression. Whatever the context, you should look like you take the assignment seriously. A good general rule is to select attire that doesn't draw attention to itself and is appropriate to the situation. In the classroom slightly more conservative and simple clothing generally works best. Visualize the impression you're creating from the audience's point of view. Would a top with a "busy" pattern or a message T-shirt be distracting? One student who normally wore a black T-shirt with an image across the front of a creature whose fangs were dripping blood, changed to a simple black shirt on speech days.

In other contexts, check out clothing expectations for the group and the occasion. For instance, a student who was invited to speak at a university staff retreat dressed as if she were going to a job interview, not realizing the retreat was located in the woods and participants would wear casual clothes. She later confessed, "I was overdressed!" If she had asked before going, she would have known.

ETHICS IN PRACTICE Managing Impressions

You can probably think of public personalities who try to appear genuinely interested in people because they want their money, time, or votes. Lawyers hire consultants to advise and coach their clients in selecting clothing, mannerisms, and nonverbal techniques to create an impression of innocence in jury members' minds. Ivy League-educated politicians wear flannel shirts or hard hats to "connect" with the working class. Using the following questions, discuss with a small group of your classmates the ethical appropriateness of these and similar actions.

Questions

1. Is it wrong to imply that a politician, an Ivy League graduate from a wealthy family, is similar to the blue-collar workers in his audience? Why or why not?
2. Are lawyers and consultants acting ethically if they try to create an image of innocence for clients they believe are guilty?
3. What if they believe in their client's innocence?
4. How do sincere lawyers and politicians contribute to the judicial or political process?
5. How do cynical lawyers and politicians contribute to the judicial or political process?

Clothing choices can affect audience impressions both positively and negatively. How might these different looks contribute to or detract from a speech on a topic such as food waste or homelessness?

Sue O'Donnell

Sue O'Donnell

Sue O'Donnell

sincere speakers presenting verbal and nonverbal messages they themselves believe

cynical speakers presenting verbal or nonverbal messages they don't believe in an attempt to create a false image

Finally, make your accessories matter. Accessories—the objects you carry or add to your clothing—include eyeglasses, jewelry, hats, and scarves. Avoid accessories that distract or draw attention to themselves. Simple is generally best.

There are ethical implications in impression management. When you try to create an impression that truly reflects who you are or when you try to deceive your audiences to one degree or another, you are making ethical choices. Presenting verbal and nonverbal messages that you actually believe is **sincere**. In contrast, intentionally choosing to create false or misleading impressions is being **cynical**, because you don't believe your own messages.[25]

Develop Effective Mannerisms

Although some aspects of your appearance are relatively fixed, to a significant degree you can control your mannerisms. Gestures and eye contact are especially important in this culture.

Control Your Gestures

Gestures are defined as the movements you perform unwittingly during speech as part of your expressive effort.[26] They range from large motions such as posture, walking, and gesturing to very small movements such as raising one eyebrow. Bodily movements function to supplement your words, display emotions, help audiences understand the structure of your speech, and, in some cases, betray nervousness.[27]

It's common to use gestures to emphasize an idea or to supplement your words. For example, you might say, "It's about this wide," and extend your hands to show the distance. Pointing out something is also common. You'd probably point to the area on the map while saying, "Look at this part of the ocean."

- To be effective, plan where you'll use gestures to make sure they are purposeful. It's easy to wave your arms about randomly or to repeat an annoying or distracting gesture.
- During one rehearsal, focus on your gestures and practice them until they seem natural. Avoid holding your elbows close to your body as you gesture.
- When possible, videotape a rehearsal and watch yourself with the sound turned off. Analyze when and how you use your hands and arms to make effective points, and when and how your movements are meaningless. Practice what to do with your hands when you are not gesturing.

Some bodily movements show emotions. Facial expressions are especially useful in conveying feelings such as disgust and contempt (appropriate for a topic such as the blood diamond industry) or humor and delight (appropriate for an awards speech). Posture can show confidence and pride or sadness and defeat (just look at the winning and losing benches on a sports team). Here are some tips for showing emotion:

- Maintain pleasant facial expressions. You don't have to smile all the time, but it's important to show a friendly attitude toward your audience throughout your speech.
- Even if you don't feel confident, you can look and act it. Stand tall; relax; hold your head erect and look directly at the audience.

A *Harvard Business Newsletter* article advises speakers to alert their audiences to the speech's high points and transitions because listeners expect such guidance and they want cues that help them listen better.[28] So consider using movements to emphasize your speech structure. Changing your posture or moving from place to place can give your audience clues about your organizational pattern. Here are a few ways to do this:

- Students on speech teams learn to "walk their points." They begin the introduction in one place and then take a couple of steps to the right to develop their first point. A few steps to the left signal the next point, and so on. The conclusion is given from the starting position. It may seem awkward to walk *every* point, but consider where and how movement could supplement your verbal transitions and signposts.
- Step back slightly or drop your hands from the podium to signal a transition.

A final way to maximize your mannerisms is to control nervous gestures. You might be tempted to fidget with your hair, bite your lip, scratch your nose, or rub your hands together during your speech. Or you might jingle keys in your pocket, twist your ring, or tap your note cards against the podium. Finally, you might use a gesture that cuts you off from your audience—like folding your arms across your chest during intense questioning. Gestures such as these suggest that you are subconsciously protecting yourself against the perceived psychological threat of the questioner.

Because these movements indicate anxiety or other stresses, especially when they appear to be nervous mannerisms, here are a few tips for eliminating them:

- Make a video of yourself rehearsing, or elicit feedback from friends. Watch the video, noting any nervous mannerism you use, and plan specific ways to avoid them. Or ask your friends to list all the movements you do that betray a lack of confidence. Discuss with them ways to improve.
- On speech day, do what you can to eliminate temptation for fidgeting. For example, if you typically twirl a pen, don't take one to the podium with you. If you constantly flip your hair out of your eyes, secure it somehow. On your speaking outline, write cues such as DON'T SCRATCH, if that is your habit.
- Be especially aware of your body language, especially during a question-and-answer period. Work to maintain an open body position, and avoid crossing your arms defensively, even if the questioning becomes pointed.

Make Eye Contact

eye contact looking audiences in the eye; communicates friendliness in the United States

In the United States, direct eye contact communicates honesty and trustworthiness. The phrase "Look me in the eye and say that" is partly premised on the cultural notion that people won't lie if they're looking at you. Here, **eye contact** also communicates that you are friendly, dynamic, extroverted, and approachable; purposely avoiding another's gaze generally signals a lack of interest.[29] This concept transfers to public speaking where the audience forms impressions of you based on your eye contact. Eye contact also helps you know if your audience is confused or bored, and you can adjust your speech accordingly.

Making eye contact is often difficult at first, because it is tempting to look at your notes, the floor in front of you, the back wall, or out the window—all gazes that communicate your discomfort. Here are some tips for developing effective eye contact:

- Look in at least three general directions: at the listeners directly in front of you, those to the left, and those to the right. Because of your peripheral vision, you can generally keep most listeners within your vision as your gaze changes direction.
- If your audience is sitting in a rectangular shape, mentally divide the group into a tic-tac-toe–like grid, and make eye contact with a friendly face in each grid.[30] This will help you look at various people within the room, not just at one or two.
- Hold your gaze with an individual for three to five seconds; finish a thought or idea before you look at someone else.[31]
- Resist the urge to make more eye contact with listeners you perceive as more powerful. In the classroom, don't just zero in on your instructor; in the workplace, don't focus on your boss's reactions at the expense of other listeners.
- Keep in mind that some people don't like to be looked at, perhaps out of shyness, perhaps for cultural reasons—they've been taught to avoid direct eye contact. If you sense your gaze makes someone uncomfortable, just scan in the general direction, but don't focus on that person's eyes.[32]

Expectations common in the United States are not universally applicable. For instance, Japanese communicators use less direct eye contact. In Japan, it is not unusual to see downcast or closed eyes at a meeting or a conference because within their culture this demonstrates attentiveness and agreement rather than rejection, disinterest, or disagreement.[33]

For additional information on gestures and eye contact, search InfoTrac College Edition for the key words *eye contact*, *nonverbal gestures*, or *body language*. What additional principles do you find in the articles there?

Vary Your Vocal Behaviors

vocalics or **paralinguistics** all aspects of spoken language except the words

Vocalics, also known as **paralinguistics**, deals with all aspects of spoken language except the words themselves—including things such as voice quality, pitch variation, and speech rate. Because of vocal cues, whenever you hear a voice on the radio, you can easily tell whether the speaker is young or old, male or female, a Southerner or Northerner, a native or nonnative speaker of English. Often you can detect moods such as boredom, hostility, or enthusiasm. This section discusses two major aspects of vocalics related to public speaking: pronunciation and vocal variation.

Work on Clear Pronunciation

articulation the way you enunciate or say specific sounds, an element of pronunciation

stress accenting syllables or words

Pronunciation, the way you actually say words, includes articulation and stress. **Articulation** is the way you say individual sounds, such as *th*ese or *z*ese, b*ir*d or b*oi*d. Some speakers reverse sounds, saying *aks* instead of *ask*, for example, or *nuculer* for *nuclear*. **Stress** is the way you accent syllables within words—*poe*-LEESE (police) or POE-*leese*,. Some people alter both articulation and stress, for instance, the word *comparable* can be pronounced two ways: COM-*purr-uh-bul* or *come*-PARE-*uh-bul*.

Your articulation often discloses your region of origin, ethnicity, and social status. For instance, regional differences include the drawn-out vowels typical of the "southern drawl" and the *r* added by many Bostonians to the end of words. Ethnic dialects such as Appalachian English or African American English have distinctive articulation and stress patterns. And the accents of nonnative English speakers reflect patterns from their first language. Links between social status and pronunciation form the premise for the classic movie *My Fair Lady*. Although Eliza Doolittle says the same words as Professor Higgins, her pronunciation marks her as a member of the lower class. By changing her pronunciation (as well as her dress and grooming), she eventually passes as a Hungarian princess.

In a multilingual world and in pluralistic classrooms and workplaces, accents are everywhere, and as travel, immigration, and technology continue to shrink the world, you'll hear even more in the future. Unfortunately, we tend to judge one another on the basis of accents that indicate social class, ethnic group membership, or status as a non-native speaker of English;[34] however, the Diversity in Practice box presents a good argument for affirming a variety of accents.

Because clear expression is essential to understanding, here are some tips for improving your pronunciation and articulation:

- When you're unsure of a word's pronunciation, consult a dictionary. Most online dictionaries now provide an audio feature so you can hear the word pronounced. Some words, such as *status* have two acceptable pronunciations—STAY-*tuhs* or STATT-*uhs*. When the dictionary provides two variations, the first is preferable.
- Work on sounds or words that cause you difficulty. Winston Churchill had a lisp, so he carefully rehearsed words that began with /s/.[35] Ralph had trouble saying the word *probably*, so he broke it into syllables (PRAW-buh-blee) and articulated each one slowly and clearly.
- During rehearsals, slow down and articulate the words clearly.
- In the speech itself, speak slowly enough to avoid slurring your words together or dropping the endings.
- If you have a serious articulation problem, a professional speech therapist can help.

Culture and Delivery

The Advice in this chapter presents norms in the United States, but different cultures have different impressions of what makes for a good delivery, and understanding and adapting to these differences will make you a more culturally sensitive communicator. Arabs and Latin Americans tend to use direct eye contact, as advised in the chapter, but Nigerian, Chinese, Puerto Rican, and Pakistani communicators tend to gaze less directly.[36]

Arabs, Italians, and African Americans tend to speak louder and more intensely than Native Americans and East Asians. North Americans tend to be uncomfortable with long pauses, but Japanese, Navajos, and speakers in India use pauses for reflection and for gathering of one's thoughts.[37]

Many immigrants take classes to improve their pronunciation, but YanHong Krompacky, herself an immigrant, tells them not to waste their money as long as their English is comprehensible and fluent. She argues, "This country is built on accents. Accent is one of the most conspicuous symbols of what makes America the free and prosperous land its own people are proud of and other people long to live in."[38]

Use Vocal Variation

Around 330 BCE, Aristotle's text on rhetoric[39] discussed variations in three important vocal components: volume, pitch, and rate (which he called rhythm).

> It is not enough to know what we ought to say; we must also say it as we ought. . . . It is, essentially, a matter of the right management of the voice to express the various emotions—of speaking loudly, softly, or between the two; of high, low, or intermediate pitch; of the various rhythms that suit various subjects. These are the three things—volume of sound, modulation of pitch, and rhythm—that a speaker bears in mind.

vocal variations changes in volume, rate, and pitch that combine to create impressions of the speaker

What kinds of impressions do **vocal variations** create? If you speak in a soft monotone instead of varying your pitch, you'll sound bored or sick; a louder monotone sounds angry. And several studies[40] conclude that audiences typically associate vocal rate and volume with the following personality traits:

Loud and fast speakers: self-sufficient, resourceful, dynamic

Loud and slow speakers: aggressive, competitive, confident

Soft and fast speakers: enthusiastic, adventuresome, confident, composed

Soft and slow speakers: competitive, enthusiastic, benevolent

Is there a relationship between your rate of speech and your credibility? Research shows that audiences associate rapid speech with intelligence and objectivity. They link a moderate rate to composure, honesty, an orientation toward people, and compassion.[41] To make vocal variations work for you, follow some of these suggestions for rehearsal:

- Put yourself into the right emotional attitude toward your material and the occasion. For example, if you want your audience to get excited about an idea, you get excited about it. If you want them to be disgusted, you be disgusted. On a ceremonial occasion, be happy; in a serious problem-solving meeting, be serious.
- Nick Morgan,[42] a professional trainer, suggests you babble during one rehearsal. That is, give your speech in nonsense syllables but use the vocalics, gestures, and body movements that express its emotional content.
- During rehearsal, record your speech and listen to your voice. Notice whether or not your tone of voice, rising or falling inflection, and stress on specific words create the meanings you want. Take notes on specific things you do well and things to improve. Rehearse the parts that could use more energy.

These suggestions apply to your actual performance:

- The most important rule is to speak loudly enough to be heard throughout the entire room.[43]
- Intentionally relax your throat before you speak and whenever you feel tense as you speak.[44]
- Use the lower range of your voice; higher pitches make you sound younger and more excitable.
- Speak naturally and conversationally. Don't force enthusiasm.
- Change vocal inflections when your audience appears to be losing interest; add pitch variation and slightly increased volume and rate to communicate enthusiasm; vary your volume and rate to add impact.[45]

For additional tips on vocal variation, search InfoTrac College Edition for the terms "vocal variety."

Pause for Effect

Finally, consider your use of pauses. Pauses can be effective or embarrassing to both you and your listeners. Effective pauses are intentional; that is, you might purposely pause

Everett Collection, Inc.

In the movie *Meet Joe Black*, William Parrish addressed the board of Parrish Communications. Watch the clip of this movie on **weblink 14.3**. Notice how his initial *um*s and nervous mannerisms give way to meaningful pauses, gestures, and movements that add emphasis to his words. (You can access this link through your CourseMate for *Public Speaking*, Chapter 14 resources.)

between major ideas or give your audience a few seconds to contemplate a difficult concept. In a speech to corporate executives, Judith Humphrey[46] advised:

> [C]onsider this: when does the audience think? Not while you're speaking, because they can't think about an idea until it's delivered. They think during the pauses. But if there are no pauses, they won't think. They won't be moved. They won't act upon what you say. The degree to which you want to involve the audience is reflected in the length of your pauses.

(This article is available on InfoTrac College Edition under the title "Executive Eloquence." Step 7 describes effective delivery.)

In contrast, ineffective pauses or hesitations disrupt your fluency and signal that you've lost your train of thought or you're searching for words. **Unfilled pauses** are silent; **filled** or **vocalized pauses** include *uh* or *um*, *like*, *okay*, and *you know*. Many professionals, as well as beginning public speakers, use *ums*. However, too many can be distracting, so work to minimize them. Here are some suggestions for using pauses effectively:

unfilled pauses silent pauses

filled (vocalized) pauses saying *um* or *uh* or other sounds during a pause

- Find places in your manuscript or outline where your audience needs you to pause so they can absorb what you just said. Use double slash marks // to mark these places.
- Then rehearse these intentional pauses. What may seem like a very long pause to you may be about right for your listeners.
- During a rehearsal, ask a friend to count the number of vocalized pauses you make and then give the speech again, and eliminate as many *um*s or *uh*s as you can.
- Use pauses as punctuation marks. For example, at the end of the body of the speech, try pausing, moving one step backward, and then saying, "In conclusion . . ." Your pause functions as a period that signals a separation in your thoughts.

A number of movies on **weblink 14.4** under "Movie Speeches" provide excellent models of good speakers who aren't afraid of pauses. (You can access this link through your CourseMate for *Public Speaking*, Chapter 14 resources.) Queen Gorgo's speech to the Spartan Council in the movie *300* and Coach Gary Gaines's speech on "Being Perfect" in the movie *Friday Night Lights* are just two examples.

Put It All Together

communicative competence the ability to communicate in a personally effective and socially appropriate manner

confident style a way of speaking characterized by effective vocal variety, fluency, gestures, and eye contact

conversational style speaking that's comparatively calmer, slower, and less intense, but maintains good eye contact and gestures

Communicative competence is defined as the ability to communicate in a personally effective and socially appropriate manner.[47] The key to a competent performance is to find the delivery that works best for you in a given situation. A **confident style** incorporates vocal variety, fluency, good use of gestures, and eye contact to create an impression of dynamism as well as credibility. If you're naturally outgoing, this style may best fit your personality. However, in some situations—somber occasions, for example—you should choose a more **conversational style**, one that's calmer, slower, softer, and less intense, but still maintains good eye contact and gestures.[48] Listeners associate this style with trustworthiness, honesty, sociability, likableness, and professionalism, and it may actually fit you better if your personality is more laid back. But more conversational speakers can adapt for an occasion, such as a rally, where excitement runs high and people expect a more enthusiastic delivery. Both styles are persuasive.

Don't worry if you are not yet dynamic or confident. Instead, begin to develop your personal delivery style, using your appearance, mannerisms, and vocal variations to your advantage.

Think Critically about Delivery

Political candidates often illustrate the link between delivery and effectiveness. For example, President Reagan was called the "Great Communicator," and Barack Obama's speaking skills are praised globally. In contrast, many politicians fail the "charismatic challenge." One presidential candidate's voice was described as "somewhere between that of a dentist's drill and the hum of a refrigerator."[49] Another's delivery was wooden, earnest, solemn, uptight, and focused more on content than on delivery. Enter the consultants. Some handlers spun their bland candidate as "authentic." Others sat beside their candidates, watching and rewatching videos of speeches, analyzing volume, rate, gestures, and facial expressions. Their overall advice was to loosen up—leave the podium, gesture widely, smile. Politicians know that no matter how wonderful their ideas, their message will be lost if their delivery annoys the audience or puts them to sleep.

In small groups, discuss the following questions:

1. What qualities are important in a president? How does presidential image matter? What do you think of the handlers' decision to spin unremarkable delivery as "authentic"?
2. Should a candidate undergo a makeover or "be herself," regardless?
3. President William Taft (1909–1914) weighed around 300 pounds. Could he be elected president today? Why or why not? Is this good or bad?
4. During the 2008 primaries, Hillary Clinton and some of her supporters claimed that media coverage was sexist. Words like "shrill," "strident," and "giggle" appeared in stories about her, but not about her male opponents.[50] Women are critiqued on their wardrobes, hairstyles, and accessories; men rarely are. In your opinion, does this constitute sexism? Why or why not?
5. Could Abraham Lincoln—with his looks and awkward mannerisms—be elected in this television-dominated society? Why or why not?

Summary

Of the four major types of delivery, memorization is common in oral cultures and in competitive speech tournaments, but it is less frequently used elsewhere. You may speak spontaneously in the impromptu style, or you may read from a manuscript. But more commonly, you'll join the ranks of extemporaneous speakers—preparing in advance but choosing your exact wording as you actually speak. Each type of delivery has its place, and each is comprised of a number of skills that you can develop through practice.

Delivery also involves nonverbal elements, and you can create a more positive impression of yourself during your delivery. The idea of managing your body and voice to affect listeners' impressions is at least as old as Aristotle—and he surely didn't invent the idea. Modern scholars continue to explore specific aspects of appearance, mannerisms, and vocal variations that create positive or negative impressions in audiences.

Your clothing, your grooming, and your accessories communicate your competence. Your mannerisms—gestures, eye contact, and vocal variation—are also important in creating impressions of dynamism, honesty, and other characteristics of credibility. As your nonverbal skills increase, your competence in public speaking increases correspondingly.

As with all attempts to influence others, the attempt to manage impressions has ethical implications. Speakers who believe in both the verbal and nonverbal messages they are sending are said to be sincere, but those who try to create false or misleading impressions are termed cynical.

STUDY AND REVIEW

Your online resources for *Public Speaking: Concepts and Skills for a Diverse Society* offer a broad range of study tools that will help you better understand the material in this chapter, complete assignments, and succeed on tests. Your online resources feature the following:

- Speech videos with critical viewing questions, speech outlines, and transcripts.
- Interactive versions of this chapter's Stop and Check activities, as well as Application and Critical Thinking Exercises.
- Speech Builder Express and InfoTrac College Edition.
- Weblinks related to chapter content.
- Study and review tools such as self-quizzes, an *interactive* glossary, and downloadable audio summaries.

You can access your online resources at the CourseMate for *Public Speaking: Concepts and Skills for a Diverse Society.* Log in at **http://www.cengage.com/login**, using the access code that came with your book or that you bought online at **http://www.cengagebrain.com**.

KEY TERMS

The terms below are defined in the margins throughout this chapter.

articulation 248
communicative competence 252
confident style 252
conversational style 252
cynical 246
delivery 241
extemporaneous delivery 243
eye contact 248
filled (vocalized) pauses 251
impression management 245
impromptu delivery 243
manuscript delivery 241
memorized delivery 242
paralinguistics 248
sincere 246
stress 248
teleprompter 242
unfilled pauses 251
vocal variations 250
vocalics 248

APPLICATION AND CRITICAL THINKING EXERCISES

1. With a small group of your classmates, make a set of guidelines for delivery that is appropriate to your classroom's unique culture. For example, would you change the advice about clothing or accessories presented in this chapter? What might you add that is not covered here?
2. According to Erving Goffman, the combination of environment, appearance, and mannerisms forms a "front."[51] Whether intentional or unwitting, this front influences the way observers define and interpret the situation. With this in mind, identify some public speakers who effectively live out their front.[52] Then discuss why some public speakers appear to be something they're not. That is, why do they present themselves as competent or trustworthy, and you later discover they aren't? What are some ethical implications of fronts?
3. If possible, make a video of one of your rehearsals or speeches and then watch it. Specifically, pay attention to your gestures, noting your use of purposeful movements and of movements that betray nervousness. Plan strategies to improve your gestures, eliminating those that create negative impressions and strengthening those that produce favorable impressions.
4. Watch the recording again. This time, evaluate your eye contact. Throughout your speech, notice the way you use your voice. Check for appropriate rate and volume; be alert for pauses, and count the number of *ums* you use, if any. Discuss with a classmate how you can improve these nonverbal aspects of delivery.
5. If you can't watch a video of your speech, create a worksheet that identifies the elements of delivery mentioned in the chapter. Give it to a classmate just before your speech, and have him or her note nonverbal aspects of your delivery; afterwards, discuss with that person strategies you can use to improve problem areas.
6. Write a script for an ad selling one of these products:
   - Used car
   - Perfume
   - Vacation to South America
   - Brand of cola

   Bring your script to class and exchange it with a classmate. Demonstrate the type of vocal variation you would use if you were delivering the ad.
7. Some colleges and universities offer public speaking courses online. With a group of your classmates, discuss the pros and cons of this practice. How do the courses work? How are speeches delivered? What are the drawbacks? Would you take one? Why or why not? (Prepare for this discussion by doing an Internet search for the words *public speaking course online*.)

SPEECH VIDEO

Log on to your online resources to watch and critique examples of memorized, extemporaneous, manuscript, and impromptu speeches.

© Tim Timmerman

CHAPTER 15

Telling Narratives

THIS CHAPTER WILL HELP YOU

- Explain how narratives function to explain, to persuade, and to entertain
- List elements of narratives
- Give guidelines for using language effectively in narratives
- Identify the parts of an exemplum
- Apply three tests for narrative reasoning

"I don't see why sleep deprivation is such a big deal."

"Neither did Brent—until one day when he found himself in the hospital because of an on-the-job injury. His story goes like this . . ."

"What happens if I donate to your organization?"

"Let me tell you about Zaur, a little boy in Azerbaijan who attends school because of a donor just like you . . ."

"What is fortitude?"

"Watch the movie, *127 Hours*; you'll see fortitude in the person of Aron Ralston . . ."

THESE ARE BUT A FEW of the ways we use stories in everyday life. The fact is we live in a "story-shaped world,"[1] because storytelling exists in every culture, throughout every era. Ordinary citizens as well as international leaders tell stories. Lawyers frame their arguments as narratives, and politicians present their political visions in story form. Coaches, teachers, members of the clergy, and comedians all routinely tell stories. Stories are so much a part of being human that Professor Walter Fisher[2] refers to us as **homo narrans**, the storytelling animal. The scholar Roland Barthes summarizes the importance of **storytelling**:

homo narrans a Latin phrase that identifies humans as storytelling animals

storytelling an oral art form we use to preserve and transmit commonly held ideas, images, motives, and emotions

> The narratives of the world are numberless. . . . Narrative is present in every age, in every place, in every society; it begins with the very history of [humankind] and there nowhere is nor has been a people without narrative. All classes, all human groups, have their narratives, enjoyment of which is very often shared by [others] with different, even opposing, cultural backgrounds. . . . Narrative is international, transhistorical, transcultural: it is simply there, like life itself.[3]

Psychologists agree that the narrative schema is the "basic cognitive principle of intelligibility"[4] because we rely on stories to make meaning. In fact, Jerome Bruner[5] says we reason in two complementary ways: narrative thinking and propositional thinking (which is described in Chapters 17 and 18). Given their importance, this text devotes a chapter to why we tell stories, how we organize them, and how we judge their merits.

Why We Tell Stories

We use narratives to inform, persuade, and entertain. They tell about our past, highlight human motivations, illuminate cultural ideals, and illustrate facets of a culture by identifying its themes and showing cultural differences. Stories preserve and transmit "ideas, images, motives and emotions with which everyone can identify."[6] Through them, audiences become more self-aware and more aware of cross-cultural issues.[7]

Informative Narratives

We use stories to provide information and cultural explanations of natural, social, and ultimate realities.[8] Listen to a group's stories and you'll better understand their perspectives and worldview.

Explaining Natural Phenomena

How did strawberries originate? The Cherokee tribe has a story about that.[9] Where do babies come from? Parents dust off the "birds and the bees" story for each new generation. How did the world come into being? Scientists weave facts and ideas into narrative accounts such as the big bang theory combined with evolutionary narratives. Others counter with alternative explanations, because the stories we tell about human origins profoundly affect our perceptions of the natural world and our place in it.[10] Narratives are essential in trials where prosecutors and defense lawyers offer competing explanations of "who did it," why, and how. Jury members must weigh and compare details before finally deciding which characters and events make the most sense to them.

Explaining Society and Institutions

Stories also explain cultural institutions or structures. Each country has its stories featuring characters who face dramatic choices, overcome hardships, invent useful as well as harmful tools, and make mistakes. US history texts explain the country's founding, its wars,

Who Should Tell Native Stories?

Lenore Keeshig-Tobias, an Ojibway poet, argues that nonnative writers and filmmakers should not borrow native stories. To do so is to commit "cultural theft, the theft of voice." She reasons:

> Stories, you see, are not just entertainment. Stories are power. They reflect the deepest, the most intimate perceptions, relationships, and attitudes of a people. Stories show how a people, a culture, thinks. Such wonderful offerings are seldom reproduced by outsiders.[11]

Within Ojibway culture, stories are considered so potent that one storyteller must ask permission to tell another's story. Consequently, Keeshig-Tobias believes that someone who wants to use a native story should come live with the storytellers for more just than a few months.

> Hear the voice of the wilderness. Be there with the Labicon, the Inmu. Be there on the Red Squirrel Road. . . . If you want these stories, fight for them. I dare you.[12]

To see and hear some Native American storytellers, search YouTube for clips of their performances. **Weblink 15.1** also links to hundreds of Native American stories from various tribes. (You can access this link through your CourseMate for *Public Speaking,* Chapter 15 resources.)

Questions

1. What do you think? Should nonnatives tell a native story? Why or why not?
2. Does this apply to other groups? For example, can only Muslims tell stories about Islam or only Christians tell New Testament stories? Can a heterosexual tell the story of a gay or lesbian? Why or why not?
3. What is "cultural theft"? Explain your answer.

blameworthy scenes (slavery), and praiseworthy events (the Constitutional Convention). However, myths and biases often obscure historical facts, and history books from other countries and from other perspectives narrate the same events quite differently. (For example, read Chief Joseph's version of US Indian relations, found in Appendix C.)

Organizations and groups have their own unique narratives. Your college or university tells a story as does your family. Because organizations rely on stories to get their messages across, hundreds of corporate trainers emphasize the importance of effective storytelling. Annette Simmons, for example, says when you represent an organization you should have a variety of stories: one to explain who you are, another to tell why you are speaking, a third to describe your vision, a fourth to teach (both positive and negative lessons), and a number of values-in-action narratives that show how your organization operates on its principles.[13]

Explaining Ultimate Things

Philosophical and religious narratives attempt to explain ultimate realities and answer questions such as, "Who are we?" "What is our purpose on Earth?" "What happens after death?" "How should I live a moral life?" Many are found in religious rituals or holidays based in historical events. Jewish people, for instance, narrate the story of Queen Esther as they celebrate Purim. Hindus celebrate the birthday of Ganesha, the deity of good fortune and prosperity during the festival of Ganesha Chaturthi. Christians remember the death and resurrection of Jesus as they celebrate Easter. In short, religious beliefs and practices are grounded in stories that followers have preserved over generations, stories that give ultimate meaning to the lives of adherents.

Persuasive Narratives

deliberative speaking a form of speaking that gives people the information and motivation they need to make wise decisions regarding future courses of action

Narrative reasoning is so effective that Aristotle classified it as a type of **deliberative speaking**—speaking that provides information and motivates people to make wise decisions.[14] Cognitive psychologists Melanie Green and Timothy Brock argue, "The power of narratives to change beliefs has never been doubted and has always been feared. Consequently, censorship has been ubiquitous for centuries."[15] Far more people absorb public narratives (such as films or news stories) than they do advocacy messages (such as sermons or political speeches). Our stories reinforce and influence our beliefs, actions, and attitudes.

Reasons for a Belief, Attitude, or Action

Narratives are especially useful for emphasizing and reinforcing a culture's significant beliefs, values, attitudes, and behaviors. Consequently, commemorative speeches honoring the lives and achievements of significant individuals often highlight values-in-action stories about those individuals. Many stories are told to provide support for our beliefs:

"Can students make a difference in their communities?"

> Yes. The November/December 2010 issue of *Civic Engagement Magazine* tells about college students who joined a SLICE team (Student Leaders in Community Entrepreneurship) and partnered with a nonprofit called Healing Spaces. Working together over one weekend, they created a dream bedroom designed for and by a 15-year-old who is battling a brain tumor. There, he can continue to recover. Their story inspired students at a nearby college to also join up with Healing Spaces to change more lives, one weekend at a time.[16]

Everett Collection, Inc.

In the movie *The Great Debaters*, little Wiley College wins a debate against mighty Harvard University. James Farmer, Jr.'s powerful narrative of a lynching exposes the wrongs of racism and supports his claim that civil disobedience is sometimes justified.

Stories also provide a rationale for our attitudes and actions. (For example, every war is justified by stories.) The following examples urge listeners toward positive goals:

"Register as a bone marrow donor."

> Little Matthew Welling is alive today because two strangers, whose bone marrow was a perfect match for his, signed up at the donor registry.[17]

"Peacemaking begins with concerned, committed individuals."

> Israeli storyteller Noa Baum's one-woman show, "A Land Twice Promised," weaves together her personal memories, the memories of a Palestinian woman she met in the United States, and their mothers' stories to provide multiple perspectives on the same places and events.[18]

Sometimes unpleasant stories expose a wrong of some sort. Emotionally moving narratives can motivate listeners to get involved in community activities—to intervene and improve the lives of others. Here's an example:

> One young mother was in tears after a photography studio told her they did not photograph "children like hers." The problem? Her child was a special needs child. Horror stories of insensitive studio responses such as this led another

mother to create Special Kids Photography of America (SKPA), an organization that uses narratives of families and photos of their children to raise awareness of the problem.[19]

Her goal was to make a difference for families who have disabled children. SKPA has trained many photographers who were moved by these stories to develop the special skills they need to be part of the solution.

Applied Storytellers

applied storytelling using stories for practical purposes, not just for entertainment

Applied storytellers are models of civic engagement because they use narratives to promote social action or better the world, not just entertain an audience.[20] They show up in prisons, homeless shelters, battered women's shelters, houses of worship and so on. You'll also find them in hospitals with patients in therapy and recovery.[21]

© 2006/Kent Miles

Laura Simms, pictured here, chooses stories from many cultures to help children who are trapped in war and conflict situations "overcome feelings of fear or powerlessness."[22] Taking inspiration from centuries-old oral traditions passed on in villages and families across the globe, she reports:

> I have gathered traditional stories from many different cultures that hopefully can provide an internal place of peace and inner nourishment for children who are dealing with tremendously overpowering feelings and images. This is what stories have done through the ages.[23]

Some applied storytellers believe that conflict arises when our stories don't match the stories of other people or groups, so they tell personal stories, as well as folktales about peace and reconciliation from many cultures to offer insights on how to transform conflict into peace. Although it's easy to avoid or discount divergent stories, we can actually learn and grow by sharing stories and by reconsidering and questioning our narratives and encouraging others to do likewise. Exchanging stories lets us look for commonalities so that we can understand and examine our differences and together co-create new narratives.[24]

Questions

1. Simms tells stories to heal emotional traumas. Can you give an example of someone who was helped emotionally through hearing a story?
2. How might storytelling function to help a person heal physically?
3. Describe a time you resolved a conflict by sharing stories with the person with whom you disagreed.
4. What conflicts on your campus result from divergent, competing stories? What opportunities, if any, are provided for sharing conflicting stories? How effective are they?
5. How might storytelling promote civility and dialogue among people who disagree?

Reasons Against an Action, Belief, or Attitude

Some stories are cautionary; they show what policies not to enact, how not to behave, or what not to believe. Cautionary tales typically use fear, shame, anger, and other strong emotional appeals.

> "Avoid tanning booths."
>
> Health professionals tell stories of people who spent hours in tanning booths as twenty-somethings; in mid-life, they face surgery and chemotherapy as they battle melanoma, the deadliest form of skin cancer.
>
> "Avoid credit card debt."
>
> A personal story about problems that resulted from a credit card spending spree can motivate listeners to use their credit cards wisely.

Persuasive stories contribute to wider policy changes as well as individual changes. For instance, on the campus level, stories about a series of computer thefts convinced administrators to tighten security policies. National stories about oil spills led to tighter regulations for oil tankers. International tales of victims of natural disasters have led millions across the globe to respond with money and muscle.

Visionary Narratives

rhetoric of possibility points out what can be, not what is

Although many stories are told in the past or present tense, others provide a vision of the future—sometimes negative, sometimes positive. The **rhetoric of possibility**[25] allows storytellers to tell what might be and to help others envision a future that they can make real. Science fiction writers often paint bleak scenarios of out-of-control technology, or they depict a bright future where machines are harnessed and controlled, allowing humans to do superhuman things. Visionary narratives also suggest ideals by presenting possibilities and expanding listeners' understandings of themselves and their lives. The most successful politicians and inspirational speakers put forth hopeful images of a better future. (The Practically Speaking feature on applied storytellers gives some examples of visionary narratives.)

In summary, persuasive stories can influence one person or millions. They provide examples of both wise and unwise behaviors; they provide a rationale for or against a policy, belief, or behavior; and they present a vision of what might be.

Entertaining Narratives

Let's face it: Not all stories are profound, and we tell many stories just to relax or have a good time. Storyteller Jackie Torrence[26] tells "Jump Tales" that end with a "BOO!" because she loves the shivers they give. Children's stories, extended jokes, situations exaggerated to the extreme, and television sitcoms are just a few examples of narratives that feature unusual or quirky characters in unusual or quirky situations.[27] Search the Internet for silly stories or jokes, for scary stories or campfire tales. The number of links you get in each category should give you some idea of the popularity of entertaining stories. (An Internet search turned up millions of links for jokes!)

Kenneth Burke, the great rhetoric scholar, summarizes story categories as "the imaginative, the visionary, the sublime, the ridiculous, . . . the satirical, every detail of every single science or speculation, even every bit of gossip."[28] We are indeed storytelling animals.

Your Narrative Purposes

Of all the stories you've told within the last twenty-four-hour period, estimate the percentage you told for the following purposes:

____ to inform
____ to persuade
____ to entertain

Will these percentages be similar in your chosen career? If so, what kind(s) of stories will you probably tell more? What kind(s) will you tell less frequently? Discuss with a small group of your classmates how you will probably use narratives to do the following in your choice of career:

- Explain natural things
- Explain organizational or social realities
- Explain ultimate things
- Motivate people to believe or act in specific ways
- Commemorate cultural beliefs, values, attitudes, or behaviors
- Provide a rationale not to believe or do certain things
- Present a vision of the future
- Entertain an audience

How We Organize Stories

Because you have been hearing and telling stories all your life, you are probably quite familiar with the basic elements of narratives. This section describes how to craft your story and choose vivid language.

Weave Narrative Elements Together

A good story has a purpose or goal that you develop by describing the setting and characters as they participate in the action or plot.

Identify Your Purpose

Whether you give a narrative speech or tell a story as part of a larger speech, consider your purpose carefully. What function do you want the narrative to fulfill? Do you want to inform, persuade, or entertain? Will you present a vision of possibilities that your audience has not yet considered? Remember that even a story told mainly for entertainment purposes needs a lesson or point.

Set Up the Story

Identifying the scene or situation provides the foundation for the overall story line. Giving time and space details about where and when the story takes place is a good way to start. (Examples: Before the newfangled invention of the telephone, the family was still living on their farm in Kansas . . . Yesterday afternoon in a suburban mall . . .) Background information on the situation or the social conditions at the time can help transport your audience into the world of the story and make them more receptive to its message.[29] (She lived in the days before the printing press, when every book was handwritten, when a single book could cost a half year's salary . . . Before the war, most of the men tended the cattle and most of the women worked in the fields . . .) Additional details also set the mood you want to convey. (Morning broke over another dry, windy day in the desert, the hundredth day without rain . . .)

Mythical stories often begin with the formulaic phrase, "Once upon a time in a faraway land." Listeners immediately pull up their mental "fairy tale schema" and listen to the story through that filter. True-life narratives draw listeners into the world of the story by starting with realistic details, "When I was a junior in high school, I was enrolled in a very small private school in the mountain country of Montana." This opening immediately activates the listeners' "personal experiences" schema. Regardless of the type of story, details about the setting help listeners place themselves psychologically in the story's space.

Develop the Characters

It goes without saying that stories contain characters, whether real or imaginary. Fictional characters include personified animals (like dogs) or natural objects (like talking trees). Clearly imaginary characters (dragons, talking trains, and other fanciful creatures) convey and reinforce important cultural values the world over. For almost 2,500 years, Aesop's fables have illustrated western cultural wisdom through animals. Coyote stories, similarly, communicate the wisdom of various Native American groups.

Depending on your purpose, realistic stories about people who act, move, speak, form relationships, and interact with others are more effective. To be believable, these characters will come with their own perspectives and will be motivated by distinctive personality traits, ethnic and religious backgrounds, educational experiences, and social connections.

Develop the Plot

plot the story's action

The **plot** is the challenge or conflict that tests the characters' assumptions, values, or actions. The way they respond to the challenges and the resulting changes in their lives form the plot, or action of the narrative. Typical plots feature characters meeting physical, psychological, and economic challenges. They have accidents, grow older, begin and end relationships, lose their possessions in a tragic manner, and so on. How they deal with these challenges provides the point or moral of the story.

Format Your Speech as a Story

Many speeches that are outlined in the common patterns described in Chapter 9 could be presented in a story format. For example, Emily's speech outline on biliary atresia appears in Chapter 11 in a topical pattern; however, she could have organized her speech as a narrative by creating a plausible story line from the elements of setting, characters, and plot.[30]

- Setting: a small town in Oregon in the late 1980s when medical breakthroughs were not as advanced as they are today. [A photograph displayed using presentation software shows the family home.]
- Characters: the parents, the very ill newborn, the doctors, the donor's family, family and friends from the community, and so on. [A photograph shows the major characters she will emphasize.]
- Plot: the crisis that was discovered when the tiny child became jaundiced. The villain is biliary atresia. [A diagram of the liver illuminates the concept.]

Presenting the speech as a narrative gives the audience a different perspective from the one outlined in Chapter 11.[31] A narrative format allows Emily to emphasize her

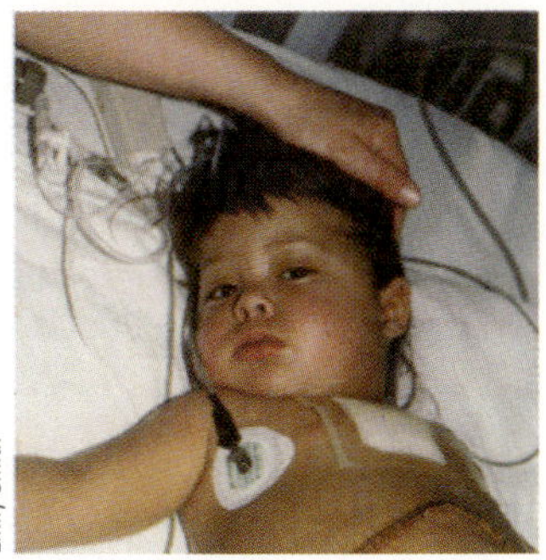
Emily Smith

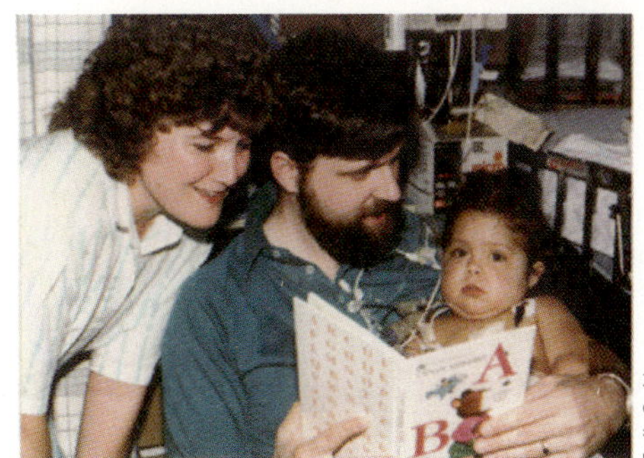
Emily Smith

Emily could have presented her speech as a narrative with a series of slides to illustrate the setting, the characters, and the plot. The character(s) chosen to play the hero(es) would depend on her speech purpose.

purpose by deciding who plays the starring role(s). If her goal is to inform the audience of medical breakthroughs, the doctors are the lead characters. To persuade listeners to become organ donors, the donor and her family play the starring roles. To emphasize the value of working together during a crisis situation, she would highlight the roles of family and community members who raised money for her treatments.

Select Vivid Language

Narrative speaking requires careful attention to language. Vivid word choices and details bring the story to life and let your listeners feel as if they are present as the events unfold. Detailed descriptions convey information, help create the scene, and provide a sense of authenticity by giving specific names, places, and times. Language includes details, constructed dialogue, and listing.

Provide Detailed Descriptions

Details are important in several places. When you first orient the audience to the plot, include enough descriptive material to give your audience the story's context. When you come to the key action points, give listeners the details they need to clearly understand the changes taking place within the characters. Finally, use a cluster of details in the climax of the story to drive home your main point.

Be careful to include just the right amount of description. Certain details are vital, but others are irrelevant for two major reasons. First, you may have too many. Just ask a child to describe a movie he saw, and he'll probably get bogged down in details. He might even miss the film's point entirely because children don't always separate details relevant to the plot from those that merely add color. Details also can be inappropriate when they reveal more than listeners want to know. For instance, disclosing intimate or shocking information might cause listeners to focus on the details and miss the story's point. For these reasons, evaluate details carefully in light of your specific audience and then edit out irrelevant or inappropriate material.

Construct Dialogue

Created or **constructed dialogue** between characters adds realism. By using vocal variety that conveys your characters' personalities and emotions, you increase both your involvement and your listener's involvement in the story. For example, here is one way to report a scene:

constructed dialogue created conversation between characters that adds realism to a story

> He told me to move my car, but I didn't, because I was only going to park for a moment. The next thing I knew, he threatened me.

Contrast the different effect it would have on your audience if you create a dialogue, then use different voices, volume, and rate for each character, like this:

> He rolled down his car window and yelled, "Hey, kid, move your pile of junk!" I turned down my radio and explained through my open window, "I'll just be here a minute. I'm waiting for my mother." He jerked open his car door, stomped over to my car, leaned into my window and said slowly through clenched teeth, "I said, (pause) 'Move . . . your . . . pile . . . of . . . junk, kid!'"

As you can see, the scene with vivid, memorable dialogue is far more likely to involve listeners. By increasing their emotional involvement in the story, you keep their attention and have greater potential for communicating your point.

Create Lists

Lists increase audience rapport because they introduce specific areas of commonality with the storyteller. If you said, "I packed my bags and checked twice to see if I had forgotten anything" you would get across the message, but adding specific details that are familiar to travelers enlivens it, as this example illustrates:

> As I packed for my trip to China, I was afraid I would forget something vital. I looked through my bag for the seventh time. Toothpaste? Check. Toothbrush? Check. Toilet paper? (I like being prepared.) Check. Deodorant? Yep. Yet something seemed to be missing—as I was to discover in an isolated village in Shanxi Province.

Analyze a Folktale

D. L. Alishman, from the University of Pittsburgh, sponsors a site of Folklore and Mythology Electronic Texts. Visit the site and download a folktale from another culture. Compare the way it's constructed with the guidelines presented here. What is the purpose of the story? Are the characters real or imaginary? What details provide clues to their personality and motivations? What is the plot of the story? How does the storyteller incorporate vivid language, use of details, dialogue, and lists?

Bob Rowan; Progressive Image/CORBIS

Storytellers universally tell folktales to pass on important cultural ideas.

How is the story similar to a typical narratives from your culture? If it's different, tell how. Jot down your analysis and prepare to discuss your conclusions with a small group of your classmates. This site is available on **weblink 15.2.** (You can access this link through your CourseMate for *Public Speaking*, Chapter 15 resources.)

Again, the details involve listeners actively, inviting them to create mental images for each item you list. As you can see, the language you choose makes a difference. Because narratives appeal to emotions, it is vital that your audience become involved in the story, and word choices that increase audience involvement make your story more powerful and memorable.

Use a Narrative Pattern

Although the various elements in the speech could be arranged by importance, interest value, or recency,[32] the chronological pattern is most commonly used for narrative speeches. Storytellers typically begin at the beginning, lead to the middle section, and wrap up the action in the conclusion, bringing in relevant information that contributes to the overall main point and editing out irrelevant facts. Often, they state the point or moral of the story explicitly at the beginning, at the end, or both. Ben Hargrove's speech at the end of this chapter and Gail Grobey's speech in Appendix C both use the chronological pattern.

The **exemplum** is another pattern that speakers have used for thousands of years.[33] This pattern has five elements: a quotation, the source, a paraphrase, a narrative that illustrates it, and an application or point. The following brief summary of the main ideas in one student's exemplum speech illustrates each element.[34]

exemplum an organizational pattern in which a narrative is used to illustrate a quotation

1. *State a quotation or proverb.* "Grant me the serenity to accept the things I cannot change, the courage to change the things I can, and the wisdom to know the difference."
2. *Identify and explain the author or source of the proverb or the quotation.* Dr. Reinhold Neibuhr wrote this in a sermon given between World Wars I and II; it was later printed on a card and distributed to soldiers. But it became famous as the slogan for Alcoholics Anonymous.
3. *Rephrase the proverb in your own words.* In other words, we should improve situations when we can or find ways to live contentedly when we know we cannot change our circumstances.
4. *Tell a story that illustrates the quotation or proverb.* Her story described how she wore hearing aids from age three on. Only when she went to school did she realize she was different, and she withdrew until years of speech therapy and training helped her accept her condition and inform others when she didn't understand them. This lessened her stress.
5. *Apply the quotation or proverb to the audience.* Everyone should learn to accept things as they are and to focus on what they have, not on what they lack.

Select your narrative from personal experiences, from historical events, or from episodes in someone else's life. Your story should represent, illustrate, or explain something important to you, perhaps a turning point in your life. Identify a lesson or point to your story and then find a quotation that supports this point. You might use a cultural saying, such as "silence is golden," or you can consult sources of quotations (listed topically and by author) in the reference section of the library or online. **Weblink 15.3** maintains links to sources for quotations. (You can access this link through your CourseMate for *Public Speaking*, Chapter 15 resources.)

A third strategy is to develop a narrative speech around a definition as explained in Chapter 16 (pages 283–284). With this pattern, a word and its denotative definition substitute for the quotation, source, and paraphrase parts of the exemplum. The story then illustrates your connotative interpretation of the word. Natasha Bevis's story of her parents' marriage illustrates what the term "intercultural marriage" means to her. (Her speech is at the end of Chapter 2.)

How We Judge Stories

Stories aren't equally valuable, so we should test them to see if they are sensible and worthy of being told. Some are true and honest; others are false, mistaken, or downright lies.[35] But how do we judge narratives? And when faced with competing stories, how do we weigh and decide which is best? To answer these questions, narrative theorists offer three major tests of narrative logic.[36]

narrative coherence deciding if a narrative is understandable or sensible

narrative fidelity testing if the narrative faithfully represents how the world works

narrative merit testing whether or not a narrative is worth telling

1. Does the story have **narrative coherence**? That is, is it understandable? Does it hang together logically? Do the events in the story follow one another in a predictable sequence? Do the characters act and interact in ways that are probable, given their personalities and cultural backgrounds? Or do some things seem out of character or out of order?
2. Does the story truly or faithfully represent what you know about the world and the way it works? In other words, does the story make sense within the larger cultural framework? If it is a myth, folktale, or hypothetical story, does it contain important truths that demonstrate appropriate ways to live? Walter Fisher[37] terms this **narrative fidelity**.
3. Does the story have **narrative merit**? Should it be told because the message is important or worthwhile? Does it motivate people to behave in ways that result in ethical outcomes for individuals and for society as a whole? Does it serve as a cautionary tale? Does it reinforce a cultural value? Before passing along a story, it is important to evaluate the desirability of doing so.

We weigh priorities and make ethical decisions when we choose whether or not to repeat a particular story. A narrative that creates problems for the individuals involved or their families can provide a good cautionary example, but the harm to innocent people may outweigh the benefits. Gossip, such as information about a political candidate's shaky marriage or the suicide attempt of a public figure's child, poses questions of narrative merit. If sensational details of the characters' private lives are merely entertaining, examine your motives. Why disclose them? However, if the story uncovers a public figure's character flaws or tendencies that don't match his or her pronouncements; then it might be appropriate to tell.

Judging Stories

Go to a current news site and select a human interest story. (For example, today's headlines feature a story about an ATM repairman who cleaned the cash out of machines and refilled the ATMs with photocopied bills; another story describes a dog whose legs were broken in a tornado but who crawled home—taking two weeks to arrive.)

Or go to the StoryCorps site where "every voice matters." This nonprofit group gives anyone with a story to tell an opportunity to tell it. Listen to a story of your choice.

Analyze the story by identifying its purpose and describing how well the characters and the plot fulfill the purpose. Use the questions about narrative coherence, narrative fidelity, and narrative merit on this page to guide your analysis.

Weblink 15.4 links you to sources for today's headlines and with the StoryCorps site. (You can access this link through your CourseMate for *Public Speaking,* Chapter 15 resources.)

Good stories aren't necessarily true—fiction has its place. But stories that are blatantly false and result in harm are wrong to tell. History provides examples of leaders who spread lies with disastrous consequences. Here's one: In the Middle Ages, people circulated false narratives about Jews poisoning the water supply of villages, stories that resulted in the murder of many Jewish people and produced irreversible negative consequences on individuals and on society in general.

Summary

In every society, narrative reasoning exists as a form of sense making. Narratives both reflect and shape cultural beliefs and values, and hearing narratives from other cultures highlights commonalities and differences between groups. Narratives in all cultures function to inform, to persuade, to commemorate cultural ideals, and to entertain. Explanatory narratives provide answers for why and how things are the way they are. Persuasive narratives provide reasons for or against a belief or course of action, and they highlight important beliefs, values, attitudes, and behaviors. Visionary narratives help us see possibilities that we had not imagined before. Finally, some narratives are just plain fun, and we tell them for entertainment purposes.

Stories have five major elements: purpose, characters, sequence, plot, and language. Vivid language is especially important because it brings characters to life and makes the action more compelling, causing listeners to identify with more elements of the story. Many speeches that are organized in traditional patterns could also be organized as narratives. Your goal determines which characters and what actions to emphasize.

Organize your story in a chronological pattern or use the exemplum pattern, a pattern with a long history that begins with a quotation, provides information about the source, and paraphrases the saying. An illustrative story forms most of the speech, which concludes with a stated lesson or moral. A speech of definition is a third way to organize a narrative. First give the denotative definition of the word and then explain its connotative meaning through a story.

Some stories are better than others, but every good story should be coherent, it should have fidelity—meaning that it represents some aspect of the real world—and it should be worthy of being told. To evaluate a story's merit, consider its effect on society, its effect on individuals, and its overall truthfulness about life.

STUDY AND REVIEW

Your online resources for *Public Speaking: Concepts and Skills for a Diverse Society* offer a broad range of study tools that will help you better understand the material in this chapter, complete assignments, and succeed on tests. Your online resources feature the following:

- Speech videos with critical viewing questions, speech outlines, and transcripts.
- Interactive versions of this chapter's Stop and Check activities, as well as Application and Critical Thinking Exercises.
- Speech Builder Express and InfoTrac College Edition.
- Weblinks related to chapter content.
- Study and review tools such as self-quizzes, an *interactive* glossary, and downloadable audio summaries.

You can access your online resources at the CourseMate for *Public Speaking: Concepts and Skills for a Diverse Society.* Log in at **http://www.cengage.com/login**, using the access code that came with your book or that you bought online at **http://www.cengagebrain.com**.

KEY TERMS

The terms below are defined in the margins throughout this chapter.

APPLICATION AND CRITICAL THINKING EXERCISES

1. What narratives do you use to explain the world of nature? The social world? Your family? Other groups to which you belong? The ultimate meanings in life? Do your stories ever clash with the narratives of others? If so, what do you do about these differences?
2. What informative narratives have you heard about your school or about an organization you work for? For example, employees at Wal-Mart hear the story about how founder and billionaire Sam Walton drove his beat-up old pick-up truck to work every day. What kind of values does this type of story teach?
3. To read another culture's explanation of its history, search InfoTrac College Edition for "Stone Camels and Clear Springs" in the journal *Asian Folklore Studies*. This drama features audience participation and feedback in the retelling of the history of the Salar people.
4. Discuss with your classmates how informative narratives help us to prepare for the unknown by sharing one of your travel stories and the advice you would give to others traveling to the same destination.
5. Share with a group of classmates a few examples of persuasive narratives you heard while you were growing up. In what ways were they intended to influence your behaviors? How successful were they?
6. To illustrate the power of persuasive narratives, visit the Urban Legends Reference page at **weblink 15.5**. Did you find any legends you had heard and believed to be true? What makes urban legends so compelling? (You can access this link through your CourseMate for *Public Speaking,* Chapter 12 resources.)

7. In what settings have you heard inspiring life stories that highlight a cultural ideal? Have you ever shared your personal saga of overcoming some challenge? If so, describe the occasion. Where might you give an inspirational personal story in the future? What would be your purpose?
8. To better understand applied storytelling, search InfoTrac College Edition for the words "healing AND storytelling." Read an article and discuss it with a small group of your classmates.
9. Think of stories that you have only heard orally. Who are the "legends" in your family, your sports team, your religious group, living group, or university? What lessons do their stories provide? What values or actions do they help you remember and perpetuate?
10. What cultural values do classic children's stories reinforce in our culture? For example, what lesson lies in the fable of "The Tortoise and the Hare"? What is the moral of "The Three Little Pigs"? Do *The Cat in the Hat* or *Finding Nemo* simply entertain or do they serve other functions as well?

11. Take one of your speech outlines and reframe the topic into narrative form by weaving setting, characters, and plot into a coherent story line.
12. Children's stories explain, persuade, and entertain. Bring in a copy of your favorite children's book. With a small group of classmates, take turns reading your books and discussing the storyteller's major goals, characters, and use of language.
13. The exemplum pattern is useful in a variety of settings. With a small group of your classmates, sketch out themes and suggest the types of supporting narratives that would be appropriate on each of the following occasions:

    - A sports award banquet
    - A luncheon meeting of a club such as Rotary or Kiwanis
    - A religious youth group meeting
    - A scholarship presentation ceremony
    - A Fourth of July celebration
    - A keynote address to a conference focusing on issues relevant to female physicians

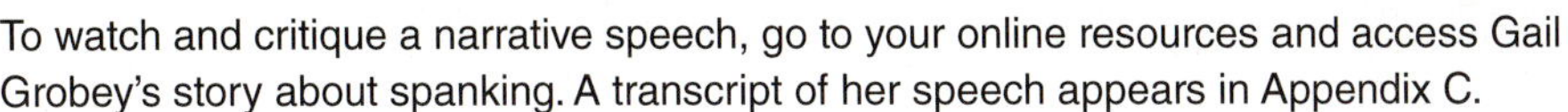

To watch and critique a narrative speech, go to your online resources and access Gail Grobey's story about spanking. A transcript of her speech appears in Appendix C.

Student Speech with Commentary

MY SEPTEMBER 11
By Benjamin Hargrove

Have any of you ever thought to yourself, "I wonder if I'll remember this for the rest of my life?" I wondered that exact thing a certain September evening as I ate waffles with my big sister. *Will I remember the waffles? Will I remember the glow of the city off the smoke? Mom's tears? My fear? My anger?* It was three months and two days before my eleventh birthday; I already had a countdown started on my baseball calendar. I always go back to the weather; it was incredible, not a cloud in sight.

Because Benjamin's experience is so unusual, he relates to the audience by asking a question about memorable moments in general.

We lived on Andrews Air Force Base, fifteen miles from the Pentagon in Washington, D.C. We lived there because my dad, an Air Force pilot, flew Air Force II, the Vice-President's plane. Dad was gone that day, flying the backup plane for President Bush on a trip to Florida. Dad traveled a lot, so a tiny trip to Florida was a familiar routine for my family.

Like any good storyteller, he sets the scene and introduces the characters before launching into the event that forms the plot.

I was doing my schoolwork as the phone rang. Mom answered and I could hear the familiar voice of Ms. Terri from down the street. The voice rattled through the earpiece. "There was a plane crash . . . you need to turn on the news." My heart froze. My throat felt stuck and my arms heavy but the instant panic absorbed my tears. My ten-year-old mind raced for an explanation. "It's not your dad's plane but something has happened," she said, "Turn it on!" As I walked over to turn on the TV, I remember looking out the window watching the warm sunshine slice through the branches of the huge oak tree in our backyard.

Here he uses a great many details to set up the plot.

I stared blankly at the TV screen as that skyline was destroyed. While I watched, another airplane, the same size as Dad's, collided with the other tower. And then the Pentagon was hit. A lot of our neighbors worked there and Dad had gone there for meetings before. Throughout the morning, I watched over Mom's shoulder, trying to piece it together.

The TV started talking about the President. Everybody wanted to know where he was because they did not think he would be safe much longer. I knew where he was. President Bush was with Dad in Florida. The TV started saying the President was a likely target and some terrorists might be trying to crash his plane. That's why Mom was upset the whole day. There was nothing I could say. I was too afraid. *I just hope Dad can fly faster than the terrorists.*

His insider's view provides a different perspective on a national event.

The day was stuck on pause. My big sister, Molly, went to school outside the Air Force Base. Mom started to worry about her too because we couldn't go out to get her. The base was shut down. No one understood what was happening. I overheard some adults talking about what would happen if terrorists attacked the city with chemicals. A lot of important people lived around us and maybe the terrorists knew. I thought about Dad and wondered if he was safe. I thought about the people dying in the fire and if I would remember this day when I was older. Afternoon finally arrived as the armored Humvees drove past our house on the main road. They had never driven by before.

My forehead smashed against the back window of the minivan as I strained to watch the soldiers with machine guns. We waited by the gate to pick up Molly once the police escort let the van of military kids come home. Sandbags and cement walls barricaded the entrance of the base. Police dogs and bulletproof vests swarmed around each car that progressed through the maze. Molly cried when she hugged Mom. She was brave. I was glad to not be alone that day.

He adds details here at the most important part of the day for him. His dad is safe.

The piercing ring of the telephone vibrated, once again, through the kitchen. Mom's hands shook a little as she walked over to the telephone against the wall. Her voice was a little raspy from all her crying that day. She said, "Hello?" and breathed a welcome sigh of relief. I knew who it was before she said anything. In about a minute, she hung up and turned to us with intent and exhausted eyes. *Dad is alive, and Dad is safe. That's all I need to know.* She could not say where he was or when he would be home.

Like millions of other Americans, he cannot explain the unexplainable in the end.

That night we had waffles, with peanut butter. Everything blends together but I remember the sunset breaking through the upstairs window and pouring down the stairwell into the kitchen, where we ate in silence. I fell asleep staring out my window. That night, lights from D.C. reflected off the Pentagon smoke and lit up that cloudless sky with a smoky amber glow.

© Tim Timmerman

CHAPTER 16

THIS CHAPTER WILL HELP YOU

- Describe the global importance of information
- Analyze your audience's knowledge of your subject
- Create several types of informative speeches including demonstrations and instructions, descriptions, reports, and explanations
- Follow guidelines that make your informative speeches more effective

Informative Speaking

TAKE A MOMENT and picture yourself fifteen years down the road. Where are you working? What information might you give your coworkers or the public? What instructions or directions are vital to your success? What information will make you healthier, happier, or more productive? Informative speeches, the "speech to teach" category, are very common, as these examples show:

- A leader of a campus club reports on a new fundraising plan.
- A firefighter explains fire safety to elementary school students.
- An accountant presents the annual audit to a client company's board of directors.

This chapter first examines the global importance of information. It then turns to audience analysis and distinguishes four levels of audience knowledge you should consider before you speak. Next, it describes several types of speeches, including demonstrations and instructions, descriptions, reports, and explanations—with skeletal outlines of speeches in these categories. General guidelines for informative speaking conclude the chapter.

Information Is Important Globally

That we live in an Information Age is a given. W. Russell Neuman, professor of media technology at the University of Michigan, reports that in the United States in the 1960s, the supply-to-demand ratio of available media was 98:1. That means there were 98 possible minutes of media available for every minute of consumption. By 2005 the ratio was an overwhelming 20,943:1 and rising, as new information sharing sources such as Digg, Reddit, and Twitter came online. Neuman reports that most people like having vast amounts information as close as their smartphones or computers, but he wonders if we are better informed as a result.[1]

Think about it. How much of the information you receive affects you personally? What's really important, and what's trivial? What must you know to live better, and what's simply interesting or distracting? Ask questions like this when you analyze your audience. Listeners can feel overwhelmed with disparate facts and ideas unless you relate the material to their lives and help them integrate new information with old. This not only helps them make sense of their world but it also provides them with data they can use to make wise decisions.[2] A clear description or explanation of new developments in genetically modified foods, effective strategies for studying, or wind power as an renewable energy source can furnish meaningful information for various audiences.

The United Nations has long affirmed that access to information is a human right with ethical implications. Article 19 of the Universal Declaration of Human Rights (1948) states:

> Everyone has the right to freedom of opinion and expression; this right includes freedom to hold opinions without interference and to seek and impart information and ideas through any media and regardless of frontiers.[3]

information imbalance some people or groups having very little access to information while others have it in abundance

Article 19 recognizes the potential dangers of an **information imbalance**, where some individuals and groups have overwhelming amounts of information and others have very little and thus lack fundamental understandings of the world. (The entire UN declaration is maintained at **weblink 16.1**. You can access this link through your CourseMate for *Public Speaking*, Chapter 16 resources.)

Events during the "Arab Spring" of 2011 show how information empowers a citizenry. Using Facebook and Twitter to share unfolding events, people took to the streets in Egypt, Libya, and other countries to protest oppressive governments. No wonder some countries try to prevent average citizens from freely accessing all the available information on the Internet.[4] Later that spring, a United Nations report declared access to the Internet as a human right for all nations.[5]

In summary, information is a valuable resource or commodity. It is abundant in the United States and many other countries; it's more restricted in a number of nations. Some groups and social classes have access to information essential to success and health; others have limited access to the same knowledge, and information imbalance has ethical implications. Finally, some individuals know how to take advantage of the available information; others do not.[6]

The Right to Information

What are the limits on our rights to know? Even in the United States, not all information is available to just anyone, and cultural values such as privacy or national security allow for "privileged" or "confidential" information in some cases. In journalism, reporters have gone to jail rather than name their sources.[7] Politicians or corporations try to protect strategy secrets. On the other hand, personal information on private citizens is widely available through Internet sites that (without asking permission) publish addresses, occupations, approximate salaries—along with street views of homes.

Because free access to information is vital to a democracy, the US federal government passed the Freedom of Information Act (FOIA) to give citizens access to federal agency records or information (including your personal FBI file, should you have one). However, it excludes records from Congress, the courts, or state and local government agencies.[8]

Wikileaks, a non-profit organization that publishes private and classified documents intended to expose unethical practices in governments and institutions globally,[9] recently tested national security restrictions by releasing highly classified State Department diplomatic cables and secret files on Guantanamo Bay prisoners. The Obama administration responded by investigating the legality of the organization's tactics and its sources.[10]

Questions

1. Can you think of instances where withholding information is a good thing?
2. Have you been deprived of information that you thought you needed? If so, describe the situation and tell the results.
3. Is there a difference between "limits on our rights to know" and "censorship"? Explain your answer.
4. Have you ever had personal information published on the Internet without your consent? Explain.
5. Julian Assange of WikiLeaks is a controversial Australian who says he wants openness in countries such as China and Russia—and the United States. Some consider him a hero; others think he's a villain. Read some news and opinion articles about him and come to class prepared to discuss his intentions and his tactics.

Analyze Your Audience's Current Knowledge

Listeners fall into four general categories: listeners who (a) know nothing about your topic, (b) have minimal information, (c) have forgotten or outdated information, or (d) have misinformation. Each level of understanding calls for different strategies.[11] To be effective, you must discover what the audience already knows and believes about your topic so that you can adjust your speech accordingly.[12] This can be challenging because a single audience often contains listeners from more than one category.

At the outset, analyze what your audience already knows about your topic. Are they totally unfamiliar with it? Do they have outdated information or misconceptions? Answering these questions helps you design speeches that will make the information more useful to your listeners.

Devan Marchbanks

Presenting New Information

When your audience is unfamiliar with your subject, your task is to provide a basic overview of the topic. For instance, what do you know about artificial gills? Mochi pounding? The Chinese New Year? Most people have never heard of them, so your information will be novel. I've heard speeches on each of these topics, and they were successful because the speakers followed these guidelines:

- Provide basic, introductory facts—who, what, when, where, and how information.
- Clearly define unfamiliar terminology and jargon.
- Give detailed, vivid explanations and descriptions.
- Make as many links as you can to the audience's knowledge by using literal and figurative analogies and by comparing and contrasting the concept with something familiar.
- Help audience members understand why they should know about your subject.

Presenting Supplemental Information

The great inventor Thomas Edison said, "We don't know a millionth of one percent about anything."[13] This means that listeners often have some information about a topic but have gaps in their knowledge. They want supplemental information, not a rehash of basic facts. An audience familiar with running marathons, for example, will be more impressed if you provide little-known facts about this type of race. Use these guidelines with audiences whose information is limited:

- Dig into your research sources to discover less familiar details and facts.
- Go beyond the obvious and add in-depth descriptions, details, and explanations.
- Narrow a broad topic and provide interesting and novel information about just one aspect of it. For example, talk about a few legendary African marathoners.

Presenting Review or Updated Information

Some listeners were once familiar with your subject, but they've forgotten some or most of what they learned, or they lack current, updated information. Your speech can function as a review to refresh their memories, reinforce their knowledge, and keep their information current. Reviews and updates are common in schools or workplace settings. For instance, employees may have learned about privacy laws a decade ago, but a workshop on new regulations keeps them updated. Peggy Kilburg, featured in the Practically Speaking box, often reviews or updates information. With these audiences, you'll be more effective using these guidelines:

- Review material by approaching the subject from different angles and different perspectives.
- Be creative; use vivid supporting materials that capture and hold attention.
- Use humor when appropriate, and strive to make the material interesting.
- Present the most recent available information. Because of the current proliferation of information generated by technology, data can quickly become outdated, and people who want to stay current must be lifelong learners.

Countering Misinformation

A third type of audience has misconceptions or misunderstandings that you can clarify by providing definitions and facts and by countering misinformation. For instance, the saying, "A dog is a human's best friend," is widely accepted in the United States. However, Stephen Budiansky[14] presents scientific evidence suggesting that dogs don't really adore their owners; instead, they fake devotion to manipulate humans. If this is true, many or most people in your audience misunderstand dog behavior.

In other examples, students from different ethnic backgrounds often counter misconceptions about their culture, or politicians sometimes clarify policy positions that their opponents have distorted. When you counter misunderstandings, your material will be inconsistent or contradictory to what listeners "know," so consider the following:

- Prepare for emotional responses—often negative. (Think about it. Who wants to hear that her beloved dog is really a con artist?) Consequently, present the most credible facts you can find, and tone down the emotional aspect.
- Look for information derived from scientific studies, especially quantification, when statistical or numerical support would be best.
- Define terminology carefully; explaining the origin of specific words or ideas is often a good strategy.
- Counter negative prejudices against and stereotypes about a topic (such as a particular culture) by highlighting positive aspects of the subject.

In summary, the amount of information your audience brings to your speech should make a difference in the way you select and present meaningful information, and various listeners can have differing levels of understanding. By assessing listeners' knowledge about your subject in advance, you can more effectively prepare a speech that meets their need to know.

Types of Informative Speeches

Informative speeches fall into several categories. Demonstrations and instructions, descriptions, reports, and explanations are common in college classrooms and in many careers. Two basic methods are useful for organizing and explaining information: division

Analyze Your Audience's Knowledge

As part of your preparation, analyze your audience's knowledge of your informative speech topic. (Chapter 6 gives guidelines for constructing a questionnaire to determine this.)

___ Most people have probably never heard of it.
___ Most people are familiar with it and need more in-depth information.
___ Most people were once quite familiar with it but need a review.
___ Most people are familiar with it but need updated information.
___ Most people have misconceptions about my topic.

Here's how I plan to show the relevance of the topic to their lives:

____

These are potentially negative feelings or attitudes they may have toward the topic:

____

I must take care to:

____

I can use these strategies if my audience is mixed (some know quite a bit, others know very little or have misconceptions):

____

division a method for presenting information by breaking the whole into parts and explaining each one

classification a method of presenting information by explaining things that are put into categories according to a principle

and classification.[15] **Division** involves breaking the whole into parts and discussing each part individually. For example, Kylie divided the topic of Asperger syndrome into causes, symptoms, and treatments. She then developed each sub-topic in more detail. **Classification** also divides a topic into categories, but it then uses a common standard to rate or rank the groups. For instance, languages are classified by how hard they are to learn. A speech on language learning might explain why Spanish is classified as a Level I language, Hindi as Level II, Turkish as Level III, and Chinese as Level IV.[16] An article maintained on **weblink 16.2** describes division and classification in more detail. (You can access this link through your CourseMate for *Public Speaking*, Chapter 16 resources.)

Doing Demonstrations and Providing Instructions

Instructions answer the question, "How do you do that?" Emeril Lagasse became famous by demonstrating cooking techniques; Suze Orman instructs people on how to put their finances in order. They're just two of thousands of teachers, coaches, and salespeople who both show (demonstrate) and tell (give instructions) how to do a procedure, how to use a specific object, or how to complete a task. Several principles can help you give these speeches effectively:

1. First, use the principle of division and break up the topic into required stages or steps. Then ask: What's absolutely essential? What comes first? Which step is easiest? Which is hardest? What does the audience already know how to do? Where will the audience most likely be confused? Which step takes the most time?[17]
2. Next, work on speech content. Organize the essential steps sequentially, and concentrate on clarifying and simplifying difficult or confusing steps. Carefully preplan the environment to facilitate learning—you might have your audience move their chairs

or stand up and spread out around the room. Or you may need to furnish supplies so they can do the project along with you.

3. Plan your visual support. If actual objects are practical, use them; if not, plan videos, diagrams, or other visuals. Then practice working with your props so you can use them and still maintain rapport with your audience.[18] Knowing that she could not simply describe how to draw a hand in words alone, Beth led her listeners through the process by actually drawing on a whiteboard as shown in the photographs.[19]

Specific Purpose: To inform my audience about six steps in drawing a hand.

Central Idea: It's easy to draw a hand if you follow six steps.

I. Step 1: block out the outline using simple, geometric shapes.
II. Step 2: identify the bone structure, including all the knuckles.
III. Step 3: draw around the basic outline in Step 1.
IV. Step 4: add details of knuckles, fingernails, creases, rings and so on.
V. Step 5: shade, using dark, medium, or light shades.
VI. Step 6: erase excess lines.

In her introduction, she had each student take out a pencil and a blank sheet of paper. (She'd brought along some blank paper and extra pencils, just in case.) Then, as she spoke, each student completed each step with her.

4. Time the entire process. If doing the process takes too long, you're better off demonstrating it and then distributing handouts with step-by-step instructions for listeners to do later. One student should have used this strategy instead of trying to teach her classmates to fold an origami crane in a seven-minute speech; twenty-two minutes later, everyone had half-folded cranes when the class period ran out. Another strategy for a lengthy process is to prepare several versions, stopping each at a different point of completion. Cooking and art instructors commonly do this. A cook, for example, begins a complicated dish, but instead of waiting twenty minutes for it to bake, he sets aside the partly finished pan, reaches for a second pan that contains a baked version of the dish and then adds finishing touches. Similarly, a sculptor shows an essential step in creating a pot; then she leaves it to dry and takes up a pot prepared in advance for the next step.

Devan Marchbanks

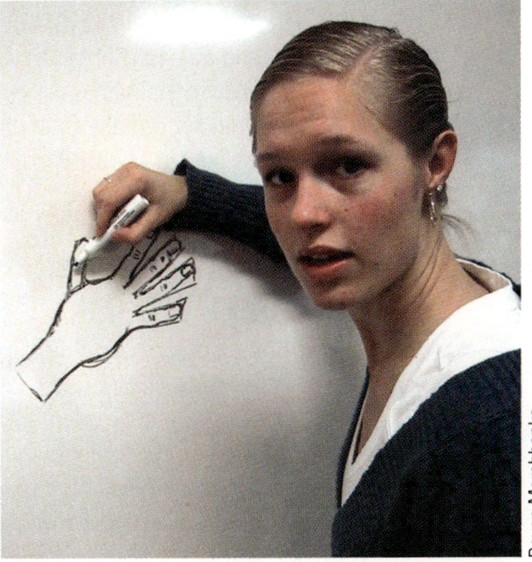

Devan Marchbanks

For her how-to speech on drawing a hand, Beth drew on the board as she explained the process. Her audience drew along with her, following her instructions step-by-step.

Not all "how-to" speeches require a demonstration. You can give tips on topics like resolving conflict, listening more effectively, or managing time wisely. In these cases, you focus on instructions or pointers that will help audience members accomplish the goal.

Giving Descriptions

Descriptions answer the question, "What's it like?" Before you can describe an object, place, or event to someone else, use the principles of division or classification to analyze it. For instance, an art museum guide might divide a painting into sections and point out details of color, form, and texture that listeners might miss at first glance. Or she might classify several paintings according to era or style and compare and contrast the details. Descriptions of places, objects, and events range from personal to global. Because listeners are generally more interested in topics close to their daily lives in location, time, and relevance, explicitly relate each topic to their perceived interests and needs.

Describing Places

People often seek information about places. A prospective student visits a campus, for example, wanting to know how it is laid out, so a college guide describes campus sites as he shows the visitor around. Descriptions of different countries or places, such as national parks or tourist attractions, similarly attract audiences, and travel agents or park rangers are just two types of professionals who describe places.

In descriptive speeches, provide vivid, precise imagery. Use visual aids including maps, drawings, slides, brochures, or enlarged photographs, and consider spatial or topical organizational patterns. Here are the main points of a speech about *Ha Noi*, given by a student from Vietnam:[20]

Specific Purpose: To inform my audience about *Ha Noi* and how it communicates.

Central Idea: *Ha Noi* is a thousand-year-old city, and its many scenic attractions reveal a lot about Vietnamese culture.

I. *Ho Hoan Kiem*, Sword Lake, reminds us of the holy sword the gods gave to protect our country.
II. *Van Mieu—Quoc Tu Giam*, the Temple of Literature, is Vietnam's first university, which was built in 1076.
III. *Lang Bac*, Ho Chi Minh's Mausoleum, honors "Uncle Ho," who brought independence to Vietnam.
IV. *Chua Mot Cot*, the One Pillar Pagoda, which honors the Buddhist goddess of mercy, was built in 1049.

For an international topic, consider geographical features (the Gobi desert) or sites (Vatican City).

Describing Objects

Descriptions of objects, including natural objects (glaciers), human constructions (the Vietnam War Memorial), huge things (the planet Jupiter), or microscopic matter (carbohydrates), are common. Students have described inanimate (wind generators) or animate (brown recluse spiders) objects by providing information such as their origin, how they are made, their identifying characteristics, how they work, how they're used, and so on.

Topic choices range from personal to international. On the personal level, students have described body features such as skin or fingernails. They've talk about campus objects like a historical tree or a memorial plaque and explained cultural artifacts such as the Golden Gate Bridge and guitars. International topics have included the Great Wall of China and London's Big Ben.

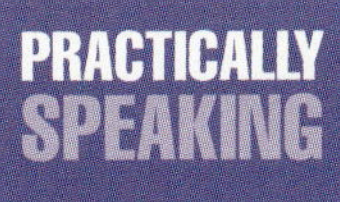

Informative Speaking on the Job

Peggy Kilburg

Peggy Kilburg has been in Human Resources for more than two decades, both in for-profit and in non-profit organizations. Most of her presentations are informative.

In your job, what types of informative topics do you speak about? Topics range from explaining policies, procedures, and benefits to prospective and/or new employees, sharing and explaining policy to (mostly) current employees, making proposals to the executive team (infrequently), making announcements at employee meetings to doing nine hours of training with new supervisors.

Recently, we had a new performance review and planning (PRP) proposal that links pay to performance, so I did several informative presentations: to the operations and budget team, the executive team, supervisors, and all the employees. Most presentations were formal, with PowerPoint slides followed by a question-and-answer session. I also prepared a handout they could take away. Workshops that trained supervisors in implementing the program lasted three hours and included discussion and group exercises.

My favorite presentations take place at the annual service award event. I prepare and present 30- or 60-second service award commentaries. These are commemorative speeches, but they include information about the honorees' job history with the organization.

How excited are your audiences about attending your speeches? I think employees are interested and curious about new processes. Some probably have a level of skepticism as well. New hires are pretty enthusiastic about listening to talks about benefits and procedures.

What are the three most important things to remember about informative presentations?

1. Know your audience in terms of their interest level, how they will use or apply the information, so that you will know what level of detail to share.
2. Organize your ideas and thoughts in advance. You may still take sidebar trips due to questions, but this ensures the basics are not skipped.
3. Make it interesting—no reading of information/notes/Power Point. Use humor, examples, and stories to make points when possible. People love stories! Be enthusiastic and appropriately engaging. I have a fairly informal style, so I think I present as if I were sharing with just a few people.
4. I know you asked for three, but above everything else is this cardinal rule: Know your information—be prepared. People have often asked me if I'm nervous about presentations. Early on I was, but experience taught me that as long as I know my stuff I can control my nerves.

Questions

1. Select two different audiences and topics that Kilburg addresses (for example, supervisors about the PRP or new hires about benefits), and try to classify the majority of listeners in each situation into one of the categories of knowledge presented earlier. Would most of them know nothing? Need additional information? Need a review? Or have misconceptions that she must counter?
2. Give examples of informative speaking in the career(s) that most interest you.

Describing Events

Events range from personal (birthday customs), community (local festivals), national (holidays), to international (the bombing of Hiroshima). At the end of this chapter, you'll find Lishan's explanation of the Chinese holiday that corresponds to St. Valentine's Day. Chronological, narrative, and topical organizational patterns are common. The first two patterns work well for step-by-step events such as the bombing of Hiroshima. The topical pattern is useful for happenings that consist of several different components. Here is an example of major subtopics for a speech describing a city event.

Specific Purpose: To inform my audience about the Portland Rose Festival.

Central Idea: The Rose Festival in Portland, Oregon, features something for everyone.

I. The Queen's Coronation features court members from each city high school.
II. The Children's Parade lets little kids get involved.
III. People from all over the region participate in the Grand Floral Parade.
IV. City Fair on the waterfront features performers, carnival rides, and other attractions.
V. The Rose Show is for flower lovers.

When you describe events in concrete detail and vivid language, your listeners can place themselves at the happening, and your speech lets them participate vicariously.

Presenting Reports

Reports answer the question, "What have we learned about this subject?" Investigative reporters search for answers to questions such as, "What are scientists learning about new treatments for melanoma?" Campus reporters pass along conclusions reached by university task forces. In classrooms and workplaces, here and abroad, people give reports. This section discusses two common topic areas: people and issues.

Reporting about People

What individuals have shaped our world? What did they accomplish? How did they live? Answer such questions by providing sketches of influential historical or contemporary characters. Biographical reports can be about thinkers (Plato), military men and women (Mongol warriors, Bodiecia), artists (Mary Cassatt), writers (Ngugi wa Thiongo), and so on. Villains (Machiavelli) as well as heroes (Harriet Tubman) make good biographical subjects.

Generally, chronological, topical, or narrative patterns best fit a biographical report. Fei Fei divided her subject into two categories: (1) Confucius's (*K'ung-fu-tzu*) life and (2) his influence. She then uses chronological subpoints to develop her first section.

Specific Purpose: To inform my audience of the life and ideas of the Chinese philosopher whose teachings influence more than a billion people globally.

Central Idea: Confucius, who lived in China about 2,500 years ago, developed a philosophy that has influenced many Asian cultures.

I. The evidence for his life is scanty, based mostly on the Analects (sayings) of Confucius.
   A. He was probably born in the feudal state of Lu, in northern China.
   B. He was concerned about war and bad rulers, and he began to gather disciples.
   C. He journeyed as a wandering scholar.
   D. He may have been a minister of state at one time.
II. Confucius's influence is widespread.
   A. His teaching method focused on growth in moral judgment and self-realization, as well as skills.

B. The concepts of *li* (maintaining proper relationships and rituals) and *jen* (benevolent, humanitarian attitudes) permeate many Asian cultures.
C. The five vital relationships include: king-subject, father-son, husband-wife, older-younger brother, and friend-friend.

Speeches about groups such as thugs, Indigenous Australians, or medieval knights are also interesting. Here are subtopics from a student speech on the Amish that is organized topically:

Specific Purpose: To inform my audience about the Amish by describing their beliefs and explaining challenges facing their group.

Central Idea: The Amish are a religious group with written and unwritten rules for living that are being challenged by education and tourism.

I. The Amish people
    A. Number and location
    B. Historical information
II. Amish beliefs
    A. Written ordinances—Dortrecht Confession of Faith (1632)
    B. Unwritten rules of local congregations—Ordnung
III. Challenges to Amish culture
    A. Education and teacher certification
    B. Tourism attention

As you develop your major points, keep in mind your audience's questions: "How is a speech about this person or group linked to my concerns?" "What impact has this subject had on society?" Answer these questions, and your listeners will better understand the relevance of the person or group. **Weblink 16.3** maintains links to biographical information on thousands of individuals, both contemporary and historical. (You can access this link through your CourseMate for *Public Speaking*, Chapter 16 resources.)

Reporting about Issues

News sources present issues currently being discussed in our communities, our nation, and our world. We deliberate about international, national, local, and campus issues that are complex and controversial. Here are a few examples:

- What have we learned about the effectiveness of alternate energy sources?
- What do we know about the various treatments for Asperger syndrome in children?
- What issues does each side emphasize as they support or oppose taxing Internet sales?

Think of your speech as an investigative report, where you research the facts surrounding an issue and then present your findings. Your goal is to help people to think clearly about a topic, so your major purpose is to provide listeners with facts they can use to formulate their own conclusions. Consequently, do not advocate one position or another, although you may decide to follow up your report with a persuasive speech on the same topic.

Periodicals databases like InfoTrac College Edition or Internet news sites can help you access up-to-date news sources. Look for answers to questions like these: What exactly is the issue? What current beliefs or theories are commonly held about the issue? What is the extent of the problem (how many people does it affect)? How did this situation develop? What solutions are proposed? What are the arguments on both sides of the issue? Generally, pro-con, cause-effect, problem-solution(s), narrative, and topical patterns are most effective for investigative reports. The following pro-con outline for a speech on wind energy used InfoTrac and Academic Search Premier databases as sources.

Specific purpose: To inform my audience about the pros and cons of wind energy.

Central idea: There are several arguments both for and against the widespread use of wind energy.

I. There are advantages to using wind turbines to produce electricity worldwide.
   A. Wind is a clean source of renewable energy that emits no greenhouse gases.
   B. Wind power can help minimize dependency on foreign oil.
   C. The technology is constantly being improved so that electricity produced during peak wind hours can be "banked" and used during peak demand hours.
II. There are a number of problems related to wind turbines.
   A. The blade/wind friction of the wind turbines emits noise and a light flicker that disturbs people who live by wind farms.
   B. Many people think wind farms destroy the beauty of the landscape.
   C. Wind farms can interfere with wild bird habitats.
   D. There are environmental impacts during the manufacturing, set up, maintenance, and dismantling of the turbines after they wear out.

Issues can be personal (eating disorders), campus (parking problems), local (potholes), national (teens and guns), or global (free trade) in scope. Many global decisions, such as what to do with nuclear waste, have broad implications. Others, although less significant, are related to larger problems. For example, cosmetic surgery on teenaged women is linked to issues of women's rights and stereotypes of female beauty.

Informative Speaking in Africa

© Sean Sprague - SpraguePhoto.com

"Knowledge is power" could be the motto of these educators who provide health and childcare information to women in Kenya.

Throughout parts of Africa, public health educators give people information that is potentially life saving. For example, women in central Africa empower one another with facts they can use to protect themselves against sexually transmitted diseases. In remote areas of Kenya, where less than 10 percent of tribal people can read and televisions and radios are not available, a few individuals travel from their villages to larger urban centers, where they learn news of the world and bring it back to their villages. In other settings, community members come together to advise newlyweds by giving the young couple practical "how-to" information they need to build an effective marriage.[21]

Explaining Concepts

The explanatory or **expository speech** is more simply called the "speech to teach." Expository speakers set forth, disclose, unmask, or explain an idea in detail.[22] Science and history teachers regularly define terms and explain concepts; parents also answer the endless "whys" of 4-year-olds with explanations. Good expository speakers can identify the hurdles listeners are likely to encounter in their attempt to comprehend the concept. They then plan ways to overcome those barriers and make meanings clear.

expository speech the "speech to teach" that explains an idea in detail

Defining Terms

Definitions answer the questions "What is it?" or "What does it mean?" Definition speeches are common in classrooms and workplaces—for example, a philosophy professor defines justice, a speech professor clarifies the concept of confirmation as it's used in that academic discipline, and an employer defines sexual harassment for new employees. Inspirational speakers also define words: a priest defines peacemakers; a commencement speaker defines character; a coach defines commitment. In short, although people act in ways we classify as *just* or as *sexual harassment*, we can neither see nor touch justice or harassment; defining those terms helps us as a society to discriminate between appropriate and inappropriate behaviors.

One effective organizational pattern for a speech of definition[23] presents first the denotative and then the connotative meaning of a word. (Chapter 12 discusses denotation and connotation in detail.)

1. **Denotative Meaning**: Focus on the definition of the word as found in reference books, such as thesauruses or etymological dictionaries. The *Oxford English Dictionary* or another unabridged dictionary provides the most thorough definitions. Books in an academic discipline show how scholars in that field define the term; for example, the definition of *confirmation* found in a dictionary is not identical to the definition you'd find in a book on interpersonal communication. Develop the denotative point of your speech by selecting some of the following ideas:

   - Provide synonyms and antonyms that are familiar to your audience.
   - Explain the use or function of what you're defining.
   - Give the etymology of the word. What's its historical source? How has the concept developed over time?
   - Compare an unknown concept or item to one your audience already knows.

   For example, "an Allen wrench" might be unfamiliar to some listeners, but "a wrench that looks like a hockey stick" or "an L-shaped wrench" helps them select the specific tool, given a line-up of wrenches.[24]

2. **Connotative Meaning:** Focus on connotative meanings, the emotional associations of words, by using realistic life experiences as creatively as possible. Here, draw from whatever you can think of that will add emotional elements to your explanation.

   - Relate a personal experience that demonstrates the idea.
   - Quote other people telling what the term means to them.
   - Tell a narrative or give a series of short examples that illustrate the concept.
   - Refer to an exemplar—a person or thing that exemplifies the term.
   - Connect the term to a familiar political, social, or moral issue.

For example, in the denotative section of her student speech on destiny, Terez first provided the dictionary definition and then explained the etymology of the word like this:

> The Roman saying *Destinatum est mihi* meant "I have made up my mind." In Rome, destiny meant a decision was fixed or determined. Later the word reappeared in both Old and Middle French in the feminine form *destiné*. Finally, from the Middle English word *destinee*, we get the modern form of the word.

Next, a transition led to her connotative section, which consisted of an extended example of a near-fatal car wreck that devastated her family.

> However, it isn't the word's etymological history that is meaningful to me. You see, destiny is a depressing reminder of a car accident.

Terez concluded with the following quotation by William Jennings Bryan:

> Destiny is not a matter of chance; it is a matter of choice. It is not a thing to be waited for; it is a thing to be achieved.

Including both denotative definitions and connotative associations provided a fuller picture of the concept of destiny.

Giving Explanations

Think of explanations as translations: You take a complex or information-dense concept and put it into common words and images that make it understandable. Explanations commonly answer questions about processes ("How does it work?") or about concepts ("What's the theory behind that?" or "Why?"). To answer such questions, you should describe stages, ordered sequences, or procedures involved in processes, both natural and cultural. You can explain how something is done (training guide dogs for the blind, international negotiations), how things work (elevators, cuckoo clocks, microwave ovens), or how they're made (mountain bikes, a pair of shoes). Not surprisingly, chronological patterns are common. Casey's speech on artificial gills at the end of Chapter 13 is an example.

In the 1941 movie *Meet John Doe,* actor Gary Cooper delivers a speech explaining the concept of "John Doe," the average person. **Weblink 16.4** maintains a link to his speech. Notice the many examples he uses to develop his definition. (You can access this link through your CourseMate for *Public Speaking,* Chapter 16 resources.)

Concepts also provide good, but challenging, topics. What do we know about intelligence? What's in the mind of a serial killer? What is Johari's Window? These questions relate to concepts or abstractions—the mental principles, theories, and ideas we form to explain both natural and social realities. For instance, although we may not know for certain what causes some people to kill repeatedly, we formulate theories or explanations for serial killers' behaviors.

Because concepts are sometimes difficult to define and explain, you must make the complex ideas and theories understandable and relevant to your listeners. Here are some guidelines for speeches about concepts, using the concept of "intelligence" as the topic:

- Simplify complex ideas by dividing them into their component parts. For example, intelligence can be broken down into categories that include social intelligence, spatial intelligence, and musical intelligence.[25]
- Carefully define your terminology, avoiding technical jargon. Exactly what falls into the category of spatial intelligence? Use examples that clarify this component of intelligence, or show the items from the tests that measure spatial intelligence.
- Clarify confusing details by using analogies, both figurative and literal, to compare the concept to something that listeners already understand. In this case, you might compare spatial intelligence to running a maze.
- Use detailed examples of concrete situations that illustrate the actions of people who test high in various kinds of intelligence.

We sometimes clash over theories, concepts, and ideas. For instance, exactly what is universal healthcare? People's ideas differ. What caused the dinosaurs to become extinct? Theories vary. What constitutes a date rape? Not everyone gives the same answer. The purpose of explanatory speaking is not to argue for one definition or another but to clarify the concept, sometimes by comparing and contrasting differing definitions and theories regarding it. Figure 16.1 summarizes the types of informative speeches and the questions each is designed to answer.

Type of Speech	Question(s) It Examines
Demonstration	How do you do that?
Description	What's it like?
Report	What have we learned about this topic?
Explanation	What is it? What does it mean? How does it work? What's the theory behind it?

Figure 16.1
Informative Speech Types

Guidelines for Informative Speaking

A common complaint about informational speaking is that it's boring.[26] To keep your audience's attention and to be both understandable and relevant, remember these guidelines for producing comprehensible messages:[27]

- **Do an "obstacle analysis" of the audience.** Identify the parts of the message they might find hard to understand and then work on specific ways to make those sections clear. Next, identify internal barriers that would prevent your audience from learning your material. You might face psychological resistance if you choose a scientific topic for an audience who thinks science is difficult and boring or if you challenge an audience's current misconceptions about a subject they hold dear. Plan ways to deal with each obstacle.[28]

- **Organize the material carefully**. Be kind to your listeners by stating your major points clearly and by building in signposts such as *next* and *in addition* that help them identify the flow of ideas. Use structures such as lists, comparisons-contrasts, or cause-effect patterns. Provide transitions, internal previews, and summaries that show how your material is linked—using words and phrases such as *because*, *therefore*, and *as a result* (see Chapter 9). **Discourse consistency** also helps; for example, you might begin every section with a question or alliterate your main points throughout the entire speech.[29]

discourse consistency using a repetitive style such as alliteration of main points throughout the speech

- **Personalize your material for your audience.** Help listeners see the connection between your topic and their experiences, goals, beliefs, and actions. When they see the information as personally relevant, they're more likely to listen and learn effectively.
- **Compare the known to the unknown.** Start with what's familiar to your audience and then build on this foundation, showing similarities and differences between your topic and what listeners already know.
- **Choose your vocabulary carefully.** To avoid bewildering listeners with technical information and incomprehensible jargon, define your terms and explain them in everyday, concrete images. Avoid trigger words with negative connotations that might set off negative reactions in audience members.
- **Build in repetition and redundancy. Repetition** means that you say the same thing more than once. **Redundancy** means that you repeat the same idea several times, but you develop it somewhat differently each time. Phrases such as in *other words* or *put simply* are ways to build in redundancy. Repeat and redefine the critical parts of the message to reinforce these crucial points in your listeners' minds.[30]

repetition saying the same thing more than once

redundancy repeating the same idea more than once, but developing it differently each time

- **Strive to be interesting**. In your preparation, occasionally try to hear your speech as if someone else was delivering it. Do you find yourself drifting off? If so, where? Search for ways to enliven your factual material. Examples and detailed descriptions, for instance, engage your audience dialogically because they invite your listeners to form mental images as you talk.

If you follow these guidelines, you will increase your listeners' motivation and interest in the topic. And your careful attention to details will help them understand the material more clearly.

Do an Obstacle Analysis and Strategic Plan

As you prepare your speech, ask yourself the following questions:

- What concepts or steps may be obstacles for this audience?
- What psychological barriers are likely?
- What is the best way to overcome these obstacles?
- Are the steps in order? Are my main ideas clear?
- Where might I use alliteration, rhyming, or another form of discourse consistency?
- Where are my signposts and transitions? Should I use more?
- How, specifically, have I connected this material to the lives of my classmates?
- What does my audience already know that I'm building upon?
- Is my language clear?
- Where should I repeat an idea verbatim?
- Which ideas have I presented in a number of different ways?

Summary

The ability to give and receive information has always been empowering; this is especially so in the Information Age. Those who lack information do not have the basic knowledge they need to perform competently in complex societies. As a result, a variety of people in a variety of settings give informative speeches. Their goals are to present new information, to supplement what's already known, to review or update material, or to correct misinformation.

There are several categories for informative speaking that answer listeners' questions such as "How do you do that?" or "What does that mean?" These include demonstrations and instructions, descriptions, reports, and explanations.

Finally, remember seven keys to informative speaking. Do an obstacle analysis that identifies elements within the topic or within the listeners that might prove to be barriers, and then work to overcome those obstacles. Organize the speech carefully, and provide links that connect the material. Relate your topic to your listeners, and make vocabulary choices that clarify your ideas. Think of creative ways to present your information, and throughout your talk, tie abstract concepts to concrete experiences that are familiar to your listeners. Finally, include repetition and redundancy to reinforce the critical points of the message and, as always, strive to be interesting.

STUDY AND REVIEW

Your online resources for *Public Speaking: Concepts and Skills for a Diverse Society* offer a broad range of study tools that will help you better understand the material in this chapter, complete assignments, and succeed on tests. Your online resources feature the following:

- Speech videos with critical viewing questions, speech outlines, and transcripts.
- Interactive versions of this chapter's Stop and Check activities, as well as Application and Critical Thinking Exercises.
- Speech Builder Express and InfoTrac College Edition.
- Weblinks related to chapter content.
- Study and review tools such as self-quizzes, an interactive glossary, and downloadable audio summaries.

You can access your online resources at the CourseMate for *Public Speaking: Concepts and Skills for a Diverse Society.* Log in at **http://www.cengage.com/login**, using the access code that came with your book or that you bought online at **http://www.cengagebrain.com**.

KEY TERMS

The terms below are defined in the margins throughout this chapter.

classification 276
discourse consistency 286
division 276
expository speech 283
information imbalance 272
redundancy 286
repetition 286

APPLICATION AND CRITICAL THINKING EXERCISES

1. Within a small group in your classroom, discuss implications of the unequal distribution of information. For example: What if only some societies knew how to make sophisticated weaponry? What if only some individuals or groups knew their cultural

history? What if only women had access to health information and men were excluded? What if only people under 35 years of age, with incomes over $80,000 a year, knew how to use computers?

2. For your classroom speech, consider a topic from the field of communication. Look for information that could help your classmates communicate better. For example, topics such as how to work through conflict, how to become independent from parents, or how to successfully navigate the early stages of a romantic relationship are useful in interpersonal communication. Nonverbal communication topics include different concepts of time or the types of touch. For mass communication, you could explain how camera angles communicate meaning or how other countries regulate the Internet.
3. Working with a small group, generate a list of speech topics for each category. The audience:

   - Is totally unfamiliar with the topic (examples: biliary atresia, *dun dun* drums).
   - Has some knowledge of the topic, but not all the details (driving while texting, pumpkins).
   - Has studied the topic, but needs a review (the five canons of rhetoric, D-Day).
   - Has outdated information (an updated computer program).
   - Has major misconceptions regarding the topic (cheerleading, tarantulas).

   Select a subject from two different categories and discuss how you would modify your speech plans to accomplish your general purpose with each topic.
4. In a small group, think of creative ways to present an informative speech that reviews audience knowledge about one of these familiar topics:

   - Good nutrition
   - What to do in case of a fire
   - How to read a textbook

5. Descriptions can be speeches in themselves, or good descriptions can be elements of larger speeches. To improve your descriptive skills, identify a place, an object, or an event and then make a list of vivid words that provide information about the look, the feel, the smell, the taste, or the sound of the item or place. Share your description with a small group of your classmates.
6. Search the Internet for the exact term "informative speaking." Read the material on a site from either a speech team (also called a forensics team) or from a university professor who provides additional information about speaking to inform.

SPEECH VIDEO

Log on to your book's online resources to watch and critique Lishan Zeng's speech "The Chinese Valentine's Day." The text of his speech is available both here and in your online resources, which also provide an online of Lishan's speech.

Student Speech with Commentary

THE CHINESE VALENTINE'S DAY
By Lishan Zeng

Lishan's assignment was to research, outline, and deliver an informative speech using a visual aid. He conducted a survey before he spoke to assess the class's familiarity with his topic. Most did not know about the Chinese counterpart to St. Valentine's Day, and they had only superficial knowledge of the American holiday. He planned his speech accordingly.

Look at this picture. What do you see? The universe? The stars? Or a romantic story? I see love in this picture. It's the story of Niulang and Zhinü, and that's the origin of Chinese Valentine's Day.

Lishan displays a photograph of the Milky Way on the left half of a slide.

According to the survey I did, eighty percent of you did not know that there is a Chinese Valentine's Day, and ninety percent did not know the origin of it. This does not surprise me. What surprises me is that ninety percent of you know the date of the Western Valentine's Day but just ten percent of you know why you have that day.

That motivates me to do the research about the Western Valentine's Day and then tell you the story of the Chinese Valentine's Day. I will compare the Western and Chinese Valentine's Day, and I hope that by the end of my speech you will get to know when the Valentine's Day is and how and why people celebrate the Valentine's Day.

He adds the title "Valentine's Day" on the right of the slide.

He adds the words, "A Comparison between Western and Chinese Culture" on the slide.

Most of you know that the Western Valentine's Day falls on February 14. But most of you do not know that the Chinese Valentine's Day falls at the seventh day of the seventh lunar month, and it falls on August the 16th this year.

Some of you know why people celebrate Valentine's Day. According to History.com, people in the West celebrate Valentine's Day to remember the death of St. Valentine. St. Valentine was a priest of the third century in Rome. At that time the Emperor of Rome forbade marriage for young men because he thought young men unmarried made better soldiers. Well, St. Valentine went against that law and performed marriages for young lovers in secret. Another version of this story is that St. Valentine's helped Christians escape the harsh Roman prisons where they were often beaten and tortured. In either story, he was bound and sentenced to death.

He projects a photo on the left half of the slide showing an icon of St. Valentine.

About the Chinese Valentine's Day. According to chinadaily.com, it's a day when Niulang and Zhinü are allowed to meet with each other. Niulang is a poor, handsome boy, living with his brother and sister-in-law. He owns nothing but an old ox that can talk and is an immortal from the Heaven.

Next to the icon of St. Valentine, he shows a romanticized image of Niulang and Zhinü.

Zhinü is the daughter of the Emperor of Heaven, who is good at handcrafting, especially in weaving clothing. Because the ox is treated nicely by Niulang, the ox wants to fulfill one of Niulang's wishes, so the ox asks Niulang what he wants. "Uh . . . I want to marry a beautiful girl," that's Niulang's answer. Then the ox takes Niulang to heaven, and there, Niulang meets Zhinü. And they fall in love. After that, they are married and have two kids.

He displays a blank slide.

But their story is not like any of the romantic Disney stories. They do not end up living happily together ever since. The marriage between a human and a god is never permitted, so the Emperor of Heaven takes Zhinü away from Niulang and her kids. But, he's touched by their love and agrees that they could meet each other once a year. And that day becomes the seventh day of the seventh lunar month.

As we can see, no matter if it's the Western or the Chinese cultures, people celebrate Valentine's Day all because of love, but they observe that in different ways. In the West, Valentine's Day is about sharing love with lovers and family members. People send gifts, like flowers, chocolates, candy, and love cards to persons they love.

His slide shows candy in a heart-shaped box. He adds flowers and then a card on the right half of the slide.

In China, Valentine's Day is more about the longing for love and in the present. Chinese girls offer fruit and incense to Zhinü, to pray to have good skills and to find a satisfactory boyfriend. Lovers pray that they could get blessed and also pray for their love and happiness. Now let's do a review about the Valentine's Day. Western Valentine's Day falls on February 14, and Chinese Valentine's Day falls on the seventh day of the seventh lunar month. And the Western Valentine's Day is about a story about St. Valentine, and the Chinese Valentine's Day is the story of Niulang and Zhinü. And people celebrated Western Valentine's day by sharing flowers, chocolate, candy, and love cards with the people they love. Chinese people spend the holiday to pray for good skills and love.

This slide shows fruit on one side and an incense burner on the other.

This table, comparing the two cultures' version of the holiday, has a "build" so that lines appear when he is talking about them. Because Lishan's first language is Chinese and he speaks with an accent, this word slide helps his listeners better understand his speech.

Valentine's Day Western Culture vs Chinese Culture		
	Western Valentine's Day	**Chinese Valentine's Day**
When	February 14	The seventh day of the seventh lunar month, falls on August 4 this year
Why	The Story of Saint Valentine	The Story of Niulang and Zhinü
How	Flowers, candy, chocolate, cards	Pray for skills and love Observe the star

In conclusion, Western Valentine's Day and Chinese Valentine's Day all contribute to love, although they celebrate that in different ways. The longing for love is a strong thing that Chinese and the Western people share. Here are more things we share, even though we come from different cultures. And there will be lots to discover.

CHAPTER 17

Foundations of Persuasion

THIS CHAPTER WILL HELP YOU

- Diagram and explain Toulmin's model of reasoning
- Explain how reasoning strategies vary across cultural groups
- Identify ways that *ethos*, or speaker credibility, functions as an element of reasoning
- Explain the role of *pathos*, or emotional proofs, in reasoning
- Explain four basic types of *logos*, or rational proofs, and know how to test each one
- Recognize several kinds of fallacious reasoning
- Identify elements of invitational rhetoric

SCHOLARS HAVE STUDIED rhetoric—the art of persuasion—for centuries, but during World War II, scholars began to focus more specifically on the conditions and strategies that could give rise to a leader such as Hitler. Why could he persuade so many otherwise ordinary people to do such horrible things? Why would others resist heroically and rescue those who were targeted by Nazis? One study of rescuers found that they were similar in most ways to nonrescuers, but they more often came from homes where parents disciplined them through reasoning, explanations, and advice.[1] In other words, their parents used persuasion, not coercion, to help them make wise choices.

persuasion the symbolic process in which a communicator intentionally creates a message in an attempt to convince others to change their attitudes or behaviors in an atmosphere of free choice

artistic proofs reasons to accept an argument that the speaker creates in the audience

Persuasion is defined as the symbolic process in which a communicator intentionally creates a message in an attempt to convince others to change their attitudes or behaviors in an atmosphere of free choice. However, persuaders can only raise a need and create a case for change; their audiences choose whether to change or to refuse their appeals.[2] What makes a message persuasive? Centuries ago, Aristotle identified three elements of rhetoric, which he called **artistic proofs** because you, the speaker, must create them in the audience:

> Of the modes of persuasion furnished by the spoken word there are three kinds. The first kind depends on the personal character of the speaker [*ethos*]; the second on putting the audience into a certain frame of mind [*pathos*]; the third on the proof, or apparent proof, provided by the words of the speech itself [*logos*].[3]

Persuasive methods are found in the canon of invention. This chapter begins with a contemporary diagram that explains how we reason and then presents ethos, pathos, and logos, which work together to form a totality of "good reasons." In other words, emotion is often reasonable; reason has emotional underpinnings; and it is both reasonable and emotionally satisfying to hear a credible speaker. Creating and evaluating arguments by using these three modes will empower you to be a more effective speaker and listener. However, "winning" an argument is neither desirable nor possible in many cases, and the chapter concludes with principles and forms of invitational rhetoric.

Use Toulmin's Reasoning Model

Every day you use reasoning to make sense of the world and to make decisions that affect your life. Based on your observations, you form conclusions that seem sensible. You may not think much about how you reason; you just "know" if something makes sense or not. However, you sooner or later find that not everyone shares your conclusions, and you often feel compelled to explain them.[4] So you build a case or create an argument to support your ideas.

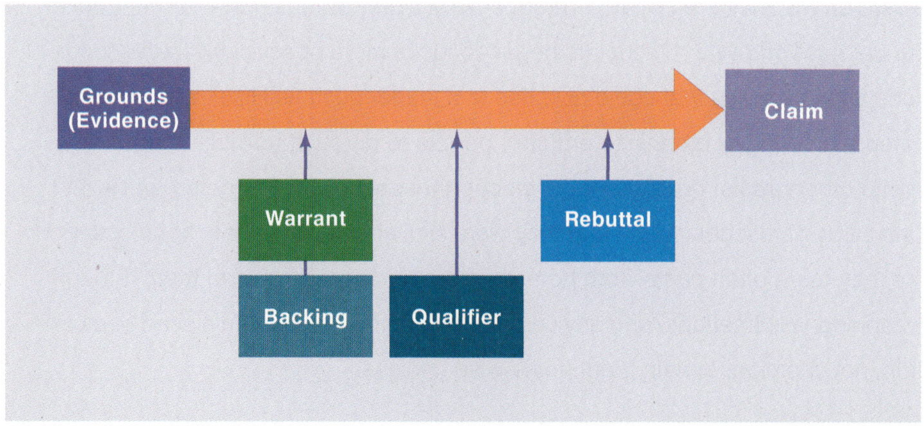

Figure 17.1
Toulmin's Model of Reasoning Stephen Toulmin developed this model as a way to visualize the elements of reasoning.

An **argument** is "an intentional, purposeful activity involving reason and judgment,"[5] and professor Stephen Toulmin[6] diagrammed six elements of arguments. His linear model, shown in Figure 17.1, helps you visualize the type of reasoning common in the United States. Learning to make a claim, qualify it, provide supporting evidence that warrants your conclusion and plan ways to deal with counterarguments will make your speeches more persuasive.

argument intentional, purposeful speaking that involves reason and judgment

Claims A **claim** is the debatable point or proposal you want your audience to accept. It is a conclusion or generalization that some people don't accept, a statement that requires some sort of evidence or backing to be believed. *Factual claims* argue about what exists, what causes a phenomenon, or what the future will bring. *Value claims* deal with the goodness, or the worth of a thing. Finally, *policy claims* argue over actions or proposals for change. Each type of claim is described in more detail in Chapter 18.

claim debatable point or proposal you want listeners to accept

Grounds, Data, or Evidence Support your claim using **grounds** (also called **data** or **evidence**) in the form of facts, examples, narratives, quotations, statistics, and literal and figurative comparisons, as described in Chapter 8. Use data from a variety of reliable sources, and arrange the evidence in the order your listeners will find most reasonable or most forceful.[7] Evidence enables your listeners to weigh your argument and decide whether or not your conclusions make sense. Without sufficient and credible data, your claims are simply unsupported **assertions**.

grounds, data, or **evidence** supporting material offered to back up a claim

assertion a claim presented without supporting evidence

Warrants The assumptions, justification, or logical links that you and your listeners use to connect your evidence with your claim are called **warrants**. They derive from rules, laws, or principles that emerge out of cultural traditions and institutions.[8] For example, requiring search warrants in criminal investigations is grounded in the Fourth Amendment to the Constitution that forbids unreasonable searches. Police officers can only get a warrant if they have sufficient evidence to connect the suspect to the crime. If a fingerprint on the gun (evidence) matches the suspect's print (additional evidence), it is logical to conclude that the suspect fired the gun (claim of fact), because our fingerprints are all unique (the warrant that connects or links the evidence to the claim).

warrant justification or reasoning that connects the claim and the evidence

In many cases, the warrants are implicit. For example, ads for vitamins use words like "perkiness," "power," and "energy." The ad makers assume that buyers want those qualities, which they will associate with the vitamins. If the audience disagrees with the warrant, they won't accept the argument.[9]

Backing When your warrant is not broadly understood or broadly accepted, you can give additional reasons, called **backing**, to support or defend it. For example, think of a trial in which blood was found on a defendant's jacket (evidence). In case the jury doesn't understand the link between the blood evidence and the defendant (warrant), the prosecution brings in several experts who explain the science of DNA (backing) and testify that the blood must belong to the victim (backing). If buyers don't associate "perkiness" with vitamins, the ad makers might bring in scientific evidence or testimonials to strengthen the link.

backing reasons given to support the warrant

Qualifiers Avoid words such as *always* or *never* when you make claims. Instead, use **qualifiers**, which are words and phrases that limit or narrow the scope of your claim. Here are some examples: *in most cases*, *in males between the ages of 7 and 9*, *usually*, and *among women with a college degree*.

qualifiers words and phrases that limit or narrow the scope of a claim

Rebuttal Because most issues are complex and have many possible solutions, not all listeners will agree with your conclusions. So, as a "listening speaker," you should try to hear their potential arguments and then prepare to deal with them directly. This is the

rebuttal arguments that counter or disagree with a claim

rebuttal part of the model. It might help if you think of rebuttals as your listeners' questions that begin with the word *But* . . . or the phrase *But what about* . . . ? Demonstrating that you've considered arguments both for and against your conclusions and that you still have good reasons for your claim enhances your persuasiveness.

In summary, if you learn to recognize the type of claim you are making, qualify it, provide evidence and backing to warrant it, and then confront potential audience rebuttals, you will be more effective in presenting your ideas to others and having them recognize your views as reasonable. (Of course, there are other methods of sense making, as the Diversity in Practice feature on cultural reasoning explains.)

The Influence of Culture on Reasoning

Culture influences our reasoning resources in a number of ways that can easily lead to misunderstandings between cultural groups.[10]

- **Topics considered appropriate for public debate vary across cultures.** Chapter 1 pointed out that topic taboos vary across cultures. Some groups, for instance, would not argue over such issues as gay rights, day care, or euthanasia. Openly speaking about sex is unthinkable in some cultures.
- **Cultures conceptualize issues differently.** It's common in the United States to think of issues as problems and solutions we can define, propose, test and then eliminate or enact; others believe problems result from fate, a bad relationship with the deity or deities, or being out of harmony with one another or the universe.[11]
- **The norms for structuring and framing a discussion vary.** Some cultures ground their discussions in the historical perspectives of the various participants or rely on narrative structures to frame their speeches, rather than seeking causes and effects or making claims and counterclaims. Also, in the highly individualistic culture of the United States we typically ask, "Who won the argument?" However, members of collectivist cultures deplore arguments that present one position as superior to another and draw attention to the rhetor.[12] They see themselves as a community of equals who must cooperate to reach consensus.
- **Levels of explicitness differ across cultures.** In the United States, we commonly state conclusions explicitly and concretely. However, other cultures tolerate much more ambiguity; their speakers exert influence through subtlety and indirectness.
- **Forms of proof are often dissimilar.** What's considered rational or irrational, what counts as evidence, and what constitutes a good reason varies across cultures. As Chapter 8 pointed out, facts, statistics, and studies by experts are typically used here, but elsewhere, cultures find good reasons in narratives, analogies, authoritative texts, and the sayings of wise, experienced elders.
- **Communication styles vary.** Mainstream US culture is biased toward linear, analytical models of reasoning, as depicted in the Toulmin model. Other cultural groups reason more holistically through drama, intuition, and emotional expressiveness.

Develop Ethos or Speaker Credibility

People place their confidence in speakers they see as personally believable, trustworthy, and of good character. Their inner reasoning runs something like this: "She really knows what she's talking about. She also seems to have good intentions, so I trust what she's saying." In contrast, audiences frequently use the speakers' ethos as a reason *not* to believe their claims when they think, "He's using one-sided material from very extreme sources! He just wants us to buy something. I don't trust him, so I don't really trust his information."

These examples illustrate the artistic proof called **ethos**—the proof that comes from your personal qualities. Aristotle believed that ethos is your most effective mode of persuasion. Here is his explanation:

ethos personal credibility or character traits that make a speaker believable and worthy of the audience's confidence

> Persuasion is achieved by the speaker's personal character [*ethos*] when the speech is so spoken as to make us think him [or her] credible. We believe good [people] more fully and more readily than others: this is true generally whatever the question is, and absolutely true where exact certainty is impossible and opinions are divided.[13]

Because ethos is your listener's perception of you as a speaker, you can shape a positive impression by paying attention to your personal appearance, showing confidence, making eye contact, using appropriate gestures, and avoiding vocalized pauses as described in Chapter 14. There are four additional components of ethos: good character, goodwill, good sense, and dynamism.

Exhibiting Good Character

Remember the Latin phrase introduced in Chapter 1? *Vir bonum; dicendi peritus.* Character counts. Your listeners will believe you more readily if they trust you, so demonstrate honesty, integrity, and trustworthiness by documenting your sources and giving facts that square with what they know to be true. Choose topics that matter to you, and stick by your convictions, even when they are unpopular. Politicians get into trouble when they appear to be poll driven and pander to different audiences, flip-flopping from position to position according to what's popular instead of holding to their core beliefs.

Expressing Goodwill

Your listeners want to know you have them in mind, that you understand their situations and their language. Kenneth Burke,[14] one of the twentieth century's most respected rhetoricians, stressed the importance of **identification**, sometimes called **co-orientation**. He argued that a variety of divisions separate us, but identification can bring people with diverse beliefs and behaviors together.

identification or **co-orientation** concerns shared among speakers and listeners that help overcome divisions and bring diverse people together

But how do you identify with your audience? One way is to find areas of **common ground**—to emphasize similarities between you and your listeners. When you share beliefs, values, attitudes, and behaviors, it's easy to find common ground. However, diversity makes identification more challenging. With a very diverse audience, you may have to search for commonalities on which to build. For instance, every audience shares with you the needs for safety and self-esteem. When she was president of the US Pan Asian American Chamber of Commerce, Susan Au Allen emphasized common goals with her largely African American audience.

common ground specific areas or concerns that both speaker and audience consider important

> So I salute you, a cherished ally. . . . We are Japanese, Filipinos, Chinese, Asian Indians, Koreans, Vietnamese, Laos, Thais, Cambodians, Hmongs, Pakistanis, and Indonesians. Each has a distinct beautiful ethnic cultural heritage, but our goals are the same as yours. We want to remove racial barriers, we want equal opportunity for our members, and we want to create greater horizons for those who follow.[15]

Developing Good Character

Quintilian

As chief educator of Rome, Quintilian distinguished oratory from rhetoric when he wrote about the education of orators.[16] Rhetoric, he proclaimed, is amoral; it can lead to both good and bad results. In contrast, oratory is a moral activity; orators defend the innocent, repress crime, support truth over falsehood, persuade listeners toward right actions, and promote positive civic action.

Evil persons cannot be effective orators because they are so bound up in greed, misdeeds, and concerns over being caught in their deceits that they neglect the tools of invention, and audiences will reject them. Instead, orators should cultivate traits of truth seeking, justice, and honor before they take to the public stage. To form moral and intellectual character, they should study philosophy, seek wisdom, and pursue sincerity and goodness. Only after they have developed character, should they study oratory. Quintilian was realistic enough to recognize that no one could be perfect, but he urged each orator to be both good and sensible.

Questions

1. What is your response to Quintilian's claim: "I do not merely assert that the ideal orator should be a good [person], but I affirm that no [one] can be a good orator unless he [or she] is a good [person]"?[17]
2. Do the same high standards hold for people like Peggy Kilburg (Practically Speaking: Chapter 16) whose speaking is mostly informative? Why or why not?
3. How might our culture be changed if the study of public speaking came during the last semester of every college student's senior year—as the culmination of his or her education—and if all other studies were considered foundational?
4. Imagine that Quintilian were somehow transported into the Internet Age. How might he advise digital citizens to prepare for participation in the "public stage" of cyberspace?

Although identification typically relies on commonalities, in some cases your differences will make you more credible, depending on the topic. For example, Gary suffered a stroke when he was seventeen years old; consequently, when he spoke about strokes and stroke victims, his words were much more persuasive because of his disability. Patricia spoke credibly about Liberia because she was born and raised in that African nation.

Demonstrating Good Sense

Good sense is a cluster of characteristics, made up of several components, including:

- **Intelligence:** Show that you have a broad understanding of your subject, complete with up-to-date information of the highest quality. Be able to discuss related historical developments, and link your topic to contemporary national and international issues. Then, listeners will recognize that you're not just bluffing your way through your speech and that you have the discernment to select only the most credible information.

- **Sound reasoning:** Support your claims with trustworthy evidence and logical connections between ideas. Avoid fallacies and unwarranted or excessive appeals to emotions.
- **Composure:** Demonstrate composure by maintaining your poise in a stressful situation. For example, if you become overly agitated, your audience may wonder why you can't control yourself. On the other hand, if you remain composed and controlled, they'll perceive you more favorably. However, note the differences in cultural expectations about composure described in the Diversity in Practice feature.

Composure in Other Cultures

CONCEPTS OF ETHOS depend on the cultural context. Thomas Kochman, author of *Black and White Styles in Conflict*, explained that credible speakers in the African American tradition are often forceful and emotional rather than calm and composed.[18] Good speakers are genuinely intense in their expression, and sometimes their emotional expressiveness contrasts greatly with the order and procedure common in the Euro-American style of public speaking. For this reason, listeners brought up in the Euro-American culture may consider them loud or aggressive.

Similarly, Janice Walker Anderson[19] found that Arabs traditionally expected effective speakers to show their emotion and to heighten the audience's emotions through the rhythm and sounds of words. In these cultures, overstating a case indicates the speaker's sincerity, not a distortion of facts; in contrast, a soft tone indicates that the speaker is weak or perhaps dishonest.

Showing Dynamism

Dynamism, or forcefulness, is a fourth trait that influences credibility. It is linked to extroversion, energy, and enthusiasm. (See Chapter 14.) This doesn't mean that you can't be credible if you are introverted; however, your visible enjoyment of your topic, your enthusiasm, and your overall liveliness contribute to your ethos. Think of it this way: aren't you more likely to believe someone who states ideas forcefully rather than apologetically?

Evaluating Ethos

Weblink 17.1 maintains a link to TED, a source for "riveting talks by remarkable people, free to the world." Read or listen to two persuasive speeches. Identify some ways each speaker demonstrates good character, goodwill, good sense, and dynamism. (You can access this link through your CourseMate for *Public Speaking,* Chapter 17 resources.)

Include Pathos or Emotional Proofs

Contrast the following situations:

- You're listening to a speaker who seems credible and who supports her claim well. However, you're unmotivated—you are neither interested in the topic nor concerned about the issue.
- You're listening to a second speaker (same topic) who also seems credible and supports her claim well. However, she links the subject to your core beliefs, values, personal goals, and emotions. You find yourself caring about it and wanting to believe and act as she proposes.

motivation internal, individualized factor that results when we understand how topics affect our lives in a personal way

pathos appeals or reasons directed toward audience emotions

The second speaker understands that **motivation** is an internal, individualistic, or subjective factor that results when listeners understand how topics affect their lives in a personal way. It's essential to persuasion. In other words, we look for emotional and psychological reasons to support our decisions. And in the end, our subjective reasons may be as influential as our logical ones. This demonstrates the power of emotions in reasoning—the proof Aristotle called **pathos**.

Although you often respond subconsciously to emotional appeals, responses can be conscious, and your thoughts may run something like this: "I feel sorry for the people who lost all their possessions in the disaster; I'm going to donate," or "Going to the career center like the speaker suggests will help me get a better job," or "I've experienced frustration just like the speaker. I can relate!" Pathos relies on appeals to emotions and to needs.

Appeals to Positive Emotions

According to Aristotle, emotions are all the feelings people have that change them in ways that affect their judgment. Modern psychologists say we "approach" pleasurable emotions such as love, peace, pride, approval, hope, generosity, courage, and loyalty. We also feel good about our core beliefs and values, such as freedom and individualism. Appeals to your listeners' positive feelings and values, can often motivate them to accept and act on your claims.

Narratives and examples are good ways to highlight emotional appeals. In this speech excerpt, Remi gives several examples showing things her university is doing to ensure that food waste has positive outcomes.

> Leftover food such as chicken, vegetables, and pasta is used in soup the following day. Unsold sandwiches and fruit from the snack bar are given away Friday nights in the dining hall. The university donates about 150 meals to Urban Services every Friday. Plant Services is working on a vermiculture (worm bins) to compost salad leftovers.[20]

These examples help students (who might feel guilty for wasting so much food) feel more hopeful by knowing that their wasteful habits are not entirely destructive. Because she is not condemning their behaviors, her listeners are not defensive, so they can more easily examine their personal eating habits.

Appeals to Negative Emotions

We try to avoid negative emotions such as guilt, shame, hatred, fear, insecurity, anger, and anxiety because they are unpleasant. However, negative emotions are often useful. Fear, anger, and guilt, for instance, can motivate us to avoid real dangers—a fact that the campaign against drunk driving uses effectively. Think of a story you've heard or an ad you've seen that shows adorable children killed by drivers who "just this once" drove while intoxicated. Don't they make you want to prevent the problem?

One way to arouse negative emotions is to use analogies. In this speech excerpt, Hillary Clinton likened the Internet to the Berlin Wall. She is arousing negative emotions toward censorship and division by showing how they violate our core values of free expression and connection.

> As I speak to you today, government censors somewhere are working furiously to erase my words from the records of history. But history itself has already condemned these tactics. . . . The Berlin Wall symbolized a world divided and it defined an entire era. Today, . . . the new iconic infrastructure is the Internet. Instead of division, it stands for connection. But even as networks spread to nations around the globe, virtual walls are cropping up in place of visible walls.
>
> Some countries have erected electronic barriers that prevent their people from accessing portions of the world's networks. They've expunged words, names, and phrases from search engine results. They have violated the privacy of citizens who engage in non-violent political speech.[21]

Appeals to negative emotions can be forceful, sometimes with disastrous results. Consider how effectively hate groups appeal to their audiences' weaknesses, rages, fears, and insecurities. In addition, speakers can easily overdo negative appeals, and excessive appeals to guilt or fear may turn off an audience. One listener responded to a famous environmentalist activist's speech in this way:

> [Her] presentation is meant to instill unease. In my case, she is succeeding, though not in the way she intends. She is making me worry . . . for the fate of this movement on which so much depends. As much as I want to endorse what I hear, [her] effort to shock and shame just isn't taking . . . . I find myself going numb.[22]

He advises environmentalist speakers to evaluate the psychological impact of their appeals to fear and guilt and to present instead a "politics of vision" that connects environmental goals to positive emotions—to what is "generous, joyous, freely given, and noble" in the audience.

Appealing to Needs

One of the most widely cited systems of classifying needs follows the work of Abraham Maslow,[23] who ranked needs into five levels, each building on the others—generally in the same order. Although he described five levels, Maslow himself believed that "most behavior is multi-motivated"[24] and that a combination of levels is active in each situation. Here is a list of Maslow's levels and some suggestions for ways to address each one:

- **Basic needs:** Link your topic to your listeners' basic survival needs for water, air, food, and shelter.
- **Security and safety:** Explain how to gain peace of mind, job security, safety, comfort, better health, physical safety, and so on.
- **Love and belonging:** Show how your topic helps your listeners be better friends, creates a stronger community, or builds ties between people.
- **Esteem**: Demonstrate that you respect your listeners, and mention their accomplishments when appropriate. Find ways to make them feel competent to carry out your proposals. Let them know that their ideas, opinions, and concerns are significant.
- **Self-actualization:** Challenge your listeners to look beyond themselves and reach out to others. Encourage them to dream big dreams and accomplish unique things. The Army slogan "Be all that you can be" is an example of an appeal to self-actualization.

Remi's speech on food waste is built around our basic need for food and our need to create a stronger community. Rob's speech on America's deteriorating infrastructure (at the end of Chapter 8) appeals to our needs for safety and comfort while we travel. Casey's speech on artificial gills (at the end of Chapter 13) shows how engineers are dreaming big dreams and creating unique inventions.

(To learn more about Maslow's work, search the Internet for "Maslow's hierarchy of needs." Look for additional levels that other scholars have added to his hierarchy.)

Understanding Complex Motivations

As you can see, using pathos is complex, because needs, wants, emotions, and values overlap. As you create emotional appeals, keep in mind four important factors that result in motivational variation from individual to individual.[25]

1. **Sometimes you must choose between two goals or feelings**. Perhaps the choice is between good things—job security or the ability to reach your potential. Or you may have to choose the lesser of two evils—higher tuition or cuts in university services.
2. **Motives vary according to our circumstances**. Someone who's just ended a significant relationship may worry more about belonging and self-esteem than someone in a long-term relationship. In some contexts, what motivates you is different from what motivates someone in a different socioeconomic group or in a different age group.
3. **Our responses often reflect mixed motives**. The person who donates out of loyalty to her school may also like the pride she feels when a building is named in her honor. An angry blogger may be writing out of underlying anxiety, fear, or frustration.
4. **Motivations are often group centered**. What we want for ourselves, we want for others, including our family, friends, religious groups, schools, towns, states, society, and world. Consequently, a speech about child abuse in other countries can motivate listeners who want security for themselves and their own families, as well as for strangers.

Testing Emotional Appeals

Emotions, although essential, are not always trustworthy, so it is important to examine them to see if they make sense. For example, if you use fear to motivate your audience, ask yourself if you are creating or playing on irrational fears or if the fear is justified? Excessive use of emotional appeals can cloud logical reasoning.

When you're listening to emotional appeals, ask questions such as these: "Why am I feeling guilty?" "Is my guilt reasonable?" "Is this speaker trying to manipulate me through my feelings?" "Although he is causing me to feel angry, is anger my primary emotion? Could my underlying emotion be fear? Does this challenge to my cherished beliefs create anxiety that I am masking with anger?"[26]

Further, make sure emotion is used ethically. Generally, it is unethical to use emotional appeals in an attempt to bypass logical reasoning. For example, an appeal to national pride may create an argument for going to war in a way that clouds more rational arguments against military involvement. A speaker may use fear to motivate listeners to act for his or her personal profit rather than for their own good. (See the Ethics in Practice Box that discusses demagoguery.)

Use Logos or Rational Proofs

logos arguments from the words of the speech itself; often called rational proofs

Logos, often called rational proofs, refers to the verbal arguments you make relating to your subject. These arguments include analogy, inductive, deductive, and causal reasoning.

ETHICS IN PRACTICE

Demagoguery

Moviestore collection Ltd / Alamy

The 2006 movie *All the King's Men* tells the story of Huey P. Long, a controversial Louisiana politician, whose enemies called him a demagogue and whose supporters called him a "champion of the common man."[27]

Ideally, good speakers blend the three artistic proofs, and the term **demagogue** is typically reserved for those who rely more on ethos and pathos than on logical reasoning. In a study of Huey P. Long, Joshua Gunn identifies a demagogue as:

> an obsessional neurotic, righteously complete, frequently obscuring or erasing audiences as mere objects at the exact moment of professing his or her love for them. [The demagogue claims] to bring order to chaos, thereby representing strength, resolve, and absolute autonomy . . . [by placing] much more emphasis on the feelings inspired by ethos and pathos, and largely at the expense of logos and reasoned argument.[28]

To Patricia Roberts-Miller, the defining characteristic of a demagogue is "polarizing propaganda that motivates members of an ingroup to hate and scapegoat some outgroup(s)"[29] by promising a coming era of stability and control; the result is an "us" and "them" mentality. Demagogues are often dynamic, dramatic, passionate speakers who inspire devotion among followers. Often they characterize themselves as just a common person fighting for the people,[30] but they also include opportunists who work for their own gain, politicians who inflame passions to gain or maintain power, and doomsayers who create a heightened sense of crisis in order to reveal their novel solutions.[31]

Was Huey P. Long a demagogue? To his critics he was, but to his credit, he used his persuasive powers to benefit people in the lower economic classes. He embraced many populist causes including free textbooks in school, new buildings and roads, construction of Louisiana State University (including a great football team), and redistribution of wealth.[32] He was assassinated at age 42.

demagogue a polarizing speaker who appeals to audiences more on the basis of emotion and personal charisma than on reasoned arguments

Questions

1. Do an Internet search for "demagoguery" or "demagogy" and make a list of people who are currently being called demagogues. Tell why each person is labeled this way. Do you think the label is appropriate? Why or why not?
2. The word "demagogue" has negative connotations. Why is demagoguery considered to be one of the most unethical forms of speaking?

Reasoning by Analogy: Figurative and Literal

Chapter 8 defines an **analogy** as a comparison between one item that is unknown or less familiar and something already familiar to the audience. You can reason by using *figurative* (metaphor) or *literal* (parallel case) analogies.

analogy comparison of one item that's less familiar or unknown to something concrete and familiar

Figurative Analogies (Metaphors)

Reasoning by metaphor figuratively compares two things that are generally different but share a recognizable similarity. This type of reasoning is fundamental and universal, practiced by cultures globally and historically,[33] and typical of African and African American speakers.[34] Aristotle associated metaphor with mental brilliance, as seen in this quotation from *Poetics*.

reasoning by metaphor comparing two things that are generally different but share a recognizable similarity

> [T]he greatest thing by far is to be a master of metaphor. It is the one thing that cannot be learnt from others, and it is also a sign of genius, since a good metaphor implies an intuitive perception of the similarity in dissimilars.[35]

Here are some examples of metaphors taken from speeches given by professionals. What images do they evoke in you?

- Good news is music to our ears; insecurity causes us to play it by ear; when we are getting along, we are in harmony or in tune with one another.[36]
- We see too many roadblocks to women's empowerment [globally]. Cultural roadblocks . . . educational roadblocks . . . political roadblocks . . . financial roadblocks, and technological roadblocks, to name a few.[37]
- The presidency is the most visible thread that runs through the tapestry of the American government.[38]

Metaphors are inherently dialogical because they require your listeners to participate actively and make sensible connections between the two things you compare. In addition, the images inherent in metaphors have emotional overtones. Contrast your feelings about *roadblocks* or *open doors*, a *harvest* of justice or the *moneyed scales* of justice; a *turkey* of a deal or a *gem* of a deal.

Our metaphors guide our actions. For example, what is the role of your college or university in your community? Is it a good neighbor, a partner, a beacon of light? The metaphor you embrace affects how you engage the community. If you choose "partner," your involvement is arguably different than if you think of yourselves as a "beacon of light."

Literal Analogies (Parallel Cases)

parallel case or **literal analogy** comparing likenesses between two similar things; arguing that what happened in a known case will likely happen in a similar case

Whereas metaphors highlight similarities between two different things, reasoning by **parallel case** or **literal analogy** points out likenesses between two similar things. We often use this type of reasoning to formulate policies by asking what another person or group decided to do when faced with a problem similar to our own. Here are some examples.

- How should your campus deal with parking needs? Look at case studies of schools similar to yours that solved similar parking problems, and then infer whether the other schools' experiences will be a good predictor of what might or might not work for yours.
- How should a local hospital keep health care costs under control? Look at cost-saving measures instituted by a similar hospital in a similar location.

In summary, we commonly use actual cases based on real experiences to formulate policies and make predictions about the future. Then we predict that what happened in a known case will happen in a similar case that we project.

Testing Analogies

Reasoning by metaphor is not generally considered a "hard" proof that can be easily tested. The best test is to make sure your listeners can sensibly connect your concept with the comparison so that the comparison does, in fact, illuminate, clarify, and illustrate your idea.

Parallel case reasoning is different; you should test it more directly by considering the following two questions.

1. Are the cases really alike? Or are you "comparing apples to oranges"?
2. Are they alike in essential details?

Reasoning Inductively

inductive reasoning starting with specific instances or examples then formulating a reasonable conclusion

In **inductive reasoning**, you begin with specific instances or examples and formulate a reasonable generalization or conclusion from them. In other words, inductive reasoning moves from the particular to the general; it is characteristic of women and speakers from a variety of ethnic groups. Patricia Sullivan,[39] for instance, explains that African American leaders typically tie knowledge to human experiences, human actions, and human interactions. Knowledge does not exist for its own sake or in the abstract. What is relevant is considered relevant because it makes a difference in people's lives.

Reasoning and the Sexes

Although both men and women reason inductively, some feminist philosophers argue that inductive reasoning is a *major* reasoning strategy for women. They say that women typically begin with specific experiences of real people, such as the rape survivor, the family without medical insurance, the student athlete whose sport was eliminated, and then generalize from these examples. This means that women's reasoning is characteristically grounded in personal experiences that arise out of their interpersonal relationships.[40]

Women are commonly stereotyped as reasoning with their hearts rather than their heads—an overgeneralization that may have some basis in fact. Studies of women's patterns of thinking show the importance of emotion in their reasoning process.[41] Although obviously different from "dispassionate investigation," emotions complement logic and intertwine with rational proofs. Feelings are not inferior to reason, and they are not something women must overcome if they are to think clearly. Instead, emotions can be a source of knowledge, and "truth" or "knowledge" without emotion is distorted.[42]

In contrast, some scholars argue against fundamental differences between men and women. They believe that use of evidence, linear thinking, and deductive logic are not inherently masculine, and that both men and women use them. Further, use of intuitive and emotional arguments are not inherently feminine; men often reason through experiences, emotions, and empathy.[43]

The Laboratory for Complex Thinking and Scientific Reasoning at McGill University[44] studied male and female scientists. They found no major differences in use of inductive, deductive, or causal reasoning processes. However, they discovered that, given an unexpected finding, men tended to assume they knew the cause, whereas women tracked it down.

Whatever differences there may be, the "difference must be viewed as a resource for—not an impediment to—meaningful dialogue."[45]

Here's how inductive reasoning works in everyday life. You eat at a new restaurant in town and have a good, reasonably priced meal. That's just one specific instance. You tell some friends. They eat there and have similar positive experiences. They pass along the name of the restaurant to more and more friends, and almost everyone says the meals are great, given the price. Word gets around, and the restaurant's reputation is established: good meals at fair prices.

Inductive reasoning is valuable in creating good arguments. Kimball used these three examples in his speech on ocean acidification.[46]

- Five years ago, oyster fishermen in Willapa Bay, Washington discovered that oyster larvae weren't building shells and growing into adults; experts blamed ocean acidification.
- Tests off of California's coast show disintegrating seashells and deterioriating shells of mollusks in the waters there.
- Corals from 69 of the reefs comprising the Great Barrier Reef off of Australia showed a drop in calcification.

Generalization: Destructive forces are at work in the Pacific Ocean.

Because you can only be sure of a conclusion only if you can observe 100 percent of a population, it is ideal to look at every example before you form a conclusion.

However, 100 percent samples are rare. (Not everyone who eats at the same restaurant has a great meal, and all the world's coastal areas cannot be easily tested.) Instead, select a representative sample, survey the characteristics of that sample, formulate conclusions and then generalize your findings to the larger population it represents. But take care: if Kimball only reported on Pacific Ocean research findings, he couldn't necessarily assume that his conclusions applied globally. Other factors may affect outcomes in different waters.

Testing Inductive Reasoning

The three major tests for inductive reasoning are all linked to the tests you used to evaluate examples in Chapter 8.

1. Are enough cases represented to justify the conclusion? Or are you forming a conclusion based on too few cases?
2. Are the cases typical? That is, do they represent the average members of the population to which the generalizations are applied? Or are they extreme cases that may show what could happen, but not what usually happens?
3. Are the examples from the time period under discussion, or are they out of date?

(The Diversity in Practice feature on page 303 provides additional information on men's and women's use of inductive reasoning.)

Reasoning Deductively

deductive reasoning starting with a principle (the premise) and applying it to a specific case

Inductive reasoning moves from specific examples to conclusions or generalizations, but **deductive reasoning** goes the other direction. It begins with a generalization or principle, called the *premise*, and moves logically to an application in a specific case. (See Figure 17.2 for an example of the relationship between inductive and deductive reasoning.) In formal logic, the deductive reasoning process is often shown in the form of a *syllogism* such as this:

Major premise: Everyone who goes through a Bar Mitzvah is Jewish.

Minor premise: Aaron just had his Bar Mitzvah.

Conclusion: Therefore, Aaron is Jewish.

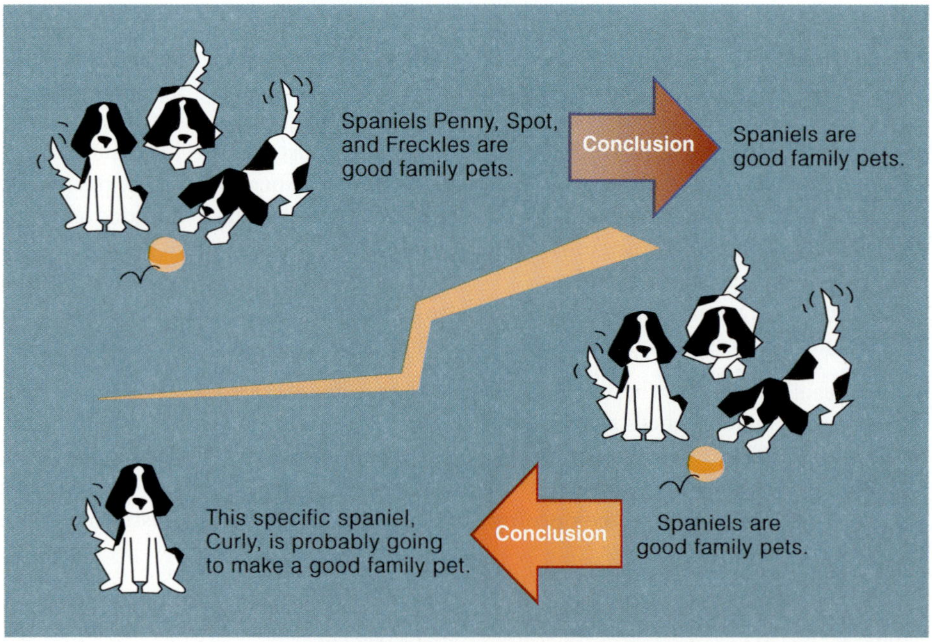

Figure 17.2 **Inductive and Deductive Reasoning** You observe a number of spaniels and inductively reason that they make good pets. Using that premise, you deduce that Curly, the specific spaniel you've chosen, will be a good family dog.

When you're sure of the major premise, you can state your conclusion with confidence. Because a Bar Mitzvah is the Jewish coming of age ceremony, only young men in that religion go through it. In contrast, many premises are less certain. Although some, such as "all people are mortal," are 100 percent true, others, such as "Each meal at the new restaurant in town is excellent," may not be valid in every case; the cook might occasionally have a bad night. So it's wise to qualify both your premises and your conclusions. Here is an example about the value of urban debate leagues:

Major premise: Participation in high school urban debate leagues helps *many* students get better grades.

Minor premise: Yolanda Baylor is a debater at an inner-city high school in the South Bronx.

Conclusion: She has *probably* improved her grades.[47]

When you reason deductively, you rarely state the entire syllogism, so your listeners must fill in the unstated premises. Aristotle called this an **enthymeme**. For example, you might say, "Is Aaron Jewish? Of course. He just had his Bar Mitzvah," and let your audience make the necessary connections. Or (talking with friends about the new restaurant in town), "You can't go wrong eating there, and you won't bust your budget." Your friends then use their generalizations about restaurants and recommendations to make sense of what you've just said.

enthymeme omitting part of the syllogism in an argument and letting listeners supply what's missing; inherently dialogical

Using enthymemes is inherently dialogical, for your listeners must form conclusions based on their knowledge of what you *don't* say. However, if they know nothing about your subject (the rules regarding Bar Mitzvahs or the connection between debating and grades, for example), they'll miss your meaning.

Testing Deductive Reasoning

There are two major tests for deductive reasoning:

1. For the conclusion to be valid, the premises must be true or highly probable.
2. To be reasonable, the conclusion must follow from the premise.

Reasoning Causally

Causal reasoning links two events or occurrences in such a way that one comes first and regularly leads to the second. Because the belief in cause-and-effect is a fundamental element of the Euro-American belief system, causal reasoning is common. Example: it is evident that the lack of oxygen to the brain (first event) causes death (second event)—this link is observed time after time.

causal reasoning linking two factors in such as way that the first occurs before the second and regularly leads to the second as a matter of rule

Cause-and-effect links are less evident in complex situations where many variables precede a condition and could be linked to it. For example, one speaker stated: "There were nine million immigrants last year, and there were nine million Americans out of work." Both facts could be verified by counting. However, if the speaker blames immigration for causing unemployment his statement might sound like this: "There were nine million Americans out of work last year *because* there were nine million immigrants." In his original statement, the two conditions exist together in time, perhaps by chance. In the second statement, the second phenomenon (unemployment) results from the first (immigration) and would not exist without it. However, most people agree that the causes of unemployment are much more complex than an influx of immigrants. When reasoning by cause, the key is to produce enough reasons to warrant the connection between the two factors.

Here are just a few of the causal claims currently being debated: Cell phones can lead to brain tumors. Ocean acidification inhibits the development of shells and skeletal structures in a variety of sea animals. Walking 10,000 steps a day is linked to longevity.

fallacy failure in logical reasoning that leads to unsound or misleading arguments

ad populum an appeal to popular opinion

ad hominem an attack on the messenger rather than the message

false analogy comparing two things too dissimilar to warrant the conclusion drawn

faulty generalization a fallacy of induction; generalizing too broadly, given the evidence

silppery slope a fallacy of causation; saying one small thing will lead to larger things without offering proof

post hoc a fallacy of causation; a false cause

false dichotomy an either-or fallacy that ignores other reasonable options

Testing Causal Reasoning

Test causation by asking a series of questions to assess whether the reasoning is valid.

1. Is there a real connection? Does one follow as a result of the first, or do the two events simply exist together in time? (Is it correlation or causation?)
2. Is this the only cause? The most important cause? Or are other factors at play?
3. Is the cause strong enough for the effect?

In summary, you have at your disposal a variety of reasoning strategies you can use to warrant your claims, including figurative and literal analogies, inductive and deductive reasoning, and causal links. All of these reasoning types fall under the category of logos, or rational proofs.

Recognizing Logical Fallacies

A **fallacy** is a failure in logical reasoning that leads to unsound or misleading arguments.[48] Fallacies have been around for thousands of years, as you can tell by the Latin names given to some of them. As a speaker or critical listener, you should examine arguments carefully to avoid using or being taken in by the common fallacies shown in Table 17.1.

Arguments can be fallacious because they fail to provide evidence or because they present faulty evidence for the claim. Fallacies also attack the messenger instead of countering the message. Fallacies of analogy, causation, induction, and false choice are common. Learning to recognize fallacies will help you think more critically about the arguments you make and those you hear every day.

Type of Fallacy	Example
Unsupported assertion	*offering a claim without any evidence* ("I deserved an A in class; why did you give me a C?")
Ad populum or bandwagon	*literally, "to the people"—an appeal to popular reason instead of offering evidence* ("We all agree . . ." or "Everyone says . . .")
Ad hominem (personal attack)	*literally, "against the person"—an attack against the source, not the evidence or reasoning* ("Of course, a liberal would think that way.")
False analogy	*comparing two things that are not similar enough to warrant the comparison* (Although three million websites use the analogy, "Animal Auschwitz," mistreatment of animals is not similar to the Nazis treatment of their enemies.)
Faulty generalization	*inductive fallacy that extends the conclusion further than the evidence warrants* ("I hate that politician; everyone in his political party is corrupt.")
Slippery slope	*stating, without proof, that if one step is taken, a snowball or domino effect will cause other negative results* ("If you take away any gun rights, pretty soon hunters won't even be able to keep their shotguns.")
Post hoc (ergo propter hoc)	*fallacy of causation; literally, "after this, therefore because of this"—assumes that, because one thing follows another, the first caused the second* ("I took my lucky rabbit's foot to the test with me, and I passed with flying colors.")
False dichotomy	*states an issue as an either-or choice, overlooking other reasonable possibilities* ("Either you get a college degree, or end up in a low-paying job.")

Table 17.1
Common Reasoning Fallacies

In conclusion, other cultures may not use Aristotle's terminology to name the proofs of ethos, pathos, and logos, but that does not mean they don't have them in some form. Across the globe, speakers follow cultural ideas about what makes a speaker trustworthy, and they address their listeners' emotional and rational responses.

Identifying Fallacies

Working alone or with a group of classmates, copy the list of common fallacies, and come up with an example of each. Use material from television shows or movies, personal experiences, letters to the editor, talk-show callers, current events, and the like. Share your examples with other class members.

For additional information, **weblink 17.2** links to a site sponsored by Dr. Robert Gass, University of California, Fullerton. He provides definitions and humorous examples of these and other common fallacies. (You can access this link through your CourseMate for *Public Speaking*, Chapter 17 resources.)

Incorporate Principles and Forms of Invitational Rhetoric

Ideas about polarizing issues such as political or religious beliefs can be so deeply rooted that marshaling your best arguments and presenting them credibly will not be persuasive. In these circumstances, a form of "sense making" called **invitational rhetoric** may be preferable.[49] Rather than focus on winning an argument, you invite your audiences to understand your world as you do, and you then invite them to present their own perspectives. Change may or may not result, but mutual understanding can be enhanced. The originators of the concept, Sonia Foss and Cindy Griffin, identify three principles and two forms associated with invitational rhetoric.

invitational rhetoric inviting audiences to enter and understand the rhetor's world and then share their own perspectives; focuses on mutual understanding and mutual influence, not winning or change per se

Combining Three Principles

Invitational rhetoric focuses on mutual understanding and mutual influence based on the principles of equality, individual value, and self-determination. It's one way you can develop a dialogical spirit as described in Chapter 3.

1. **Equality**: Instead of imposing your "superior" views on others, you view your listeners as equals. You don't select strategies to overcome their resistance; however, you do identify possible barriers to understanding and try to minimize or neutralize them. In short, you open yourselves to one another's viewpoints.

   For example, say it's an election year. Your classroom contains active supporters of three different candidates. You all have formulated good reasons for your choices. As an invitational rhetor, you share the path you've traveled in making your decision, and you invite your classmates to share theirs.

2. **Nonhierarchical value of all**: This means you approach your audience as equaling you in rank; you respectfully look for the value in their conclusions as well as your own. You don't attempt to demean their position and point out their deficiencies, and you try to maintain a positive relationship with those who differ from you.

Back to the election. By not considering yourself intellectually or morally superior by virtue of your viewpoint, you can respect your classmates' conclusions, because you work hard to see the point of their reasoning. There's no yelling, no put-downs, and no character assassination of the various candidates.

3. **Self-determination**: Invitational rhetoric may or may not result in change. If your listeners change their opinions or their behaviors, it won't be because you shamed or scared them into accepting your views. And you may modify your own positions by considering their insights. In some instances, you and your listeners may agree to disagree while remaining mutually respectful.

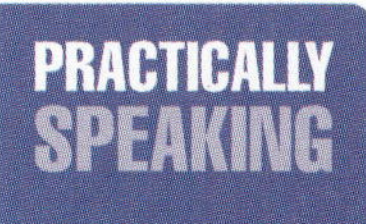

Jeanne M. Edwards, Accountant

Jeanne M. Edwards/KPMG

Jeanne M. Edwards is a partner with KPMG, a major international accounting and consulting firm based in New York City. While earning her university degree in business administration with an emphasis in accounting and economics, she participated on her university's debate team. She now travels all over the world helping clients solve problems.

Of what value was your training in debate? I apply skills from debating every day. In debating, I learned to look at a broad issue or problem and break it into sections or smaller pieces that I could then sort through and analyze. Debating also taught me to listen to other perspectives on the same issue. By listening carefully, I learned which types of evidence would be most persuasive to different audiences.

In consulting, I generally find that there is an organizational position on the problem and there is a mandate for change—which can be either negative or positive. I help clients identify the various elements of the issue and then find compelling, unique reasons to support the decisions they must make.

Having to debate both sides of issues taught me that there are a variety of perspectives on any issue. With each new problem, I look for the weaknesses and the strengths of the various positions. The issues that keep coming up again and again are the most important, and identifying them allows the common threads to eventually become evident. Clients can then come to a solution based on common interests that makes sense for their organization.

Questions

1. How does the ability to look at an issue from a variety of perspectives make a person more persuasive?
2. Edwards doesn't tell clients what to do, she helps them reason their way through difficult issues and find conclusions that work for them. In what other occupations are consulting skills vital?
3. Edwards doesn't use the words "invitational rhetoric," but where do the principles and forms of invitational rhetoric show up in her approach?

You and your classmates eventually split your votes, but regardless of who's elected, you have insights into the reasoning involved in each position, and you have learned more about working effectively in the political climate that will follow the election.

Including Two Forms

How does invitational rhetoric look in real situations? This alternative way of approaching issues typically takes two forms: offering perspectives and creating conditions that result in an atmosphere of respect and equality.

1. **Offering perspectives**: You explain what you currently understand or know, and you show a willingness to yield, examine, or revise your conclusions if someone offers a more satisfying perspective. When confronted with hostile or very divergent viewpoints, **re-sourcement** is one way to respond creatively by framing the issue in a different way.

   If this sounds complicated, read Gail Grobey's speech in Appendix C. In a narrative format, Gail offers her perspective on not spanking children (to listeners most of whom believed in spanking), and she reframes her daughter's discovery of a prescription pill as an *act of heroism* (saving the dogs from danger) rather than buying into the *ownership frame* (it's mine, and you can't take it away) her daughter presents.

re-sourcement creatively framing a divisive issue or viewpoint in a different way that may be less threatening

2. **Creating conditions**: You can create conditions in which your audiences feel safe, valued, and free to offer their own perspectives in two ways. First, use **absolute listening**, which means you listen without interrupting or inserting yourself into the talk; don't criticize or counter argue. This allows others to discover their own perspectives. Second, use **reversibility of perspectives.** While others are sharing their ideas, try to think from their perspectives instead of only your own. The Native American saying "Don't judge people until you've walked a mile in their moccasins" demonstrates perspective taking.

   Invitational rhetoric, a form of reasoning often associated with women, is a model of cooperative, dialogical communication in which you and your audiences generate ideas. Because it is rooted in affirmation and respect, it's arguably an ethical way of coming to conclusions. Further, because you're not intent on controlling the ideas of others, you can disagree without figuratively going to war.

absolute listening listening without interrupting or inserting oneself into the talk

reversibility of perspectives an attempt to think from the other's perspective as well as one's own

Summary

Whether you are making simple daily decisions or arguing about complex national policy questions, the canon of invention provides you with many resources for making sound decisions. Although it is often impossible to prove a claim beyond any doubt, you can at least interweave a variety of reasoning strategies to support your ideas.

Toulmin's linear model of reasoning shows that claims of fact, value, and policy are based on various kinds of evidence, with a connecting link or warrant and backing that justifies them. Listeners weigh the evidence, data, or grounds to see if it is sufficient and trustworthy enough to lead to the conclusion. To avoid overstating your claim, it is important to limit its scope by using qualifiers. Further, your arguments are more persuasive if you can rebut or counter the objections your listeners have. Doing so shows that you are familiar with a variety of perspectives on the issue.

Aristotle presented three kinds of artistic proofs thousands of years ago. They are artistic because you, the speaker, must create them within the audience. He considered the first proof, *ethos* or personal credibility, to be the most important.

A believable speaker should have good character, goodwill, good sense, and dynamism, but ideas about credibility vary across cultures.

Pathos or emotional proofs involve appeals to your listeners' positive and negative emotions as well as their needs. The chapter presented five basic needs: survival, security, belonging and love, esteem, and self-actualization. Emotions combine to form motivations that are both complex and mixed, and emotional appeals need to be tested to see if they make sense.

The final proof, *logos* or rational proof, comes from your words. Analogies, both figurative and literal, involve reasoning by comparison. Inductive reasoning draws generalizations or conclusions from a number of examples. Then, deductively, generalizations are applied to particular cases. Finally, causal or cause-to-effect reasoning links things that exist in time in such a way that the second results from the first. All these methods require the application of specific tests; otherwise, they can lead to fallacious or faulty conclusions.

An alternative way to make sense of complex issues is to practice invitational rhetoric based on equality, individual value, and self-determination rather than on control. You offer your perspectives and create conditions in which others are free to offer theirs. Absolute listening and reversibility of perspectives let you hear and learn from the viewpoints of others. Change may or may not result.

STUDY AND REVIEW

Your online resources for *Public Speaking: Concepts and Skills for a Diverse Society* offer a broad range of study tools that will help you better understand the material in this chapter, complete assignments, and succeed on tests. Your online resources feature the following:

- Speech videos with critical viewing questions, speech outlines, and transcripts.
- Interactive versions of this chapter's Stop and Check activities, as well as Application and Critical Thinking Exercises.
- Speech Builder Express and InfoTrac College Edition.
- Weblinks related to chapter content.
- Study and review tools such as self-quizzes, an *interactive* glossary, and downloadable audio summaries.

You can access your online resources at the CourseMate for *Public Speaking: Concepts and Skills for a Diverse Society.* Log in at **http://www.cengage.com/login,** using the access code that came with your book or that you bought online at **http://www.cengagebrain.com.**

KEY TERMS

The terms below are defined in the margins throughout this chapter.

absolute listening 309
ad hominem 306
ad populum 306
analogy 301
argument 293
artistic proofs 292
assertion 293
backing 293
causal reasoning 305
claim 293
common ground 295
deductive reasoning 304
demagogue 301
enthymeme 305
ethos 295
evidence, data, or grounds 293
fallacy 306
false analogy 306
false dichotomy 306
faulty generalization 306

identification or co-orientation 295
inductive reasoning 302
invitational rhetoric 307
logos 300
motivation 298
parallel case or literal analogy 302
pathos 298
persuasion 292
post hoc 306
qualifiers 293
reasoning by metaphor 301
rebuttal 294
re-sourcement 309
reversibility of perspectives 309
slippery slope 306
warrant 293

APPLICATION AND CRITICAL THINKING EXERCISES

1. Watch a movie or television show about a trial, and see if you can diagram the argument or case against the suspect using Toulmin's model. Who is arrested? For what (the claim)? On what evidence (the data or grounds)? What's the warrant (the link: causal reasoning, inductive reasoning, deductive reasoning, parallel case reasoning, testimony by a credible source, emotional arguments)? Is there backing for the warrant? Is the claim or charge limited or qualified? How? What are the rebuttal arguments (the defense)?
2. Stephen Toulmin is a major figure in argumentation. Search the Internet to find out more about this important thinker whose work is studied by beginning speakers across the nation and the globe. Be prepared to contribute to a class discussion about his ideas.
3. Find a political cartoon or an advertisement for a product that interests you. How does it appeal to emotions (both positive and negative)? To needs?
4. With a small group of classmates, make a list of possible speech topics that relate to each of the levels of need in Maslow's hierarchy.
5. Find a letter to the editor in your local newspaper about a controversial topic, or read a comment that follows an online news article. Identify the types of reasoning the author uses and then evaluate his or her arguments. Do they pass the tests for reasoning given in the text? Assess the overall effectiveness of the argument.
6. Watch the movie, *Twelve Angry Men*, or watch clips of some of the movie's speeches found YouTube. Focus on the persuasiveness of the arguments stemming from logical and emotional appeals and from the credibility of the speaker(s).
7. **Weblink 17.3** maintains a link to Debatepedia: The International Debate Education Association website. Under the category "The Debate Digest" link to the featured debate. Working with a partner and, each one taking a side, read through the major arguments and the supporting materials. Decide which position has the most compelling arguments and why. (You can access this link through your CourseMate for *Public Speaking,* Chapter 17 resources.)

8. Read the speech at the end of this chapter. Stop and answer the questions posed throughout.

SPEECH VIDEO

Read the following speech, "The Benefits of Hunting," for examples of sensible and of faulty reasoning. For more examples of persuasive reasoning, go to your online resources to watch and critique one or more of the following: "Cyber-Bullying," Carrie Weichbrodt's "Grief Counseling on Campus," "Immediate Action," "Cultural Sensitivity and the Peace Corps," or Gail Grobey's "Spanking" (invitational rhetoric).

Student Speech with Questions

This speech contains both sound and faulty reasoning. To guide your analysis, stop throughout your reading and answer the questions inserted between points in the text.

THE BENEFITS OF HUNTING
By Anonymous

Animals, I'm sure, have a place in everyone's heart. No one would like to see animals live pitiful lives and die by the hundreds from overpopulation and starvation. Well, this has happened before, and it could very well happen again if hunting is once again abolished by people who are uneducated about its true benefits.

If the welfare of animals means anything to you, it is essential that you listen closely to the biological facts that support hunting as being beneficial to wildlife, for in order to conserve wildlife, we must preserve hunting.

In the next few minutes, I will tell you about the damages resulting when people's right to hunt in certain areas is taken away. I will inform you of the uneducated ideas of animal activists and, finally, explain the differences between hunters and poachers.

a. *What do you think about the use of the phrases "I'm sure," "everyone," and "no one"? What effect does the use of the term "uneducated" have?*
b. *What claim is the speaker making?*

So many people are unaware of the damage that occurs to wildlife when hunting is taken away from a particular area. The best example of this happened in the state of Massachusetts. There, an animal rights group rallied and petitioned against deer hunting. Their efforts led to the banning of hunting in Massachusetts. During the period in which deer hunting was allowed, the deer population was around 100,000. Within the first year after the law was enacted, the population soared to 150,000.

Sounds good? Well, it wasn't! The overabundance of deer created a famine. Deer began to eat forest trees, gardens, and roots. They ate down to the foliage, leaving the plants unable to grow back the next year. Three years after the law went into effect the deer population went from 150,000 to only 9,000. It took the state ten years to return the deer population to normal. Eventually, the hunting ban was reversed, and the deer population has remained at its carrying capacity. I think it is hunting that plays a major role in keeping species from overpopulation.

c. *What kind of reasoning is the speaker using? Does it pass the tests? Do you think her conclusion is obvious? Why or why not?*
d. *She says in her introduction that she will present biological facts about hunting. Does she do so to your satisfaction?*

People often argue that animals were fine before man invented guns. However, before the white men came over here with guns, there weren't sprawling cities like Los Angeles and Portland to take up most of the animals' habitat. In those days, there was far more land for the animals to live on. Today, modernization has pushed the animals into a smaller wildlife area, leaving them less food and less room for breeding. Therefore, it is easier for the animals to overpopulate. Hunting has played a major role in keeping the animal population at a normal number. If hunting is taken away, the animals are sure to overpopulate.

It has been proven that humankind, even in its earliest form, has always hunted animals. Here in North America, before white people and guns came over, Indians hunted animals on a consistent basis. They killed hundreds of buffalo by herding them over cliffs every year. They caught school after school of salmon that migrated up the rivers. These hunts have always played a major role in population management, whether or not you choose to label it as a law of nature.

e. What argument does the speaker attempt to rebut? Does she do so to your satisfaction?

However, people argue that Indians needed to hunt animals to live, whereas today's North Americans don't need to kill animals to survive. So what if we can survive on fruit and vegetables? Humans are born omnivorous, meaning it is natural for us to eat both meat and plants. What is inhumane about eating an animal for food? Weren't we designed to do so?

f. Here is the second argument she attempts to counter or rebut. How well does she succeed? Explain your answer.

People also argue that the laws of nature will take care of animals. Hunting has always been a major part of the laws of nature. Without mountain lions to kill rabbits, the rabbit population would be a long-gone species because of overpopulation. Humans as well as mountain lions are animals. Our predation is as important to other animals, such as deer, as the mountain lion's predation is to rabbits.

g. What is the third argument the speaker attempts to refute? What kind of reasoning does she use?
h. Which of the three arguments do you think she did the best job of refuting? Which argument did she refute the least adequately?

Animal activists harass hunters all the time. These people have false perceptions of what hunting really is and who hunters really are. At a rally against deer hunting, a woman speaker argued, "Hunters are barbarians who are in it for the kill. Hunters would use machine guns if they could. Plus, the deer are so cute." I think that argument is pathetic and holds absolutely no validity.

Another instance of hunter harassment occurred at Yellowstone National Park. An animal activist was not satisfied with only verbal harassment, so he struck the hunter on the head twice. Are animal activists really the peaceful and humane people they claim to be? And they still believe that hunters are bloodthirsty, crazy, and inhumane!

i. Do these two examples pass the tests for their use? Are they typical? How does the speaker generalize from them? How might she make her point instead?

Many of these misperceptions about hunters come from the association of hunters with poachers. Hunters are not poachers! Poachers are people who kill animals when they want, regardless of laws and regulations that were set to protect the animals. These are the kind of people who hunt elephants for their ivory tusks or kill crocodiles for their skins. Poachers kill deer in areas that are off-limits, during off-limit hunting seasons. These people are criminals who are extremely harmful to wildlife. Hunters would turn in a poacher in an instant if they caught one. Poachers give hunting a bad image in the eyes of the public. It's too bad that the animal activists don't go after the poachers who are extremely harmful to animals, and stop pointing a finger at hunters who follow the laws and regulations.

j. Why does the speaker contrast hunters to poachers? In what ways, if any, is this an effective argument?

If hunting is banned, just imagine a drive through the mountains on a road covered with emaciated skeletons of cadaverous deer who died of starvation. No longer can you take a picture of Bambi, your favorite deer that you saw every year at Yellowstone National Park. For Bambi and his family were overpopulated, and they slowly wilted away until their final day. Too bad there weren't a few healthy bucks taken by hunting that year to keep Bambi and family at a cozy carrying capacity where there was plenty of delicious food for all of them.

k. Here, the speaker uses a great deal of pathos. Identify emotional language and images. Is this effective? Why or why not?

The argument that animal activists use against hunting is fabricated mainly from emotions. If they are personally against killing an animal, I can respect that. But they have no place trying to ban hunting. It is proven by biological facts that hunting is necessary for wildlife management. It provides millions of dollars that fund the construction of programs that help wildlife. It keeps species from overpopulating and starving to death. In order for wildlife to flourish at an optimum population number, hunting must continue to be a major part of wildlife management.

CHAPTER
18

THIS CHAPTER WILL HELP YOU

- Find a subject for a persuasive speech
- Decide on a claim of fact, value, or policy
- Analyze your audience's attitude toward your topic
- Develop a speech to convince
- Create a speech to actuate

Persuasive Speaking

IN ANCIENT ATHENS, Aristotle identified three areas in which rhetoric—the art of finding the available means of persuasion—enabled democracy to thrive: law courts, governing assemblies, and ceremonial or ritual occasions that reinforce cultural beliefs and values.[1] Today, speakers in the United States continue to present divergent viewpoints in legal settings and decision making bodies, and ceremonial speakers still reinforce and emphasize cultural values on ritual occasions. Because US culture values civic engagement and free speech, you, too, can be a person of influence who attempts to persuade others to believe or to act in ways you find desirable. (The role of persuasive speaking varies cross-culturally, as the Diversity in Practice feature illustrates.)

This chapter provides information about selecting a topic, deciding on a claim, and analyzing your audience's attitude toward it. Then it gives guidelines for creating speeches to convince and to actuate behaviors.

DIVERSITY IN PRACTICE

Persuasion in China

Yin-yang (Tai Chi) in Chinese art, the symbol

As China rapidly becomes a global superpower, interactions between China and the West highlight some fundamental assumptions about influence and persuasion. Li Liu,[2] a professor at Beijing Normal University, contrasts the Western model of persuasion with the more collectivist model typical of Chinese persuaders. For centuries, persuaders in the West have combined ethos, pathos, and logos into their speeches with the intent of swaying others. However, Chinese persuasion has been dialogical and inherently interdependent—reflecting Confucian ideals of harmonious relationships that balance *yang* (power, light, masculinity) and *yin* (passivity, darkness, femininity).

In China, a person's sense of self is embedded in family and social relationships; consequently, persuasion is grounded in these interdependent associations. Within the family, influence or persuasion is based in filial piety (respect for parents) and in maintaining family harmony. Outside the family, influence is grounded in *guanxi*, or relationships that operate on reciprocity; the obligations that emerge from these relationships become tools of influence.

How does this work out in practice? Researchers have found that messages are more persuasive when they are tailored to embedded cultural frames, when they include culturally relevant themes, and when the recipients are thinking about cultural distinctions. One study found that European Americans were more likely to believe that caffeine posed risks and they should alter their behaviors when the message was framed as hurting them personally. However, Asian Americans were more persuaded by messages that focused on their relational obligations.[3]

Questions

1. Go to **weblink 18.1** and watch the video in which two Chinese people explain the concept of *guanxi*. Then talk with a few classmates about how *guanxi* might affect an American business representative who is doing business in China. (You can access this link through your CourseMate for *Public Speaking*, Chapter 18 resources.)

Select Your Persuasive Topic

Choosing a persuasive topic can be challenging. Even if you have ideas for subjects, you may not know how to focus clearly on one claim and one specific purpose. Your topic should be disputable, significant to others, and important to you; it's arguably more ethical to influence others toward a viewpoint or action that you personally believe, care about, and actually practice. So begin your topic search by asking yourself several questions.[4]

- *What do I believe strongly?* What do I hold to be true that my audience might dispute? What ideas and issues would I argue against?
- *What arouses strong emotions in me?* What makes me angry? What are my pet peeves? What arouses my pity? When am I happiest? What do I fear?

- *What social ideals do I support?* What changes would I like to see in society? What current problems or conditions could improve if we were convinced there is a problem, that solutions exist, and that we can be part of those solutions? Are there any causes for which I would sign a petition or join a protest?
- *What practices enrich my life?* What have I discovered that makes life more meaningful? What activities will expand our horizons? What improves our health? What leads to more fulfilling personal relationships?

Carrie's speech about grief counseling on campus, found in Appendix C, is just one example of a classroom topic that reflects strong beliefs about issues related to her personal and social concerns. Other students have spoken about rap music (to convince the audience that it reinforces male dominance), photoshopped images in ads (to convince listeners that this is unethical), the joys of opera (to motivate listeners to attend an opera), learning another language (to reinforce the practices of people taking a language course or to motivate others to study another language), and so on.

Select Your Topic

Fold a piece of paper into fourths, and label each quarter with one of the following categories:

- My strong beliefs
- My strong feelings
- My social ideals
- My personal ideals

Make a list of topics in each category.

Next, circle the topics in each section that you think would be most appropriate for this particular group.

Analyze the circled topics, and put an X by those you could discuss within the allotted time.

Finally, select the best topic, given your audience and the time constraints.

Make a Claim

After you have chosen a topic, your next step is to identify a claim you can support. Chapter 17 described Toulmin's model of argumentation and identified three kinds of claims: fact, value, and policy, which generally build on one another. In other words, we don't enact a policy without first considering the facts involved and without building on important values. We now turn to each type of claim.

Claims of Fact

factual claim argument about existence, causation, or predictions

Factual claims address controversial questions about what, when, where, why, or how something happened or will happen. We assess their validity by using terms such as *true* or *false*, *correct* or *incorrect*, *yes* or *no*. These claims are common in courtrooms, religious institutions, and educational settings such as history or science classes. The three general categories of factual claims are debatable points, causal relationships, and predictions.

Debatable points are disputable statements about things that do or do not exist (existence) or things that did or did not happen (history). Here are three examples about which reasonable people disagree:

debatable point disputable statements about facts of existence or history

There is life after death.

The defendant murdered her daughter.

JFK won the 1960 presidential election only because of widespread voter fraud.

Causal relationships argue that a particular phenomenon is the result of something that came before it and led to it. Often two things are correlated, meaning that they occur together with a degree of regularity. The question then arises: are they linked in such a way that the second would not occur—at least in the form it does—without the first? In other words, **correlation** and causation are not synonymous. For example, skipping breakfast and poor grades may occur together in elementary schools (correlation), but does skipping breakfast actually lead to poor grades (causation)? Children who skip breakfast also tend to be tardy and absent more often; attendance may have more impact on grades than breakfast.[5] Causal claims such as these are commonly reported:

causal relationship links one phenomenon to another that preceded it and led to it

correlation two things occur together, but one does not necessarily lead to the other

Certain meat marinades reduce carcinogens in grilled chicken.[6]

Too much time spent on Facebook causes depression in young girls.

The price of textbooks is so high because too many students resell used texts.

Claims of prediction contend that something will or will not happen in the future. We make decisions today based on what we think will happen tomorrow. For example,

claim of prediction claim that something will or will not happen in the future

Advergaming will become the marketing tool of choice for many corporations.

A deadly strain of flu will become a pandemic in the coming year.

The Mariners will win the World Series this year.

All these claims generate differences of opinion that advocates support with various types of evidence. Is there life after death? People disagree. The media and protesters outside courtrooms protest many jury decisions. Did JFK really "steal" the election from Richard Nixon? Historians have formed different conclusions, but no one has proven this. What causes high textbook prices? Is the resale market the major cause? Or are more complex factors involved? What links a particular meat marinade to reduced carcinogens? How, specifically, does Facebook cause depression in young girls? Finally, predictions about the future are open to debate. Advergaming may be replaced by a more effective technique. Pandemics may be prevented. And, of course, arguments about sports teams fuel many a conversation.

Debatable points, causal questions, and predictions often exist in the same issue. Take climate change, for example. Someone might argue that (1) *unnatural* climate change exists; (2) *human activity* caused it, and (3) if we don't do something, there will be *dire consequences* for the planet.

Claims of Value

When you evaluate something using terms such as *right* or *wrong*, *good* or *better* or *best*, *beautiful* or *ugly*, *worthwhile* or not *worthwhile*, you're making a **value claim**. Here are some value claims (with the evaluative term in italics):

value claim argument about right or wrong, moral or immoral, beautiful or ugly

It's *unfair* for giant corporations to avoid paying taxes.

Boxing is an *inhumane* sport.

National security is *more important* than personal privacy during airport screenings.

Note that both national security and personal privacy are important in the third claim, but the argument is over which value should take priority in that specific context. The pro-choice/pro-life debate is similar. Pro-choice people are not anti-life, nor are pro-lifers anti-choice. However, the two sides disagree over which value should have precedence in the abortion issue.

criteria the standards used for making evaluations or judgments

Value conflicts are difficult to resolve without agreement on the **criteria** or standards for deciding how to judge moral or immoral, fair or unfair, humane or inhumane. That's why it's vital to state the criteria on which you base your judgment. If you can convince listeners to accept your standards, they'll more readily accept your judgment; even if you fail to convince them, they can at least understand the reasonableness of your argument.

Consider a movie you liked and your friend didn't. Why did you reach different conclusions about it? Because each of you set up different criteria for "good" movies. Let's say your friend likes romance, beginning-to-end action, and stunning visual effects, which this movie lacked. However, your criteria might include realistic characters and an unpredictable plot, and this one met your standards. You can argue for hours about the merits of the movie, but unless one (or both) of you adjusts your criteria, you'll never agree.

Claims of Policy

policy claim argument about the need or the plan for taking action

status quo Latin phrase that means "the existing state of affairs"

burden of proof responsibility of the speaker who argues against the status quo to make the case for change

We make decisions regarding our behaviors both as individuals and as members of groups—decisions about *whether* or *not* we should act and about *how* we should proceed. **Policy claims** are the statements we make about desirable actions. To identify them, look for the terms *should* or *would*. There are basically three types of policy claims: policies should change, behaviors should change, and policies (or actions) should remain the same.

Status quo is a Latin phrase that means the existing state of affairs. Consequently, arguments against the status quo are arguments for change, ranging from international or national issues to local or campus issues. When you argue against the status quo, the **burden of proof** is your responsibility because, as the cultural saying puts it, "If it ain't broke, don't fix it." Consequently, it's up to you to prove that there is a significant problem and that it can and should be fixed by the solution you propose. Examples include the following:

Congress should adopt a flat tax system.

Our campus should create a grief support system.

Year-round schooling should be required in all school districts.

Some policy claims aim at personal behaviors. Here, your goal is to have your audience change their actions, as these examples illustrate:

Every student should get involved in a civic engagement project.

You should sign up to volunteer in either the Boy's Club or the Girl's Club.

Americans should cut up all their credit cards.

presumption assumption that change is not necessary until proven otherwise

In contrast, arguments supporting the status quo are arguments in favor of the current situation and against change. These claims have what's called **presumption**; this means that the status quo is presumed to be workable and not in need of alteration. (In courts of law, presumption of innocence lies with the defendant. The prosecution must prove guilt beyond a reasonable doubt, or the defendant goes free.) Here are some claims supporting the status quo:

The university should not raise tuition.

The current tax system is adequate.

You should stay in school instead of dropping out.

Often people will agree that there is a problem, and they may even agree on its causes. However, they argue over different solutions. For example, many educational reformers agree that education within the United States needs improvement, and they similarly argue against the status quo, but their solutions become debatable points.

Table 18.1
Any or all of these claims can be made about the topic, "Ocean Acidification."

Type	Goal	Claim
Fact	Argue a debatable point	The chemistry of oceans worldwide is now off balance.
	Prove a cause-effect relationship	Increasing CO_2 emissions since the beginning of the Industrial Revolution is causing coral reefs to die.
	Make a prediction	Rising ocean acidity levels between now and the year 2100 could create areas of ocean territory void of organisms that would not reverse for 1,500 to 2,000 years.
Value	Argue something is right or wrong, good or bad, beautiful or ugly	It is immoral to continue the current rate of CO_2 emissions.
Policy	Propose a policy change	The United Nations should create a network of protected ocean areas to help degraded marine habitats recover.
	Propose a behavioral change	You should go to www.oceana.org to join the discussion and push legislation forward.
	Argue against a policy change	Creating a network of protected ocean areas is unnecessary.

Some argue for smaller classes. Others advocate for alternative schools; still others think vouchers are the way to solve specific problems.

Although we separate claims of fact, value, and policy for analysis, in reality a persuasive speech includes a combination of claims as Table 18.1 shows. Effective speakers skillfully blend various types of claims in order to successfully persuade an audience.

Rich Carey/Shutterstock

Is something bad happening to plant and animal life in our oceans? If so, what caused this? What can we do about it? These questions lead to claims of fact, value, and policy that can be interwoven into a single speech.

Make Fact, Value, and Policy Claims

To better understand how discussions surrounding a controversial topic combines fact, value, and policy claims, work alone or with a small group of classmates and choose a controversial topic such as doctor assisted suicide, gay marriage, Internet privacy, or sex education.

- (fact) Write at least one factual claim (debatable point, causation, or prediction).
- (value) Assess questions of good or bad, and develop criteria for a decision.
- (policy) Decide whether or not the status quo needs to be changed, and frame your policy claim accordingly.

Share your claims with the class as a whole.

Finally, go back to the topic you've selected for your own speech and list several fact, value, or policy claims you could make about it. Choose one claim you will develop, and write it out.

Assess Your Audience's Attitude

You have your topic and your claim. To better identify how listeners will respond to your goal, you need to assess their attitude. Much of the persuasion-related research focuses on attitudes, which Chapter 6 described as our positive or negative evaluations of the behavior in question; attitudes include a mental (what we believe about it) and an emotional (how we feel about it) component, and they form the basis for our actions. The Princeton University Cognitive Science website summarizes attitudes as complex mental states "involving beliefs and feelings and values and dispositions to act in certain ways."[7]

Chapter 6 showed how to measure the components of attitudes along a scale ranging from strong agreement or acceptance to strong disagreement or nonacceptance. Table 18.2 illustrates how the beliefs, emotions, and behaviors that comprise an audience's attitude can range from strong support to strong opposition to your claim. In between, are neutral listeners—often because they lack information to form an opinion either way or because they are apathetic and lack motivation to care or to do something about the issue. Obviously, it's most difficult to persuade someone who is strongly opposed to the position you are advocating.

Table 18.2

Audience attitudes involve a combination of their beliefs, emotions, and actions regarding your topic.

	strongly	moderately	neutral	moderately	strongly
BELIEFS	disagree	disagree	no beliefs either way	agree	agree
EMOTIONS	hostile	negative	no evaluation either way	positive	favorable
ACTIONS	never act	rarely act	unaware of need to act	sometimes act	always act
ATTITUDE	negative	negative	neutral	positive	positive

<——convince first, then motivate to act——> <—reinforce or motivate to act—>
most difficult———————————————————————easiest

In general, the following guidelines will help you plan effective speeches that are sensitive to audience attitudes:

- When listeners are neutral toward your claim, ask why. Do they lack information? Are they apathetic? With uninformed audiences, present factual information early so they have enough knowledge to form an opinion. Then use emotional appeals to create either a positive or negative attitude toward your topic. With apathetic audiences, use emotional appeals by linking the topic to listeners in as many ways as you can, and appeal to values such as fairness and justice.
- When differences are mild, approach your audience directly. Use objective data to make a clear case; present the positive facets of your subject; and make links to personal and community values your audience accepts. This way, although they might still disagree with you, they can understand why you hold your position.
- When your listeners are negative toward your proposal, rethink your options. With mildly or moderately negative audiences, try to lessen the negative so they can see positive aspects of your proposal. If they're strongly opposed, you face a hostile audience. So set modest goals and aim for small attitudinal changes. Present your points clearly so that they will at least understand how you came to your conclusions.
- When audiences reject your proposals, approach the subject indirectly by establishing common ground. For instance, begin with a statement with which everyone agrees, and explain why there is agreement. Then make a statement that most would accept, and explain why this is so. Move gradually to the point about which they disagree. By this time, they will have seen that they agree with you on many points, and as a result, they may be less negative toward your ideas.[8]
- Perhaps the most distressing situation arises when your audience is hostile toward you personally. Then, it's vital to emphasize common ground between yourself and your listeners.

Generally, attitudes change incrementally, so expect change to be gradual. Each new encounter with the subject may bring about only a slight change, but eventually, the small changes can add up.

Christoph Kadur/iStockphoto

Assessing your audience's attitude toward your speech helps you choose strategies that will make your message more persuasive.

Adapt to the Audience's Attitude

Analyze the following public speaking situation. An anthropology major prepares a speech on government funding for archaeological digs. Her claim is that the study of archaeology is important enough to receive government funding because knowledge of other human cultures helps us to better understand our own.

Divide into three groups within the classroom. Each group will discuss how the speaker should prepare for one of the following audiences:

1. A group of anthropology majors who agree with her and are highly positive toward her topic.
2. An audience that knows nothing about anthropology but expresses concern about how their tax money is spent.
3. Listeners who consider archaeology to be a waste of time.

Questions

1. How will the speaker analyze the particular audience?
2. What purpose should she select for that group?
3. What specific strategies will she use to make her points?
4. What kinds of reasoning and evidence should she use?
5. What should she emphasize, and why?

Choose a Specific Purpose

After you better understand your audience's attitude and how that affects your strategies, consider the specific response you want from your listeners. Do you want them to mentally accept your ideas? Do you want to motivate them to act? Each specific purpose requires different strategies.

Persuasive Goal: To Convince About Facts, Values, and Policies

Some audience members don't believe your claim or accept your value judgment, either because they hold a different viewpoint or because they haven't thought much about the subject. Consequently, when you want mental agreement with your claim—whether it is a claim of fact, value, or policy—you design a speech to **convince**.

convince a persuasive purpose that targets audience beliefs

Convincing about Facts

Some general strategies are effective when you want to convince someone to believe a disputed fact, accept a causal relationship, or believe you when you make a prediction.

- Define important terminology and provide a history of the issue.
- Build your case carefully, using only high quality evidence that passes the tests for credible supporting material. Research studies show that statistics are particularly useful for lending credibility to an argument.[9]
- Rely more on logical appeals than on emotional appeals.
- Prove your competence by being knowledgeable about the facts; cite sources for your information.
- Show respect for your listeners' intelligence and divergent beliefs.

For example, Kelli decided to argue this factual claim (causation): Playing with fashion dolls leads to poor body images in young girls. Many females in her audience disagreed somewhat; they grew up playing with these dolls and they didn't feel particularly harmed. Others—especially the males—hadn't thought much about the topic. So most of her audience was neutral or moderately opposed to her claim. Her burden was to prove the link, and her best strategies were logos or rational proofs. Here is how she built her case:[10]

- First she provided a brief history of the most famous fashion doll of all: Barbie.
- She countered a common myth ("You may have heard that Barbie's body would be bent in half constantly if she were alive because her lower body could not support her upper body") by reporting, "I couldn't find any facts to support this, but I did find a study in *Sex Roles Journal* of 1996 that discussed the proportions of Barbie's body."[11]
- After supplying novel facts about the dolls, she cited a study reported by developmental psychologists in the journal *Adolescence* that showed the importance of toys in children's development.[12]
- Her next cited study, from the journal *Developmental Psychology*, showed that children internalize images from dolls and become aware of their body image at around age six, and some girls at this age have body dissatisfaction.[13]
- The same study compared girls who played with Barbie to girls who played with Emme, a larger-sized fashion doll and found the former had more negative body images.[14]
- Her final study reported that adolescent females believed fashion dolls were images of perfection, and both males and females believed they affected girls' self-image. Most said they were bad role models.[15]
- She concluded by saying she is not calling for a ban on these dolls, but she wants people to recognize their impact.

Overall, the studies by experts provided Kelli's listeners with good reasons to see a link between playing with fashion dolls and lower body image in developing girls. Her speech would have been more convincing if she had defined "body image" more precisely.

Convincing about Values

Because we make different judgments about people, objects, policies, and so on, we often try to convince others to share our evaluations. Here are two value claims: (1) embryonic stem cell research is wrong; (2) finding cures for people who are currently alive is more important than preserving an embryo. The first comes to a judgment about the issue; the second argues that both values are important, but one supersedes the other.

For a variety of reasons, value judgments within a single audience may vary so widely that some judge a topic, such as gay marriage, as unethical whereas others consider it a moral necessity. Furthermore, because values are assumptions about what is good, value questions often generate deep emotional responses. It is nearly impossible to move listeners from judging a topic as unethical to evaluating it as highly ethical because of a single speech, but here are some tips for arguing value claims:

- Use emotional appeals. Examples are a good way to help listeners identify with those involved in the issue. Also, link the topic to related values that everyone can agree on, such as fairness or freedom.
- Appeal to authority if your audience accepts your source as authoritative. (See Chapter 8.) Some audiences will be moved by appeals to cultural traditions, words of poets, philosophers, scientists, or scriptural texts; others will discount those same authorities.

One useful organizational strategy is the **criteria-satisfaction pattern** in which you first establish the standards you're using to evaluate the topic and then show how

criteria-satisfaction pattern good for value or definition speeches; sets forth standards for judgment or for inclusion in a category and then shows how the proposal meets or exceeds these standards or fits into the category

Gay marriage is a value-laden topic that people judge differently based on different criteria. Opponents often appeal to tradition, natural law, or religious texts to support their views. Advocates often appeal to shared values and examples to convince people to change their views.

govicinity/iStockphoto

your subject meets those standards. Set audience-centered criteria[16] by answering questions such as these:

- How do we make and apply judgments regarding this issue?
- What criteria do we use?
- Where do these criteria come from?
- Why should we accept these sources?

For example, Helene faced a hostile or at least moderately negative crowd when she presented her value claim: Snakes make good pets.

So she first set up some criteria people commonly look for in a pet:

- A pet should be interesting.
- Pets should be easy to care for.
- You should be able to read a pet's emotions.

She then linked each point to snakes.

- She presented several fascinating facts about snakes.
- She described how easy they were to care for.
- She explained how to read a snake's emotions.

At the end of her speech, no one was ready to run out and buy a snake, but listeners were more willing to evaluate snakes positively—at least as pets for someone else!

Convincing about Policies

stock issues the questions a reasonable person would need to have answered before forming a reasoned decision about a topic

In order to convince an audience that a policy claim is workable, you must adequately answer some critical questions, called **stock issues**, which are defined as

> the fundamental questions that must be answered if a proposition is to be accepted or rejected. Stock issues are generally presumed to be the set of questions a thinking, reasonable person would ask and would need to have answered to make a reasoned decision about a particular issue.[17]

The four stock issues related to policy claims are harm (or ill), blame, cure, and cost.

- *Harm* is sometimes called *ill*. Here you define the problem, explain its history, and show that it is significant enough to call for a solution. Develop the quantitative effects (the number of people affected) by using statistics or studies that show how widespread it is. Also include qualitative effects (how it affects an individual's or group's quality of life), by using examples or testimony from people involved with the problem.

- *Blame* is the "cause" part of the problem where you link a cause or causes to the effects you established in the harm section. What elements of the status quo contribute to the problem or allow it to remain unsolved? Some causes may be structural, meaning that laws or organizations are either in place and should be removed, or that structures are lacking, and the problem exists because they are not there. Other causes may be attitudinal, meaning that individuals or groups lack the understanding or the will to solve the problem. Either way, support your causal claims by using scientific studies, plausible explanations, and testimony from experts who have investigated the problem in depth.[18]
- *Cure* is the "solution" section of the speech where you provide a plan and describe how it will create **solvency**, an effective solution to the problem. What must happen for the problem to be solved? Who will do it? How? Through what agency? At what price? How will the plan eliminate or work around the structural or attitudinal causes? Clear and detailed answers to these questions will help convince your listeners that your plan will actually solve the problem.
- *Cost* is the "feasibility" part of the plan in which you do a cost-benefit analysis and weigh the advantages against the disadvantages. You must show that the plan will actually work. Some plans look good on paper, but they are too costly in time or money to be practical.

solvency the proposed plan will actually solve the problem

In summary, you must convince your audience that a problem exists and that it affects a significant number of people and alters their quality of life. You then convince them that it was caused by factors that can either be eliminated or circumvented by the plan you propose. Give enough details of the plan so that listeners can understand how it will work, and provide a cost benefit analysis so they are convinced that it is practical.

US citizens got a lesson in policy debating when the federal government enacted a policy known as "Obamacare" to reform healthcare.

- [Harm] Almost everyone agreed that problems existed in the status quo. Health costs were high; insurance rates were skyrocketing; not everyone had access to the treatments and medications they needed, and so on.
- [Blame] Congress pointed to structural causes including (depending on who you asked) for-profit health insurance companies, too many malpractice lawsuits, the lack of a single-payer government system, and so on. Attitudes also contribute. Too many people demand unnecessary procedures from costly specialists.[19]
- [Cure] Congress passed a giant plan that most members of Congress had not actually read. Critics disputed details of the plan; some thought it went too far; others thought it didn't go far enough.
- [Cost] Furthermore, the cost of the overhaul was hotly debated. The cost-saving benefits, touted by its supporters, were disputed by its detractors.

The task of convincing citizens that the plan is legal and has merits is ongoing, and adjustments continue to be made as elements of the plan are implemented.

Convincing Arguments

Identify a time when you changed your mind about something you previously believed or valued. What arguments caused you to change? Who made them? What evidence was the most convincing? Why?

How can you adapt persuasive strategies that were effective with you to support convincing claims of fact, value, or policy?

Persuasive Goal: To Actuate

actuate motivate the audience to do something

Sometimes you want your audience to change their actions. Then your specific purpose is to **actuate** behavior. This requires you to consider your listeners' beliefs about your topic, their motivations, and their opinions about whether or not they can and should act as you suggest. This section discusses two theories that explain motivations to act: cognitive dissonance theory and the Theory of Reasoned Action (TRA). It then provides an organizational pattern commonly used to motivate behaviors.

Cognitive Dissonance Theory

cognitive dissonance theory says that humans seek stability or equilibrium; when faced with inconsistency they seek psychological balance; this may motivate them to change in order to be consistent

dissonance inconsistency or clash

Often people behave in ways that are inconsistent with their beliefs or values. Leon Festinger[20] developed the **cognitive dissonance theory** to explain the resulting inconsistency or **dissonance** we experience. He originally studied smokers who continued to smoke even though they knew that it harmed their bodies. This theory states that living organisms, including humans, seek balance or equilibrium. When challenged with inconsistency, we try to return to a balanced psychological state. If our behaviors fail to match our beliefs, we typically experience discomfort until we either alter our beliefs to match our behaviors or alter our behaviors to match our beliefs.

Inconsistency between action and belief is one of the best motivators for change. For example, it is easier to persuade you to consult an employment counselor if you are stuck in a job you hate than if you love everything about your current workplace. If you strongly support a political party's ideas but do nothing, it's easier to persuade you to vote than if you care nothing about politics. (For additional information, do an Internet search for "cognitive dissonance theory" and follow a couple of links that have .edu in their URL.)

The Theory of Reasoned Action

Theory of Reasoned Action links behavioral intentions with attitudes, subjective norms, and perceived behavioral control; assumes we rationally weigh costs and benefits of our actions

subjective norms our perceptions of what significant people think we should do

perceived behavioral control our opinion about our ability to do a behavior

The **Theory of Reasoned Action** (TRA) is another good way to think about the process of motivating an audience because it adds a social component. It assumes that humans are rational and that we systematically weigh the costs and benefits of acting, given an opportunity to do so.[21] We also act in ways that allow us to meet the expectations of others. In short, our actions line up with (1) our *attitudes*, including both our beliefs and feelings about the topic, (2) our **subjective norms**, which are our perceptions of what people who are important to us think we should do, and (3) our **perceived behavioral control**—our opinion about our ability to accomplish the behavior in question.[22] All three factors influence our intentions to act, although our attitudes generally carry more weight. Interestingly, one study found that people in a collectivist culture scored higher on subjective norms, but this did not necessarily predict their intention to act.[23]

For illustration, let's say a speaker urges listeners to support the campus speech team by attending a debate being held on campus, and she wants them to perceive that this is something they can easily do. So, in addition to appeals to foster positive attitudes about competitive debate, she includes details about where and how to act. An audience member might reason like this:

> I think I'll watch the debate (intention) in the student union building tonight (opportunity). I dislike taking time from study (negative attitude/cost), but I like the idea of supporting our university's team (positive attitude/benefits). My friends and family like to debate ideas (subjective norms), and they'd admire me for attending this function (benefits). Therefore, I'll do it.

In contrast, another listener might respond differently:

> I don't intend to attend this debate (intention). A debate sounds boring (negative attitude/cost), and I support other teams on campus. None of my friends or family would care (subjective norms) whether or not I went. So don't ask again.

(You can read more about TRA by searching the Internet or looking on InfoTrac College Edition for "theory AND reasoned AND action.")

PRACTICALLY SPEAKING *Gayathri Ramprasad*, A Mental Health Ambassador

Gayathri Ramprasad

Gayathri Ramprasad,[24] *who speaks about mental illness, answered some questions about her persuasive goals.* I was born and raised in India in a loving family. But by age 18, I was debilitated by anxiety and panic attacks. As a young mother in America, I struggled with depression and found myself in a hospital's psychiatric ward. There, I promised to become a harbinger of hope and healing—to fight for myself and others like me. Today, I've spoken to more than 25,000 people nationally and internationally.

I started sharing my journey one-on-one. Many who had been touched by mental illness thanked me for bringing hope. However, some people within my Indian community found it hard to imagine why a woman with a loving husband, beautiful children, and a fabulous future could be depressed.

My first public speech was as an MBA student, when I told my story in a five-minute exemplum based on the quotation, "Courage is fear that has said its prayers." The response was positive. I later became associated with the National Alliance on Mental Illness. After I spoke as a keynote speaker at one of their luncheons, a girl about 18 years old thanked me. "Tonight was the night I was going to kill myself. But now, I have hope that I too shall recover and reclaim my life. Thank you for saving my life." I vowed then to share my story for the rest of my life.

I have presented in prisons, mental hospitals, graduate classes, and conferences. My most memorable speech was at the same hospital where I was once locked up. Now I promote global mental health awareness and cultural competency among cultural minorities.

What are your basic themes? There are five: (1) mental illnesses are brain disorders; (2) treatment works; (3) recovery is possible; (4) have hope; and (5) seek help. My ultimate speaking goal is to promote mental health awareness, stop stigma, and save lives. Monroe's Motivated Sequence works well for me.

What must you overcome with listeners? There is wide cultural variance in beliefs, attitudes, values, and behaviors pertaining to mental illness, and cultural stigma is one of my greatest barriers. Many think mental illness is a sign of personal weakness or a character flaw. Others believe that medications and hospitalizations are the only treatment options. I must dispel these myths to present my arguments. My program integrates three approaches the UCLA School of Medicine developed to reduce stigma:

1. *Educate* about the neurobiological nature of mental disorders. This changes knowledge.
2. *Give cases* of citizens who recovered and lived normally. This changes attitudes.
3. *Have people actually interact* with recovered and functional mentally ill persons. This is an anti-stigma impact at the behavioral level.

What already supports your topic in listeners' minds? There is a growing awareness of mental health issues, locally and globally, as more people share their testimonials of recovery. Tremendous scientific breakthroughs in understanding and treating mental illness support my arguments. Finally, my greatest advantage is my personal testimonial, which I have found is far more powerful in changing people than any number of papers in scientific journals.

Questions

1. How does Gayathri's story show the importance of strong beliefs, strong feelings, personal ideals, and social ideals in finding a topic?
2. What would be her biggest challenge if she were to present her story on your campus or in your community?
3. Think of another topic that is surrounded by stigma. Discuss within a small group how you might apply the principles from UCLA for reducing that stigma.

Monroe's Motivated Sequence

Monroe's Motivated Sequence a call to action in five steps: attention, need, satisfaction, visualization, and action

Alan Monroe, legendary speech professor at Purdue University, developed and refined a commonly used persuasive pattern that is especially effective when your purpose is to actuate behavior. **Monroe's Motivated Sequence** is a modified problem-solution format.

Before people act, they must be motivated to do what they know they should do. Consequently, it's important to provide emotional as well as logical reasons for behaviors. This pattern includes the word motivated, because it builds in several steps that increase motivational appeals. (Note that this pattern is not a formula in the sense that you must include each element. Rather, Monroe suggests various ways to develop your points.) Here are the five easily remembered steps in the sequence, as explained by Monroe himself.[25]

1. **Attention Step:** As with any other speech, you begin by gaining the audience's attention and drawing it to your topic.
2. **Need Step:** This step is similar to the problem part of a problem-solution speech. Monroe suggests four elements: (a) *statement*—tell the nature of the problem; (b) *illustration*—give a relevant detailed example or examples; (c) *ramifications*—provide additional support such as statistics or testimony that show the extent of the problem; and (d) *pointing*—show the direct relationship between the audience and the problem.
3. **Satisfaction Step:** After you demonstrate the problem or need, show its extent and its effects on the audience, you then propose a solution that will satisfy the need. This step can have as many as five parts: (a) *statement*—briefly state the attitude, belief, or action you want the audience to adopt; (b) *explanation*—make your proposal understandable (visual aids may help at this point); (c) *theoretical demonstration*—show the logical connection between the need and its satisfaction; (d) *practicality*—use facts, figures, and testimony to show that the proposal has worked effectively or that the belief has been proved correct; and (e) *meeting objections*—show that your proposal can overcome your listeners' potential objections.
4. **Visualization Step:** This step is unique. Here, you ask listeners to imagine the future, both if they enact the proposal and if they fail to do so. (a) *Positive*—describe a positive future if your plan is put into action. Create a realistic scenario showing good things your solution provides. Appeal to emotions such as safety needs, pride, pleasure, and approval. (b) *Negative*—have listeners imagine themselves in an unpleasant situation if

they fail to put your solution into effect. (c) *Contrast*—compare the negative results of not enacting your plan with the positive results your plan will produce.

5. **Action Step:** In the final step, call for a specific action: (a) *name* the specific, overt action, attitude, or belief you are advocating; (b) *state* your personal intention to act; and (c) *end* with impact.

Terah, a nursing major, wanted to give an organ donor speech, but a survey of her classmates revealed that they had a lot of information and a good attitude toward donation, so she focused on motivating them to put their good intentions into action by giving specific details they could easily do. Here are her major points:[26]

Attention: My survey showed that you want to be organ donors but have not yet signed up.

I. It's easy and accessible.
II. From my research, I will give you specific steps to take to become an organ donor.

Need: My survey showed that I don't need to convince you of a need for organ donor, and I don't have to clear up misconceptions.

Satisfaction: My survey revealed that you need how-to information about signing up.

I. For $34 and proof of identity, the Department of Motor Vehicles can mark your driver's license.
II. You can get a free donor card from www.organdonor.gov/donor/index.htm.
III. You can sign up for free at www.donatelifenw.org or on the online donor registry at www.organdonor.gov/donor/registry.shtm.
IV. Tell your family your wishes because they may have to tell doctors who ask about donating.

Visualization:

I. Imagine you sign up, a tragedy happens, and Josh in New Mexico gets your heart; Mary in Colorado has a new kidney, Glen in North Dakota receives your liver, and many more have improved lives from other tissues.
II. Now imagine you don't follow up, a tragedy happens, and several very sick people can't benefit from your organs.
III. Which choice is ideal?

Action

I. Follow one of the easy procedures and sign up to be a donor.
II. I did this last year, and I'm very glad I did.
III. No more procrastination; do it today!

As you might imagine, this pattern is good for sales speeches when your goal is to create a need and get people to purchase a product.

Use Monroe's Motivated Sequence

Working alone or with a small group, plan a short outline for a speech intended to motivate your audience to action. Choose one of these general topic categories:

- **Sales**: Convince your classmates to buy a specific product.
- **Public service**: Ask your listeners to donate time or money to a worthy cause.

Summary

The best subjects for persuasive speeches come from the things that matter most to you personally. For this reason, ask yourself questions such as "What do I believe strongly?" "What arouses my strong feelings?" "What would I like to see changed?" "What enriches my life?" Your answers will generally provide you with topics that you're willing to defend. Choosing your subject is only the first part of topic selection. You must then decide whether you will focus on developing a claim of fact, value, or policy.

Understanding the strength of the audience's attitude—comprised of their beliefs, emotions, and actions regarding your topic—will help you develop specific strategies for audiences who are hostile or somewhat opposed to your ideas, for audiences who are neutral, and for audiences who are generally supportive of your claim.

This chapter explained how to develop speeches around two specific goals: to convince or to actuate behaviors. A speech to convince aims to gain audience agreement with your conclusions, whether they are about facts, value judgments, or the wisdom and feasibility of specific policies. A speech to actuate tries to motivate the audience to act in the ways you propose. According to cognitive dissonance theory, motivation to act comes when our beliefs and actions don't match up; aligning them helps us regain balance or equilibrium. The Theory of Reasoned Action adds the social component. We act when our beliefs and attitudes are favorable toward the behavior in question, when we believe that we can accomplish it, and when we think others are supportive of our actions.

STUDY AND REVIEW

Your online resources for *Public Speaking: Concepts and Skills for a Diverse Society* offer a broad range of study tools that will help you better understand the material in this chapter, complete assignments, and succeed on tests. Your online resources feature the following:

- Speech videos with critical viewing questions, speech outlines, and transcripts.
- Interactive versions of this chapter's Stop and Check activities, as well as Application and Critical Thinking Exercises.
- Speech Builder Express and InfoTrac College Edition.
- Weblinks related to chapter content.
- Study and review tools such as self-quizzes, an *interactive* glossary, and downloadable audio summaries.

You can access your online resources at the CourseMate for *Public Speaking: Concepts and Skills for a Diverse Society.* Log in at **http://www.cengage.com/login**, using the access code that came with your book or that you bought online at **http://www.cengagebrain.com**.

KEY TERMS

The terms below are defined in the margins throughout this chapter.

actuate 326
burden of proof 318
causal relationship 317
claim of prediction 317
cognitive dissonance theory 326
convince 322
correlation 317
criteria-satisfaction pattern 323
criteria 318
debatable point 317
dissonance 326
factual claim 316
Monroe's Motivated Sequence 328

perceived behavioral control 326
policy claim 318
presumption 318
solvency 325
status quo 318
stock issues 324
subjective norms 326
Theory of Reasoned Action 326
value claim 317

APPLICATION AND CRITICAL THINKING EXERCISES

1. Scan a current news source and identify at least two news items of the day that address issues in each category: fact, value, and policy. Bring the list to class and discuss it with your classmates.
2. Watch a crime show and identify the types of evidence required to prove the facts of the case: the defendant did the crime. How does the evidence required for legal cases differ from the evidence you use to support factual claims in the classroom? How is it similar?
3. Listen to at least one persuasive speech by a professional speaker, taking notes on the speaker's arguments. (C-SPAN or ted.com are good sources for such speeches.) What kinds of claims does the speaker make? How does he or she support the claims? Who are the intended audiences? How effectively does the speaker adapt to audience attitudes? **Weblink 18.2** maintains links to these sites. (You can access this link through your CourseMate for Public Speaking, Chapter 18 resources.)

4. To explore hostile speaking in greater depth, go to **weblink 18.3**. The author is a professional consultant. Compare his list of ten typical responses to hostile audiences with his six positive alternative strategies. This is a .com website. How credible do you think the author is? Why? (You can access this link through your CourseMate for *Public Speaking,* Chapter 18 resources.)
5. With a small group in your classroom, identify areas in which national attitudes have changed regarding a controversial issue. How did persuasive public speaking contribute to those changes?

SPEECH VIDEO

Critique Linnea Strandy's speech "Fair Trade Coffee," which is organized according to Monroe's Motivated Sequence. The text of her speech is provided next. Also see Bonita Persons' policy speech, "Don't Drive Drowsy" (featured at the end of Chapter 10), or watch the video of Carol Godart's value speech, "Fat Discrimination." The videos, transcripts, and outlines of all these speeches are available in your online resources.

Student Speech with Commentary

FAIR TRADE COFFEE
By Linnea Strandy

Attention Step

The first step in Monroe's Motivated Sequence is similar to other speeches; it requires Linnea to draw attention to the topic and show its relevance to the audience. She has a fairly easy task with this topic, because almost all her listeners are coffee drinkers, and her town has many coffee venues. However, she should be aware that some people avoid coffee for religious, dietary, or personal reasons.

Fair . . . Trade . . . Coffee. These three words are not hard to understand, yet Fair Trade is a complex issue of which we are all a part. Did you purchase some sort of coffee this week? Or did someone you know purchase coffee last week? Whenever you purchase a product, it's a sign of support—a vote, if you will. We should all be voting Fair Trade.

Catherine Dolan, author of *Ethical Sourcing in the Global Food System,* says that Fair Trade is a social movement and model of international trade. It promotes paying a fair price to the farmer for his goods all the while maintaining social and environmental standards related to the production of those goods.

OK. So you're not a coffee drinker. Bananas, flowers, and sugar—these should also be Fair Traded, but I will use coffee as the example in this speech, because, according to www.blackgoldmovie.com, it is an $88 billion industry, second only to oil as the most highly traded commodity globally. According to Global Exchange, it was the first product to become Fair Trade Certified.

Need Step

This section shows that information often precedes persuasion. Before people are motivated to act, they need to know about a problem.

Citing sources bolsters her credibility and keeps her from plagiarizing material.

Clearly there is a need for Fair Trade in the global marketplace. Global Exchange, an organization for Fair Trade worldwide, reports that local coffee growers rely on middlemen who purchase coffee beans for about 50 cents per pound. Compare that to the world price of about $1 per pound and the consumer price of $3 to $5 per *cup*. This means that coffee bean farmers barely scrape by while large corporations and importers take millions in profits.

According to Tim Harford, from *The Undercover Economist*, this is how it works. Small family farmers grow 50 percent or more of the world's coffee. Most of these farmers are unorganized, so middlemen or estate owners buy their beans at merely 2–4 percent of the retail price.

Beans are initially processed at farms and estates where the local middlemen take advantage of the growers' lack of information, transportation, and access to credit, and force them to sell at low prices, while demanding high interest rates on loans.

Exporters then buy from these middlemen who try to buy low and sell high. Brokers sell to importers who sell to roasters who sell to distributors or retailers.

Retailers sell to consumers, who enjoy their daily beverage oblivious to the injustice currently in the system. According to the coffee calculator at blackgoldmovie.com, a person who drinks one medium latte daily for a year pays the growers between $14 and $40; the traders get $91. And the coffee shops, roasters, and importers in our country? About $1200.

Clearly there is a need for economic justice in this, and other products like it.

Satisfaction Step

The satisfaction step describes the solution. In this case, it's a policy that consumers don't have much control over, but listeners can decide whether or not to support it through their "vote."

A proposed solution is Fair Trade Certified (FTC) coffee that meets the following international criteria as given by Trans Fair USA:

- Pay enough to sustain farmers.
- Provide credit and technical assistance.
- Use organic farming practices (no harmful chemicals, protection of land and habitat, water conservation).
- Maintain fair labor conditions (safety rules, no child labor).
- Empower through direct trading.
- Develop the community businesses, healthcare, and education.

You can have a part by choosing to buy only FTC coffee. If you're not a coffee drinker, urge your friends to buy certified coffee or you can buy other FTC products. As a result there will be higher living standards for farmers, thriving communities, and more sustainable farming practices.

Visualization Step

The visualization step is a good place to include emotional appeals such as stories of real people and how their lives are affected.

Imagine that Fair Trade Certified coffee becomes the norm: Tim Harford in *The Undercover Economist* envisions small farmers working in trade cooperatives where they earn three to five times as much on their coffee. The co-ops help farmers to sell directly to importers. Because they are democratically organized, they invest a portion of the premium into community development and environmental protection programs, and they offer credit to farmers at reasonable rates.

- Importers buy directly from cooperatives and pay Fair Trade prices.
- Roasters roast coffee with Fair Trade labels.
- Distributors sell this coffee to their accounts.
- Retailers sell Fair Trade coffee in their establishments.

Consumers still enjoy their coffee, but this time they feel safe knowing that they've helped people like Edgar. Edgar's story is featured in *Brewing Justice: Fair Trade Coffee, Sustainability and Survival*, by Daniel Jaffee. Edgar says, "All my life, all I have ever done is work, work, work—only work. I had no choice. I wanted my children to have an education so that they could choose what they want to do."

Today all his children have completed secondary school. One son is finishing medical school, helped by Edgar's living wage and a scholarship from the coffee cooperative. Two other children have also received scholarships through the cooperative. Edgar clearly hopes you and your friends will drink more Fair Trade Certified coffee.

Imagine if you don't insist on FTC coffee. People like Edgar continue to receive low wages, and their children continue to be trapped in low paying jobs with no incentive to help their environment or the community.

Action Step

You can do a lot to support economic justice in the coffee industry and other FTC commodities. Spread the word; tell your friends; read materials, and be aware. Think before you drink, and patronize companies that only use Fair Trade Certified products. Even if you don't drink coffee, you can pressure politicians to change the trade rules. You can also join an organization like OXFAM America, the FAIRTRADE foundation, Trade Justice Movement, or World Development Movement.

In the conclusion, Linnea gives her audience a number of things they can do, and she briefly states her own intentions to act before ending with the "vote" metaphor she introduced in the beginning section.

Personally, I seek out FTC coffee.

David Ransom states in *The No-Nonsense Guide to Fair Trade* that more and more consumers are like me—and hopefully you. They are not only asking "Is this good for me?" but also "Is this good for others and the environment?" The growth of Fair Trade products proves that many of us are voting for a better world with our purchases.

SPEAKING IN SMALL GROUPS

Throughout the world, the ability to work well in small groups is essential in classrooms, businesses, and other organizations that regularly accomplish their tasks through cooperative teams and groups. In fact, recent college graduates said that the ability to work in teams is the most important skill that employers seek.[1] Task-oriented teams often produce excellent results, but working in them can be frustrating, especially for participants who are unaware of group dynamics. This appendix first presents some advantages and disadvantages of group work. Next, it gives tips for working in two types of groups: investigative groups and problem-solving groups. A description of formats commonly used to present the group's final product concludes this appendix.

Advantages and Disadvantages of Group Work

You've probably heard the saying "Two heads are better than one." However, if you're trying to accomplish a task with a group plagued by scheduling conflicts, dominating members, or nonparticipants, you may be tempted to work alone. Truth be told, the many advantages of group work must be balanced against the disadvantages.

Advantages of Group Work

Working in groups and teams has several advantages:[2]

- **Groups have access to more information and knowledge than do individuals working alone.** It's only reasonable that more people equal more experiences and more combined knowledge. For example, a group member who has expertise in one area but lacks it in another needs other people to balance those weaknesses. Together, group members can pool resources and generate more information than an individual could produce.
- **Participants bring various viewpoints to the group that can help more creative ideas emerge.** By combining personalities and thinking style preferences, the group as a whole can respond more creatively to an issue than if the solution relies on only one person's ideas. Diversity within a group also increases the members' understandings of various cultural perspectives that bear upon the issue.
- **Group work provides a deeper level of involvement and learning.** When everyone participates, the group can do three to four times as much research in approximately the same time as a single person working alone. Discussions also let group members ask and answer questions that clarify confusing ideas and sharpen critical thinking skills. Consequently, many people learn better in small groups.

- **Many people enjoy working in small groups.** Some people are more motivated and have more positive attitudes when they don't deal with a subject or problem alone. Social interactions can make teamwork satisfying because group members learn about one another while analyzing the issue.
- **Working in small groups results in the co-creation of meaning.** Because of the nature of information sharing and decision making, small groups are inherently dialogical. Ideally, members form conclusions by bouncing their ideas off one another.

Disadvantages of Group Work

Despite these advantages, group work has disadvantages that you should anticipate.

- **Working in groups takes more time.** Scheduling meetings and working around the schedules of other busy people takes time, which often frustrates the more task-oriented group members.
- **Some members do more work than others.** Sometimes team members work less than they would if they were responsible for the entire project. This can result in tension and resentments among members.
- **Some group members monopolize the discussion and impose their ideas on others.** Dominators can take over a group if the members aren't careful. One reason is linked to personality: some people are extroverted and expressive. Another is linked to gender: women often defer to men in mixed groups.[3]
- **There is a tendency toward groupthink.**[4] Groupthink happens when members try to avoid conflict by subtly pressuring themselves and others to conform to a decision (which may be irrational and unwise). On a national and international level, several world leaders convinced their respective teams that Iraq had weapons of mass destruction and that war was necessary to eradicate them. As we now know, they relied on incorrect intelligence gathering; no weapons were found. Most decisions your group makes won't have such widespread implications, but you should strive to ensure that you aren't making a bad decision out of politeness or unwillingness to challenge the group's decision.

In summary, although group work offers many advantages, it also has disadvantages. Groups cannot avoid the time factor, but they can make attempts to use their available time together wisely. However, most disadvantages can be minimized if group members are accountable to one another, if all members have a chance to voice their opinion, and if they avoid agreement simply for the sake of peace.

Investigative Teams

Educators commonly ask students to team up to study a subject and present their findings to the entire class. According to one study,[5] biology students learn to do "science thinking" in small groups, and their classroom presentations hone the organizational and speaking skills they will use throughout their careers as scientists.

Investigative reporters, students and professionals alike, also team up to probe complex social issues. Because a seven- to ten-minute informative speech (described in Chapter 16) can only present an overview of a controversy, many instructors ask students to team up and study a significant issue in greater depth. Students typically learn more and become more involved in a subject when they investigate it with others.[6] The group shares the research burden, which allows a particular student to focus mainly on one area. Not only do team members learn more, others in the class benefit from the variety of perspectives they hear and the in-depth coverage they get when the group shares its findings publicly.

Male and Female Tendencies in Group Interactions

In her book, *You Just Don't Understand: Women and Men in Conversation*, Deborah Tannen[7] identifies several differences in the conversational styles associated with males and females. John Cowan[8] traces these differences to boys' and girls' playground experiences, which he suggests are "at least a light-year apart." Male- and female-associated characteristics are tendencies, not absolutes, and men and women, especially college students, are probably more alike than different.[9] Nevertheless, Tannen's conclusions are widely discussed, and the following tendencies have implications for small group communication.

- Men tend to use *Report Talk*—informative speaking that relies more on facts, figures, and definitions and less on personalized information. In contrast, women tend to use *Rapport Talk*—speaking that stresses relationships and personalizes information with examples and stories.
- Men tend to pursue interactional goals aimed at gaining power, status, and respect, whether or not they offend others. Women, in contrast, tend to help others and build relationships between people. They are less concerned about winning an argument.
- Men tend to speak in a *dominant way*, meaning that they interrupt and display their knowledge and expertise. They also set the agenda. On the other hand, women express more agreement, make connections, and smooth relationships. Men offer "assertion followed by counterassertion," and women offer "inquiry followed by counterinquiry."[10] Although women suggest more topics than men, men choose which topic to discuss.
- Men explain more than women, and their explanations are lengthy. Women can and do explain, but they have fewer opportunities to do so in mixed gender groups.
- Men speak more in mixed gender groups. Conversational time is one-sided in their favor. Women listen more and speak less in these settings.

To learn more about this topic, search the Internet for *Deborah Tannen*. You'll find interviews, excerpts from her books, and other interesting information about gender differences that affect the way males and females talk in small groups.

To research and report a topic effectively, the team should have several meetings that progress from an initial get-acquainted session through the research stage to the final presentation.

First Meeting: Getting Acquainted

In your initial meeting, find out each person's interest, knowledge, and expertise regarding your topic. Exchange phone numbers or email addresses. Leadership can develop informally, or you can designate someone to guide the meeting and keep people on task. An important role is *gatekeeper*, the person who makes sure that quiet people participate and that no one dominates the discussion. Another important role is *recorder*, the member who takes notes or minutes on what transpires during the meeting.

During this meeting, divide your subject into subtopics, and have each member select specific aspects to research in depth. For instance, you might decide to include a definition, the history, numbers and types of people affected, regions or areas affected, proposed solutions, or arguments for and against each solution.

Successful groups find ways to hold members accountable. Consequently, before you adjourn, have group members identify what they will do before the next meeting. Then set a date, place, and a time (beginning and ending) to meet again.

Additional Meetings: Discussing the Subject

Start each new meeting by approving the minutes of the previous meeting. Organize your group's work by writing out an explicit *agenda*, an ordered list of the items you'll discuss. Ask all members to summarize their work and answer questions the others ask. After everyone has contributed, discuss the following: What questions do we still have as a group? Are there gaps in our research? If so, where? What patterns or recurring themes are we finding? Are we beginning to detect a way to organize our final presentation?

Continue to use the gatekeeper and recorder roles. In every meeting, focus on your final goal: to present your material publicly. To achieve this objective, cooperate on organizing ideas and outlining materials into a coherent form. Review the organizational patterns presented in Chapter 9, and think of creative ways to introduce and conclude your presentation (Chapter 10). Identify possible visual aids (assigning a person to create each one), and put someone in charge of any equipment needs.

Before the group separates, have all participants describe what they will do before the next meeting to forward the group's goals. Then set a date, place, and time for your next meeting.

Final Meeting: Polishing the Presentation

Meet one last time to finalize all the details. Give each group member a written outline or record of what you've done. Rehearse the actual presentation so that everyone knows her or his role, and iron out any glitches that arise. Check that visuals are made and equipment is ordered, and then congratulate one another on a job well done.

Problem-Solving Teams

Professor Jack Henson[11] defines a "problem" as the difference between *what is* (the present condition) and *what should be* (the goal). In other words, it's the gap between what we have and what we want. Problem solving teams discuss campus, local, national, and global problems. Campus or local issues include such things as military recruitment on campus, challenges to free speech, parking problems, and alcohol abuse. National and international issues such as environmental protection, global trade imbalances, childhood obesity, and safe water gain our attention.

In most contexts, a structured, rather than a random, approach results in more effective teamwork, and groups often use a problem-solving method described a hundred years ago by the educator John Dewey and modified several times since. Dewey's analytical, linear process of appraising problems and generating solutions is typical of Euro-American culture, but similar methods are used globally. For example, the Africa Region's Knowledge and Learning Center reported that women's groups in Senegal also use a five-step process to solve community problems.[12] This process is not strictly linear, proceeding from point to point in one direction only; your group may circle back to previous steps, and you may revise as you go along. What follows is a modification of John Dewey's original five steps.

Step One: Define the Problem

At the outset state the problem clearly, or your task will be more difficult later because it is hard to find a solution for a vague problem. Some problems are simple to define: "Whom shall we hire as the new basketball coach?" is an obvious problem to solve after a coach resigns. However, for most problems, you need to narrow the topic and follow these three general suggestions:

- State the issue as a policy question, using the word *should*. For example, "What should we do to enhance nighttime safety in campus parking lots?"
- Leave the question broad enough to allow for a variety of answers—that is, use an open rather than a closed question. The yes or no closed question "Should the student council repair acts of vandalism in the student union building?" leads to less effective discussion than the open question "How should the student council ensure that campus buildings remain free from vandalism?"
- State the question as objectively as possible, avoiding emotionally charged language. "How can we get rid of this unfair grading system?" is less useful than "What changes, if any, should be made in the current methods of assigning grades?"

Step Two: Analyze the Problem

Next, begin collecting pertinent information using the guidelines described in Chapters 7 and 8. Look for the facts, values, and policies that relate to your topic. Divide the relevant issues among group members and have them consult a variety of sources for information. Asking questions such as these will be helpful:

- What are the factual issues involved? What's the history of the problem?
- What causes the problem? Which are primary causes? What secondary factors contribute to it?
- What effects result from the problem?
- What values apply? Are ethical issues involved? In what respects?
- Are any relevant policies involved? Any historical precedents?

After completing these two steps, you're ready as a group to explore possible solutions.

Step Three: Set Criteria for Deciding on a Solution

Because solutions must be realistic in terms of time, money, and ease of enactment, set standards for determining an acceptable solution before you even begin to suggest possible solutions. Ask yourselves two vital questions:[13] (1) What must we do? That is, what is *required*? (2) What do we want to do? In other words, what is *desired*? For example, we must solve the problem with less than $10,000; we want to solve it with less than $5,000. We must have the policy in effect by the beginning of the next school year; we want it implemented by the end of the spring term. Budget and time constraints automatically rule out some solutions as too costly or too time consuming.

Step Four: List Possible Solutions

During this period, your group should generate as many ideas as possible. A common method is brainstorming, in which group members offer any idea that pops into their minds, regardless of its practicality. Consider using a mind map as described in Chapters 5 and 7 to record these ideas.

Here are some tips for a successful brainstorming session:

- Have a recorder write down all the suggestions on a whiteboard or flip chart.
- Record each idea without evaluating it.
- Make sure each person in the group has an opportunity to contribute at least once.
- Piggyback off one another's ideas—that is, encourage group members to use one proposal as a jumping-off point for another.

After everyone has contributed, begin to evaluate each idea against the criteria you decided upon earlier. Your brainstorming session may lead you to rethink your criteria, so don't hesitate to go back and make necessary revisions.

Step Five: Select the Best Solution

After your group defines and analyzes the problem, sets criteria for a solution, and generates a number of ideas, it's time to select the best solution. Evaluate the suggested solutions against the criteria you set. You'll easily eliminate some ideas because they're too expensive, too time consuming, or don't fit your criteria for other obvious reasons. After you have pared down your options, analyze and weigh the merits of those that remain to find the one that group members can agree on.

Presenting Your Group's Findings

In general, there are three basic ways to present your conclusions: a final report, a panel, and a symposium. To illustrate, we'll look at how a group that formulated a new nighttime campus parking policy might announce their recommendations.

A Final Report

In this format, one member presents for the entire group, although everyone has gathered data and helped formulate the new policies. To communicate with the college leadership as well as the public, the task committee works together to write a final report that details the procedures used and gives the underlying rationale for the proposed policy. The committee chair then presents it to the student council and to the board of trustees for approval. A press release generated from the final report goes out to area news sources. Television stations might pick up the story and send reporters to interview the committee spokesperson who provides additional information about the policy recommendations. (Although this format is common in businesses and organizations, most instructors don't assign it because speech classes are settings where everyone is expected to speak.)

A Panel Discussion

After group members have gone through the investigative research or the problem solving process that came up with a series of recommendations, they then plan several discussion questions. To actually present their ideas, the entire problem-solving group might appear in a "town hall" type session on campus. There, in a free-flowing, dialogical manner, each committee participant discusses the recommended safety policies and the process the group went through to formulate them. A leader or moderator asks a series of questions, and members take turns providing insights, with everyone contributing from his or her store of information and opinions. Afterward, the moderator may open the discussion to the audience and encourage listeners to talk with panelists during a question-and-answer period. In this way, the group and the audience cooperate in cocreating meaning.

A Symposium

In this format, each group member selects one aspect of the issue and prepares and delivers a speech that is organized using informative or persuasive speech strategies presented throughout the text. After everyone has spoken, the moderator opens up the floor for a question-and-answer period. Group members would divide the campus parking topic into sub-points, and assign each person one topic. The first speaker might lead off by describing the problem; the second overviews possible solutions. The third explains the chosen solution, and the fourth relates a case study of a college that implemented a similar policy. The final speaker provides a summary. After they finish, a moderator invites audience questions.

To inform parents of the new nighttime safety policies, the committee might present a symposium during Parents' Weekend. Interested family members would come to hear the task group members discuss their recommendations. One discusses the history of the problem. The next describes the campus-wide discussions that took place over a two-year period. A third details the specifics of the new policy, and the final speaker tells why the committee believes this solution is workable. Parents can then ask questions.

In summary, although teamwork is a vital part of modern life, working in teams and groups offers advantages as well as disadvantages. Whether you work on an investigative team or in a problem-solving group, organize each meeting so that everyone participates and all group members understand and carry out their responsibilities. Keep a record of what takes place in each meeting. Problem-solving teams typically go through several steps in which they identify and analyze a problem and formulate a workable solution. Both investigative and problem-solving groups present their findings, whether in a group report, panel discussion, or symposium format.

SPEAKING ON SPECIAL OCCASIONS

Celebrations, solemn occasions, and occasions that reaffirm group values are the settings for special occasion speeches. Their general purpose is to commemorate. They also have an integrative function that helps connect people to one another and to their shared goals.[1] Special occasion speeches reinforce and maintain the common belief-attitude-value cluster that influences the group's behaviors.

This appendix provides guidelines for speeches of introduction, farewell, announcement, award presentation and acceptance, nomination, commemoration or goodwill, and eulogy. The Diversity in Practice feature describes some aspects of organizational culture that affect your speech.

Introductions

When strangers first meet, they ask questions such as "Who is this person?" "What do we have in common?" "What brings her here?" Introductions are short informative speeches that provide the facts people need to interact effectively with a newcomer. You might introduce a classmate, a new co-worker, or a speaker at a special event. In each situation, keep your introduction brief. Chapter 2 provided guidelines for introducing a classmate. Here are some tips for introducing an unfamiliar person to your school or work environment:

- Provide the newcomer's name and job title.
- Give a few details about the person's educational and occupational background as well as personal characteristics or accomplishments that will help the audience know a little more about him or her.
- Close by welcoming the newcomer to the group.

Here is a sample introduction of a new faculty member in an elementary school. Notice that it briefly presents her qualifications and provides the current faculty and staff with enough information about her background and some of her interests that they can relate to her.

> This year, we are pleased to welcome a new faculty member, Cornelia Baily-Hunter, who will be joining us as our music specialist.
>
> Cornelia received her B.A. in Music Education from Indiana University, South Bend, and her Master's of Music Education from Penn State. Her passion for music in a child's life dates back to her elementary school days when a very patient orchestra teacher introduced her to the joys of playing the oboe. She marched in the band in high school, joined the university's orchestra, and earned tuition money by playing in a woodwind quartet that performed at weddings and other social functions. Before moving here to the Southwest to be closer to family, she taught for six years in Pennsylvania.
>
> Cornelia, we're glad you're here. We know you will be a great addition to the faculty.

To introduce a guest speaker, include some information about the occasion that precipitated the invitation as well as about the actual speaker. Here are some elements to include in such speeches:

- Greetings and/or a welcome to the group.
- A statement about the occasion.
- Announcement of the speaker's name and topic.
- A brief account of the speaker's background, education, training, achievements, personality, or any other salient information that relates to the topic or the audience.

After the talk, be prepared to make a few closing remarks. Briefly thank the speaker, and make a simple, short reference to the central idea of the speech.

Farewells

Saying good-bye is never easy because departures cause disruptions that affect those left behind to a greater or lesser degree. This is true whether or not the person was well liked. For example, consider the emotions that arise when a popular professor takes a position in another university, a beloved rabbi retires, an unpopular manager joins another company, or the seniors on the football team graduate. Because all these departures signal changes in an organization's social patterns, farewell speeches function to ease the inevitable adjustments that both the departing individual and the group must make.

Individuals who are leaving bid the group or organization farewell, and a group member says good-bye on behalf of those who remain. Both speakers should express emotions—especially appreciation, sadness, affection, and hope for the future. Balance the sadness inherent in the occasion by speaking about happy times. Telling humorous stories is one way to do this.

When you are the person leaving, include some or all of these elements in your farewell:

- Remind group members of what they've meant to you personally.
- List some lessons you learned from being with them.
- Tell stories that you'll carry with you as happy memories.
- Express both your sadness at leaving and your hopes for the future.
- Encourage them to continue upholding the mission values of the organization.
- Invite people to write or visit you in your new location.

When you bid farewell to someone who is departing, you speak not only for yourself but also for the group. Include these elements in your speech:

- Recognize the person's accomplishments in the group.
- Identify positive personal characteristics that you will remember.
- Use humorous anecdotes.
- Express your personal sadness and the group's sense of loss.
- Wish the person well in his or her new location.
- When appropriate, present a gift as a remembrance.

Announcements

Announcements provide facts about upcoming events or developments of interest. In clubs and organizations, businesses and faculty meetings, announcements are an agenda staple because they answer the questions "What's happening?" or "What's new?" Essential to these short speeches are details regarding who, where, when, and how much it costs, as the following outline shows:

- First, draw your listeners' attention to the event.
- Provide such details as who, what, when, and where the event takes place.
- Give both the costs and the benefits of attending.
- End with a brief summary of important information.

Here's a sample announcement:

> Have fun and do good at the same time by attending the third annual Oregon Food Bank Benefit which will be held Tuesday, August 2nd, from 5:30–9:00 P.M. at McMenamins Grand Lodge in Forest Grove. Listen to the Big Band sounds of Swing DC and meet some representatives of the Oregon Food Bank, who will be there to take donations of cash or canned goods. The restaurant will donate half of all food and beverage receipts to the food bank. Children are welcome.
>
> So help stop hunger in Oregon a week from Tuesday, from 5:30–9:00 P.M. in Forest Grove. The Internet provides a map and directions to the lodge or call 503-992-9533 for details.

Organizational Culture

It's common to think of organizations as small cultures within the dominant culture; for example, we use the term *corporate culture* to talk about specific businesses. Your school or workplace has an ethos or personality that derives from its core beliefs, values, attitudes, and behaviors and is often encoded in its mission statement. Organizational culture is comprised of many elements that organizational members know and newcomers must learn. Here are just a few:[2]

- History—the founders, the founding date, the founding mission.
- Political system—the way power is distributed, who leads and who follows, and when.
- Distribution of wealth—pay equity, merit pay, bonuses, stock options, and dues or collections.
- Art, music, and dress—logos, songs, or uniforms.
- Language—jargon or special in-group terminology.
- Rituals—banquets, picnics, award ceremonies, installations, commencements.
- Folklore—narratives and myths, heroes and villains, described in the stories passed from person to person within the organization.[3]

These last two aspects of culture are particularly relevant to public speaking. In *Theory Z: How American Business Can Meet the Japanese Challenge*, W. B. Ouchi[4] explains that organizational symbols, ceremonies, and myths communicate a group's beliefs and values. The stories that are told and retold and passed from generation to generation explain organizational values, beliefs, and memories. Knowing these symbols and stories is important in understanding the organization; using them in public speaking can be a powerful form of proof to members of the organization.

Awards

Award rituals express the common values of a group; individualistic cultures recognize meritorious work or character traits that embody these ideals. It's common to present recipients with a permanent memento of some sort. When you present an award, emphasize the group's shared beliefs, values, and commitments. In general, award presentations include these elements:

- Name the award and describe its significance. What personal traits or accomplishments does it honor? In whose name is it being presented? Why is it given? How often is it awarded? How are the recipients selected?
- Summarize the selection criteria and reasons the recipient was chosen.
- Relate the appropriateness of the award to the traits of the recipient.
- Express good wishes to the recipient.

In contrast, more collectivist cultures rarely single out one individual to praise over others. (New Zealanders, for instance, have the saying "The tall poppy gets mown down.") Consequently, members of these cultures may feel uncomfortable if their personal characteristics are publicly acknowledged. In these situations, honor the entire group rather than a single individual.

Accept an award with a brief speech that reinforces the cultural values that the award demonstrates, as these guidelines and sample acceptance speech show:

- Thank those who honored you.
- Acknowledge others who helped you.
- Personalize what it means to you.
- Express appreciation for the honor.

> Thank you Professor Geffner for those kind words, and thank you committee for selecting me as the Outstanding Speech and Hearing Student this year. As you know, many other students are deserving of honor for their scholarship and their service to the clients in our speech clinic, and I know that each one deserves recognition.
>
> Of course, no student can accomplish anything were it not for the support of a dedicated faculty—and the faculty here at St. John's University is outstanding. I have been impressed not only with their wisdom and skills, but also with the personal interest they all take in the life of each student who majors in speech pathology and audiology. Thanks also to my parents, who supported me both financially and emotionally through these past four years. I appreciate you all.
>
> Next year I will attend graduate school at Northwestern University. I'm sure that when I'm homesick for New York I will remember this honor and be inspired by your confidence in me.
>
> Thank you once again.

For an excellent example, read Martin Luther King, Jr.'s Nobel Peace Prize acceptance speech. You can easily find it on the Internet.

Nominations

Nominations are short persuasive speeches that do two things: (1) introduce your candidate to the group, and (2) present brief arguments explaining why he or she should be elected. Be sure to include the following elements:

- Name the office, and tell its importance to the organization as a whole.
- List the reasons the candidate is right for the office.

Two persuasive organizational patterns are especially effective: (1) a statement of reasons pattern, where you list and explain the reasons one-by-one; and (2) a criteria satisfaction pattern, where you set up criteria for the office and then show how the candidate meets the criteria. When he nominated Sonia Sotomayor for a Supreme Court vacancy, President Obama set the following criteria:[5]

> First and foremost is a rigorous intellect, a mastery of the law, and ability to hone in on the key issues and provide clear answers to complex legal questions. Second is recognition of the limits of the judicial role. . . . Yet these qualities alone are insufficient. . . . It is experience that can give a person a common touch and a sense of compassion and understanding of how the world works and how ordinary people live. And that is why it is a necessary ingredient in the kind of justice we need on the Supreme Court.

He then explained why his nominee met the criteria. Along with her academic preparation he noted:

> Walking in the door, she brings more experience on the bench and more varied experience on the bench than anyone currently serving on the US Supreme Court had when they were appointed.

He concluded with details of her life to show that she understands how society works and how common people live.

Commemorative Events

Commemorative speeches emphasize the audience's ideals, history, and memories; they are common at breakfast, luncheon, and dinner meetings, as well as at conventions and commencement ceremonies. Although their basic purpose is to inspire and to reinforce beliefs and values, these special occasion speeches are often entertaining as well. Each speech is different; however, the following characteristics are typical:

- **Build the speech around a theme.** Find out in advance if one has already been selected for the occasion; if so, prepare your remarks around it. If not, select your own inspiring theme. Here are some titles of recent commemorative speeches that show the speaker's theme: "If I Were to Sing Tonight"[6] (by an Irish-American governor at the American Irish Fund gala); "I Was a Teenage Scientist"[7] (by a university president at a science talent search dinner); and "From Tentative Twig to Mighty Branch"[8] (by a university vice chancellor at a welcoming ceremony for new students and their parents).
- **Inspire listeners.** Inspiration is often linked to positive emotions and values such as hope, courage, respect, perseverance, and generosity. Notice the many positive emotions and values in this excerpt from the Prime Minister of Australia Julia Gillard's[9] address to the US Congress:

  > For my parents' generation, the defining image of America was the landing at Normandy. Your "boys of Point-du-Hoc"—risking everything to help free the world. For my own generation, the defining image of America was the landing on the moon. My classmates and I were sent home from school to watch the great moment on television. I'll always remember thinking that day: Americans can do anything. Americans helped free the world of my parents' generation. Americans inspired the world of my own youth. I stand here and I see the same brave and free people today. I believe you can do anything still. There is a reason the world always looks to America. Your great dream—life, liberty and the pursuit of happiness—inspires us all.

- **Pay special attention to language.** To make your speech both inspiring and memorable, choose vivid, moving, and interesting words and phrases. Describe scenes in detail so that your hearers can form images in their minds; select words that are rich in connotative meanings. Some of the most famous inspirational lines come from Martin Luther King, Jr.'s speeches (available online) or from John F. Kennedy's inaugural address, which you can read at the end of Chapter 12. The following excerpt comes from a commencement address:[10]

> This planet came with a set of instructions, but we seem to have misplaced them. Important rules like don't poison the water, soil, or air, don't let the earth get overcrowded, and don't touch the thermostat have been broken. Buckminster Fuller said that spaceship earth was so ingeniously designed that no one has a clue that we are on one, flying through the universe at a million miles per hour, with no need for seatbelts, lots of room in coach, and really good food—but all that is changing.
>
> There is invisible writing on the back of the diploma you will receive, and in case you didn't bring lemon juice to decode it, I can tell you what it says: You are Brilliant, and the Earth is Hiring. . . .

- **When appropriate, use humor.** For certain events, such as after-dinner speeches whose major purpose is to entertain, humor is almost essential. This example comes from the opening of psychiatrist Mark Servis's[11] commencement address at the UC Davis School of Medicine:

> I want to talk to you, soon-to-be-full-fledged doctors, about mystery, myth and meaning in medicine. But first I'd love to hear you explain to me the mystery, myth, and meaning of choosing a psychiatrist to speak to you at your graduation. What does it say about this class that a psychiatrist, a shrink, is your choice of speaker? I'm not sure, but I think, in part, it is because you are a daring and bold group, unafraid—and I commend you. But what is going to happen now when someone asks you, or your family members and friends who are here today, "Have you ever seen a psychiatrist?" Think about it, you could be in trouble. Let me encourage you all to not be too literal in your answer to that question.

- **Be relatively brief.** These speaking occasions are generally not times to develop an extensive policy speech or to provide detailed information. Rather, they are times to state major themes that reinforce important values.

For further examples, go to **weblink B.1** and read the transcripts of commencement addresses from a variety of speakers. (You can access them through your CourseMate for *Public Speaking*, Appendix B resources.)

Tributes

Tributes are commemorative speeches that highlight and reinforce important cultural beliefs, values, and behaviors. A tribute (called an *encomium* in Latin) praises the qualities of a person (the Basque artist, Jorge Oteiza), thing (dogs), idea (love), organization (NASA), event (D-Day), or group (members of a legendary sports team). Subjects may be living or deceased. A tribute for a living subject should focus on the person's character and achievements; tributes to historical characters should balance the subject's virtues and accomplishments. George Graham Vest, Missouri lawyer and U.S. Senator, gave this tribute to dogs during a lawsuit over a foxhound killed by a sheep farmer[12]

> Gentlemen of the Jury: The best friend a man has in the world may turn against him and become his enemy. His son or daughter that he has reared with loving care may prove ungrateful. . . . The money that a man has, he may lose. . . . The people who are

> prone to fall on their knees to do us honor when success is with us, may be the first to throw the stone of malice when failure settles its cloud upon our heads.
>
> The one absolutely unselfish friend that man can have in this selfish world, the one that never deserts him, the one that never proves ungrateful or treacherous is his dog. A man's dog stands by him in prosperity and in poverty, in health and in sickness. He will sleep on the cold ground, where the wintry winds blow and the snow drives fiercely, if only he may be near his master's side. He will kiss the hand that has no food to offer. . . . He guards the sleep of his pauper master as if he were a prince. When all other friends desert, he remains. . . .
>
> If fortune drives the master forth, an outcast in the world, friendless and homeless, the faithful dog asks no higher privilege than that of accompanying him, to guard him against danger, to fight against his enemies. And when the last scene of all comes, and death takes his master in its embrace and his body is laid away in the cold ground, no matter if all other friends pursue their way, there by the graveside will the noble dog be found, his head between his paws, his eyes sad, but open in alert watchfulness, faithful and true even in death.

Needless to say, Vest won the case. Here are some guidelines for a tribute:

- In the introduction, tell why the subject is significant or worthy of honor.
- Tributes are intended to highlight praiseworthy characteristics, ideas, and behaviors that benefit society. So at the outset, identify a few ideals the subject represents.
- Consider using a statement of reasons pattern. For example, a student tribute to the baseball great Ted Williams, gives three reasons to praise Williams: patriotism, perseverance, and charity.[13]
- Develop each point with illustrative incidents from the person's life.
- This is not primarily an informative speech, although you probably need to include information about the subject.

One of the most famous speeches in this category is President Reagan's Tribute to the Challenger Crew which is available on **weblink B.2**. (You can access it through your CourseMate for *Public Speaking*, Appendix B resources.) See also St. Paul's famous tribute to love found in the Bible (I Corinthians 13).

Eulogies

Because they commemorate someone who has died, eulogies are perhaps the most difficult kind of speeches to give. Don't worry about summarizing the person's entire life; instead, highlight things that celebrate the person's personality and the virtues she or he embodied and then focus on sharing your feelings and your experiences to comfort other mourners. For example, here are some lines from Jonah Goldberg's eulogy for his father:[14]

> I think it would be a mistake to think my dad's wisdom and his humor were different facets of his personality. For him, "humor" and "wisdom" were different words for the same thing. After all, a sense of humor is merely the ability to see connections between things we haven't noticed before (while laughter is what we do when we realize that those connections should have been obvious all along). Is wisdom really such a different thing?
>
> Maybe it is, but it never really seemed to be in my dad.
>
> Call it wisdom or humor, my dad saw the world through different lenses. . . . what was obvious for my dad was often insightful, profound, or hilarious to the rest of us. And, conversely, what was obvious to most people could be a complete mystery to him. To call my dad "handy" or overly burdened with street smarts would be a stretch.

Here are some guidelines for preparing a eulogy:

- If you're the only person giving a eulogy, consult family members and friends for insights and anecdotes that capture essential personal characteristics or positive traits. This also gives you an opportunity to learn if there is information the family prefers you *not* mention.
- Draw from your memories, and share appropriate feelings and experiences.
- Keep in mind your goal, which is to appropriately celebrate the deceased person's life by focusing on positive, memorable characteristics and accomplishments.
- Humor, used sensitively, can be appropriate and comforting.
- Consider using the wave pattern and organize your eulogy around a repeated theme like "Harry was an honest, honorable man . . ." or "John was a devoted friend . . ." or "Molly had enough energy for three people . . ." Support each crest of the wave with an illustrative example.
- Lines from poetry or the deceased's favorite lyrics often work well.
- Don't worry about delivery. If you break down or otherwise show your emotions, your audience will be sympathetic. If you think losing control will be a problem, write out and read your eulogy, or speak with the person officiating beforehand and ask him or her to take over if you simply cannot continue. (For an example of appropriate emotion in a eulogy, watch Cher's speech at the memorial service for Sonny Bono, her former husband. It's available on **weblink B.3**. (You can access it through your CourseMate for *Public Speaking*, Appendix B resources.)

- Keep it short. Unless you're told otherwise, limit your remarks to five to ten minutes.

In summary, special occasion speeches function to integrate the members of the group with one another and with the community in which they exist. You'll hear these talks in a variety of organizations—from clubs and volunteer associations to business, educational, and religious institutions. You may have numerous opportunities to introduce newcomers, present awards, give announcements, and make other short speeches on special occasions.

APPENDIX C

SAMPLE SPEECHES

Student Speeches

Narrative Speeches

Self-Introduction (Chapter 2)

By Mona Bradsher

Mona was assigned to introduce herself by telling something unique. You can watch a video of her delivering her speech through your CourseMate for Public Speaking, *Appendix C Resources.*

My name is Mona Bradsher. I'm a junior, although I'm older than most juniors at our school. In my speech, I want to introduce you to a very persuasive 6-year-old. Through her, you'll learn why I have come back to finish my college degree after a ten-year break from school.

When I was 18, I started college like many of you. But, unlike most of you, I dropped out when I was 20—in the middle of my sophomore year. I left school because I wanted to get married to a man named Jason. I'd met him the summer before, and we had fallen in love. Jason and I did get married and we had a daughter, Sasha.

In my case, the fairy tales were wrong: Jason and I didn't live happily ever after. We divorced just before our fifth wedding anniversary. So there I was—a 25-year-old single mom with a child to raise. My income was pretty low because I didn't have enough education to get a job that paid well. It was hard to get by on what I could make and the small amount of child support that Jason paid each month. We didn't go out for dinners or movies, but we did eat healthy meals at home. We didn't have money for a nice car, so we used the bus system. When Sasha was sick, I'd have to work extra hours to pay the doctor's bill and the cost of prescriptions. So it was tough, and I worried that as my daughter got older I wouldn't be able to support her on what I made. I felt really trapped.

Last year Sasha started school. One day she came home and told me her teacher had taught them about the importance of education. Sasha's teacher had put up a chart showing the difference between what high school graduates and college graduates make. Her teacher also talked about how education helps every person fulfill his or her individual potential and lead a fuller life. The teacher told all the children that education was the most important gift they could give themselves. So Sasha said to me, "Mommy, now that I'm going to school, why don't you go too?" At first I told Sasha that mommy had to work to pay for our apartment and food, but Sasha would have none of that. She insisted that I should go to school. I don't know how many of you have tried to argue with a very insistent 6-year-old, but take my word for it: You can't win! Because my daughter was so persistent, I checked around and found out there is an educational loan program specifically for older students who want to return to school and complete their education. I qualified, and I'll keep getting the loan as long as I maintain a B average. So far, my average is above that because Sasha and I have a deal: We study together for three hours every night.

And that's why I'm here now. That's why I've come back to finish my degree after a ten-year break. I'm here because my daughter reminded me of the importance of education.

If I can learn an important lesson from a 6-year-old, then I can learn other important lessons from the teachers at our university.

Spanking? There's Gotta Be a Better Way (Chapters 15 and 17)

By Gail Grobey

Gail was assigned to give a short narrative speech that made a point. This is also an example of invitational rhetoric because she invites her audience, which is generally supportive of spanking, to share her perspective. You can watch a video of her delivering her speech through your CourseMate for Public Speaking, *Appendix C Resources.*

My daughter Celeste [*displays a photograph*] has always been a rather precocious child. She's picked up all kinds of concepts and language from listening to her future-English-teacher mom talk and has learned how to apply them. When given the opportunity, she'll wax lyrical in her piping 4-year-old voice at some length about the Joker's role as antagonist in Batman and how Robin functions as a foil or why the conflict between the villain and the hero is necessary. She's constantly telling me when I'm stressed about school or work or the mess in the kitchen, "Mom, just breathe. Just find your center and relax in it."

Yes, she's a precocious child, but this time let me place the emphasis on child. Her temper is fierce and daunting, like her mother's! She can get very physical in her anger, striking out destructively at anything she can get her hands on. She can also be manipulative, which is really more like her father!

At times, my patience is driven to the very end, and so I can understand why some parents turn to spanking. There are times when there seems to be no other alternative, when I can't think of any other way to get through to this completely irrational being. And there are a lot of things about me that would make me the ideal spanking parent: my temper, my impatience, my obsessive need to control. And after all, I was a spanked child. But when she was born, and I saw that tiny body and the light in her eyes, I made a conscious commitment never to strike my child.

As she's grown, that commitment has been challenged. About a year ago, she pranced into my room chanting in the universal language of preschoolers, "Look what I found! You can't have it." I looked down and in her hand was a large, inviting, bright red pill with irresistible yellow writing on it. I recognized it at once as one of my mother's blood pressure pills, and quite naturally, my first impulse was to snatch it.

I also recognized, however, that she was looking for just such a reaction from me. She had lately begun establishing clear patterns of button-pushing. I would say, "Give it to me." To which she would naturally reply, "No!"

And so it would begin. She was prepared to throw and fully enjoy the temper tantrum that would inevitably follow and tax me to the end of my patience. I repressed my impulse to aggressively take command and instead, bent down on one knee and asked her with casual awe, "Wow. Where'd you find it?"

She eyed me suspiciously, backing up. She said, "On the kitchen floor. It's mine. I'm keeping it."

All I could think of was how easy it would be to tip her over the edge into a major fight. The big ones always begin over something small and silly—me attempting to exercise control over something and her asserting that this is not acceptable. We both get lost in our rage. It would have been so easy to just grab the pill and move into fight mode. But I held firm to creativity over violence.

"Oh, Celeste," I said, "thank you so much. You are a real hero. You found that dangerous pill and picked it up before the dogs could eat it and make themselves sick. You saved them! What a hero!"

The change on her face was instant. She voluntarily and proudly relinquished the pill and dashed off to tell her grandma what a noble deed she'd just done. I remember saying out loud, "Whew. That was close!" It seems like such a small thing, but I see it as representative of the greater whole.

It's one of my proudest moments as a parent: Celeste and I both walked away with the feeling that we had accomplished something important. She experienced a boost in self-esteem, and I ended up holding firm to my commitment and reinforcing to myself my belief that there is always an alternative way to deal with children, no matter how small the situation or problem. One never needs to resort to violence.

El Equipo Perfecto (The Perfect Team) (Chapter 13)

By Uriel Plascencia; interpreter, Kelly Bilinski

Uriel's first language is Spanish, so he prepared a narrative speech in Spanish; before the speech, he went over his speech with a fellow student. On the day he spoke, she translated his words as he paused between ideas. You can view a video of Uriel and Kelly delivering this speech through your CourseMate for Public Speaking, *Appendix C Resources.*

Cuando estaba en mi último año de Preparatoria, yo tuve buenos amigos. Nuestra amistad era muy fuerte que estábamos juntos mucho tiempo. (When I was a senior in high school, I had some very good friends. Our friendship was so strong that we spent a lot of time together.) *Nosotros éramos como un equipo en todos los aspectos porque estábamos en las mismas clases, hacíamos juntos nuestra tarea, practicábamos deportes y platicábamos mucho. Nosotros nunca tuvimos problemas serios.* (We were like a team in all aspects because we spent time in classes doing our homework, playing sports, and talking. We never seemed to have any serious problems.)

En el principio del segundo semestre, se abrió un campeonato de vóleibol. (In the beginning of the second semester, there were openings for intramural volleyball.) *Yo no pensaba estar en estos juegos porque yo estaba muy ocupado con mis estudios.* (I didn't think about being in those games because I was very busy with my studies.) *Dos de mis amigos hicieron un equipo y me invitaron a formar parte del equipo, yo acepté estar en el equipo.* (Two of my friends made a team and they invited me to be a part of the team; I decided to play with them.) *Ellos me dijeron la hora y el día de nuestros partidos.* (They told me the time and the days that we were supposed to play.) *Un día, ellos me llamaron por teléfono para saber si yo iba a venir al partido y yo les dije que sí.* (One day, they called me to find out if I was coming to the game, and I said yes.)

Antes del partido, ellos me dijeron que yo iba a jugar el segundo juego. (Before the game, they told me that I was going to play the second set.) *Cuando ellos terminaron de jugar el primer juego, yo fui a la cancha para hacer cambios y ellos no quisieron cambiarme.* (When they finished playing the first set, I came to the court to switch players, and they didn't want to switch the team.) *Ellos no quisieron que yo jugara con ellos.* (They didn't want me to play with them.) *Yo me sentí un poco mal y traté de entenderlos porque nosotros teníamos planes para el futuro.* (I felt a little bad, and I tried to understand because we had plans for the future.) *Ellos ganaron el juego y nos fuimos juntos de ahí. Ellos no se disculparon y no me dijeron nada acerca de esto.* (They won the game and we left from there together. They didn't apologize or even talk to me about it.)

Ellos me volvieron a llamar por teléfono para saber si yo iba a venir a los juegos finales y yo dije que sí. Yo fui muy emocionado a los juegos finales porque yo quería que fueramos los campeones. (They called me again to find out if I was coming to the finals, and I said yes again. I came to the game very excited because I wanted to win the finals.) *Antes del juego, ellos me dijeron qua yo iba a jugar el segundo juego. Ellos me volvieron hacer la misma cosa que última vez.* (Before the game, they told me that I was going to play the second set. They made me the same promise as the last time.) *Yo fui a la cancha para hacer cambios y ellos no quisieron cambiarme.* (I came to the court to switch with another player, but then they didn't want to switch.) *Ellos me rechazaron enfrente de muchas personas porque había mucha gente durante los juegos finales.* (They rejected me in front of many people because there were a lot of people during the finals.) *Ellos insinuaron que no me necesitaban.* (They meant they didn't need me.) *Yo estaba muy decepcionado y me sentí muy estúpido enfrente de ellos. Yo me fui de la cancha y no pude entender por qué ellos me hicieron esto.* (I was very disappointed, and I felt so stupid in front of them. I left the court, and I couldn't understand why they made this promise.) *Nosotros no habíamos tenido problemas y no supe cuál era el problema.* (We hadn't had any problems, and I didn't know what was wrong.) *Yo me esperé para ver si ellos ganaban* (I waited there to see if they would win) *pero no ganaron y me fui inmediatamente de ahí.* (but they didn't, and I left immediately.)

Yo estaba pensando todo el día acerca de cuál fue el problema porque yo pensaba que nuestra amistad era más fuerte que un estúpido juego. (I thought the whole day about what was wrong because I believed our friendship was stronger than a stupid game.) *Ellos no podían decir que yo era un mal jugador porque yo era mejor que ellos.* (They couldn't say that I was a bad player, because I was actually a better player.) *Yo me sentí muy triste porque ellos no me habían hecho algo como esto antes.* (I felt very bad because they had made a promise like this before.) *Yo traté de entender la situación pero no pude.* (I was trying to understand the situation but I couldn't.)

Al siguiente día, (The next day,) *uno de mis amigos me estaba buscando para disculparse. El sabía lo que hizo y trató de explicarme y disculparse.* (one of these friends was looking for me to apologize. He knew what he had done, and he tried to explain to me and apologize.) *Yo lo perdoné.* (I forgave him.) *Cuando me amigo trató de disculparse, yo no lo estaba escuchando. Yo estaba escuchando mi corazón y a Dios.* (When my friend was trying to apologize, I didn't listen to him. I was listening to my heart and God.) *Yo aprendí de Dios a perdonar y esta es la razón por que yo lo perdoné.* (I learned from God to forgive, and this is the reason why I forgave him.) *Nosotros somos amigos otra vez.* (We are friends again.) *El aprendió una lección y estoy seguro que él no lo volverá a hacer a nadie.* (He learned a lesson, and I am sure that he won't do this again to anybody.)

Informative Speech with Presentation Aids

(Chapters 13 and 16)

Music-Thanatology (Outline)

By Abby Rine

Abby was assigned to do an informative speech with visual aids.

Specific Purpose: To inform my audience about comforting music that is played to terminally ill patients as they die.

Thesis Statement: Music-thanatology, playing comforting music to dying patients, differs from music therapy; it is an ancient practice that is being revived today.

Introduction

[*A recording of harp music plays softly during the introduction.*]

I. During Salvatore Villalobos' final battle with throat cancer, he became increasingly anxious until he was offered comfort music through his hospice (Trujillo, 2011).
  A. Judith Shotwell, a harpist and music-thanatologist, soothed his final days by playing for him.
  B. In order to keep dying patients comfortable and give them peace, many hospitals and hospices now provide a similar service.
    1. According to MTAI, Music-Thanatology Association International (2011), music-thanatology is the prescriptive use of music—harp and voice—to help aid mental, physical, and spiritual symptoms of those approaching death.
    2. The word thanatology comes from the Greek word *thanatos*, which means death.
    3. The music is live, not recorded, so the musician can be attuned to the patient's and family's specific needs.

II. Death is inevitable, but no one wants pain and suffering.

III. I first heard about music-thanatology as a news item; my curiosity was piqued, and I wanted to know more about the technique.

IV. I will explain the difference between music-thanatology and music therapy, then I'll give a brief history of the practice and show how it is currently being revived.

Body

I. Music-thanatology (MTAI, 2011) is not the same as music therapy according to the American Music Therapy Association website (2011).

[*A PowerPoint list has two columns comparing therapy to thanatology.*]

  A. Music therapy is designed to aid life-supporting processes, but music-thanatology aims to help people "unbind" and move toward the completion of life.
  B. Music therapists engage people actively, often using words; music-thanatologists typically eliminate words.
  C. The rhythms and beats vary; music therapy is often upbeat and peppy, but music-thanatology is calm and slow; it includes periods of silence.
  D. Music therapy aids the quality of life; music-thanatology aids the quality of death.
    1. Music-thanatology is classified as palliative medicine; the Latin root *pallium* means "cloak" or "shelter."
      a. The World Health Organization defined palliative care as ". . . the active total care of patients whose disease is not responsive to curative treatment. Control of pain, of other symptoms, and of psychological, social, and spiritual support is paramount. The goal of palliative care is the achievement of the best quality of life for patients and their families" (quoted in Fins, p. 17).
      b. When medical procedures fail in an irreversible illness, caregivers shift attention from the disease to the welfare of the whole person and provide palliative care until death.
      c. Mary K. Sheehan, MSN, MBA, RN, and CEO of a palliative care center, states, "Music-thanatology brings a new spiritual dimension to the dying process. It is transformative for everyone present. . . . [It is] an amazing gift to the family, an event they will remember in a positive manner" (quoted in Baker, 2010).
    2. Thanatologists adapt music to each patient's needs by using rhythms that correspond with the patients' vital signs.
      a. As the thanatologist learns more about the patient, such as his medication and his handling of his illness, she adapts the music's tone and rhythm.
      b. "You meet the patient where the patient is," says Rebecca Hazlitt, a music-thanatologist from Estes Park, Colorado (Harvey, 2010).

II. Music-thanatology is not a new medical technique.

[*A Gregorian chant plays softly in the background during point II.*]

- A. According to Donald Heintz in *The Last Passage: Recovering a Death of Our Own* (2011), the monks of Cluny, France, in the tenth century practiced music to give spiritual, emotional, mental, and physical comfort for the dying.
- B. They began to use "infirmary music," which usually consisted of Gregorian chants.
  - 1. These chants are characterized by highly developed melodic content and lack of rhythmic accent and pulse.
  - 2. Chants are closely related to respiration and can be connected to the brain processes and central nervous system.
  - 3. [*Pause to listen to a few seconds of the chant.*]

III. Music-thanatology was neglected until Therese Schroeder-Sheker experienced the death of a patient while working as a nurse's aid in a geriatric home.

- A. Her 2001 book, *Transitus: A Blessed Death in the Modern World,* tells how she came into a patient's room as he was dying; she instinctively put her head beside his and sang to him until he died.
  - 1. Later, she studied ways that music could aid the dying, and she added the harp to her vocals.
  - 2. She founded the Chalice of Repose Project (C.O.R.P) to awaken the dormant practice of music-thanatology.
- B. Two educational centers now certify music-thanatologists.
  - 1. The C.O.R.P. (April 2010, last updated) offers the Contemplative Musicianship Program, the Music-Thanatology Program, and the Masters Degree Program in Music-Thanatology, which is affiliated with The Catholic University of America.
  - 2. Lane Community College in Eugene, Oregon, also offers a two-year non-degree training program.
- C. Currently, music-thanatologists work in the US and in the Netherlands.
  - 1. They conduct a 30 to 60 minute vigil in the weeks, days, or hours before death.
    - a. Vigils are especially helpful during crises periods when hard decisions are made or life-supports are removed (League for Innovation, 2010).
      - 1) Thanatologists play harps because they are easy to transport and they are polyphonic (meaning they can play more than one note at a time) (Chalice of Repose Project, 2009, last updated).
      - 2) They play unfamiliar tunes, because they don't know what associations a patient might make with a particular melody (Trujillo, 2011).
    - b. Patients, families, and care facilities benefit.
      - 1. Patients typically experience decreased pain, reduced anxiety, deeper slumber, and lessened fear (League for Innovation, 2010).
      - 2. Families have opportunities to have closure.
        - a) For example, music at Kathleen Corcoran's bedside encouraged her friends and family to sit by her, "pour out their hearts, and verbally express themselves," according to Sister Vivian Ripp, her music-thanatologist (McGowan, 1998).
        - b) Each person thanked Kathleen for what she had brought into his or her life, and she died peacefully.
        - c) "It was strikingly, overwhelmingly beautiful," her husband said (McGowan, 1998).
    - c. Facilities report a decrease in pain and delirium medications (Baker, 2010).
  - 2. Music-thanatology has proven effective with cancer, respiratory and infectious diseases, AIDS, dementia, Alzheimer's, and multiple sclerosis patients.

3. Rebecca Hazlett (Harvey, 2010), who has played for hundreds of dying persons, processes her emotions by talking with other thanatologists and by crying in her hot tub.
   a. Thanatologists must have a self-care program such as meditating.
   b. "The key is you have to have made some sort of peace with the idea of dying," Hazlett says.

Conclusion

[*Replay the harp music from the introduction.*]

I. Today we have looked at the ancient but also contemporary practice of music-thanatology as a way of assisting dying patients.

II. We contrasted it with music therapy, noted its roots in medieval infirmaries, and heard some of its proponents' claims.

III. Death is inevitable, but music-thanatologists do their best to soothe and comfort those who are going through it.

IV. Although Salvatore Villalobos died, his wife said, "Judith and her music were a great inspiration in our lives. She made the last days of my husband's life very comfortable and he found peace" (Trujillo, 2011).

References

American Music Therapy Association. (2011). A career in music therapy. Retrieved from www.musictherapy.org/handbook/career.html.

Baker, R. C. (2010, July 21, last updated). Music-thanatology. Advance for Nurses. Retrieved from http://nursing.advanceweb.com/Regional-Articles/Features/Music-Thanatology.aspx.

Chalice of Repose Project. (2010, April, last updated). Overview of all educational programs offered. Retrieved from http://chaliceofrepose.org/ed-overview/.

Chalice of Repose Project. (2009, July 30). Why the harp for music-thanatology and prescriptive music? Retrieved from http://chaliceofrepose.org/why-the-harp/.

Fins, J. (2006). *A palliative ethic of care: Clinical wisdom at life's end.* Sudbury, MA: Jones & Bartlett.

Harvey, J. (2010, March 9). The sound of angels moving matter—music and medicine at the end of life. *Estes Park Trail-Gazette*. Retrieved from www.eptrail.com/ci_14641088.

Heinz, D. (1999). *The last passage: Recovering a death of our own.* Oxford, UK: Oxford University Press.

League for Innovation in the Community College. (2010, June). Musical prescriptions for end of life care. *League Connections, 11*(6). Retrieved from www.mtai.org/index.php/press_full/2010/06/.

McCowan, K. (1998, December 24). An exceptional death recalled. *The Register-Guard*, Eugene, OR. Retrieved from www.mtai.org/index.php/press_full/1998/12/.

MTAI. (2008). What is music-thanatology? Music-Thanatology Association International. Retrieved from www.mtai.org/index.php/what_is.

Trujillo, A. M. (2011, February 19). Harpist uses music to soothe hospice patients. *The New Mexican*. Retrieved from www.santafenewmexican.com/Soothing-sounds.

Persuasive Speeches

Come Watch Lacrosse (Chapters 17 and 18)

By Andrés Lucero

Andrés was assigned to make one claim and support it by giving three reasons.

Have you ever sat and watched a long, boring baseball game? You all know the deal: ball . . . strike . . . ball . . . strike . . . ten minutes later, a pop up. Well, if you've endured such "entertainment" and agree that there might be more exciting things to do with your time, you should try watching a sport created by Native Americans—one that is fast and exciting, hard hitting, and very strategic. A sport like lacrosse. As you may know, I play lacrosse for the university. Today, I will explain why you should watch a lacrosse game.

Lacrosse is fast and exciting. In fact, it is called the fastest sport in the world, because the clock runs constantly and only stops for a few seconds when the ball goes out of bounds. Unlike baseball or football, players never have time to rest. For that reason, there are many substitutions during the game. Since there is always action on the field, there is never a boring moment. Watching lacrosse is similar to watching a long rally in a tennis match, yet the game itself is as hard hitting as football.

A second reason to watch lacrosse is because it is a very physical game. Since it is a contact sport, not surprisingly, there is lots of rough contact. If I am not careful, I can be seriously injured. I know this from experience. In my first month of college play, I had a painful introduction to Division I lacrosse. On too many occasions, I found myself lying flat on my back, with nothing but sky in view. I discovered that there are many lacrosse players who set up a kill and look to just cream a guy. However, a player does not have to be roughed up. Some players—myself included—try to use strategy to outsmart the opponent.

And this is a third reason you should watch a lacrosse match. Good players and good teams do not just go out and run around the field, they plan what they will do and then they execute their plan. When you watch a game, you can see how the entire team works together to make goals. Most of the finesse teams, those who concentrate on strategy, win more often than those who look for ways to injure their opponents.

In conclusion, you now have three good reasons to watch a lacrosse game: it is a fast, hard-hitting sport that requires much strategy to win. So the next time you find yourself in front of the TV watching a ball . . . then a strike . . . then a ball . . . then ten minutes later, a pop up, get up and go watch a lacrosse game—experience it first hand.

Needed: A Grief Support System on Campus (Chapter 17)

By Carrie Weichbrodt

Carrie's assignment was to give a persuasive speech about a campus problem that needed a solution. Her goal is to convince her audience of a need; she is not formulating a policy.

The phone rings. You answer it, and suddenly the world stops. You have just become one of the thousands of college students experiencing the grief of losing a loved one.

On September 13th, 2006, my life changed forever when it was my phone that rang. My dad was gone. I was 18.

As a student and Resident Assistant, I know many other people on our campus who are grieving. Somehow we find each other.

To deal with my grief, I went to the Health and Counseling Center and asked for a grief specialist. There were no resources for me. I got a doctoral student in psychology who told me I was fine.

Freud did not believe that normal bereavement is a pathological disturbance requiring professional intervention. In his 1917 essay, "Mourning and Melancholia," he argued that mourning is our reaction to a loss, but we eventually form new attachments and move on without professional help. But I believe he was wrong, and today, I will prove it. I will show that there is a significant and compelling need for grief specialists in the campus Health and Counseling Center. Then I'll outline a plan that will solve this problem.

How extensive is the problem? The number of undergraduates dealing with grief is substantial. In a Spring 2008 article in the journal *New Directions for Student Services*, David Balk, the leading researcher in the field of college student bereavement, asserts that at any given time, 20–30 percent of college undergraduates are in the first twelve months of grieving the death of a family member or friend. The National Students of Ailing Mothers and Fathers (AMF) Support Network, initiated at Georgetown University, says that between 35 and 48 percent of college students are dealing with a death that occurred within the previous two years. Counselors at Kansas State University, Oklahoma State University, City University of New York, and the University of Arizona estimate that grief is a defining issue in the lives of no fewer than 50 percent of the students on their respective campuses.

One reason is the mortality rates on college campuses. The numbers are somewhat difficult to assess, but 5,000 to 18,750 students nationwide die annually. That's about 4 to 15 per 10,000. Most deaths are vehicle accidents. Our own small campus has had two traffic fatalities, plus one drowning in recent years. And last year, a popular professor died of cancer. In addition, many students have parents or other close relatives and friends who are struggling against terminal illnesses.

In an often-cited article, "College Student Loss and Response, Coping with Death on Campus," Louis E. LaGrand, professor of health science at the State University of Arts and Science, Potsdam, New York, argues that colleges and student communities too often dismiss the serious and continuing impact of unresolved grief among young adults.

My goal today is not to depress you with staggering statistics, but to assure you that there *is* a need that we should address. Irreparable loss can devastate any young adult.

Now that we know some of the numbers, let's look at five areas affected by grief: physical, behavioral, interpersonal, cognitive, and spiritual.

Physical effects include insomnia and exhaustion. Insomnia is especially significant during the first twenty-four months of bereavement. That's the first two years! Grieving students also suffer from exhaustion as a result of the emotional struggle they are going through.

There are *behavioral* effects as well. Students struggle to stay organized, manage their time, and meet deadlines. They lose their typical patterns of conduct as they try to absorb the loss of the loved one.

Interpersonal effects result when friends dismiss the intensity and duration of the grief cycle and begin to shun the griever. Let's face it, ongoing grief is uncomfortable to be around.

There are also *cognitive* effects. Grieving students have problems concentrating, studying, and remembering what they've studied, which has obvious effects on grades and test taking. They typically experience a drop in test scores in the first six months of bereavement, and a timely response by institutions is warranted.

Finally, there are *spiritual* effects. Bereaved students ask "why?" and begin to question their assumptions about reality, fairness, and goodness.

Now that we understand the extent of the problem and its effect on students, let's discuss what can be done.

First, I propose that the university hire a bereavement specialist who would work with campus personnel to design a program for educating professors, Residence Life personnel, and Resident Assistants in ways they can assist grieving students. This would include annual professional workshops on grief and grieving.

Second, many students feel more comfortable expressing their grief in an informal environment with someone who has had a similar experience. The bereavement specialist would recruit students who have skillfully walked through grief to be peer counselors; these students can further process their own experience when they mentor fellow students.

There is a model for this. Georgetown University is the home of the National Students of Ailing Mothers and Fathers (AMF) Support Network. It was started by David Fajgenbaum, whose phone call came July 17, 2003. His mother had stage four brain cancer, and she died while he was still a student. The group's name Ailing Mothers and Fathers (AMF) includes his mother's (Anne Marie Fajgenbaum) initials: A.M.F. The group's Web site says its mission is to support all grieving college students, to empower them to fight back against terminal illnesses, and to raise awareness about the needs of grieving college students.

Our university's Health and Counseling Center's Web page states its goal as, "Helping students stay healthy so they may achieve the highest personal growth and intellectual success." Providing effective resources for grieving students, allows these students to achieve their highest personal growth and intellectual success. David Balk says:

> Rather than deciding that bereaved college students are on their own and merely wish them good luck, we should make the effort to determine whether appropriate institutional responses can be put in place to help students get beyond a life event that can obstruct their best academic performance and may ultimately affect a school's retention and graduation rates.

So we have the opportunity to make a difference in the lives of hundreds of students on our campus. This number may be as high as 720 undergraduates each year. Creating a grief support program would further the university's commitment to holistic health for all students.

Today we've seen there is a significant need and that grief affects a student's ability to be a competent scholar. However, specialists can make a difference, and it's been done before.

I hope that none of you get that devastating, life-changing phone call during your college career. But I hope that if you do, a program will be in place to help you work through the grief that inevitably follows.

References

Balk, D. (2001). College student bereavement, scholarship and the university: a call for university engagement. *Death Studies, 25*, 67–84.

Balk, D. (2008, Spring). Grieving: 22 to 30 percent of all college students. *New Directions for Student Services, 121*, 5–14.

Berson, R. (1988). A bereavement group for college students. *Journal of American College Health, 37*.

Cusick, A. (2007). Death response plans in universities: a structural approach. Unpublished Manuscript.

Floerschinger, D. (1991). Bereavement in late adolescence: interventions on college campuses. *Journal of Adolescent Research, 6*.

Freud, S. (1957). Mourning and melancholia. *The complete psychological works of Sigmund Freud, Vol. 14*. London: Hogarth Press.

LaGrand, L. (1986). College student loss and response: coping with death on campus. *New Directions for Student Services, No. 31*. San Francisco: Jossey-Bass.

McGowan, K. (2008, March 7). OPTIMISM: Make the road by walking. Retrieved March 12, 2008, from www.studentsofamf.org/National_Students_of_AMF_featured_in_Psychology_Today_Magazine!-nid-39.html

National Students of AMF. (n.d.) AMF mission statement. Retrieved March 12, 2008, from www.studentsofamf.org/

Commemorative Speech: Tribute

Jorge Oteiza (Appendix C)

By Ryan McGonigle

Ryan was assigned to pay tribute to a cultural hero. As a student of Basque descent, he praises the life of a famous Basque artist who is revered in his culture.

The name Jorge Oteiza may not exactly raise any eyebrows or provoke any curiousity among the American public, but to the Basque people and to me—an American of Basque descent—he is a legend. Oteiza was arguably the greatest Basque artist and poet of the twentieth century.

Jorge Oteiza was born in Guipuzcoa Province in Spain, near the famous coastal Basque city of San Sebastian at the beginning of the twentieth century. As a child he was raised according to Basque tradition: Honor your father and mother; persevere under hardships; give generously to your neighbors; speak respectfully to others; and most of all, keep your word—which is better than gold. These ideals, centuries old, were later reflected in Oteiza's poetry and art.

As the son of a sheepherder, Oteiza was accustomed to adversity. At home he worked what seemed to be eternities every day. At school he struggled to learn Castilian Spanish—which, by the way, no one in his family spoke. He had no choice in learning it, however; it was either learn it or get whipped by the teachers. Later, he would write poetry in this, his second language. Ironically, it was through that very same school system that he became interested in art—his first love.

Following the death of his father, he was obliged to continue in his father's footsteps as a sheepherder. Traditionally, in Basque country, sons follow the family occupation. If your father was a fisherman, most likely you will be one too. Breaking with tradition is not only very hard to do, but it is also dishonorable. Fortunately for Jorge, his sister soon married, and the sheep became part of the dowry given to his brother-in-law. This released Oteiza to realize his true potential as an artist. His style of sculpture became well known in the area, and soon his work was in demand. Oteiza made sculptures for the city in which he lived, San Sebastian, as well as for other cities throughout the Basque area.

In the mid 1930s during the Spanish Civil War, three major events occurred for Oteiza. First, he married Itziar Carrieco Etxendia. Throughout his life, she was the inspiration for much of his work. Not only did she support him, she encouraged him to create both poetry and art. The second event happened when the Bask region declared its independence from Spain. This resulted in a war, and his home came under fire. In the conflict, he lost his best friend, the photographer Nicolas de Lekuona. Finally, Oteiza was incarcerated in a mass roundup of Basque intellectuals, priests, and artists. He spent almost two years in jail.

It was in one of Spain's infamous prisons that Ortiza became a man worthy of his surname. "Oteiza" in the Guipuzcoan dialect of Basque sounds very much like the word that means "prickly bush," and like a thorn—or a prickly bush in the side of the Spaniards—he caused a bit of irritation. In prison, he became nationalistic, and his later sculpture and poetry shows the positive and negative effects of his identification with the revolutionary Basque movement. He frequently put his neck on the line by sculpting pro-Basque and/or anti-Spain works. For example, some of his work portrays the hardships of the Basque people that resulted from the policies of the Spanish dictator Franco. Eventually, the regime of Franco got to him, and he took a hiatus from sculpture to work on his poetry.

In his poetry, the pro-Basque theme or the Basque experience is prominent. One phrase recurs throughout his work—"*Gora Euzkadi Ederra*" or "Long live the beautiful Basque country." This is a strongly nationalistic phrase that arouses Basque emotions. It is somewhat similar to the African-American slogan from the 1960s: "Black is Beautiful."

During this time, he took on an apprentice—a man by the name of Eduardo Txillida.* Oteiza put all of his efforts into teaching Txillida his art form, but all Txillida could do was to copy or imitate his master. Eventually, the two split and to this day Oteiza accuses his pupil of not being able to do anything original. All Txillida's works resemble Oteiza's, just on a grander scale. He copied his master without permission instead of developing his own style, and in Oteiza's eyes, he failed to keep his word.

Basque critics consider Oteiza to be a true master because he maintained traditional art forms. He received honors from the Basque school *Euskertz Aindia*, the official academy of the Basque people. He did not care so much about money or fame—although he had both. Instead, he cared about his people and their welfare. Throughout the long ordeal

*Txillida is sometimes spelled Chillida.

of the war and in the ensuing years, Jorge Oteiza persevered under hardships. For these reasons, he is the true master.

Professional Speech

A Global Agenda for Interfaith Dialogue: Tolerance, Love, and Cooperation

By Fahri Karakas[1]

Fahri Karakas is on the Faculty of Management at McGill University in Montreal, Canada. Here's how he opens his goodwill speech (Appendix A), given at the Interfaith Dinner of Dialogue Foundation in Montreal, December 2004. It illustrates oral style (Chapter 12) and the wave pattern (Chapter 9).

It is a great pleasure to share this celebration and dinner with you. We are hundreds of people here from various races, different religions, and diverse backgrounds. All of us united, committed, excited, and together under one roof. This is a vivid portrait of the cosmopolitan and multicultural Canadian society. A model of richness as a result of diversity. A living model of democracy and peaceful coexistence. I want to convey my sincere congratulations and thanks to Dialogue Foundation of Montreal for preparing this special occasion for us. I am especially impressed with our friends' sincerity, kindness, generosity, openness, and eagerness to learn. They have been very effective in educating me and others about international religious topics, as well as in promoting an open interfaith dialogue in Montreal.

In the first part, as a practicing Muslim, I would like to share with you a few words on my personal reflections on the month of Ramadan, Ramadan practices, and fasting experiences. Ramadan is commonly called the "Lord of Eleven Months." It is a very special month for Muslims filled with lots of blessings, happiness, love, and sharing.

Personally, I always remember missing Ramadan throughout the year. Ramadan is accepted as our lovely, kind, valued guest. Ramadan is welcomed with great joy, excitement, tranquility, and peace. When I think of Ramadan, I remember all values, people, times, and contexts—all very valuable to me.

When I think of Ramadan, I remember Turkey—my beloved country—the home bed (cradle) of 27 different civilizations. When I think of Ramadan, I remember Istanbul—the city I am in love with, with all its grandeur and mystery.

When I think of Ramadan, I remember special *iftar* (dinner) tents built on every corner in Istanbul—throughout the streets of Uskudar, Sultanahmet, and Eyup. *Iftar* tents are ready, welcoming you everywhere with great warmth. All people eat there as a family, as brothers and sisters, without any borders. Regardless of your status, wealth, race, and religion. All people experiencing perfect equality and sincerity. You are busy? In traffic? Could not reach home? Not have enough money? You just break your fast or have your dinner in the streets.

When I think of Ramadan, I remember my dear mother . . . who cooked a lot of meals, so delicious Turkish cuisine, *tarhana* soups, *boreks*, and *kebaps*, for me. When I think of Ramadan, I remember being awakened by my father in the middle of the night at 4 A.M. for *sahur* (midnight supper). I remember having, sharing our meal as well as our compassion and love together, in an original context in the middle of the night.

When I think of Ramadan, I remember fasting. And I remember—during the day of fasting—especially just before fast breaking, feeling so elevated, so purified, so excited, so awkward, so happy, like a baby. It is a peak experience. . . .

Historical Speeches

An Indian's View of Indian Affairs

By Chief Joseph[2]

In-mut-too-yah-lat-lat, also known as Chief Joseph of the Nez Percé Indian tribe, told this story on January 14, 1879, before a large gathering of Cabinet officers, congressional representatives, diplomats, and other government officials. His speech argues that Congress should act in behalf of his people for a number of good reasons.

My name is *In-mut-too-yah-lat-lat* (Thunder Traveling Over the Mountains). I am chief of the *Wal-lam-wat-kin* band of *Chute-pa-lu*, or *Nez Percés* (nose-pierced Indians). I was born in eastern Oregon, thirty-eight winters ago. My father was chief before me. When a young man, he was called Joseph by Mr. Spaulding, a missionary. He died a few years ago. There was no stain on his hands of the blood of a white man. He left a good name on the earth. He advised me well for my people.

Our fathers gave us many laws, which they had learned from their fathers. These laws were good. They told us to treat all men as they treated us; that we should never be the first to break a bargain; that it was a disgrace to tell a lie; that we should speak only the truth; that it was a shame for one man to take from another his wife, or his property without paying for it. We were taught to believe that the Great Spirit sees and hears everything, and that he never forgets; that hereafter he will give every man a spirit-home according to his deserts: if he has been a bad man, he will have a bad home. This I believe, and all my people believe the same.

We did not know there were other people besides the Indian until about one hundred winters ago, when some men with white faces came to our country. They brought many things with them to trade for furs and skins. They brought tobacco, which was new to us. They brought guns with flint stones on them, which frightened our women and children. Our people could not talk with these white-faced men, but they used signs which all people understand. These men were Frenchmen, and they called our people *Nez Percés* because they wore rings in their noses for ornaments. Although very few of our people wear them now, we are still called by the same name. These French trappers said a great many things to our fathers, which have been planted in our hearts. Some were good for us, but some were bad. Our people were divided in opinion about these men. Some thought they taught more bad than good. An Indian respects a brave man, but he despises a coward. He loves a straight tongue, but he hates a forked tongue. The French trappers told us some truths and some lies.

The first white men of your people who came to our country were named Lewis and Clark. They also brought many things that our people had never seen. They talked straight, and our people gave them a great feast, as a proof that their hearts were friendly. These men were very kind. They made presents to our chiefs and our people made presents to them. We had a great many horses, of which we gave them what they needed, and they gave us guns and tobacco in return. All the *Nez Percés* made friends with Lewis and Clark, and agreed to let them pass through their country, and never to make war on white men. This promise the *Nez Percés* have never broken. No white man can accuse them of bad faith, and speak with a straight tongue. It has always been the pride of the *Nez Percés* that they were the friends of the white men. When my father was a young man there came to our country a white man (Rev. Mr. Spaulding) who talked the spirit law. He won the affections of our people because he spoke good things to them. At first, he did not say anything about white men wanting to settle on our lands. Nothing was said about that until about twenty winters ago, when a number of white people came into our country and built houses and made farms. At first our people made no complaint. They thought there was room enough for all to live in peace, and they were learning many things from the white men that seemed to be good. But we soon found that the white men were growing rich very fast, and were greedy to possess everything the Indian had. My father was the first to see through the schemes of the white men, and he warned his tribe to be careful about trading with them. He had suspicion of men who seemed so anxious to make money. I was a boy then, but I remember well my father's caution. He had sharper eyes than the rest of our people.

Next there came a white officer (Governor Stevens), who invited all the *Nez Percés* to a treaty council. After the council was opened he made known his heart. He said there were a great many white people in the country, and many more would come; that he wanted the land marked out so that the Indians and white men could be separated. If they were to live in peace it was necessary, he said, that the Indians should have a country set apart for them, and in that country they must stay. My father, who represented his band, refused to have anything to do with the council, because he wished to be a free man. He claimed that no man owned any part of the earth, and a man could not sell what he did not own.

Mr. Spaulding took hold of my father's arm and said, Come and sign the treaty. My father pushed him away, and said: Why do you ask me to sign away my country? It is your business to talk about spirit matters, and not to talk to us about parting with our land. Governor Stevens urged my father to sign his treaty, but he refused. I will not sign your paper, he said; you go where you please, so do I; you are not a child, I am no child; I can think for myself. No man can think for me. I have no other home than this. I will not give it up to any man. My people would have no home. Take away your paper. I will not touch it with my hand.

My father left the council. Some of the chiefs of the other bands of the *Nez Percés* signed the treaty, and then Governor Stevens gave them presents of blankets. My father cautioned his people to take no presents, for after a while, he said, they will claim that you have accepted pay for your country. Since that time four bands of the *Nez Percés* have received annuities from the United States. My father was invited to many councils, and they tried hard to make him sign the treaty, but he was firm as the rock, and would not sign away his home. His refusal caused a difference among the *Nez Percés* . . .

Chief Joseph continues the speech, detailing years of treaty negotiations between the Nez Percé and the whites. His conclusion recognizes that the inevitable has happened; his people are powerless against the white settlers. But his final plea is for equal justice under law for the Indian as well as for whites.

Ain't I a Woman?[3]

By Sojourner Truth [Isabella Van Wagenen] (1797–1883)
Men in the audience at the Women's Convention (Akron, Ohio, 1851) argued against woman suffrage for three reasons: (1) man's superior intellect; (2) Christ was a man; and (3) the sin of the first woman, Eve. No manuscript exists of Sojourner's speech refuting each point. However, History of Woman Suffrage (1902) gave an eyewitness summary of the points, including Truth's dramatic delivery. This is the most commonly published version:

> Well, children, where there is so much racket there must be something out of kilter. I think that between the Negroes of the South and the women at the North, all talking about rights, the white men will be in a fix pretty soon. But what's all this here talking about?
>
> That man over there says that women need to be helped into carriages, and lifted over ditches, and to have the best place everywhere. Nobody ever helps me into carriages, or over mud-puddles, or gives me any best place!
>
> And ain't I a woman? [*Said raising herself to her full height and her voice to a pitch like rolling thunder.*]

Look at me! Look at my arm! [*She bared her right arm to the shoulder, showing her muscles.*]

I have ploughed and planted, and gathered into barns, and no man could head me!

And ain't I a woman?

I could work as much and eat as much as a man—when I could get it—and bear the lash as well!

And ain't I a woman?

I have borne thirteen children, and seen them most all sold off to slavery, and when I cried out with my mother's grief, none but Jesus heard me!

And ain't I a woman?

Then they talk about this thing in the head; what did they call it? [*someone whispered* "Intellect"]

That's it, honey. What's that got to do with women's rights or Negro's rights? If my cup won't hold but a pint, and yours holds a quart, wouldn't you be mean not to let me have my little half-measure full? [*To loud cheers, she pointed and gave a "keen glance" at the minister who made the argument.*]

Then that little man in black there, he says women can't have as much rights as men, 'cause Christ wasn't a woman! Where did your Christ come from? [*In deep, wonderful tones, outstretched arms and eyes ablaze*]

[*Still louder.*] Where did your Christ come from? From God and a woman! Man had nothing to do with Him.

[*Turning to another man*] . . . If the first woman God ever made was strong enough to turn the world upside down all alone, these women together [*glancing across the platform*] ought to be able to turn it back, and get it right side up again! And now they are asking to do it, the men better let them. [*Sustained cheering*]

Obliged to you for hearing on me, and now old Sojourner has got nothing more to say. [*Roars of applause*]

[Note: originally reported in dialect and translated into Standard English.]

GLOSSARY

A

absolute listening listening without interrupting or inserting oneself into the talk

Academic Invisible Web (AIW) scholarly databases in the Invisible Web that librarians are identifying

academic journals journals that pertain to specific areas of academic research

accidental plagiarist plagiarist who lacks knowledge about the rules

accommodation response to diversity in which you listen and evaluate the views of others; both sides adapt, modify, and bargain to reach mutual agreements

actuate motivate the audience to do something

ad populum reasoning fallacy, an appeal to popular opinion

ad hominem an attack on the messenger rather than the message

affective effects influences on listeners' feelings

ageist language language that negatively influences the way listeners think about older people

alternation varying numbers and letters in a consistent pattern for different levels of points

alliteration words with recurring initial sounds

ambiguous word identifies more than one object or idea; its meaning depends on the context

analogies stating similarities between two things

analogy comparison of one item that's less familiar or unknown to something concrete and familiar

anticipatory speech anxiety tension experienced at the mere thought of giving a speech

antimetabole saying words in one phrase, and reversing them in the next phrase

annotate to summarize a book or article's contents on a source card

applied storytelling using stories for practical purposes, not just for entertainment

archetypal symbols recurring metaphors and similes that arise from shared human and natural experiences

argument intentional, purposeful speaking that involves reason and judgment

articulation the way you enunciate or say specific sounds, an element of pronunciation

artistic proofs reasons to accept an argument that the speaker creates in the audience

assertion a claim presented without supporting evidence

assimilation response to diversity in which you surrender some or most of your ways and adopt cultural patterns of another group

attitude our tendency to like or dislike something or to have positive or negative feelings about it

audience analysis identifying audience characteristics to communicate more effectively

B

backing reasons given to support the warrant

bar graphs compare data from several groups by using bands of various lengths

behavioral effects influences on audience actions

bicultural knowing and applying different rules for competent behaviors in two cultures

burden of proof responsibility of the speaker who argues against the status quo to make the case for change

C

canon a set of principles, standards, norms, or guidelines

canon of delivery rules or standards for presenting a speech

canon of disposition or **arrangement** guidelines for organizing a speech

canon of invention principles for designing a speech that meets a need of a specific audience

canon of memory guidelines to help you remember your ideas

canon of style principles for choosing effective language

canons of rhetoric principles, standards, norms, or guidelines for creating and delivering a speech

causal reasoning linking two factors in such as way that the first occurs before the second and regularly leads to the second as a matter of rule

causal relationship links one phenomenon to another that preceded it and led to it

cause-effect pattern presents reasons (causes) and implications (effects) of a topic

central idea a synonym for thesis statement

chronological pattern presents points in a sequential or time order

civic engagement working with others to help solve issues of public concern

civility self-control or moderation, contrasts with arrogance; civil speakers persuade, consult, and compromise rather than coerce and manipulate

claim debatable point or proposal you want listeners to accept

claim of prediction claim that something will or will not happen in the future

clarification questions requests to clear up confusing ideas

classification a method of presenting information by explaining things that are put into categories according to a principle

closed questions requests for brief, specific answers

co-cultures subgroups of culture, characterized by mild or profound cultural differences, that coexist within the larger culture

code switching changing from one dialect to another

cognitive dissonance theory says that humans seek stability or equilibrium; when faced with inconsistency they seek psychological balance; this may motivate them to change in order to be consistent

cognitive effects influences on beliefs, understandings, and other mental processes

cognitive modification identifying negative thoughts and replacing them with positive ones

cognitive preference the ways you prefer to perceive, reason, remember, and solve problems; it's culturally influenced but unique to you

collectivist cultures members of these cultures are integrated into an in-group that protects them throughout their lives.

comments information added from personal experience or research

common ground specific areas or concerns that both speaker and audience consider important

communication apprehension (CA) the fear or dread of negative responses you might experience because you speak out

communication style a culture's preferred ways of communicating, given its core assumptions and norms

communicative competence the ability to communicate in a personally effective and socially appropriate manner

comprehensive listening listening to learn, understand, or get information

concrete words specific, rather than general or abstract, terms

confident style a way of speaking characterized by effective vocal variety, fluency, gestures, and eye contact

connectives words, phrases, and sentences used to lead from idea to idea and tie the parts of the speech together smoothly

connotative meaning emotional overtones, related feelings, and associations that cluster around a word

constructed dialogue created conversation between characters that adds realism to a story

content outline formal record of your major ideas and their relationship to one another in your speech

conversational style speaking that's comparatively calmer, slower, and less intense, but maintains good eye contact and gestures

convince a persuasive purpose that targets audience beliefs

coordination arranging points into levels, giving the points on a specific level the same basic value or weight

core cultural resources beliefs, attitudes, and values (BAV) along with behaviors that provide a logical basis for a culture to define what is necessary, right, doubtful, or forbidden

correlation two things occur together, but one does not necessarily lead to the other

creative works poems, dances, paintings, writings, and other aesthetic creations

credibility listeners' impressions of your character, intentions, and abilities that make you more or less believable

criteria the standards used for making evaluations or judgments

criteria-satisfaction pattern good for value or definition speeches; sets forth standards for judgment or for inclusion in a category and then shows how the proposal meets or exceeds these standards or fits into the category

critical listening listening that requires you to reflect and weigh the merits of messages before you accept them

critical thinking the ability to think analytically about ideas

culture an integrated system of learned beliefs, values, behaviors, and norms that include visible (clothing, food) and underlying (core beliefs, worldview) characteristics of a society

cultural allusions references to historical, literary, and religious sources that are culturally specific

cut-and-paste plagiarism copying material word-for-word and then patching it together without quotation marks or citations

cynical speakers presenting verbal or nonverbal messages they don't believe in an attempt to create a false image

D

debatable point disputable statements about facts of existence or history

deductive reasoning starting with a principle (the premise) and applying it to a specific case

deliberate fraud knowing, intentional plagiarism

deliberative speaking a form of speaking that gives people the information and motivation they need to make wise decisions regarding future courses of action

delivery the verbal and nonverbal behaviors you use to perform your speech

demagogue a polarizing speaker who appeals to audiences more on the basis of emotion and personal charisma than on reasoned arguments

demographic analysis identifying audiences by populations they represent, such as age or ethnicity

demonstrated or **intrinsic credibility** obvious knowledge the speaker shows during the speech

denotative meaning what a word names or identifies

diagrams drawings or designs that explain, rather than realistically depict, an object or process

dialogical theory of communication theory proposing that face-to-face conversation is the prototype that is foundational to all other communication

digital object identifier (DOI®) series of numbers and letters that locate intellectual property online

dialect a variant form of a language

direct methods asking audience members directly for their opinion by questionnaires, interviews, and so on

discourse consistency using a repetitive style such as alliteration of main points throughout the speech

dismissive language put-downs; language that discounts the importance of someone's viewpoint

dissonance inconsistency or clash

division a method for presenting information by breaking the whole into parts and explaining each one

D-R-E method a feedback method that describes content, shares personal responses, and gives evaluation

document cameras high-resolution cameras that display documents and three-dimensional objects

domain the type of site such as .com, .edu, or .org that tells the site's purpose and tax status

dual coding theory (DCT) theory that our brains process material two ways: through language and through images

dual processing combining words and images to create meanings

E

empirical facts data verifiable by observation

enthymeme omitting part of the syllogism in an argument and letting listeners supply what's missing; inherently dialogical

enumeration a count

epithets words or phrases with powerful negative connotations, used to describe some quality of a person or group

established facts data verified consistently by many observers

ethical communication the conscious decision to speak and listen in ways that you, in light of your cultural ideals, consider right, fair, honest, and helpful to all parties involved

ethnicity heritage and cultural traditions, usually stemming from national and religious backgrounds

ethos personal credibility or character traits that make a speaker believable and worthy of the audience's confidence

exemplum an organizational pattern in which a narrative is used to illustrate a quotation

experts people whose knowledge is based on research, experience, or occupation

expository speech the "speech to teach" that explains an idea in detail

expressive cultures cultures that encourage members to give their opinions, speak their minds, and let their feelings show

extemporaneous delivery preparing and rehearsing a speech carefully in advance, but choosing the exact wording as you deliver the speech

euphemisms words or phrases that substitute an inoffensive term for a potentially offensive, embarrassing, or unpleasant thing

eye contact looking audiences in the eye; communicates friendliness in the United States

F

fabrication making up information or repeating information without sufficiently checking its accuracy

factual claim argument about existence, causation, or predictions

Fair Use provision the provision in the federal Copyright Act that allows free use of materials for educational and research purposes

fallacy failure in logical reasoning that leads to unsound or misleading fallacy arguments

false analogy comparing two things too dissimilar to warrant the conclusion drawn

false dichotomy an either-or fallacy that ignores other reasonable options

faulty generalization a fallacy of induction; generalizing too broadly, given the evidence

fight-or-flight mechanism physiological mechanism your body automatically activates when threatened; helps you fight or flee

figurative analogies stated similarities between two otherwise dissimilar things, requires an imaginative connection

filled (vocalized) pauses saying *um* or *uh* or other sounds during a pause

flip charts tablets you prepare in advance or create on the spot; turn to a new page or tear off and display pages as you finish them

flowcharts show the order or directional flow in which processes occur; may simply be a series of labeled shapes and arrows

G

gender clusters of traits culturally labeled as masculine, feminine, or androgynous

general purpose four general purposes are: to inform, to persuade, to entertain, or to commemorate

geographic maps show mountains, deserts, and other natural features; not easily outdated

grounds, data, or **evidence** supporting material offered to back up a claim

H

habituation lessening anxiety by successfully repeating an experience over time

hearing physical process involving sound waves, eardrums, and brain receptors

heckler listener who disrupts a speech or confronts a speaker during a speech

homogeneous audiences listeners who are similar in attitude

homo narrans a Latin phrase that identifies humans as storytelling animals
hostile audiences listeners who are negative toward the topic or the speaker
hypothetical example not a real incident or person, but true-to-life

I

identification or **co-orientation** concerns shared among speakers and listeners that help overcome divisions and bring diverse people together
image-based visuals carry meaning in visual images; written words are secondary
impression management self-presentation, using the metaphor of a staged drama in which we use props and personal mannerisms to create and maintain impressions of ourselves
impromptu delivery speaking with little advanced preparation
improper paraphrase changing some words of a source but keeping the basic structure and ideas intact without citing the source
inclusive language ethical terminology that affirms and includes, rather than excludes, persons or groups of people
indentation formatting by spacing various levels of points inward
indirect methods assessing audiences by observation or secondhand sources
individualistic cultures members of these cultures depend mainly on themselves and are judged on personal merits
inductive reasoning starting with specific instances or examples then formulating a reasonable conclusion
information card card for recording and categorizing important data
information imbalance some people or groups having very little access to information while others have it in abundance
interactive whiteboards connect to other technology; you can overwrite material and then save your markups
internal monologue (I-M) self-talk
internal preview brief in-speech summary that foretells the subpoints you'll develop under a major point
internal summary restatement of the ideas within a subpoint
Invisible Web or **Deep Web** the vast number of Web pages that are not seen by computer spiders
invitational rhetoric inviting audiences to enter and understand the rhetor's world and then share their own perspectives; focuses on mutual understanding and mutual influence, not winning or change per se

J

jargon a specialized, technical vocabulary that serves the interests and activities of a particular group

K

key words important words and phrases that will jog the speaker's memory

L

languages verbal codes consisting of symbols that a speech community uses for communication
lecture capture use of technology to upload class materials in digital formats
line graphs display in a linear form one or more variables that fluctuate over a time period
listening active process that receives, distinguishes, attends to, assigns meaning, and remembers what you hear
listening speaker dialogical speaker who hears audience interests and concerns before, during, and after a speech
literal analogies comparisons between two actual things that are alike in important ways
literal image shows the actual subject
loaded questions questions containing implications intended to put the speaker on the defensive
logical elements a speech's major ideas with supporting materials and their relationship
laypeople or **peers** ordinary people whose knowledge comes from everyday experience
logos arguments from the words of the speech itself; often called rational proofs

M

manuscript delivery reading a speech
memorized delivery giving a speech you've learned word for word
metaphors comparison of two dissimilar things
median middle number in a set of numbers arranged in a ranked order
memorized delivery learning the speech by heart, then reciting it
metaphorical image implies the subject
mixed metaphor combining metaphors from two or more sources, starting with one comparison and ending with another
mode most frequently occurring number
model a facsimile of an object you can't easily bring to the speech
mean average of a group of numbers
Monroe's Motivated Sequence a call to action in five steps: attention, need, satisfaction, visualization, and action
motivated audiences listen for a reason
motivation internal, individualized factor that results when we understand how topics affect our lives in a personal way
multivocal society society that actively seeks expression of a variety of voices or viewpoints

N

narrative coherence deciding if a narrative is understandable or sensible
narrative fidelity testing if the narrative faithfully represents how the world works

narrative merit testing whether or not a narrative is worth telling
nonexpressive cultures cultures that value privacy and encourage members to keep their emotions and ideas to themselves rather than to express them publicly
nonparallel language language that does not treat the two sexes equally

O

open questions requests for more lengthy responses
oral culture culture with no writing and no technology for recording messages apart from face-to-face interactions
oral style characteristics of spoken language compared to written language
organic pattern alternative pattern that provides a clear speech structure in a less linear form
organizational culture the way of life of a specific organization, which includes its history, traditions, heroes, folklore, vocabulary, rituals, and ways of doing things
original documents evidence recorded by a primary source such as letters or autobiographies
organizational charts show hierarchies and relationships
OPACs online public access catalogs

P

parallel case or **literal analogy** comparing likenesses between two similar things; arguing that what happened in a known case will likely happen in a similar case
parallel points creating points that are similar in kind and length
participatory questions questions that listeners answer overtly
passive audiences unmotivated listeners who listen to accomplish other goals
pathos appeals or reasons directed toward audience emotions
percentage figure that shows the relationship of the part to the whole, which is represented by the number 100
perceived behavioral control our opinion about our ability to do a behavior
performance anxiety fear of forgetting or of poorly presenting a speech
personification giving human characteristics to nonhuman entities
perspective taking trying to imagine something from another person's point of view
persuasion the symbolic process in which a communicator intentionally creates a message in an attempt to convince others to change their attitudes or behaviors in an atmosphere of free choice.
picture graphs or pictographs present data in pictures, each representing a certain number of individual cases
pie graphs represent parts of the whole or divisions of a population by circles divided into portions
physical factors bodily conditions that can limit your desire or ability to listen
physiological anxiety bodily responses to a perceived threat (increased heart rate, adrenaline rush)
plagiarism presenting the words, images, or ideas of others as if they were your own
plot the story's action
policy claim argument about the need or the plan for taking action forming a reasoned decision about a topic
political maps show current borders for states and nations; can be outdated in a fast-changing world
post hoc a fallacy of causation; a false cause
prejudice preformed biases or judgments, whether negative or positive
presentation aids Visual, audio, and multimedia support that helps audiences understand and remember information.
presentation software programs computer software to create a package of lists, tables, graphs, and clip art
presumption assumption that change is not necessary until proven otherwise
preview short summary of the major points you'll develop in the speech
primary sources information from people actually involved in the event
prior or **extrinsic credibility** credibility that speakers bring to the speech because of their experience and reputation
problem-solution pattern describes a problem and a possible solution to it
process anxiety fear due to lack of confidence in knowing how to prepare a speech
process speech describes a sequence of steps or stages that follow one another in a fairly predictable pattern
pro-con arrangement presents arguments in favor of and arguments against an issue
psychological anxiety mental stress about a perceived threat
psychological factors mental stressors or distractions that take away from your desire or ability to focus
psychological profile assessment of an audience's beliefs, values, and attitudes
public speaking a person delivers a presentation to a group that listens, generally without interrupting the speaker's flow of ideas
public speaking anxiety (PSA) fear or dread specifically related to speaking in public

Q

qualifiers words and phrases that limit or narrow the scope of a claim

R

race categories, often associated with stereotypes, based on physical characteristics
racist language language that privileges one racial or ethnic group over another
random audiences listeners who are initially doing something else but are attracted by a message that catches their attention

rate of increase or decrease percentage that uses an earlier baseline figure to compare growth or decline
ratio relationship shown by numbers, such as 1 in 10
reasoning by metaphor comparing two things that are generally different but share a recognizable similarity
rebuttal arguments that counter or disagree with a claim
redundancy repeating the same idea more than once, but developing it differently each time
receiver apprehension (RA) anxiety that people experience while listening
reference librarian librarian at the reference desk who is specifically trained to help people find information
relics or **artifacts** culturally significant creations such as buildings, jewelry, or tools
repetition saying the same thing more than once
requests for elaboration questions asking for more information
resistance response to diversity in which you refuse to change, and you defend your own positions or attack others
re-sourcement creatively framing a divisive issue or viewpoint in a different way that may be less threatening
***respons*-ibility** speakers' and listeners' mutual engagement with ideas, which allows them to jointly forge meanings
reversibility of perspectives an attempt to think from the other's perspective as well as one's own
rhetoric the study of persuasion in its various forms; this helps develop critical thinking skills
rhetoric of possibility points out what can be, not what is
rhetorical questions questions that listeners answer in their minds
rhymes words that end in the same sound
"rightsabilities" phrase coined by Professor Vernon Jensen to highlight the tension between our right to free speech and our responsibility for our speech

S

salient relevant or significant
sans serif font a simple font with no cross lines on each letter
scaled questions asking for responses along a continuum, used to assess attitudes
schemas mental models that guide your perception, interpretation, storage, and recollection of a speech
scholarly books books based on research that advances knowledge in an academic field
script writing out every word of the speech
search engine created by computer robots (spiders), matches search terms to words in its database
secondary sources summaries or interpretations of an event or a person provided by nonparticipants
self-selected audiences choose to listen to a selected subject or speaker
serif font a font with cross lines at the top and bottom of letters
sexist language language that privileges males and their activities and interests
signpost connective such as *first*, *most importantly*, and *consequently* that links ideas, lends emphasis, and helps listeners keep their place in the speech
similes short comparisons that use the word *like* or *as* to compare two items that are alike in one essential detail
sincere speakers presenting verbal and nonverbal messages they themselves believe
six-by-six rule limit information to six lines, six words per line
social category culturally constructed category such as race or gender
solvency the proposed plan will actually solve the problem
source cards cards used to record bibliographic information
spatial pattern presents points by place or location
speaking notes the notes you use to deliver your speech
specialized databases databases on thousands of topics, can be accessed by searching specifically for them
specialized encyclopedias texts that summarize information in specific subject areas
specific purpose the cognitive, affective, or behavioral responses a speaker desires
speech genres cultural forms we rely upon when we participate in a specific type of communication
speech-thought differential the difference between the rate you think (about 500 words per minute) and the average speaking rate (about 150 words per minute)
spiral pattern repetitive pattern with a series of points that increase in drama or intensity
Standard English the English dialect most commonly used in public speaking and in US institutions
star pattern presents relatively equally weighted speech points within a thematic circle that binds them together; order of points may vary
status quo Latin phrase that means "the existing state of affairs"
stereotype place someone in a category and then assume the person fits the characteristics of that category
stock issues the questions a reasonable person would need to have answered before forming a reasoned decision about a topic
storytelling an oral art form we use to preserve and transmit commonly held ideas, images, motives, and emotions
stress accenting syllables or words
structural elements a speech's introduction, body, and conclusion
style in rhetoric, style refers to language
subject directory created by humans; searches the Internet by subject categories
subject librarian librarian who also has an advanced degree in a particular subject such as law or medicine
subjective norms our perceptions of what significant people think we should do
subordination placement of supporting points under major points
systematic desensitization process designed to lessen physical reactions to stress; teaches how to relax while thinking about frightening speech events

T

taboo topics a culture considers inappropriate

teleprompter screen, located beneath the camera lens, on which the words of the speech scroll up during a filmed speech

terminal credibility final impression listeners have of a speaker

text-based visuals carry meaning in the written words rather than in visual images

Theory of Reasoned Action links behavioral intentions with attitudes, subjective norms, and perceived behavioral control; assumes we rationally weigh costs and benefits of our actions

thesis statement a single sentence that names the subject and establishes its significance

topical arrangement divides a subject into subtopics, each of which is part of the whole

trade books books aimed at a general audience

trade journals journals that pertain to specific occupations

transactional model of communication represents communication as a process in which speakers and listeners work together to create mutual meanings

transition summary of where you've been and where you're going in your speech

U

unfilled pauses silent pauses

unmotivated audiences listeners who lack a listening purpose or goal

V

vague words imprecise terms that have indefinite boundaries

value claim argument about right or wrong, moral or immoral, beautiful or ugly

values standards used to make evaluative judgments such as good or bad

verbiage nonessential language

visualization rehearsing by using your imagination to envision your speech from start to finish

vocal variations changes in volume, rate, and pitch that combine to create impressions of the speaker

vocalics or **paralinguistics** all aspects of spoken language except the words

W

warrant justification or reasoning that connects the claim and the evidence

wave pattern repetitive pattern that presents variations of themes and ideas, with major points presented at the crests

words verbal symbols that stand for or represent ideas

REFERENCES

CHAPTER 1

1. TED. (n.d.) Majora Carter: Activist for environmental justice. TED: Ideas Worth Spreading. Retrieved from www.ted.com/speakers/majora_carter.html.
2. Jensen, K. K., & Harris, V. (1999). The public speaking portfolio. *Communication Education, 48*, 221–227.
3. California State Senate. (2002, January 20, last updated). Definition of critical thinking. Quoted on B. Dowden, Philosophy 4, California State University Sacramento. Retrieved from www.csus.edu/indiv/d/dowdenb/4/ct-def/def-of-ct.htm.
4. Lunsford, A. (2008, last updated). Scholarly definitions of rhetoric. Retrieved from www.americanrhetoric.com/rhetoricdefinitions.htm.
5. Hillary for President. (2008, January 7). Morning HUBdate: Rhetoric vs. reality. Press Release. Retrieved from www.hillaryclinton.com/news/release/view/?id=5065.
6. The first three definitions and others can be found on Lunsford, A. A. (2008, last updated). Some definitions of rhetoric. *Rhetoric and Composition.* Retrieved from www.stanford.edu/dept/english/courses/sites/lunsford/pages/defs.htm.
7. Quoted in Xing, L. (1998). *Rhetoric in ancient China, fifth to third century, B.C.E.: A comparison with classical Greek rhetoric*. Columbia, SC: University of South Carolina Press. p. 88.
8. Allen, M., Berkowitz, S., Hunt, S., & Louden, A. (1999). A meta-analysis of the impact of forensics and communication education on critical thinking. *Communication Education, 48*, 18–30.
9. Rhodes, T. (2010, November). Learning across the curriculum: Communication departments hold vital role. *Spectra, 46*(1): 12–15.
10. Peterson, M. S. (1997). Personnel interviewers' perceptions of the importance and adequacy of applicant's communication skills. *Communication Education, 46*, 287–291.
11. Darling, A. L., & Dannels, D. P. (2003). Practicing engineers talk about the importance of talk: A report on the role of oral communication in the workplace. *Communication Education, 52*, 1–16.
12. Waugh, T. (2004, June). The tide is turning. Are you ready? *The Practical Accountant, 37*, 16–17.
13. Goldfinger, J. (2009). Democracy Plaza: A campus space for civic engagement. *Innovative Higher Education, 34*, 69–77. doi 10.1007/s10755-009-9096-1.
14. See the definition of "dialogist publicity" in K. Wahl-Jorgensen. (2001). Letters to the editor as a forum for public deliberation: Modes of publicity and democratic debate. *Critical Studies in Media Communication, 18*, 303–320.
15. Roper Starch. (1999). How Americans communicate. Poll commissioned by the National Communication Association. Retrieved from www.natcom.org/research/Roper/howamericanscommunicate.htm.
16. Witt, P. L., & Behnke, R. R. (2006, April). Anticipatory speech anxiety as a function of public speaking assignment type. *Communication Education, 55*, 167–177.
17. Smith, D. (1996, February). Globalization of the general education curriculum. Discussion leader. George Fox University, Newberg, OR..
18. Galvin, K. M., & Cooper, P. J. (2000). Perceptual filters: Culture, family, and gender. In K. M. Galvin & P. J. Cooper (Eds.). *Making connections: Readings in relational communication* (2nd ed., pp. 32–33). Los Angeles: Roxbury.
19. Collier, M. J. (2006). WSCA presidential address: Cultural positioning, reflexivity, and transformative third spaces. *Western Journal of Communication, 70*, 263–269.
20. Orbe, M. P. (1998). *Constructing co-cultural theory: An explication of culture, power, and communication*. Thousand Oaks, CA: Sage.
21. Conrad, C. (1994). *Strategic organizational communication: Toward the twenty-first century* (3rd ed., p. 31). Fort Worth: Harcourt Brace.
22. Gray, G. W. (1946). The precepts of Kagmenmi [sic] and Ptah-hotep. *Quarterly Journal of Speech, 31*, 446–454.
23. Halledén, P. (2005). What is Arab Islamic rhetoric? Rethinking the history of Muslim oratory art and homiletics. *Int. J. Middle East Studies, 37*, 19–38. DOI: 10.1017.S0020743805050038.
24. *Dao De Jing* 81.185 is quoted in Xing, *Rhetoric in ancient China*, p. 87.
25. Pearce, W. B. (1989). *Communication and the human condition.* Carbondale: Southern Illinois University Press.
26. Pearce, *Communication and the human.*
27. Ong, W. J. (1982). *Orality and literacy: The technologizing of the word.* New York: Methuen.
28. Hofstede, G. (n.d.). Dimensions of national cultures. Geert Hofstede website. Retrieved from www.geerthofstede.nl/culture/dimensions-of-national-cultures.aspx.
29. Oddou, G. (2006, Spring). Hofstede's dimensions of culture. California State University, San Marcos. MGMT 461. Retrieved from courses.csusm.edu/mgmt461go/Hofstede correlations.doc.
30. FIU Oral Presentation Lab. (n.d.). Cultural issues and public address. Florida International University, Miami, FL. Retrieved from http://opl.fiu.edu/cultural.htm.
31. Lai, A. (2006, June). Eye on religion: Cultural signs and caring for Chinese patients. *Southern Medical Journal,* 99, 688–610.
32. Sallinen-Kuparinen, A., McCroskey, J. C., & Richmond, V. P. (1991). Willingness to communicate, communication apprehension, introversion, and self-reported communication competence: Finnish and American Comparisons. *Communication Research Reports,* 8, 54–65.

33. Marsella, A. J. (1993). Counseling and psychotherapy with Japanese Americans: Cross-cultural considerations. *American Journal of Orthopsychiatry, 63*, 200–208. ISSN: 00029432.

34. Klopf, D. W. (1997). Cross-cultural apprehension research: Procedures and comparisons. In J. A. Daly, J. C. McCroskey, J. Ayers, T. Hopf, & D. M. Ayres. (1997). *Avoiding communication: Shyness, reticence, and communication apprehension* (2nd ed., pp. 269–284). Creskill, NJ: Hampton Press.

35. Messenger, J. (1960). Anang proverb riddles. *Journal of American Folklore, 73*, 235.

36. Weider, D. L., & Pratt, S. (1990). On being a recognizable Indian. In D. Carbaugh (Ed.), *Intercultural communication and intercultural contacts* (pp. 45–64). Hillsdale, NJ: Lawrence Erlbaum.

37. Jenefsky, C. (1996). Public speaking as empowerment at Visionary University. *Communication Education, 45*, 343–355. See also M. A. Jaasma. (1997, summer). Classroom apprehension: Does being male or female make a difference? *Communication Reports, 10*, 218–228.

38. Clasen, P., & Lee, R. (2006). Teaching in a sanitized world: An exploration of the suburban scene in public communication pedagogy. *Communication Education, 55*, 438–463.

39. Stewart, E. C., & Bennett, M. J. (1991). *American cultural patterns: A cross-cultural perspective* (rev. ed.). Yarmouth, ME: Intercultural Press.

40. Evans, R. W., & Avery, P. G. (1999, Sep/Oct). Taboo topics: Cultural restraint on teaching social issues. *Social Studies, 90*(5), 218–225. ISSN: 00377996.

41. DeJong, J., Jawad, R., Mortagy, I., & Shepard, B. (2005). The sexual and reproductive health of young people in the Arab countries and Iran. *Reproductive Health Matters, 13*(25), 49–59. doi: 10.1016/S0968-8080(05)25181-9.

42. Sayer, D. (2010). Who's afraid of the dead? Archaeology, modernity, and the death taboo. *World Archaeology, 42*(3), 481–491.

43. Ugwu-Oju, D. (1993, November 14). Pursuit of happiness. *New York Times Magazine.*

44. Arnett, R. C., & Arneson, P. (1999). *Dialogic civility in a cynical age: Community, hope, and interpersonal relationships.* Albany, NY: SUNY Press.

45. Schwandt, B., & Soraya, S. (1992, August 13–15). Ethnography of communication and "*Sprechwissenschaft*"—merging of concepts. Paper presented at the Ethnography of Communication Conference, Portland, OR.

46. Bavelas, J. B., Hutchinson, S., Kenwood, C., & Matheson, D. H. (1997). Using face-to-face dialogue as a standard for other communication systems. *Canadian Journal of Communications, 22*, 14 pp. [Online.] Retrieved from http://info.wlu.ca/,wwwpress/jrls/cjc/BackIssues/22.1/bavel.html.

47. Bahktin is quoted in A. Wierzbicka. (1991). *Cross-cultural pragmatics: The semantics of human interaction* (p. 149). Berlin: Mouten de Gruyter.

48. Bevelas, Using face-to-face.

49. Barnlund, D. (1962). Toward a meaning-centered philosophy of communication. *Journal of Communication, 12*(4), 197–211.

50. Stoner, M. R. (2007, July). PowerPoint in a new key. *Communication Education, 56*, 354–381.

51. The transactional model appears in almost every communication text.

52. Crooks, R. (1998, May 11, last modified). Noise. English Department, Bentley College. Retrieved from http://web.bentley.edu/empl/c/rcrooks/toolbox/common_knowledge/general_communication/noise.html.

CHAPTER 2

1. Bodie, G. D. (2010). A racing heart, rattling knees, and ruminative thoughts: Defining, explaining, and treating public speaking anxiety. *Communication Education, 59*(1), 40–105.

2. McCroskey, J. C. (1977). Oral communication apprehension: A summary of recent theory and research. *Human Communication Research, 4*, 78–96.

3. Richmond, V. P., & McCroskey, J. C. (1995). *Communication: Apprehension, avoidance, and effectiveness* (4th ed.). Scottsdale, AZ: Gorsuch Scarisbrick.

4. Beatty, M., McCroskey, J. C., & Heisel, A. D. (1998). Communication apprehension as temperamental expression: A communibiological paradigm. *Communication Monographs, 65*, 197–219.

5. Bodie, A racing heart.

6. Robinson, T. E. (1997). Communication apprehension and the basic public speaking course: A national survey of in-class treatment techniques. *Communication Education, 46*, 188–197.

7. Witt, P. L., & Behnke, R. R. (2006). Anticipatory speech anxiety as a function of public speaking assignment type. *Communication Education, 55*(2), 167–177.

8. Bippus, A. M., & Daly, J. A. (1999). What do people think causes stage fright? Naïve attributions about the reasons for public speaking anxiety. *Communication Education, 48*, 63–72.

9. Duff, D. C., Levine, T. R., Beatty, M. J., Woolbright, J., & Park, H. S. (2007). Testing public anxiety treatments against a credible placebo control. *Communication Education, 56*(1), 72–88.

10. Cicero, M. T. (1981). *Ad herennium: De ratione dicendi. (Rhetorica ad herennium).* (H. Kaplan, Trans.) The Loeb Classical Library. Cambridge, MA: Harvard University Press.

11. Staley, C. C., & Staley, R. S. (2000). Communicating in organizations. In K. Galvin & P. Cooper (Eds.). *Making connections: Readings in relational communication,* (2nd ed., p. 287–294). Los Angeles: Roxbury.

12. Quintilian. (1920–1922). *The instituto oratoria of Quintilian* (4 vols., H. E. Butler, trans.) The Loeb Classical Library. Cambridge, MA: Harvard University Press.

13. Style. (2008). *Compact Oxford English Dictionary.* Accessed June 3, 2008, from www.askoxford.com/concise_oed/style?view5uk.

14. Pearson, J. C., Child, J. T., & Kahl, D. H., Jr., (2006). Preparation meeting opportunity: How do college students prepare for public speeches? *Communication Quarterly, 54*(3), 351–366.

15. Sawyer, C. R., & Behnke, R. R. (1999). State anxiety patterns for public speaking anxiety and the behavior inhibition system. *Communication Reports, 12*, 33–41.

16. Behnke, R. R., & Sawyer, C. R. (2001). Patterns of psychological state anxiety as a function of anxiety sensitivity. *Communication Quarterly, 49*, 84–95. See also M. J. Young, R. R. Behnke, & Y. M. Mann. (2004). Anxiety patterns in employment interviews. *Communication Reports, 17*, 49–57.

17. McGlynn, F. D., Smitherman, T. A., & Gothard, K. D. (2004). Comment on the status of systematic desensitization. *Behavior Modification, 28*(2), 194–205. doi: 10.1177/0145445503259414.

18. This process came from Richmond, R. L. (2011). Systematic desensitizatio A guide to psychology and its practice. Retrieved from www.guidetopsychology.com/sysden.htm.

19. Howell. W. (1990). Coping with internal-monologue. In J. Stewart (Ed.) *Bridges not walls: A book about interpersonal communication* (5th ed., pp. 128–138). New York: McGraw Hill.

20. Mount Sinai Medical Center. (2007). Stress: Diseases and Conditions. Retrieved from http://www.mssm.edu/cvi/stress.shtml#q2.

21. Bippus & Daly, What do people.

22. Kane, L., & Helmer, L. (2006, October 6). Conquering podium paralysis: Public speaking skills for doctors. *Medical Economics, 83*(19), 31–32.

23. Ayers, J., & Sonandre, D. M. A. (2003). Performance visualization: Does the nature of the speech model matter? *Communication Research Reports, 20*(3), 260–268.

24. Mount Sinai Medical Center, Stress.

25. Ayres and Hopf have been studying visualization for many years. See J. Ayres & T. S. Hopf. (1989). Visualization: Is it more than extra-attention? *Communication Education, 38*, 1–5.; see also J. Ayres, T. S. Hopf, & D. M. Ayres. (1994). An examination of whether imaging ability enhances the effectiveness of an intervention designed to reduce speech anxiety. *Communication Education, 43*, 256.

26. Ayers, J. (2005, April). Performance visualization and behavioral disruption: A clarification. *Communication Reports, 18*(1), 55–63.

27. Ayres, J., Hopf, T., & Edwards, P. A. (1999). Vividness and control: Factors in the effectiveness of performance visualization? *Communication Education, 48*, 287–293.

28. MacIntyre, P. J., & MacDonald, J. R. (1998). Public speaking anxiety: Perceived competence and audience congeniality. *Communication Education, 47*, 359–365.

29. Finn, A. N., Sawyer, C. R., & Behnke, R. R.(2003). Audience-perceived anxiety patterns of public speakers. *Communication Quarterly, 51*, 470–482.

30. Stockstill, C. J., & Roach, K. D. (2007). Communication apprehension in high school athletes. *Texas Speech Communication Journal, 32*(1), 53–64.

CHAPTER 3

1. U.S. Constitution Online. (2010, January 24, last updated). Amendment 1: Freedom of religion, press, expression. Retrieved from http://www.usconstitution.net/xconst_Am1.html.

2. Jensen, J. V. (1997). *Ethical issues in the communication process.* Mahwah, NJ: Lawrence Erlbaum.

3. Jensen, *Ethical issues.*

4. Pearson, J., Child, J. T., Mattern, J. L., & Kahl, D. H. (2006). What are students being taught about ethics in public speaking textbooks? *Communication Quarterly, 54*(4), 504–521.

5. Porter, R. E., & Samovar, L. A. (1994). An introduction to intercultural communication. In L. A. Samovar & R. E. Porter (Eds.). *Intercultural communication: A reader* (7th ed., p. 4–25). Belmont, CA: Wadsworth.

6. Pearce, W. B. (1989). *Communication and the human condition.* Carbondale: Southern Illinois Press.

7. Berger, P. (1969). *A rumor of angels: Modern society and the rediscovery of the supernatural.* Garden City, NY: Doubleday.

8. Berger, *A rumor.*

9. Tannen, D. (1998). *The argument culture: Moving from debate to dialogue.* New York: Random House.

10. Gates, H. L. (1992). *Loose cannons: Notes on the culture wars.* New York: Oxford University Press.

11. Pearce, W. B., & Pearce, K. A. (2000). Combining passions and abilities: Toward dialogic virtuosity. *Southern Communication Journal, 65*, 161–175.

12. Barker, B. (2011, February 12). Interview. *CNN Saturday, Live.* 7:29 a.m. PST.

13. Tannen, *The argument culture*, 289.

14. Quoted in Bartanen, M., & Frank, D. (1999). Reclaiming a heritage: A proposal for rhetorically grounded academic debate. *Parliamentary Debate: The Journal of the National Parliamentary Debate Association, 6*, 31–54.

15. Barrett, H. (1991). *Rhetoric and civility: Human development, narcissism, and the good audience.* Albany, NY: SUNY Press.

16. Obama, B. H. (2011, January 12). Remarks by the President at a memorial service for the victims of the shooting in Tucson, Arizona. McKale Memorial Center, University of Arizona, Tuscon, AZ. Retrieved from www.whitehouse.gov/the-press-office/2011/01/12/remarks-president-barack-obama-memorial-service-victims-shooting-tucson.

17. Jensen, *Ethical issues.*

18. Khadaroo, S. T. (2011, February 24). Does Facebook boost civic engagement among American youths, too? *The Christian Science Monitor.* InfoTrac College Edition. (Article CJ249927176)

19. Jensen, *Ethical issues.*

20. Yankelovich, D. (1999). *The magic of dialogue: Transforming conflict into cooperation.* New York: Simon & Schuster.

21. The mission statement is quoted on the group's home page at www.seedsofpeace.org.

22. Seeds of Peace. About us.

23. Seeds of Peace. (2011, February 14). Egyptian Seeds respond to 2011 revolution. Seeds of Peace in the News. Retrieved from www.seedsofpeace.org/story/2011/02/situation_in_egypt_follow_reflections_of_seeds_of_peace_graduates

24. Shalhoub-Kevorkian, N. (2001, March). Using the dialogue tent to break mental chains: Listening and being heard. *Social Service Review, 75*, 135.

25. Pearce & Pearce, Combining passions.

26. Etzioni, A. (1996). *The new golden rule: Community and morality in a democratic society* (pp. 104–106). New York: Basic Books.

27. Seeds of Peace. About us. Retrieved from www.seedsofpeace.org/site/PageServer?pagename5aboutus.

28. Annan, K. (2001, February 5). Idea of "dialogue among civilizations" rooted in fundamental UN values, says Secretary-General in Seaton Hall address [Press release and text of address]. Seton Hall University, School of Diplomacy and International Relations, South Orange, NJ. Retrieved from www.un.org/Dialogue/pr/sgsm7705.htm.

29. Mallory, B. L., & Thomas, N. L. (2003, Sept–Oct). When the medium is the message: Promoting ethical action through democratic dialogue. *Change, 2–9.* Retrieved from www.collegevalues.org/pdfs/galleyproofsCHANGEfinal.pdf.

30. Adamy, J., & Bendavid, N. (2009, August 8). Lawmakers rethink town hall meetings. *Wall Street Journal*, A5.

31. Jonsson, P. (2011, February 18). Wisconsin protests: Why "week of

rage" matters to rest of America. *Christian Science Monitor*. Retrieved from www.csmonitor.com/USA/Politics/2011/0218/Wisconsinprotests-why-week-of-rage-matters-to-rest-of-America.

32. CQ Transcriptwire. (2008, June 10). McCain delivers remarks at the National Small Business Summit. *The Washington Post*. Retrieved from www.washingtonpost.com/wp-dyn/content/article/2008/06/10/AR2008061001509.html.
33. Hexham, I. (1999). Academic plagiarism defined. University of Calgary Department of Religious Studies. Retrieved from www.ucalgary.ca/hexham/study/plag.html.
34. UCDavis Student Judiciary Affairs. (Updated 2001, October-25). Avoiding plagiarism. Retrieved from http://sja.ucdavis.edu/avoid.htm#guidelines.
35. UCDavis Student Judiciary Affairs. (Updated 2008, February 25). Why academic integrity matters. Retrieved from http://sja.ucdavis.edu/academic-integrity-page2.html.
36. Plagiarism.com (2011). Plagiarism and the Internet. Retrieved from http://plagiarism.org/plag_article_plagiarism_and_the_internet.html.
37. Plagiarism.com, Plagiarism and the Internet.
38. Many Internet sites explain plagiarism. See Online Writing Lab. (2011, January 14, last edited). Avoiding plagiarism. Purdue University. Retrieved from http://owl.english.purdue.edu/owl/resource/589/03/. See also Writing Center. (2007). See also, Plagiarism. University of North Carolina. Retrieved from www.unc.edu/depts/wcweb/handouts/plagiarism.html.
39. Mason, W. (2005, May). Make it newish: E. E. Cummings, plagiarism, and the perils of originality. (E.E. Cummings: A biography) (Book Review). *Harper's Magazine*, *310*, 92–102.
40. Kennedy, R. S. (1980). *Dreams in the mirror: A biography of E. E. Cummings.* Quoted in Mason, Make it.
41. Sawyer-Laucanno, C. (2004). *E.E. Cummings, a biography*. Quoted in Mason, Make it, p. 100.
42. Purdue Online Writing Lab.
43. Writing Center, Plagiarism.
44. UCDavis Student Judiciary Affairs. (2001). Avoiding plagiarism.
45. Gilday, B. (2010, Fall). The dark side of product placement [Student Speech]. George Fox University, Newberg, OR.
46. Valentine, J. (2004). The *dun dun* drum [Student Speech]. George Fox University, Newberg, OR.
47. Stern, J. (2009, August). Making smarter movies. Speech delivered June 20, 2009, at the Los Angeles Film Festival, Los Angeles, CA. *Vital Speeches of the Day*, *75*(8), 347–352.
48. A video on YouTube demonstrates the WorldCat.org Citation Tool advises this. Retrieved from www.youtube.com/watch?v=X8W7kWMrVNk.
49. The material in this box draws from N. Carbone. (2001, December 3). Thinking and talking about plagiarism. Bedford St. Martins Technotes. Retrieved from http://bedfordstmartins.com/technotes/techtiparchive/ttip102401.htm.
50. Hunter, J. (1997). Confessions of an academic honesty lady. Grinnell College Writing Lab. [Online.] Retrieved from www.grinnell.edu/academic/writinglab/forum/con_hj.pdf.
51. Reuters. (2011, January 6). Journal says doctor faked data linking autism to vaccines. *The Washington Post*. Retrieved from www.washingtonpost.com/wp-dyn/content/article/2011/01/05/AR2011010507052.html.
52. Department of Journalism. (n.d.). Academic Integrity Handbook. University of Arizona. Retrieved from http://journalism.arizona.edu/publications/academic_integrity/integrity_handbook.pdf.
53. Hunter, Confessions.

CHAPTER 4

1. Janusik, L. (2011). Listening facts. Paragon Resources. Retrieved from www.paragonre sources.com/library/listen.pdf.
2. CACHE'. (n.d.). Cyprus 20 cents 2011. CACHE' Historical and World Coins. Retrieved from www.cachecoins.org/cyprus01.htm.
3. The 25 percent efficiency rate is widely quoted. See C. A. Roach & N. J. Wyatt. (1995). Listening and the rhetorical process. In J. Stewart. (Ed.). *Bridges not walls: A book about interpersonal communication* (9th ed., pp. 171–176). New York: McGraw-Hill.
4. Maes, J. D., Weldy, T. B., & Icenogle, M. L. (1997, January). A managerial perspective: oral communication competency is more important for business students in the workplace. *Journal of Business Communication*, *34*, 6–14.
5. Treuer, P. (2006, July 17, last updated). Listening skills. *Student Handbook*. University of Minnesota Duluth. Retrieved from www.d.umn.edu/kmc/student/loon/acad/strat/ss_listening.html.
6. Salopek, J. J. (1999). Is anyone listening? *Training and Development*, *53*(9), 58–60. See also R. D. Ramsey. (2007, November). The most important skills for today's supervisors. *Supervision*, *68*(11), 3–5.
7. Lenckus, D. (2005, November 28). Physician apologies, listening skills found to reduce med mal claims. *Business Insurance*, *39*(48).
8. Burley-Allen, M. (2001). Listen up: Listening is a learned skill and supervisors need it to improve their employee relationships. *HR Magazine*, *46*(11), 115–117.
9. Swanson Jaecks, K. M. (2009, Spring). Current perceptions of the role of dental hygienists in interdisciplinary collaboration. *Journal of Dental Hygiene*, *83*(2), 84–91.
10. Owen, J. (2007, June 2). Interior decorator cites listening skills as key to satisfying clients. *The Walton Sun* (Santa Rosa Beach, FL). Retrieved from InfoTrac College Edition database.
11. Olsztynski, J. (2008, December). Master the art of listening. *Roofing Contractor*, *28*(12), 18–19.
12. Golen, S., & Lynch, D. H. (2008, September). The importance of listening skills in tax preparation. *The CPA Journal*, *78*(9), 56–59.
13. This quotation is public domain. It is available on many quotation collections online.
14. Janusik, Listening facts.
15. TAMU Student Counseling Service. (2008). Listening skills. Texas A & M University. Retrieved from http://scs.tamu.edu/selfhelp/elibrary/listening_skills.asp.
16. Santos, F. (2008, July 23). Mayor orders New York to expand language help. *New York Times*. Retrieved from www.nytimes.com/2008/07/23/nyregion/23translate.html.

17. Lundsteen, S. W. (1993). Metacognitive listening. In A. D. Wolvin & C. G. Coakley (Eds.). *Perspectives on listening* (pp. 106–123). Norwood, NJ: Ablex.

18. Lundsteen, Metacognitive listening.

19. Imhof, M. (1998). What makes a good listener? Listening behaviors in instructional settings. *International Journal of Listening, 12*, 81–105.

20. Edwards, R., & McDonald, J. L. (1993). Schema theory and listening. In Wolvin & Coakley, *Perspectives*, 60–77.

21. Imhof, M. (2001). How to listen more efficiently: self-monitoring strategies in listening. *International Journal of Listening, 15*, 2–19.

22. Lundsteen, Metacognitive listening.

23. Imhof, M. (2003). The social construction of the listener: Listening behaviour across situations, perceived listener status, and culture. *Communication Research Reports, 20*(4), 357–366.

24. Educause. (2008). 7 things you should know about lecture capture. EDUCAUSE Learning Initiative. ELI 7044.pdf.

25. Tannen, D. (1989). *Talking voices: Repetition, dialogue, and imagery in conversational discourse.* Cambridge: Cambridge University Press.

26. Sitkaram, K. S., & Cogdell, R. T. (1976). *Foundations of intercultural communication.* Columbus, OH: Charles E. Merrill.

27. Sitkaram & Cogdell, *Foundations of intercultural.*

28. Daniel, J., & Smitherman, G. (1990). How I got over: Communication dynamics in the black community. In D. Carbaugh (Ed.), *Intercultural communication and intercultural contacts* (pp. 45–64). Hillsdale, NJ: Lawrence Erlbaum. See also A. L. Smith (Molefi Asanti). (1970). Socio-historical perspectives of black oratory. *Quarterly Journal of Speech, 61*, 264–269.

29. Kiewitz, C., Weaver, J. B. III, Brosius, H-B., & Weimann, G. (1997). Cultural differences in listening style preferences: A comparison of young adults in Germany, Israel, and the United States. *International Journal of Public Opinion Research, 9*, 233–248.

30. Ridge, A. (1993). A perspective of listening skills. In Wolvin & Coakley, *Perspectives*, 1–14.

31. Read, B. (2006, April 7). A law professor bans laptops from the classroom. *The Chronicle of Higher Education, 52*(31).

32. OrinKerr.com. (2006, March 23). More on laptops in class [email from June Entman]. Retrieved from www.orinkerr.com/2006/03/23/more-on-laptops-in-class/.

33. Bone, J. (2010, March 11). American lecturers banning laptops from the classroom. *The Sunday Times*, London. Archive article. Retrieved from www.timesonline.co.uk/tol/news/world/us_and_americas/article7057511.ece.

34. Bone, American lecturers.

35. Bone, American lecturers.

36. Boyd, S. D. (2001, October). The human side of teaching: Effective listening. *Techniques, 76*(7), 60.

37. Goodman, G., & Esterly, G. (1990). Questions—the most popular piece of language. In J. Stewart. (Ed.). *Bridges not walls: A book about interpersonal communication* (9th ed., pp. 171–176). New York: McGraw-Hill p. 69–79.

38. Becker, C. B. (1986). Reasons for the lack of argumentation and debate in the Far East. *International Journal of International Relations, 10*(1), 75-92. doi: 10.1016/0147-1767(86)90035-0; See also Sueda, K. (1995). Differences in the perception of face: Chinese *mien-tzu* and Japanese *mentsu. World Communication, 24*(1), 23–31.

39. Anonymous reviewer. (2004).

40. Winiecki, K. L., & Ayers, J. (1999). Communication apprehension and receiver apprehension in the workplace. *Communication Quarterly, 47*(4), 431–440.

CHAPTER 5

1. Christensen, M. D. (1998, March). An idea is only the bait. *The Writer, 111*, 20–21.

2. Bitzer, L. F. (1999). The rhetorical situation. In J. L. Lucaites, C. M. Condit, & S. Caudill. (Eds.), *Contemporary rhetorical theory: A reader* (pp. 217–225). New York: Guilford; see also R. E. Vatz. (1999). The myth of the rhetorical situation. In Lucaites, Condit, & Caudill, *Contemporary rhetorical theory*, 226–231.

3. McKeon, R. (1998). Creativity and the commonplace. In T. B. Ferrell (Ed.), *Landmark essays on contemporary rhetoric* (pp. 33–41). Mahwah, NJ: Hermagoras Press.

4. American Peanut Council. (n.d.). About the peanut industry. Retrieved from www.peanutsusa.com/USA/index.cfm?fuseaction=home.page&pid=12.

5. Weinstein, B. (2008, January 15). The ethics of talking politics at work. *BusinessWeek*. Retrieved from www.businessweek.com/managing/content/jan2008/ca20080115_994641.htm.

6. Murray, D. M. (1998, May). Write what you don't know. *The Writer, 111*, 7–9.

7. Christensen, An idea.

8. Carrell, L. J. (1997). Diversity in the communication curriculum: Impact on student empathy. *Communication Education, 46*, 234–244.

9. Grant, H. (2007, January). Sabina Xhosa and the new shoes. Address delivered November 1, 2006, at the IBM Lecture, Westminster College, Fulton, Missouri. *Vital Speeches of the Day, 73*(1), 36–40.

10. Scofield, S. (1999, August). An end to writer's block. *The Writer, 111*, 7–9.

11. Augustine. (397–426, 1958). *On Christian doctrine: Book IV* (D. W. Robertson Jr., Trans.). New York: Liberal Arts Press.

12. Campbell, G. (1963). *The philosophy of rhetoric* (L. Bitzer, Ed.). Carbondale: Southern Illinois University Press. (Original work published 1776)

13. Porrovecchio, M. (2005, March 29). Personal email.

14. Monroe, A. H. (1962). *Principles and types of speech* (5th ed.). Chicago: Scott Foresman.

15. Gwynne, R. (2005, March 12, last updated). Topic organization. University of Tennessee Knoxville. Accessed from http://web.utk.edu/gwynne/topic_organization.html.

16. Gwynne, Topic organization.

17. Anonymous reviewer. (2005). College of Marin.

18. Griffin, C. W. (1998). Improving students' writing strategies; Knowing versus doing. *College Teaching, 46*, 48–52.

CHAPTER 6

1. Media Release. (2007, November 27). OSU's Wright named Oregon's "Professor of the Year" by CASE, Carnegie Foundation. News and Communication Services: Oregon State University. Retrieved from http://oregonstate.edu/dept/ncs/newsarch/2007/Nov07/dawnwright.html.

2. Media Release, OSU's Wright.

3. Holman, P. (1970). *The psychology of speakers and audiences.* Glenview. IL: Scott Foresman.

4. Bitzer, L. F. (1999). The rhetorical situation. In J. L. Lucaites, C. M. Condit, & S, Caudill. (Eds.), *Contemporary rhetorical theory: A reader* (pp. 217–225). New York: Guilford. See also M. Garrett, & X. Xiao. (1993, Spring). The rhetorical situation revisited. *RSQ: Rhetorical Society Quarterly, 23*(2), 30–40.
5. Garret & Xiao, The rhetorical situation.
6. Psychologists have written about audience motivations for decades. An early book was H. L. Hollingsworth. (1935). *The psychology of audiences.* New York: American Book Company.
7. Editorial. (2006, July 3). Pander-monium: Our view: Congress is angling for votes, not solving problems. *Spokesman-Review* (Spokane, WA). Retrieved from InfoTrac College Edition.
8. Simon, P., quoted in Editorial, Pandermonium.
9. Reider, J. (2008). *The Word of the Lord is upon me: The righteous performance of Martin Luther King, Jr.* Cambridge, MA: The Belknap Press of Harvard University Press.
10. Reider, J. (2008, May 22). Interview. Tavis Smiley. PBS. Retrieved from www.pbs.org/kcet/tavissmiley/archive/200805/20080522_rieder.html.
11. Reider, Interview.
12. New London Group (1996) A pedagogy of multiliteracies: Designing social futures. *Harvard Educational Review 66*(1), 60–92.
13. Collier, M. J. (1994). Cultural identity and intercultural communication. In L. A. Samovar & R. E, Porter. (Eds.). *Intercultural communication: A reader* (7th ed., pp. 36-45). Belmont, CA: Wadsworth.
14. Rothenberg, P. S. (Ed.). (1998). *Race, class, and gender in the United States.* New York: St. Martin's Press.
15. O'Neil, D. (2006, July 5, last updated). Overview. Ethnicity and Race Tutorial. Palomar College, San Marcos, CA. Retrieved from http://anthro.palomar.edu/ethnicity/ethnic_1.htm.
16. Crowley, S. (2011, January 29). Black? White? Asian? More young Americans choose all of the above. *New York Times*. Retrieved from www.nytimes.com/2011/01/30/us/30mixed.html?pagewanted=all.
17. Marmor, J. (1996, December). Blurring the lines. *Columns, 16*(8), 22–27.
18. Jameson, D. A. (2007, July). Reconceptualizing cultural identity and its role in intercultural business communication. *The Journal of Business Communication, 44*(3), 199(37).
19. Halstead, T. (1999, August). A politics for generation X. *Atlantic Monthly, 284*(2), 33ff.
20. Oblinger, D. (2003, July/August). Boomers & Gen Xers & millenials: Understanding the new students. EDUCAUSEreview. Retrieved from net.educause.edu/ir/library/pdf/erm0342.pdf.
21. Jameson, Reconceptualizing cultural.
22. Jeanes, W. (2010, December 3). Does where you live determine what you drive? The Garreau Group. Retrieved from http://autos.aol.com/article/what-people-drive-where/.
23. Rokeach, M. (1972). *Beliefs, attitudes, and values.* San Francisco: Jossey-Bass.
24. Jaffe, C. I. (1995). Chronemics: communicating mainstream cycles to Russian Old Believer children. *World Communication, 15*, 1–20.
25. Levine, R. (1997). *A geography of time.* New York: Basic Books.
26. McCroskey, J. C. (1993). *An introduction to rhetorical communication* (6th ed.). Englewood Cliffs, NJ: Prentice-Hall.
27. Habitat for Humanity. (2011). Fact sheet (FAQs). Retrieved from www.habitat.org/how/factsheet.aspx.
28. Weider, D. L., & Pratt, S. (1990). On being a recognizable Indian. In D. Carbaugh. (Ed.). *Intercultural communication and intercultural contacts* (pp. 45–64). Hillsdale, NJ: Lawrence Erlbaum.
29. Miller, A. N. (2002). An exploration of Kenyan public speaking patterns with implications for the American introductory public speaking course. *Communication Education,* 5(2), 168–182.
30. Charlesworth, D. (2009). Assign this: Considering lyrics as public speeches: Extending the application of audience analysis. *SPECTRA, 45*(7), 10.

CHAPTER 7

1. *Internet Wire.* (2006, November 14). College students fall short in demonstrating the ICT skills necessary for success in college and the workplace. Market Wire via Comtex. Retrieved from InfoTrac College Edition database.
2. Badke, W. (2010, May/June). Getting past resistance. *Online Magazine*. 51–53.
3. Lieggi, L. (1999, July 20). Personal interview. George Fox University, Newberg, OR..
4. Rolfe, A. (2008, May 21). Personal interview. George Fox University, Newberg, OR.
5. Miller, A. N. (2002). An exploration of Kenyan public speaking patterns with implications for the American introductory public speaking course. *Communication Education*, 5(2), p. 174.
6. Leiggi, Personal interview.
7. Orwell, M. (n.d.). Job description of a reference librarian. eHow Money. Retrieved from www.ehow.com/facts_5548214_job-description-reference-librarian.html.
8. Head, A. J., & Eisenberg, M. B. (2009, December 1). Lessons learned: How college students seek information in the digital age. Project Information Literacy Progress Report. The Information School. University of Washington. Downloaded from projectinfolit.org/pdfs/PIL_Fall2009_Year1Report_12_2009.pdf.
9. Yu, H., & Young, M. (2004). An impact of Web search engines on subject searching in OPAC. *Information Technology and Libraries, 23*, 168–181. See also S. Abram & J. Luther. (2004, May-1). Born with the chip: The next generation will profoundly impact both library service and the culture within the profession. *Library Journal, 129*, 34–38.
10. Leiggi, Personal interview.
11. University of Maryland. (2006, August, last revised). Primary, secondary, and tertiary sources. Guides to Information Resources. University Libraries. Retrieved from www.lib.umd.edu/guides/primary-sources.html.
12. This is the slogan of TED: Ideas Worth Spreading. www.ted.com.
13. Head & Eisenberg, Lessons learned; see also N. J. Schweitzer. (2008). Wikipedia and psychology: Coverage of concepts and its use by undergraduate students. *Teaching of Psychology, 35*, 81–85.
14. Lever, T. (2009, Autumn). Wikipedia: What's in it for teachers? *Screen Education*, 53, 38–42.
15. Economist Intelligence Unit N.A. Incorporated. (2011, January 15). Wikipleadia: User-generated content. *The Economist US, 398*(8716), 69. Retrieved from www.economist.com/node/17911276.
16. Reuters. (2005, April 8). Yahoo backs Wikipedia. Retrieved from http://today.reuters.co.uk/news/newsArticle.aspx?type5internetNews&storyID52005-

04-08T013855Z_01_HOL805922_RTRIDST_0_OUKIN-TECH-YAHOO.XML.

17. Lever, Wikipedia.
18. Lever, Wikipedia.
19. Shaw, D. (2008, February/March). Wikipedia in the newsroom. *American Journalism Review*, 40–45.
20. This is the slogan of FedStats. www.fedstats.gov.
21. Head & Eisenberg, Lessons learned.
22. Unless noted otherwise, the information in this section comes from University of California, Berkeley. (2004, August 18, last updated). Finding information on the Internet: A tutorial. UC Berkeley—Teaching Library Internet Workshops. Retrieved from www.lib.berkeley.edu/TeachingLib/Guides/Internet/FindInfo.html.
23. Lewandowski, D., & Mayr, P. (2006). Exploring the Academic Invisible Web. E-Lis: Reprints in Library and Information Science. Retrieved from http://eprints.rclis.org/handle/10760/9203.
24. Tenopir, C. (2010, May 1). Online databases: Abundance of information. *Library Journal*, p. 22.
25. O'Neill, A. B., & Everhart, C. (1997). Trash or treasure: Teaching students how to evaluate Internet resources. Retrieved from www.bcpl.net/~dcurtis/psd/handouts/s3-67/. This resource is old, but a more recent article says the questions posed earlier are still valid; see S. Calkins & M. R. Kelley. (2007, Fall) Evaluating Internet and scholarly sources across the disciplines: Two case studies. *College Teaching*, *55*(4), 151–156.
26. Calkins & Kelley, Evaluating Internet.
27. Hawkes, L. (1999). *A guide to the World Wide Web.* Upper Saddle River, NJ: Prentice-Hall.
28. Wolfe, R. M., & Sharp, L. K. (2005). Vaccination or immunization? The impact of search terms on the Internet. *Journal of Health Communication*, *10*, 537–551.
29. Anonymous reviewer. (2008).
30. Paragraph 107: Fair use. (2004, April 30). Copyright Law of the United States of America. Title 17. Circular 92. Chapter 1. Retrieved from www.copyright.gov/title17/92chap1.html.
31. The International DOI Foundation. (n.d.). Frequently asked questions about the DOI system: What is a DOI name? Retrieved from www.doi.org/faq.html#1.
32. APA Style. (n.d.). Basics of APA Style tutorial. Retrieved from http://flash1r.apa.org/apastyle/basics/index.htm.
33. For a case study using the Mozart Effect, see Calkins & Kelley, Evaluating Internet.

CHAPTER 8

1. InfoTrac College Edition has many articles that support environmentalists' claims.
2. InfoTrac College Edition has many articles about dissenters such as Bjorn Lomborg. Some issues are outlined in S. Elmhirst. (2010, September 27). I didn't want to be the gay guy who talks about the environment. *New Statesman*, *132*(5020), 30–31. See also R. Bailey. (2008, October). The rational environmentalist: Bjorn Lomborg on the priorities that should come before global warming. *Reason*, *40*(5), 46–54.
3. Sayer, J. E. (2007, March). A good speech is "a good man speaking well." Commencement address delivered January 12, 2007, at the Ohio Institute of Photography and Technology, Dayton, OH. *Vital Speeches*, *73*(3), 265–269.
4. Griffiths, D. (2008, May 17). Uncertain times for quake survivors. BBC News [Online]. Retrieved from http://news.bbc.co.uk/2/hi/asia-pacific/7406459.stm.
5. BreakTheChain.org. (2001, July 26, last updated). That's one dumb shrub. Retrieved from www.breakthechain.org/exclusives/bushiq.html.
6. MacIntyre, A. (1981). *After virtue: A study in moral reasoning* (2nd ed.). South Bend, IN: University of Notre Dame Press.
7. Craig, K. (2010–2011). Ocean acidification [Competitive speech]. Northwest Forensics Conference: Mount Hood Community College.
8. Weichbrocht, C. (2008, Spring). Needed: A grief support system on campus [Student Speech]. George Fox University, Newberg, OR.
9. Miller, A. N. (2002). An exploration of Kenyan public speaking patterns with implications for the American introductory public speaking course. *Communication Education*, 5(2), 168–182.
10. DiMaggio, M. (2008, last updated). You have my deepest condolences: You just won the lottery [Student Speech]. St. John's University, Jamaica, NY.
11. Associated Press. (2008, March 4). Gang memoir is a total fabrication. CBS News. Retrieved from www.cbsnews.com/stories/2008/03/04/entertainment/main3903246.shtml.
12. Perkins, J. (2011, April 22). Letter to the Editor. *Virginia Law Weekly*, *63*(26). University of Virginia. Retrieved from www.lawweekly.org/?module=displaystory&story_id=3368&edition_id=180&format=html; See also Press Release. (2011, May 6). Law student who alleged police misconduct recants story, clears university police. UVA Today. Retrieved from www.virginia.edu/uvatoday/newsRelease.php?id=14982.
13. The Smoking Gun. (2008, January 8). The man who conned Oprah. Retrieved from www.thesmokinggun.com/archive/0104061jamesfrey1.html.
14. Springen, K. (2004, June 7). Drastically downsized. *Newsweek*, 78. Retrieved from InfoTrac College Edition.
15. Berger, J. (2008, June 1). Prison puppies. *New York Times.* Retrieved from www.nytimes.com/2008/06/01/nyregion/nyregionspecial2/01Rpuppies.html.
16. Slade, C. (2003). "Seeing reasons": Visual argumentation in advertisements. *Argumentation*, *17*, 14–160. ISSN: 0920-427X.
17. Jeong, S-H. (2008, March). Visual metaphor in advertising: Is the persuasive effect attributable to visual argumentation or metaphorical rhetoric? *Journal of Marketing Communication*, *14*(1), 59–73.
18. Jeong, S-H. (2006). Persuasive effect of visual metaphor in advertising: Is it attributable to metaphorical rhetoric or visual argumentation? Conference Paper. International Communication Association. Communication and Mass Media Complete database.
19. LaWare, M. R. (1998). Encountering visions of Aztlan: Arguments for ethnic pride, community activism and cultural revitalization in Chicano murals. *Argumentation and Advocacy*, *34*, 140–153.
20. Wilson, P. (1983). *Second-hand knowledge: An inquiry into cognitive authority.* Westport, CT: Greenwood.
21. Lanier, J. (2008, March 12). Compound puppies: Prisoners learn to train dogs. *Independent Tribune.* Retrieved from InfoTrac College Edition.
22. Florida/Metro. (1999, May 30). Prison puppies: Ices, Spirit, Moby, and Heather may be locked up, but they aren't criminals—they're learning to be guide dogs. *The Tampa Tribune (Tampa, FL)*. Retrieved from InfoTrac College Edition.

23. Tembo, M. S. (1999, April). Your mother is still your mother. *World and I, 14*, 4. Retrieved from InfoTrac College Edition.

24. Odom is quoted in D. McMenamin. (2011, February 11). Lamar Odom gets stitches to close gash. ESPN. Retrieved from http://sports.espn.go.com/los-angeles/nba/news/story?id=6111516.

25. McArdle, M. (2011, May 3). Anatomy of a fake quotation. *The Atlantic.* Retrieved from www.theatlantic.com/national/archive/2011/05/anatomy-of-a-fake-quotation/238257/.

26. Gentry, R. (2010). The prevalence and implications of food waste [Student Speech]. George Fox University, Newberg, OR.

27. Sepich, R. (2010–2011). America's infrastructure problem [Competitive speech]. Northwest Forensics Conference: Mount Hood Community College.

28. *Business Week*. (2005, March 21). It must be winter in New York: Top 20 local markets. Retrieved from www.businessweek.com/technology/tech_stats/topnet050321.htm.

29. Stephenson, S. (2011, May 19). Pile of debt would stretch beyond stratosphere. Reuters News. Retrieved from www.reuters.com/article/2011/05/19/us-usa-debt-size-idUSTRE74I5TL20110519.

30. FactCheck.org. (2011, April 8). Dems, GOP fight over homeless vets. Annenberg Public Policy Center. Retrieved from http://factcheck.org/2011/04/dems-gop-fight-over-homeless-vets/.

31. FactCheck.org, Dems, GOP.

32. National Center for Victims of Crime. (2004, February 26). *Crime and victimization in America, statistical overview* [Online]. Retrieved from http://www.ncvc.org.

33. Darling, A. L., & Dannels, D. P. (2003). Practicing engineers talk about the importance of talk: A report on the role of oral communication in the workplace. *Communication Education, 52*(1), 1–16.

34. Darling & Dannels, Practicing engineers.

35. Dannels, D. P. (2002). Communication across the discipline and in the disciplines: Speaking in engineering. *Communication Education, 51*(3), 254–268.

36. Dannels, Communication across, 263.

37. U.S. Department of Labor. (2005, June 5). Bureau of Labor Statistics. Retrieved from www.bls.gov/cps/wlf-table17-2005.pdf.

38. Szalavitz, M. (2010, October 12). The marijuana number that was too good to check. *Time*. Retrieved from http://healthland.time.com/2010/10/12/the-marijuana-number-that...

39. National Center for Victims of Crime. (2000). Crime and victimization in America: Statistical overview. Retrieved from www.ncvc.org.

40. Khan, L. A. (2002, January 15). A century of great awakenings: "We have learned much about ourselves." Speech delivered May 4, 1950, at the U.S. Senate, Washington, DC. *Vital Speeches of the Day, 68*(7), 222–225.

41. Sepich, America's infrastructure.

CHAPTER 9

1. Miller, G. A. (1956). The magical number seven, plus or minus two: Some limits on our capacity for processing information. *The Psychological Review, 63*, 81–97.

2. Anonymous reviewer. (2010).

3. Norwood, K., & Duck, S. W. (2009). Relationship dissolution processes. In H.T. Reis & S. Sprecher. (Eds.). *Encyclopedia of relationships* (pp. 414–419). Thousand Oaks, CA: Sage.

4. Fekkes, T. (2010). Negative political advertisements [Student Speech]. George Fox University, Newberg, OR.

5. Gentry, R. (2010). Perceptions of beauty: The media's influence over Asian women [Student Speech]. George Fox University, Newberg, OR.

6. Gentry, R. (2010). The prevalence and implications of food waste [Student Speech]. George Fox University, Newberg, OR.

7. See B. Alexander. (2009, January 12). Direct-to-consumer drug ads losing their punch. Health care on msnbc.com. Retrieved from www.msnbc.msn.com/id/28584952/; see also, I. D. Spatz. (2011, February 9). Better drug ads, fewer side effects. Op-Ed. *New York Times*. Retrieved from www.nytimes.com/2011/02/10/opinion/10spatz.html?_r=1.

8. Gandy, D. (2007, July). The secret to becoming very wealthy. Commencement address delivered May 5, 2007, at St. Leo University, St. Leo, FL. *Vital Speeches of the Day, 73*(7).

9. McMinn, M. (2011, March 1). Faculty lecture. George Fox University, Newberg, OR.

10. Bloch, M. (1975). *Political language and oratory in traditional society.* London: Academic Press.

11. Miller, A. N. (2002). An exploration of Kenyan public speaking patterns with implications for the American introductory public speaking course. *Communication Education*, 5(2), 168–182.

12. Engen, D. E. (2005). The civic awareness and imagination assignment. *Communication Teacher, 10*(3), pp. 80–83.

13. Jorgensen-Earp, C. (n.d.), "Making other arrangements": Alternative patterns of disposition [Unpublished course handout]. Lynchburg, VA: Lynchburg College.

14. Jorgensen-Earp, Making other arrangements.

15. Zediker, K. (1993, February). Rediscovering the tradition: Women's history with a relational approach to the basic public speaking course. Panel presentation at the Western States Communication Association, Albuquerque, NM.

16. Truth, S. (1997). Ain't I a Woman? *Modern History Sourcebook*. [online]. Retrieved from www.fordham.edu/halsall/mod/sojtruth-woman.html. (Original speech delivered 1851, Women's Convention, Akron, OH.)

17. Giovanni, N. (2007, April 17). We are Virginia Tech: Remarks at the memorial ceremony for Virginia Tech shooting victims. Retrieved from www.americanrhetoric.com/speeches/nikkigiovannivatechmemorial.htm.

18. Tiffin, T. (2010, August 12). Celebration of life service: Patsy Whittenberg Engel. Newberg, OR.

19. Anonymous reviewer. (2010).

CHAPTER 10

1. Quintilian. (1920–1922). *The instituto oratoria of Quintilian* (4 vols., H. E. Butler, trans.) The Loeb Classical Library. Cambridge, MA: Harvard University Press.

2. Veninga, R. L. (2010, June 22). Floods, oil spills, tornados: The psychology of resilience. Speech delivered June 9. 2010, at the Detroit Economic Club, Detroit, MI. *Vital Speeches of the Day, 76*(9), 390–392.

3. Holiday, A. (2010, Fall). Infomercials: Do they deserve any respect? [Student

Speech]. George Fox University, Newberg, OR.

4. Holiday, A. (2010, Fall). ACL injuries in the female athlete [Student Speech]. George Fox University, Newberg, OR.
5. Lapahie, H., Jr., (2001). Diné clans. LAPAHIE 5.1. www.lapahie.com/Dine_Clans.cfm; see also Office of Diné Culture, Language, and Community Services. (n.d.) Unit 11: NAHAT'/ / Division of Diné Culture. Retrieved from www.nmcn.org/heritage/dine_culture/nahatagvt.pdf.
6. Braithwaite, C. A. (1997). *Sa'ah Naaghái Bak'eh Hòzhóón:* An ethnography of Navajo educational communication practices. *Communication Education, 46*, 219–233.
7. Ferriero, D. (2011, February). The state of the National Archives. Speech delivered December 2, 2010, at the National Archives, College Park, MD. *Vital Speeches*, 77(2), 76–80.
8. Dodge, L. (2010, Fall). Homelessness in Portland [Student Speech]. George Fox University, Newberg, OR.
9. Dodge, Homelessness in Portland.
10. Gilday, B. (2010, Fall). The dark side of product placement [Student Speech]. George Fox University, Newberg, OR.
11. Loop, F. D. (2009, September). Pro-longevity: Practicing smarter medicine. Speech delivered June 3, 2009, to the Treatment of Cardiovascular Disease: Legacy and Innovation, Cleveland Clinic, Cleveland, OH. *Vital Speeches of the Day*, 75(9), 412–416.
12. Nevils, B. (2010, Fall). Retirement planning [Student Speech]. George Fox University, Newberg, OR.
13. Bernard, R. (2010, Spring). Dressage [Student Speech]. George Fox University, Newberg, OR.
14. Moncrief, M. (2010, August). The length of 100 years. Speech delivered May 8, 2010, at the commencement ceremony, Texas Christian University, Fort Worth, TX. *Vital Speeches of the Day*, 76(8), 342–345.
15. Persons, B. (2004, Fall). Driving while drowsy [Student Speech]. George Fox University, Newberg, OR.
16. Anonymous Reviewer. (2010).
17. Geck, R. (2010, Fall). United States' pandemic preparedness [Student Speech]. George Fox University, Newberg, OR.

CHAPTER 11

1. Wood, N. (1979). The classical canons in basic speech and English classes. *RQS: Rhetoric Society Quarterly*, 9(4), 188–193.
2. Streicher, J. (1996, 1999, updated). The five stages of culture shock [Student Speech]. George Fox University, Newberg, OR.
3. Gentry, R. (2010). Perceptions of beauty: The media's influence over Asian women [Student Speech]. George Fox University, Newberg, OR.
4. Erian, H. (2002). Overconsumption of sugar [Silver Medalist; Informative Speech]. Phi Ro Pi Tournament, Fort Worth, TX.
5. Riverdale School. (1999, December 14). Preparing the delivery outline. Riverdale School speech class, upper grades. Retrieved from www.teleport.com/beanman/english/delivout.html.
6. *SNOW.* (1999). Thinking and learning skills. University of Toronto. Retrieved from http://snow.utoronto.ca/learn2/introll.html.
7. Irvine, J. J., & York, D.E. (1995). *Learning styles and culturally diverse students: A literature review*. (ERIC Document Reproduction Service No. ED382 722 UDO3046)
8. Riding, R., & Cheerman, I. (1991). Cognitive styles—an overview and integration. *Educational Psychology, 11*, 193–215.
9. Tomlinson, C. A. (2009, February). Learning profiles and achievement: Do learning preferences have a place in promoting student success in the classroom? *School Administrator, 66*(2), 28–34.
10. Hermann-Nehdi, A. (2010, May). Whole brain thinking: Ignore it at your peril. *T+D, 64*(5), 36–42.
11. Jorgensen-Earp, C. (n.d.), "Making other arrangements": Alternative patterns of disposition [Unpublished course handout]. Lynchburg, VA: Lynchburg College.

CHAPTER 12

1. Ahmed, A. R. (2009, April). Safety margins in resection of sacral chordoma: Analysis of 18 patients. *Archives of Orthopaedic & Trauma Surgery, 129*(4), 483–487. doi: 10.1007/s00402-008-0674-y.
2. Trudgill, P. (2000). *Sociolinguistics: An introduction to language and society, 4th ed.* New York: NY: Penguin Books.
3. Gozzi, R. (1990). *New words and a changing American culture.* Columbia, SC: University of South Carolina Press.
4. Cited in R. Engnell. (2010). Senior capstone: Ethical and spiritual dimensions of communication. George Fox University, Newberg, OR.
5. Pattinson, G. (2005, September 26). Tingo, nakkele, and other wonders. BBC News. Retrieved from http://news.bbc.co.uk/2/hi/uk_news/magazine/4248494.stm.
6. Liberman, M. (2004, February 15). 46 Somali words for camel. *Language Log*. Retrieved from http://itre.cis.upenn.edu/myl/languagelog/archives/000457.html.
7. Whorf, B. L. (1956). *Language, thought, and reality*. Quotations from Benjamin Lee Whorf. Retrieved from http://mtsu32.mtsu.edu:11072/Whorf/blwquotes.html.
8. Gozzi, *New words*.
9. Dialects doing well. (1998). InSCIght on Apnet. Retrieved from www.apnet.com/inscight/02181009/graphb.htm.
10. Pot. (2002). Merriam-Webster online. Retrieved from www.merriam-webster.com/dictionary/pot.
11. Bennett, J. (2008, June 7). Revenge of the nerdette. *Newsweek Magazine*. Retrieved from www.newsweek.com/id/140457.
12. Delwiche, A. (2002, September 29). Propaganda: Euphemisms. Propaganda Critic. Retrieved from www.propagandacritic.com/articles/ct.wg.euphemism.html.
13. Oral Communication Center. (2011). Spoken vs. written language. Hamilton College, Hamilton, Clinton, NY. Retrieved from www.hamilton.edu/oralcommunication/spoken-language-vs-written-language.
14. DeVito, J. A. (1965). Comprehension factors in oral and written discourse of skilled communicators. *Speech Monographs, 32*, 124–128.
15. Ferraro, V., & Palmer, K. C. (n.d.). Differences between oral and written communication. Retrieved from www.mtholyoke.edu/acad/intrel/speech/differences.htm.
16. Greidanus, S. (2007). *Preaching Christ from Genesis: Foundations for expository*

sermons. Grand Rapids, MI: Wm. B. Eerdmans Publishing.

17. Stern, J. D. (2009, August). Making smarter movies. Speech delivered June 20, 2009, to the Los Angeles Film Festival, Los Angeles, CA. *Vital Speeches of the Day, 75*(8), 347–352.
18. Lessing, D. (2008, February). Not winning the Nobel Prize: Lecture given December 7, 2007, to the Nobel Peace Prize Committee, Oslo, Norway. *Vital Speeches of the Day, 74*(2), 72–73.
19. Reagan, R. (1986, January-31). Address on the Challenger disaster. Nationally televised speech. Available on www.youtube.com/watch?v=gEjXjfxoNXM.
20. Scherer, J. J. (2010, August). Go for tov: Learning to "come home to yourself." Speech delivered May 1, 2010, at the commencement ceremony for Roanoke College, Salem, VA. *Vital Speeches of the Day, 76*(8), 351–354.
21. Examples came from www.americanrhetoric.com.
22. Lamm, R. D. (2005). How to make an environmentalist. Speech delivered January 27, 2005, at the Thorne Ecological Institute 50th Anniversary, *Vital Speeches of the Day, 71*(10), 304–306.
23. Carnahan, J. (1999, June 15). Born to make barrels: Women who put their stamp on history. Speech delivered March 31, 1999, at the Trailblazer's Awards Ceremony, University of Missouri, St. Louis, MO. *Vital Speeches of the Day, 65*, 529–531.
24. Brody, W. J. (2007, November). What's promised, what's possible. Speech delivered September 7, 2007, to the National Press Club. Washington, DC. *Vital Speeches of the Day, 73*(11).
25. Peters, D. (2000, May). Sweet seduction. *Chatelaine, 73*(5), 53.
26. Osborn, M. (1997). The play of metaphors. *Education, 118*, 1, 84–87.
27. Panelist. (2008, June 12). *Life on the Rock* (Encore). EWTN Television.
28. Seattle. (1971). The Indian's night promises to be dark. In W. C. Vanderwerth. (Ed.). *Indian oratory: Famous speeches by noted Indian chieftains* (pp. 118–122). Norman, OK: University of Oklahoma Press. (Original work published 1853).
29. Osborn, M. (1967). Archetypal metaphor in rhetoric: The lightdark family. *Quarterly Journal of Speech, 53*, 115–126. See also M. Osborn. (1977). The evolution of the archetypal sea in rhetoric and poetic. *Quarterly Journal of Speech, 63*, 347–363.
30. Sorensen, A. (2010, October 31). JFK advisor Theodore Sorensen. (1928–2010). *Time* [online]. Retrieved from www.time.com/time/politics/article/0,8599,2028527,00.html.
31. James, S. D. (2008, February 8). Passing the torch: Kennedy's touch on Obama's words. ABCNews [online]. Retrieved from http://abcnews.go.com/Politics/Vote2008/story?id=4259093&page=1.
32. James, Passing the torch.
33. Seattle. The Indian's night.
34. Reider, J. (2008). *The Word of the Lord is upon me: The righteous performance of Martin Luther King, Jr.* Cambridge, MA: The Belknap Press of Harvard University Press.
35. Johannesen, R. L., Valde, K. S., & Wheedbee, K. E. (2008). *Ethics in human communication*, 6th ed. Long Grove, IL: Waveland Press.
36. Emory University Department of Religion. (2001, December 6). *Statement on inclusive language*. Retrieved from www.emory.edu/COLLEGE/RELIGION/about/statement.html.
37. Seiter, J. S., Larsen, J., & Skinner, J. (1998). "Handicapped" or "handicapable"? The effects of language about persons with disabilities on perceptions of source credibility and persuasiveness. *Communication Reports, 11*(1), 21–31.
38. Currey, J., & Mumford, K. (2002, September 18). Just talk: Guide to inclusive language. University of Tasmania. Retrieved from http://student.admin.utas.edu.au/services/just_talk/Disability/disability.htm.
39. Frida, D. O. (2007, May 9). Revenge of the muses: Could it be that finally women have had it with demeaning language?" *New York Daily News/Latino*. Retrieved from www.nydailynews.com/latino/2007/05/09/2007-05-09_revenge_of_the_muses.html.
40. Lustig, M. W., & Koester, J. (1993). *Intercultural competence: Interpersonal communication across cultures*. New York: HarperCollins; see also G. F. Simons, C. Vazquez, & P. R. Harris. (1993). *Transcultural leadership: Empowering the diverse workforce*. Houston: Gulf.
41. Thiederman, S. (1991a). *Bridging cultural barriers for corporate success: How to manage the multicultural workforce*. New York: Lexington; see also S. Thiederman. (1991b). *Profiting in American multicultural market places: How to do business across cultural lines*. New York: Lexington.
42. Kennedy, J. F. (1961, January 20). Inaugural address. Retrieved from www.presidency.ucsb.edu/ws/index.php?pid=8032#axzz1Qo8B25xq.

CHAPTER 13

1. Widder, E. (2010, April). Glowing life in an underwater world. Retrieved from www.ted.com/talks/lang/eng/edith_widder_glowing_life_in_an_underwater_world.html.
2. Clark, J. (2008, Winter). PowerPoint and pedagogy: Maintaining student interest in university lectures. *College Teaching, 56*(1), 39–45.
3. Reynolds, S. (1996, December). Selling to another language. *Communication World, 14*, 11.
4. Hartland, W., Biddle, C., & Fallacaro, M. (2008, June). Audiovisual facilitation of clinical knowledge: A paradigm for dispersed student education based on Paivio's dual coding theory. *AANA Journal, 76*(3), 194–198.
5. Comtex. (2009, October 7). m62 highlights difference between visual aids and useless photos. *Marketwire/Canada*. Infotrac College Edition database. (Article CJ210053995)
6. Mackeiwicz, J. (2008). Comparing PowerPoint experts' and university students' opinions about PowerPoint presentations. *J. Technical Writing and Communication, 38*(2), 149–165.
7. Wall, T. (2004, October). PowerPoint pitfalls that can kill an audience's will to stay awake. *Presentations, 18*(10), 46.
8. Quoted in M. Martinez. (2010, November). New literacies for a new era: Learning to read words is no longer enough; students must learn to be visually literate too. *Phi Delta Kappan, 92*(13), 72–74.
9. Wall, PowerPoint pitfalls; Comtext, m62 highlights.
10. Muhovic, E. (2000). Visual aids for presentations. Center for Managerial Communications, Denver University. Retrieved from www.du.edu/emuhovic/visualpresentations.html.
11. Clark, PowerPoint and pedagogy.
12. Mackiewicz, Comparing PowerPoint.
13. Katt, J., Murdock, J., Butler, J., & Pryor, B. (2008). Establishing best practices

for the use of PowerPoint as a presentation aid. *Human Communication, 11* (1), 193–200.

14. Ezekiel 4:1–3.
15. Cicero, De Orator 2:266267. Summarized in Beacham, R. C. (1999). *Spectacle entertainments of early imperial Rome* (p. 38). New Haven: Yale University Press.
16. Wall, PowerPoint pitfalls.
17. Anonymous reviewer (1994).
18. AV Technology. (2009, March 6). Document cameras. NewsBay Media. Retrieved from http://avtechnologyonline.com/article/27094.aspx.
19. Presentation tips: "Document camera." (2004, February 18). University of Wisconsin–Madison. Retrieved from www2.fpm.wisc.edu/support/PresentationTips.htm. See also Put more power in your next presentation: Use a document camera. (2005). Presenters Online. Retrieved from www.presentersonline.com/technical/tools/documentcamera.shtml.
20. Doumont, J-L. (2005, Feb.). The cognitive style of PowerPoint: Slides are not all evil. *Technical Communication, 52*(1), 64–71.
21. Radel, J. (1999, July). *Effective presentations*. The University of Kansas Medical Center on-line tutorial series. Retrieved from http://KUMC.edu/SAH/OTEd/jradel/effective.html.
22. Hernandez, T. (2004, Dec.). Digital whiteboards allow design teams to capture plan markups. *Building Design & Construction, 45*, 19–21.
23. Zielinski, D. (2003, Sept.). Go! Part two: Planes, trains and presenting: Secrets and strategies of speakers on the go. *Presentations, 47*(4), 17–28.
24. Anonymous reviewer. (1994).
25. Five keys to effective handouts. (1997, October 13). *Buffalo Business First* [online]. Retrieved from http://buffalo.bizjournals.com/buffalo/stories/1997/10/13/smallb3.html.
26. Katt, et. al., Establishing best practices.
27. Reynolds, G. (2006, August 30). From design to meaning: A whole new way of presenting? Retrieved from www.presentationzen.com/presentationzen/2006/08/from_design_to_.html.
28. Glazer, E. (2009, Summer). A process for Web design. TC801. Retrieved from https://www.msu.edu/~glazered/tc801/index.html.
29. Reynolds, G. (2005, September 5). What is good PowerPoint design? Retrieved from http://presentationzen.blogs.com/presentationzen/2005/09/whats_good_powe.html.
30. Poole, A. (2010). Which are more legible: Serif or sans serif typefaces? Retrieved from http://alexpoole.info/which-are-more-legible-serif-or-sans-serif-typefaces.
31. The facts about fonts. (2003, December). *PR Newswire*. Retrieved from InfoTrac College Edition database.
32. Bennett, J. (2008, April 7). Just go to Helvetica. (Design). *Newsweek, 151*(14), 54.
33. Great FX Business Cards. (2005, March-21). Using color to your marketing advantage. Accessed from www.greatfxbusinesscards.com/colorandemotions.htm.
34. Great FX Business Cards, Using color.

CHAPTER 14

1. ESPN News. (2010, July 11). R.I.P. Bob Sheppard. Retrieved from www.youtube.com/watch?v=hlmuWrniEF0.
2. Eisen, M. (2010, July 12). Lasting impression. NYGiants.com. Retrieved from www.giants.com/news/headlines/story.asp?story_id=44086.
3. Hypes, M. G., Turner, E. T., Norris, C. M., & Wolfferts, L. C. (1999, January). How to be a successful presenter. *Journal of Physical Education, Recreation & Dance, 70*(1), 50–53.
4. Unless noted otherwise, most suggestions in this section come from Schwartz, A. E. (1988, August). Rehearsing: Key to avoiding training chaos. *Training and Development Journal, 42*(8), 15–17.
5. Kaye, S. (1999, March). Make an impact with style: Presentation tips for leaders. *IIE Solutions, 31(3)*, p. 26(2). Retrieved from InfoTrac College Edition database.
6. Schwartz, Rehearsing.
7. Kampmann, M., & Rosen, J. (1991, January). Speaking with confidence. *Supervisory Management, 36*(1), 3.
8. Lee, C. E. (2009, March 5). Obama's safety net: The TelePrompter. Politico. Retrieved March 5, 2009, from www.politico.com/news/stories/0309/19663.html.
9. McDonald, C. A. (2008, June). Email interview.
10. Most of the recent work on the canon of memoria is linked to cultural memory, but see W. E. Hoogestraat. (1960). Memory: The lost canon? *Quarterly Journal of Speech, 46*(2), 141–148.
11. Schwartz, Rehearsing.
12. Kaye, S. (1999, March). Make an impact with style: Presentation tips for leaders. IIE Solutions, *31*(3), p. 26(2).
13. These tips draw from Schwartz, Rehearsing.
14. Reider, J. (2008). *The Word of the Lord is upon me: The righteous performance of Martin Luther King, Jr*. Cambridge, MA: The Belknap Press of Harvard University Press.
15. Anonymous reviewer. (2010).
16. Hoogestraat, Memory.
17. Anonymous reviewer. (2008).
18. Keefe, J. (1988, August) Drama lessons for speakers. *Meetings & Conventions 33*(9), *30*.
19. Schwartz, Rehearsing.
20. Keefe, Drama lessons.
21. Montalbo, T. (1980). Churchill: A study in oratory. Seven lessons in speechmaking from one of the greatest orators of all time. The Churchill Centre. Retrieved from www.winstonchurchill.org/i4apages/index.cfm?pageid+814.
22. Goffman, E. (1959). *The presentation of self in everyday life*. Garden City, NY: Doubleday Anchor.
23. Bippus, A. M., & Daly, J. A. (1999). What do people think causes stage fright? Naïve attributions about the reasons for public speaking anxiety. *Communication Education, 48*, 63–72.
24. Arthur, A. (1997, July). Keeping up public appearances: Master the fine art of public-speaking and give a great presentation every time. *Black Enterprise*, 27(12), 54.
25. Goffman, *The presentation of self*.
26. Gullberg, M., & Holmqvist, K. (2006). What speakers do and what addressees look at: Visual attention to gestures in human interaction live and on video. *Pragmatics & Cognition, 14*(1), 53–82.
27. Ekman, P., & Friesen, W. V. (1969). The repertoire of nonverbal behavior: Categories, origins, usage, and coding. *Semiotica, I*, 49–98.
28. Morgan, N. (2004, Winter). Preparing to be real. *Harvard Management Communication Letter, 1*(1), 3–5.
29. Hansen, J. (2010, September). Teaching without talking: Teachers need to

be aware of more than just the words they speak to children. They also need to monitor the nonverbal messages that they're sending to students through proximity, eye contact, gestures, and touching. *Phi Delta Kappan, 91*(10), 35–41.

30. Kempmann & Rosen, Speaking with confidence.
31. Brody, M. (1998, August). Delivering your speech right between their eyes. *American Salesman, 43*(8), 29–31.
32. Brody, M. (1994, June). Delivering your speech right between their eyes. *Supervision, 55*(8), 18.
33. Richmond, V. P., & McCroskey, J. C. (2000). *Nonverbal behavior in interpersonal relations* (4th ed.). Scottsdale, AZ: Gorsuch Scarisbrick.
34. Lev-Ari, S., & Keysar, B. (2010). Why don't we believe non-native speakers? The influence of accent on credibility. *Journal of Experimental Social Psychology, 46,* 1093–1096. doi: 10.1016/jesp2010.05.025.
35. Montalbon, Churchill.
36. Richmond, V. P., McCroskey, J. C., & Payne, S. K. (1991). *Nonverbal behavior in interpersonal relations (2nd Ed.).* Englewood Cliffs, NJ: Prentice Hall. See also FIU Oral Presentation Lab. (n.d.) Cultural issues and public address. Florida International University, Miami, FL. Retrieved June 2, 2011, from http://opl.fiu.edu/cultural.htm.
37. FIU Oral Presentation Lab, Cultural issues.
38. Krompacky, Y. H. (1993, March 21). Immigrants, don't be in such a hurry to shed your accents. *The New York Times.* Sec. 4, p. 16.
39. Aristotle, (1954, 1984). *The Rhetoric.* (H. R. Roberts, Trans.). New York: The Modern Library.
40. Summarized in Burgoon, J. K., Buller, D. B., & Woodall, W. G. (1989). *Nonverbal communication: The unspoken dialogue.* New York: Harper & Row; see also G. B. Ray. (1986). Vocally cued personality prototypes: An implicit personality theory approach. *Communication Monographs, 53,* 266–276.
41. Burgoon, Buller, & Woodall, Nonverbal communication.
42. Morgan, Preparing to be real.
43. Morgan, Preparing to be real.
44. The next three suggestions come from Toastmasters International. (n.d.). Vocal variety. Retrieved from www.angelfire.com/tn/bektoastmasters/Toastmasters5.html.
45. Davidson, W., & Kline, S. (1999, March). Ace your presentations. *Journal of Accountancy, 187*(3), 61. See also Hypes, Turner, Norris, & Wolfferts, Successful presenter.
46. Humphrey, J. (1998, May 15). Executive eloquence: A seven-fold path to inspirational leadership. Speech delivered November 25, 1997, to the Board of Trade, Metropolitan Toronto, Canada. *Vital Speeches, 64*(15), 468–471.
47. Hart, R. P., & Burks, D. O. (1972). Rhetorical sensitivity and social interaction. *Speech Monographs, 39,* 90.
48. Branham, R. J., & Pearce, W. B. (1996). The conversational frame in public address. *Communication Quarterly, 44*(4), 423–439.
49. Brookhiser, R. (1999, November 22). Weird Al: A troubled and alarming vice president. *National Review, 60*(22), 32–34. See also Shipman, C. (2000, December/January). Searching for Al. *George Magazine, 102,* 9.
50. Democracy in America (blog). (2008, June 23). Sexism at the *Times*? *The Economist.* Retrieved from www.economist.com/blogs/democracyinamerica/2008/06/sexism_at_the_times.cfm.
51. Goffman, *The presentation of self.*
52. Anonymous reviewer, 2004.

CHAPTER 15

1. Wicker, B. (1975). *The story-shaped world: Fiction and metaphysics, some variations on a theme.* South Bend, IN: University of Notre Dame Press.
2. Fisher, W. R. (1984). Narration as a human communication paradigm: The case of public moral argument. *Communication Monographs, 51,* 1–22; see also W. R. Fisher. (1984). The narrative paradigm: An elaboration. *Communication Monographs, 52,* 347–367.
3. Barthes is quoted in D. E. Polkinghorne. (1988). *Narrative knowing and the human sciences* (p. 14). Albany, NY: SUNY Press.
4. Bundgaard, P. F. (2007). The cognitive import of the narrative schema. *Semiotica, 165*(1/4), 247–261.
5. Bruner, J. (1986). *Actual minds, possible worlds.* Cambridge, MA: Harvard University Press.
6. Cassady, M. (1994). *The art of storytelling: Creative ideas for preparation and performance* Colorado Springs, CO: Meriweather p. 12.
7. Anokye, A. D. (1994, Fall). Oral connections to literacy: The narrative. *Journal of Basic Writing, 13,* 46–60.
8. Keeshig-Tobias, L. (1990, January 26). Stop stealing native stories. Downloaded from web.uvic.ca/vv/stolo/Tobias.pdf.
9. Keeshig-Tobias, Stop stealing.
10. Coste, D. (1989). *Narrative as communication.* Minneapolis: University of Minnesota Press.
11. Cherokee. (n.d.). The origin of strawberries. Native American Lore. Retrieved from www.ilhawaii.net/~stony/lore148.html.
12. Spangler, D., & Thompson, W. I. (1992). *Reimagination of the world: A critique of the new age, science, and popular culture.* New York: Bear & Company.
13. Simmons, A. (n.d.). Six stories you need to know how to tell. International Storytelling Center. Retrieved from www.storytellingcenter.com/resources/articles/simmons.htm.
14. Aristotle, (1954, 1984). *The Rhetoric.* (H. R. Roberts, Trans.). New York: The Modern Library.
15. Green, M. C., & Brock, T. C. (2000). The role of transportation in the persuasiveness of public narratives. *Journal of Personality and Social Psychology, 79*(5), 701–721.
16. Kim, M. (2010, November/December). Healing spaces: Volunteers create "dream rooms" for seriously ill children. *Civic Engagement.* Rutgers University School of Public Affairs and Administration, 10–11. Retrieved from http://publicservice.newark.rutgers.edu/home/civic-engagement.html.
17. CBS News. (2008, December 17). Thanks to the kindness of strangers. *The Early Show.* Retrieved from www.cbsnews.com/stories/2008/12/16/earlyshow/health/main4671829.shtml
18. Baum, N. (2003). A land twice promised. Retrieved from www.noabaum.com/land.html.
19. Dorame, K. (2011, February/March). Supporting smiles. *Civic Engagement.* Rutgers University School of Public Affairs and Administration, 16–17.
20. Neile, C. S. (2005). Can storytelling save the world? Florida Storytelling Association. Retrieved from www.flstory.org/can_storytelling_save.html.
21. Heuer, A. B. (2001). Storytelling and health care: Applied storytelling with stroke survivors. *Diving in the Moon,*

Trust the Power of Story, 2. Retrieved from www.andreheuer.com/articles/storytelling_health_care_stroke.html.

22. Vergnani, S. A. (2003, March 14). Healing through storytelling. Columbia News Service. Retrieved from www.jrn.columbia.edu/studentwork/cns/2003-03-14/16.asp.
23. Quoted in Vergnani, Healing through.
24. Neile, C. S. (2005). International Storytelling Center internship. The Woodrow Wilson National Fellowship Foundation. Retrieved from www.woodrow.org/phd/Practicum/neile.html; See also, C. S. Neile. (2003). War and peace and story. *Words of Wing, 6.* [online]. Healing Story. Retrieved from www.healingstory.org/articles/healing-story-articles.html.
25. Kirkwood, W. G. (1992). Narrative and the rhetoric of possibility. *Communication Monographs, 59,* 30–47.
26. Torrance, J. (1998). *Jackie tales: The magic of creating stories and the art of telling them.* New York: Avon Books.
27. Cassady, *The art of storytelling.*
28. Burke, K. (1983, August 12). Dramatism and logology. *The Times Literary Supplement,* p. 859.
29. Green & Brock, The role of transportation.
30. Cyphert, D. (2007). Presentation technology in the age of electronic eloquence: from visual aid to visual rhetoric. *Communication Education, 56*(2), 168–172.
31. Cyphert, Presentation technology.
32. Tannen, D. (1989). *Talking voices: Repetition, dialogue, and imagery in conversational discourse.* Cambridge: Cambridge University Press.
33. McNally, J. R. (1969). Opening assignments: A symposium. *The Speech Teacher, 18,* 18–30.
34. Steph. B. (2010, January 29). Growing up deaf [Student Speech]. George Fox University, Newberg, OR.
35. Burke, Dramatism and logology.
36. Fisher, Narration as a human communication.
37. Fisher, The narrative paradigm; Fisher, Narration as a human communication.

CHAPTER 16

1. Neuman, W. R. (2010, February 4). Appraising information abundance: The Chronicle review. *Chronicle of Higher Education.* Retrieved from http://chronicle.com/article/Appraising-Information/63744/.
2. Davidson, J. (2005, January 15). Bombarded on all sides: Handling everyday information. Speech delivered September 29, 2004, to Land America, Las Vegas, NV. *Vital Speeches of the Day, 71*(7), 212–217.
3. General Assembly of the United Nations. (1948, December 10). Universal Declaration of Human Rights. Retrieved from www.un.org/Overview/rights.html.
4. Gluckman, R. (2004, October 18). Beyond the Net's reach: A German firm says it has connected North Korea to the Web, only Pyongyang won't throw the switch. *Newsweek,* 40. Retrieved from www.newsweek.com/2004/10/17/beyond-the-net-s-reach.html.
5. LaRue, F. (2011, May 16). Report of special rapporteur on the promotion and protection of the right to freedom of opinion and expression. United Nations General Assembly, Human Rights Council, Seventeenth Session, Agenda item 3. A/HRC/17/27. Downloaded from http://latimesblogs.latimes.com/technology/2011/06/united-nations-report-internet-access-is-a-human-right.html.
6. Maxwell, L., & McCain, T. A. (1997, July). Gateway or gatekeeper: The implication of copyright and digitalization on education. *Communication Education, 46,* 141–157.
7. Associated Press. (2005, July 7). Reporter jailed for refusal to name leak source. Retrieved from www.msnbc.msn.com/id/8417075/.
8. U.S. Department of State (2008). Freedom of Information Act (FOIA). Retrieved from http://www.state.gov/m/a/ips/.
9. WikiLeaks. (2011, June 2, last updated). WikiLeaks. Retrieved from http://mirror.wikileaks.info/.
10. Greenwald, G. (2011, June 9). WikiLeaks grand jury investigation widens. *Salon.* Retrieved from www.salon.com/news/opinion/glenn_greenwald/2011/06/09/wikileaks/.
11. Fillible, R. (1988). Public speaking course handout. Oregon State University, Corvallis, OR.
12. Edwards, R., & McDonald, J. L. (1993). Schema theory and listening. In A. D. Wolvin & C. G. Coakley. (Eds.) *Perspectives on Listening* (pp. 60–77). Norwood, NJ: Ablex.
13. Quotation retrieved from www.quotedb.com/quotes/1382.
14. Budiansky, S. (1999, July). The truth about dogs. *Atlantic Monthly, 284*(1), 39–41, 44+.
15. Connelly, M. (n.d.). Division and classification. InfoTrac College Edition. Retrieved from http://infotrac.thomsonlearning.com/infowrite/ex_division.htm.
16. ACTFL. (n.d.) ACTFL certified proficiency testing programs (oral and written). American Council on the Teaching of Foreign Languages. Retrieved from www.actfl.org/i4a/pages/index.cfm?pageid=3642.
17. Patterson, M. (n.d.). Demonstrative speech (how to). Brazosport College. Retrieved from www.brazosport.cc.tx.us/,comm/demon.html.
18. Flynn, K, R, (n.d.). Demonstration or "how to" speech topics. Copia-Lincoln Community College. Retrieved from www.colin.edu/flynn/Speech/Demo_Speech.htm.
19. Kuzmovich, E. (2005). How to draw a hand [Student Speech]. George Fox University, Newberg, OR.
20. Nguyen, N. (2005, March). *Ha Noi, Thanh pho yeu dau* (my beloved city) [Student Speech]. George Fox University, Newberg, OR.
21. Miller, A. N. (2002). An exploration of Kenyan public speaking patterns with implications for the American introductory public speaking course. *Communication Education,* 5(2), 168–182.
22. Rowan, K. (1995). A new pedagogy for explanatory public speaking: Why arrangement should not substitute for invention. *Communication Education, 44*(3), 235–250.
23. von Till, B. (1998, November). Definition speech. San Jose State University. Poster session. National Communication Association meeting, New York City.
24. Boerger, M. A., & Henley, T. B. (1999). The use of analogy in giving instructions. *Psychological Record, 49*(2), 193.
25. Gardner, H. (1993). *Multiple intelligences: The theory in practice.* New York: Basic Books.
26. Goodall, H. L., & Waaigen, C. L. (1986). *The persuasive presentation: A practical guide to professional communication in organizations.* New York: Harper & Row.
27. Rubin, D. L. (1993). Listenability 5 oral-based discourse + considerateness. In Wolvin & Coakley, Perspectives, 261–268.

28. Rowan, A new pedagogy.
29. Rubin, Listenability 5 oral-based.
30. Thompson, F. T., & Grandgenett, D. J. (1999). Helping disadvantaged learners build effective learning skills. *Education 120*(1), 130–135.

CHAPTER 17

1. Oliner, S. P., & Oliner, P. M. (1988). *The altruistic personality: Rescuers of Jews in Nazi Germany.* New York, NY: The Free Press.
2. Perloff, R. M. (2003). *The dynamics of persuasion: Communication and attitudes in the 21st century* (2nd ed.). Mahwah, NJ: Lawrence Erlbaum Associates, p. 8.
3. Aristotle, (1954, 1984). *The Rhetoric.* (H. R. Roberts, Trans.). New York: The Modern Library 1356, 356, 20.
4. Anonymous reviewer. (1994).
5. Stewart, R. A., & Roach, K. D. (1998). Argumentativeness and the Theory of Reasoned Action. *Communication Quarterly, 46*(2) 177–193.
6. Toulmin, S. (1958). *The uses of argument.* Cambridge, UK: Cambridge University Press; Toulmin, S., Rieke, R., & Janik, A. (1984). *An introduction to reasoning* (2nd ed.). New York: Macmillan.
7. Rex, L. A., Thomas, E. E., & Engel, S. (2010). Applying Toulmin: Teaching logical reasoning and argumentative writing. *English Journal, 99*(6), 56–62.
8. Horne, M. P. (2008). Teaching religious doubt with Toulmin's Model of Reasoning. *Teaching Theology and Religion, 11*(4), 203–212. ISSN 1368-4868.
9. Anonymous reviewer. (2011).
10. Hilliard, A. (1986). Pedagogy in ancient Kemet. In M. Karenga & J. Carruthers (Eds.). *Kemet and the African world view* (p. 257). London: University of Sankore Press.
11. Combs, S. C. (2004). The useless-/usefulness of argumentation: the DAO of disputation. *Argumentation and Advocacy, 41*(2), *58*(13).
12. Combs, The useless-/usefulness.
13. Aristotle, (1954, 1984). *The Rhetoric.* (H. R. Roberts, Trans.). New York: The Modern Library.
14. Burke, Dramatism and logology.
15. Allen, S. A. (1993, February 15). To be successful you have to deal with reality: An opportunity for minority business. Speech delivered October 20, 1992, to the National Minority Supplier Devellopment Council, Cleveland, OH. *Vital Speeches, 59,* 271–273.
16. Quintilian. (1920–1922). *The instituto oratoria of Quintilian* (4 vols., H. E. Butler, trans.) The Loeb Classical Library. Cambridge, MA: Harvard University Press.
17. Quintilian, *The instituto oratoria.*
18. Kochman, T. (1990). Cultural pluralism: Black and white styles. In D. Carbaugh (Ed.). *Cultural communication and intercultural contacts* (pp. 219–224). Hillsdale, NJ: Lawrence Erlbaum.
19. Anderson, J. W. (1991). A comparison of Arab and American conceptions of "effective persuasion." In L. A. Samovar & R. E. Porter (Eds.). *Intercultural communication: A reader* (5th ed., pp. 96–106). Belmont, CA: Wadsworth.
20. Gentry, R. (2010). The prevalence and implications of food waste [Student Speech]. George Fox University, Newberg, OR.
21. Clinton, H. R. (2010, March). A new nervous system for our planet. Speech delivered January 21, 2010, at the Newseum, Washington, DC. *Vital Speeches of the Day, 76*(3), 108–114.
22. Roczak, T. (1992, June 9). Green guilt and ecological overload. *New York Times,* A23.
23. Maslow, A. H. (1987). *Motivation and personality* (3rd ed.). San Francisco: Harper & Row.
24. Maslow, A. H. (1943). A theory of human motivation. Originally published in *Psychological Review, 50,* 370–396. Posted by C. D. Green. (2000, August). Classics in the history of psychology website. http://psychclassics.yorku.ca/Maslow/motivation.htm.
25. Brigance, W. N. (1961). *Speech: Its techniques and disciplines in a free society* (2nd ed.). New York, NY: Appleton-Century-Crofts.
26. Anonymous reviewer. (1994).
27. Huey Long Official Website. (2010). Long legacy project. Retrieved from www.hueylong.com
28. Gunn, J. (2007). Hystericizing Huey: Emotional appeals, desire, and the psychodynamics of demagoguery. (Huey Pierce Long). *Western Journal of Communication, 71,* 1–27.
29. Roberts-Miller, P. (2005). Democracy, demagoguery, and critical rhetoric. *Rhetoric & Public Affairs, 8*(3), 462. Retrieved from Communication and Mass Media Complete database.
30. Roberts-Miller, Democracy, demagoguery.
31. Gunn, Hystericizing Huey.
32. Gunn, Hystericizing Huey.
33. Wicker, B. (1975). *The story-shaped world: Fiction and metaphysics, some variations on a theme.* South Bend, IN: University of Notre Dame Press.
34. Hilliard, Pedagogy in ancient, p. 287.
35. Aristotle. (1984). *Poetics* (1459, 5). (I. Bywater, Trans.) New York: The Modern Library. (Original translation published 1954).
36. McClain, F. J. (2001, November 1). The music in your soul: A celebration of life. Speech delivered September 18, 2001, at the Fall Convocation, Queens College, Charlotte, NC. *Vital Speeches of the Day, 68*(2), 59–61.
37. Kent, M. (2010, December 1). Women's equality: "A battle for . . . the world's economic, environmental and social fabric." Speech delivered October 4, 2010, as the Yale World Fund Lecture, New Haven, CT. *Vital Speeches of the Day, 76*(12), 558–562.
38. Pence, M. (2010). My subject today is the presidency. Speech delivered September 20, 2019, at Hillsdale College, Hillsdale, MI. *Vital Speeches of the Day, 76*(11), 504–508.
39. Sullivan, P. A. (1993). Signification and African-American rhetoric: a case study of Jesse Jackson's "Common Ground and Common Sense" speech. *Communication Quarterly, 41*(1), 1–15.
40. Griffiths, M. (1988). Feminism, feelings, and philosophy. In M. Griffiths & M. Whitford (Eds.). *Feminist perspectives in philosophy* (pp. 131–151). Bloomington: Indiana University Press; see also A. Jaggar. (1989). Love and knowledge: Emotion in feminist epistemology. In A. Garry & M. Pearsall (Eds.). *Women, knowledge, and reality: Explorations in feminist philosophy* (pp. 129–155). London: Unwin; McMillan, 1982).
41. Jaggar, Love and knowledge.
42. Griffiths, Feminism, feelings.
43. Frank, D. A. (1997). Diversity in the public space: A response to Stepp. *Argumentation and Advocacy, 33,* 195–197.
44. Dunbar, K. (2000). Gender, science & cognition [Online]. Retrieved from www.psych.mcgill.ca/perpg/fac/dunbar/women.html.
45. Asen, R. (1999, Winter). Toward a normative conception of difference in

public deliberation. *Argumentation and Advocacy, 35*(3), 115–116.

46. Craig, K. (2010–2011). Ocean acidification [Competitive speech]. Northwest Forensics Conference: Mount Hood Community College.
47. Morris, H. J., (2002, June 17). League of their own. *U.S. News & World Report, 131*(21), 50–51.
48. Gass, R. (1999). Fallacy list: SpCom 335: Advanced argumentation [Online]. California State University, Fullerton. Retrieved from http://commfaculty.fullerton.edu/rgass/fallacy31.htm.
49. Foss, S. K., & Griffin, C. (1995). Beyond persuasion: A proposal for an invitational rhetoric. *Communication Monographs, 62*, 2–18.

CHAPTER 18

1. Aristotle, (1954, 1984). *The Rhetoric.* (H. R. Roberts, Trans.). New York: The Modern Library.
2. Mullins, D. (1993). Guest lecture. St. John's University, Jamaica, NY.
3. Liu, L. (2008). *Yang* and *yin* in communication: Towards a typology and logic of persuasion in China. *Diogenes, 217*: 120-132. ISSN 0392-1921.
4. Uskul, A. K., & Oyserman, D. (2010). When message-frame fits salient cultural-frame, messages feel more persuasive. *Psychology and Health, 25*(3), 321–337. ISSN 1476-8321.
5. STATS. (n.d.). What's the difference between correlation and causation? Statistical Assessment Services. Affiliated with George Mason University. Washington, DC. Retrieved from http://stats.org/in_depth/faq/causation_correlation.htm.
6. Kaufman, W. (2011, July 14). Google announces Global Science Fair winners. NPR News. Retrieved from www.npr.org/2011/07/12/137783968/google-announces-global-science-fair-winner.
7. "Attitude." (n.d.). Definition retrieved from www.cogsci.princeton.edu/cgi-bin/webwn2.1.
8. Anonymous reviewer. (1994).
9. Boster, F. J., Kenzie, A. C., Campo, S., Liu, W-Y., Lillie, J. K., Baker, E. M., & Yun, K. A. (2000). The persuasive effects of statistical evidence in the presence of exemplars. *Communication Studies, 51*(3), 296–306.
10. Hoecker, K. (2010, Fall). A doll's effect on young girls' concepts of beauty. [Student Speech.] George Fox University, Newberg, OR.
11. Norton, K. I., Olds, T. S., Olive, S., & Dank, S. (1006). Ken and Barbie at life size. *Sex Roles, 34*(3–4), 287–294. doi: 10.1007/BF01544300.
12. Kuther, T. L., & McDonald, E. (2004, Spring). Early adolescents' experiences with, and view of, Barbie. *Adolescence, 39*(153), 39–51.
13. Dittmar, H., Halliwell, E., & Ive, S. (2006). Does Barbie make girls want to be thin? The effect of experimental exposure to images of dolls on the body image of 5- to 8-year-old girls. *Developmental Psychology, 42*(2), 283–292. doi: 10.1037/0012-1649.42.2.283.
14. Dittmar, Halliwell, & Ive. Does Barbie make.
15. Kuther & McDonald. Early adolescents' experiences.
16. Bartanen, M. D. (n. d.). Application of the issues-agenda paradigm to speaker duties and stock issues in value debates. Cross Examination Debate Association. Retrieved from cedadebate.org/CAD/index.php/CAD/article/view/115/101.
17. Hill, B., & Leeman, R. W. (1997). *The art and practice of argumentation and debate.* Mountain View, CA: Mayfield Publishing Company, 163–164.
18. Tobin, S. J., & Weary, G. (2008). The effects of causal uncertainty, causal importance, and initial attitude on attention to causal persuasive arguments. *Social Cognition, 26*(1), 44–56.
19. Editorial. (2007, November 25). The high cost of health care. *New York Times.* Retrieved from www.nytimes.com/2007/11/25/opinion/25sun1.html?pagewanted=1.
20. Festinger, L. (1957). *A theory of cognitive dissonance.* New York: Row, Peterson.
21. This theory, developed by Fishbein and Ajzen, is summarized in D. Trafimow & K. A. Finlay. (2001). Evidence for improved sensitivity of within-participants' analyses in test of the theory of reasoned action. *The Social Science Journal, 38*(4), 629–638. See also L. A. Muse & C. L. Stamper. (2007). Perceived organizational support: Evidence for a mediated association with work performance. *Journal of Managerial Issues, 19*(4), 517–538.
22. Poss, J. E. (2001, June.) Developing a new model for cross-cultural research: Synthesizing the health beliefs model and the theory of reasoned action. *Advances in Nursing Science, 23*(4), 1–16.
23. Park, H. S. (2000). Relationships among attitudes and subjective norms: Testing the theory of reasoned action across cultures. *Communication Studies, 51*(2), 162–175.)
24. Ramprasand, G. (2008). E-mail interview. (Edited)
25. Monroe, A. H. (1962). *Principles and types of speeches* (5th ed.). Chicago: Scott Foresman.
26. Pugh, T. (2007, Fall). Organ donation. [Student Speech.] George Fox University, Newberg, OR.

APPENDIX A

1. Burbach, M. E., Matkin, G. S., Gambrell, K. M., & Harding, H. E. (2010, September). The impact of preparing faculty in the effective use of student teams. *College Student Journal, 44*(3), 752–761.
2. Beebe, S. A., & Masterson, J. T. (1990). *Communicating in small groups: Principles and practices* (3rd ed.). New York: Harper Collins; See also, P. J. Cooper. (1995). *Communication for the classroom teacher* (5th ed.). Scottsdale, AZ: Gorsuch Scarisbrick.
3. Tannen, D. F. (1990). *You just don't understand: Men and women in conversation.* New York, NY: William Morris.
4. Janik, I. (1971, November). Groupthink. *Psychology Today*, 43–46.
5. Eisen, A. (1998). Small group presentations in teaching "science thinking" and context in a large biology class. *Bioscience, 48(1)*, 54–57.
6. Burbach, Matkin, Gambrell, & Harding, Impact of preparing.
7. Tannen, *You just don't.*
8. Cowan, J. (2000). Lessons from the playground. In K. Galvin & P. Cooper (Eds.). *Making connections: Readings in relational communication*, (2nd ed., p. 307). Los Angeles: Roxbury.
9. Grob, L. M., Meyers, R. A., & Schuh, R. (1997). Powerful/powerless language use in group interactions: Sex differences or similarities? *Communication Quarterly, 45(3)*, 282–303.
10. Cowan, Lessons from.
11. Henson, J. (n.d.). Problem solving using group challenges. Retrieved from www.bvte.ecu.edu/ACBMEC/p1998/henson.htm.

12. Sengalese women remake their culture. (1998, December). *IK Notes World Bank, No. 3*. Retrieved from www.africapolicy.org.

13. Kepner, C. H., & Tregoe, B. B. (1965). *The rational manager: A systematic approach to problem solving and decision making.* New York: McGraw-Hill.

APPENDIX B

1. Goodall, H. L., & Phillips, G. M. (1984). *Making it in any organization.* Upper Saddle River, NJ: Prentice-Hall.

2. Pacanowsky, M. E., & O'Donnell-Trujillo, N. (1983). Organization communication as cultural performance. *Communication Monographs, 50*, 126–147.

3. Bormann, E. G. (1985). Symbolic convergence theory: A communication formulation. *Journal of Communication, 35*, 128–138.

4. Ouchi, W. B. (1998, Fall). The concept of organizational culture in a diverse society. SIETAR International. Retrieved from http://208.215.167.139/sij-98-12/keynote03.htm.

5. Obama, B. H. (2009, May 26). Remarks by the President in nominating Judge Sonia Sotomayor to the United States Supreme Court. Retrieved from www.whitehouse.gov/the-press-office/remarks-president-nominating-judge-sonia-sotomayor-united-states-supreme-court.

6. O'Malley, M. (2011, May). If I were to sing tonight. Speech delivered March 16, 2001, at the American Ireland Fund's National Gala, Washington, DC. *Vital Speeches of the Day*, 77(5), 166–167.

7. Coleman, M. S. (2011, May). I was a teenage scientist. Speech delivered March 11, 2011, at the Intel Talent Search Alumni Dinner, Washington, DC. *Vital Speeches of the Day*, 77 (5), 181–184.

8. McCardell, J. M. (2011, November). From tentative twig to mighty branch. Speech delivered August 22, 2010, at the welcoming ceremony, University of the South, Sewanee, TN. *Vital Speeches of the Day, 76* (11), 492–495.

9. Gillard, J. (2011). I always remember thinking: Americans can do anything. Speech delivered March 9, 2011, to a Joint Session of Congress, US House of Representatives, Washington, DC. *Vital Speeches of the Day, 76* (11), 492–495.

10 Hawken, P. (2009, May 3). The Earth is hiring. Commencement address delivered at the University of Portland, Portland, OR. Retrieved from www.humanity.org/voices/commencements/speeches/index.php?page=hawken_at_uportland.

11. Servis, M. (2007, July). Myth, mystery, and meaning in medicine. Speech delivered June 9, 2007, Commencement, UC Davis School of Medicine, Davis, CA. *Vital Speeches of the Day, 73* (7), 309–311.

12. Vest, G. G. (1870). Tribute to the dog. Retrieved from www.historyplace.com/speeches/vest.htm.

13. Howlett, S. (2003, Fall). Beyond batting [Student Speech]. Radford University. Radford, VI. Retrieved from www.radford.edu/~llanc/manuscriptsample.htm.

14. Goldberg, J. (2005, June 17). The hop bird: My dad, 1931–2005. *National Review Online*. Retrieved from www.nationalreview.com/goldberg/goldberg200506170746.asp.

APPENDIX C

1. Karakas, F. (2005, April 1). A global agenda for interfaith dialogue: Tolerance, love, and cooperation. Speech delivered December 2004 at the Interfaith Dinner of Dialogue Foundation. Montreal, Canada. *Vital Speeches of the Day, 71*(12), 373–376.

2. Joseph. (1879, April, original publication date). An Indian's view of Indian affairs. *North American Review, 128*(269). 412–433. Retrieved from www.washington.edu/uwired/outreach/cspn/sense/part1%20pages/texts/josephview.htm.

3. Truth, S. (1997). Ain't I a Woman? *Modern History Sourcebook*. [online]. Retrieved from www.fordham.edu/halsall/mod/sojtruth-woman.html. (Original speech delivered 1851, Women's Convention, Akron, OH.)

INDEX